Encyclopedia of
Caribbean Literature

Advisory Board

Encyclopedia of Caribbean Literature

Edited by

D. H. FIGUEREDO

Greenwood Press
Westport, Connecticut • London

Library of Congress Cataloging-in-Publication Data

Encyclopedia of Caribbean literature / edited by D.H. Figueredo.
   p. cm.
  Includes bibliographical references and index.
  ISBN 0-313-32742-4 (set : alk. paper) — ISBN 0-313-32743-2 (v. 1: alk. paper) — ISBN 0-313-32744-0 (v. 2 : alk. paper)
  1. Caribbean literature—Encyclopedias.   2. Authors, Caribbean—Biography—Encyclopedias.
I. Figueredo, D.H., 1951– .
  PN849.C3E53   2006
  809'.89729—dc22   2005025483

British Library Cataloguing in Publication Data is available.

This book is included in the *African American Experience*
database from Greenwood Electronic Media. For more
information, visit: www.africanamericanexperience.com.

Library of Congress Catalog Card Number: 2005025483
ISBN: 0-313-32742-4 (set)
    0-313-32743-2 (vol. 1)
    0-313-32744-0 (vol. 2)

First published in 2006

Greenwood Press, 88 Post Road West, Westport, CT 06881
An imprint of Greenwood Publishing Group, Inc.
www.greenwood.com

Printed in the United States of America

The paper used in this book complies with the
Permanent Paper Standard issued by the National
Information Standards Organization (Z39.48-1984).

10 9 8 7 6 5 4 3 2 1

Every reasonable effort has been made to trace the owners of copyrighted materials in this book, but in
some instances this has proven impossible. The editor and publisher will be glad to receive information
leading to more complete acknowledgments in subsequent printings of the book and in the meantime
extend their apologies for any omissions.

Contents

List of Entries

Guide to Related Topics

In addition to biographical entries, the *Encyclopedia* includes entries on numerous special topics. The following list conveniently groups these topical entries in broad categories.

Drama:
Carreta, La

Fiction:
Brown Girl, Brownstones
Cecilia Valdés o La Loma del Àngel; novela de costumbres cubanas
Charca, La
Compère Général Soleil
Farming of Bones, The
Gouverneurs de la rosée
Hills Were Joyful Together, The
House for Mr. Biswas, A
In the Castle of My Skin
New Day
Palace of the Peacock, The
Paradiso
"*Viaje a la semilla*"
Wide Sargasso Sea

Genres *and* Types of Literature:
Abolitionist Literature
Anancy Stories
Anti-Castro Literature
Barrack Yard Literature
Barroco/Baroque
Children's Literature in the English-Speaking Caribbean
Children Literature in the Hispanic Caribbean
Costumbrismo
Detective Fiction
Dub Poetry

Exile Literature
Gay and Lesbian Literature
Historical Novel
Immigrant Literature
Indianist Literature
Literatura Comprometida/Socially Engaged Literature
Magical Realism
Negrista Literature
Noismo
Nuyorican Literature
Peasant Novel, The
Performance Poetry
Plantation Society in Caribbean Literature, The
Slave Narratives
Testimonio
Trujillo Era

Cultural or National Identity:
Ainsi parla l'oncle
Bovaryism
Caliban
Code Switching
Créolité
Indigènisme
Insularismo
Negrista Literature
Négritude

Journals:
Asomante
Beacon, The

Bim
Caribbean Quarterly
Casa de las Américas, journal
Ciclón
Focus
Kyk-Over-Al
Linden Lane Magazine
Lunes de Revolución
Mariel, journal
*Notas y Letras; semanario de
    literatura y bellas artes*
Orígenes
Revista Chicano-Riqueña
Revista de Avance
Revue Indigène, La
*Savacou, Journal of the Caribbean
    Artists Movement*
Sin Nombre
Tropiques

Literary Generations:
Generación del 48
Generación del 45, or the Desperate
    Generation
Generación del 60
Generación del 30
Generation de la Ronde, La
Griots, Les
Independentistas del 40
Mariel Generation

Movements:
Atalayismo
Barroco/Baroque
Boom, The Latin American
Créolité
Diepalismo
Indigènisme
Insularismo
Joven Poesía Dominicana
Modernismo/Modernism
Naturalism/Naturalismo
Négritude
Noismo
Novísimos
Pluralismo, El
Poesía Sorprendida, La
Posnovísima

Postumismo
Realismo/Realism
Romanticismo/Romanticism
Spiralist Movement
Surrealism
Vedrismo

National Literatures:
Anglophone Caribbean Literature,
    History of
Cuban American Literature
Cuban Literature, History of
Dominican American Literature
Dominican Republic Literature,
    History of
Francophone Caribbean Literature,
    History of
Guyanese Literature, History of
Haitian Literature, History of
Haitian Literature in Kreyòl (the Haitian
    Language)
Jamaican Literature, History of
Martinique, History of the Literature of
Nuyorican Literature
Puerto Rican Literature, History of
Trinidadian and Tobagonian Literature,
    History

Organizations and Institutions:
Ateneo Puertorriqueño
Caribbean Artists Movement (CAM)
Caribbean Voices
Casa de las Américas
Conference of the Association for Com-
    monwealth Literature and Language
    Studies (1971)
Messenger Group, The
Poetry League of Jamaica
Seis, Los
Tertulia/Cénacle/Literary Salon/Soirée
Unión de Escritores y Artistas de Cuba
    (UNEAC)

Poetry:
Aguinaldo puertorriqueño
Cahier d'un retour au pays natal
"Dessalinienn, La," The National
    Anthem of Haiti

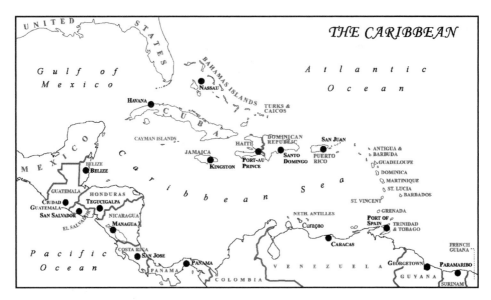

Map by Armando H. Portela.

Macouba, Auguste (1939–)

Macouba is a controversial poet and playwright from Martinique who criticizes France's ruling of the island. His actual name is Auguste Armeth.

Macouba was born in Case-Pilote, Martinique, on August 17, 1939. His family was poor and he attended vocational school in Fort-de-France. At the age of nineteen, he went to France to work in a factory. Two years later, he was drafted into the French army and served in Algeria. Finishing his tour of duty, he returned to Paris. In 1964, he published the poetry collection *La cri antillais*, a criticism of colonialism.

In 1965, he matriculated at the University of Paris, majoring in sociology. In 1968, he wrote the drama *Eïa! Man-maille-là*, which was staged in Paris and then published in 1970. Once again, the theme was colonialism and racism. In 1970, he finished his studies at the university. That same year, he published a book-length essay, *Esquisse d'une sociologie politique de la Martinique*, a study of the departmentalization of Martinique, the process through which the island became a French department—a state. Through the 1970s, he published numerous essays on topics ranging from poetry to political evaluation of the administrations of **Aimé Césaire**, the poet who was the mayor of Fort-au-France for decades and promoter of departmentalization.

Macouba's writings were not always well received in Martinique and in France. His play *Eïa! Man-maille-là*! was eventually published due to the influence of the well-known Haitian poet **René Depestre**.

Further Reading

Corzani, Jack. "West Indian Mythology and Its Literary Illustrations." *Research in African Literatures* 25, no. 2 (Summer 1994): 131.

—*D. H. Figueredo*

Madiou, Thomas (1814–84)

Madiou was Haiti's first historian. His five volumes on the history of his country, according to Patrick Bellegarde-Smith, in *Haiti: The Breached Citadel*

(1990): "argued against white racial supremacy" (56). Madiou was also a public servant who vigorously defended his country's right to govern itself in the manner it chose.

Madiou was born in Port-au-Prince on April 30, 1814, the son of an artillery colonel who was also a pharmacist. When his mother died, Madiou's father married the niece of Haitian President Jean-Pierre Boyer (1776–1850). At the age of six, Madiou was sent to study in France, where he eventually attended the Collège Royal D'Angers. When he was twenty-one, he became an attorney. While in France, he realized not only how little the French knew about his country and about Haiti's revolution but the low opinion they held of the newly established nation. This was a condition that disturbed Madiou and that would influence him later on to write his famous histories of the country.

In 1833, he met the niece of Haitian's liberator Toussaint L'Ouverture (1744–1803). Their recollections about Haiti made him nostalgic, and in 1836 he returned home. When he asked for books on the history of the country, he was told that there were none. Thus, he decided to become the nation's first historian. Appointed secretary to a minister, he had full access to the national archives. In 1843, he started to teach history at the Lycée; a year later, he was appointed the school's director.

In 1847, Madiou published the first volume of his *Histoire d'Haïti*. The next few years, he was appointed to several governmental posts, serving as personal secretary of President Nicholas Fabre Geffrard (1806–79) and then as ambassador to Great Britain, France, and Spain. Upon his return to Haiti in 1866, a fire destroyed Port-au-Prince. Madiou lost his home and, what was more important to him, his manuscripts. While rewriting his history, he was appointed minister of public education. In 1884, he arranged to have his manuscripts published in France. That same year, he suffered a stroke and passed away.

His history, based on interviews with survivors of the revolution, narrates in great detail the revolutionary period in Haiti, highlighting the contribution of the women who fought alongside men. Sometimes dramatic and often romantic, the volumes offer the flow of fiction. Like other historians of the period, Madiou, according to Bellegarde-Smith, was attracted to European culture and was something of an elitist: "therefore [he] favored rapid cultural assimilation to Western norms and advocated class harmony under elite tutelage" (56).

Further Reading

Bellegarde-Smith, Patrick. *Haiti: The Breached Citadel*. Boulder, San Francisco, and London: Westview Press, 1990.

Berrou, Raphaël, and Pradel Pompilus. *Histoire de la littérature haïtienne*. Tome 1. Port-au-Prince: Editions Caraëbes, 1975.

—*D. H. Figueredo*

Magical Realism

There are several versions of how and when this term originated. Consensus would indicate, however, that "magical realism" was first used by German art critic Franz

Roh (1890–1965) as a means of defining the work of German visual artists, in particular their representation of reality, in the decade from 1920 to 1930.

In the 1940s, the term—*lo real maravilloso*, in Spanish—reappeared in association with Latin American and Caribbean literature, most notably in the prologue to **Alejo Carpentier**'s novel of the Haitian Revolution, *El reino de este mundo* (1949). In that prologue he takes European surrealism to task for its artificiality, its "attempting to arouse the marvelous at all costs." Carpentier found "the real marvelous" in Haiti, in the fantastic juxtaposition of cultures, the baroque layering that is the product of Latin America's history. The other Latin American novelist closely associated with the term and the theory is Ecuadorian Demetrio Aguilera Malta (1909–81). Gabriel García Márquez (1927–) has repeatedly attributed the "magical realism" so closely associated with his work to history, specifically, to the history of the region where he was born and of which so much of his literature explores.

In addition to García Márquez, Carpentier, and the lesser-known Demetrio Aguilera Malta, other contemporary Latin American writers considered to fall within the mode of "magical realism" are Guatemalan Miguel Angel Asturias (1899–1974) and Chilean Isabel Allende (1946–). Because of the popularity of the film *Like Water for Chocolate* (1992), North American readers became familiar with the work of Mexican novelist Laura Esquivel (1950–), on whose novel of the same name it is based. *See also* Alexis, Jacques Stephen; Boom, the Latin American.

Further Reading

Zamora, Lois Parkinson, and Wendy B. Faris, eds. *Magical Realism: Theory, History, Community*. Durham: Duke University Press, 1995.

—Pamela María Smorkaloff

Magloire, Clement. See Magloire-Saint-Aude, Clément.

Magloire-Saint-Aude, Clément (1912–71)

Haitian journalist and poet born in Port-au-Prince as Clément Magloire fils. Magloire fils eventually rebelled against his authoritarian father, Clément Magloire, who had founded the daily *Le Matin* in 1907 and was on a first-name basis with the presidents of Haiti. In 1941, the son added his mother's maiden name to his own and became Magloire-Saint-Aude.

As early as 1930, the younger Clément published articles in *Samedi Littéraire*, *Le Matin*, *La Relève*, and **Les Griots**. He was associated with **Carl Brouard**, **Lorimer Denis**, and **François Duvalier**. With them, he signed the "Déclaration"—the famous manifesto of Les Griots—published in the first issue of the journal *Les Griots*, June 23, 1938, but he does not seem to have been active on the political scene and did not assume the *Noiriste*—black power—doctrine that Duvalier made the basis of his regime. **Philippe Thoby-Marcelin** was the first to call Magloire-Saint-Aude a "surrealist." The name stuck, and the Haitian poet was called on to introduce the French surrealist poet and theoretician André Breton (1896–1966) when he visited Haiti in December 1945.

Following two small volumes of poetry, *Dialogue de mes lampes* and *Tabou*, both published in 1941, Magloire-Saint-Aude published only two prose texts, *Parias* (1949), a novel termed a "documentaire," and *Ombres et reflets* (1952) along with a scattering of articles and poems. More to the point than the term *surrealist* is Maximilien Laroche's suggestion that Magloire-Saint-Aude is a "hermetic" poet. Laroche states, in the journal *Présence Francophone* 1975, that the poet's "drama is that he interiorizes the elements of the conflict that characterizes his situation." The poet's failure to publish between 1956 and 1971 might be seen as a kind of "zombification," a state in which he could not give voice to any critical views of President Duvalier, following his election in 1957, with whom he had been so closely associated. Magloire-Saint-Aude lived a rather bohemian and solitary life. Beginning in 1967, Duvalier gave him a monthly stipend and, at the poet's death, he received a state burial at the hands of the younger president Jean-Claude Duvalier (1951).

In a dialogue with his own persona (*Le goût des jeunes filles*), writer **Dany Laferrière** says that Magloire-Saint-Aude remains "the greatest American poet." *See also* Haitian Literature, History of.

Further Reading

Coates, Carrol F. "In the Father's Shadow: Dany Laferrière and Magloire-Saint-Aude." *Journal of Haitian Studies* 8, no. 1 (2002): 40–55.

Magloire-Saint-Aude. *Dialogue de mes lampes et autres textes. Oeuvres complètes.* Édition établie et présentéé par François Leperlier. Paris: Jean-Michel Place, 1998

—*Carrol F. Coates*

Mais, Roger (1905–55)

Jamaican novelist Roger Mais was also an artist, playwright, and political activist who wrote the first Jamaican ghetto novels, *The Hills Were Joyful Together* (1953) and *Brother Man* (1956), and achieved notoriety in 1944 with his essay "Now We Know," where he criticized Winston Churchill's (1874–1965) position that despite the war and Jamaica's participation in the British effort against Hitler's Germany, England would not reward the colony with independence. Sentenced to six months in prison for seditious behavior, his experience behind bars and the prisoners he met there laid the foundation for the writing of *The Hills Were Joyful Together*.

Mais was born on August 11, 1905, in Kingston, Jamaica, the son of a pharmacist and a school teacher. As a child he grew up in the countryside, where his father had taken up farming. Homeschooled, he attended Calabar High School, in Kingston, when he was fourteen years old. But instead of pursuing further schooling after graduation, as expected of a light-skinned black who was a member of the middle class, Mais worked at different jobs, from selling insurance to journalism. Though he wanted to write, it was not until the labor and social unrest of 1938 that he found his calling: writing about the plight of the urban poor. A socialist, Mais supported Norman Manley (1883–1969), the leader of the People's National Party, and wrote for the party's official organ, *Public Opinion*. It was in this journal that he published the anticolonialist essay that led to his imprisonment. Disappointed with the poor reception his novels received, Mais left Jamaica in 1951 and traveled to Paris, where he befriended American novelist Richard Wright (1908–60). In 1955, he returned to Jamaica, where he succumbed to cancer on June 15.

Between 1949 and 1950, Mais wrote at least seven plays and two unpublished novels, *Blood on the Moon* and *Storm Warning*. In 1952, he wrote the novel *Black Lightning*; a year later he wrote *The Hills Were Joyful Together*, followed by *Brother Man* in 1954. The latter two works are **barrack yard** novels, narratives that take place in a tenement yard; the naturalist elements of the novels manifest themselves in the characters: prostitutes and thieves doomed to fail. There are no protagonists in *The Hills Were Joyful Together*; the emphasis is on the community, the residents of the yard. In *Brother Man*, however, there is a hero: a Christlike Rastafarian who is betrayed by the poor people he has helped and is beaten up by a mob. The choice of a Rastafarian as a protagonist was a revolutionary step taken by Mais, for in the 1940s and 1950s, Rastafarians were feared and disliked by Jamaican society. *Black Lightning* is a retelling of the Samson story, wherein the protagonist, a physically strong sculptor, loses his sight and ability to rely on himself; the novel, set in the countryside of Mais's youth, is essentially a character study of an artist in search of his identity.

Literary studies of Mais's works dispute as to which is his best novel. Numerous critics prefer *Black Lightning*, suggesting that the story of the sculptor's struggles can take place anywhere in the world, and thus carrying a universal meaning, while the "yard" novels are too localized, too Jamaican for a wider audience. But other critics conclude that *The Hills Were Joyful Together*, which combines Jamaican dialect and innovative narrative strategies, is the far richer work. Some critics believe that Mais was a flawed author, but poet and scholar **Edward Kamau Brathwaite** points out that Mais was a developing writer who by dying relatively young didn't get the opportunity to perfect his craft. *See also* Barrack Yard Literature; Jamaican Literature, History of.

Further Reading

Brathwaite, Edward. "Introduction." *Brother Man* by Roger Mais. Oxford: Heinemann, 1974.

Hawthorne, Evelyn J. *The Writer in Transition: Roger Mais and the Decolonization of Caribbean Culture*. New York: P. Lang, 1989.

—*D. H. Figueredo*

Maloney, Merton. See Roach, Eric Martin.

Mañach Robato, Jorge (1898–1961)

———————————— ■ ————————————

The author of the best written biography of Cuban poet and martyr **José Martí** and a student of the uses of humor in Cuba, this university professor is representative, along with **Juan Bosch** in the Dominican Republic, **Aimé Cesairé** in Martinique, and **Eric Williams** of Trinidad-Tobago, of the intellectual who is active both in cultural matters and in the political arena. Like many Caribbean writers throughout the centuries, Mañach Robato spent many years of his life in exile.

Mañach was born in Cuba on February 14, 1898, of a Spanish father and a Cuban mother. He spent his childhood in Spain, returned to Cuba, and then in 1915 went to the United States to study at Cambridge High School and at the prestigious Boston Latin School, both in Massachusetts. Graduating from Harvard University in 1921, he went to France to study law at the University of Paris. Back in Cuba in 1922, he earned a doctorate in philosophy and letters and a law degree from the Universidad de la Habana.

In 1923, Mañach joined the Grupo Minorista, a gathering of Cuban intellectuals who were critical of Cuba's political situation and lack of culture. He served as assistant attorney general of the Supreme Court of Havana from 1925 to 1926. In the early 1930s, he joined in a conspiracy to overthrow the dictatorship of Gerardo Machado (1871–1939), who ruled Cuba from 1924 to 1933. In 1934, he was appointed minister of education but resigned to protest political corruption and then left for New York, where he taught at Columbia University. He returned to the island in 1939, and a year later he was elected to the Cuban Senate, where he helped to draft the liberal constitution of 1940. In 1944, he served as minister of state. Eight years later, he found himself fighting against the dictatorship of General Fulgencio Batista (1901–73), who had taken over the government by military force, and, in 1957, went into exile for the second time. He returned to Cuba in 1959 to lend support to **Fidel Castro** and the Cuban Revolution. When he grew disappointed with the revolutionary government, he went into his final exile in 1960. He died in Puerto Rico a year later.

While pursuing these political and civic activities, Mañach worked as a university professor, created an innovative educational program on the radio, which taught Cuban history and culture, and founded and moderated a television show called *Ante la prensa—Meet the Press*. He also wrote scores of articles and numerous books, including *Glosario* (1924), *Estampas de San Cristóbal* (1926), *Pasado vigente* (1939), *Historia y estilo* (1944), and *Teoría de la frontera*, published posthumously (1970). But the two volumes that brought him fame throughout Latin America were *Indagación del choteo* (1928) and *Martí, el apóstol* (1933).

Indagación del choteo is a study of how Cubans use humor, wordplay, and moderate disrespect when confronting social and economic adversities or when dealing with authority figures; he concludes that "choteo," meaning to make fun of everything, is an effective tool used to confront oppressive regimes. This conclusion applies to the use of humor throughout the Caribbean, regardless of language. *Martí, el apóstol*, is a novelized biography of the poet in which Mañach re-creates

Marti's personality, probably the first attempt in Cuba to depict Martí as a man rather than a myth and a symbol. Scholar Nicolás Álvarez, in *La obra literaria de Jorge Mañach*, considers the Cuban author one of the best essayists in Latin America.

Further Reading

Álvarez, Nicolás Emilio. *La obra literaria de Jorge Mañach*. Potomac, MD: J. Porrúa Turanzas, North American Division, 1979.

Rexach, Rosario. *Dos figuras cubanas y una sola actitud: Félix Varela y Morales (Habana, 1788–San Agustín, 1853), Jorge Mañach y Robato (Sagua la Grande, 1898–Puerto Rico, 1961)*. Miami, FL: Ediciones Universal, 1991.

—*D. H. Figueredo*

Manicom, Jacqueline (1938–76)

A feminist, Manicom published only one novel, *Mon examen de blanc* (1972). However, her analysis of racial relations in Martinique, and France's attitude toward the island, has earned her recognition decades after the work was first published.

A native of Guadeloupe, Manicom was a midwife and the founder, with her husband, of a family-planning clinic in Martinique. She promoted the legalization of abortion and advocated equal rights for women. Sensitive to the racial issues on her island, she explored the theme in her novel, *Mon examen de blanc*, published in Paris.

In this novel, Manicom suggested that an indication of success in Martinique was the ability of an individual either to pass as white or to be accepted within a circle of white friends. In the novel, she also criticized the French authorities, who did not want independence for Guadeloupe. Though written with a political message, the novel was essentially a love story. The work, however, was not welcomed initially by many of her compatriots. In 1974, she wrote a study of midwifery as a memoir: *La graine; journal d'une sage-femme*.

Manicom died in a car accident, in either April or May of 1976. The accident and her death remain a mystery. *See also* Feminism in Caribbean Literature; Francophone Caribbean Literature, History of.

Further Reading

Manicom, Jacqueline. *La graine; journal d'une sage-femme*. Paris: Presses de la Cité, 1974.

Paravisini-Gebert, Lizabeth. "Feminism, Race, and Difference in the Works of Mayotte Capécia, Michèle Lacrosil, and Jacqueline Manicom." *Callaloo* 15, no. 1 (1992): 66–74.

—*D. H. Figueredo*

Manley, Edna (1900–87)

The founder—alongside **Philip M. Sherlock, Vic Reid,** and **Roger Mais**—of *Focus,* Jamaica's first literary magazine, Edna Manley was a sculptor, a mentor, and a promoter of Jamaican culture. She was the wife of Norman Manley (1893–1969), a politician and labor leader, and the mother of Michael Manley (1924–97), who was elected prime minister of Jamaica in 1972.

Edna Swithenbank Manley was born in England on January 29, 1900, the daughter of an English minister and a Jamaican mother. At the age of fourteen, she met and fell in love with her cousin Norman Manley. In 1921, the couple was married and relocated to Jamaica. In Jamaica, she supported her husband's political activities and fostered the friendship of artists and writers. She was involved with the editing of the weekly *Public Opinion,* the organ of the People's National Party, which featured a literary supplement. As *Public Opinion* began to fail due to administrative problems, the members of its board, which included Manley and the poet **Una Marson,** decided to publish a literary journal, entitled *Focus.* In the first issue, Manley observed that Jamaica was changing and that the journal would address those changes by expressing an interest in developing a nationalist approach to culture as well as criticizing social conditions on the island; a major preoccupation was that of a national identity and the poems, short stories, and essays published addressed that concern from both a European and an African perspective.

During this period, Manley also funded the work of many young artists. Her activities led to the eventual establishment of the Jamaican School of Art. Many of the writers she knew and helped went on to international acclaim, including **George Campbell, John Hearne,** and **Roger Mais.**

A sculptor, Manley exhibited her works in Jamaica and England. She gained numerous honors, including the Order of Merit (1980) and Jamaica's Woman of Distinction Award (1985). Today, the national school of art is called the Edna Manley School of the Visual Arts.

Further Reading

Breiner, Laurence A. *An Introduction to West Indian Poetry.* Cambridge: Cambridge University Press, 1998.

Manley, Edna. *Edna Manley: The Diaries.* Edited by Rachel Manley. London: A Deutsch, 1989.

—*D. H. Figueredo*

Manzano, Juan Francisco (1797–1853)

Poet and slave Juan Francisco Manzano was born in the city of Matanzas, Cuba, in 1797. He was the child of two slaves of the Cuban Marquise of Santa Ana, who treated the slave boy as if he were her own child. She sent him to catechism school to learn Catholic doctrine and took him to the theater. Unfortunately for Juan Francisco Manzano, the Marquise of Santa Ana died, and all her property, including her slaves, was inherited by the Cuban Marquise of Prado Ameno, who turned out to be as wicked as his previous mistress was benevolent. But Manzano was a domestic slave in a city with a certain cultural life, such as the theater, and he learned to read and write by watching the son of his mistress do his school exercises. By age twenty, Manzano was writing poems in the neoclassic style of the first decade of the nineteenth century.

In the 1830s, Manzano came to the attention of the aristocrat and man of letters **Domingo Del Monte**, who held gatherings of writers and prominent members of the Cuban-born white elites of Matanzas. Domingo Del Monte encouraged Manzano to write his own autobiography, and when it was finished, he gave a copy of the first part of this work to R. R. Madden (1798–1886), a representative of the British government in Matanzas, who translated it into English and published it in London under the title *The Life and Poems of a Cuban Slave*. The Spanish original of Manzano's autobiography was not published until 1937, but the regular attendees to Del Monte's salon were moved by the plight of the Afro-Cuban poet; they collected funds and bought his freedom from the Marquise of Prado Ameno. As a freedman Manzano practiced the trade of pastry baker and continued writing poems, which were published in such newspapers and magazines as *La aurora de Matanzas, El album, El aguinaldo habanero*, and *La moda o recreo de las damas*. In 1848, he and Domingo Del Monte were accused of participating in a conspiracy for a rebellion of slaves and freed blacks known in Cuban history as Conspiración de la Escalera (the Ladder Conspiracy). Del Monte was safely abroad, but Manzano was imprisoned for two years. After this event he was no longer active in Matanzas literary circles. He died in Havana on July 19, 1853.

Juan Francisco Manzano wrote mainly poetry; aside from his celebrated autobiography, he also wrote the play *Zafira*. Most of his poetry was published in newspapers and magazines, but he also published two books of poems, in 1821 and 1831. His poetry is uneven, but what has been preserved is inspired, although framed in the poetic forms prevalent in his times. Some of his poems are personal and emotive, like "Mis treinta años," a poem bewailing his status as a slave, written upon his thirtyeth birthday, and "La Música," inspired by and written for a professional pianist named Celia. Juan Francisco Manzano has been accused of being unauthentic by critics who assume that because he was a descendant of Africans he should have written in an African language and upheld African culture and have said that he was imitative. Those critics should consider that he was born in Cuba, several generations removed from his African ancestors; that the neoclassic literary style was prevalent in the island and the so-called Western World when he began to write poetry; and that the language of Castile was for all practical reasons his native language. Although uneven, his poetry is significant on account of its craftsmanship, his play *Zafira* has more than ordinary merit, and his autobiography is one of the first autobiographies written by a Cuban literary author. *See also* Abolitionist Literature; Equiano, Olaudah; Negrista Literature; Slave Narratives; Tertulia/Cénacle/Literary Salon/Soirée.

Further Reading

Azougarth, Abdeslam. *Juan Francisco Manzano: Esclavo poeta de la isla de Cuba*. Valencia: Episteme, 2000.

Friol, Roberto. *Suite para Juan Francisco Manzano*. Habana: Editorial Arte y Literatura, 1977.

Manzano, Juan Francisco. *Obras*. Habana: Instituto del Libro Cubano, 1972.

—*Rafael E. Tarrago*

Maran, René (1887–1960)

Called a precursor of **Négritude**, a black consciousness movement, and also criticized for espousing assimilation, René Maran was a controversial award-winning novelist, short-story writer, and poet. He was the first black writer to win the prestigious French literary award the Goncourt Prize in 1921.

René Maran was born on November 5 (some sources indicate the 15th) in Fort-de-France, Martinique. His father was a public servant, and in 1890, the family traveled to Gabon, Africa, where his father was offered a colonial post. A few years later, Maran was sent to Paris to study. Upon graduation from the Lycée de Talance in Bordeaux, France, Maran returned to Africa to work as colonial officer. The years in Africa provided him with the information and inspiration for his most famous work, the novel *Batouala* (1921). However, before writing the novel, he had written a book of poetry, *La maison du bonheur* (1909), and a collection of short stories *La vie intérieure* (1912). It was *Batouala*, however, that made him a celebrity.

Described as the first real black novel, *Batouala* takes place in the Congo and depicts the traditional life of Africans, the abuses they suffered at the hands of white colonists, and the oppressive nature of French colonial rule. Though the novel was well received for its literary merits, it provoked an angry reaction with many French readers, who resented Maran's criticisms of the colonial system. As a result, Maran resigned his post and returned to Paris in 1923. In Paris, he befriended several American expatriates, including Langston Hughes (1902–67) and Gwendolyn Bennett (1902–81). He also joined the Universal League for the Defense of the Black Race.

Maran alternated between novels and poetry, writing a total of eight novels and three volumes of poetry. He also contributed short stories and essays to numerous anthologies and periodicals, such as *Le Monde illustre* and *Candide*. If he started his writing career involved in controversy, he ended in the same state: with the publication of the interracial love story *Un Homme pareil aux autres* (1947). The story of a black man who falls in love with a French beauty and who feels validated as a man when she returns his affection provoked the ire of Martinican writer **Frantz Fanon**. In his work, *Peau noire, masques blancs* (1952), Fanon called Maran neurotic for wanting to have sexual relationships with a white woman and for considering such an activity as a superior achievement. Fanon believes that Maran needed to be corrected: "He is a neurotic who needs to be emancipated from his infantile fantasies" (79).

Maran did not write many books after the publication of *Un Homme pareil aux autres*. His fame, however, rests on his colonial novel *Batouala*. This novel has been translated into fifty languages.

Further Reading

Fanon, Frantz. *Black Skin, White Masks.* New York: Grove Press, 1967.

———. *Peau noire, masques blancs.* Paris: Editions Du Seuil, 1952.

Kesteloot, Lilyan. *Les écrivains noirs de langue française: naissance d'une littérature.* Bruxelles: Editions de Sociologie de l'Université Libre de Bruxelles, 1971.

Ojo-Ade, Femi. *René Maran, the Black Frenchman: A Bio-Critical Study.* Washington, DC: Three Continents Press, 1984.

—*D. H. Figueredo*

Marcelin Family

Two brothers, Phillipe and Pierre, and a cousin, Frédéric, who were instrumental in developing a national Haitian literature that rejected foreign models and looked to Haitian history, culture, and traditions for inspiration, the Marcelins were key cultural and political figures in twentieth-century Haiti.

Marcelin, Frédéric (1848–1917). Frédéric was born on January 11, 1848, in Port-au-Prince. Educated in Paris, he became involved in Haitian politics as a youth and was elected to the Haitian parliament when he was in his twenties. He served in political offices on and off throughout his life, and from 1892 to 1894 he was the director of Haiti's Treasury Department.

Rejecting European influences and Haitian writers' tendency to imitate French authors, he advocated for a true representation of Haiti in literature. In 1903, he published *Autour de deux romans*, wherein he proposed the need for a national literature. In 1905, he founded the journal *Haïti Littéraire et Sociale*, which he directed until his death.

His two best-known works are the novels *Thémistocle Épaminondas Labasterre* (1901), a spoof of politicians and political activities in Haiti, and *La vengeance de Mama* (1902), in which he promotes the use of education to change society. These novels draw realistic portrayal of Haiti and present the author's preoccupation with a national identity. His other works include the technical volumes *La politique* (1987) and *Finances d'Haïti* (1911) as well as the autobiographical ventures *Au gré du souvenir* (1913) and *Bric à Brac* (1913). He passed away in Paris in 1917.

Marcelin, Pierre (1908–). Pierre was born on August 6, 1908, in Port-au-Prince, Haiti, where he attended private schools. Pierre grew up surrounded by writers and books. With his brother Phillipe, he became interested in celebrating Haiti's culture, specifically the traditions of the rural poor. The two brothers set out to write several works that belonged to the genre of the **peasant novel**, a genre that attempted to depict the customs, suffering, and hard work of Haitian peasants. In 1944, they published their first novel *Canapé-vert*; the work won the 1943 Farrar and Rhinehard Latin American fiction contest. In 1946, the two brothers published *La Bête du Musseau*, translated into English as *The Beast of the Haitian Hills* (1946). Success accompanied their third novel, *La Crayon de Dieu*, which was published first in English as *The Pencil of God* (1951), with an introduction by the influential American critic Edmund Wilson (1895–1972); the original French version was published in France in 1952. In 1970, they published *Tous les hommes sont fous*, also issued the same year in English as *All Men Are Mad*.

Thoby-Marcelin, Phillipe (1904–75) was born on December 11, 1904, in Port-au-Prince, Haiti, and added his mother's surname to his name. He attended the Petit Seminaire College Saint-Martial in Port-au-Prince, earning a law degree. Starting to write poetry as an adolescent, he associated himself with the leading writers and intellectuals of his country, helping to found the journal *La Revue indigène*, in 1927, and becoming one of the prominent members of the literary movement called **indigènisme**, which promoted nationalism and Haiti's history and culture. During this time, Thoby-Marcelin was writing poetry as a protest against the American intervention of the nation in 1915, encouraging his compatriots to reject American influence and to celebrate Haiti's culture and history. In 1932, he published the book of poems *La négresse adolescente*, followed nearly a decade later by *Dialogue avec la femme endormie* (1941). These poems revealed two favorite themes: the poet's love of his country and a sense of nostalgia and melancholy. In the 1940s, Thoby-Marcelin switched to the writing of fiction, which he viewed as more lucrative. He and his brother Pierre Marcelin cultivated the genre of the **peasant novel**, which honored and celebrated Haiti's rural poor.

Thoby-Marcelin favored the use of standard French rather than Kreyòl. But he also advocated for a return to the original traditions and Haitian folklore. He migrated to the United States in 1949, where he passed away in 1975. *See also* American Occupation of Haiti, Literature of the; Haitian Literature, History of; Haitian Literature in Kreyòl (the Haitian Language).

Further Reading

Dumas, Pierre-Raymond. *Frédéric Marcelin, économiste, ou, Les riches dépouilles d'u ministr des finances: essai*. Port-au-Prince, Haïti: Imprimeur II, 2000.

Fowler, Carolyn. *Philippe Thoby-Marcelin, écrivain haïtien, et Pierre Marcelin, romancier haïtien*. Sherbrooke, Québec, Canada: Naaman; Atlanta, GA: Hakim's Book Store, 1985.

Garret, Naomi. *The Renaissance of Haitian Poetry*. Paris: Présence africaine, 1963.

—*D. H. Figueredo*

Marcelin, Frédéric. See Marcelin Family.

Marcelin, Pierre. See Marcelin Family.

Marchena de Leyba, Amelia Francasci (1850–1941)

The first Dominican woman novelist, Marchena de Leyba was born in Santo Domingo of a father from a Hispanic-Dutch Sephardic background and of a Dominican mother. She was the fourth in a family of nine children. For many years, Marchena de Leyba ran a general store from the back rooms in her house. Throughout her long life she enjoyed the friendships of many Dominican politicians and intellectuals.

Marchena de Leyba wrote for the newspaper *El eco de la opinión* and for the literary supplement of the Monday editions of the prestigious daily *Listín Diario*. It was in this supplement where her first novel, *Madre culpable* (1983), was published in installments. The novel was so popular that it was one of the few books of the period to come out in two editions. She followed this work with *Duelos del corazón* (1901), *Recuerdos e impresiones: historia de una novela* (1901), and *Francisca Mortinoff* (1901), romantic novels set in Cuba and in Spain. In 1925, she wrote the essay *Miriño, íntimo*, where she draws intimate portraits of the leading public figures of the nineteenth and early-twentieth centuries and depicts the political conflicts at the turn of the twentieth century.

Marchena de Leyba has the distinction of being a published Dominican writer at a time when men dominated the field. She passed away in Santo Domingo on February 27, 1941.

Further Reading

Cocco de Filippis, Daisy. *Documents of Dissidence: Selected Writings by Dominican Women*. New York: CUNY Dominican Studies Institute, 2000.

—Daisy Cocco de Filippis

Margenat, Alfredo (1907–87)

Margenat was a Puerto Rican poet known for his involvement with the vanguard movement **Atalayismo**, which advocated experimental but political poetry.

A native of San Juan, where he was raised and where he died, Margenat wrote poems, short stories, and essays that were published in such influential journals as *Alma Latina* and *El Mundo*. Interested in a type of poetry that expressed political statements, especially of a nationalist vein, in the 1920s, he befriended likeminded poets **Clemente Soto Vélez** and **Graciany Miranda Archilla**. In 1928, he cofounded, with Vélez and Miranda Archilla, the vanguard movement called "El Hospital de los Sensitivos." Later on, the movement became known as Atalayismo. The movement's objective was to break from traditional poetic forms and themes and emphasize experimentation. As a member of the Atalaya group, Margenat wore long hair and colorful clothes.

In the 1930s, he continued writing for newspapers while exploring a poetry that manifested his doubts and unhappiness about political change on the island and the potential for independence from the United States. In 1932, he received a literary prize from the **Ateneo Puertorriqueño** for the book of aesthetic essays, *Estar sentado es un placer*. Over the years, he parted company with his earlier companions and did not become as well known as Soto Vélez. Margenat's poems have not been collected into books and his poetry beckons study.

Further Reading

Díaz Rivera, Carmen. "Luego de dos décadas de espera el Instituto de Cultural publica libro del atayalista Clemente Soto Vélez." http://www.radiouniversidad.org (accessed 1/17/05).

Toro-Sugrañes, José A. "Biografías." *Nueva enciclopedia de Puerto Rico.* Hato Rey, Puerto Rico: Editorial Lector, 1994.

—*D. H. Figueredo*

Margenat, Hugo (1933–57)

A Puerto Rican poet who died at a young age, Margenat wrote political poetry representative of the **literatura comprometida**—socially engaged literature—movement. His writings advocated for Puerto Rican independence.

Born and raised in San Juan, Margenat expressed concerns for the political fate of Puerto Rico at a very early age, identifying with the political movements that sought independence from the United States. As a teenager, he began to write poetry, which he published in local publications. Drafted into the U.S. Armed Forces, he matriculated at the Universidad Católica de Ponce upon the conclusion of his tour. At the university he was one of the founders of the political group, Acción Juventud Independentista.

In 1954, he published his first book of poetry, *Lampara apagada*. His second book came out in 1955, *Intemperie*. The two volumes protested against social inequality and rallied the reader to fight against poverty, racism, and discrimination. At the time of his death in 1957, he left numerous poems that were published posthumously as *Mundo abierto* (1958) and *Ventana hacia lo último* (1961). Critics feel that had Margenat reached maturity, he would have emerged as one of the Caribbean's great poets. To honor his memory and work, the Instituto de Cultura Puertorriqueña in 1974 gathered all his poems, published and unpublished, into one volume *Obras completas*.

Further Reading

Medina López, Ramón Felipe. *Hugo Margenat, poeta agónico.* San Juan, Puerto Rico: Ediciones CIBA, 1999.

—*D. H. Figueredo*

Mariel, journal (1983–85)

Literary and political journal founded in 1983 by novelist **Reinaldo Arenas** and a group of friends who, like him, had participated in the Mariel Boatlift. This was an event that occurred in the summer of 1980, when Castro invited Cuban American exiles to sail to the port of El Mariel, in northern Cuba, to pick up relatives who wished to migrate. The invitation resulted in the flight of over 110,000 Cubans. Arenas and a score of young writers were among the refugees.

The journal was conceived to promote the idea of a generation. The emphasis was primarily on publishing works written by writers who had left Cuba through El Mariel. But within a couple of issues, the journal started to publish works written by such older and more established Cuban writers as **Guillermo Cabrera Infante**, who had left the island in the 1960s. Though all the works published were of literary quality, most of the pieces were clearly anti-Castro: these included essays, poems, and short stories.

Mariel, revista de literatura y arte, was the first Cuban publication that presented a negative view of Fidel Castro written by established writers as opposed to the works of the exiles who in the decade of the sixties had edited literary magazines with limited literary merits. Due to the lack of financial support and editorial conflicts, the journal ceased publication in 1985. In 2003, a special anniversary edition was published and edited by Reinaldo García Ramos, one of the original editors. *See also* Anti-Castro Literature; Cuban American Literature; Literary Journals; Mariel Generation.

Further Reading

Arenas, Reinaldo. *Antes que anochezca: autobiografía*. Barcelona: Tusquets, 1992.

Villaverde, Fernando. *Crónicas del Mariel*. Miami, FL: Ediciones Universal, 1992.

—*D. H. Figueredo*

Mariel Generation

This term describes a group of young writers who arrived in the United States through the Freedom Flotilla of 1980. The boatlift originated from the port of El Mariel, where thousands of Cuban American had anchored in rented vessels of all types, from shrimpers to luxury yachts, to pick up relatives and friends. Dozens of young writers, many of whom had been political prisoners, climbed aboard the boats; the most famous was the novelist **Reinaldo Arenas**.

Once they reached the United States, these writers, who had not been allowed to publish in Cuba, began to write short stories and novels, most of which were autobiographical and rendered testimony to the oppression they had experienced on the island. The Mariel writers also penned poems and essays. Typical works include *El jardín del tiempo* (1984), by Carlos Díaz, about a talented young man who is denied the prestigious **Casa de las Américas** award because of his anti-Castro views, and the book of poetry *El fin, la noche* (1984) by Roberto Valero, about the departure from the island and the poet's sudden separation from his family and relatives. These writers founded three publications, *Mariel*, *Término*, and *Unveiling Cuba*; of the three, *Mariel* was the most significant.

As a group, the Mariel writers were influenced by the likes of Jorge Luis Borges (1899–1986), Carlos Fuentes (1928–), and Gabriel García Márquez (1927–), icons of Latin American letters. In their novels and poems, the Mariel writers used experimental techniques, such as a lack of clear chronology, multiple narrators, and linguistic games. The most literary innovator, and the best known, was Reinaldo Arenas.

Consisting mostly of men, the Mariel Generation also included artists and scholars. The generation did not create a literary movement, and their output was within the framework of the creative literature of the time, especially Latin American literature. What united these writers was their experiences in Cuba, their opposition to Fidel Castro, and their desire to leave a literary legacy. *See also* Anti-Castro Literature; Literary Journals; *Mariel*, Journal.

Further Reading

Arenas, Reinaldo. *Antes que anochezca: autobiografía*. Barcelona: Tusquets, 1992.

Bertol, Lillian. *The Literary Imagination of the Mariel Generation*. Miami FL: Endowment for Cuban American Studies, Cuban American Studies, Cuban American National Foundation, 1995.

—D. H. Figueredo

Marín, Francisco Gonzalo "Pachín" (1863–97)

Poet, short-story writer, and journalist, Francisco Gonzalo Marín Shaw, known as "Pachín" Marín, a mulatto, was born in Arecibo, Puerto Rico, the first of seven brothers of a humble family. He attended elementary and secondary schools in his hometown. In high school, he learned Latin, typography, and how to play the violin and the guitar. In 1883, he worked as a bookkeeper for a printer and for the newspaper *El Universo*. He published his first book of poetry, *Flores nacientes*, in 1884; in these poems he revealed romantic influences. From 1885 to 1886 he edited the newspaper *El Publicista*. In 1887, he participated in the Autonomy Assembly convened by Puerto Rican patriot Roman Baldorioty de Castro (1822–89), in Ponce, and upon his return to Arecibo, Pachín Marín founded the newspaper *El Postillón*, which served as a podium to combat colonialism.

Persecuted by rural colonial guards, he fled on a steam liner to the coastal town of Mayagüez, and from there to Santo Domingo, Dominican Republic. In that country, he taught at a school in the town of Azua and became director of a school in Santiago de los Caballeros, but his opposition to the dictatorship of the Dominican ruler Ulíses Heureaux (1845–99) resulted in his arrest and deportation to Curaçao. While in the Dominican Republic, he wrote the patriotic drama *27 de Febrero*.

In 1889, Pachín Marín established himself in Venezuela but was soon expelled from that country by dictator Andueza Palacio (1846–1900). He sailed to Martinique and then returned to Puerto Rico in 1890, publishing again his newspaper

El Postillón. In his editorials he demanded the end of colonial rule, rallied all Puerto Ricans to battle, and asked for the Spaniards to leave the island. Pachín Marín was censured and insulted, and finally his newspaper was shut down by the authorities. He fled to New York City.

In New York City, he was one of the first writers from the Caribbean to fight against racism in the United States. Ten days after his arrival, in September in 1891, he wrote in a letter: "Though this is my country, for mysteries I can't explain, my race is solely despised." In the same letter, he also declared: "I'm still unemployed. Finding employment is not easy, yet is not perceived so in this country. There are infinite numbers of people unemployed. Winter is nearing and with its arrival snow will fall on the streets and cold will reign in the homes and death will await those who can't afford a miserable coat."

In New York City, Pachín Marín attended meetings of Cuban pro-independence groups and befriended **José Martí**. Pachín Marín immediately understood Martí's new approaches to the revolutionary war and embraced his cause, participating in patriotic activities with Puerto Ricans and Cubans, émigrés and patriots. Martí wrote an article in the newspaper *Patria*, on July 2, 1892, about Pachín Marín's musical sensibilities and talent as a singer. On November 4, 1893, Martí wrote about Pachín Marín's political activities—by this time the Puerto Rican youth was serving as secretary of the patriotic organization Club Borinquen—and about his poetry. Martí said: "[Pachín Marín] spoke with sincerity of a house where there is only discrimination against bigotry, intrigue, and hatred, and then recited his verses, of a mysterious vein with sparks of marshal poetry." Pachín Marín participated in numerous cultural activities sponsored by Cubans and Puerto Ricans.

From 1891 to 1892, he published a new edition of his newspaper *El Postillón* and in the publication *La Gaceta del Pueblo* wrote a chronicle of New York City, entitled "Nueva York from its depth; a face of Bohemian life," which was one of the first Puerto Rican texts on immigration. In the article, he depicted a tragi-comic vision of those on the margin of society, their hopelessness, and the inhospitable future awaiting Puerto Rican immigrants. These were themes that would appear in the twentieth century in the works of such major Puerto Rican authors as **Pedro Juan Soto** and **José Luis González**. During 1892, Pachín Marín wrote numerous poems and published a collection titled *Romances*.

In 1893, he relocated to Haiti, where he continued his revolutionary activities, founding with other compatriots living in Haiti a patriotic organization. He established a hotel, but when the building burned down, financial difficulties forced his return to New York City in 1896. When he learned that a brother, Wenceslao, perished fighting in the Cuban jungles, he enlisted with the insurgents and arrived in Cuba on March 24, 1896, with an expeditionary force led by Cuban general Calixto García (1839–98). His courage and skills as a soldier earned him recognition, and he was promoted to sergeant and then lieutenant. Overcome with malaria, he was sent to the province of Camagüey to recover. Pursued by Spanish soldiers, Pachín Marín and the other Cuban soldiers hid in a swamp. Pachín Marín told his comrades to leave him in the swamp without food and water. When the Cuban soldiers were able to return a few days later, they found him dead on a hammock, holding on to his rifle.

Pachín Marín's literary works reflect his adventures. His poetry, evocative of his vitality and filled with the passion characteristic of his political endeavors, address his love affairs, express his separatist ideals, his quest for liberty, and his opposition to colonialism in Cuba and Puerto Rico. Poems, such as "En el álbum de una desconocida," were gallant and patriotic. His political rebelliousness, expressed with great sincerity, caused him persecution. His last book of poems, *En la arena* (1898), was written while fighting in the Cuban jungles; it was published posthumously.

Further Reading

Acevedo, Ramón Luis. *Pachín Marín: poeta en libertad. Cuadernos de Cultura*, no. 4, (2001): 46.

Babín, María Teresa. "Vida y poesía de Pachín Marín." In *Antología de Pachín Marín*. San Juan: Ateneo Puertorriqueño, 1958.

Ojeda Reyes, Félix. "Todas las estrella del universo. Francisco Gonzalo Marín Shaw." In *Peregrinos de la libertad*. Río Piedras, Puerto Rico: Editorial de la Universidad de Puerto Rico, 1992.

—*Emilio Jorge Rodríguez*

Marlow, Max. See Nicholson, Christopher R.

Marqués, René (1919–79)

■

One of Latin America's greatest dramatists and gifted short-story writer, the Puerto Rican René Marqués is the author of a seminal drama about the woes and pain of Latino immigration. His play *La Carreta* was the first Latino drama to chronicle the uprooting of a rural family from its ancestral lands in the mountains of Puerto Rico and its pilgrimage, first to the slums of San Juan, and then to New York City, where disillusionment and the loss of family members send the survivors back to the island.

Marqués René was born on October 4, 1919, in Arecibo, Puerto Rico, into a family of agrarian background. He studied agronomy at the College of Agriculture in Mayagüez and actually worked for two years for the Department of Agriculture. But his interest in literature took him to Spain in 1946 to study the classics. Upon his return, Marqués founded a little theater group dedicated to producing and furthering the creation of Puerto Rican theater. In 1948, he received a Rockefeller Foundation fellowship to study playwriting in the United States, which allowed him to study at Columbia University and at the Piscator Dramatic Workshop in New York City. After his return to San Juan, he founded the Teatro Experimental del Ateneo—the Atheneum Society Experimental Theater. From that time on, Marqués maintained a heavy involvement not only in playwriting but also in the development of Puerto Rican theater. He also produced a continuous flow of short stories, novels, essays, and anthologies. He passed away on March 22, 1979.

While Marqués's best-known work is *La Carreta*, which debuted in 1953, was published in 1961, and translated as *The Oxcart* in 1969, he had been writing since 1944, when he published his first collection of poems, *Peregrinación*. His published plays include *El hombre y sus sueños* (1948), *Palm Sunday* (1949), *Otro día nuestro* (1955), *Juan Bobo y la Dama de Occidente* (1956), *El sol y los MacDonald* (1957), and a collection, *Teatro* (1959), which includes three of his most important plays: *Los soles truncos, Un niño azul para esa sombra*, and *La muerte no entrará en palacio*.

There are many other published plays, novels, collections of short stories, and essays. Marqués is one of the few Puerto Rican writers who has had international audiences and impact. The style, philosophy, and craft of his works, as produced in New York, have had long-lasting influence on the development of Latino theater in the United States. *See also* Acosta, Iván; Nuyorican Literature; Puerto Rican Literature, History of.

Further Reading

Caballero Wangüemert, María M. *La narrativa de René Marqués*. Santurce: Editorial Playor, 1986.

Reynolds, Bonnie Hildebrand. *Space, time, and crisis: the theater of René Marqués*. York, SC: Spanish Literature Pub. Co., 1988.

—Nicolás Kanellos

Marrero Aristy, Ramón (1913–59)

A journalist, novelist, and historian, this Dominican author is famous in Latin America for the novel *Over* (1939), about the American presence in the sugar industry in the Dominican Republic and for his death at the hands of Trujillo henchmen.

Born in San Rafael del Yuma, Dominican Republic, on June 14, 1913, Marrero Aristy moved with his family to the town of La Romana when he was a young child. In La Romana, he attended primary school but also worked at a general store that serviced the workers of a nearby sugarmill; his experiences there would server later on as background for the novel *Over*.

When he was twenty-two years old, Marrero Aristy relocated to Santo Domingo, where he was able to complete his high school education. He matriculated at the university, interested in studying journalism, but due to financial restraints had to withdraw. Nevertheless, his gift as a writer enabled him to work as a journalist for several newspapers, including *La Nación, El Caribe*, and *Listín Diario*. In 1938, he published a collection of short stories that belonged to the **costumbrismo** genre, that is, stories of local color, and in 1939, he published his famous novel. The novel criticized American and European business enterprises in the Dominican Republic.

It is believed that politically Marrero Aristy espoused socialist ideals and identified with workers. However, the need to make a living forced him to accept a government position from Rafael Leónidas Trujillo and even became friendly with the ruler. Marrero Aristy held several posts for the next two decades, including labor secretary and foreign representative in the United States and Europe. While abroad, he led the life of a bon vivant and was known for frequenting night clubs.

In the 1940s, Marrero Aristy published several books of essays, including *En la ruta de los libertadores* (1943), about Dominican patriots, and *Trujillo, síntesis de su vida y obra* (1949), a complementary biography. In the late 1950s, Marrero Aristy accepted an assignment from Trujillo: an official history of the Dominican Republic, to be titled *La República Dominicana: origin y destino del pueblo cristiano más antiguo de América*. Out of the three planned volumes, Marrero Aristy wrote two. He did not finish the third because in 1959 he accused Trujillo, in a *New York Times* article, of being a corrupt leader. The article was published on July 12. Five days later, Marrero Aristy was shot to death, his body was placed inside a car, and the car was pushed off a cliff.

Upon his death, Marrero Aristy left an unfinished novel, *El camión rojo*. Today, a street in Santo Domingo carries his name. His son Rafael is a well-known artist in Latin America. *See also* Trujillo Era.

Further Reading

Alcántara Almánzar, José. "Ramón Marrero Oristy: *Over.*" In *Narrativa y sociedad Hispanoamérica*, 55–57. Santo Domingo, República Dominicana: Instituto Tecnológico de Santo Domingo, 1984.

Crassweller, Robert D. *Trujillo: The Life and Times of a Caribbean Dictator*. New York: Macmillan 1966. pp. 398–400.

—*D. H. Figueredo*

Marryshow, Theophilus Albert (1887–1958)

A pioneer journalist and poet from Grenada, Marryshow was active in politics and in the promotion of the West Indian Federation.

With limited primary education—he did not go to school beyond the fourth grade—Marryshow planned to become a carpenter. However, in 1903, he found a job as office boy at the newspaper the *Grenada Federalist*, where he demonstrated a talent for writing. He began to write articles for the newspaper, and by the time he was in early twentyies he was appointed editor of a competing publication, the *Grenada Chronicle*.

In 1915, he set up his own journal, the *West Indian*, where he published his early poetry under his name and under the pen name Max T. Golden. Becoming interested in politics, in 1918, he helped to set up the Representative Government Association, and in 1925 he was elected to the Legislative Council. He wrote a series of articles commenting on the island's social ills and advocating for political change. These articles were published posthumously as *Cycles of Civilization* (1973). In 1958, he was elected to the West Indies Senate.

His poetry has yet to be collected. In Grenada, he is remembered for his work as an editor and the social commentaries he published in the press.

Further Reading

Sheppard, Jill. *Marryshow of Grenada: An Introduction*. Barbados, West Indies: Letchworth Press, 1987.

—*D. H. Figueredo*

Marshall, Paule (1929–)

Though born in the United States, and often described as an African American writer, Paule Marshall has written predominantly about the Caribbean and the lives of West Indian immigrants in the United States. Her most famous novel, **Brown Girl, Brownstones** (1959), is an autobiographical narrative about a talented young girl encountering discrimination at several levels: as a woman, a black person, and a Caribbean native.

Marshall was born on April 9, 1929, in Brooklyn, New York, as Valenza Pauline Burke, the daughter of Barbadian parents. As a child she was captivated by the accents and sounds of the West Indian women she heard in the neighborhood; from the way these women spoke she would later on develop her sense of narrative and the liveliness of her dialogues.

After graduating from Brooklyn College in 1953, she was hired as staff writer by the magazine *Our World*. In 1957, she married Kenneth Marshall. In 1959, she published *Brown Girl, Brownstones*. Though the novel was soon out of print and went unnoticed for a few years, it was reprinted in 1971 and since then, it has never been out of print. The memorable portrayal of a strong mother determined to be successful in the United States, the idealistic father drawn to a romantic Barbados that was more an exercise in nostalgia rather than reality, and the emotional tension experienced by a girl torn between her mother and her father have made the novel a favorite in college campuses.

In 1962, Marshall received the Rosenthal Award from the National Institute of Arts and Letters for her collection of short stories, *Soul Clap Hands and Sing*, which depicts the lives of four women from Barbados, Brooklyn, Guyana, and Brazil. In 1969, she wrote *The Chosen Place, the Timeless People*, an exploration of race and class in the fictional island of Bourne—a stand-in for Barbados—as seen through the eyes of a Caribbean woman and an American anthropologist visiting the island.

For the next two decades, Marshall experienced changes in her life—divorce and a second marriage—and was a visiting professor at numerous universities, including Yale, Columbia, and the University of California–Berkeley. In the early

1980s, she returned to writing, publishing *Praise Song for the Widow* in 1983. The novel revealed a preoccupation with identity and ethnicity as it tells the story of a middle-aged widow returning to her African and Caribbean roots. Marshall followed this work with several others: *Reena and Other Stories* (1983), *Daughters* (1991), and *The Fisher King* (2000).

Though Marshall's realistic prose widens her readership, it hinders academic analysis as some critics find her style somewhat commercialized. Some writers and scholars from the Caribbean consider Marshall ambivalent about her own heritage, observing that on one hand she emphasizes her American birth, seldom mentioning her Barbadian ancestry, and on the other she writes about heroines in search of Caribbean roots. It might be that Marshall is challenging a "monolithic view of black culture," as Heidi Slettedahl Macpherson suggests in "Perceptions of Place" in the volume *Caribbean Women Writers* (1999), moving "beyond the depiction of one's character identity to the exploration of cultural identity and cultural conflicts" (91). *See also* Feminism in Caribbean Literature; Mother-Daughter Relationships.

Further Reading

DeLamotte, Eugenia C. *Places of Silence, Journeys of Freedom: The Fiction of Paule Marshall*. Philadelphia: University of Pennsylvania Press, 1998.

Denniston, Dorothy Hamer. *The Fiction of Paule Marshall: Reconstructions of History, Culture, and Gender*. Knoxville: University of Tennessee Press, 1995.

Macpherson, Heidi Slettedahl. "Perceptions of Place: Geopolitical and Cultural Positioning in Paule Marshall's Novels." In *Caribbean Women Writers: Fiction in English*. New York: St. Martin's Press, 1999.

—*Angela Conrad and D. H. Figueredo*

Marson, Una (1905–65)

Called "Britain's first feminist" and Jamaica's first major woman poet, Marson promoted West Indies culture, was a literary mentor, and the creator and first editor of **Caribbean Voices**, the legendary BBC radio program that introduced to the world the talent of dozens of writers from the Anglophone Caribbean. She was also a prototype of the English-speaking Caribbean writer who, frustrated with limited opportunities at home, sought self-exile in England.

Marson was born in Sharon Village, Jamaica, on February 6, 1905, the daughter of a prominent preacher—Reverend Solomon Isaac Marson—who decades after his death was still remembered by parishioners all over Jamaica. Though she did not exceed at her studies in school, at home she was introduced to European literature, classical music, and art, and displayed an early talent for writing. In the 1920s, she moved to Kingston, where she was the first woman editor and publisher of the feminist journal, *The Cosmopolitan*, was involved in the **Jamaica Poetry League**, and penned essays advocating equality for Jamaican women. She also wrote the play *At What Price Glory* (1931), about a love affair between a stenographer and her boss. The play offered a twist for the era: after being impregnated by her lover, the heroine decides to rely on herself for financial and spiritual support rather than on her lover. The drama was staged in Kingston in 1932.

Hungering for a wider cultural horizon, Marson traveled to London in 1932. In England she worked for exiled Ethiopian emperor Haile Selassie (1892–1975) and befriended such intellectuals and writers as Paul Robeson (1898–1976), George Orwell (1903–50) and T. S. Eliot (1888–65). Through her contacts, she became a BBC broadcaster in 1940, writing for and coordinating a radio program entitled *Calling the West Indies*, which was meant to boost the morale of Caribbean men in the British armed forces. This program was the seed for the legendary *Caribbean Voices*, which Marson suggested as a way to promote the region's culture and literary talent. The BBC appointed her the first editor-producer of the show. While working for the BBC, Marson gave a series of conferences on Jamaican culture, was secretary of the League of Coloured Peoples, and wrote dozens of poems that were eventually published in 1945 under the title *Towards the Stars*. The poems addressed the discrimination and racial isolation she had experienced in London, a theme that would be explored a decade later by a generation of younger writers, including **George Lamming** and **Samuel Selvon**.

Suffering from mental fatigue, Marson returned to Jamaica in 1946. In 1949, she was a cofounder of the publishing house the Pioneer Press, which specialized in children's and young-adult literature. After participating in local politics and promoting social and economic equality for Jamaicans, Marson traveled to the United States, where she was briefly married to a successful dentist. In the early 1960s, she represented Jamaica at an international conference on women's integration into economics and politics in Israel and spent a few months in that nation, helping to train women advance in professional and political circles. Returning to Jamaica, she passed away on May 6, 1965.

Langston Hughes (1902–67) included some of her poetry in his volume *Poetry of the Negro, 1746–1949* (1949) as did Arthur J. Seymour in the anthology *Kyk-Over-Al* (1951). In 1986, Marson was included in the *Penguin Book of Caribbean Poetry*. Ten years later she was again anthologized in *The Routledge Reader in Caribbean Literature*. In the 1970s, radical critics dismissed her work as derivative and too conservative, failing to notice that Marson was intensely nationalistic and critical of colonialism at a time when most Jamaicans viewed themselves as faithful British subjects. With most of her work still unpublished, Marson awaits further critical evaluation and study. *See also* Collymore, Frank; Exile Literature; Jamaican Literature, History of.

Further Reading

Donnell, Alison, and Sarah Lawson, Welsh. *The Routledge Reader in Caribbean Literature* London: Routledge, 1996.

Jarrett-Macauley, Delia. *The Life of Una Marson: 1905 to 65*. Manchester: Manchester University Press, 1998.

—*D. H. Figueredo*

Martí, José (1853–95)

∎

Symbol of the Cuban nation, independence leader, and a founder of Latin American **modernismo**, José Martí managed to fit all of this into a relatively short life of fourty-two years. His life was an intense drama, and his writings reflect the multiple causes to which he was dedicated, most significantly the struggle for Cuban independence from Spain. Martí's body of writing is as diverse as his life and fills many volumes, including hundreds of journalistic articles, poems, plays, children's stories, literary critiques, social commentaries and political treatises.

Born in Havana, he started writing at an early age, publishing several anti-Spanish political articles and letters in 1869 that led to his imprisonment and a sentence of hard labor. Two years later, Martí was exiled to Spain, where he earned two academic degrees, one in law and the other in philosophy, while at the same time continuing his advocacy for Cuban independence with the publication of the essay *El presidio político en Cuba*. In 1875, Martí moved to Mexico, where he began a fledgling career in journalism with a poem dedicated to the memory of his late sister. During a two-year stay in Mexico he translated Victor Hugo's (1802–85) work *Mes Fils* (1874) from French into Spanish, wrote the play *Amor con amor se paga*, and met his future wife, Carmen Zayas Bazán (1853–1928). With the end of the first Cuban war of independence—the Ten Years' War (of 1868–1878)—Martí returned to his beloved island, where his political activism once again led to a clash with Spanish authorities and a second forced exile.

After a brief stay in Europe, Martí moved to New York City in 1880, where he lived for most of the remainder of his life. It was in New York that Martí distinguished himself as a journalist for Latin American newspapers. In hundreds of articles, Martí sought to interpret life in the United States for Latin American audiences. He covered dozens of newsworthy events, including the opening of the Brooklyn Bridge, the installation of the Statue of Liberty, the career of bank robber Jesse James (1847–82) and the presidency of Ulysses S. Grant (1822–85). He sought to capture the struggles within U.S. society and wrote frequently about the discrimination suffered by African Americans, Native Americans, and Chinese immigrants. By shedding light on American society and culture, Martí sought to define a unique political and cultural space for Latin America, which he called *Nuestra América* (1891), in a series of essays on the subject. In these writings, he cautioned Latin America against succumbing to the economic, cultural, and political influence of the United States. On the literary side, Martí wrote extensively about United States authors such as Walt Whitman (1819–92), Ralph Waldo Emerson (1803–82) and Henry Wadsworth Longfellow (1807–82) and helped introduce their work in Latin America.

It was during his New York exile that he wrote his most famous literary work, *Versos Sencillos* (1891), a collection of forty-six poems, none of which he gave titles, identified simply by roman numerals. Many of his most famous poems are included in this work including "La niña de Guatemala (IX)", "**La rosa blanca** (XXXIX)," and the opening poem (I), frequently used in the lyrics of the popular Cuban folk song *Guantanamera*. The beginning words to the poem and the song are as follows:

> Yo soy un hombre sincero
> De donde crece la palma,

Y antes de morirme quiero
Echar mis versos del alma.

(I am an honest man / From where the palms grow; / Before I die I want my soul / To shed its poetry.)

Throughout *Versos Sencillos*, Martí used powerful images found in nature to write about injustice, friendship, liberation, and romance. Interspersed in the poems are references to the struggle for Cuban independence and the fight of men and women in general for freedom from oppression. Some of the most powerful poems deal with slavery, such as poem number XXX, an excerpt of which reads as follows:

Rojo, como en el desierto
Salió el sol al horizonte:
Y alumbró a un esclavo muerto,
Colgado a un seibo del monte.

Un niño lo vio: tembló
De pasión por los que gimen:
Y, al pie del muerto, juró
Lavar con su vida el crimen!

(Red as a desert sun / The sun rose at the horizon / And shone upon a dead slave hanged / From a mountain ceiba.

A small boy witnessed it / And trembled for the groaning men; / At the victim's feet he vowed to cleanse / That crime with his life.)

Martí's mixture of poetry and politics is viewed as controversial by some who believe that one detracts from the other. As a result, his influence as a modernist poet is sometimes a subject of debate. A decade earlier, Martí penned *Ismaelillo* (1882), an affectionate collection of poems dedicated to his son, whom he rarely saw because of an estranged marriage and years in political exile. After his death, two additional books of poetry were published: *Versos libres* (1913) and *Flores del destierro* (1933).

Martí dedicated the last years of his life, almost completely, to the cause of Cuban independence, organizing the military and political campaign against the Spanish. In 1892, he founded the Partido Revolucionario Cubano. On April 11, 1895, two months after the start of the independence war, Martí arrived in Cuba as part of a rebel force. He died in battle on May 19, ambushed by Spanish snipers. *See also* Children's Literature in the Hispanic Caribbean; Cuban Literature, History of; Marín, Francisco Gonzalo "Pachín."

Further Reading

Foner, Philip S., ed. *José Martí, Major Poems: A Bilingual Edition*. Translated by Elinor Randall. New York: Holmes & Meier Publishers, 1982.

Fountain, Anne. *José Martí and U.S. Writers*. Gainesville: University Press of Florida, 2003.

Rodríguez-Luis, Julio, ed. *Re-Reading José Martí (1853–1895): One Hundred Years Later*. Albany, State University of New York Press, 1999.

—*Frank Argote-Freyre*

Martin, Egbert "Leo" (1862–90)

The first Guyanese poet, Martin achieved notoriety in England with his addition of two stanzas to "God Save the Queen," written in 1887. His poems, romantic in vein, celebrated and glorified the natural beauty of Guyana.

A self-taught writer, Martin was a product of his time: He read and studied British literature, was influenced by the romantic poet William Wordsworth, and sought the approval of the white colonists. In 1883, he published a book of poetry, *Leo's Poetical Works*, which he dedicated to the governor of British Guiana. In 1887 he participated in a contest to write additional lines to the British national anthem. His entry won the contest and his verses were printed in England:

> And, like a bird at rest
> In her own ample nest,
> Let Britain close
> Far-reaching wings and strong
> O'er her colonial throng
> Guard, keep and shield them long
> From all their foes
>
> While o'er the Empire's bound
> The Sun shall skirt his round,
> Shining serene
> On one broad amity
> Holding from sea to sea
> Free rule and subjects free:
> God Save the Queen.

Martin used Victorian language and imagery to describe Guyana's landscape. Though it could be said that he was writing for European readers, nevertheless, his poems reveal a love of Guyana and Guyanese: "Bold front whose eyes give way to none / Clean, honest hands tho' hard and black / . . . to him all praise." Very little is known of this poet, and there seems to be only one copy available of his book, housed at the New York Public Library. *See also* Anglophone Caribbean Literature, History of; Romanticismo/Romanticism; Williams, Francis.

Further Reading

Breiner, Laurence A. *An Introduction to West Indian Poetry*. Cambridge: Cambridge University Press, 1998.

Martin, Egbert. "National Anthem." In *The Penguin Book of Caribbean Verse in English*, edited by Paula Burnett. London: Penguin Books, 1986.

—*D. H. Figueredo*

Martínez Álvarez, Rafael (1882–1959)

A respected and brilliant Puerto Rican jurist, Martínez Álvarez was also a poet, playwright, and novelist. In his writings, he displayed something of a contradictory nature: his novels were pessimistic whereas his plays tended to be humorous and celebratory of Puerto Rico and Puerto Ricans. He was the author of legal texts as well.

Born in San Juan on June 13, 1882, Martínez Álvarez studied law at the Albany Law School of New York. He spent the first ten years of his professional life earning recognition as an attorney: he was a member of the Civil Service Commission, a federal judge, and dean of the Law School at the Universidad de Puerto Rico. Literature, however, beckoned him, and he soon cultivated all the genres: poetry, fiction, and drama.

His first book of poem, *Del verdín de mis jardines*, was published in 1914; these poems were influenced by the **modernismo** movement. In 1919, he published a verse drama, *Tabaré*, and in 1921 and 1922, he wrote several legal texts, including *Texto de derecho internacional privado* and *Prontuario de código civil*.

In the 1920s, he was attracted by **naturalismo**, where the protagonists belong to the lower socioeconomic levels of society and are the victims of circumstances beyond their control. His naturalist novels were *Don Cati* (1923), *El loco del Condado* (1925), *Madre, ahí tienes a tu hijo* (1927), and *Pancho Ibero* (1935). The novels were set in an urban setting and addressed such social ills as adultery, political corruption, inadequate public education, and sexual deviance. To escape this gloomy world, Martínez Álvarez often depicted the countryside as the place for salvation.

For his drama, Martínez Álvarez cultivated **realismo** and **costumbrismo**, scenes of local color. His play *La convulsive* (1917) is a political drama, whereas *la madreselva enflorecia* (1926) takes place in the countryside. He also wrote a comedy, *Don Cati y Doña Doro* (1925).

Further Reading

Rivera de Álvarez, Josefina. *Diccionario de literatura puertorriqueña*. Tomo I San Juan: Instituto de Cultura Puertorriqueña, 1970.

—*D. H. Figueredo*

Martínez Capo, Juan (1923–95)

This Puerto Rican poet and literary critic was best known for his articles on culture published in popular newspapers. Through his columns on literature and Puerto Rican writers, Martínez Capo introduced the general population to the world of letters.

A native of Aibonito, Puerto Rico, in the 1940s he attended the Universidad de Puerto Rico, majoring in humanities and business. He took graduate courses at Columbia University, New York. In that city, he worked as a journalist for the popular daily *La Prensa*. Returning to San Juan, he worked in the equally popular and influential *El Mundo* as a writer and editor. In the 1950s, his poetry appeared in the journals *Asomante* and *Orbe*, and in 1954, he published his first poetry collection, *Fénix*. In 1961, his second volume, *Viaie*, was published. His poetry borrowed from several movements, from **romanticismo** to **modernismo**, expressing both the highly personal and the philosophical.

In the 1960s, his columns "La escena literaria" and "Libros de Puerto Rico," published in *El Mundo* and *Puerto Rico Ilustrado*, served as major vehicles for news, information, and commentary on Puerto Rico's literature. He was praised for writing accessible articles filled with historical, philosophical, and social commentary. Through his columns, the average reader learned about new authors on the island.

Martínez Capo was the editorial director of the Universidad de Puerto Rico press from 1986 to 1988.

Further Reading

Rodríguez Correa, Awilda. *Juan Martínez Capó, crítica literaria: índice bibliográfico*. San Juan, Puerto Rico: Instituto de Cultura Puertorriqueña, 1997.

Toro-Sugrañes, José A. "Biografía." In *Nueva enciclopedia de Puerto Rico*, 134–35. Hato Rey, Puerto Rico: Editorial Lector, 1994.

—*D. H. Figueredo*

Martínez-Fernández, Luis (1960–)

Historian and essayist Luis Martínez-Fernández was born in the turbulent context of 1960 Havana. Two years later his family sought exile; and he grew up in Lima, Peru, and San Juan, Puerto Rico. In his early twenties, while being trained as a professional historian at the Universidad de Puerto Rico, he cultivated the essay genre and contributed frequently with incisive columns for *El Reportero* and *El Mundo*. In recent years, Martínez-Fernández has returned to the essay as a vehicle for self-reflection and social and political commentary in the poignant tradition of Cuban political satirists. His essays have appeared in *Hopscotch*, *Diálogo*, *El Nuevo Día*, and *Academe*, among other venues.

As a historian, Martínez-Fernández has challenged both traditional and contemporary ways of writing history by purposely remaining independent from the dominant historical trends of American academia by holding on to an unmuffled Cuban voice and by navigating the intersections between history and storytelling. One of his most salient contributions to Latin American and Caribbean historiography is his pioneering regional and comparative approach to the history of the Hispanic Caribbean. His books *Torn between Empires* (1994) and *Protestantism and Political Conflict in the Nineteenth-Century Hispanic Caribbean* (2002) have served as models of comparative history. Upon publication of his *Fighting Slavery in the Caribbean* (1998), writer and critic **Antonio Benítez Rojo** commented: "Luis Martínez-Fernández has the rare virtue of reconciling both the analytical incisiveness of a mature historian and the sweeping breadth of an impassioned storyteller."

Martínez-Fernández also edited the award-winning two-volume *Encyclopedia of Cuba* (2003). Currently he serves as director of the Latin American, Caribbean, and Latino Studies program of the University of Central Florida in Orlando. He is at work on an essayed history of Cuba.

Further Reading

Adams, Michele. "The Cuban Stories of Luis Martínez-Fernández." *The Hispanic Outlook I Higher Education* (October 1998): 14–15.

Martínez-Fernández, Luis. *Contemporary Authors Online*. Thomson, Gale, 2005. http://www.galenet.galegroup.com (accessed 6/20/05).

—Frank Argote-Freyre

Martínez Tolentino, Jaime (1943–)

—

A Puerto Rican author who cultivates the genre of the supernatural, Martínez Tolentino has received recognition as a short-story writer and expert on the structure of the ghost-story narrative.

Born in Salinas, Puerto Rico on January 10, 1943, Martínez Tolentino was attracted to literature and the French language. In the mid 1960s, he studied at New York University, where he earned a BA and an MA in French literature. After conducting further studies on the French language at the Sorbonne, he relocated to Spain, obtaining a PhD in literature and philosophy.

Influenced by the writings of Honoré De Balzac (1799–1850), the supernatural tales of Edgar Allan Poe (1809–49), and the psychological perspective of Henry James (1843–1916), Martínez Tolentino began to write ghost stories and narratives with fantastical and unexplained events. In 1970, his short story "La Tormenta," about a drowned sailor terrifying a group of people who had sought shelter from a storm in a beach house, received a literary prize from the Encuentro Europeo de Universitarios, in Lisbon. Subsequently, he published numerous stories in literary reviews.

In 1983, he gathered several of his short stories into the volume *Cuentos Fantásticos*. In the introduction to the volume he wrote, "What man knows about the world is limited: only the tangible. But of the beyond . . . of dreams and nightmares . . . of the transit between life and death . . . of insanity . . . of that which takes us away from this world . . . of that we know little" (1–2).

Martínez Tolentino teaches French at the Universidad de Puerto Rico. He has written for the stage, *La imagen del otro: drama en tres actos* (1980), and has published a collection of stories inspired by Amerindian legends, *Desde el fondo del caracol y otros cuentos taínos* (1992).

Further Reading

Martínez Tolentino, Jaime. "Introduction." *Cuentos Fantásticos*. Río Piedras, Puerto Rico: Universidad de Puerto Rico, 1983.

Puleo, Gus. "El cuento fantástico en Puerto Rico y Cuba: Estudio teórico aplicación a varios cuentos contemporáneos." *Hispanic Review* 65, no. 1 (Winter 1997): 128–83.

—*D. H. Figueredo*

Martinique, History of the Literature of
■

During the seventeenth and eighteenth centuries, the literature of Martinique consisted of folk stories and legends shared by the slaves and their descendants. It was based on oral traditions, and as such, these works were not written down. Observes Mickaëlla L. Pèrina in *African Caribbeans: A Reference Guide* (2003): "At first, this oral literature referred exclusively to Africa, but its contact with European literary norms transformed not only its themes but its language—into Creole" (133).

The first major works to appear were the book of poetry *La maison du honheur* (1909) and the collection of short stories *La vie intérieure* (1912), both written by **René Maran**. In 1921, Maran wrote the novel that made him famous, *Batouala*. Though the setting was Africa, the attention the novel received made the readers aware of Maran and his birthplace.

In the 1940s, a group of teachers and friends revolutionized Martinican culture and attracted the world's attention. The friends **Aimé Césaire**, his wife, **Suzanne Roussy Césaire**, and the philosopher **René Ménil** published the journal *Tropiques*, which from 1941 to 1945 propagated throughout the francophone Caribbean the ideas of **Négritude** as well as encouraging an anticolonialist stance.

Négritude became a major philosophical and cultural force that helped to shape political and literary movements in the Caribbean, Africa, and even the United States. The best-known poem to emerge from the movement was *Cahier d'un retour au pays natal*, written by Aimé Césaire in 1938 and then edited to its present form in 1947. In the poem, Césaire proclaimed his African heritage, celebrated Africa's natural condition over a mechanized Europe—seeing in virginal Africa the beginning of the world and in Europe a tired, dying world—and glorified the color of his skin. The poem and his advocacy of Négritude made Aimé Césaire the one force to contend with in Martinique for next seven decades.

In 1948, **Mayotte Capécia** wrote the romance *Je suis Martiniquaise*, a controversial love story wherein the heroine sees salvation for her and her children only through marriage to a white person. In 1950, what would become a popular international novel was published: *La rue cases nègres*. Written by **Joseph Zobel**, the novel depicted the lot of the poor and abused sugarcane workers who lived on a plantation in Martinique. The novel was banned in Martinique and was not available until twenty years later. In 1983, *La rue cases nègres* became a successful movie.

In 1955, a collection of poems, entitled *Poemes de l'une et l'autre terre*, followed three years later by the novel *La Lezarde* (1958), brought fame and recognition to a young writer, **Edouard Glissant**. The poems, which were metaphysical and challenging, illustrated the author's preoccupation with a Caribbean identity. The novel told of a plot to assassinate a Martinican official and the hero's development as an adult. Both works explored the significant theme of the legacy of colonialism. As Glissant matured as a man and a writer, he challenged Césaire's Négritude movement, claiming that Martinican identity was not only African and black, but also European, Asian, and Latin American. He called this mixing of races and culture, **Créolité**.

In 1952, **Frantz Fanon**, a psychiatrist, wrote a philosophical text that studied the psychological roots of racism: *Peau noire, masques blancs* (1952). That was only the beginning for the young writer. In 1961, shortly before his death, Fanon published *Les damnés de la terre*, a key document in Third World studies and a revolutionary text that called for armed struggle against colonialism and imperialism. The two volumes made Fanon the most famous writer from Martinique.

The 1970s and 1980s were decades of questioning the island's departmentalization, which made Martinique something akin to a French province, and of promoting creolization. **Vincent Placoly**, a novelist and a playwright, used novels (*L'Eau-de-Mort-Guildive*, 1973) and dramas (*Dessalines, ou, La passion de l'indépendance 1983)* to criticize the island's semicolonial status. In 1989, the volume *Éloge de la créolité* by Jean Bernabé, **Patrick Chamoiseau**, and Raphaël Confiant, picked up on Glissant's advocacy for creolism and defined the Caribbean persona as composed of all of the races and people in the region, not just black. The volume, a manifesto, also proposed the use of Creole, which derived from the French and several African languages, as the true language of the francophone Caribbean. Of these three writers, Chamoiseau is considered one of the greatest living writers of the francophone Caribbean, writing a variety of award-winning novels, memoirs, and essays, as well as a volume of folk tales. His innovative technique—a blending of French and Creole, oral and written literary styles—has been dazzling readers since the early 1980s. Complex works, such as his novels *Solibo Magnificent* (1988) and *Texaco* (1992), have prompted critics to compare him to such diverse and outstanding writers as François Rabelais (1483–1553), James Joyce (1882–1941), Gabriel García Márquez (1927–), and Salman Rushdie (1947–).

In the late 1980s and 1990s, another Césaire gained prominence: **Ina Césaire**, Aimé and Suzanne's daughter. Believing that the island's oral traditions were best expressed through the theater, Ina Césaire turned to drama, writing *Memoirs d'isle* (1985), about two women recalling their lives in Martinique; *D'infant du passages ou Le Epic du Ti-Jean* (1987), about a teenager and an orphan; *La mansion close* (1991), based on the true story of six women in jail; and *Rosanie Soleil* (1992), about a labor strike. Unlike her father, who only writes in French, Ina Césaire uses both French and Creole.

Her use of Creole, almost in direct defiance of her father, underlines the cultural debate occurring in Martinique at the beginning of the new century. But the debate extends beyond academic discourse. Pèrina points out: "At stake are issues of national identity, race, and political representation that affect cultural policy, immigration, language, economics, and politics, and how Martinicans view themselves" (135). *See also* Francophone Caribbean Literature, History of; Haitian Literature in Kreyòl (the Haitian Language).

Further Reading

Bernabé, Jean et al. *Eloge de la créolité.* Paris: Gallimard; Presses Universitaires créoles, 1989.

Césaire, Aimé. *Cahier d'un retour u pays natal.* Paris: Présence africaine, 1951.

Murdoch, H. Adlai, ed. *Creole Identity in the French Caribbean Novel.* Miami: University of Florida Press, 2001.

Ormerod, Beverley. "The Representation of Women in French Caribbean Fiction." *In An Introduction to Caribbean and Francophone Writing: Guadeloupe and Martinique*, 101–17. New York: Berg, 1999.

Pèrina, Mickaëlla L. "Martinique." In *African Caribbeans: A Reference Guide*, edited by Alan West Durán, 127 to 39. Westport, CT: Greenwood Press, 2003.

Sharpley-Whiting, T. Denfan. *Negritude Women.* Minneapolis: University of Minnesota Press, 2002.

—*D. H. Figueredo*

Martis, Jose Antonio. See Lauffer, Pierre A.

Matamoros, Mercedes (1851–1906)

Early erotic writer, Matamoros was a Cuban poet who in 1902 wrote twenty sonnets under the title of "El último amor de Safo," which shocked masculine sensibilities of the time when women were meant to be prudish and discreet. Matamoros was also a patriot who supported Cuba's independence from Spain. Under the name of Ofelia, she wrote numerous articles describing local customs and traditions.

Mercedes Matamoros y del Valle was born in Cienfuego, Cuba. She lost her mother when she was three years old, and her father relocated with her to Havana. She was exposed to literature at an early age, and her father, who came from an affluent family and was well educated, taught her English, French, and German.

At the age of fourteen, Matamoros submitted to the local press *costumbristas* articles, pieces on local events and characters. When she was twenty she began to translate into Spanish the poetry of Lord Byron (1788–1824), Geoffrey Chaucer (1343–1400), and Johann Wolfgang Goethe (1749–1832). In 1869, during a political rally against Spanish rule she wore the red-and-white colors of the Cuban flag, a daring act that could have provoked the ire of Spanish soldiers.

In 1882, she published her first collection of poems, *Sensitivas.* In the 1890s, her father died and left her penniless. Two years later, a group of friends funded the publication of her next book, *Poesías completas;* the copies she sold and her work as a private tutor helped to support her. In 1902, she published *Sonetos*, which contained the controversial Safo sonnets. Both the *Sonetos* and *Poesías completas* brought certain national recognition.

Matamoros died on August 25, 1906. The cultural institution the Ateneo de la Habana paid for her funeral. In 1997, her poems were published in a single volume, *La poesía de Mercedes Matamoros. See also* Costumbrismo; Feminism in Caribbean Literature.

Further Reading

Jiménez, Luis, ed. *La voz de la mujer en la literatura hispanoamericana fin-de-siglo.* San José, Costa Rica: Editorial de la Universidad de Costa Rica, 1999.

Romeo, Raquel. "En Torno al Discurso Poético de Mercedes Matamoros." In *La voz de la mujer en la literatura hispanoamericana fin-de-siglo*, compiled by Luis Jiménez, 145–56. San José, Costa Rica: Editorial de la Universidad de Costa Rica, 1999.

—*D. H. Figueredo*

Mateo Palmer, Ana Margarita (1950–)

An award-winning literary critic from Cuba, Mateo Palmer is an internationally recognized scholar, professor, and documentarian. Her works examine Cuba from a nationalist perspective, but within a Caribbean-at-large framework, as well as the relationship between literature and immigration.

Born in Havana, Cuba, on October 28, 1950, she attended Cathedral School and Tomás David Royo Valdés, both in Havana, and Carlos J. Finlay high school. Though she loved literature, she did not think of the formal study of the subject until her sister, who was majoring in literature at the university, convinced her to take such studies. Thus, in 1974, Mateo Palmer earned a BA in Hispanic literature and language from the Universidad de la Habana. She taught at diverse schools and universities in Cuba before accepting the position of professor of Cuban studies at the Instituto Superior de Arte, in Havana, in the late 1980s.

In 1988, she published the study *Del bardo que te canta*, about the development of the "trova," a highly poetic music form, popular in Cuba since the nineteenth century. In 1991, she earned a PhD from the Universidad de la Habana. Her research on the Caribbean novel served as the basis for her book, *Narrativa caribeña: reflexiones y progonósticos* (1991). Her writings on the development of national literatures throughout the Caribbean earned her recognition, and she was rewarded with scholarships to study at the University of Georgetown, Guyana, in 1984 and 1986; Summer Institute for the Study of American Literature at University of California in Santa Barbara, 1988; Harvard University, 2002; among others. She was also visiting professor at universities in Brazil, Italy, and Spain, among others. At these institutions, she taught courses on Cuban literature.

In 1995, Mateo Palmer published *Ella escribía poscrítica*, a study on the Cuban culture of the 1990s and artistic manifestations that were traditionally marginalized: tattoos and graffiti artwork. An innovative text, *Ella escribía po-scrítica* combines essay discourse with fiction and testimonial narratives. That same year, Mateo Palmer directed the documentary *De la piel y la memoria.* In 2002, she published *Paradiso: la aventura mítica,* an analysis of the use of classical myths in the novel *Paradiso* (1966) by **José Lezama Lima.** In 2004, she published *El Caribe en su discurso literario.*

She indicates that her interest in the Caribbean emerges from the fact that she is from the Caribbean and that any interpretation of the region must also address immigration, a topic of great interest to her, since many of her relatives have left Cuba. For *El Caribe en su discurso literario,* Mateo Palmer was awarded Cuba's National Literary Prize for literary criticism.

Further Reading

Mateo Palmer, Margarita. 2005. Interview with D. H. Figueredo, April 5.

———. "Signs After the Last Shipwreck." *Boundary* 28, no. 3 (Fall 2002): 149.

—D. H. Figueredo

Matos Bernier, Félix (1869–1937)

A Puerto Rican journalist and poet, Matos Bernier was a patriot who criticized the Catholic Church and Spanish colonial rule. His only novel, *Puesta a sol* (1903), is a parable about Puerto Rico and the political events that occurred at the end of the nineteenth century.

A native of Coamo, Puerto Rico, Matos Bernier was homeschooled by his father. After working a few years as a bookkeeper, he switched to journalism and poetry, fields that were his passion. He wrote for the publications *La Juventud Liberal* and *Revista de Puerto Rico.* His articles were of a political nature, attacking colonialism and the Catholic Church's authoritarianism.

In 1886, he published his first collection of poems, *La salvación de un ángel,* poems typical of the genre known as **romanticismo.** Two years later, during a period of increased suppression by the Spanish government, Matos Bernier left for the Dominican Republic. From there he traveled to Venezuela and finally Martinique before returning to Puerto Rico in 1890. During these years, he collected his political writings into the volume *Ecos de propaganda* (1889). In Puerto Rico, he worked for the journal *Revista de Puerto Rico* and founded his own political review *La libertad* (1894). For his criticism of the Church, he was sentenced to three months imprisonment.

The end of the century proved a fruitful period for Matos Bernier, who published several books of poetry, including *Margarita Gautier* (1894), *Recuerdos benditos* (1895), *Canto a la patria* (1898), and a collection of prose and poetry, *Páginas sueltas* (1897). Many of the poems expressed patriotic sentiments.

At the turn of the century, he intensified his labor as a journalist and editor. In 1903 he wrote the novel, *Puesta a sol,* which in style and content differed from his tendency to write romantic poetry and political essays. The novel reflected his somber mood at the time when the United States had taken over the island after the Spanish-Cuban-American War of 1898. Written in a naturalistic mold, where society controls the events of the people, the novels explored Puerto Rico's inability to control its own destiny. With autobiographical elements, the novel also recounted the author's experience in the Spanish prison.

Matos Bernier spent the last years of his life as a columnist for the daily *El Mundo* and a journalist for the publications *La Democracia* and *Puerto Rico Ilustrado*, among others. *See also* Naturalism/Naturalismo.

Further Reading

Díaz de Olano, Carmen R. *Félix Matos Bernier, su vida y su obra*. San Juan, Puerto Rico: Biblioteca de Autores Puertorriqueños, 1956, 1955.

Rivera de Álvarez, Josefina. "Novela: la novela puertorriqueña desde sus orígenes hasta el presente." In *La gran enciclopedia de Puerto Rico*, edited by Vicente Báez, 21. San Juan: Puerto Rico en la Mano and La Gran Enciclopedia de Puerto Rico, Inc. 1980.

—*D. H. Figueredo*

Matos Paoli, Francisco (1915–2000)

Nominated in 1977 for a Nobel Prize in Literature, Matos Paoli was a Puerto Rican poet whose abundant poetic productivity expanded several literary movements, from **Romanticismo** to the **Atayalismo** school of poetry, and from the national to the universal. A political activist and fervent supporter of independence for Puerto Rico, he suffered imprisonment during the 1950s. He was a literary critic as well.

Matos Paoli was born on March 9, 1915, in Lares, Puerto Rico. He lived on a farm but spent as much time reading the classics as roaming the countryside. When he was a teenager he met revolutionary Pedro Albizu Campos (1893–1965), who wanted the island to achieve full autonomy and not be dependent on the United States, and as a result Matos Paoli joined the Nationalist Party. In 1931, his mother passed away and his mourning resulted in his first book of poetry, *Signario de lágrimas*.

In 1937, he matriculated at the Universidad de Puerto Rico. Upon graduating in 1941, he worked as a translator and scriptwriter for radio programs produced by Puerto Rico's Department of Education. At the age of twenty-six he married Isabel Freire Meléndez, who was his inspiration for numerous love poems—published in 1997 under the title *Bajo el signo del amor*.

In 1943, he was appointed literature professor at his alma mater. The following year, he published two books of poems, *Habitante del eco* and *Teoría del olvido*. The books reveal a mystical preoccupation expressed in a poetry that is hermitical and personal. As his poetic and scholarly works gained him recognition, in 1950 he increased his political activism: he was elected secretary of the Nationalist Party and delivered pronationalist speeches, justifying the actions taken by two Puerto Rican militants who had attempted to assassinate President Harry S. Truman (1884–1972) in Washington, D.C. This posture brought about his arrest. In prison, in 1951, he wrote the collection of poems *Luz de los héroes*, patriotic poems that celebrated Puerto Rican heroes and the natural beauty of the island. One of his best-known poems, "Canto a Puerto Rico," was included in this collection.

In 1955, the governor of Puerto Rico, the poet **Luis Muñoz Marín**, exonerated Matos Paoli, and he was able to return to his professorial post at the university. The period in prison, though, affected him emotionally, and he was further attracted to mysticism. In 1958, he published *Criatura del rocío*, poems about ideas and symbols that transcended his nationalism. Three years later, his *Canto de la locura* reaffirmed his commitment to social causes while still expressing his need to remove himself from society and to seek solitude. *Canto de la locura* became one of his most popular works, often performed in theaters in Puerto Rico.

During the 1960s, Matos Paoli contributed letters to several publications expounding on his literary theories; the letters were addressed to three Puerto Rican writers: **Luis Palés Matos, Francisco Arriví,** and **Francisco Lluch Mora.** In the 1970s, he intensified his poetic activities, publishing nineteen volumes of poetry; many of these later poems revealed sarcasm and a sense of irony. In the 1980s, he revised and enlarged many of the poems he had written in the 1950s and 1960s, including "Canto nacional a Borinquen," which he had written while in prison. During this phase of his life he received several international awards, including the International Certificate in Poetry from the University of Colorado (1981), the prestigious José Vasconcelos Prize from Mexico (1986), and the Prometheus Poetry Prize from Spain (1987). His colleagues at the university also campaigned for his Nobel Prize nomination.

Matos Paoli died on July 10, 2000. Critics **Margot Arce de Vázquez,** Laura Gallego, and **Luis de Arrigoitia,** in *Lecturas puertorriqueñas: Poesía* (1968), considered Matos Paoli a unique lyrical poet who attempted to create a world and a language that was private and who used poetry as a tool for mysticism while still evoking his love for Puerto Rico.

Further Reading

Arce de Vázquez, Margot, et al. *Lecturas puertorriqueñas: Poesía*. Sharon, CT: Troutman Press, 1968.

Bourne, Louis, et al. *Poesía esencial de Francisco Matos Paoli: Estudio y antología*. Madrid: Verbum, 1994.

—*D. H. Figueredo*

Mauvois, Georges (1922–)

Mauvois is a politically engaged dramatist from Martinique who chooses to write in Creole to affirm his Martinican roots and reject French colonialism. He is the winner of the 2004 **Casa de las Américas** prize for literature.

Mauvois wrote his first play at the age of forty-four after having worked as a postmaster, an attorney, and a trade unionist in Fort-de-France. The comedy, *Agénor Cacoul*, was staged by a student group in Paris in 1967. It tells the story of a strike on a sugar plantation and the efforts undertaken by the ambitious and corrupt mayor to end the labor dispute in favor of the plantation owners. The protagonist, Cacoul is depicted as a complex character with personal and political desires, thus allowing Mauvois to flesh out the political message with psychological insight and credible behavior. The dialogue is written in French and Creole with ongoing change, or **code switching**, from one language to the other. The French language is symbolic of colonialism, whereas Creole is representative of the people.

Though the play had a limited performance, it brought some recognition to Mauvois. The dramatist, however, did not pursue writing again until his retirement in the late 1980s. He translated into Creole Molière's *Don Juan* (1996) and the Greek classic *Antigone*, which he titled *Antigòn* (1997). In 2003, he wrote *Ovando* about the colonization of the Caribbean by the Spanish; this historical drama served also as a parable of the suffering experienced by his compatriots in Martinique throughout the centuries.

Mauvois' daughter submitted *Ovando* to the Casa de las Américas literary competition, thus the notification of the award surprised the author. Mauvois's plays are regularly performed in Martinique.

Further Reading

Jones, Bridget. "Theatre and Resistance? An Introduction to some French Caribbean Plays." In *An Introduction to Caribbean Francophone Writing: Guadeloupe and Martinique*, edited by Sam Haigh, 83–100. New York: Berg, 1999.

—*D. H. Figueredo*

Maxwell, Marina Ama Omowale (194?–)

Novelist, poet, playwright, lecturer, and producer, from San Fernando, Trinidad, Maxwell has made a substantial contribution to the literary movements and the arts in the Caribbean. She attended Michigan State University, where she earned a BA in sociology, an MA in telecommunications and television production, an MS in sociology, and is currently completing a PhD dissertation on a culturally relevant Caribbean television theater. Maxwell has traveled extensively in the Caribbean, Africa, United States, Britain, and Latin America, conducting research and giving seminars and presentations.

The founder of the yard theater in Jamaica in the 1960s, as well as the Writers Union of Trinidad and Tobago in the 1980s, Maxwell has been a lecturer for over thirty years at the Cipriani Labour College in Trinidad and Tobago. Her varied working career includes stints as a reporter and journalist for the *Daily Gleaner*, the Jamaican influential newspaper, and the BBC in London. In addition, she has functioned as secretary to the **Caribbean Artists Movement (CAM)** in London. Under the aegis of her own company, Omnamedia TV Ltd, she has produced directed, presented, and voiced over a hundred cultural and educational video programs, series and teaching tools. Marina Maxwell conducts courses in television production, creative writing, business communications, journalism, and radio, writing and production. She is a strong advocate for Caribbean television and videography.

Maxwell has written ten plays and two novels: *Chopstix in Mauby: a Metaphor in Magical Realism* (1996) and *The Drumless Tribe*. She is currently working on *The 8th Octave; Creatures of Fire;* and *She Is a Clock of Flowers, My Mother* (poetry). Her poems have been published in ten anthologies. Maxwell's novels are rooted in **magical realism**—a realm of the fantastic rooted in a hybrid Caribbean mythology that expresses the sensibility of "all races of the diaspora, all creeds of the baroque Caribbean, shaping and reshaping itself always like mud temples in the rains," as she writes in "Devil Beads." Maxwell, who frequently conducts creative writing workshops, passionately believes in the rich and distinctive contribution of the Caribbean literary voice to world literature. She states: "I'd like writers to find their own unique voices instead of copying past and especially foreign writers. We have such immense local creativity and writing potential here and across the Caribbean. . . . It is our region which is now producing the most magical writers, poets, playwrights, TV and film/video producers and directors . . . we are producing the next generation of pathfinders of expression and consciousness."

Maxwell was awarded a research study grant to the Smithsonian Institution, in Washington, D.C., and was invited to be a Commissioner (Caribbean) of the Schomburg Center of the New York Public Library.

Further Reading

Clarke, George Elliot. "Contesting Model Blackness: A Meditation on African-Canadian African-Americanism, or the Structure of African Canadianite." *Essays on Canadian Writing* no. 3 (Spring 1998): 1–55.

—*Paula Morgan*

Mayard, Constantin (1882–1940)

Mayard was a Haitian poet, essayist, and orator. He was also a government official and politician.

Mayard was born in Port-au-Prince, Haiti, on November 27, 1882. Of a well-to-do family, he was educated at the Petit Séminaire Collège Saint-Martial, where he demonstrated an interest in literature and politics. In his early twenties, he contributed poems and essays to the journal *La Ronde*, the leading cultural publication of the day.

At the age of thirty, he was elected to the Haitian Congress. In 1915, he was appointed Minister of Interior. Three years later, he published the book-length essay, *De la solidarité*, his observations of Haitian politics. His skills as an orator and administrator, and his friendship with government officials, earned him a series of foreign appointments, including Haiti's delegate before the League of Nations and serving as Haitian Minister in France and in Chile.

While an active participant in the work of the League of Nations, sitting in committees that oversaw the admittance of new members and political conflicts in Europe, Mayard still managed to write. In 1933, he published his best-known collection of poems, *Trente poémes*. These poems addressed such popular subjects as the Caribbean's natural beauty and Haiti's social needs. The poems expressed his sentiments in an emotional but refined manner. In 1934, he published the book-length essay *Haiti*.

A world traveler, either for his own pleasure or on behalf of his Haiti, Mayard was in Santiago, Chile, when he passed away on December 27, 1940.

Further Reading

Herdeck, Donald, ed. *Caribbean Writers: A Bio-Bibliographical-Critical Encyclopedia.* Washington, DC: Three Continents Press, 1979.

Lehmann, Gérard. *Pages retrouvées de Constantin Mayard, poète haïtien.* Saint-Malo, Coëtquen éd.: Corlet, 2005.

—*D. H. Figueredo*

McDonald, Ian A. (1933–)

The second editor, after **A. J. Seymour**, of the influential Guyanese literary journal *Kyk-Over-Al*, McDonald is a poet who was born in Trinidad but has lived most of his life in Guyana. A successful businessman, he has nevertheless dedicated his energy, talent, and money to the promotion of West Indian literature and culture.

Ian Archie McDonald was born on April 18, 1933, in Trinidad. He graduated from Queens Royal College, Trinidad, in 1951. He continued his studies at Cambridge University, earning an MA in 1959. In 1955, he relocated permanently to Guyana, where he worked in the sugar industry and traveled throughout the region, charmed by Guyana's wilderness. The years he spent in his native Trinidad form the basis for his novel *The Hummingbird Tree* (1969). His love of Guyana is evidenced in the book of poetry *Essequipo* (1992), a celebration of the country's natural beauty.

In 1984, A. J. Seymour asked him to edit *Kyk-Over-Al*, and McDonald was instrumental in reviving the journal. He reprinted many of the pieces that had been published decades before by the likes of **Martin Carter** and **Wilson Harris** while also looking for fresh talent. In 1990, he published a combined version of *Bim*, the seminal literary review from Trinidad, with *Kyk-Over-Al*. The recipient of Guyana's Golden Arrow of Achievement in 1986 and an honorary doctorate from the University of West Indies in 1997, McDonald also wrote the following books: *Mercy Ward* (1988), *Jaffo the Calypsonian* (1994), *Terminal Cafe* (1994), and *Evolution's Shore* (1995).

Further Reading

Oloizia, Richard. "Word of mouth: Terminal Café by Ian McDonald." *Library Journal* 120, no. 10 (June 1, 1995): 208.

—D. H. Figueredo

McFarlane, Basil. See McFarlane Family.

McFarlane Family

Father and two sons from Jamaica who promoted a national culture, mentored Jamaican writers, and wrote essays on Jamaican literature. The three were also poets and public servants.

McFarlane, Basil (1922–). Poet and journalist, Basil spent his life in Jamaica, unlike many of the emerging writers and intellectual of the period who often migrated to England. He worked for Radio Jamaica and was subeditor of the *Daily Gleaner*.

The son of J. E. Clare McFarlane, he was born in St. Andrew Parish and served in the Royal Air Force from 1944 to 1946. In 1956, he wrote *Jacob and the Angel and Other Poems*. His poems sketch routine incidents in life, such as the body of a dead animal on a curbside, depicting it with the simplicity of a haiku poem and assigning it philosophical significance.

McFarlane has also written film criticism published in *Daily Gleaner* and other local publications.

McFarlane, John Ebenezer Clare (1894–1962). The most famous of the threesome, poet and literary mentor J. E. Clare McFarlane wrote *A Literature in the Making* (1965), the first critical study of Jamaican literature. He was the founder of the **Poetry League of Jamaica**.

Born in Spanish Town, McFarlane was interested in promoting a national literature and in offering Jamaican writers a space where they could read and discuss their works. In such spirit, he established in 1923 the Poetry League of Jamaica, a chapter of the Empire Poetry League, and wrote a series of critical studies on the poetry of his contemporaries that would be published in 1956 under the title of *A Literature in the Making*. He also published the first anthology of Jamaican poetry, *Voices from Summerland*, in 1929. Twenty years later he published a second anthology, *A Treasury of Jamaican Poetry*. Both volumes became part of the Jamaican school curriculum from the 1930s to the 1950s.

McFarlane befriend and mentored such poets as **Vivian Virtue**, who was the league's secretary, and **Una Marson**. Opinionated, conservative, and of a colonialist mentality—he promoted a national culture but opposed political nationalism—McFarlane favored the use of standard English and was critical of poetry written in dialect. For instance, he did not invite the popular poet and performer **Louise**

Bennett to the league and excluded her poems from his anthologies because of her preference for Jamaican dialect.

McFarlane published five books of poetry, *Beatrice* (1918), *Poems* (1924), *Daphne* (1931), *Selected Poems* (1953), and *The Magdalen* (1958). He was the first Jamaican to serve as the island's financial secretary.

McFarlane, R. L. Clare (1925–). Like his father and brother, R. L. Clare has served in Jamaica's civil service, has written poetry, and has promoted Jamaican culture and literature. Born in Kingston, he is the author of *Selected Poems 1943–1952* and *A Gift of Black Mangoes (Poems 1989–1995)*. His poetry celebrates Jamaica's natural beauty, expressing pride in being Jamaican. *See also* Jamaican Literature, History of.

Further Reading

Donnell, Alison, and Sarah Lawson Welsh. *The Routledge Reader in Caribbean Literature*. London: Routledge, 1996.

Jarrettt-Macauley, Delia. *The Life of Una Marson: 1905–65*. Manchester: Manchester University Press, 1998.

McFarlane, J. E. Clare. *A Literature in the Making*. Kingston, Jamaica: The Pioneer Press, 1956.

—*D. H. Figueredo*

McFarlane, John Ebenezer Clare. See McFarlane Family.

McFarlane, R. L. Clare. See McFarlane Family.

McKay, Claude (1889–1948)

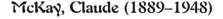

Claude McKay has written very powerful verse about race and oppression that prefigured and strongly influenced writers of the Harlem Renaissance and throughout the Caribbean. McKay first received recognition for his poems written in traditional British formats that, however, employed the melodious vernacular of Jamaica. After he emigrated to the United States, a number of his sonnets and ballads became some of the strongest and most eloquent statements of the subjugation of people of African origin in the New World. For part of his career he worked as an editor and journalist for socialist publications in the United States and Britain. His most famous sonnet, "If We Must Die" (1919), captures a dignity and defiance that has long spoken to readers faced with prejudice and violence. During his career he published many volumes of poetry, many short stories, three novels, and several autobiographical works. Though he never returned to his island home, McKay still represents the dignity of the Afro-Caribbean voice throughout the world.

Born Festus Claudius McKay in Sunny Ville, Clarendon Parish, Jamaica, he grew up as one of eleven children whose proud parents taught them to respect peasant work and life. He worked briefly in a variety of jobs, including woodwork and law enforcement at the Constabulary. He became interested in poetry as a young man and found his voice first in the *patois* of his native island. With the encouragement of British linguist Walter Jekyll (1849–1929), he published two volumes in 1912, *Songs of Jamaica* and *Constab Ballads*. In the former, McKay versified his love for the natural beauty of Jamaica. The work is filled with lush images of spiritual con-

Representative of the Afro-Caribbean voice in the world, Claude McKay wrote numerous poems, short stories, and novels that influenced 20th-century African American writers. *Source: Schomburg Center for Research in Black Culture, The New York Public Library, Astor, Lenox, and Tilden Foundations. Courtesy of Lisa Finder.*

nection with the land and its grandeur. The latter collection addresses one of McKay's more recent discoveries, the racial hatred and inequalities in the urban life he found when he moved from predominantly black Sunny Ville to white-controlled Kingston.

That same year, McKay moved to the United States, first to study agriculture at Tuskegee Institute in Alabama, then to Kansas State College, and finally to New York City, where he abandoned his formal studies. By 1917, he had become acquainted with important literary persons in New York, and two of his best-known poems were published in major periodicals, "To the White Fiends" (1919) in *Pearson's Magazine* and "If We Must Die" in Max Eastman's (1883–1969) *The Liberator*. From these contributions, McKay's position on the literary landscape could be plotted. Politically, it was clear that he was going to address issues of race and class. Both poems employed images of racial pride and opposition to the powers that would attempt keeping men and women oppressed by race. Further, he allied himself with the leftist Eastman and made clear a commitment to the peasant and working class. In addition, McKay staked out territory in the literary world by adopting a traditional European form, the sonnet, and simultaneously transforming it into a powerful voice of the masses. The voice in the sonnets is strong, direct, plain-spoken and yet elegant in its economy of language.

Between 1917 and 1921, McKay traveled to Europe. He worked in London as an editor for the socialist paper *The Worker's Dreadnought*. He published his third poetry volume, *Spring in New Hampshire*, in 1920 and his fourth, *Harlem Shadows*, in 1921, when he returned to the United States. Between 1922 and 1934, McKay traveled and worked on fiction. He first stayed in the Soviet Union until he lost his interest in the

Communist Party, and then sojourned through France, Germany, North Africa, and Spain. During this period he published three novels and a collection of short stories. These were not all well received by critics, however. The best-selling and most widely reviewed of these was *Home to Harlem* (1928), which remained problematic for many black critics. The novel was praised for its evocative depiction of the seamy side of Harlem life, yet leaders like WEB Du Bois (1868–1963), writing in the journal *The Crisis* in June 1928, found it too "dirty" and he claimed that McKay had"set out to cater for that prurient demand on the part of white folk for a portrayal in Negroes of . . . utter licentiousness" (202). McKay was defended by some of his contemporaries, who found the book true to the working class life of Harlem. McKay, too, defended his work on the grounds of its authenticity in the essay "A Negro Writer to His Critics", countering that "a sincere artist . . . *will* see characters through his predilections and prejudices, unless he sets himself deliberately to present those cinema-type figures that are produced to offend no unit" (132).

McKay continued to be an influential voice in world literature until his death, in 1948, and beyond. His verse captured both a love of the nature and simplicity of peasant life and a seething hatred brought on by racial injustice. He influenced 1930s poets trying to capture African cultural heritage in the **Négritude** movement and 1960s Black Arts Movement figures such as Amiri Baraka (1934–). His use of the Jamaican dialect reversed the trend in dialect poetry in the United States as practiced by reconstruction-era poets like Paul Laurence Dunbar (1872–1906). Rather than adopting a minstrel-show voice that was intrinsically connected with anti-black sentiment, he captured and immortalized the beauty and uniqueness of a regional Caribbean voice.

Further Reading

Du Bois, WEB. "Review of *Home to Harlem*." *The Crisis* no. 6 (June 1928): 202.

Hathaway, Heather. *Caribbean Waves: Relocating Claude McKay and Paule Marshall.* Bloomington: Indiana University Press, 1999.

McKay, Claude. "A Negro Writer to His Critics." *The Passion of Claude McKay: Selected Poetry and Prose, 1912–1948*, edited by Wayne F. Cooper, 132–39. New York: Schocken Books, 1973.

Tillery, Tyrone. *Claude McKay: A Black Poet's Struggle for Identity.* Amherst: University of Massachusetts Press, 1992.

—Angela Conrad

McNeill, Anthony (1941–96)

McNeill was a Jamaican poet who addressed social issues as well as universal themes in his writings. Though he often experimented with poetic forms, he was praised for writing in a style that was elegant and accessible. McNeill was also a journalist.

Born in Kingston, Jamaica, on December 17, 1941, McNeill was the son of an elected member of the Legislative Council. During his youth he worked at a variety of jobs that ranged from a civil service clerical post to a trainee manager of a Playboy resorts in Ocho Rios, Jamaica. He was also a failed encyclopedia salesman and a successful pool hustler. But he also managed to study, traveling to the United States, where he earned an MA in Art from Johns Hopkins University, in Maryland, in 1971, and an MA and a PhD from the University of Massachusetts in 1976.

McNeill worked as a journalist and a radio scriptwriter during the 1960s. In the 1970s, he was assistant director of publications for the Institute of Jamaica. He was also a columnist for *The Gleaner*, the influential Jamaica daily. While studying and working, McNeill wrote poetry, winning in 1966 the first prize in the Jamaica Festival Literary Competition. He published his first book of poetry, *Hello Ungod*, in 1971. This was followed by *Reel from "The Life Movie"* in 1972, which expressed his commitment to social causes. The latter book brought him recognition; that same year he was awarded the Silver Musgrave Medal for poetry.

In 1979, McNeill published *Credences at the Altar of Cloud*. While the poems in *Reel* were more controlled, even conventional in their format, the poems in *Credences* were of an experimental nature, a combination of prose poetry and short verses. Observes critic Daryl Cumber Dance, in *New World Adams*, of the poet's overall style: "[it] ranges from the familiar and traditional to the highly innovative and experimental; one might even occasionally label bizarre the blurred type, the unusual layout, the unconventional punctuation, and the consciously retained typographical errors;" (160).

During the 1970s, McNeill experienced emotional problems: he suffered a breakdown and became an alcoholic. He wrote prolifically but did not publish a book for two decades. Sensing an early death, he published in 1998 *Chinese Lanterns from the Blue Child*, in which he said

> I wonder who sings
> sad
> from the ruins
> Somebody with wings.

Further Reading

"Anthony McNeill." http://www.peepaltreepress.com (accessed 5/6/05).

Dance, Daryl Cumber. *New World Adams: Conversations with Contemporary West Indian Writers*. Yorkshire, England: Peepal Tree, 1984, 1992.

—*D. H. Figueredo*

Medina, Pablo (1948–)

■

Pablo Medina is a memoirist, poet, and novelist whose works echo the loneliness and melancholia of exile. He was one of the first Cuban American writers to switch from writing in Spanish to English.

Medina was born in Havana in 1948 into a middle-class family of Spanish descent. He spent the winters and summers of his childhood visiting the farm where his grandparents lived. There, he tailed the sugarcane workers, idled away hours in the fields or riding horses, and observed such practices and traditions as pig slaughtering and cockfighting. At home, he lived in an affluent neighborhood surrounded by aunts, uncles, and cousins. Growing up in Havana during the 1950s, events of the Cuban Revolution unfolded before him: sabotages, dictator Fulgencio Batista's (1901–73) henchmen rounding up suspects, and dead bodies lying in a park. All of these images he depicts in his memoir *Exiled Memories: A Cuban Childhood* (1990).

Pablo Medina is one of the first Cuban American poets to write in English rather than in Spanish. *Courtesy of Pablo Medina.*

After **Fidel Castro**'s triumph in 1959, Medina and his parents went into exile, settling in New York City. He attended public school for one year and then went to Fordham Preparatory School, a Jesuit institution located in the Bronx. After graduation, he matriculated at Georgetown University, where he earned a BA and an MA. Early on in New York City, he experienced the emptiness that other exiles from the Caribbean have experienced in the United States and elsewhere and have written about, a knowledge that he belonged neither to Cuba, which was the past, nor the United States, which was the present and the future. He began writing poetry that expressed those sentiments.

In 1975, Medina wrote, according to Virgil Suárez in *Little Havana Blues* (1996), the first collection of poems written directly into English by a Cuban-born writer; it was titled *Pork Rind and Cuban Songs*. This was followed by the poetry collections *Arching Into the Afterlife* (1991) and *Floating Island* (1999). In 1994, he wrote the novel *The Marks of Birth*. Though he doesn't identify the country as Cuba, it is a novel about the revolution and Castro's dictatorship. In 2000, he wrote his second novel, *The return of Felix Nogara*. Other titles include *Todos me van a tener que oir/Everyone Will Have to Listen* (1990), a translation from the Spanish, with poet Carolina Hospital, of Cuban dissident Tania Diaz Castro; *Puntos de Apoyos (2002)*: poems written in Spanish; a new and updated edition of *Exiled Memories (2002), The Cigar Roller: A Novel (2005)*; and *Points of Balance*, a bilingual poetry collection *(2005)*.

Medina's poetry is clear, accessible, and heart-wrenching. The experience of exile has made him aware of the uncertainties of life and the ending of all things. But through words he attempts to delay that ending by recapturing the past, preserving his boyhood home in Cuba in vivid memories: "As long as there is blood in my veins, as long as there are words on my tongue, stories to be told, the house stands." In 2005, Medina and other Cuban intellectuals visited Cuba to lend support to librarians and writers establishing independent libraries that collect books not approved by the revolutionary government. *See also* Cuban American Literature; Exile Literature.

Further Reading

Medina, Pablo. *Exiled Memories: A Cuban Childhood*. Austin: University of Texas Press, 1990.

———. Interview by D. H. Figueredo, March.

Suárez, Virgil. *Little Havana Blues: A Cuban-American Literature Anthology*. Houston, TX: Arte Público Press, 1996.

—D. H. Figueredo

Medina López, Ramón Felipe (1935–)

Medina is a Puerto Rican poet and novelist. In his poetry, he expresses religious and mystical concerns, whereas in his novel he explores Puerto Rican nationalism and the island's failure to achieve independence from the United States. He is also a professor at the Universidad de Puerto Rico.

Born and raised in Santurce, Medina studied at elementary and secondary schools in his hometown before traveling to Minnesota to enroll at the University of Saint John, where he studied art. In 1956, he published the book of poems *El ruiseñor bajo el cielo* while also submitting short stories and poems to such literary journals as *Alma Latina*, *Asomante*, *Guajana*, and *Prometeo*. In 1965, he received an MA in arts from the Universidad de Puerto Rico. Through the late 1960s and 1970s, he taught literature at the Universidad de Puerto Rico and wrote several books of poetry, *Canto de Dios airado* (1969), *Te hablo a ti* (1971), *Del tiempo a tiempo* (1973), and *Andina de la alborada* (1978). The poems, written in traditional rhyming stanzas as well as free verse, revealed his mystical and contemplative tendencies.

In 1973, his novel *El 27* was published. Well received by the critics and Puerto Rican intellectuals, the novel detailed the mental processes of a Puerto Rican revolutionary who was sent to an insane asylum and then prison for participating in a plot against the island's governor. The novel, a study of the protagonist's initial rebellion and final submission to colonialism, was seen by many as a parable of Puerto Rican politics.

During the 1980s, Medina prospered in his career as a college professor, assuming the administration of the Department of Hispanic Studies at the university of Puerto Rico. He also continued writing poetry, publishing *Un árbol de palabras* (1987) and *A quien contigo va* (1987). In 1984, he wrote the literary study *Juan Antonio Corretjer, poeta nacional puertorriqueño* (1984).

Further Reading

Figueroa, Javier. "Diccionario: Diccionario Histórico-Biográfico." In *La gran enciclopedia de Puerto Rico,* edited. by Vicente Báez, 118–19. San Juan: Puerto Rico en la Mano and La Gran Enciclopedia de Puerto Rico, 1980.

—D. H. Figueredo

Mejía Soliere, Abigail (1895–1941)

A historian, essayist, and feminist from the Dominican Republic, Mejía Soliere used her writings to promote women's equality and the right to vote.

Born in Santo Domingo to a family of intellectuals, Abigail Mejía Soliere went to Spain at the age of thirteen to attend classes at the Colegio de la Compañía de Teresa de Jesús in Barcelona. After graduation, she traveled to Italy and France, returning to the Dominican Republic, where she participated in cultural and political activities. The American invasion of 1916 fueled some of the passion in her writings.

In 1927, Mejía Soliere founded the Club Nosotras and in 1931 she became the founding president of Acción Feminista Dominicana. She then lobbied for the establishment of the National Museum, which was founded in 1933 and where she worked as its first director. She also taught literature at the Escuela Normal—Normal School—and organized the women's movement in the Dominican Republic. She advocated for public high school instruction for women as well.

Though Mejía Soliere wrote a novel in 1927, entitled *Sueña Pilarín*, she was essentially an essayist. Her prose, infused with quotes, dates, statistics, logic, flattery, anger, and excitement, presents a veritable tour de force of the art of persuasion, as illustrated in her introduction to her book *Ideario feminista y algún apunte para la historia del feminismo dominicano* (1939) : "We would say that FEMINISM, far from aspiring to MAKE US MASCULINE, aspires to the contrary, to MAKE men a little bit FEMININE, to soften them, to make them sweeter" –as quoted in the anthology *Documents of Dissidence*, published 2000 (87). Mejía Soliere was not afraid to confront men who ridiculed feminist ideas, often engaging them in letters and editorials published in the press. She was, however, lured by dictator Rafael Leónidas Trujillo's (1891–1961) promise to grant women the vote in 1932 and became a supporter of his regime.

Mejía Soliere died in 1941, one year before women were granted the right to vote. Her works include *Por entre frivolidades* (1922), *Historia de la literatura castellana* (1929), *Historia de la literatura dominicana* (1936), *Vida de Máximo Gómez en Santo Domingo* (1936), among others. A selection of her writings was published in 1995 under the title *Obras escogidas*. *See also* Trujillo Era.

Further Reading

Cocco de Filippis, Daisy. *Documents of Dissidence: Selected Writings by Dominican Women.* New York: CUNY Dominican Studies Institute, 2000.

—Daisy Cocco de Filippis

Meléndez, Concha (1895 or 1904–1983)

■

Meléndez was a Puerto Rican literary critic and scholar who devoted her life to re-searching and writing about Caribbean and Latin American literature. For her writings, promotion of Caribbean culture, and her role as one of the first academic administrators in Latin America, Meléndez was awarded numerous prizes and honors.

A native of Caguas, Puerto Rico, she attended primary and secondary schools in her hometown. After graduating from high school, she matriculated at the Universidad de Puerto Rico, earning a teachers certificate in 1924. She then went to New York City, where she earned an MA from Columbia University. In 1932, she was awarded a PhD in philosophy and literature from the Universidad Nacional de México, the first woman in the history of that country to earn a doctorate. In 1934, she published her best-known work, *La novela indianista en Hispanoamérica*, a major and comprehensive study of Indian themes in Latin American literature. In 1936, she published *Pablo Neruda*, considered one of the best studies ever written on the great Chilean poet (1904–73).

In 1940, she helped to found the Department of Hispanic Studies at the Universidad de Puerto Rico. She was appointed director of the department, a post she maintained for nearly twenty years. She researched the lives and works of eminent Caribbean and Latin American writers, including the Cuban **José Martí**, **José De Diego**, her compatriot, and Jorge Isaacs (1837–95), from Colombia, publishing the volumes *Figuraciones de Puerto Rico y otros estudios* (1958) and *José De Diego en mi memoria* (1966).

In 1964, she was a visiting scholar at Middlebury College, in Vermont, and in 1971, the Venezuelan government recognized her labor on the study and promotion of Latin American literature, awarding her the Andres Bello Medal. That same year, she was elected as Puerto Rico's Woman of the Year.

The first woman admitted to the Puerto Rican Academy of Languages, her work as mentor and promoter of women in academia is honored every year when the Coalition of Hispanic American Women of Miami awards a high school girl a college scholarship. A school in San Juan, Puerto Rico, bears her name. Her other works include *Entrada en el Perú* (1941), *El arte del cuento en Puerto Rico* (1961), *Moradas de poesía en Alfonso Reyes* (1973), and *Cuentos hispanoamericanos* (1985).

Further Reading

Ciarlo, Héctor Oscar. *El escritor y su obra: al encuentro de Concha Meléndez y otros ensayos*. Río Piedras, Puerto Rico: Editorial de la Universidad de Puerto Rico, 1982.

Meléndez, Concha. *Antología y cartas de sus amigos*. San Juan, Puerto Rico: Editorial Cordillera Editorial de la Universidad de Puerto Rico, 1995.

—*D. H. Figueredo*

Meléndez Muñoz, Miguel (1884–1966)

Meléndez Muñoz was a Puerto Rican novelist and journalist who expressed a social concern for rural poverty. His stories evoked the vernacular of the jíbaro, the Puerto Rican farmer.

Born on July 22, 1884, in Cayey, Puerto Rico, Meléndez Muñoz was the son of a Spanish military officer and a Puerto Rican mother. He spent his childhood with his family in Madrid, Spain, and upon their return to Puerto Rico, his father passed away. Finishing elementary school in 1888, Meléndez Muñoz went to work at a general store near the farm where he lived. Around this time, Meléndez Muñoz started to write articles for the newspapers *El Heraldo Español*.

In the early 1900s, he moved to San Juan. The poet and political figure **Luis Muñoz Rivera** mentored him and introduced him to other writers. Submitting his articles to numerous newspapers, Meléndez Muñoz began a forty-year relationship with the influential journal *Puerto Rico Ilustrado*. During the 1940s, he worked for Puerto Rico's Department of Education and was president of the **Ateneo Puertorriqueño** from 1943 to 1945. He also owned a firm that specialized in agricultural products.

Meléndez Muñoz wrote novels, short stories, and articles. He championed the poor farmers and residents of the countryside. Wrote historian Ribes Tovar, in *100 Outstanding Puerto Ricans* (1976): Meléndez Muñoz "believed that a more just distribution was necessary [in Puerto Rico]. He aimed at the creation of more jobs . . . and he was obsessed with the desire to do away with the hunger of the rural class" (232). These ideas were expressed in his works, including the volumes *Estudio social del campesino puertorriqueño* (1916) and *Cuentos de la carretera central* (1941).

In 1958, the Universidad de Puerto Rico awarded Meléndez Muñoz an honorary doctorate. He spent the last years of his life in the quietness of the Puerto Rican countryside and mountains. He passed away on November 27, 1966, in Cayey.

Further Reading

Cuaderno de homenaje a don Miguel Meléndez Muñoz. San Juan, Departamento de Instrucción Pública, Estado Libre Asociado de Puerto Rico, 1957.

Ribes Tovar, Federico. *100 Outstanding Puerto Ricans*. New York: Ultra Plus, 1976.

—*D. H. Figueredo*

Melville, Pauline (1948–)

A Guyanese actress and author, Melville has spent most of her life away from Guyana, yet her experiences in that country and her contact with her countrymen inform her writings. Describing herself as British-Guyanese, Melville sees herself as the product of creolization, of the mixing of many races and cultures.

The daughter of an English woman and an African-Amerindian-European father, Melville was raised in England, where she became an actress. Her recollection of Guyana included the experiences of the people in that country leading ordinary lives while confronting such barriers as poverty and racism. The diction and accent of her compatriots also lingered in her memory. These experiences formed the bases for the short stories she began to write in the late 1980s.

In 1990, she published the collection of stories *Shape-shifter*. The twelve pieces in the volume tell the stories of Guyanese immigrants in London as well as in Guyana. *Shape-shifter* was reviewed by the mainstream press in England and United States. The *New York Times Book Review*, in November 1991, praised Melville for her ability to depict realistic and engaging characters. Other reviews admired her ear for dialects and diction.

In 1997, Melville published the novel *The Ventriloquist's Tale*, which was also well received by critics on both side of the Atlantic. The novel, a love story that takes place in Guyana during the 1930s, received the Whitebread First Novel Award (1997). In 1999, Meville wrote *The Migration of Ghosts*, which the journal *Booklist* described as magic tales that exist "outside of the sort of time we know and anguish over in our machine-ruled culture. They move to a more organic, subtly female rhythm set to a river's flow, or the roll and sway of the generous hips of the bronze women."

Further Reading

Ott, Bill. "Shape-shifter." *New York Times Book Review*, November 10, 1991.

Robinson-Walcott, Kim. "Claiming an identity we thought they despised: Contemporary white West Indian writers and their negotiation of race." *Small Axe* 7, no. 2 (September 2003): 93.

Seaman, Donna. "The Migration of Ghosts." *Booklist* 15, no. 18 (May 15, 1999): 1670.

—*D. H. Figueredo*

Mendes, Alfred H. (1897–1991)

Influential Trinidadian editor, novelist, and political activist, Alfred H. Mendes was a member of the Beacon Group, an informal gathering of intellectuals who were intent on changing the Victorian atmosphere of Trinidadian letters during the 1930s. His novel *Black Fauns* (1935) is a classic of **barrack yard literature**, or stories of the slums.

Of Portuguese descent, Mendes was born on November 18, 1897. He studied at Queens College in Port of Spain and at Hitchin Grammar School and Mill Hill Public School in England. During World War I, he served in the British infantry brigade. In 1922, he returned to Trinidad, where he welcomed into his home a literary group led by writer and historian **CLR James**. In 1929, he and James founded the cultural journal *Trinidad*, which was published for one year. The journal published a commentary, which can be described as a generational manifesto, by Mendes contesting the conservative views of readers who were scandalized by the journal's publication, of the short story "Triumph" by CRL James. The story, which helped to establish the genre of barrack yard literature, or slums, reveals the life of the urban poor, who are far removed from the educated middle classes, of which Mendes and James were representatives; the story also challenged the affected code of behavior promoted by Victorian literature. *Trinidad* was followed by the journal *The Beacon*. On this influential publication, Mendes and the young contributors attempted to erase the aesthetics of a literary canon and a Victorian morality they perceived as obsolete; this auto-de-fe was evident in the published fiction, but Mendes could not free the journal's poetry from its conventional nature.

In 1933, Mendes relocated to New York City, where he socialized with the members of the intellectual community: Malcom Lowry (1909–57), Ford Maddox Ford (1873–1939), Richard Wright (1908–60), **Claude McKay**, and Countee Cullen (1903–46). Mendes wrote for several journals published in the United States, France, and Great Britain. It was in London that he published his two novels, *Pitch Lake* (1934) and *Black Fauns*. The first tells the story of a Portuguese youth so intent in climbing the social ladder of Port of Spain, Trinidad, that he destroys himself; the novel had an introduction by Aldous Huxley. The second novel, which depicts local color, follows the lives and tragedies of several women who live in a barrack yard; to write this novel, the middle-class Mendes spent six month living in the yard. The two novels proved highly influential in the works of Anglophone Caribbean writers.

Returning to Trinidad in 1940, Mendes gave up his literary career to accept administrative positions in the government—Deputy General Manager (1947), General Manager of the Port Services Department (1953). He was also a member of the United Front, a political party of socialist leanings. Upon his retirement, he lived in Majorca and in Canary Islands before settling in Barbados. In 1972, the University of West Indies awarded him an honorary degree. Mendes's grandson, Sam Mendes, after a successful theatrical career in London, was awarded the Oscar for directing the film *American Beauty* (1999). Other books by Alfred H. Mendes include *The Wages of Sin* (1925), *Pablo's Fandango and Other Stories* (1998), and *The Autobiography of Alfred H. Mendes, 1897–1991* (2002).

Further Reading

James, CLR. "Discovering Literature in Trinidad: The Nineteen Thirties." *Savacou* 2 (1970): 54–60

Levy, Michele. "C.L.R. James, Alfred H. Mendes, and La Diablesse." *Journal of West Indian Literature* 1, no. 5 (April 2001): 1–3.

Sander, Reinhard W. "Alfred H. Mendes: The Sympathetic Observer." In *The Trinidad Awakening: West Indian Literature of the Nineteen-Thirties*. Westport, CT: Greenwood Press, 1988.

—*Emilio Jorge Rodríguez*

Méndez Ballester, Manuel (1909–2003)

∎

A major Puerto Rican dramatist whose works express the conflicts and tensions experienced by ordinary people trying to understand Puerto Rico's change during the

1930s and 1940s from an agricultural society to an industrial environment. Méndez Ballester was a self-taught writer who won numerous awards.

Born in Aguadilla, Puerto Rico, he attended elementary school in his hometown, went to high school in New York City, where his parents were living for a brief time, and, upon their return, matriculated at the Universidad de Puerto Rico. Unable to complete his college education, due to financial restraints, he found employment at a sugar mill where he witnessed the economic uncertainties experienced by sugarcane workers and the authoritarianism of foremen and sugar mill owners. These conflicts would serve as the basis of his first successful play, *Tiempo muerto* (1940).

From the sugar mill, Méndez Ballester returned to San Juan, where he worked as an office clerk. Again, he sympathized with the plight of the average worker. He began to write articles for local publications and befriended writers **Fernando Sierra Berdecía** and **Francisco Manrique Cabrera**; the three founded a traveling theater that staged productions in the countryside. In 1937, Méndez Ballester published a historical novel, *Isla cerrera,* a chronicle of the island during the conquest and colonization by the Spanish. During this period, he worked for a public educational radio station.

In 1938, he wrote the play *El clamor de los surcos*, which was staged in 1939 and was awarded a drama prize by the **Ateneo Puertorriqueño**. Most scholars agree that this play was amateurish; however, it served as a training ground for his second play, *Tiempo muerto*. Written in a realistic vein, *Tiempo muerto* is the story of a patriarch who unable to find a job allows his daughter to work for the company's foremen, who seduces her. However, with the seduction comes a job offer for the patriarch, who quietly accepts the situation. His son, however, is not willing to accept their fate. A series of events bring death to the family. The drama was successfully staged, and his popularity allowed Méndez Ballester to devote all his time to writing.

Méndez Ballester wrote eleven dramas and several short stories. His work explored the Americanization of Puerto Ricans on the island and in the United States as well as the political conflicts between those who want independence and those who settle for a more comfortable life. But there is also a lighter side to the playwright. In works such as the comedy *El milagro* (1958), he makes fun of superstition and religious hypocrisy.

Though not as well known, Méndez Ballester wrote scripts for three Zarzuelas, Spanish operettas: *El misterio del castillo* (1946), *Un fantasma decentito* (1950), and *Es de vidrio de la mujer* (1952). He also wrote a column, often humorous, for the daily *El Nuevo Día* and served in the Puerto Rican Congress from 1964 to 1968. In 1988, a museum—Sala Méndez Ballester—was established in Puerto Rico to honor his memory and preserve his manuscripts. *See also* Realism/Realismo.

Further Reading

Cazurro García de Quintana, Carmen. *Medio Siglo de Periodismo Humorístico-Satírico: el Humor Como Fórmula Artística de Significación en el Periodismo de Manuel Méndez Ballester*. San Germán, Puerto Rico: Universidad Interamericana de Puerto Rico, 1993.

Yin, Philippa Brown. "Puerto Rico." In *Encyclopedia of Latin American Theater*, edited by Eladio Cortés and Mirta Barrea-Marlys, 398–416, 433. Westport, CT: Greenwood Press, 2003.

—*D. H. Figueredo*

Ménil, René (1907–2004)

Martinican philosopher who cofounded, with **Aimé** and **Suzanne Césaire**, the seminal journal *Tropiques*, Ménil was an early promoter of **Négritude**. Later on though, he rebuked the movement as too exclusive.

Ménil was born in Fort-au-France, Martinique. He attended the École Normale Superieure of Paris, where he concentrated on philosophy. He was influenced by Marxism and *surrealism* and explored the African roots of the Caribbean. Upon his return to Martinique, just before the outbreak of World War II in Europe, he became a teacher at the prestigious Lycée Victor Schoelcher in Fort-au-France. At the Lycée he worked with faculty members Aimé and Suzanne Césaire. The trio lamented the cultural vacuum in Martinique, which they saw as the result of French colonialism and racism. In 1941, they founded *Tropiques*, for which Ménil and the Césaires paid out of their pockets. While Aimé Césaire cultivated poetry, Ménil wrote philosophical essays, informed by surrealism, of Caribbean culture and politics.

After the journal ceased publication, Ménil parted company from the Césaires. Suzanne devoted herself to raising her family and Aimé became a major Caribbean poet, a deputy in France, and the mayor of Fort-De-Prince. Ménil continued teaching at the Lycée. The essays he wrote during the 1940s and 1950s were critical of Négritude. He believed that Négritude promoted an exotic image of blacks that functioned as a reaction to European values and which advocated class differences.

In 1981, Ménil published *Tracées: identité, négritude, esthétique aux Antilles*. His second book was *Antilles déjà jadis: Précédé de Tracées* in 1999.

Further Reading

Richardson Michael, ed. *Refusal of the Shadow: Surrealism and the Caribbean*. London and New York: Verso, 1996.

—*D. H. Figueredo*

Messenger Group, The

Founded in 1972, the Messenger Group was a novelty in Guyana: a cultural group that promoted Indo-Guyanese culture and the development of East Indian literature in that nation. The group was founded by cultural activist and poet **Rajkumari Singh**, who attracted artists, stage performers, poets, and novelists to the meetings. These writers and artists met in Singh's house, where they held literary salons.

The Messenger Group, which was active throughout the 1970s, encouraged the career of several poets who achieved national and international recognition, including **Mahadai Das** and **Rooplall Monar**. Other established figures that attended the gatherings were the poet **Martin Carter** and numerous professors and journalists. *See also* Tertulia/Cénacle/Literary Salon/Soirée.

Further Reading

Naidu, Janet A. *Indian Women of Guyana: reflections of their existence, survival and representation.* http://www.guyanajournal.com/women (accessed 6/15/05).

—*D. H. Figueredo*

Métellus, Jean (1937–)

A physician and a mathematics professor, Métellus is a Haitian novelist and poet. His poetry is often compared to the works of **Aimé Césaire**. In his writings, Métellus evokes Haiti's links to Africa.

Born on April 30, 1937, in Jacmel, Haiti, Métellus graduated from secondary school—College Pinchinat—in 1957 and worked as a teacher for two years. In 1959, he emigrated to France, where he attended Faculté des Sciences de Paris, earning a medical degree in 1970. During the 1970s, he combined his knowledge of medicine and math with articles and essays he contributed to medical journals. During the 1980s, he started to write novels: *Jacmel au crepuscule* (1981), *La famille Vortex* (1982), *Une eau-forte* (1983), *La parole prisonnière* (1986), *L'année Dessalines* (1986), and *Les cacos* (1989). These works earned him several literary awards, including the 1982 prize André Barré de l'Académie française, and the 1984 prize Fondation Roland de Jouvenel de l'Académie française.

In 1975, his book-length poem "Au pipirite chantant," published in the journal *Les Lettres Nouvelles*, attracted the attention of French writer Andre Malraux (1901–76), who promoted Métellus's poetry. Three years later, Métellus published the poem as a book, but while critics compared the poem (about a Haitian bird that rises in the morning and sings, symbolizing Haiti's struggles and hope for the future), to Césaire's famous work *Cahier d'un retour au pays natal*, it was not until another edition twenty years later that Métellus received international acclaim. The later volume was entitled *Au pipirite chantant et autres poemes*.

Métellus has also written historical plays that have been staged in France, including *Anacaona* (1985) and *Colomb* (1995). He currently works at the Hôpitaux de Paris and Centre Hospitalier Émile Roux as a neurologist who is particularly interested in how the brain responds to words. His other works include *Les dieux pèlerins* (1997), *L'archevêque* (1999), *Voix nègres, voix rebelles* (2000), *La vie en partage* (2000), and *Toussaint Louverture, le précurseur* (2004).

Further Reading

Naudillon, Françoise. *Jean Métellus*. Paris: L'Harmattan, 1994.

—*D. H. Figueredo*

Mieses Burgos, Franklin (1907–76)

A lyrical poet from the Dominican Republic, Mieses Burgos was one of the founders of the literary movement known as **La Poesía Sorprendida**. His poetry tends to be metaphysical, though written in a language that is accessible and unpretentious.

Mieses Burgos was born in Santo Domingo on December 4, 1907. He attended public schools in the capital and started to write as teenager as a way of escaping his family's poverty. Influenced by the poetry of the Dominican **Enrique Henríquez** and the Nicaraguan Rubén Darío (1867–1916), Mieses Burgos chose to express his creative desires primarily through poetry.

In 1943, he cofounded with Mariano Lebrón Saviñón, **Freddy Gatón Arce,** and Alberto Baeza Flores (1914–98), an influential critic and scholar from Chile, the literary movement known as La Poesía Sorprendida—surprised or bewildered poetry. This movement favored symbolism and **surrealism**, rejecting realism; it was also a method used by the writers to create a type of poetry that could not be censored during the dictatorship of Rafael Leónidas Trujillo (1891–1961). The group published a journal of the same title but with the addition of a subtitle: *La poesía con el hombre universal.* The subtitle, meaning the poetry for the universal man, was coined by Mieses Burgos who wanted to deemphasize national influences, which he believed limited poetry's appeal.

In 1944, Mieses Burgos published *Sin mundo ya y herido por el cielo*, a volume of poetry that he considered his best. The poetry in this collection was musical, lyrical, and passionate:

> Esa ventana tuya por donde yo he querido lanzar mi último grito
> mi más pesada piedra de soledad crecida!

(Through that window that is yours I want to pitch my last shout / the heaviest rock of grown silence!)

Though he refrained from criticizing Trujillo's dictatorship, Mieses Burgos also wrote poetry of social protest such as the collection *Clima de eternida* (1944). His other books of poetry include *Seis cantos para una sola muerte* (1948), *Antología poética* (1952), and *El héroe* (1954). He has been described as the Dominican Republic's best lyrical poet.

He was an affable man who liked to frequent **tertulias**, literary salons. He died in Santo Domingo on December 11, 1976. Poet and critic Marcio Veloz Maggiolo, in *Cultura, teatro y relatos en Santo Domingo* (1972) described Mieses Burgos as a poet that introduced the language of surrealism to the Dominican Republic. *See also* Trujillo Era; Literatura Comprometida/Socially Engaged Literature.

Further Reading

Piña Contreras, Guillermo. *Doce en la literatura dominicana.* Santiago de los Caballeros, República Dominicana: Universidad Católica Madre y Maestra, 1982.

Veloz Maggiolo, Marcio. *Cultura, teatro y relatos in Santo Domingo*. Santiago de los Caballeros, República Dominicana: Universidad Católica Madre y Maestra, 1972.

—*D. H. Figueredo*

Miller, Jeannette (1944–)

Miller is a poet and art critic from the Dominican Republic. She belongs to a group of poets who emerged during the 1960s and who often wrote about the lifestyle of the nation's middle class.

Jeannette Miller was born in Santo Domingo on August 4, 1944. After attending elementary and secondary schools, she matriculated at the Universidad Autónoma de Santo Domingo, majoring in Spanish literature. An expert on Spanish grammar, she conducted numerous seminars on the subject while writing poetry. In 1972, she published her first book of poetry, *Fórmulas para combatir el miedo*. Her second book of poetry, *Fichas de identidad/Estadía,* was published in 1985. Her poetry, written in a free verse that contains a certain musicality, often captures an instance in daily life, such as accidentally colliding with a person on the way to the store or commenting on friends who cry when they drink beer. Under the clear and accessible language, there is the hint, though, of female repression in a society controlled by men. Much of Miller's poetry has been anthologized and appears in Caribbean journals and in such American publications as *Callaloo,* published in Charlottesville, Virginia.

Miller is also a well respected art critic. In 1975 she won the Premio de Investigación Teatro Nacional award for research in art. Other awards honoring her work as a critic are the Premio a la Crónica y Crítica de Arte (1976) and the Supremo de Plata Joyces (1977). Her books on art include *Paisaje dominicano: pintura y poesía* (1992) and *Arte dominicano, artistas españoles y modernidad: 1920–1961* (1996), among others.

Further Reading

Brown, Isabel Zakrzewski. *Culture and Customs of the Dominican Republic*. Westport, CT: Greenwood Press, 1999.

"Answer to a Masochistic Note from My Friends." *Callaloo* 23, no. 3 (Summer 2000): 976–71.

—*Daisy Cocco de Filippis*

Milscent, Jules S. (1778–1842)

The founder of the first literary journal in Haiti, Milscent wrote fables, inspired by the European model, which were based in Haiti. As a patriotic poet, he called for the union of all Haitians in order for the nation to prosper.

Jules Solime Milscent was born 1778 in Grande-Rivière du Nord, Haiti. He was the son of a Frenchman and freed black woman. He studied in France, and upon his return to Haiti, founded in 1817 the country's first literary journal, *L'abeille haytienne*. In this journal he published his poetry, which consisted predominantly of two types: the odes and one he called the "épitre." The latter was a celebratory poem that praised the accomplishments of Haiti's patriots. But Milscent also ventured into other genres, such as fables, love poetry, and madrigals. In his writings, Milscent demonstrated his knowledge of Greek mythology and French literature.

In 1818, President Jean-Pierre Boyer (1776–1850) appointed Milscent member of the commission responsible for the writing of the country's civil code. In 1832, Milscent was elected deputy to congress and six years later he was elected president of that body.

Milscent perished during the earthquake that devastated the nation in 1842. *See also* Haitian Literature, History of.

Further Reading

Berrou, Raphaël, and Pradel Pompilus. *Histoire de la littérature haïtienne*. Tome 1. Port-au-Prince: Editions Caraëbes.

—*D. H. Figueredo*

Mir, Pedro (1913–2000)

Pedro Julio Mir Valentín, known simply as Pedro Mir, was born in San Pedro de Macorís, in the Dominican Republic, on June 13, 1913. One of the great voices of Latin American protest poetry, Mir is also a pan-Caribbean figure. His identification with the populations of all the islands that have suffered the tragedy of sugar and monoculture, as well as his personal history, makes him the son of all the Antilles.

Pedro Mir was born on Dominican soil to a Cuban sugar technician who took up residence in San Pedro de Macorís at the turn of the twentieth century and a Puerto Rican woman, Vicenta Valentín. Mir grew up around sugarcane, in San Pedro de Macorís, and the rich multicultural and multiracial atmosphere it gave rise to. He attended elementary and secondary school in his hometown, where he also attained a teaching degree. Mir's first poems were published individually, while he was working as a schoolteacher there. In 1941, he completed a doctorate in law at the Universidad de Santo Domingo.

In 1947, Pedro Mir departed for Cuba. His exile in Cuba would last twenty years. It was there that he published *Hay un país en el mundo* (1949), a book-length poetic tribute to his native land, then the captive of dictator Rafael Leónidas Trujillo (1891–1961) and the sugar mill, and his best-known poem. From that same period dates "Contracanto a Walt Whitman" (1952), a poem in which Mir establishes a dialogue with the American poet, taking him to task for the degeneration of an earlier "we" into an egotistical and imperial "I."

Mir returned to the Dominican Republic in 1968, and his "Amén de mariposas" was published the following year. Dominican American novelist and poet **Julia Alvarez**, author of *In the Time of the Butterflies* (1994), cites Pedro Mir in the epilogue to her novel and credits his poem to the butterflies—code name for the Mirabal sisters, leaders of the underground resistance to Trujillo—for having informed and inspired the novel. Like the writings of Julia Alvarez, who came after him, all of Pedro Mir's literary texts, whether poetry, short story, or novel, bear witness to history; Dominican, Caribbean, Latin American history. His only novel, *Cuando amaban las tierras comuneras* (1978), now sadly out of print, is an epic narrative of the life of the nation over the course of a half century. Set between the first and second U.S. occupations of the island in 1916 and 1965, respectively, Mir's novel chronicles the aftermath of the American invasion and its effect on national consciousness.

Upon his return to the Dominican Republic, Mir joined the faculty of the Universidad Autónoma de Santo Domingo. In addition to his literary efforts, Mir now also devoted himself to historical research and aesthetics. He published numerous collections of essays, winning a prize for his essay on the Monroe Doctrine, in 1974. That essay was entitled "Las raíces dominicanas de la doctrina Monroe," or "The Dominican Roots of the Monroe Doctrine," and chronicled in essay form, as did his poetry and prose fiction, the complex relations between his nation and the United States. In addition to the novel, Mir authored a collection of short stories, *La gran hazaña de Límber y después otoño* (1977). A prolific essayist as well, Mir published inquiries into literary and aesthetic theory as well as Dominican history.

Best known and loved for his poetry, Pedro Mir, poet laureate of the Dominican Republic, died in July of 2000 at the age of eighty-seven; then president Leonel Fernández declared three days of national mourning. *See also* Dominican Republic Literature, History of; Hispanic Caribbean Literature, History of; Trujillo Era.

Further Reading

Beiro Álvarez, Luis. *Pedro Mir en familia*. Dominican Republic: Fundación Espacios Culturales, 2001.

Mir, Pedro. "There Is a Country in the World." *Callaloo* 23, no. 23, (Summer 2000): 850–57.

—*Pamela María Smorkaloff*

Miranda, Luis Antonio (1896–1975)

A Puerto Rican poet and essayist, Luis Antonio Miranda was also a politician and public servant.

Born in Ciales, he began to work in the local press as a teenager, becoming an editor in his early twenties. Miranda was director of several dailies and reviews: *Florete*, *El Mundo*, and *El Imparcial*, among others. He also founded the review *El Poliedro*.

A supporter of the proindependence movement from the United States, he was an active member of the political parties Partido Nacionalista and Popular Democrático.

Miranda began to write poetry in his teens, publishing his first book at the age of twenty-two, *Abril florido*. Several other volumes followed: *El rosario de doña Inés* (1919), *Albas sentimentales* (1923), *Música prohibida* (1925), and *El árbol lleno de cantos* (1945). His poetry belongs within the **Modernismo** movement of the early twentieth century, which cultivated an intense awareness of aesthetics, a preference for a metaphorical language, and the controlled expression of emotions, though the Puerto Rican version also reflected on a national identity and nationhood.

After the decade of the 1920s, Miranda concentrated on political matters. In 1943, his collection of essays and articles, published in newspapers, *La justicia social en Puerto Rico*, expressed his concern with social and economic development on the island. In 1960, he wrote a literary study, *El negrismo en la literatura de Puerto Rico*.

Further Reading

González, José Emilio. "Poesía: La poesía en Puerto Rico." In *La gran enciclopedia de Puerto Rico*, edited. by Vicente Báez, 22. San Juan: Puerto Rico en la Mano and La Gran Enciclopedia de Puerto Rico, 1980.

Toro-Sugrañes, José A. "Geografía, historia y cultura." In *Nueva enciclopedia de Puerto Rico*. Tomo 4, 141. Hato Rey, Puerto Rico: Editorial Lector, 1994.

—*D. H. Figueredo*

Miranda Archilla, Graciany (1908–91)

Graciany Miranda Archilla was a Puerto Rican poet, journalist and essayist, and co-founder of an important literary movement called **Atayalismo**. The founder of the Association of Puerto Rican Journalists, he also was the director of the Sunday edition of the influential Spanish daily *El Diario*, the principal Spanish language paper published in New York City.

Miranda Archilla was born in Morovis, Puerto Rico on June 2, 1908, the sixth of nine children of Francisco Miranda, a businessman, and his wife Celsa Archilla, a writer of poetry and fiction. He developed a talent for writing and an interest in literature as a young boy. When he was twenty years old, he moved to San Juan to be near the **Ateneo Puertorriqueño**, where poets and writers gathered, and to hone his craft as a poet. In 1928, he joined fellow poets **Clemente Soto Vélez, Alfredo Margenat,** and Fernando González Alberty to found a new poetic movement called Atalaya de los dioses. Atalayismo, as it came to be known, was one of the most debated of the vanguard movements in Puerto Rico, becoming also one of the most prolific. Its members, basically young men, kept their hair long, wore wild clothes, and adopted strange pseudonyms. Their intent was to revolutionize Puerto Rican poetry by breaking with decades of **romanticismo**, both in content and form.

Theirs was to be a different kind of lyric poetry using new themes, imagery, and rhythms.

Several of the island's magazines and newspapers opened their pages to the works of the Atalayistas. The magazine *Gráfico* allowed them a weekly page to publish their poetry. *El Diluvio, La Linterna*, and *Índice* also were receptive to their works. Miranda Archilla became director of the poetry section of *Alma Latina*, where the Atalayistas gave voice to their literary theories. They quickly attracted numerous poets to their group, such as Antonio Cruz y Nieves, **Luis Hernández Aquino**, and Pedro Carrasquillo, among others. The Atalayistas established a press called Atalaya de los dioses and published a book of poetry by Miranda Archilla entitled *Responso a mis poemas náufragos* (1931), considered the classic Atalayista text.

The Grupo Atalaya expressed a need for a more socially conscious and politicized poetry. During the 1930s, under

An editor of the influential daily *El Diario*, Graciany Miranda Archilla was a poet and cofounder of the literary movement Atayalismo. *Source: Centro de Estudios Puertorriqueños.*

the influence of the charismatic leader of the Nationalist Party, Pedro Albizu Campos (1893–1965), the Atalayistas writings began to manifest nationalistic tendencies and to incorporate the Nationalists' ideology. A number of them became followers of Albizu and in fact suffered imprisonment and persecution for their political convictions.

During the 1930s and through the 1940s, Miranda Archilla worked as a writer for various magazines and newspapers. He was a founder of the magazines *Alma Latina, Surco, Sindicales*, and a newspaper, *Juan Caliente*. For numerous years he was the editor of the Sunday section of Puerto Rico's major newspaper, *El Mundo*, and worked for another important newspaper, *El Imparcial*.

In 1933 Miranda Archilla married Julia Carmen Marchand, with whom he had two sons, Graciany and Andrenio. He was divorced in 1946, and in 1951 married Estrella Laboy. As Puerto Rico's political climate became increasingly repressive, Miranda Archilla migrated to New York City with his new wife in search of better job opportunities as well as a more open political environment. Once in the city, he began working as the director of the Sunday section of *El Diario*. He also participated in the cultural and political activities of the Puerto Rican community in New York and in organizations such as the Instituto de Puerto Rico, Círculo de Autores, and Vanguardia Betances. Using the pseudonym Oscar Blanco, Miranda Archilla wrote numerous articles for *Vanguardia Betances*, reaffirming his strong support for Puerto Rican independence from the United States.

Miranda Archilla was the author of several books of poetry as well as of essays, short stories, and novels. Among these are *Cadena de ensueños, Responso a mis poemas náufragos, Sí de mi tierra* (1937), and *El oro en la espiga*. A selection of his historical essays is included in *Clamores antillanos*. He was also an avid translator, and some of his own works, such as *Matria & Monody with Roses in Ash November* (1978) and *Hungry Dust*, are in English. In addition to his creative writing and translating, he devoted time in the last twenty years to writing the history of the Atalayista movement. His unfinished and unpublished manuscript, housed at the Center for Puerto Rican Studies, Hunter College, has been used by researchers to develop dissertations and other works on Puerto Rican literature. He was honored by the Asociación Puertorriqueña de Escritores de Nueva York (1983), the Puerto Rican Institute of New York (1991), La Casa de la Herencia Puertorriqueña (1989), and by the Comité de Afirmación Puertorriqueña 1991), among other organizations for his political and literary contributions.

Further Reading

Miranda Archilla, Graciany. *Poesía vanguardista: 1929–1988*. San Juan, Puerto Rico: Editorial de la Universidad de Puerto Rico, 2002.

—Nélida Pérez and Nelly Cruz

Miss Lou. See Bennett, Louise.

Mittelhölzer, Edgar Austin (1909–65)

Best known for his Kaywana trilogy, historical novels about a Guyanase family, Mittelhölzer was a prolific writer often described as the "father" of the novel in the Anglophone Caribbean. The creator of a national novel, he was the first Anglophone author to become a professional writer. Melancholic by nature, Mittelhölzer predicted his death by suicide in one of his early novels, *Corentyne Thunder*, published in 1941.

Mittelhölzer was born on December 16, 1909 in New Amsterdam, British Guiana. Of Swiss, French, English, and African ancestry, his dark complexion, according to his autobiography *A Swarthy Boy* (1963), displeased his European-looking father. This conflict shaped Mittelhölzer's attitudes as he tried to identify with his European and African heritages. The psychological and cultural tensions he experienced became one of the main themes of his writings.

Mittelhölzer attended the prestigious Bernice High School but was expelled when he kicked a teacher who sarcastically referred to the Guyanase people as "natives." Out of school, he wrote in earnest, submitting short stories to journals in London. Since the stories were usually rejected, the young writer published his own first novel, *Creole Chips*, in 1937, which he attempted to sell door-to-door. Four years later, however, a British publisher accepted and published the novel *Corentyne Thunder*, about a wealthy mulatto in love with a Hindu peasant girl.

Rich in the descriptions of the Guyana countryside, vivid characterizations, and the romantic portrayal of love and passion, the novel, regarded in England as both exotic and erotic, proved successful. From then on, Mittelhölzer didn't stop writing, producing twenty novels in less than twenty-five years.

In 1941 Mittelhölzer moved to Trinidad. Looking for better opportunities as a writer, he relocated to London in 1947, thus being one of the first English-speaking Caribbean authors to go into self-exile. In 1952 he was awarded a Guggenheim fellowship and moved to Canada. From Canada, he traveled to Barbados and then back to England in 1956. Though his novels were generally well received, allowing him a comfortable living, marital tensions, conflict with editors who considered his work pornographic, and mental stress plagued Mittelhölzer and in 1965, he set himself on fire.

Mittelhölzer has been described as a realistic writer, a historical novelist, and a fantasy writer. But it is his family and historical saga, *The Children of Kaywana* (1952), *The Harrowing of Hubertus* (1954), and *Kayana Blood* (1958) that are his best-known works. The trilogy tells the story of the Van Groenweggel family from their arrival at Guyana in the seventeenth century to independence in 1953. The dozens of characters in the novels allowed Mittelhölzer to explore a variety of themes: racial identity, sexual obsessions, family conflicts, colonialism, and postcolonialism. An undercurrent in the stories is the attraction toward death and suicide felt by many of the characters.

Critics from the Caribbean charged that Mittelhölzer sacrificed his art for the sake of popularity and earning royalties. Other critics were vexed by the author's political views and his admiration of such figures as Nero and Benito Mussolini. However, serious and comprehensive study of Mittelhölzer novels and the evolution of his place in the development of Caribbean literature awaits. *See also* Anglophone Caribbean Literature, History of.

Further Reading

Gilkes, Michael. *Racial Identity and Individual Consciousness in the Caribbean Novel.* Georgetown, Guyana: Ministry of Information and Culture, National History and Arts Council, 1975.

Gilkes, Michael. *The West Indian Novel.* Boston: Twayne Publishers, 1981.

Seymour, A. J. *Edgar Mittelholzer: The Man and His Work.* Georgetown, Guyana: privately printed, 1968.

—*D. H. Figueredo*

Modernism. See Modernismo.

Modernismo/Modernism

Though Nicaraguan poet Rubén Darío (1867–1916) is dubbed the father of this major literary movement, Modernismo had its beginning in the writings of the

Cubans **Julián del Casal** and **José Martí** and the Mexican Manuel Gutiérrez Nájera (1863–93). Modernismo embraced prose as well as poetry but it is the latter that became the most popular; its main characteristics were an intense awareness of aesthetics; a preference for a metaphorical language; the controlled expression of emotions; a cultivated longing for the past; a heightened sense of duality or dualism; allusions to paintings, sculptures, and the plastic arts; and the belief that beauty was the only absolute in life. Modernismo rejected sentimentalism, as was sometimes the case with **romanticismo**, the movement which preceded it and from which it emanated. Though initially influenced by French literature and philosophy, Modernismo was the first literary movement that originated in Latin America and then went on to influence Spanish literature in Spain, reversing the usual literary trajectory.

The movement had two phases. The first began in the 1880s and ended at the turn of the century, with the deaths of Martí and Casals, as poet and critic **Eugenio Florit** suggested in *Literatura hispanoamericana: Antología e introducción histórica* (1970). The second phase, which Ruben Dario dominated, ended in 1915. An illustration of the first phase of modernismo can be found in one Marti's verses from the collection *Versos sencillos* (1891):

> Sueño con claustros de mármol
> Donde en silencio divino
> Los heroes, de pie, reposan:
> De noche, a la luz del alma,
> Hablo con ellos: de noche!

(I dream of marble clusters / Where in divine silence / The heroes, repose while standing: / At night with the light from the soul / I speak with them: at night!)

It is Martí who is also considered the first to pen a modernista novel, *Amista funesta* (1895). Despite its romanticism, this tragic love story contained all the elements of Modernismo. Written in a controlled yet poetic language, the novel used the dualism of light and shadow, love and hate, life and death throughout the text, emphasizing the importance of the senses. Equally controlled was the poetry of Casal, who in collections of poems such as *Nieve* (1892) and *Bustos y rimas* (1893), wrote on erotic love and unfulfilled desires, constantly alluding to nonliterary works of art, such as sculptures and paintings. In the Dominican Republic Tulio Manuel Cestero wrote two modernistas novelettes, *Sangre de primavera* (1908) and *Ciudad romántica* (1911). In Puerto Rico, intellectuals embraced Modernismo to combat the growing American influence and the threat of losing of Spanish heritage and language. These writers did not respond to the aesthetic and artistic affectation of this literary movement but to the modernist notion of culture as an artificial entity that could be shaped, that could be created. For writers like **José de Diego, Luis Llorens Torres**, and **Nemesio Canales**, Modernismo became a mechanism to define the particularity of Puerto Rican culture.

The modernistas believed that the writer had to be heroic, if not in deed at least in words. They also longed for a dramatic death, if not heroic at least while still young. Their wishes proved true. For the three writers most identifiable with movement did not reach the age of fifty: Casal, Dario, and Martí.

Modernismo was primarily influenced by the French writers Ferdinand Brunetière (1849–1906) and Theophile Gautier (1811–72). It was practiced in just about every nation in Latin America, though in Brazil it took a different form, as its authors tended to concentrate on developing a literature reflective of Brazilian arts and history. Modernismo was not the same as the modernism movement practiced in Europe, except for Spain, by writers like Joseph Conrad (1857–1924), and by Ernest Hemingway (1899–1961) and William Faulkner (1897–1962) in the United States. Though minor writers from the Spanish-speaking Caribbean continued to write modernista works well into the first half of the twentieth century, Modernismo ceased to exert influence after the advent World War I. *See also* Cuban Literature, History of; Dominican Republic Literature, History of; Puerto Rican Literature, History of.

Further Reading

Anderson Imbert, Enrique and Florit, Eugenio. *Literatura hispanoamericana: Antología e introducción histórica.* 2nd ed. 2: 38–112. New York: Holt, Rinehart and Winston, 1970.

Cardwell, Richard and McGuirk, Bernand. *¿Que es el modernismo? Nueva encuesta, nuevas lecturas.* Boulder, CO: Society of Spanish and Spanish-American Studies, 1993.

Henríquez Ureña, Max. *Breve historia del modernismo.* México, D.F,: Fondo de Cultura Económica, 1954.

—*D. H. Figueredo*

Mohr, Nicholasa (1938–)

Best known as an author of fiction for children and young adults, Mohr has had a wide-ranging career in literature and the fine arts. Her parents migrated from Puerto Rico to New York City, where she was born and raised as one of seven children. In high school she sought a career in art. Despite a lack of encouragement from her family, who believed women were supposed to assume traditional roles, and from her teachers, who placed little faith in the ambitions of a Puerto Rican girl from an impoverished background, she studied fashion illustration, painting, and printmaking in New York City and Mexico. An editor encouraged her to write about her difficult childhood, and her autobiographical novel, *Nilda*, written for young people, and which she illustrated herself, was published in 1973. Set in the early 1940s, the novel follows Nilda for three years, from age ten to thirteen, as she experiences the death of both parents and confronts poverty, the humiliating welfare system, and insensitive teachers. These and other themes of Puerto Rican life in "el barrio" inform her next books, the collections of short stories *El Bronx Remembered* (1975) and *In Nueva York* (1977), the novel *Felita* (1979), and its sequel, *Going Home* (1986). Mohr began writing for young people because she saw a dearth of books that presented the complex lives and struggles of Puerto Rican children living in the United States. She wanted children like herself to recognize themselves in her fiction and to find hope in the endurance of her characters.

In the 1980s, Mohr turned to writing for adult readers, with a sharper focus on the challenges facing Puerto Rican women within a paternalistic culture. *Rituals of Survival: A Women's Portfolio*, published in 1985, contains five stories and a novella featuring women who overcome childhoods marred by parental death and abusive relatives, who confront controlling husbands and the prospect of living alone after their husbands' deaths, and who endeavor to give their children happier lives than the ones they had. She explores similar themes in the short story collection, *A Matter of Pride and Other Stories* (1997). Her 1994 autobiography, *In My Own Words: Growing Up Inside the Sanctuary of My Imagination*, depicts the first fifteen years of her life in Spanish Harlem. In poetic language that is understandable to middle-school readers yet can be appreciated by adults, she describes life as the only girl with six brothers, her crowded apartment and the streets of the barrio, the emergence of her creative ambitions, her conflicts with teachers from kindergarten on, and the death of her parents—her father when she was eight and her mother when she was fourteen.

Mohr has continued to write books for children, including *The Song of El Coquí and Other Tales of Puerto Rico* (1995), a bilingual collection of folktale adaptations illustrated by Puerto Rican artist Antonio Martorell, and *The Magic Shell* (1995) about a child from the Dominican Republic who emigrates with his family to a cold and unfamiliar New York. She has also written plays based on her short stories and autobiography. *See also* Nuyorican Literature.

Further Reading

Hernández, Carmen Dolores. *Puerto Rican Voices in English: Interviews with Writers.* Westport, CT: Praeger, 1997.

Kanellos, Nicolás. "Nicholasa Mohr (1935–)." In *Herencia: The Anthology of Hispanic Literature of the United States*, 241–44. Oxford: Oxford University Press, 2002.

—Lyn Miller-Lachman

Monar, Rooplall Motilal (1945–)

An Indo-Guyanese writer, Monar is a poet and a short-story writer. His works document the traditions and customs of East Indians in the Caribbean and depict the daily struggles of the Indian peasant community in Guyana.

Monar was born in a sugar plantation in Guyana, where both his parents worked as sugarcane cutters. In 1953, the family moved to Annandale, where they settled in house with its own plot. There, his mother planted vegetables for the family. Monar attended a government elementary school and went on, eventually, to Hindu College. He also studied at the Annandale Evening College.

As a youth he wrote poetry, and, in 1967, he won a contest with the poem "The Creole Gang." Other poems were then included in journals and several anthologies of Guyanese writers. In 1971, he published his first volume of poetry,

Meanings, where he analyzed the cultural duality of being an Indian and Guyanese and of the conflicts between traditional Indian values and the modernization of Guyana. In 1983, he published his second book of poems, *Patterns*.

During the early 1970s, he recorded Indian and Guyanese legends and interviewed elderly Indians, discovering that despite the oppressive regime of the sugar plantations, the workers maintained a fierce individuality and a spirit of rebellion. These stories were collected in the volume *Backdam People* in 1985. The two books that followed, *Koker* (1987), and the novel *Jahjhat* (1989), solidified his reputation as a Guyanese writer.

Further Reading

"Rooplall Motilal Monar." http://www.peepalpress.com (accessed 4/10/05).

—*D. H. Figueredo*

Montaner, Carlos Alberto (1943–)

Carlos Alberto Montaner is a Cuban journalist whose columns and articles are published throughout the Spanish-speaking world except for Cuba, where he is banned by the government. He is also a short-story writer, a novelist, and a publisher.

Carlos Alberto Montaner Surís was born in Havana on April 3, 1943. His father was a journalist and his mother a teacher. While a student at the Universidad de la Habana in 1960, he organized a student strike against the revolutionary government. He was arrested and sentenced to twenty years' imprisonment but managed to escape and seek asylum in the Venezuelan embassy. At the age of seventeen, he left for the United States.

He lived in Miami and earned an MA in Spanish at the University of Miami before moving to Puerto Rico. From the island, he relocated to Madrid, Spain, where he founded a publishing company, Editorial Playor. While running the publishing house he became a syndicated columnist for over fifty newspapers in Spain and Latin America. Montaner has appeared on and hosted television programs, has taught at numerous universities in South America and the United States, and has participated in many international conferences. In 1990, he established the organization Unión Liberal Cubana with the objective of helping a democratic transition in Cuba. Fidel Castro's regime has accused Montaner of being a CIA operative and a terrorist.

Montaner has written several books of fiction and two novels. His most famous nonfiction work is *Manual del perfecto idiota latinoamericano* (1996), wherein he comments on what he perceives as the double standards held by Latin American intellectuals who condemn dictatorships all over the hemisphere but refrain from calling **Fidel Castro** a dictator. Montaner's best known novel is *Perromundo* (1972). Though Montaner situates the novel in a prison in an unnamed country, *Perromundo* is a study of political oppression in Cuba and can be placed within the genre known as **anti-Castro literature**. His second novel, *1898: La trama*

(1987), is a playful exploration of the mystery surrounding the explosion of the battleship in Maine in Havana's harbor in 1898.

His other books include *Poker de bruja y otros cuentos* (1968), *Instantáneas al borde del abismo* (1973), *Doscientos años de gringos* (1976), *Raíces torcida de América Latina* (2001), *Viaje al Corazón de Cuba* (1999), *Fabricantes de miseria* (1999).

Further Reading

Fernández de la Torriente, Gastón, ed. *La narrativa de Carlos Alberto Montaner: estudios sobre la nueva literatura hispanoamericana.* Madrid: Cupsa, 1978.

D. H. Figueredo

Montes Huidobro, Matías (1931–)

Matías Montes Huidobro is a Cuban writer who explores Cuban literary history, the revolution, and life in exile in his essays, plays, and fiction. In Spanish, he is best known for his numerous plays. In English, his reputation is based on his novel *Qwert and the Wedding Gown* (1992), about a Cuban exile emotionally paralyzed by his departure from the island.

Born on April 26, 1931, in Sagua La Grande, Cuba, Montes Huidobro seemed destined for a successful career as a dramatist: he began writing as a teenager, won a writing contest for a play he wrote when was eighteen years old, and had his second play, *Sobre las mismas rocas* (1951), staged by the age of twenty. The young playwright embraced the triumph of the Cuban Revolution in 1959 and wrote three plays that celebrated the political change on the island: *La botija, El tiro por la culata,* and *Las vacas,* all written between 1959 and 1960. By 1961, Montes Huidobro realized that the revolutionary government expected Cuban authors to support a socialist political agenda and that dissent would not be tolerated. Such was the theme of his next three plays, written in 1961, *Gas en los poros, La sal de los muertos,* and *La madre y la guillotina,* only the last was staged in Cuba. Shortly after, Montes Huidobro went into exile; the Cuban government soon confiscated copies of *La sal de los muertos.*

In 1962, Montes Huidobro, who had earned a PhD in education from the Universidad de la Habana in 1952, found work as teacher in Philadelphia before relocating to Hawaii, where he taught Spanish drama at the University of Hawaii–Manoa. While he was active in numerous cultural organizations, such as the New York–based Círculo de Cultura Latinoamericana, he did not write a play again until 1979, almost twenty years after his promising beginning. The play was titled *Ojos para no ver,* and it was a symbolical and experimental retelling of the rise to power of **Fidel Castro**, though the ruler's name is never mentioned. In 1988, Montes Huidobro wrote *Exilio,* which follows the trajectory of friends who meet in New York while in exile from Fulgencio Batista's (1901–73) dictatorship in the 1950s, return to Cuba after Castro seizes power, and flee the island one more time.

Exile was also the theme of his collection of short stories, *La anunciación y otros cuentos* (1967) and the novels *Desterrados al fuego* (1975) and *Segar a los muertos* (1980). The first novel is considered his best. It is an autobiographical story about a novelist who is unable to adapt to his exile in the United States while his wife embraces her new life in her new home; while she works in a factory, the novelist idles his days away in the park, longing for the past. The novel follows a stream-of-consciousness narrative with elements of **magical realism**—birds who speak—and erotic passages. The English translation *Qwert and the Wedding Gown* garnered praise. Scholar Ilan Stavans, writing in *The Review of Contemporary Fiction*, celebrated the novel's publication in English: "Matías Montes Huidobro has unjustifiably been forgotten . . . his work should be known better in the English-speaking world."

Montes Huidobro has written dozens of essays, including the prologue to the 1995 reissue of the Cuban classic poetry collection *El Laúd del Destarrado*, originally published in 1858 in the United States, and *Persona, vida y máscara en el teatro cubano* (1973), an authoritative theoretical analysis of Cuban theatre. *See also* Anti-Castro Literature; Cuban Literature, History of; Exile Literature.

Further Reading

Escarpanter, José A. "Una confrontación con trama de suspense." In *Teatro Cubano Contemporáneo: Antología*, edited by Moisés Pérez Coterillo, 623–29. Madrid: Fondo de Cultural Económica, 1992.

Febles, Jorge M. Matías Montes, and Armando González-Pérez. *Huidobro: acercamientos a suobra literaria*. Lewiston, NY: E. Mellen Press, 1997.

Stavans, Ilan. "Qwert and the Wedding Gown." *The Review of Contemporary Fiction* 13, no. 1 (Spring): 264.

D. H. Figueredo

Mooto, Shani (1958–)

Born in Ireland in 1958 of Trinidadian Presbyterian parents, novelist Shani Mootoo left her parental birthplace for Canada at the age of nineteen, where she became a visual artist and filmmaker. Her videos, paintings, and photo-based works have been exhibited internationally. Fiction became for her an avenue for exorcising the pain of childhood sexual abuse and for questioning her multifaceted identities.

Mootoo published her first collection of short stories, *Out on Main Street*, in 1993. The title story explores the relationship between individuals, genders, ethnicities, and migrants and their identification with cultural artifacts such as language, food, dress. The first-person narrative voice, speaking on behalf of the collectivity, frames a multiplicity of potential responses to the central issue of "who are we?" In terms of ancestral belonging, her first person narrator confesses: "We ain't good grade A Indians." In relation to New World acculturation, the declaration is, "We is kitchen Indians." Similarly, Mooto disallows her protagonist any fixed gender identity. Instead, the first-person narrator is a butch lesbian, who is jealous when men eye her excessively femme lover, and a femme jiggly-wiggly identity, geared to attract the same men.

Mootoo's next novel, *Cereus Blooms at Night* (1996), which was short-listed for both the 1997 Giller Prize and the Chapters/Books in Canada First Novel Award, is her haunting contribution to Caribbean writers' recurrent theme: Narratives of Caribbean childhood, with nostalgic associations of paradise lost, innocence defiled, environmental harmonies disrupted. Set in the post indentureship period in Lantacamara, a thinly veiled evocation of Trinidad, the novel is harshly critical of the colonizing and Christianizing agenda of the Presbyterians among the Indians. The main character, Mala Ramchadin, becomes a surrogate wife to her father after he loses his wife to her lesbian lover, who is also his ultimate love object. Mala eventually murders her father and abuser. Silenced by abuse and anguish, she fragments into multiple, voiceless personalities, more at home in nature than in society. The narrative questions which sexual transgression—incest, homosexuality, transvestism, gender fluidity—should be "hyper normalized" and which should be rejected as perverse and why?

Mootoo's fictional voice emanates clearly from her location as an Irishwoman, Canadian, West Indian—the first by virtue of birth, the second by adoption—naturalization—and the third by virtue of childhood upbringing and parental birthplace. Yet Mootoo, a lesbian who "comes out" in the metropolis, masterfully wields her exquisitely crafted fictional tool with activist intent, to slay many a sacred cow. Her works can be read as a symbolic pilgrimage that must come to terms with the landscape, politics, memory, and desire. She reframes the issue of "who am I?" into "who and how and why am I becoming?" Mootoo formulates representational strategies to rescue queer, postcolonial subjectivities from narrative erasure. She unearths her silenced characters and roots them in a rearticulated version of the Caribbean physical and sociocultural landscape. *See also* Gay and Lesbian Literature.

Further Reading

Ghosh, Dipti. "Baigan Aloo Tabanka Bachanal: Writer, Artist, Filmmaker Shani Mootoo in Her Own Words," *Trikone Magazine* 9, no. 4 (1994): 5–6.

—*Paula Morgan*

Morales, Jacobo (1934–)

The first Puerto Rican film director to be nominated for an Oscar and one of Puerto Rico's most successful and popular film actors and producers, Morales is a poet, a dramatist, and a scriptwriter.

A native of Lajas, he conducted his elementary and secondary studies in his hometown. In the early 1950s, he studied theater at the Universidad de

Puerto Rico, though by that time he was already familiar with the performing arts: he had been a radio child actor and had written radio scripts in the 1940s. While at the university, he also appeared in many television programs, becoming a favorite comedic actor. His training and experience helped him later on to secure roles in such American films as *Bananas* (1971), with Woody Allen, where he spoofed **Fidel Castro** (1935–), and *Up the Sandbox* (1972), starring Barbra Streisand (1942–).

In the 1970s, Morales wrote several plays, staged in Puerto Rico: *Muchas gracias por las flores; cinco alegres tragedias* (1973), *Cinco sueños en blanco y negro* (1975), *Aquella, la otra, este y aquel* (1978), and *Una campana en la niebla* (1979). In the same decade, he cultivated political poetry, which criticized colonialism and racism. Collections of poetry such as *100 x 35* (1973) and *409 metros de solar y cyclone fence* (1978), were praised for the accurate and humorous depiction of the Puerto Rican vernacular.

In 1989 his film, *Lo que le paso a Santiago*, a romance about a widower and a beautiful woman he meets, was nominated for an Oscar in the foreign film category.

Further Reading

Fernandez, Ronald, et al., eds. *Puerto Rico: Past and Present; an Encyclopedia*. Westport, CT: Greenwood Press, 1998.

Zurita, Pedro. "El Cine Latinoamericano Desenreda Sombras." *Impacto*. September 29, 1998.

—*D. H. Figueredo*

Morales Cabrera, Pablo (1866–1933)

Morales Cabrera was a Puerto Rican journalist and historian. His two most famous works are *Cuentos populares* (1910) and *Cuentos criollos* (1925), which popularized legends and folklore from the countryside. In his writings, Morales Cabrera celebrated his love of the island and his compatriots.

Born in Toa Alto, Puerto Rico, on August 17, 1866, Morales Cabrera grew up in the countryside, surrounded by farmers whose stories and legends captivated the would-be writer. He submitted stories and articles to the publications *El Buscapié* and *La Correspondencia de Puerto Rico*. He often signed his submissions under the pseudonyms of Tirso de la Torre and José Balsamo.

Through the 1880s and 1890s, he was a rural teacher, and from this experience, he wrote the volume *La disciplina escolar en Puerto Rico* (1903), which won a prize from the **Ateneo Puertorriqueño**. In 1910, he wrote a biography of the nineteenth-century patriot and politician Baldorioty de Castro (1822-1889), *Biografía de Don Román Baldorioty y Castro*. That same year he published the book that brought him national recognition, *Cuentos populares*. The book was a retelling of the stories he had heard from the countryside, duplicating the rhythm and diction of Puerto Rican farmers.

In 1917, he was elected to the Puerto Rican Congress; three years later, he was reelected. During the 1920s, he founded the Asociación de Agricultores de Puerto Rico, editing its journal *El Agricultor Puertorriqueño*. In 1925, he wrote a sequel to *Cuentos populares*, entitled *Cuentos criollos*, a collection of stories that celebrated Puerto Ricans. In 1932, he wrote the history volume, *Puerto Rico indígena: Preshistoria y protohistoria de Puerto Rico*.

Morales Cabrera passed away on February 24, 1933, in San Juan.

Further Reading

Morales Cabrera, Pablo *Cuentos. Con un estudio biográfico-crítico de Esther Melón Porta-latín.*San Juan de Puerto Rico, Instituto de Cultura Puertorriqueña, 1966.

D. H. Figueredo

Moravia, Adeline. See Moravia Family.

Moravia, Charles. See Moravia Family.

Moravia Family

Father and daughter writers and cultural figures from Haiti. Of the two, the father, Charles Moravia, was the most famous.

Moravia, Adeline (1907–78). A native of Port-au-Prince, Adeline Moravia attended elementary and secondary school in her hometown. She then traveled to France, Italy, and the United States. Though she was always interested in writing, she did not actively pursue publishing until late in life.

In her late sixties, she began writing the novel *Aude et ses fantôme*. She submitted it to the contest Prix des Caraïbes in 1976, winning first prize. The novel was published a year later. In 1978, Moravia passed away.

Moravia, Charles (1876–1938). Charles Moravia was born on June 17, 1876, in Jacmel, Haiti. He graduated from the Petit Séminaire Collège Saint-Martial in Port-au-Prince, where he studied literature and politics. While in school, he wrote poetry, which he eventually published as a book in 1903 under the title of *Roses et camélias*. That same year, he published his tribute to patriot **Toussaint Louverture**, *Ode à la mémoire de Toussaint Louverture*. While the first volume consisted of poems written in a romantic vein, the second book was representative of nationalistic poetry.

Moravia was also attracted to theater, influenced by the French playwright Edmond Rostand (1868–1918), the author of *Cyrano de Bergerac* (1897). Writing verse-plays evocative of Rostand, Moravia published *La Crête-à-Pierrot*

(1908) and *Le fils du tapissier: épisode de la vie de Molière* (1923). Both plays were staged in Port-au-Prince. In 1943, he wrote the drama, *L'amiral Killick*. All three plays reproduced historic moments and portrayed historic figures, expressing Moravia's desire to inspire his compatriot by imitating the deeds of great men from history.

Moravia coupled his writing career with duties as a public servant. He was a senator and an officer of the Haitian Academy of Arts and Sciences. He was also the director of the daily newspapers *La Plume* and *Le Temps*

Further Reading

Herdeck, Donald, ed. *Caribbean Writers: A Bio-Bibliographical-Critical Encyclopedia.* Washington, DC: Three Continents Press, 1979.

D. H. Figueredo

Morejón, Nancy (1944–)

Nancy Morejón is one of Cuba's most prominent living poets. Grounded in her Afro-Cuban heritage as well as in the Cuban Revolution and daily Cuban life, Morejón's spare, lyrical poems explore themes that include race, history, the family, and social justice. Broadly speaking, her poetry "gives voice to a chorus of silenced voices," expressing hope for "a tangible utopia," as she expressed in a speech in Cuba in February 2002.

She was born August 7, 1944 in Havana and was raised in the Los Sitios district of Central Havana, where she was surrounded by manifestations of Afro-Cuban culture, such as itinerant musicians and street rumba. She enjoyed a close relationship with her parents. Her mother, formerly a tobacco worker and a seamstress, became a housewife after Nancy's birth. Her father worked as a merchant marine, traveling to the United States for long periods—particularly, to

Prominent Cuban poet Nancy Morejón is inspired by her African heritage and commitment to the Cuban revolution. *Courtesy of William Luis.*

New Orleans—before he settled down as a stevedore in Havana. His experience stimulated Nancy's interest in the United States and in jazz. Both parents encouraged her poetic endeavors from an early age.

Morejón began writing poetry when she was nine years old. She was fourteen at the time of the Revolution, an event that profoundly shaped her life as well as her poetic vision. She studied French language and literature at the Universidad de la Habana, graduating magna cum laude, and subsequently worked at the Cuban Union of Writers and Artists, **Unión de Escritores y Artistas de Cuba (UNEAC)**, with **Nicolás Guillén**. She presently directs the Caribbean Studies Center at **Casa de las Américas**. Morejón maintains an active dialogue with the international literary community and has traveled to Africa, Europe, Latin America, and to the United States, where she has participated in conferences hosted by the Smithsonian Institution, University of California at Berkeley, and Yale University. In 2001 she took part in the Fourth Caribbean Writers Conference at York College in New York City.

She has published thirteen collections of poems—beginning with *Mutismos* (1962)—three monographs, a play, and four volumes of critical studies on Cuban and Caribbean history and literature, most notably, *Recopilación de textos sobre Nicolás Guillén* (1974) and *Nación y mestizaje en Nicolás Guillén* (1982). Translated into more than ten languages, her poems have been compiled into several bilingual anthologies in English and Spanish, among them, *Where the Island Sleeps Like a Wing* (1985) and *Looking Within* (2003). She received the UNEAC essay award for *Nación y Mestizaje* (1980); the Premio de la Crítica, for her collection *Piedra pulida* (1986); and the National Prize for Literature (2001). Morejón is also a translator, having rendered the work of Paul Eluard (1895–1952), **Aimé Césaire**, and **Edouard Glissant** from French into Spanish.

Nancy Morejón's work, which continues the legacy of Nicolás Guillén, draws upon African religion and heritage as an integral component of Cuban culture. In "The Eyes of Eleggua" (1967), the poet combines drama, voice, and vibrant imagery to evoke the Yoruba god's presence. "Black Woman" (1974), her most widely anthologized poem, opens with the line "I can still smell the foam of the sea they made me cross"; the poem majestically details a history of black women—and by extension, of black men—from their arrival in Cuba as slaves to their newfound equality with the triumph of the Revolution, symbolized by "the tree [of] communism whose prodigal wood resounds."

While many of her poems extol the ideals of the Revolution, others reveal a tension between the political and personal spheres. In "At a Meeting" (1993), for example, the speaker daydreams about Cellini (1500–1571) and the splendors of Renaissance Florence until she is brought back to the mundane reality of the meeting that [she] "attend[s] with discipline." Her best poems transcend ideology, building metaphors out of objects such as carnations, clams in a market, or a wine bottle washed up on the shore.

Nancy Morejón incorporates her heritage, life-experiences, and faith in a greater society into a lyrical poetry that reflects the multiple facets of Cuban reality. Her poems distill experience, capturing the immediacy of the moment while speaking to universal themes.

Further Reading

Behar, Ruth, ed. *Bridges to Cuba/Puentes a Cuba*. Ann Arbor: University of Michigan Press, 1995.

Decosta-Willis, Miriam, ed. *Singular Like a Bird: The Art of Nancy Morejón.* Washington, DC: Howard University Press, 1999.

Morejón, Nancy. "Palabras por el Premio Nacional de Literatura," February 2002 http://www. afrocubaweb.com/nancymorejon.htm (accessed 1/15/05).

—Daniel Shapiro

Moreno Jimenes, Domingo (1894–1986)

One of the founders of the literary movement known as **postumismo**, Moreno Jimenes was a popular poet from the Dominican Republic who believed poetry belonged to all people and was not the sole province of the rich and educated. To prove this point, Moreno Jimenes traveled throughout the Dominican Republic, often on foot, to read his poems in schools, clubs, and plazas. He was called the Sumo Pontíco of the postumismo movement.

Moreno Jimenes was born in Santiago de los Caballeros on September 7, 1894. He began to write poetry at the age of seventeen when he fell in love with a girl of Spanish descent; he courted her through his poems, and when her parents rejected him, he used poetry to mourn the separation. In 1911, he published his first book of poems, *Promesa.* This was followed four years later with *Vuelos y duelos.* In 1921, he published *Psalmos.* This was also the year when, along with his friends Andrés Avelino Garcia and Rafael Augusto Zorrilla, he founded the postumismo movement, which was a rejection of **costumbrismo**, regional or local writing, and of European influences in national letters.

During the 1920s and 1930s, Moreno Jimenes wrote eighteen volumes of poetry. He toured the republic, reading from his works and selling the volumes himself. One of his best-known poems was "Mi vieja se muere" (1925), a meditation on his mother's death. Mortality was a dominant theme for the poet, and he visited it again in 1934 when his daughter passed away: his grief inspired him to write "El poema de la hija reintegrada," one of his most popular poems. In 1929, he became director of the journal *El día estético*, and in 1950, he was appointed director of the Instituto de la Poesía Osvaldo Bazil, a cultural institution. Throughout the 1940s and 1950s, he wrote small volumes of poetry, usually about thirty pages long, which were published as pamphlets that he continued to sell himself. He was active in numerous cultural activities, always promoting a poetry that was nationalistic and accessible to all. In 1974, he was awarded the National Poetry Prize. He passed away on September 23, 1986.

In a language that reflected the vernacular of common folks, Moreno Jimenes wrote about his family, the people he met, and the landscape he saw on his travels, always in harmony and unison with his subject, as reflected in the poem "El diario de la aldea" (1925):

> ¡Quién fuera madreselva!
> ¡Quién fuera río!
> ¡Quién fuera cañada!

(Wish that I were a honeysuckle! / Wish that I were a river! / Wish that I could be a canyon!)

Further Reading

Moreno García, Bárbara. *El recorrido poético de Domingo Moreno Jimenes*. [Germany]: B. Moreno García, 2001.

Piña Contreras, Guillermo. *Doce en la literatura dominicana*. Santiago de los Caballeros, Republica Dominicana: Universidad Católica Madre y Maestra, 1982.

D. H. Figueredo

Morisseau-Leroy, Félix (Feliks Moriso Lewa) (1912–98)

This Haitian playwright, poet, novelist, journalist was born in Grand-Gosier in 1912. In a special issue of the magazine *Finesse* (1992), dedicated to Morisseau-Leroy, the poet **Paul Laraque** wrote, "Moriso monchè, Ou se Legba. Se ou ki louvè baryè-a pou nou" ("Dear Morisseau, you are Legba. You are the one who opened the gate for us"). This was a heartfelt tribute from one of the most active poets writing in **Kreyòl** in the second generation. Working under the intellectual inspiration of **Jean Price-Mars** and **Jacques Roumain**, Morisseau must be remembered first as one of the pioneers who wrote in Kreyòl in order to communicate with the people and to prove that it was possible to produce theater, and print literature, in the national language of Haiti. Along with Jacques Roumain and **Jacques Stephen Alexis**, Morisseau made a lifelong effort to communicate with the people, in Africa as well as in Haiti and the United States.

In 1953, Morisseau published the text of his *Antigone en créole*—now available with standard Kreyòl orthography as *Antigòn in Teyat kreyòl*. The following year, Morisseau and colleagues constructed a theater on the Mòn Ekil-Morne Hercule-, close to Morisseau's house in Pétionville. *Antigòn* was produced followed by **Franck Fouché**'s version of *Œdipe Roi*. Although the plays in Kreyòl were publicized and sometimes criticized as "translations," they were in fact new creations with Haitian settings and problems as their context. All aspects of Haitian culture—Kreyòl language, vodou, traditional wisdom, etc.—were central in this theater. **Franketienne's** theater and writings in Kreyòl are deeply indebted to Morisseau's pioneering work.

Morisseau wrote for newspapers and literary journals, including *La Relève*. In protest against the United States occupation of Haiti of 1915–34, he published his first poem, "Debout les jeunes!" in *La Presse* (1929). He finished a "Licence en droit"—law degree—in Port-au-Prince in 1934. After some teaching at the secondary level, Morisseau was given an important appointment in the Ministry of Education in 1941. During World War II, he studied and traveled in the United States for several years, receiving an MA in education from Columbia University in 1943. He published a first novel, *Récolte* (1946), seen by Gouraige as a fictional example of the "primacy of collective action" (435). A second novel, based on an early dramatic sketch, appeared in 1995—*Les Djons d'Aïti tonma*. The first volume of Morisseau's best-known collection of poems was published in Port-au-Prince in 1953: *Diacoute*. This volume included what is perhaps Morisseau's most famous poem, "Mèsi, Desalin"—Thanks, [Papa] Dessalines.

Morisseau's popular appeal, combined with his outspoken opposition to dictatorial tendencies among the Haitian presidents and the continued domination of the United States, quickly put his life in danger following the election of **François Duvalier** in 1957. About one year later, he left Haiti for Paris, where his *Antigòn* was produced at the Théâtre des Nations in 1959.

Morisseau spent some twenty one years in Africa, first in Nigeria, then as a UNESCO consultant in Ghana, and finally as an invited consultant of President Léopold Senghor (1906–2001) in Sénégal. In 1981, Morisseau left Africa, with failing eyesight, and established residence in Miami, where he lived until his death. For years, he continued to produce almost weekly articles for *Haïti en Marche*, published in Miami, as well as to oversee the collecting and reprinting of plays, poetry, and fiction. The collective volumes below—*Dyakout, Teyat, Kont*—include many of Morisseau's earlier writings. Only selections of his poetry have appeared in English to date.

Morisseau-Leroy passed away in Miami in 1998. *See also* Haitian Literature in Kreyòl.

Further Reading

"A mighty voice is stilled." *Miami Times*, September 17, 1998.

Morisseau-Leroy, Félix. *Dyakout 1, 2, 3, 4*. Jamaica, NY: Haïtiana Publications Inc., 1990.

———. *Haitiad & Oddities*. Translated by Jeffrey Knapp, et al. Miami: Pantaleón Guilbaud, 1991.

———. *Les Djons d'Aïti Tonma, roman*. Paris: L'Harmattan, 1996.

———. *Teyat kreyòl*. Delmas, Haiti: Éditions Libète, 1997.

———. *Kont kreyòl*. Port-au-Prince: Imprimerie Le Natal, 2001.

—*Carrol F. Coates*

Morris, Mervyn (1937–)

A Jamaican poet who is described as writing a controlled and intimate poetry, Mervyn Morris is also a respected professor, critic, and literary mentor. He was one of the first to recognize the literary importance of such performance poets as **Louise Bennett** and **Jinta "Binta" Breeze**.

Morris was born in Kingston, Jamaica, on February 21, 1937. As a child his father read him the works of British writers such as P. G. Wodehouse (1881–1975) and works of Jamaican writers, including the popular-oriented poetry of Bennett. Morris attended, with would-be writer **Jean D'Costa**, the Half-Way-Tree Elementary

School, where his mother was a teacher. He won a scholarship to attend secondary school at Munro College, where he began to write short stories and poetry. After high school, he was awarded a scholarship to the University College of West Indies; he studied English, French, and History. In 1957, he won a Rhodes Scholarship and went to St. Edmund Hall, in Great Britain. Upon his return, he assumed teaching and administrative roles at Munro College and at the University of West Indies, where he was mentored by poet and critic **Edward Baugh.**

His first book of poetry was *The Pond* (1973). This volume was followed by *On Holy Week* (1976). The verses in these two collections were written in a simple, direct language that described settings and sentiments with clarity. His third collection, however, consisted of more evasive poems, written in the haiku format of three lines with the last line carrying the message of the piece. The book was entitled *Shadowboxing*, and it was published in 1979. His fourth book of poetry was *Examination Centre* (1992).

Morris's poetry tends to examine the personal and the private. Unlike many Caribbean writers—**Martin Carter** of Guyana, for example—Morris prefers to address not political issues but the complexities of family and domestic life instead. One of his best-known poems is "Family Pictures" (1973). In the poem, Morris vividly and realistically draws a portrait of a happy family and the contented head of the house. But in his mastery of the subtle, Morris suggests that the happy husband and father might also be a prisoner of his family:

> to go alone
> to where . . .
> no one knows
> which man is
> father, husband,victim,
>   . . . the master of one cage.

Writer Pamela C. Mordecai, in *Fifty Caribbean Writers*, observes of Morris: "[he] leaves us in little doubt . . . that he knows perfectly well what he is doing, has careful control of how much he is letting on at any one time, and is quite deliberately carving out the poem" (344).

Morris also spent much of his academic energy promoting the writing of new Jamaican authors, such as Louise Bennett and Jinta Binta Breeze. In that capacity, he edited several seminal volumes that introduced Jamaican writers to readers in Great Britain and in the United States: *Seven Jamaican Poets: An Anthology of Recent Poetry* (1971), *Jamaican Woman: An Anthology of Poems* (1980), and *The Fabor Book of Contemporary Caribbean Short Stories* (1990).

A recipient of the prestigious Musgrave Medal (1976), Morris retired from teaching in 2002. On the occasion of the retirement, such important literary figures as the poet **Mutabaruka** and the critic Baugh participated in a cultural event that rendered tribute to Morris, the poet and the professor.

Further Reading

Chang, Victor L., ed. *Three Caribbean Poets on Their Work*. Mona, Jamaica: Institute of Caribbean Studies, 1993.

Mordecai, Pamela C. "Mervyn Morris (1937–)." In *Fifty Caribbean Writers: A Bio-Bibliographical-Critical Sourcebook*, edited by Daryl Cumber Dance, 343–56. Westport, CT: Greenwood Press, 1986.

D. H. Figueredo

Morrison Fortunato, Mateo (1947–)

A poet from the Dominican Republic, Morrison Fortunato is also a promoter of national culture and identity. He is known for his work as a literary critic and for the many conferences he has organized in the Dominican Republic.

Born in Santo Domingo on April 14, 1947, Morrison Fortunato was raised in that city. At the Universidad Autónoma de Santo Domingo he majored in literature and after obtaining a BA in 1964, he traveled to Venezuela to conduct studies in administration at the Centro Latinoamericano y del Caribe. Returning to the Dominican Republic, he was director of the literary journal *Aquí* and organized numerous cultural and literary conferences. His reputation as a cultural activist and journalist made him a well-known figure in the Dominican Republic.

He published his first book of poems, *Aniversario del dolor*, when he was twenty-six years old. The poems expressed his political commitment to social change in his country and in Latin America. He published his second collection in 1983, *Visiones del transeúnte*. The decade between the two books he devoted to cultural activities, organizing and supervising literary events at the Universidad Autónoma. He served on the board of the Unión de Escritores, an organization for writers, and was a member of a similar group based in Venezuela.

In 1986, he published *A propósito de imagenes*, and in 1991, *Nocturnidad del viento*. Many of these poems he read at public readings and conferences. In 1999, he celebrated three decades of cultural activity and of writing with the publication of *30 años de poesía y otros escritos*.

Further Reading

"Mateo Morrison Fortunato." Escritores dominicanos. http://www.geocities.com (accessed 5/20/05).

D. H. Figueredo

Morúa Delgado, Martín (1857–1910)

Journalist, newspaper editor, and novelist Martín Morúa Delgado was born in Matanzas, Cuba, on November 11, 1857. His father was the Basque Francisco

Morúa and his mother the African Isabel Delgado. Morúa Delgado went to primary school and then learned the trade of barrel maker. He began to write at a young age and, in 1880, founded in Matanzas the newspaper *El Pueblo*. Intended for an Afro-Cuban readership, *El Pueblo* was dedicated to the defense of the rights of Africans and Cubans of African ancestry as allowed by an order established in 1878 by the Spanish authorities as part of the peace agreement—the Pact of El Zanjón—which ended the first Cuban war of independence in 1878.

Becoming active in insurrectionist conspiracies for the renewal of the separatist struggle, in 1884, Morúa Delgado left for New York City, where worked in the newspaper *La Repúlica*. An avid reader, he studied several languages and also worked as a reader, "lector," at cigar factories. Owned by Cubans, the cigar factories hired Cuban cigar workers who had developed in their native island the tradition of hiring someone to read to them while they worked. Morúa Delgado read to the workers Spanish translations of the works of Henrik Ibsen (1828–1906), Fyodor Dostoyevsky (1821–81), Leo Tolstoy (1828–1910), and he himself translated into Spanish the biography of Toussaint Louverture (1743?–1803) by John Beard, and the book *Called Back*, by Hugh Conway.

Until 1886, Morúa Delgado was active in the various insurrectionist projects of Cuban exiles in Jamaica, Central America, Mexico, and the United States. In that year he wrote a letter to General Máximo Gómez (1836–1905)—acknowledged as the supreme military leader of the disbanded Cuban Liberation Army—telling him what he considered to be the main problems with those insurrectionist projects. After that, he withdrew from Cuban insurrectionist activities and settled in Key West, where he married the Cuban Elvira Granados and published the magazine *Revista Popular*.

In 1890, he returned to Cuba and embraced the ideology of the Cuban Liberal Party, known as Cuban Autonomist Party. He worked as a reader for a Havana cigar factory and wrote the novel *Sofía* (1891). He wrote literary criticism for prestigious periodicals such as *Revista cubana, El Figaro,* and *La Habana elegante*, including a controversial critical essay on the novel **Cecilia Valdés**, by the Cuban **Cirilo Villaverde**. In 1892, he began publishing the magazine *La Nueva Era*, addressed to an Afro-Cuban readership, and where he published a series of insightful articles on the Cuban political and social scene. During this time his rivalry with the Afro-Cuban political leader and journalist Juan Gualberto Gómez (1854–1933) intensified. He opposed Gomez's project of a consortium of Afro-Cuban mutual aid associations to wrest from the colonial government the application of desegregationist laws passed in 1878, arguing that the project would foster animosities between black and white Cubans. This rivalry was mirrored by their professional careers as men of letters. In 1891, Juan Gualberto Gómez was inducted into the prestigious Cuban Sociedad Económica; three years later, Morúa Delgado was inducted as well.

When the Cuban war of independence broke out in 1895, Morúa Delgado opposed it, fearing the conflict would only elongate the process of attaining home rule under Spain. But he was disillusioned by the failure of the Madrid government to implement decentralizing laws passed by the Spanish Parliament in 1895, just before the uprising, and the repressive policies implemented in Cuba by the governor appointed in 1896. In July of that year, Morúa Delgado left for the United States where he supported Cuban separatism once again. In 1898, he returned to Cuba as an officer of the Cuban Liberation Army; in the battle fields, he published the newspaper *La Libertad*.

In 1901, he participated in the Constitutional Assembly that drafted the Cuban Constitution of that year, and published the novel *La familia Unzúazu*, a continuation of *Sofía*. After the establishment of the Republic of Cuba in 1902, Morúa Delgado became active in politics as a member of the Liberal Party. As member of the Cuban Senate, he opposed class- or race-based political organizations and sponsored an amendment forbidding the formation of race-based political parties. He was Secretary of Agriculture, Commerce and Labor in the Cabinet of President José Miguel Gómez (1858–1921) when he died at Havana on April 28, 1910. *See also* Negrista Literature.

Further Reading

Hadley, George, "Reading Behind the Face: Corrective Revisions in Martín Morúa Delgado, Charles W. Chestnut, and Frances E. W. Harper." In *Reading Between the Black and White Key: Deep Crossings in African Diaspora Studies, Proceedings of the St. Clair Drake Graduate Culture Studies Forum*, Series 2, edited by Ve A. Clark, 63–80. Berkeley: African American Studies Department. University of California at Berkeley, 1994.

Morúa Delgado, Martín. *Obras Completas de Martín Morúa Delgado, 6 vols.* Habana: Publicaciones de la Comisión Nacional del Centenario del don Martín Morúa Delgado, 1957.

—Rafael E. Tarrago

Mother-Daughter Relationships

Much of the writing of women authors of the Caribbean highlights relationships between generations of women in the same family: mothers, aunts, and grandmothers. A common theme is the struggle of a younger generation of women to break away from traditions held sacred by their mothers without casting off the close connections they have to them as strong survivors and positive role models. At times, it is only by learning the history of their mothers from their aunts or grandmothers that characters come to understand fully the challenges and rewards of their mothers' choices.

Many variations on this theme exist, and it crosses national, racial, and generational boundaries. In an historical example, **Wide Sargasso Sea** (1966), by white novelist **Jean Rhys**, from Dominica, Antionette Cosway Mason fights against, but ultimately is forced to follow, the same unhappy road her mother trod: she uses her beauty to ensnare a husband of high status. Subsequently, she is driven mad by his disregard for what she really is—and is eventually taken away to England, where she becomes the madwoman in the novel *Jane Eyre*.

Sometimes the mother-daughter relationship is complicated by the clash of cultures that occurs when families emigrate to the United States or Great Britain. For instance, **Esmeralda Santiago**'s autobiography, *When I Was Puerto Rican* (1993) shows her younger self, Negi, as she first rejects her mother's choices to bear lots of children and to continue living with her father despite his affairs with other women. After her move with her mother to New York, she discovers a respect for her mother's resilience and great capacity for love. When she asserts herself and talks her way into a better school, she and her mother learn that submission does not work to the advantage of a young Spanish-speaking woman in New York.

In these stories of migration, mothers sometimes are so strict with their adherence to the old ways that they drive their daughters away, to disconnect from their Caribbean roots. A highly emotional example comes from Haitian American writer **Edwidge Danticat** in her novel *Breath, Eyes, Memory* (1994). Sophie, the protagonist, is subjected to the traditional Haitian practice of mothers "testing" their daughters—that is, a mother pushing her fingers against the daughter's hymen as a way of verifying virginity. The humiliation of this practice leaves Sophie with sexual phobias. It is not until she returns to Haiti with her own baby daughter that she learns her mother's whole history and understands her strength: when Sophie discovers that her own birth resulted from her mother's rape, she understands more fully her mother's fears about sexuality as well as the reason why her mother partially rejects her. Similarly, the West Indian mother appears unduly harsh in **Audre Lorde**'s autobiography, *Zami: A New Spelling of My Name* (1982). Young Lorde tries desperately to unite with her mother's heritage through the practice of pounding spice with a mortar and pestle, but her mother keeps her at arm's length so as not to spoil her.

In **Paule Marshall**'s novel ***Brown Girl, Brownstones*** (1959), she demonstrates conflict between mother and daughter for inverse reasons. Here, it is the Barbados-born mother who pushes for an American life of getting and spending, while her daughter, Selina Boyce, yearns for the sunshine and slower ways of the islands, which she finds represented in her father. Likewise, in **Cristina Garcia**'s novel *Dreaming in Cuban* (1992), the daughter rejects her mother's anti-Castro stance and conservative views while demonstrating admiration for the Cuban Revolution.

Ultimately, though, these writers and characters struggle against their mothers, they come to see their histories as unique and important. Their mothers represent getting out from under an oppressive colonial life and a repressive political regime, taking pride in their heritage and origin. *See also* Feminism in Caribbean Literature; Grandparents in Caribbean Literature.

Further Reading

Danticat, Edwidge. *Breath, Eyes, Memory*. New York: Random House, 1994.

García, Cristina. *Dreaming in Cuban*. New York: Knopf, 1992.

Lorde, Audre. *Zami: A New Spelling of My Name*. Freedom, CA: Crossing Press, 1982.

Santiago, Esmeralda. *When I Was Puerto Rican*. New York: Random House, 1993.

—*Angela Conrad*

Moya Pons, Frank (1944–)

A Dominican Republic historian who wrote the first history of that nation in English, Frank Moya Pons is the typical Caribbean scholar who is also an activist and a political figure. His books are standard texts used in the Dominican Republic's secondary schools.

Frank Moya Pons was born on March 13, 1944, in La Vega, Dominican Republic. In 1966, he earned a BA from the Universidad Autónoma de Santo Domingo, an MA from Georgetown University, and a PhD from Columbia University. He taught at numerous universities, including New York University, Columbia University, and City University of New York. He was secretary of state for the Dominican Republic, in charge of the environment and his name has been suggested as a potential presidential candidate in the near future.

Moya Pons has written over twenty books on the history and culture of the Dominican Republic. His analyses are driven by an agenda: reaffirming Dominican culture and heritage and pointing out the errors of the past, even those made by icons of the Dominican Republic. In his famous *The Dominican Republic: A National History* (1995), originally written in Spanish, he criticizes former president **Joaquin Balaguer** for his corruptive regime and censorship of the press. In *El choque del descubrimiento* (1992) he was one of the first established scholars to challenge the celebrations of the quintessential arrival of Columbus, describing it as a commemoration of slavery and the annihilation of the Amerindians. In *La sociedad taína* (1973), he demonstrated that during the sixteenth century, Spanish conquistadores and African slaves had sexual relations with the surviving Amerindians, an idea that had not been fully explored by other historians. Moya Pons is known for writing in an accessible style aimed at a general readership.

Moya Pons's books include *La dominación haitiana, 1822–1844* (1972), *Futuro dominicano* (1980), *Después de Colón: trabajo, sociedad y política en la economía del oro* (1987), *Pioneros de la banca dominicana: una historia institucional del Banco Popular Dominicano y del Grupo Financiero Popular* (1989), *Breve historia contemporánea de la República Dominicana* (1999).

Further Reading

Martínez, Carlos T. "Frank Moya Pons." *Grandes dominicanos*. Santo Domingo: Editora Centenario, 2000.

—*D. H. Figueredo*

Mulata in Caribbean Literature, The

The mulata, or mulatto woman, in English, is usually the offspring of a white man and a black woman. Beautiful and desirable, she is perceived as inheriting the best physical features of her parents. The offspring of an illicit liaison, she embodies lust, sexuality, and abandonment, and as such she is a highly sought possession. To be able to seduce her is a testament of a man's power over a woman, be it through courtship, financial rewards, or force.

The mulata in Caribbean literature is either an object of desire or disdain. Puerto Rican poet **Luis Llorens Torres** expresses her sheer sexuality, and his own lusting, in the poem "Copla mulata" (1929):

> Esta criolla pelinegra y ojinegra,
> boquirroja y dientiblanca;
> . . . temblorosa en el pecho,
> temblorosa en las ancas . . .

(A dark-haired and dark-eyed Creole woman / of red lips and white teeth / . . . of trembling breasts / trembling buttocks . . .).

A couple of lines down the poem, he compares her to a filly that he must mount. Probably, the best-known mulata in literature is the tragic **Cecilia Valdés** (1879, 1882) from the novel of the same name by the nineteenth-century Cuban writer **Cirilo Villaverde**. Valdés is in love with a white aristocrat, whom she hopes to marry. Her tragedy lies in the fact that to her lover she is only a sexual entity and certainly not a woman to marry.

Some writers disdained the racial mixing of the mulata. For **Aimée Césaire**, in his play *Une tempête; d'après "La tempête" de Shakespeare. Adaptation pour un théâtre nègre* (1969), mulata signifies weakness, a reduction of the essential power of blackness. For him, **Caliban**, who is black, represents rebellion and self-assertion; light-skinned Ariel, on the other hand, is indicative of submission and the desire to please the master. More virulent on the subject was **Frantz Fanon**. In his book *Peau noire, masques blancs* (1952) he attacked the Martinican writer **Mayotte Capécia** for writing a novel, *Je suis Martiniquaise* (1948), in which the heroine wants to marry a white man to improve her lot and that of her children. Fanon called this longing "lactification" and interpreted it as a sort of mental illness and of cultural inferiority.

More benign was the Cuban poet **Nicolás Guillén**. In his poem "Mulata" (1930), he expresses his love for a black woman and rejects the so-called attraction of the light-skinned mulata:

> Tanto tren con tu cuerpo
> . . . tanto tren con tu boca
> . . . yo con mi negra tengo,
> y no te quiero pa na!

(Such a fuzz over your figure / . . . such a fuzz over your lips / . . . with my black woman I have everything / and I don't need you for anything.)

For other writers still, the mulata was representative of the many cultures of the Caribbean. That is how **Tomás Hernández Franco**, from the Dominican Republic, conceived of his character Yelidá (1942) in the epic poem of the same name. Yelidá, the daughter of a European sailor and a black slave, is symbolic of the birth of the Dominican Republic. And for **Manuel del Cabral**, also from the Dominican Republic, the mulata, which he describes in the poem "Trópico suelto" (1941) as musical notes—"tu carcajada de maracas . . . tu carne de cuero de tambora (your laughter of maracas . . . your flesh of drums' skins)"— is the essence of the Caribbean.

Further Reading

Mejía Núñez, Guadalupe. "La Mulata en la expresión artística." http://sincronia. cucsh.udg.mx/lamulata.htm (accessed 6/1/05).

Tandt, Catherine Den. "All That Is Black Melts Into Air: Negritude and Nation in Puerto Rico." In *Caribbean Romances: The Politics of Regional Representation*, edited by Belinda J. Edmondson. Charlottesville: University Press of Virginia, 1999.

—*D. H. Figueredo*

Mulatta. See Mulata in Caribbean Literature, The.

Muñoz, Elías Miguel (1954–)

A Cuban American novelist and poet who writes in English and Spanish about intergenerational conflict within Cuban American families and the pressures experienced by male adolescents to adhere to the machismo, or male-driven, code. He has been praised for his complex but sympathetic portrayals of father and son relationships.

Muñoz was born in Cuba and reached his teen years during the decade when the Cuban government was sending gay men, like the novelist **Reinaldo Arenas**, to labor camps, and though Muñoz himself did not suffer such a fate, he would recall the fearful ambiance in his writings years later. In 1969, he and his family migrated to the United States, settling in California. He earned a PhD in Spanish from the University of California–Irvine and taught at Wichita State University. In 1988, he resigned teaching to devote time exclusively to writing.

His two best-known novels are *The Greatest Performance* (1991) and *Brand New Memory* (1998). The first novel is a sensitive study of the relationship between a young boy on the verge of embracing his sexuality and his father: the boy fears the father will reject him upon discovering he is gay. *Brand New Memory* is a coming-of-age novel about a young girl who discovers her heritage when her Cuban grandmother comes to visit her and introduces her to Latin traditions and customs. The girl's parents, successful members of the middle class, are representative of American materialism; the grandmother is a symbol of a spiritual and artistic life, where success is measured by appreciating the beauty in relationships. Comments novelist **Virgil Suárez** of Muñoz, in *Little Havana Blues* (1996): Muñoz adds "layers of complexity to the ethnic [experience] by occupying the space of the . . . marginalized both within the community and externally because of sexual practices" (14). *See also* Grandparents in Caribbean Literature.

Further Reading

Kanellos, Nicolás. *Hispanic Literature of the United States*. Westport, CT: Greenwood Press, 2003.

Suárez, Virgil, ed. *Little Havana Blues: A Cuban-American Literature Anthology*. Houston, TX: Arte Público Press, 1996.

—*D. H. Figueredo*

Muñoz Family

Father and son poets and politicians from Puerto Rico: Luis Muñoz Rivera was a nineteenth-century patriot who fought for Puerto Rico's independence from Spain; his son, Luis Muñoz Marín, was the island's first elected governor.

Muñoz Marín, Luis (1898–1980). Though known as Puerto Rico's first democratically elected governor and the principal creator of the Commonwealth status for the island, Muñoz Marín thought of himself as writer. In fact, the title of his biography, written by Thomas Aitken, is *Poet in the Fortress* (1964). Like the Martinican **Aimé Césaire** and the Trinidadian **Eric Williams**, Muñoz Marín is a prototype of the Caribbean politician who is also a writer.

José Luis Alberto Muñoz Marín was born on February 18, 1898, in San Juan. After spending his childhood in Puerto Rico, he relocated to the United States when his father was appointed Puerto

Representative of the politician who is also an author, Luis Muños Marín (at left in photo) viewed himself more as a poet than a public figure. *Source: Centro de Estudios Puertorriqueños.*

Rico's Resident Commissioner in Washington, D.C. Muñoz Marín attended Georgetown University Preparatory School until he was sixteen years old. After his father's death in 1916, Muñoz Marín traveled back and forth between San Juan and New York City, enrolling for a short while at Columbia University.

In 1917, he wrote a collection of short stories, *Borrones*, while writing for the newspaper *La Democracia*. He befriended Puerto Rican poet **Luis Palés Matos**, and together they toured the Puerto Rican countryside, allowing Muñoz Marín the opportunity to witness the struggles of the peasants who were abused by their employers at the sugar mill and coffee plantations. Around this time, his interest in politics began to grow, and in 1920 he joined the Socialist Party. He became involved with the Pan-American labor movement and in 1929 served as secretariat of the

Pan-American Union. In 1931, he switched to the Liberal Party and a year later was elected to the Puerto Rican Senate, advocating economic and social reforms for the rural poor. During this period, he wrote for several American periodicals, including *The Nation*, the *New Republic*, and The *New York Herald Tribune*.

In 1938, he founded the Popular Democratic Party, campaigning for the reduction of the work day to eight hours, improving the educational system, and establishing laws permitting collective bargaining between employees and employers. During the 1940s, he was president of the Puerto Rican Senate, economic commissioner, and chairperson of the commission on the island's political status. In 1949, he was elected governor. Choosing whether to promote full independence or to concentrate on an economic infrastructure that would improve conditions for all Puerto Ricans, he opted for instituting the commonwealth status which allowed Puerto Rico to enact its laws—as long as they didn't violate the U.S. Constitution—and to receive federal benefits and protection. He also initiated Operation Bootstrap to encourage the presence of American corporations on the island. These initiatives have remained controversial with critics accusing Muñoz Marín of giving up independence in favor of a semicolonial status. This is how author **Edgardo Rodríguez Julia** interpreted it in his book *Tribulaciones de Jonas*, a fictional biography of the governor.

Though political life limited Muñoz Marín's creative energy, he wrote scores of speeches and an autobiography, *Memorías: Autobiografía pública, 1898–1940* (1982), and a follow-up, *Memorías: 1940–1952* (1999). Some of his other works include *Diario, 1972–1974* (1999), *Historia del Partido Popular Democratico* (1984), and *Discursos* (1999). His poetry and prose were collected in 1999 under the title of *La obra literaria de Luis Muñoz Marín: poesía y prosa, 1915–1980*. His nonfiction work details his development as a politician and documents the political process on the island. He passed away on April 30, 1980.

Muñoz Rivera, Luis (1859–1916). He was one of the Puerto Rican patriots who convinced Spain to grant autonomy to the island. However, the Spanish-Cuban-American War of 1898 terminated the potential transition as a defeated Spain yielded Puerto Rico to the United States.

A journalist, Muñoz Rivera founded in 1880 the newspaper *La Democracia*, which published the writings of emerging Puerto Rican authors. In 1899, he founded a second periodical, *El Territorio*, and in 1901, he established The *Puerto Rican Herald*. He favored greater autonomy from the United States but did not openly ask for independence and was instrumental in the legislation known as the Jones Act, which granted American citizenship to Puerto Ricans. He passed away on November 15, 1916.

Despite his political activities, Muñoz Rivera devoted time to the writing of poetry. "Las Campanas" (1887) is one of his best-known poems and is typical of his production. In the poem, he rallies Puerto Ricans to fight for their freedom with "polvora estruendo y choques de espada" (thundering powder and the clash of swords). His poetry typifies the patriotic fervor and literary style of the nineteenth century. His works include *Tropicales* (1902) and *Obras Completas* (1968).

Further Reading

Fernández Méndez, Eugenio. *Luis Muñoz Rivera, hombre visible*. San Juan, Puerto Rico: Biblioteca de Autores Puertorriqueños, 1982.

Lluch Vélez, Amalia. *Luis Muñoz Marín: poesía, periodismo y revolución, 1915–1930.* Santurce: Universidad del Sagrado Corazón; Puerto Rico: Fundación Luis Muñoz Marín, 1999.

—*D. H. Figueredo*

Muñoz Marín, Luis. See Muñoz Family.

Muñoz Rivera, Luis. See Muñoz Family.

Mutabaruka (1952–)

Mutabaruka is probably Jamaica's best-known contemporary **Dub** poet. His poetry is political, advocating an end to racism. He is also an activist.

Mutabaruka, which is a Rwandan word meaning "One who is always victorious," was born Allan Hope on December 26, 1952, in Rae Town, Jamaica, a small enclave of Kingston. After four years at Kingston Technical High School and a brief stint at a job in electronics, his field of study, Mutabaruka joined the Jamaica Telephone Company. During his time there he began to explore Rastafarianism.

Rastafarianism joined two very powerful themes in Mutabaruka's life at this time: political radicalism and spirituality. For Mutabaruka, the Rastafarian movement contextualized the global movement toward independence from European colonial powers in the early 1960s that many Caribbean countries experienced and an international black power movement in the late 1960s and early 1970s that had developed in the wake of a similar movement in the mid-1960s in the United States of America.

Like many Jamaican youth growing up in the aperture between colonial rule by England, and national independence, Mutabaruka had a strong foundation in Western conceptions of Christianity and grew up a Roman Catholic. This religious centering was difficult to reconcile with the black power movement with which he saw himself very much connected through his high school teachers, like Marcus Garvey Jr., and intellectual teachers like Stokely Carmichael, who provided a theoretical framework for his social radicalism. He began to see Rastafarianism as a complete expression of his personal spiritual center and his sociopolitical outlook. Rastafarianism showed Mutabaruka a "visible God," that is to say, man *as* God and showed the importance of an "African perspective" on spirituality, intellectuality, and social consciousness. For Mutabaruka, it is in the milieu of this dynamic political awareness that his poetry comes into being.

While he values reggae music in its own right, and has an intimate relationship with it as the vehicle of much of his work, he nevertheless draws a clear distinction between himself as poet and the musical form this poetry has traditionally taken, "Dub, "which he sees as"dressing to appeal to the people. The message is in the words" Indeed, he sees the term *Dub* as limiting in many ways, as it "refers to only one aspect of my work."

The message of his poetry is clear and consistent. He sees the philosophy of white supremacy, perpetrated by white middle-class men as responsible for much of the global turmoil we see around us today. As he says, "The artist has a responsibility to bring this message to the people." While he concedes the class nature of this turmoil, he sees the politics of the skin very much informing that of social class formation, even in Jamaica where the population is ostensibly black; color discrimination persists to this day, though in very subtle ways. Indeed, his poem "Sitting on the Fence" was informed by both the politics of the skin and the politics of social class. He says of this poem "This was actually based on a man I used to see in my neighborhood when I was growing up. He never said anything to me, I never said anything to him we just watched each other." He continues, "I take that experience and come to the conclusion that poor people are paranoid of rich people, rich people are paranoid of poor people . . . everybody's paranoid." His work has gone some way to reveal, analyze, and address this paranoia. As an advocate for the rights of the oppressed and a voice against injustice, few could find a more original and distinctive poetic voice than Mutabaruka's.

Today, Mutabaruka and his friend Yvonne live in the Potosi District, in St. James. They have two children and live in the house that he built. His books include *Outcry* (1973), *Sun and Moon*, cowritten with Faybienne (1976), and *First Poems, 1970–79* (1980). *See also* Breeze, Jinta "Binta"; Dub Poetry.

Further Reading

Mutabaruka. Home page. http://www.mutabaruka.com/ (accessed 11/12/04).

———. 2004. Interview by Ian Marshall, Nov 15.

Oumano, Elena. "Mutabaruka Presides over 'Spirits.'" *Billboard* 110, no. 205 (June 20, 1998):13–15.

—Ian H. Marshall

N

Naipaul Family

Father and sons from Trinidad, Seepersad Naipaul—the father—was a successful journalist, Shiva Naipaul, a novelist and world traveler, and V. S. Naipaul, the recipient of the 2001 Nobel Prize in Literature. Of the three, V. S. Naipaul is the best known.

Naipaul, Seepersad (1906–53). Seepersad was a brilliant journalist and short-story writer. He served as the basis for the character of Mr. Biswas in the novel *A House for Mr. Biswas* (1961), written by his son V. S. Naipaul.

Seepersad Naipul was born in Longdenville, Caroni, Trinidad, of possibly Brahmin descent. Determined to be successful, Naipul became a journalist. In 1929, he was hired by the *Trinidadian Guardian*.

In 1938, Seepersad Naipaul moved his family from the town of Chaguanas to Port of Spain. He read extensively, from the high literary-minded works of D. H. Lawrence (1885–1930) to the more popularly oriented William Somerset Maugham (1874–1965). His dream was to be a successful writer of fiction, and in 1943, he published a collection of stories and folktales, *The Adventures of Gurweda*. Two schools of thought exist as to whether the collection was successful: In one version, the book sold out in Trinidad; in another version, just a few copies were sold.

Since Naipaul had to support a family of seven, he could not make a living as a writer of fiction. Thus, he concentrated his energy in encouraging his favorite son, V. S. Naipaul. He taught him how to write creatively and referred him to the classics of world literature, especially British literature. Seepersad once told his son that he could use him as model for a novel—which V. S. Naipual did decades later.

Seepersad died of heart failure at age of forty seven. He did not see V. S's and Shiva's successes as writers.

Naipaul, Shiva (1945–83). Shiva Naipaul was born on February 25, 1945, in Port of Spain, Trinidad. After attending elementary and secondary schools in his hometown, he traveled to England to attend University College at Oxford. He graduated in 1968.

Shiva Naipaul followed in his father's and brother's footsteps: he loved literature and was a gifted writer. He submitted short stories to journals and to such anthologies as *Penguin Modern Stories* (1970). In 1971, the novel *Fireflies* brought him fame and recognition. The novel, a study of a family falling apart as a result of internal conflicts and an over ambitious drive to succeed, earned him the John Llewellyn Rhys Memorial Prize and the Winifred Holtby Prize. The novel was widely reviewed in such major publications as the *New York Times Book Review*.

Partly as a result of the novel's success, Shiva Naipaul was appointed lecturer at Aarhus University in 1972. A year later, he published his second novel, the equally successful *The Chip-Chip Gatherers*, which was also set in Trinidad and depicted the adversarial relations of two Hindu families. In 1978, he published a controversial travelogue of Africa, *North of South: An African Journey*. While reviewers praised his writing abilities, scholars felt that Naipaul did not portray Africa accurately.

In the 1980s, Shiva Naipaul wrote several successful novels and a work of nonfiction, *An Unfinished Journey* (1987). The latter was a study of the infamous Jonestown mass suicide: in 1978, a crazed pastor named Jim Jones (1931–78), who had taken his followers from Los Angeles, California, to the jungles of Guyana, ordered all the members of his congregation to commit suicide. Shiva Naipaul's volume is an attempt at understanding the sociological and psychological factors that led to such a tragedy.

Like his father thirty years before, on August 13, 1985, Shiva Naipaul suffered heart failure. His reputation as a writer suffered because of the constant comparisons with his more famous brother, V. S. Naipaul.

Naipaul, V. S. (1932–). Regarded as one of the greatest writers in the English language, Naipaul is a prolific novelist, essayist, and writer of travelogues. In 1990, he was knighted by the Queen of England.

Born in Chaguanas, Trinidad, on August 17, 1932, Vidiahdar Surajprasad Naipaul was introduced to literature and the idea of writing at an early age by his father, who was a journalist. Over the years, son and father would encourage each other in their literary pursuits. Intelligent and gifted, V. S. Naipaul perceived Trinidad as a stifling society with little creativity or social and academic opportunities. Even before his teen years, he had promised himself to leave for England.

At the age of seventeen, Naipaul won a scholarship to study at University College, Oxford. A year later, he finished a novel, which he submitted to a publisher but was rejected. His father consoled him, telling the young Naipaul to keep on writing and to use his father's life as a potential source for a novel.

In Oxford, Naipaul experienced loneliness and probably discrimination: he was dark-skinned and poor. He was determined to be a brilliant student and a brilliant author. He was both, and two years after his graduation in 1953, he published his first novel, *The Mystic Masseur*. The novel presented a humorous, and sarcastic, portrayal of Trinidad, including family members and such well-known figures as **Albert Gomes**, founder of the journal **The Beacon**. Two other novels followed in rapid succession: *The Suffrage of Elvira* (1958) and *Miguel Street* (1959). The latter, a series of connected short stories, proved popular as a young-adult book in the United States. The three works rewarded Naipaul with fame, money, and recognition. His one regret was that his father had died just before the publication of *The Mystic Masseur*.

His father was the subject and inspiration for his next book, *A House for Mr. Biswas* (1961), his most famous and probably his best work. The novel is a complex study of a man intent on achieving success at all costs, in this case, the purchase and ownership of a home in Trinidad. *A House for Mr. Biswas* was soon regarded as one of the best novels in English literature.

Restless and feeling homeless, for Naipaul could not identify with Trinidad and was not completely at home in Great Britain, he accepted a nonfiction assignment: the writing of a travelogue of the Caribbean. The result was *The Middle Passage* (1962), in which he wrote the controversial statement that "nothing was created in the British West Indies" (19). While in one fundamental sense the comment was an attack on colonialism and how it stifled creativity, generations of writers have been insulted by the observation, feeling that Naipaul was belittling the Caribbean and was echoing racist views.

Through the 1960s, Naipaul wrote several novels and collections of short stories, including *Mr. Stone and the Knight's Companion* (1963) *A Flag on the Island* (1967), and *The Mimic Men* (1967). Collectively, the works explored human isolation and exploitation. He traveled throughout Europe and Africa, writing essays and journals and commenting on political and social development. In 1975, he published *Guerrillas*, his first successful novel in the United States. In 1979, he published *A Bend in the River*, where he again wrote a memorable sentence, reflective of his pessimistic nature: "The world is what it is; men who are nothing, who allow themselves to become nothing, have no place in it" (3).

The death of his younger brother Shiva affected V. S. Naipaul, who in the 1980s experienced some emotional and mental distress. The sense of personal loss inspired *The Enigma of Arrival* (1987), where in Naipaul contemplates the futility and brevity of life while also studying the ending of British colonialism. As if to seek escape from personal examination, Naipaul turned to nonfiction and to traveling. He visited the southern United States, seeking comparisons between the region and the Caribbean, *A Turn in the South* (1989), and then toured India, writing *India: A Million Mutinies Now* (1991). Other nonfiction works followed: *Bombay, Gateway of India* (1994) and *Beyond Belief* (1998). In 2000, he published the letters he and his father had written to each other while V. S. was in Oxford. *Between Father and Son* served as a monument to the man who believed in the talent and future of the young son.

In 2001, V. S. Naipaul was awarded the Nobel Prize for Literature. In a press release, the Academy explained the choice: "for having united perceptive narrative and incorruptible scrutiny in works that compel us to see the presence of suppressed histories." The Academy felt that though at times Naipaul had been criticized for controversial observations, his writings provoked readers into a wider view of the human experience and a questioning of all assumptions.

Since winning the Nobel Prize, Naipaul has continued to anger some readers and to challenge all who read his words in works such as *Half a Life* (2001), *The Writer and the World* (2002), and *Magic Seeds* (2004). Concludes critic Rajesh C. Oza in *India Currents* (2005): "While Naipaul has always been full and fierce and sharp and sly, for me he turns light onto darkness, shining his particular brilliance on the world's darkness. He dourly demands that we see the shadows. . . . I usually leave his books shaken and troubled, my sunny optimism braced for the challenges of our changing and unchanging world"(30). *See also* Anglophone Caribbean Literature, History of; Trinidadian and Tobagonian Literature, History of; Immigrant Literature.

Further Reading

Bala, Suman. *V. S. Naipaul: A Literary Response to the Nobel Laureate*. New Delhi: Khosla Pub. House, in association with Prestige Books, 2003.

Barnouw, Dagmar. *Naipaul's Strangers*. Bloomington: Indiana University Press, 2003.

Feder, Lillian. *Naipaul's Truth: The Making of a Writer*. Lanham, MD: Rowman & Little-field Publishers, 2001.

Hughes, Peter. *V. S. Naipaul*. London: Routledge, 1988.

Naipaul, V. S. *The Middle Passage: The Caribbean Revisited*. New York: Random House, 1962, 1990.

"The Nobel Prize in Literature 2001: V. S. Naipaul." *Svenska Akademien*. http://nobelprize.org/literature/laureates/2001/press.html (accessed 4/10/05).

Rajesh C., Oza. "Naipaul's Lives: Half and Whole." *India Currents* 18, no. 10 (Feb. 2005): 30.

—*D. H. Figueredo*

Naturalism/Naturalismo

A movement that reached the Caribbean from France, where its champion was Émile Zola (1840–1902), whose essay "Le Roman experimental" (1880) rallied writers to interpret life and nature with the detached eye of a scientist.

Naturalismo, which was an expansion of **realismo,** or the realistic movement, preferred the seedier side of life and held the belief that man acted by instincts rather than reason; furthermore, naturalismo saw the world as chaotic and interpreted man's behavior as merely a reaction to the chaos. The heroes and heroines were often members of the lower social classes and were usually portrayed as criminals and prostitutes; when the character was highborn, the character was generally a hypocrite.

The Puerto Rican **Manuel Zeno Gandía**, who was a physician, is probably the best known practitioner of naturalism in the Spanish-speaking Caribbean. He conceived a series of novels titled *Crónica de un mundo enfermo* wherein the world was essentially divided into good people and villains with the former usually losing to the latter. The novels in this series were *La charca*—the most famous of the group—(1894), *Garduña* (1896), *El negocio* (1922), and *Los redentores*, written in 1925 but published after the author's death.

In Cuba, **Carlos Loveira** wrote the naturalist novel *Juan Criollo* (1927), and **Miguel Carrión** wrote *Las honradas* (1917) and *Las impuras* (1919). In the Dominican Republic Andrés L. Requeña wrote *Cementerio sin cruces* (1952). Collectively, these novels reflected a preoccupation with history and the effects of political and social events on the individual. Elements of naturalism are present in the works of many twentieth-century writers, including the brothel scenes Haitian **Jacques Stephen Alexis** depicted in his classic *L'espace d'un cillement* (1959), the drama *Short Eyes* (1975) by Nuyorican playwright **Miguel Piñero,** and Nuyorican **Piri Thomas**'s memoir *Down These Mean Streets* (1967). *See also* Romanticismo/Romanticism.

Further Reading

Darbouze, Gilbert. *Dégénérescence et régénérescence dans l'oeuvre d'Émile Zola et celle de Manuel Zeno Gandía: étude compare*. New York: Lang, 1997.

Molina, Sintia. *El naturalismo en la novela cubana.* Lanham, MD: University Press of America, 2001.

—Sintia Molina and D. H. Figueredo

Nau Brothers

Émile and Ignace were nineteenth-century Haitian writers who contributed to the history and literature of the emerging nation. Émile was a historian and Ignace was a poet. Through their writings they affirmed Haiti's right to chart its own political course and to create its own cultural identity.

Nau, Émile (1812–60). Émile Nau believed that through literature Haiti could gain the recognition the world was reluctant to offer the emergent nation. His history of Haiti, *Histoire des caciques d'Haïti* (1854), is an impassioned affirmation of Haitian nationalism.

Émile Nau was born in Port-au-Prince on February 26, 1812. He was part of a group of writers, which included his own brother **Ignace Nau** and the **Ardouin brothers,** who in 1836 met regularly in "cénacles" to discuss the evolution of Haitian literature. During that period, he edited two journals, *Le Républicain* and *L'Union.*

In 1842, Nau was elected administrative deputy of the city of Port-au-Prince. In 1847, he was reelected deputy, and, in 1858, he was appointed to the commission of public education. President Faustin Élie Soulouque (1785–1867) awarded him the title of baron.

In 1854, Nau published *Histoire des caciques d'Haïti,* a combination biography of Christopher Columbus (1451–1506), geography of Haiti, and a study of the Amerindians who lived in Haiti. The work has been criticized for its absence of documented sources but this history, often described by Nau as written in his heart, was an emotional account of Haiti's beginnings and a manifestation of Haitian nationalism at a time when the nations of the world chose to ignore the black republic.

Émile Nau died of high fevers on February 27, 1860.

Nau, Ignace (1808–1845). Ignace Nau was one of the first romantic poets in Haitian Literature. His poetry was vibrant, sorrowful, and nostalgic: he mourned his wife's loss but was consoled by the beauty of the Haitian countryside. He is regarded, with **Coriolan Ardouin,** as the father of Haitian poetry.

Ignace Nau was born in Port-au-Prince, Haiti. For his elementary schooling, he attended L'Institution Jonathas Granville, where he studied ancient Greek literature and such French writers as François Villon (1431–?); he also spent a few years in New York City, where he enrolled at a Catholic secondary school. Because of his intellect and erudition, he served in the government of President Jean-Pierre Boyer (1776–1850), first as the president's personal secretary and then as secretary of the Bureau of Finances.

In 1836, Nau, his brother Émile, and the **Ardouin brothers,** founded the journal *Le Républicain,* which the government regarded as too critical of the republic and shut down. A year later, Nau and his friends founded *L'Union*, which concentrated more on literary matters than on politics.

In the 1830s, the poet's wife, Marie, passed away. The bereaved poet wrote *Livre de Marie*, which consisted of poems of laments and mourning. He also wrote *Pensées du Soir*, in which he recalled the happiness he and his wife had experienced before her death. Nau, however, did not limit himself to his private life: he also celebrated nature in such poems as "A la Belle-de-Nuit" and "Le Tchite et l'Orange." His Catholic faith inspired poems such as "Au Tombeau," about Christ.

Nau, who never recovered from the loss of his wife, lived the rest of his life in relative seclusion. He passed away in 1845. Scholars Raphael Berrou and Pradel Pompilus, in *Histoire de la littérature haïtienne*, called Ignace Nau the first lyrical poet of Haiti; his descriptions of Haiti's natural beauty would influence, a century later, the more nationalist poems of **Émile Roumer**. A complete collection of his poems, *Poésies complètes*, was published in 2000. *See also* Haitian Literature, History of.

Further Reading

Berrou, Raphaël, and Pradel Pompilus. *Histoire de la littérature haïtienne*. Tome 1. Port-au-Prince: Editions Caraëbes. 1975.

Garret, Naomi M. *The Renaissance of Haitian Poetry*. Paris: Présence africaine, 1963.

—*D. H. Figueredo*

Negrismo. See Negrista Literature.

Negrista Literature

During the 1920s a number of writers in Cuba, Puerto Rico, and the Dominican Republic began to write works inspired by African deities and by the dances, customs, and speech patterns of the popular sectors of African ancestry. These writers were echoing the **Négritude** proclaimed by the French-speaking Martinican **Aimé Césaire** and the vogue for African art and culture sweeping through Paris and popular with the European artists and intellectuals of the time. In 1926, the Cuban newspaper *El Diario de la Marina* began publishing the weekly supplement "Ideales de una Raza," addressed to and featuring contributions by Afro-Cubans. Around the same time in Puerto Rico, the group **Los Seis** began to turn to social and racial issues as part of their war on romantic poetry while in the Dominican Republic, **Manuel de Cabral** wrote his impressive collection of poems *12 Poemas Negros*.

In Cuba, the first authors of what came to be called Poesía Negrista were white: **Emilio Ballagas**, Ramón Guirao, José Talle, and **Alejo Carpentier**. But in 1930, the Afro-Cuban **Nicolás Guillén** took the Cuban literary world by storm with his collection of poems *Motivos de Son*. The first writer to popularize Poesía

Negrista in Puerto Rico was **Luis Palés Matos**. Although Palés Matos was white, he celebrated the African elements in Puerto Rican culture, which he considered to be an inseparable part of Puerto Rican identity.

Early Poesía Negrista in Cuba, and in the rest of the Spanish-speaking Caribbean, was picturesque, almost folkloristic, in its evocation of African religion and the dances, customs, and speech patterns of African descendants. But by the second half of the 1930s, Negrista poets began to criticize the exploitation of the African ancestry that had been depicted in a light, almost ridiculing manner. At this time the Afro-Cuban Marcelino Arozarena began to write his class-conscious "sones" and craddle songs. In 1937, Nicolás Guillén joined the Communist Party and published in Mexico his radical collection *Cantos para soldados y sones para turistas*.

The international reputation of Negrista poets like Guillén and Palés Matos has eclipsed Negrista narrative. In the first half of the twentieth century, Venezuela witnessed a veritable explosion of fiction-evoking African themes. Two notable Venezuelan Negrista novelists were Juan Pablo Sojo (1907–1948), author of *Nochebuena Negra* (1943), and Ramón Díaz Sánchez (1903–1968), author of *Cumboto* (1950). Quince Duncan (1940–) in Costa Rica, Cubena (1941–) in Panama, and Carlos Arturo Trunque in Colombia wrote fiction portraying the lives of descendants of Africans in those countries, emphasizing their struggles.

Since 1959, most of the comprehensive critical studies of Negrista/Afro-Hispanic literature have come out of the United States, where significant monographs have been written. These include Richard Jackson's *Black Image in Latin American Literature* (1976), Miriam de Costa's *Blacks in Hispanic Literature* (1977), and William Luis's *Voices from Under: Black Narrative in Latin America and the Caribbean* (1984). *See also* Indianist Literature.

Further Reading

Jackson, Shirley. *La Novela Negrista en Hispanoamérica*. Madrid: Editorial Pliego, 1986.

Mansour, Mónica. *La Poesía Negrista*. México: Ediciones Era, 1973.

Morales, Jorge Luis. *Poesía Afroantillana y Negrista (Puerto Rico-Republíca Dominicana-Cuba)*. Río Piedras: Editorial Universitaria de Puerto Rico, 1981.

—*Rafael E. Tarrago*

Negrista Poetry. See Negrista Literature.

Négritude

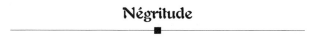

Négritude was a literary and political movement that reaffirmed African heritage while rejecting European values; its first proponents were Léopold Sédar Senghor, from Senegal, **Léon-Gontran Damas**, from French Guiana, and the Martinican **Aimé Césaire**. It was Césaire who coined the term and was the first to use it in writing, including it in his book-length poem *Cahier d'un retour au pays natal*, penned in 1939:

> Ma Négritude n'est pas una pierre
> sa surdité.
> Ruée contre la clameur de jour
> Ma Négritude n'est pas une taie d'eau
> Morte sur l'oeil mort de la terre

(My Négritude is not a stone / deaf. / Against the clamor of the day / My Négritude is not dead water / On the defunct eye of the soil).

Senghor, Damas, and Césaire criticized Europe in general and France in particular for its brutal colonization of Africa and Latin America; they condemned Europeans for promoting the belief that the white race was superior to all the other races; and then dismissed Europeans' contention that Africa was primitive and without culture. Instead, they glorified the mystical bond between Africans and nature and celebrated Africans' physique, spirituality, family ties, and ancestral worship. These authors rallied the black men all over the world to embrace their African roots, advocating a return to Africa.

These ideas were expressed in journals such as *Tropiques* edited by Césaire with his wife, **Suzanne Césaire**, and *Présence africaine*, and in books of poetry and novels published over a period of four decades. Some of the most famous and representative works include the book of poems *Pigments* by Damas (1930); the novels *Gouverneurs de la rosée* by **Jacques Roumain** (1944) and *Rue Cases Negres* by **Joseph Zobel** (1950); the tomes of essays *Ainsi parla l'oncle* by Dr. **Jean Price-Mars** (1928) and *Discours sur le colonialisme* by Césaire (1953).

In the 1960s a new generation of Caribbean writers veered away from Négritude. Some claimed that Négritude mythologized an Africa that never was and negated the Caribbean's colonial experience. Others, like **Patrick Chamoise**, viewed the Caribbean not just as a home for people of African descent but as a multicultural universe where people from France, India, and China, and their descendants, forged rich and complex cultural identities. Still others feared that Négritude could flame an extreme form of black nationalism, such as practiced by dictator **François Duvalier**, that could result in the repression of people not considered black. And in the 1970s, Caribbean feminists criticized Césaire and his colleagues for not acknowledging the role played by women authors, such as Suzanne Césaire, in the early stages of the movement.

According to G. R. Coulthard, in *Race and Colour in Literature* (1962), the roots of Négritude may be traced to Haiti, where the awareness of a black consciousness first flourished in the nineteenth century and in the writing of Haitian intellectual Jean Price-Mars. However, Césaire and Senghor were influenced by the writers of the Harlem Renaissance, particularly **Claude McKay**, who wrote about the fragmentation that existed within the black community as a result of skin color, the popularity of African art and culture in the Paris of the 1920s, and Marxist ideals that sided with the oppressed and marginalized people. In the Spanish-speaking Caribbean, Négritude manifested itself as poetic movement called Poesía Negrista. In the Anglophone Caribbean, however, Négritude was more a political than a literary movement, though there were individual authors, such as **Una Marson**, from Jamaica, who explored and expressed an interest in the Caribbean's African heritage.

The word *Négritude* is French, and its use indicated a preference for its root *negres* rather than *noir*, meaning black. The latter was the polite term used by whites in France while *negres* was derogatory, akin to "nigger" but not as virulent. The conscious selection of *negres* was a defiant act: it meant the authors where choosing what to call themselves. *See also* Caliban; Créolité; Indianist Literature; Negrista Literature.

Further Reading

Berrian, Albert H., and Richard A. Long, eds. *Négritude: Essays and Studies*. Hampton, VA: Hampton Institute Press, 1967.

Coulthard, G. R. *Race and Colour in Caribbean Literature*. London: Oxford University Press, 1962.

Sharpley-Whiting, T. Denean. *Negritude Women*. Minneapolis: University Of Minnesota Press, 2002.

—*D. H. Figueredo*

Negrón Muñoz, Mercedes. See Lair, Clara.

Nettleford, Rex M. (1933–)

An influential cultural figure in Jamaica, Rex Nettleford is a renaissance man who has achieved recognition as a dancer, choreographer, and scholar. As an author, he writes about the culture and politics of the region. His essays, speeches, and studies reflect a commonsense approach that makes him popular with general readers.

Rex Milton Nettleford was born in Falmouth, Jamaica, on February 3, 1933. He received his primary education in his hometown and attended Cornwall College for his secondary studies. In 1952, he attended the University of West Indies. After graduation four years later, he was a Rhodes Scholar at Oxford. At Oxford, his love of music, dance, and theater intensified, and he choreographed several productions, including a rock version of *The Birds*, by Aristophanes (440–380 BCE). At Oxford, he also befriended musician and actor Dudley Moore (1935–2002).

When he returned to Jamaica, he worked for the National Dance Theater Company, where he established the Jamaica School of Dance. A tutor at the University of West Indies, he ascended the academic ranks, eventually becoming director of Extra Mural Studies and of the School of Continuing Education. While dancing and teaching, he began to write in the late 1960s. In 1963, he wrote, with **John Hearne**, *Our Heritage*, and in 1969, he published *Roots and Rhythms: The Story of the Jamaica Dance Theater*. He followed this work with several volumes on the culture and politics of Jamaica—*Caribbean Cultural Identity: The*

Case of Jamaica (1979) and *Inward Stretch Outward Reach: A Voice from the Caribbean* (1992), among them—and edited Norman Manley's (1893–1969) speeches: *Manley and the New Jamaica: Selected Speeches and Writings, 1938–1968.*

In 1998, he was named vice chancellor, and eventually chancellor, of the University of West Indies. A promoter of Jamaican culture, his writings reveal a universal vision of his island and the Caribbean. He shies away from supporting one particular racial definition of the West Indies, promoting instead an all-inclusive perspective of the history and culture of the region. An article in the Jamaican *Gleaner* described Nettleford as "unmatched in the learning and the acuteness of his understanding of the lives of his people."

Further Reading

"Rex M. Nettleford. 1933-." *Contemporary Authors Online*, Gale, 2002. http://www.galenet.galegroup.com (accessed 5/5/05).

"Rex Nettleford." *The Weekly Gleaner* (North American edition). July 23, 2003.

—D. H. Figueredo

New Day (1949)

∎

Written by **Vic Reid**, *New Day* was the first nationalistic novel in Jamaica. The narrative retells the history of the island from 1865, when the Morant Bay rebellion occurred, to 1944, when Jamaica achieved self-rule. The events are seen through the eyes of eighty-seven-year-old John Campbell, recalling his family's involvement with the emerging nation. The novel is not meant to be a historical treatise. The author phrases it thus in the prologue: "I have attempted to transfer to paper some of the beauty, kindliness, and humor of my people, weaving characters into the wider framework of these eighty years and creating a tale that will offer an . . . impression . . . of the way which Jamaica and its people came to today"(viii).

New Day is divided in three parts. Part one begins in 1865, when drought and taxation is crippling the poor farmers, servants, and laborers of the region. An aristocrat named George William Gordon is advocating for the recalling from England of the inefficient governor while a radical preacher called Deacon Bogle insists that war is the only way to release Jamaicans from colonial oppression. John Campbell's older brother David favors Bogle's approach, and one Sunday morning, David, along with some of Bogle's supporters, is arrested. The following day, Bogle's men rescue David, but the confrontation results in a shootout in which forty unarmed Jamaicans are killed by the soldiers. Angered, Bogle leads a full scale rebellion, butchering the mayor and burning the courthouse. When the rebels proclaim that they will destroy whatever belongs to the white settlers, David helps his father's friend, Dr. James Creary, and his beautiful daughter, Lucille, escape. In the meantime, hundreds of British soldiers arrive with orders to kill anyone who is black. In rapid succession, Bogle and Gordon are hanged, and John's father is shot dead. David runs to a cay—a key—off Jamaica, taking with him Lucille and his brother.

In part two, which begins in 1865 and ends in 1882, the queen of England orders an investigation into the rebellion and David, accompanied by Lucille and John, sails to Jamaica to testify before an inquiry board. The board grants him amnesty and the right to build a home on the cay and to cultivate bananas. Before leaving Morant Bay, David marries Lucille, and they have a son, whom they name Creary. On the cay, the banana plantation prospers, but life is monotonous and Lucille grows bored, longing for the social life she had left behind in Jamaica. She befriends the American sea captain who is David's sole buyer and transporter of bananas, and while visiting him on his ship, a hurricane lashes the cay. The captain is forced to set sails, seeking refuge in Cuba, where he dies in an accident. Stranded, Lucille is raped by Spanish soldiers. Ashamed, she decides not to return to the cay, opting for Morant Bay, where she becomes a prostitute, unaware that her husband was killed during the hurricane by a falling palm tree and that John Campbell is raising her son.

In the last part of the novel, covering the years 1882 to 1944, John Campbell rears Creary, who invests the money his uncle and father had made importing bananas, becomes wealthy, marries a woman from England, and leads the life of an aristocrat. He and his wife have a son, whom they name Garth. But their happiness is short-lived: for both die of smallpox, and John is left alone to raise Garth, whom he calls Son-son. After teaching Garth everything he knows about Jamaica, John sends Garth to England to study law. When Garth returns home, he promotes unionism, builds a hospital on his farm for his laborers, and provides scholarship to those who want to attend college. In the early 1940s, Garth founds a political party whose platform is self-rule for Jamaica. He tours the island, promoting his agenda and cultivating businessmen with similar ideas. Through speeches and the use of influential liberal friends from England, Garth is able to convince the British Crown to permit self-government for the island. The novel ends the day the new constitution is to be signed.

New Day was the first Jamaican novel written in Jamaican dialect but edited so that English readers anywhere could understand it. It was also one of the first books to present the Morant Bay rebellion, called a "riot" by British historians, in a favorable light.

Further Reading

Dance, Daryl Cumber. *New World Adams: Conversations with Contemporary West Indian Writers*. Yorkshire, England: Peepal Tree, 1984, 1992.

Reid, Vic. *New Day*. New York: Alfred A. Knopf, 1949. (Reissued by Chatham Bookseller, Chatam, New Jersey, 1972.)

—*D. H. Figueredo*

Nichols, Grace (1950–)

Considered one of the leading poets in Great Britain, Grace Nichols is a Guyanese writer who explores Afro-centrism as well as the need to remember the past in order to succeed in the present. She is also a novelist and children's author.

Nichols was born in Guyana on January 18, 1959, and graduated from the University of Guyana with a degree in communications. She taught for three years before working as a journalist for the newspaper the *Chronicle*. From 1973 to 1976, she was as an information assistant for the Government Information Service. During the 1970s, her first short stories were read over a local radio program, and her first poems appeared in the journal *Focal*. In 1977, she and her partner, the writer **John Agard**, moved to Great Britain, where the separation from her homeland inspired Nichols to write. In 1983, she published *I Is a Long Memoried Woman*, haunting poems about the atrocities committed on black people by racists, illustrated by the role of the master during slavery. But the poems also affirm the need to remember and to rectify the errors of the past: in the poem "I'm Coming Back," the narrator tells the master that she will bend before him, as expected by the master, but only "to rise and strike." The book received wide acclaim and earned Nichols the Commonwealth Poetry Prize.

The recognition brought about invitations to read at schools, colleges, and libraries. In 1985, she published *The Fat Black Woman's Poems*, wherein she challenges the concept of physical beauty imposed by white Europeans:

> If my fat
> was too much for me
> . . . I would have lost a stone.

A year later, Nichols published the novel *Whole of a Morning*, which she had first started writing in Guyana in the early 1970s. In 1989, she published the book of poems *Lazy Thoughts of a Lazy Woman and Other Poems*. In 1996, she received the Guyana Prize for the collection of poems *Sunris*.

In the 1980s, Nichols noticed the need for children books dealing with Afro-Caribbean themes, and to that end she wrote *Baby Fish* and *Other Stories from Village to Rainforest*, which she printed herself in 1983; this effort was followed by several other children's books, all published by such major houses as Macmillan and Viking: *The Discovery* (1986), *No Hickory No Dickory No Dock*, with John Agard (1990), and *Give Yourself a Hug* (1994).

Writer and scholar **Kwame Dawes**, in the book *Talk Yuh Talk* (2001), describes Nichols's style as containing "the terseness of language, the sparseness of adjectival indulgence, and the constant quest for the simply rendered and resonating image that suggests both dream and stubborn reality" (135). M. J. Fenwick, writing in *Sisters of Caliban*, sees Nichols's poetry as socially engaged and "moving toward revolution" (xxx). *See also* Literatura Comprometida/Socially Engaged Literature.

Further Reading

Dawes, Kwame. *Talk Yuh Talk: Interviews with Anglophone Caribbean Poets*. Charlottesville: University Press of Virginia, 2001.

Webhofer, Gudrun. *Identity in the Poetry of Grace Nichols and Lorna Goodison*. Lewiston, NY: E. Mellen Press, 1996.

—*D. H. Figueredo*

Nicholson, Christopher R. (1930–)

A widely successful author from Guyana who is nevertheless not well known be-cause of the many pen names he uses, Nicholson is the creator of the spy hero Jonas Wilde, called "the Eliminator," written under the name of Andrew York. In his spy novels, Nicholson often spoofs Ian Fleming (1908–64) and James Bond. Nicholson has also written dozens of historical novels and thrillers.

The son of a Scottish police officer, C. R. Nicholson was born in Georgetown, British Guiana—now Guyana—on December 7, 1930. After attending primary and secondary schools in Georgetown, he began to work as a clerk at the age of seven-teen at a branch of the Royal Bank of Canada, a position he maintained for nine years. Nevertheless, he still had a desire to study, relocating to Barbados to matricu-late at Harrison College. He also studied at Queen's College, in British Guiana. However, it seems that he did not earn a diploma.

An ardent reader of Arthur Conan Doyle (1859–1930) and Sir Walter Scott (1771–1832), Nicholson began writing in the late 1950s, publishing several histori-cal romances—*Ratoon* (1962), *Dark Noon* (1963), and *Amyot's Cay* (1964). He also wrote a history of Guyana and neighboring islands, *The West Indies: Their People and History* (1965). As the exploits of James Bond revolutionized the espi-onage genre in film, Nicholson opted to cultivate the spy genre. Writing under the name of Andrew York, he created a secret agent named Jonas Wilde, a more soulful James Bond type. From 1966 to 1995, Nicholson wrote over a dozen spy adven-tures. One novel in the series was filmed in 1968, *Danger Route*, starring British actor Richard Johnson (1927–) as the super spy.

The Andrew York novels proved profitable for Nicholson, who relocated to England. He continued writing under his own name but also used other names: Leslie Arlen, Robin Cade, Peter Grange, Mark Logan, and Alan Savage. Combined, he wrote thrillers and historical romances set in such exotic locations as Paris dur-ing the French Revolution: *Tricolour: A Novel of the French Revolution* (1976) and *French Kiss* (1978). With his wife, Diana Bachman, he wrote mysteries and thrillers using the name Max Marlow.

His many pseudonyms have made him an elusive figure, and his body of work does not always reveal his Caribbean roots. Nicholson lives in Channel Islands, England, where is also known as Christopher Nicole.

Further Reading

"C. R. Nicholson." *Contemporary Authors Online*. The Gale Group, 2001. http://www.galenet.galegroup.com (accessed 5/10/05).
St. James Guide to Crime and Mystery Writers. Detroit: St. James Press, 1996.

—*D. H. Figueredo*

Nicole, Christopher. See Nicholson, Christopher R.

Niger, Paul (1915–62)

A writer from Guadeloupe, Niger is the pseudonym of Albert Beville, who took his pen name from the great African river Niger. He was a poet and a political activist. He was also a hero of the French underground during World War II.

A native of Basse-Terre, Guadeloupe, Niger completed secondary studies at the Lycée Carnot in the town of Pointe-à-Pitre before traveling to Paris to attend the École de la France d'Outre-mer, a school established to train colonial officers. At the school, he met writer and compatriot **Guy Tirolien** and other students and intellectuals who were supportive of **Négritude**, the black consciousness movement founded by **Aimé Césaire, Léon-Gontran Damas**, and Léopold Senghor (1906–2001). When World War II broke out and France was invaded by the Nazis, Niger remained in Paris, working for the underground.

At the end of the war, he served as a colonial administrator in West Africa. His experiences in Africa inspired him to write poetry, with his poems appearing in 1948 in the anthology *Anthologie de la nouvelle poésie negre et malgache*, edited by Senghor. In 1956, he wrote the novel *Les puissants*. In 1960, he participated in France in Guyana's independence movement. In 1962, he published an essay rejecting assimilation and promoting an affirmation of the African roots of the Caribbean, "L'assimilation, forme suprême du colonialisme." Two years later, on June 22, 1962, Niger died in plane crash in Guadeloupe. His last novel, *Les grenouilles du mont-kimbo*, was published posthumously in 1964.

Niger's major theme was Africa and the pride he felt in being a descendant of Africans. His poetry is described by Edward A. Jones, in *Voices of Negritude* (1971), as "at once violent and tender, like the land of his ancestors" (82).

Further Reading

Jones, Edward A. *Voices of Negritude*. Valley Forge, PA: Judson Press, 1971.

Kesteloot, Lilyan. *Black Writers in French*. Translated by Ellen Conroy Kennedy, 279–80, 302–3. Philadelphia: Temple University Press, 1974.

—*D. H. Figueredo*

Noismo

Noismo was a short-lived literary movement from Puerto Rico, founded in 1925 by Vicente Geigel Polanco, Enrique Lervold, Vicente Palos Matos, **Samuel R. Quiñones**, Antonio Colorado, and Jose Arnaldo Meyners. Other collaborators included **Juan Antonio Corretjer, Fernando Sierra Berdecia**, and **Cesáreo Rosa Nieves**. These writers were known as the "Grupo No" or "Los Nos." Their manifesto, published in the journal *El Imparcial* in 1926, claimed a rejection of foolish and effeminate literature, while endorsing utilitarianism and puritan values. Much

Noista poetry was published in periodicals. By 1928 the group had ceased to exist, though most of its members became prolific writers and participants in the development of modern Puerto Rican culture.

Further Reading

"Poesía." In *La gran enciclopedia de Puerto Rico*. Vol. 3, 140–141. San Juan, Puerto Rico: Puerto Rico en la Mano y La Gran Enciclopedia de Puerto Rico, 1976.

—*D. H. Figueredo*

Nolla Family

Mother and daughter writers and poets from Puerto Rico. Members of a prominent family, the mother is known as Olga Ramírez de Arellano and the daughter as Olga Nolla.

Nolla, Olga (1938–2001). Nolla was a feminist and controversial Puerto Rican writer. Her poems and novels criticized macho culture and advocated for sexual equality.

Nolla was born on September 18, 1938, in Río Piedras, Puerto Rico. Her uncle was Luis A. Ferré (1904–2003), governor of Puerto Rico, and her cousin is the novelist **Rosario Ferré**. Upon graduation from high school in Mayagüez, she attended Manhattanville College, New York. In the 1960s, she began to write, and during the 1970s, she and her cousin Ferré, founded the journal *Zona, carga y descarga*, where she published some of her early poems.

In 1973, Nolla published her first collection of poems, *De lo familiar*. Other works followed: *El sombrero de plata (1976)*, *El ojo de la tormenta (1976)*, *Clave de sol (1977)*, *Dafne en el mes de marzo (1989)*, *y Dulce hombre prohibido (1994)*. The poems revealed an elegant but frank sexuality; often erotic illustrations accompanied the text.

In the 1990s, Nolla began to write prose, first the collection of short stories *Porque nos queremos tanto* (1990) and then the novels *La segunda hija* (1992), about a family in Puerto Rico during the 1950s; *El castillo de la memoria* (1996), a historical novel about explorer Juan Ponce de León and his family; and *Rosa de papel* (2002), about an ambitious Puerto Rican politician. *La segunda hija* was deemed pornographic in Puerto Rico. Once, when Nolla was invited to read the novel at a school, she was forced away by armed guards.

Nolla passed away in New York City in 2001. Her other works include *El manuscrito de Miramar* (1998), *El caballero del yip Colorado* (2000), and *Unicamente míos* (2001).

Ramírez de Arellano de Nolla, Olga (1911–). A native of San Germán, Olga Ramírez de Arellano attended Catholic schools before conducting her secondary studies at the Escuela Superior de Mayagüez. In 1936, she earned a BA in humanities from the Universidad de Puerto Rico. While a student, she wrote poems that were published in the journal *La Torre*. In 1937, she married José Nolla, a scientist and author of several botanical studies. While raising her family, she continued writing, achieving recognition with the publication of her first book of poems *Cauce hondo* (1947). This volume was followed by *El rosal fecundo* (1955).

Throughout the 1960s and 1970s, she wrote over eight volumes of poetry—including *Te entrego, amor* (1962), *Mar de poesía* (1963), and *Orbe* (1966)—numerous short stories and theatrical pieces that were staged in San Juan but had not been published yet. While her work, consisting primarily of love poetry or verses that celebrate and affirm a Puerto Rican identity, have proved popular on the island, she has yet to achieve recognition in Latin America.

Further Reading

Enciclopedia puertorriqueña: Siglo XXI. Vol. 5. Santurce: Caribe Grolier, Inc. 1998.

"Olga Nolla." http://www.suagm.edu/umet/olga_nolla/pages/bio.html (accessed 9/9/05).

Santos Febres, Mayra. "Adiós a una gran poeta: Olga Nolla." *El Diario La Prensa*, Aug. 2, 2001.

—*D. H. Figueredo*

Notas y Letras; semanario de literatura y bellas artes (1886)

This was the first literary journal published in Curaçao. It was founded and directed by Ernesto Romer, a Hispanist, and the poet **Joseph Sickman Corsen**, and printed by Agustin Bethencourt, a local businessman. The three financed and distributed the publication, which published seventy-two issues.

Notas y Letras came out weekly and it contained articles written in Spanish, thus serving the Sephardic Jews, Venezuelans, and Colombians who lived there as well as migrants from the Dominican Republic who had settled in Curaçao mainly for political reasons. *Notas y Letras* published poems and stories written by writers from the Caribbean and Latin America. It also printed articles that had been published elsewhere.

The journal demonstrated to colonial authorities that there was an interest in literature and in the arts in Curaçao. Later on, the poet Corsen went on to achieve fame as the first writer to publish in the Papiamentu language.

The journal ceased publishing in 1886. *See also* Literary Journals.

Further Reading

Haas, F. de. "Notas y Letras vornde band met Midden-en Zuidamerikaanse dichters." *Beurs-en-Nieuwsberichten*, May 5, 1969.

—*Emilio Jorge Rodríguez*

Novas Family

Father and daughter writers from Cuba. Together their literary output spanned the twentieth to the twenty first centuries.

Novas, Himilce (1944–). The daughter of Cuban novelist **Lino Novas Calvo,** Himilce Novas was born on June 19, 1944, in Havana. Growing up in a home surrounded by books and frequented by writers, her household served as something of a writers workshop. In fact, she and her parents often communicated through writing. At the age of twelve she began to write poetry, publishing some of her poems in a literary journal edited by Nobel Prize winner José Camilo Cela (1916–2002), from Spain.

In 1960, she and her parents left Cuba, settling in New York. She went to Julia Richman High School, where she was feature editor of the school paper

Lino Novas Calvo was a novelist and short-story writer who was one of the earliest creators of Magical Realism. *Courtesy of the photographer, Himilce Novas.*

and wrote a regular column, which won a Columbia School of Journalism Award. She attended Hunter College and the City University Graduate Center (CUNY). She worked as a journalist for such publications as the *New York Times* and the *Christian Science Monitor.* Ascending through the ranks of publishing, she was appointed editor in chief of *L'Officiel/USA.* From 1990 to 1994, she hosted and produced a radio talk show, *The Novas Report.* She has taught at numerous universities, including Wellesley College and the University of California–Santa Barbara.

While leading an active professional life as a journalist and producer, Novas has written several works of fiction and nonfiction, earning the distinction of being one of a handful of Latino writers whose output is regularly reviewed and featured in such major periodicals as the *Los Angeles Times* and the *Philadelphia Inquirer* and on such radio stations as National Public Radio.

Her best-known work of nonfiction is *Everything You Wanted to Know About Latino History* (1994), a clever and accessible compilation of facts, this book has been reprinted several times and is on the list of books recommended by the New York Public Library and the Smithsonian Institution, among others. It is her fiction, however, that has attracted critical attention. Her first novel, *Mango, Bananas, and Coconuts: A Cuba Love Story* (1997), is a satirical and innovative reinterpretation of the popular genre of romance and of **magical realism,** in which the fantastic is combined with the routine. Her second novel, *Princess Papaya* (2004), challenges traditional Latin American views on gender and sexual relationships while still exploring such political issues as oppression and marginalization.

Himilce Novas has also written dramas, her play *Scrips* was produced by legendary Broadway producer Joseph Papp (1921–1991). She is an actor and an artist as well, using the name Supernovas.

Novas Calvo, Lino (1905–83). One of the early creators of **magical realism,** where the fantastical and the ordinary exist side by side, Novas Calvo was a Cuban novelist and short-story writer praised for his in-depth studies of marginalized characters, such as peasants and the urban poor, doomed to tragic endings. The Spanish translator of William Faulkner (1897–1962) and Ernest Hemingway (1899–1961), he was influenced by these two American writers, evoking emotions rather describing them and hinting at a darker meaning beyond simple and straightforward dialogues. His best-known work is *El negrero: Vida novelada de Pedro Blanco Fernández de Trava* (1933), a realistic historical novel about a slave trader.

Novas Calvo was born in Spain and was sent to Cuba by his parents to be reared by an uncle. Self-educated, Novas Calvo worked at various jobs, from factory work to sugarcane cutter, eventually finding a position at a prestigious Havana bookstore, where he befriended writers and professors. During his free time, he studied French and English at night school and through correspondence courses.

In 1927, he wrote the poem "El camarada", which was published in the influential literary journal *Revista de Avance*, and in 1929, he published the short story "Un hombre arruinado." Both works were well received by the literary circles of the time and established his reputation as a gifted writer. As a result, in 1931, he returned to Spain as a journalist for a Cuban periodical. While in Madrid, the journal *Revista de Occidente* published three of his short stories. Describing the religious practices of Afro-Cubans and conjuring a landscape that seemed exotic to the Spaniards, Novas Calvo became a favorite among Madrid's literary critics and intellectuals.

He went back to Cuba in 1940. Two years later, he received the Hernández Cata Award for fiction. During the 1940s and 1950s, he wrote numerous short stories, which were included in the collections *Cayos Canas* (1946) and *El otro cayo* (1959). The stories were noted for their reproduction of Cuban speech and mannerisms. A year after **Fidel Castro** came to power, Novas Calvo left for the United States, where he taught at Syracuse University. Despondent over the political change in Cuba and nostalgic for the island, he didn't have the same creative drive of his youth. During this period he edited a collection, titled *Maneras de contar* (1970), of previously published stories and new pieces; the latter were essentially within the genre of **anti-Castro literature.** Perhaps his most memorable anti-Castro short story is "Un bum," a retelling of Poe's "Cask of Amontillado," in which an exile plots the assassination of a Castro supporter who has sent to prison and to death many victims falsely accused of conspiring against the revolutionary government.

Novas Calvo passed away in New York City. In 1983, the literary journal **Mariel** devoted an issue to his creative output. Though many of his short stories are included in anthologies of Latin American literature and his novel *El negrero* has never been out of print, Novas Calvo is still a neglected and underestimated Caribbean writer. *See also* Cuban American Literature, History of; Negrista Literature; Santería in Literature.

Further Reading

"Himilce Novas." http://www.supernovas.org/index13.htm (accessed 6/15/05).

Roses, Lorraine Elena. *Voices of the Storyteller (Contributions to the Study of World Literature, no. 14)*. Westport, CT: Greenwood Press, 1986.

Souza, Raymond D. *Lino Novás Calvo*. Boston: Twayne, 1981.

—*D. H. Figueredo*

Novelas gaseiformes. See Labrador Ruiz, Enrique.

Novísimos

This term refers to young Cuban writers who cultivated the short-story genre during the 1990s. Most of these writers were born in the 1970s, were not from Havana, and were not interested in living in the capital, as most Cuban writers had tended to do in the past. Some of the writers in this group include **Marylin Bobes, Adelaide Fernández de Juan, Pedro Juan Gutierrez,** and **Ángel Santiesteban.**

These writers addressed such themes as the difficulties of living in Cuba after the fall of the former Soviet Bloc, the propagation of prostitution, the exodus of the "balseros"—the would-be exiles who left the island on home-made rafts—and the war in Angola. The style used by these writers is testimonial, realist, naturalist; the prose is often lyrical and oblique, hinting rather than expressing sentiments. Collections of short stories representative from this period are *Alguien tiene que llorar* (1995) by Bobes and *Sueño de un día de verano* (1998) by Santiesteban. *See also* Cuban Literature, History of; Naturalism/Naturalismo; Posnovísima.

Further Reading

Conner, Olga. "La generación de los posmarieles: Germán Guerra." *El Nuevo Herald*, April 14, 2002.

Valle, Amir. "La narrativa cubana de los 90." http://www.literaturas.com/IslasAmirvalle-cuba2003.htm (accessed 6/10/05).

—*Rolando Pérez and D. H. Figueredo*

Nuyorican Literature

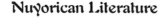

Nuyorican literature is produced by Puerto Ricans born or raised in the continental United States. While the term *Nuyorican* derives from the combination of the words *New York* and *Puerto Rican*, today the term follows Puerto Ricans wherever they live in a bilingual and bicultural environment outside of the island. Author **Jaime Carrero** even promoted the term *Neo-Rican* as a further denotation of bicultural evolution.

Puerto Rican writing in New York dates back to the end of the nineteenth century, and creative writing in English dates back to the 1940s, when newspaper columnist **Jesús Colón** made the transition to English for the *Daily Worker*. This seems to be a rather appropriate beginning for Nuyorican writing and identity, given that Colón was highly identified with the Puerto Rican working class and staking out a piece of Manhattan as part of Puerto Rican cultural identity. Many of the writers who followed him were influenced by his highly regarded book *A Puerto Rican in New York and Other Sketches* (1961). Unlike the writers of the island of Puerto Rico, who are members of an elite, educated class and many of whom are employed as university professors, the New York writers who came to be known as Nuyoricans are products of parents transplanted to the metropolis to work in the service and manufacturing industries. These writers are predominantly bilingual in their poetry and English-dominant in their prose; they hail from a folk and popular tradition heavily influenced by roving bards, storytellers, "salsa" music composers, and the popular culture and commercial environment of New York City.

Nuyoricans are generally bilingual and bicultural, as is their literature. During the search for ethnic roots and the civil rights movement of the 1960s, young Puerto Rican writers and intellectuals began using the term *Nuyorican* as a point of departure in affirming their own cultural existence and history as divergent from that of the island of Puerto Rico and that of mainstream America. A literary and artistic flowering in the New York Puerto Rican community ensued in the 1960s and early 1970s as a result of greater access to education and the ethnic consciousness movements. By the early 1970s, a group of poet-playwrights working in the Lower East Side of Manhattan—"Loisaida"—gathered around a recitation and performance space, the Nuyorican Poets' Café, and generated exciting performances and publications. Included in the group were **Miguel Algarín**, the founder of the café, Lucky Cienfuegos, **Jesus Abraham "Tato" Laviera**, and **Miguel Piñero**, with frequent participation from **Victor Hernández Cruz**, Sandra María Esteves, **Pedro Juan Pietri**, and **Piri Thomas**, all of whom became published writers and literary activists. Three of the core Nuyoricans, Cienfuegos, Piñero, and Thomas, were ex-convicts who had begun their literary careers while in prison and associating with African American prison writers; all three influenced the development of Nuyorican writing by concentrating on prison life, street culture and language, and their view of society from the underclass. Algarín, a university professor, contributed a spirit of the avant-garde for the collective and managed to draw into the circle such well-known poets as Allen Ginsberg (1926–1997), and the Nuyorican Poets' Café was often successful at reestablishing the milieu and spirit of the Beat Generation cafés. **Tato Laviera**, a virtuoso bilingual poet and performer of poetry, "declamador," contributed a lyrical, folk, and popular-culture tradition that derived from the island experience and Afro-Caribbean culture but cultivated specifically in and for New York City.

It was Miguel Piñero's work and life, which has been memorialized in the Hollywood film *Piñero*, however, that became most celebrated, his prison drama *Short Eyes* having won an Obie and the New York Drama Critics Circle Award for Best American Play in the 1973–74 season. His success, coupled with that of fellow

Nuyorican Piri Thomas, as well as that of Pedro Pietri, who developed the image of street urchin always high on marijuana, resulted in Nuyorican literature and theater often being associated with crime, drugs, abnormal sexuality, and generally negative behavior. Thus, many writers who in fact were asserting Puerto Rican working-class culture did not want to become associated with the movement. Still, others wanted to hold onto their ties to the island and saw no reason to emphasize differences, preferring to stress similarities.

What exacerbated the situation was that the commercial publishing establishment in the early 1970s was quick to take advantage of the literary fervor in minority communities, and issued a series of ethnic autobiographies that insisted on the criminality, abnormality, and drug culture of the New York Puerto Ricans. Included in this array were Piri Thomas's *Down These Mean Streets* (1967, issued in paper in 1974), his *Seven Long Times* (1974) and *Stories from El Barrio* (1978); Lefty Barreto's *Nobody's Hero* (1976); and a religious variation on the theme, Nicky Cruz's *Run Nicky Run*. So well worn was this type of supposed autobiography that it generated a satire by another Nuyorican writer, **Ed Vega**, who comments in the introduction to his novel *The Comeback* (1985):

> I started thinking about writing a book, a novel. And then it hit me. I was going to be expected to write one of those great American immigrant stories, like *Studs Lonigan*, *Call It Sleep*, or *Father*. . . . Or maybe I'd have to write something like *Manchild in the Promised Land* or a Piri Thomas's *Down These Mean Streets*. . . . I never shot dope nor had sexual relations with men, didn't for that matter, have sexual relations of any significant importance with women until I was about nineteen. . . . And I never stole anything. . . . Aside from fist fights, I've never shot anyone, although I felt like it. It seems pretty far-fetched to me that I would ever want to do permanent physical harm to anyone. It is equally repulsive for me to write an autobiographical novel about being an immigrant. In fact, I don't like ethnic literature, except when the language is so good that you forget about the ethnic writing it.

More than anything else, the first generation of Nuyorican writers was dominated by poets, many of whom had come out of an oral tradition and had found their art through public readings. Among the consummate performers of Nuyorican poetry were Victor Hernández Cruz, Sandra María Esteves, Tato Laviera, and Miguel Piñero. Like many of his fellow poets, Cruz's initiation into poetry was through popular music and street culture; his first poems have often been considered jazz poetry in a bilingual mode, except that English dominated his bilingualism and thus opened the way for his first book to be issued by a mainstream publishing house: *Snaps: Poems* (Random House, 1969). Tato Laviera's inventive use of **Spanglish**, the mixing of English and Spanish, has risen to the level of virtuosity. The inheritor of the Spanish oral tradition, with all of its classical formulas, and the African oral tradition, which emphasizes music and spirituality, Laviera brings together Manhattan and Puerto Rico. His first book, *La Carreta Made a U-Turn* (1979), uses **René Marqués's** classic play *La carreta* (1952) as a point of departure, but instead of suggesting a return to Puerto Rico, he affirms that Puerto Rico can be found in Manhattan.

One of the few women's voices to be heard in this generation is a very strong and well-defined one, that of Sandra María Esteves, who from her teen years has been very active in the women's struggle, Afro-American liberation, the Puerto Rican independence movement and the performance of poetry. In 1973, she joined

El Grupo, a New York-based collective of touring musicians, performing artists, and poets associated with the Puerto Rican Socialist Party. By 1980, she had published her first collection of poetry, *Yerba Buena*, which involves the search for identity of a colonized Latina of color in the United States, the daughter of immigrants from the Caribbean. Her three books—*Yerba Buena, Tropical Rains: A Bilingual Downpour* (1984), and *Bluestown Mocking Bird Mambo* (1990)—affirm that womanhood is what gives unity to all of the diverse characterizations of her life.

Nicholasa Mohr is one of the most productive Nuyorican prose writers. Her works include *Nilda* (1973), *El Bronx Remembered* (1975), *In Nueva York* (1986), *Rituals of Survival: A Woman's Portfolio* (1985), and *A Matter of Pride and Other Stories* (1997), in addition to numerous works for children. Her best known novel, *Nilda*, traces the coming of age of a Puerto Rican girl living in New York during World War II. Highly autobiographical, the novel depicts a girl who gains awareness of the plight of her people and her own individual problems by examining the racial and economic oppression that surrounds her and her family. In *El Bronx Remembered* and *In Nueva York*, Mohr examines through a series of stories and novellas various Puerto Rican neighborhoods and draws sustenance from the common folks' power to survive and still produce art, folklore, and strong families in the face of oppression and marginalization. In *Rituals* and *A Matter of Pride*, Mohr portrays women who take control of their lives, most of them by liberating themselves from husbands, fathers or families that attempt to keep them confined in narrowly defined female roles. In the 1990s, these themes were revisited in **Esmeralda Santiago's** memoir, *When I Was Puerto Rican* (1993) and her autobiographical novels *America's Dream* (1997) and *Almost a Woman* (1999).

A Nuyorican writer who has not benefited from the collective work done by the Nuyoricans is **Judith Ortiz Cofer**, who grew up in New Jersey and has lived most of her adult life in Georgia and Florida. Cofer is the product of university creative writing programs, and her poetry and prose are highly crafted as well as capturing some of the magic and mystery of the Latin American Boom. Her first book of poems, *Reaching for the Mainland* (1987), is the chronicle of the displaced person's struggle to find a goal, a home, a language, and a history. In *Terms of Survival* (1987), she explores the psychology and social attitudes of the Puerto Rican dialect and how it controls male and female roles; in particular she carries on a dialog with her father. In 1989, Cofer published a highly reviewed novel of immigration, *Line of the Sun*, and in 1990 an even more highly received collection of autobiographical essays, stories, and poems, *Silent Dancing: A Remembrance of Growing Up Puerto Rican*. Cofer followed with another highly regarded novel, *The Latin Deli*, in 1994, and a collection of stories for young adults, *The Year of Our Revolution*, in 1999. *See also* Code Switching; Kanellos, Nicolás; Realismo/Realism.

Further Reading

Algarín, Miguel, and Miguel Piñero. *Nuyorican Poetry: An Anthology of Puerto Rican Words and Feelings.* New York: Morrow, 1975.

Algarín, Miguel, and Bob Holman. *Aloud: Voices from the Nuyorican Poets Café.* New York: Holt, 1994.

—Nicolás Kanellos

O

Obeah Practices in Literature

Early European accounts of obeah in the Caribbean typically conflated it with other syncretic African-based practices and religions such as **vodou, Santería,** or Shango. In general, these accounts would use *obeah*, or one of the other terms, to indicate a form of magic that Africans and their Caribbean-born descendants would practice in defiance of colonial authority. Obeah does differ significantly, however, from these other practices in that it is not a religion centered on the life of the community but is rather an individualized practice and system of beliefs employing the clandestine use of charms, fetishes, and pharmaceutical plants to gain power over a person or a situation.

The word *obeah* (also spelled obi, obia, and obiah) has its etymological roots in the Ashanti word *obayifo*: a wizard or witch. The word traveled to the Caribbean from the Gold Coast of Africa—modern-day Ghana—by means of the Middle Passage. The slave trade between the British and the Gold Coast created a strong presence in the British Caribbean colonies of Ashanti and related ethnic groups, who brought with them a set of beliefs concerning spirituality and the natural world, including the belief that the obayifo has the power to use both spirits and nature to further human ambitions and purposes. The nature of the use of this power is ambiguous. According to some sources, it is a neutral power with the potential for both good and evil; according to others, it is inherently malignant. In contrast, the reaction of the British colonial authority to obeah betrays no ambiguity whatsoever. The colonial government associated obeah with slave rebellions, and they believed leaders such as Tacky, who spearheaded a Jamaican revolt in 1760, to be obeah men. British government officials and plantation owners also feared being poisoned, a well-known tactic in the arsenal of obeah practitioners. After the 1760 revolt, the Jamaican government made the practice of obeah a capital offense, a law which the other British-controlled islands soon instituted.

Caribbean literature makes occasional reference to obeah practice; obeah men and women appear in both early colonial descriptions of Caribbean culture and later postcolonial drama, fiction, and poetry. A good source of early accounts is Roger Abrahams and John Szwed's *After Africa: Extracts from British Travel Accounts and Journals of the Seventeenth, Eighteenth, and Nineteenth Centuries concerning the Slaves, their Manners, and Customs in the British West Indies.* Alan Richardson's article "Romantic Voodoo: Obeah and British Culture, 1797–1807" provides an overview of romantic British texts that focus thematically on obeah and obeah practitioners. Caribbean literature that makes implicit or explicit reference to obeah includes the following representative examples: Jamaica Kincaid's novel *Annie John* (1985), Jean Rhys's poem *Obeah Night* (1964), Derek Walcott's poem *Omeros* (1990), and Phyllis Shand Allfrey's novel *The Orchid House* (1953).

Further Reading

Abrahams, Roger, and John Szwed, eds. *After Africa: Extracts from British Travel Accounts and Journals of the Seventeenth, Eighteenth, and Nineteenth Centuries concerning the Slaves, their Manners, and Customs in the British West Indies.* New Haven, CT: Yale University Press, 1983.

Bisnauth, Dale. *History of Religions in the Caribbean.* Trenton, NJ: Africa World Press, Inc., 1996.

Olmos, Margarite Fernandez, and Lizabeth Paravisini-Gebert, eds. "Religious Syncretism and Caribbean Culture." Introduction. *Sacred Possessions: Vodou, Santería, Obeah, and the Caribbean.* New Bruswick, NJ: Rutgers University Press, 1997.

Richardson, Alan. "Romantic Voodoo: Obeah and British Culture, 1797–1807." *Sacred Possessions: Vodou, Santería, Obeah, and the Caribbean,* edited by Margarite Fernandez Olmos and Lizabeth Paravisini-Gebert, 171–94. New Bruswick, NJ: Rutgers University Press, 1997.

Williams, Joseph J. *Voodoos and Obeahs: Phases of West India Witchcraft.* New York: Dial Press, 1932.

—Paula Makris

Obejas, Achy (1956–)

Achy Obejas is a Cuban Jewish American writer who questions what it means to be Cuban, in the United States and on the island, while also exploring the themes of gay identity and Jewishness within the context of the Cuban experience.

Achy Obejas was born in Havana, Cuba on June 28, 1956. When she was six years old, her parents emigrated to the United States. Obejas grew up not in Miami, where most Cuban exiles live, but in Michigan City, Indiana, where her family settled. In 1979 she moved to Chicago, where she currently resides. She is a journalist, novelist, short-story writer, and essayist. As a journalist, Obejas has been publishing in mainstream, gay, and other alternative media for over two decades. She began at the *Sun-Times* in Chicago in 1980 as a staff writer, moving to the *Chicago Tribune* in 1991 as a record reviewer. In 1996, she was offered a full-time job there. Obejas has stated that, as a journalist, the alternative press is her real love. She wrote for the *Chicago Reader* from 1981 to 1996 and presently contributes book reviews to the *Village Voice.*

Along with the central themes of cubanía—or Cubanness—and queerness explored in her fiction, Obejas admits to being intrigued and influenced by Chicago, even as she was growing up in Michigan City. From Michigan City she could see the lights of the big city and read the works of Nelson Algren (1909–81), Richard Wright (1908–60), and Lorraine Hansberry (1930–65). Her fiction, set in Chicago, involves gays, Cubans, and Cuban Americans. Her most recent novel, *Days of Awe* (2001), deals with Chicago, Cuba, being gay, and Jewish culture. In preparation for writing the novel, Obejas researched her Jewish heritage and explored her Sephardic roots.

In 1995, at the age of thirty-nine, Obejas returned to Cuba, and she has retained that connection to the place of her

Achy Obejas is one of the first writers to explore gay themes in Cuban American literature. *Courtesy of Achy Obejas.*

birth, independent of politics. It is the connection to Cuba that has, perhaps, allowed her to engage in a dialogue with the Cuban canon and to explore, existentially, in her works what it means to be Cuban, what it means to be American, and what it means to be Cuban American in the social landscape of the present. It is her engagement with the Cuban present that marks Obejas as one of the new voices in an engagé **Cuban American literature**.

Obejas's first book, the short-story collection, *We Came All the Way from Cuba So You Could Dress Like This?* (1994), deals with displaced people, Latinos and gays, people living on the margins. The story, which lends its title to the collection, deals with intergenerational conflict among Cuban Americans, shattering many of the myths of exile. She continues on this trajectory with her second book, *Memory Mambo* (1996), winner of the Lambda Literary Award. The novel considers exile to be equivalent to false memory, and in it Obejas takes on all of the false memories held dear by her Cuban American characters. The trajectory of her fiction from the earliest short story to her latest novel, *Days of Awe*, examines what it means to be Cuban American in the same way that **Alejo Carpentier**'s oeuvre examines what it means to be Cuban. *See also* Exile Literature; Gay and Lesbian Literature.

Further Reading

Smorkaloff, Pamela María. *Cuban Writers on and off the Island: Contemporary Narrative Fiction.* New York: Twayne, 1999.

—*Pamela María Smorkaloff*

Ofelia. See Matamoros, Mercedes.

Oliver Frau, Antonio (1902–45)

A short-story writer who depicted the Puerto Rican countryside with a sense of nostalgia, Oliver Frau was an attorney.

A native of Lares, Oliver Frau grew up in the countryside, admiring the coffee plantations that sprawled on the sides of the mountains. In 1926, he earned a law degree from the Universidad de Puerto Rico. That same year, he published the collection of short stories *Cuentos y leyendas del cafetal*.

The volume consisted of local legends he had heard as a child as well as his own stories. Some of the stories depicted supernatural tales, such as one of a man who sells his soul to the devil, while others were love stories or portrayals of country folks. The stories collected in the volume had been written many years before its publication. After 1926, Oliver Frau submitted stories and articles to numerous journals, including *Puerto Rico Ilustrado* and *El Mundo*, but he never published another volume.

Oliver Frau died in Ponce. His one book of stories serves as a link to an agricultural era and a landscape that no longer exists, a world, as he described in the introduction to his stories, "of forgotten coffee plantations."

Further Reading

Oliver Frau, Antonio. *Cuentos y leyendas del cafetal*. Yauco, Puerto Rico: Tipografía El Eco de Yauco, 1938.

Vázquez, Margarita, and Daisy, Caraballo. "Cuento: El Cuento en Puerto Rico." In *La gran enciclopedia de Puerto Rico*. Tomo 4, edited by Vicente Báez, 91. San Juan: *Puerto Rico en la Mano and La Gran Enciclopedia de Puerto Rico*. 1980.

—*D. H. Figueredo*

Oliver Labra, Carilda (1922–)

A Cuban poet known for her love and erotic poetry, Carilda Oliver Labra was awarded the island's National Literary Prize in 1997 and was the guest of honor at the prestigious 2004 Feria International del Libro—International Book Fair—held in Havana; the fair was dedicated to her poetic achievements. Oliver Labra also wrote patriotic and revolutionary poems that celebrate the Cuban flag and hero Ernesto "Che" Guevara (1928–67).

Carilda Oliver Labra was born in Matanzas, Cuba, on July 6, 1922—some sources say 1924. She earned a teaching degree from the Instituto de Segunda Enseñas in Matanzas in 1943. Two years later, she graduated from the law school of the Universidad de la Habana. In the late 1940s, she studied art at the Escuela de Artes Plásticas, in Matanzas. During the 1950s, she taught literature and art at diverse schools. After the triumph of the Cuban Revolution in 1959, she participated in the national campaign to end illiteracy; during the 1960s she worked as an art instructor, held several government offices related to art and culture, and organized and hosted dozens of literary conferences.

In 1946, Oliver Labra published her first erotic poem, "Me desordeno, amor, me desordeno," a lyrical description of the act of lovemaking:

> Te toco con la punta de mi seno
> y con mi soledad desamparada;
> y acaso sin estar enamorada;
> me desordeno, amor, me desordeno.

(I touch you with the point of my breast / and with my orphaned loneliness; / and though I'm not yet in love; / I lose myself.) In 1949, she published the book of poetry *Al sur de mi garganta*, which received critical attention and was awarded the 1950 National Poetry Award. Not all her poems, however, are erotic. In 1953, she wrote "Canto a Martí," a tribute to the beloved nineteenth-century poet and patriot **José Martí**, and in 1957, while **Fidel Castro** was leading the war against dictator Fulgencio Batista (1901–73), she wrote "Canto a Fidel," a celebration of Castro's heroism. Other titles include *Canto a Matanzas* (1956), *Memoria de la fiebre* (1958), *Desaperece el polvo* (1984), and *Sonetos* (1993).

Oliver Labra is widely read in Europe, where she has been translated into English, French, and German. French singer and actor Yvés Montand (1921–91) recorded some of her poetry. In Spain, a cultural foundation bears her name.

Further Reading

González Castro, Vicente. *Cinco noches con Carilda*. Habana: Editorial Letras Cubanas, 1997.

Oliver Labra, Carilda. *Antología de la poesía heroica y cósmica de Carilda Oliver Labra*. Introducción, Salvador Bueno Menéndez; prólogo y análisis arquetípico, Fredo Arias de la Canal. México: Frente de Afirmación Hispanista, 2002.

—*D. H. Figueredo*

Ollivier, Émile (1940–2002)

Ollivier was a Haitian writer who, like many Caribbean authors, lived most of his life in exile in Canada. Exile, immigration, and the cultural duality of being from the Caribbean but feeling at home in Canada served as the inspiration for his novels.

Ollivier was born in Port-au-Prince, Haiti, on February 19, 1940, the son of an attorney. His family spoke Kreyòl, Haiti's national language, as well as French. He attended the École Normale Supérieure d'Haïti and became involved in the National Union of Haitian Students. As a result of his activism against the dictatorship of **François Duvalier**, Ollivier had to seek exile in France in 1964. A year later, he moved to Canada with his wife, settling in Montreal.

Ollivier taught at the University of Montreal. He also worked as a consultant for the government's Office of the French Language and directed multimedia projects for the Immigration Council. In the 1970s and 1980s, he published collections of essays addressing such topics as Haitian politics, immigration, literacy, and adult educations: *Haïti, quel développement?* (1976), *Analphabétisme et alphabétisation des immigrants haïtiens à Montréal* (1981), and *Penser l'éducation des adultes, ou fondements philosophiques de l'éducation des adultes* (1983).

Haiti, as seen through the eyes of a family, was the subject of his first novel, *Mère-solitude* (1983), which was an immediate best-seller, earned him the 1985 Prix **Jacques Roumain** prize and was quickly translated into Italian and English. In 1986, he published his second novel *La discorde aux cent voix*. His third novel, *Passages* (1991), which was well received by the critics, told the story of a Haitian immigrant jumping off a boat to reach Florida before moving on to Canada. Other works followed, all depicting either political conditions in Haiti or life in exile: *Les urnes scellées* (1995), *Mille eaux* (1999), and *La brûlerie* (2004); the last was published posthumously.

Involved in civic and education activities, Ollivier was the president of Institut canadien d'éducation des adultes, and an active member of l'Union des Écrivains et Écrivaines du Québec and the l'Académie des Lettres du Québec at the time of his sudden death on November 20, 2002. Some of his other awards include the 1987 Grand Prix de la prose du Journal de Montréal, the 1991 Grand Prix du Livre de Montréal, the Chevalier de l'Ordre national du Québec, in 1993, and Prix Carbet de la Caraïbe, in 1996. *See also* Exile Literature; Haitian Literature in Kreyòl (the Haitian language).

Further Reading

Dumas, Pierre-Raymond. *Panorama de la litterature haïtienne de la diaspora*. Tome. II. Port-au-Prince, Haiti: Promobank, 1996.

—*D. H. Figueredo*

Omeros (1990)

∎

This epic poem and narrative by **Derek Walcott** is a retelling of the Iliad and the Odyssey but on the island of St. Lucia. Helen, a waitress, is a seductive woman, "a beauty that left, like a ship, eyes in its wake," over whom two men, Hector and Achilles, a fisherman and a taxi driver, fight; one dies, the other survives. The Helen motif serves as the background for several parallel narratives: the British expatriates who live on the island, Major Plunkett and his wife, Maud, who is terminally ill; the old man Philoctete, who is nursing an ulcer on his leg; the figure of Omeros, also called Seven Seas, an old island man; and the narrator, who might be Walcott himself. The narrative is also a panoramic history of oppression across continents and times, from the plains of Africa, where free men are enslaved, to the plains of the American West, where Native Americas are annihilated or imprisoned. It is not presented in a straightforward manner but shifts chronologically from the eighteenth to the twentieth centuries, moving across islands and continents. Ultimately, though, the reader discovers that the true Helen of the story is the island of St. Lucia, over whom Europeans murdered the original inhabitants and then fought each other to possess this Caribbean Eden.

It took Walcott four years to write this epic. Initially, he contemplated writing *Omeros* in French but then opted for English, though the epic alternates between English, the island's vernacular, and some French. In the tradition of Greek epics, Walcott uses the hexameter, a metrical line of verse that employs stressed and unstressed, long and short syllables. Unlike Homer, Walcott does not celebrate mythological heroes but the common people—waitresses, farmers, fishermen—and does not narrate spectacular battles but the daily struggles faced by the inhabitants of the Caribbean. Walcott substitutes the battles "with the action of hurricane, tree felling or fishing," (527) observed Isabella Maria Zoppi in the article "Derek Walcott and the Contemporary Epic Poem," in *Callaloo* (Spring 1999).

The publication of *Omeros* secured Walcott's selection for the 1992 Nobel Prize for Literature.

Further Reading

Callahan, Lance. *In the Shadows of Divine Perfection: Derek Walcott's Omeros*. New York: Routledge, 2003.

Walcott, Derek. *Omeros*. New York: Farrar, Straus and Giroux, 1990.

Zoppi, Isabella Maria. "Derek Walcott and the Contemporary Epic Poem." *Callaloo* 22, no. 2 (Spring 1999): 509–28.

—D. H. Figueredo

Orígenes (1944–56)

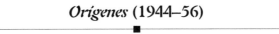

Orígenes was a Cuban literary journal that featured the writings of such important figures as **Gastón Baquero, Cintio Vitier, Virgilio Piñero,** and **Lydia Cabrera,** among others. While influenced by the Catholic convictions of the contributors and its editor, **José Lezama Lima,** the journal emphasized abstract poetics, lyricism, and modern art, expressing an aesthetic appreciation of diverse movements from the baroque to **surrealism.** Though the journal did not broadcast a political viewpoint, it criticized the government's lack of interest in a national culture and in supporting the arts. Most of the writers published in *Orígenes* went on to achieve recognition beyond Cuba and the Caribbean. *See also* Barroco/Baroque; Literary Journals.

Further Reading

Barquet, Jesús J. *Consagración de La Habana: las peculiaridades del grupo Orígenes en el proceso cultural cubano*. Miami: Iberian Studies Institute, University of Miami, 1992.

—Peter T. Johnson

Ortea, Virginia Elena (1866–1903)

Ortea was the first woman dramatist, novelist, and journalist in the Dominican Republic. A short-story writer and poet as well, she was also an early feminist who promoted the education of all women.

Ortea was born in Santo Domingo on June 17, 1866. When she was thirteen years old, her father was expelled from the Dominican Republic and the family settled in Puerto Rico, where they lived for eleven years. She began to write in the Puerto Rican town of Mayagüez, publishing her poetry in the local press under the pseudonym of Elena Kennedy. Upon her return to the Dominican Republic, she wrote poems and short stories, which were published in the daily *Listín Diario* and the journals *La Cuna de América, Letras y Ciencias* and *Revista Ilustrada*. Ortea also wrote theatrical pieces, including a musical entitled *Las femeninas* (1899), which was staged, and a novel, *Mi hermana Catalina*, which she began in 1896 but did not complete. In 1901, she published a collection of short stories, *Risas y lágrimas*. Ortea's style was realistic and controlled, though at times somewhat sentimental, and much of the action was propelled through dialogue. With restraint, Ortea criticized the mores of the time.

Writing at a time when women were expected not to demonstrate intellect, Ortea felt marginalized. She passed away at the age of thirty-seven. By the 1920s, scholars began to study her work. Today, a school in the Dominican Republic bears her name.

Further Reading

Adams, Clementina R. "Rescatando la obra de Virginia Elena Ortea: una voz combativa en pro de la mujer fin-de-siglo." In *La voz de la mujer en la literatura hispanoamericana fin-de-siglo*. Compiled by Luis Jiménez, 115–26. San José, Costa Rica: Editorial de la Universidad de Costa Rica, 1999.

Brown, Isabel Zakrzewski. *Culture and Customs of the Dominican Republic*. Westport, CT: Greenwood Press, 1999.

—*D. H. Figueredo*

Ortiz Cofer, Judith (1952–)

Award-winning Puerto Rican novelist, short-story writer, and poet Judith Cofer Ortiz was born in Hormigueros, Puerto Rico, on February 24, 1952. During her childhood, her father was in the navy, and so her family moved back and forth between Puerto Rico and Paterson, New Jersey. Upon her father's retirement, the family settled in Augusta, Georgia, where Cofer attended both high school and Augusta College. After college, she obtained an MA from Florida International University and received a fellowship for graduate work at Oxford University in England. Throughout her education, Cofer was a writer and, in 1980, began to receive recognition for her work, first with a fellowship from the Florida Arts Council, then other awards from the Bread Loaf Writers Conference (1981) and from the

National Endowment for the Arts (1989). After holding a distinguished career as a Creative Writing Professor at the University of Georgia, in 2000, Judith Ortiz Cofer accepted an endowed chair at Vanderbilt University in Nashville.

Cofer became the first Latina writer to receive a Special Citation from the PEN Martha Albrand Award for *Silent Dancing: A Remembrance of a Puerto Rican Childhood* (1990), which is a collection of autobiographical essays and poems. The book was also awarded the Pushcart Prize in the essay category, the New York Public Library System List of Best Books for the Teen Age, and its title essay was chosen by Joyce Carol Oates for the Best American Essays (1991). Cofer was also the first Latina to win the O. Henry Prize (1994) for the short story. In 1994, she also won the Anisfield-Wolf Award in Race Relations for her novel *The Latin Deli*. Cofer's two major works of poetry are *Reaching for the Mainland* and *Terms of Survival*, both published in 1987.

Cofer's well-crafted poetry reflects her struggle as a writer to create a history for herself out of the cultural ambiguity of a childhood lived between two lands, two cultures, and two languages. Through her poetry and her essays, such as those in *Silent Dancing*, she explores from a feminist perspective her relationships with her father, mother, and grandmother, while also considering the different expectations for males and females in both Anglo-American and Latino cultures. Her novel *Line of the Sun* (1990) is based on her family's gradual immigration to the United States, chronicling the years from the Great Depression to the 1960s. Her young-adult story collection, *The Year of Our Revolution* (1999), picks up where *Silent Dancing* left off, examining a young Latina's coming of age in Paterson and her rebellion against the old ways of her family.

About her identity as a writer, Cofer has stated, "Some people try mightily to forget who they are and where they came from, and those people seem a little lost to me. It's important for the artist to retain some hold on her original self even if it is painful or unattractive. . . . How can you inject passion and purpose into your work if it has no roots?" *See also* Code Switching; Feminism in Caribbean Literature; Nuyorican Literature.

Further Reading

Derrickson, Teresa. "Cold/Hot English/Spanish: The Puerto Rican Divide in Judith Ortiz Cofer's Silent Dancing." *Melus* 28, no. 2 (Summer 2003): 120–37.

Ortiz Cofer, Judith. *Woman in Front of the Sun: On Becoming a Writer.* Athens: University of Georgia Press, 2000.

—*Nicolás Kanellos*

Ortiz Fernández, Fernando (1881–1969)

Fernando Ortiz was a voracious thinker, researcher, writer, and political activist—a dominant figure in Cuban culture and letters throughout the first two-thirds of the twentieth century. He began his career by vilifying the culture and wisdom of Africa. His final work, in the late 1960s, celebrates African contributions to the beauty and strength of Cuba. Ortiz's long and incredibly prolific career, exemplifies his own core concept of transculturation, or the process through and by which a marginalized culture selects some of the language used by the dominant culture.

Born in Havana in 1881, Ortiz was educated in Barcelona, where he graduated from the Universidad de Barcelona with a law degree at age nineteen. His doctoral thesis was a controversial interpretation of law, a liberal view within a positivist framework, called "neocorrectionalist penal theory." He was an optimist who believed that science could bring progress. These traits persisted in his work through a long life, but the pursuit of truth led him far from the ideas and beliefs of his youth.

In 1902, Ortiz returned to Cuba and joined the law faculty at the Universidad de la Habana. There he began a research program on African criminality, strongly influenced by the Italian phrenologist, Cesare Lombroso (1835–1909). Pseudoscience and social Darwinism captivated many European-trained scholars in the postcolonial Americas. Ortiz's first publications condemned what he regarded as the malevolent effects of Africans in the Cuban body politic. He viewed their cultural traditions, the unfortunate baggage that accompanied slavery, as atavistic and dangerous. The context in which his ideas were produced included an aborted uprising of mainly Afro-Cuban veterans during 1906, followed by a series of high-profile criminal cases of witchcraft and child murder and the bloody Cuban race war of 1912. During this period, Ortiz's scholarship followed the reactionary conventions of the academy and the political aims of the Liberal Party, to which he belonged, and which was in power during the massacres of black Cubans in 1912. Through the teens, Ortiz continued to publish on themes of African-derived criminality. However, his meticulous research on African religion, slavery, slave uprisings, secret societies, folklore, and other topics brought together a compendium of data that began to speak to him and encourage doubt. His politics became increasingly egalitarian, and his interpretation of African culture grew more celebratory. As editor of *Revista Bimestre Cubana*, a position he held from 1910 to 1959, his work gathered the cross-currents of many disciplines and contemporary ideas.

During the 1920s, Ortiz was a leader in the "Grupo Minorista," a leftist political group opposed to conservative and racist intellectual traditions and political despotism in Cuba and elsewhere. Ortiz's home, near the Universidad, became a major salon, gathering radical writers, artists, and academicians. He organized and participated in conferences and wrote prodigiously on folklore, history, geography, archaeology, and anthropology, all within the context of a political agenda promoting progressive change. In 1930, he wrote a political manifesto, "Base para una Effectiva Solución Cubana," condemning the dictator Gerardo Machado (1871–1939). Official reaction caused his immediate exile. From 1931 to 1933, he lived in Washington, D.C., and was part of the revolutionary junta headquartered in New York. He returned to Cuba in 1933, following the ouster of the dictator. He continued his research on African folklore, directed and founded journals, organized speaker series, traveled widely, and began a radio broadcast that brought his ideas to the Cuban public.

Contrapunteo cubano del tabaco y del azúcar, Ortiz's massive and mysterious interrogation of Cuban nationhood, was published in 1940. This work intricately blends folklore, chemistry, history, geography, economics, and, most of all, ethnology into a dense postmodern representation of cubanidad. Sugar and tobacco—Cuba's major export products—embody metaphorical distinctions that pivot around the issues of race, class, gender, and culture. The text is a sequence of chapters on the dialectical relations between these two products, following a theoretical concept he labeled "transculturation." The ambivalently reciprocal influences of Africa and Spain, darkness and light, labor and capital, and so forth, are traced in this remarkably farsighted work. The racial subtext of Cuban counterpoint was made explicit in Ortiz's well-known address to the Club Atenas of Havana in 1942, entitled "Por la integración cubana de blancos y negros." Through the 1950s, he continued work at collecting folklore and theorizing on race and culture; and he never abandoned his interest in politics. Ortiz remained in favor, and he chose to remain in Cuba following the ouster of Batista. He was named president of the Cuban Academy of Sciences in 1961. He died in 1969; at the time he was working on the third part of *Hampa afro-cubana, los negros brujos.* This volume was published posthumously in 1986. In 1995, Ortiz's house near the Universidad de la Habana was opened as the Fundación Fernando Ortiz. **Miguel Barnet,** well known Cuban anthropologist, serves as director. *See also* Negrista Literature; Négritude; Santería in Literature; Schomburg, Arthur.

Further Reading

Castellanos, Jorge. *Pioneros de la etnografía afrocubana: Fernando Ortiz, Rómulo Lachatañeré, Lydia Cabrera* Miami, FL: Ediciones Universal, 2003.

Iznaga, Diana. *El estudio de arte negro en Fernando Ortiz.* Habana: Editorial de la Academia de Ciencias de Cuba, 1982.

—*Susan Greenbaum*

P

Pachín Marín. See Marín, Francisco Gonzalo "Pachín."

"Padilla Case." See Padilla, Heberto.

Padilla, Heberto (1934–2000)

Padilla was a Cuban poet, novelist, and memoirist who was the target of the notorious "Padilla Case," an event that marked the official marginalization of culture and the censorship of intellectuals in Cuba. Padilla's spare, ironic poetry and his autobiographical prose explore the theme of the artist's position in relation to the state.

Born in Pinar del Rio, Cuba, on January 20, 1934, Padilla grew up in the small town of Puerta de Golpe, in the province of Pinar del Río. He later studied law at the Universidad de la Habana. He lived in the United States from 1949 to 1952, from 1956 to 1959, and from 1980 until his death. During his second stay there, he worked as a Spanish teacher at Berlitz in New York. With the fall of the Fulgencio Batista (1901–73) dictatorship and the triumph of the Cuban Revolution in 1959, Padilla returned to Cuba, where he helped found the literary magazine **Lunes de revolución.** In 1960, he was named London correspondent of Prensa Latina, the official press agency of the Cuban government; he subsequently worked in the same position in Moscow before being recalled to his native country in the early 1960s.

Cuban poet Heberto Padilla suffered imprisonment and persecution for writing poems that were deemed anti-revolutionary. *Source: Americas Society. Courtesy of Elsa M. Ruiz.*

Padilla's second book of poems, *Justo tiempo humano* (1962), received honorable mention from **Casa de las Américas**. In 1968, an international jury awarded first prize to his book of poems *Fuera del juego* in the annual literary contest sponsored by the **Unión de Escritores y Artistas de Cuba** (UNEAC). The award piqued the Cuban authorities, who believed that the book was critical of Cuba's political system. Unable to prevent its publication, they inserted an appendix in the book declaring it a counterrevolutionary work.

In April 1971, after being arrested, jailed, and tortured for several weeks, Padilla was forced to conduct a self-criticism at a meeting at UNEAC. In that meeting, he accused himself of holding counterrevolutionary beliefs and named other intellectuals—including **Guillermo Cabrera Infante, José Lezama Lima**, and even his wife, the poet **Belkis Cuza Malé**—as enemies of the Revolution. Known as the "Padilla Case," this incident provoked an international protest by writers such as Susan Sontag (1933–2005), Jean-Paul Sartre (1905–80), and Mario Vargas Llosa (1936–), and caused many intellectuals worldwide to break with the Cuban Revolution. Thereafter, Padilla was placed under house arrest; his books were banned, and he was forbidden to publish his work. He spent the next ten years working as a translator. In 1980, finally allowed to leave Cuba, he went into exile in the United States. He taught at several universities there, finally settling in Princeton, New Jersey, where he and Cuza Malé edited the literary journal *Linden Lane*—a publication that has continued since his death.

In addition to his first books of poems published in Cuba, Padilla authored works that were published outside the country, including the poetry collection *Legacies* (1982), the novel *En mi jardín pastan los héroes* (1982)—Padilla had smuggled the manuscript out of Cuba when he went into exile—and the memoir *La mala memoria* (1989). He also translated the poetry of John Keats (1795–1821), Percy Bysshe Shelley (1792–1822), William Blake (1757–1827), and T. S. Eliot (1888–1965) into Spanish.

Heberto Padilla's poetry, while essentially self-reflective, expresses skepticism toward "the system"—its ideological fervor, regimentation of the individual, and notion of "official" art. The title poem of his collection *Fuera del juego* employs the refrain, "al poeta, despídanlo! / Ese no tiene aquí nada que hacer." (The poet! Kick him out! / He has no business here.) In the poem "En tiempos difíciles" (in *Legacies*), the speaker addresses an everyman who is asked to renounce the respective parts of his body—and, by extension, his individuality and dignity—for the purported good of the people. "A Prayer for the End of the Century" (*Legacies*) explores a familiar theme: While one age may look back "with tolerant irony" at a previous one, it very well may end up resembling it. "The Birch Tree of Iron" (*Legacies*), set in Russia, also meditates on history. Later poems such as "The Gift" (*Legacies*) treat the subject of domesticity in exile and celebrate the quotidian. Padilla also wrote homages to the poets José Lezama Lima, Octavio Paz (1914–98), Rainier Maria Rilke (1875–1926), and Wallace Stevens (1879–1955). His autobiographical novel *Heroes Are Grazing in My Garden* presents a group of characters representing once-idealistic individuals—Gregorio, Julio, and Luisa—all former revolutionaries who have become disenchanted with the Revolution. Prisoners of the system as well as of their own illusions, they are driven to alcoholism, isolation, and personal ruin. The memoir *Self-Portrait of the Other*, which overlaps material treated in the novel, details Padilla's early support of the Cuban Revolution, his experiences in Russia and Europe and his contacts with other writers there—Yevgeny Yevtushenko (1933–) and Albert Camus (1913–60), among them—his disillusionment with the Revolution, his vilification by the regime, and his exile. The memoir includes harrowing scenes of Padilla's interrogations as well as memorable portraits of **Fidel Castro, José Lezama Lima,** and Gabriel García Márquez (1927–). It is ultimately a portrait of the author's dissent against a regime intent on crushing his free will and means of self-expression.

Heberto Padilla was a participant and ultimately a victim of the extraordinary political circumstances of his country. His experience and literary output stand not only as a testament to the vulnerability and fortitude of the artist in the face of totalitarianism but as a metaphor of the individual as an existential figure. As he modestly states in "No fue un poeta del porvenir" (He Wasn't a Poet of the Future): "He spoke a lot about trying times and analyzed its ruins" [translated by Shapiro].

Further Reading

Casal, Lourdes, comp. *El caso Padilla; literatura y revolución en Cuba; documentos. Introd., selección, notas, guía y bibliografía.* Miami, FL: Ediciones Universal, 1971.

Lolo, Eduardo. *Las trampas del tiempo y sus memorias.* Coral Gables, FL: Iberian Studies Institute, North-South Center, University of Miami, 1991.

Yglesias, José. "The Case of Heberto Padilla." *New York Review of Books* 16, no. 10 (June 3, 1971).

—*Daniel Shapiro*

Padura Fuentes, Leonardo (1955–)

Cuban novelist, essayist, and journalist, Leonardo Padura has achieved fame in a genre not too commonly pursued by writers from the Caribbean: detective fiction. He is a leading figure in a generation of writers who grew up under Fidel Castro's regime and who questions some of the Revolution's accomplishments.

Leonardo Padura Fuentes was born in Havana. Graduating from the Universidad de la Habana in 1984, he began to write essays and literary criticism, which were compiled in the volume *Con la espada y la pluma* (1984). In the mid-1980s, he worked as a journalist and was stationed in Angola from 1984 to 1985 when the Cuban army was helping the Angolans fight off an invasion from South Africa. Returning to Cuba, he wrote the novel *Fiebre de caballos* (1988), followed by the collection of short stories *Según pasan los años* (1989). It was in the 1990s, however, that he achieved international recognition with his tetralogy "Las cuatros estaciones," consisting of the novels *Pasado perfecto* (1991), *Vientos de cuaresma* (1994), *Máscaras* (1995), and *Paisaje de otoño* (1998). The protagonist in these novels is police detective Mario Conde, an alcoholic would-be writer somewhat disillusioned with the revolutionary regime. In 2002, Padura wrote *La novela de mi vida*, about the lost autobiography of the romantic poet **José María Heredía y**

Heredía. In 2003, the fifth Mario Conde novel was released: *Adiós a Hemingway*, about a skeleton found in Hemingway's old farm in Havana.

Padura's works of nonfiction include *El alma en el terreno* (1989), *El viaje más largo* (1994), *Los rostros de la salsa* (1997), *Un camino de medio siglo: Alejo Carpentier y la narrativa de lo real maravilloso* (2002), and *José Marí Heredia, la patria y la vida* (2003). Unlike many Cuban writers who have chosen exile, Padura has decided to remain on the island. He has claimed, in an interview in *El Nuevo Herald* in 2001, that the government's censorship inspires him to find new ways of perfecting his craft and of offering indirect criticism of the revolution. *See also* Detective Fiction.

Further Reading

Alfonso, Pablo. *El Nuevo Herald*, December 27, 2001.

Braham, Persephone. *Crimes against the State, Crimes against Persons: Detective Fiction in Cuba and Mexico*. Minneapolis: University of Minnesota Press, 2004.

—*Wilfredo Cancio Isla*

Palace of the Peacock, The (1960)

The first novel of Guyanese author **Wilson Harris,** *The Palace of the Peacock* exemplifies the author's signature style: cerebral, **baroque,** oblique, and philosophical. The novel tells the story of a crew that travels into Guyana's interior to kidnap and force into labor an Arawak tribe. When the crew, captained by a man named Donne, arrives at the village, the Arawaks flee into the jungle. Donne leads a chase upstream on a treacherous river. One by one the men perish or vanish, and Donne is left alone. Reaching a waterfall, Donne climbs a cliff. The novel ends with Donne contemplating the vastness of the Guyanese jungle.

The adventure component of the novel frames a poetic and philosophical narrative composed of interior monologue and shifting viewpoints. The excursion is a duplicate of an earlier expedition that had occurred years before: even the names of the crew are identical. Therefore it is not always evident if the author is telling the story of the current or previous crew. The novel poses questions but offers no answers. It is, however, a meditation on the ill effects of the conquest and colonization of the Caribbean; the journey becomes a historical exposé of the past. *See also* Pasos Perdidos, Los.

Further Reading

Harris, Wilson. *Palace of the Peacock*. London: Faber and Faber, 1960.

Maes-Jelinek, Hena. *The Naked Design: A Reading of Palace of the Peacock*. Denmark: Dangaroo Press, 1976.

—*D. H. Figueredo*

Palés Family

The Palés were father and three brothers from Puerto Rico who achieved distinction as poets. The father was Vicente Palés Anés, a teacher. The brothers were Gustavo, Luis, and Vicente Palés Matos. Luis Palés Matos emerged as the best writer in the family, becoming an internationally recognized poet.

Palés Anés, Vicente (1865–1913). A native of Guayama, Palés Anés was a teacher. He was active in Puerto Rico's Masonic Fraternity, which created a space where Puerto Ricans could discuss intellectual and political topics, often assuming an anticolonial stance. His loyalty to the fraternity was evident in his book of poetry *A la masonería* (1886). In this volume, Palés Anés included poems that he had previously published in reviews such as *Revista Masónica, El Buscapié*, and *El Carnaval*. In 1889, he published his second volume of poetry, *El cementerio*.

Through the 1890s, he continued publishing works in diverse journals and newspapers. Almost a hundred years later, in 1981, some of those poems were gathered for a special issue of the literary journal *Al margen*. The issue was entitled *Selecciones palesianas*.

A street and a school in Guayama, where Palés Anés passed away, were named to honor him.

Palés Matos, Gustavo (1907–63). Born in Guayama, Palés Matos studied agriculture at the Colegio de Agricultura de Mayagüez around 1916. In the 1920s, he worked for the Puerto Rican government and began to write poems and short stories that were published in such influential newspapers as *El Mundo* and *El Imparcial*. His love of Puerto Rican history and legends resulted in the book of poems, *Romancero de Cofresí* (1942), named after the famous Puerto Rican pirate who in the early 1800s robbed from the rich, according to legend, to give to the poor. Cofresí's life once again inspired him to write the operetta *Cofresí* which was staged in San Juan in 1949.

During the 1940s and 1950s, Palés Matos worked for Puerto Rican radio and television as a translator and scriptwriter. He also wrote hundreds of poems that were not published. Twenty years after his death, the journal *Al margen* published a supplement entitled *Selecciones palesianas* (1981), dedicated to his family and their poetic works

Palés Matos, Luis (1898–1959). Alongside the Cuban **Nicolás Guillén**, Palés Matos was one of the creators of **Negrista literature**, a genre that celebrates the African presence in the Caribbean. He was one of the first poets to celebrate Afro-Caribbean feminine beauty and to poke fun at people who refused to acknowledge their African roots. Though he only published two volumes of poetry, his work is considered seminal in the development of contemporary Latin American literature and culture

Palés Matos was born on March 20, 1898, in Guayama, Puerto Rico, a town with a large population of African Puerto Ricans whose traditions and rituals charmed the young boy and probably influenced his poetic development years later. When his father died, Palés Matos was forced to leave secondary school and work at a variety of jobs, from clerical to post office work. Despite the responsibility of providing for his mother, he wrote his first book of poetry at the age of seventeen,

Azaleas (1915), a modernist exercise with allusions to classical Greek literature that nevertheless celebrated local colloquialism and the Puerto Rican countryside.

At the age of twenty, Palés Matos married for the first time. A year later, his wife passed away and he remarried. In 1921, he and poet **José de Diego Padró** created a literary movement that they named **diepalismo**—the combination of their names. Diepalismo, which essentially consisted of onomatopoetic poems, was short-lived, resulting only in one published poem, written by both poets. However, the movement's intent—that of creating meaningless words that resembled sounds with a certain musicality—manifested itself in the body of work that made Palés Matos famous: Negrista poems, poems that celebrated black culture and imitated the sound of black Puerto Rican speech.

Palés Matos began to publish Negrista poems in newspapers and journals in the mid-1920s, making him, if not the first to write in the genre at the very least one of the firsts to do so in the Caribbean, certainly before the Martinican **Aimé Césaire** coined the term **Négritude** in 1939. The poems vividly portrayed the culture and lifestyles of blacks, using black expressions and words invented by Palés Matos, as seen in the poem "Danza Negra" (1926):

> Calabo y bamboo
> Bamby y calabo
> Es el sol de hierro que arde . . .
> El alma Africana que vibrando esta
> En el ritmo gordo del mariyanda

(Calabo y bamboo / Bamby y calabo / The iron sun that burns . . . / The African soul that quivers / In the opulent beat of mariyanda). The lines contain words created by the poet, such as "calabo" and "bamboo," and allusions to African-Puerto Rican themes, such as *mariyanda*, an African dance.

These poems were collected in the volume *Tuntún de pasa y grifería*, published in 1937 and received with great acclaim by critics and readers. The playfulness, creativity, and the affirmation of a black consciousness, at a time when many Caribbean poets were shying away from the subject, spread Palés Matos's fame throughout the region and even in Spain. Though some critics thought that the poems were not genuine, since Palés Matos was white and of European descent, the poems became quite popular and remain so today.

On the strength of his poetic genius, Palés Matos was appointed poet in residence at the Universidad de Puerto Rico in 1944. At the university, he fell in love with a student for whom he wrote love sonnets. In 1949, he published the autobiographical novel *Litora; reseña de una vida inútil*. The last ten years of his life were a sad period, as the poet lost his son and grandchildren and developed heart disease. He died of a heart attack on February 23, 1959. Much of his poetic work was left unpublished.

Palés Matos, Vicente (1903–63). Born in Guayama, Vicente Palés Matos joined his brothers in the pursuit of poetry, though he was not as prolific. As a teenager, he founded a literary movement that he and a friend, Tomás L. Batista, named "enforismo," which promoted experimental literature. Three years later, he joined writers **Samuel R. Quiñones, Cesáreo Rosa Nieves,** and **Fernando Sierra Berdecía** in creating the movement known as **noismo**, which promoted the use of breaks in poetic lines and experimental punctuations. The movement was short-lived.

In 1945, Vicente Palés Matos published *Viento y espuma*, which included poetry and short stories. In 1967, his second and final collection, *La fuente de Juan Ponce de León y otros poemas*, was published. *See also* Puerto Rican Literature, History of.

Further Reading

López-Baralt, Mercedes. *El barco en la botella: la poesía de Luis Palés Matos*. San Juan Puerto Rico: Editorial Plaza Mayor, 1997.

———. "Luis Palés Matos." In *Spanish American Authors: The Twentieth Century*, edited by Angel Flores 641–43. New York: H. Wilson Company, 1992.

López Román, Juan Edgardo. *La obra literaria de Vicente Palés Matos*. Río Piedras, Puerto Rico: Editorial de la Universidad de Puerto Rico, 1984.

—D. H. Figueredo

Palma, Marigloría (1921–94)

Palma was a Puerto Rican poet, children's writer, and short-story author. Her actual name was Gloría María Pagán Ferrer.

Born in Canovanas on September 6, 1921, Palma spent her youth in the United States and in Europe, where she married Austrian philosopher Alfred Stern. From cities like New York and Vienna, she submitted her poems to journals in Puerto Rico. At the age of twenty-one, she published her first book of poems, *Agua suelta*, which won a literary prize from the Instituto de Literatura Puertorriqueña; a similar honor awaited her second volume of poetry, *San Juan entre dos azules* (1965). The distance from Puerto Rico colored her poetry with a longing for the past and a desire to return.

In 1968, Palma did return to Puerto Rico. Through the 1960s and 1970s, she published several poetry collections, including *Palomas frente al eco* (1968), *La razón del cuadrante* (1969), and *Los cuarenta silencios* (1973). She was also attracted to children's literature, writing several plays—*Teatro para niños* (1968) and *Teatro infantile* (1970)—which were staged in San Juan. In 1973, she published the novel *Amy Kootsky*, and in 1975, a collection of short stories, *Cuentos de la abeja encinta*. Her prose is characterized by a sense of the grotesque, presented through a humorous perspective.

In the late 1970s, she studied Puerto Rican folklore, publishing the volume *Muestras de folklore puertorriqueño* in 1981. She also published in newspapers and journals essays and articles on contemporary culture. In 1982, the Casa del Autor Puertorriqueño named her author of the year.

Further Reading

Palma, Marigloría. *Cuentos de la abeja encinta*. Río Piedras, Puerto Rico: Universidad de Puerto Rico, 1975.

"Gloria M. Pagán Ferrer." *Contemporary Authors Online*, Gale, 2003. http://galenet.
galegroup.com (accessed 9/23/05).

—*D. H. Figueredo*

Papillon, Margaret (1958–)

Papillon is a popular Haitian novelist. In her writings, she focuses on Haitian culture
and politics. She is one of the few Haitian women writers to have achieved recognition in the francophone Caribbean.

Margaret Papillon was born on November 14, 1958, in Port-au-Prince, Haiti.
She started to write as a young child but was attracted to sports and preferred playing
volleyball rather than writing. She became a gym teacher and married a successful
artists, Albert Desmangles (1957–) before coming across the stories she had written
as a child and had put away. She was surprised to see how well she wrote and
decided to attempt a novel. Titled *Marginale*, the novel was published in 1987 to
great acclaim in Haiti. She followed this work with several successful publications:
Martin Toma (1991), *La saison du pardon* (1997), and *La légende de Quisqueya*
(1999). The latter work, a historical novel, was particularly popular, and in 2001,
Papillon adapted it for the stage.

By the late 1990s, Papillon dedicated herself to writing full-time. For inspiration, she turned to Haitian history and culture. In her novels, she explored sexual
relationships in Haiti, challenging male-driven conceptions of women's behavior
and role in society. While achieving recognition in her country, much of Papillon's
work has yet to reach European and American audiences. Her other works include
Terre Sauvage (1999), *Mathieu et le vieux mage au regard d'enfant* (2000),
Innocents fantasmes (2001), and *Sortilèges au carnaval de Jacmel* (2002).

Further Reading

"Margaret Papillon." http://www.lehman.cuny.edu//ile.en.ile/paroles/papillon-terreNOT.
html April 2005 (accessed 9/23/05).

—*Jayne R. Boisvert and D. H. Figueredo*

Paradiso (1966)

A Cuban novel considered one of the first to introduce a homosexual character
who is neither stereotyped nor ridiculed, as was usually portrayed in the popular
literature of the times. The novel also vividly depicted erotic encounters, both heterosexual and homosexual, but rendered in a poetic style.

Written by **José Lezama Lima**, *Paradiso* was published in 1966. It tells the story of José Cemí, from his childhood to his university days, and his search for a spiritual father. Cemí is mentored by an enigmatic figure named Oppiano Licario and befriended by university students Fronesis, a likable young man, and Foción, a gay man in love with Fronesis. When the latter leaves for Paris, Foción goes mad. Missing his two friends and feeling desolate, Cemí learns that his spiritual guide, Oppiano, has passed away. At the wake, Cemí realizes that his purpose in life is to become a writer.

Over six-hundred hundred pages long and written in a **baroque** style, *Paradiso* served as platform for Lezama Lima to expound on his complex ideas about art and aesthetics as well as to engage on philosophical discussions about sexuality in general and homosexuality in particular. The work has drawn comparisons between its author and James Joyce (1882–1941) and Marcel Proust (1871–1922). The novel's sexual frankness broadcast an erotic freedom that would manifest itself a generation later in the works of the Cuban writers **Reinaldo Arenas, Pedro Juan Gutiérrez**, and **Zoé Valdés**. The novel was briefly censored by the Cuban government but **Fidel Castro** authorized its release. Lezama Lima was working on a sequel when he passed away in 1976. *See also* Barroco/Baroque; Gay and Lesbian Literature.

Further Reading

Álbala, Eliana. *El paraíso de Lezama y el infierno de Lowry: dos polos narrativos*. Morelos, Mexico: Publicaciones del Instituto de Cultura de Morelos, Fondo Estatal para la Cultura y las Artes de Morelos, 2000.

Lezama Lima, José. *Paradiso; novela*. Habana: Unión Nacional de Escritores y Artistas de Cuba, 1966.

—Emilio Bejel and D. H. Figueredo

Pasos Perdidos, Los (1953)

Critic **Roberto González Echevarria** considers *Los pasos perdidos*, by **Alejo Carpentier**, one of the major works of Latin American literature. The novel tells the story of a musicologist who leaves New York City for an expedition to the jungles of South America, sailing on the Orinoco River, located in Venezuela. The novel was the result of the author's two excursions into the jungles, one which took place in 1947 and the second a year later, and the articles he wrote about the expeditions in 1948, published in the Cuban journal *Carteles*.

In the novel, the narrator is asked to track down the origin of music and in doing so, he feels that each phase of the journey takes him back in time, from the modern to the primeval. This element of the novel echoes an earlier attempt by Carpentier, who had written a short story, entitled **"Viaje a la semilla"** (1944), in which the protagonist ages backward, from old age to the womb. But in *Los pasos* *perdidos*, however, the journey back into time is an illusion, and the narrator finds himself in New York City once again. *Los pasos perdidos* is a philosophical study of the nature of time, the creative process, and the relationship between explorers, who were usually white Europeans, with the colonized natives, whom the explorers viewed as savages. It is also an adventure and a love story, for the narrator falls in love with a companion, Rosario, who reminds him of what is natural and genuine, as opposed to his wife, an actress who lives in New York City.

The publication of this novel made Carpentier something of a celebrity, with a critic from the *New York Times*, according to González Echevarria, advocating for Carpentier to receive the Nobel Prize for Literature and with the popular American actor Tyrone Power (1914–57) wanting to make the novel into a film. The novel influenced the depiction of the jungle created a decade later in the novels of such Latin American writers as Gabriel García Márquez (1927–) and Mario Vargas Llosa (1936–). In the Anglophone Caribbean the companion piece to this novel is *Palace of the Peacock* by Guyanese novelist **Wilson Harris**.

Further Reading

Carpentier, Alejo. *Los pasos perdidos*. Edición de Roberto González Echevarria. Madrid: Ediciones Cátedra, 1985.

———. *The Lost Steps*. Translated by Harriet de Onís. New York: Knopf, 1967.

—Wilfredo Cancio Isla and D. H. Figueredo

Patient, Serge (1934–)
∎

Patient is a poet and short-story writer from French Guiana.

Born in Cayenne, Guiana, on March 24, 1934, Patient studied in his hometown and then went to Paris at the end of World War II. He earned from the University of Paris a teaching certificate, in Spanish. Returning to Guiana, he taught Spanish through the 1950s and was then promoted to several administrative posts, culminating with the appointment of headmaster of the Lycée de Kourou in 1973.

Patient was also involved in political activities, emerging as one of the leaders of the Union du Peuple Guyanais. In 1973, he was elected general councilor in Kourou. In 1968, he published his first book of poetry, probably his most famous work, *Le mal du pays*, which examined colonial conditions in Guiana. In the 1970s, he wrote for journals and submitted several poems to the anthology, *New Writing in the Caribbean* (1972), edited by **A. J. Seymour.**

Patient also cultivated the genre of short stories. In collections such as *Le negre du gouverneur* (1972), he evoked African traditions and explored the supernatural elements of African religion. His short stories are closer to prose poems than to actual narratives.

Further Reading

Jones, Bridget. "Serge Patient and Le mal du Pays." *French Caribbean Literature*. Toronto: Black Images, 1975.

Melon-Degras, Alfred. Preface. *Guyane pour tout dire; Le mal du pays*, by Serge Patient. Paris: Éditions caribéennes, 1980.

—*D. H. Figueredo*

Patterson, Orlando (1940–)

Combining the gift of writing with scholarly research and a passion for the human condition, Jamaican novelist and scholar Orlando Patterson has written compelling sociological studies and novels about the horrors of slavery in the Caribbean and its legacy in modern society. His novels have been anthologized in numerous textbooks, and his academic work is required reading in colleges across the United States and the Caribbean.

Horace Orlando Lloyd Patterson was born on June 5, 1940, in Frome, Jamaica. As a child he spent hours at the local library and soon began to write short stories that were published in the local press. In his early twenties he attended Kingston College, in Jamaica, and in 1963, he went to England to study at the London School of Economics, earning a PhD. He taught in Great Britain before relocating to the United States, where he was appointed professor at Harvard University. In 1967, he published his dissertation, *The Sociology of Slavery: Jamaica 1655–1838*, a seminal study on the relationships between personal and systemic power in the culture of slavery. While he was working on this volume, he was also working on two novels: *The Children of Sisyphus* (1964) and *An Absence of Ruins* (1967), naturalistic depictions of poverty in Jamaica. In 1972, Patterson reshaped the research he had conducted for his doctoral degree into the novel *Die the Long Day*.

The novel tells the story of a slave woman in eighteenth-century Jamaica and her efforts to stop her master from raping her daughter. It is an episodic narrative rich in details about the daily life of the slaves and in sociological insight about the relationship between master and slave. A dominant theme is the study of the process by which an individual dehumanizes another to convert that person into property. This is a theme that Patterson pursued further in his study *Slavery and Social Death: A Comparative Study* (1991). In the mid-1990s, Patterson refuted the notion that integration had been successful in the controversial study *The Order of Integration: Progress and Resentment in America's "Racial" Crisis* (1997).

Patterson holds the post of John Cowles Professor of Sociology at Harvard University. He has been honored with numerous awards and fellowships, including the National Endowment for the Humanities awards several times, a Guggenheim fellowship in 1978–79, the scholarship award from the American Sociological Association in 1983, and the National Book Award in 1991 for his volume *Freedom in the Making of Western Culture*. *See also* Slave Narratives.

Further Reading

Ifill, Max B. *Slavery, Social Death or Communal Victory: a Critical Appraisal of Slavery and Social Death by Dr. Orlando Patterson*. Port of Spain, Trinidad: Economics and Business Research, 1996.

—*D. H. Figueredo*

Pau-Llosa, Ricardo (1954–)

Cuban poet, art critic, curator, short-story writer, Ricardo Pau-Llosa brings together words and images like few contemporary writers and artists can do. He defies facile ethnic categorizations while remaining faithful to his "Cuban-American-ness." While he writes primarily in English, neither Cuba nor the Miami of his exile are ever far from his visual imagination. He shares with other writers of his generation, like Dionisio D. Mártinez and **Gustavo Pérez Firmat**, a mastery and love of the English language that does not exclude but rather embraces both sides of a culturally rich, hyphenated life. As Dionisio Mártinez writes in his preface to *Bread of the Imagined* (1992), Pau-Llosa's work reflects a "new sensibility and a new phenomenon" (11) for both the Latino and Anglo community.

Pau-Llosa was born in Havana in 1954. In 1960, he emigrated with his family to the United States, and today he is a professor of creative writing in the English Department of Miami-Dade College. A winner of the 1983 Anhinga Poetry Prize for his book *Sorting Metaphors*, he has also won in recent years the English Language Poetry Prize from *Linden Lane* (1987) and the Simon Daro Davidowicz Award for his poem "Mulata" (1992). In 1984, he was awarded the prestigious Cintas Fellowship for his poetry.

A talented and versatile writer, he has written and edited several books on Latin American and Cuban art. *Dirube* (1979) and *Rafael Soriano: The Poetics of Light* (1998) are seminal monographs on Cuban masters. *Rogelio Polesello* (1984) and *Fernando de Szyszlo* (1991) are major works on masters from Argentina and Peru, respectively. *Outside Cuba/Fuera de Cuba* (1989), to which he was contributor and coeditor, featured the work of Cuba American artists whose works were exhibited between 1987 and 1989 in museums in Georgia, Florida, New Jersey, New York, Ohio, and Puerto Rico. Pau-Llosa was also one of the curators of that exhibition. That same year he also coedited and contributed to *Clarence Holbrook Carter* (1989). The year 1991 saw the publication of *Humberto Calzada: A Retrospective of Work From 1979–1990*, an exhibition Pau-Llosa curated, while his most recent critical contribution can be found in *Olga de Amaral: El Manto de la Memoria* (2000). From 1982 to 1994 he was a contributing editor of *Art International* (Lugano, later Paris), and he was a contributor and adviser to *The Dictionary of Art*, (1996). He is currently North American editor of *Southwart Art*, published in Buenos Aires. His articles have also appeared in *Drawing, Sculpture, Connaissance des Arts*, and other journals. He was a guest curator at the Lima Biennial in 1997 and 1999 and a juror in the major international exhibition Eco-Art at the Museum of Modern Art in Rio in 1992.

He has published five books of poetry: the award winning *Sorting Metaphors* (1983), *Bread of the Imagined* (1991), *Cuba* (1993), *Vareda Tropical* (1998), and, in 2003, *The Mastery Impulse*. His poetry has also appeared in the *American Poetry Review, TriQuarterly, Manoa, Denver Quarterly, Partisan Review, New England Review, Ploughshares,* and the *Kenyon Review*. His short stories have appeared in various magazines and anthologies, most notably in *Sudden Fiction* (1996).

"The question is not what you look at, but what you see," said Henry David Thoreau (1817–62). And whether Pau-Llosa is writing about art, or writing poetry; it is *seeing*, that informs his work. "[E]ven when I'm not writing directly about painting, or a poem that is inspired by a painting, being around painters and being around art educated my eyes—educated me to see formal and symbolic correspondences in the visual world," says Pau-Llosa in *Poet's Truth* (138). In *The Mastery Impulse*, Pau-Llosa pays homage to the Cuban American painter, Humberto Calzada, in a poem aptly entitled "Years of Exile." For Pau-Llosa the exile's imagination is always visual; it belongs to that theater of images we call memory: "In the case of Cuba, the imagination of exile artists and exile poets is the imagination of the culture. Only this imagination has been able to choose freely its freedom and expression," he wrote in *Outside Cuba* (59). Hence, it is precisely because the freedom to imagine is the exile's remaining treasure that Pau-Llosa can equate the life-world of *his* Miami with *his* Delft in *Mastery Impulse* (86). But he leaves it up to us not merely to read, or to look, but to see the connection between the two cities. *See also* Cuban American Literature; Exile Literature.

Further Reading

Dick, Bruce Allen. "A Conversation with Ricardo Pau-Llosa." *A Poet's Truth: Conversations with Latino/Latina Poets*. Tucson: University of Arizona Press, 2003.

Milian, Alberto. "Defying Time and History: Interview with Ricardo Pau-Llosa." *Manoa* 15, no. 1 (2003).

———. *Sorting Metaphors*. Tallahassee, FL: Anhinga Press, 1983.

Milian, Alberto, Ileana Fuentes Perez, and Graciella Cruz Gaura. *Outside Cuba: Contemporary Cuban Visual Artists*. New Brunswick, NJ: Office of Hispanic Arts, Mason Gross School of the Arts, Rutgers University, 1989.

Shapard, Robert, and James Thomas, eds. *Sudden Fiction (Continued): 60 New Short Stories*. New York: Norton, 1996.

—*Rolando Pérez*

Paz, Senel (1950–)

Cuban short-story writer, Senel Paz achieved international recognition with the film *Fresa y Chocolate*, an adaptation of his short story "El lobo, el bosque y el hombre nuevo." Paz is also a screenwriter.

Paz was born in Las Villas, Cuba. As a child he lived in the countryside but spent his teen years as an interned student at the Universidad de la Habana, the beneficiary of a government scholarship. Paz was the first in his family to go to college and, as he told critic **Emilio Bejel** in *Escribir en Cuba* (1991), the Cuban Revolution made him "a person . . . a thinker . . . an intellectual" (307). At the university, he met such writers as **Jesús Díaz** and studied writing techniques and literary theories. In 1970, he published his first short story in a literary magazine published at the university. Majoring in journalism, he worked as editor of the journal *Revolución y Cultura*. In 1979, he received the David Award, given to unpublished writers, for a collection of short stories entitled *El niño aquel*. The volume was published in 1980.

In 1983, Paz published the novel *Un rey en el jardín*, which proved a best seller in Cuba. In 1985, he wrote the film script *Una novia para David*. But it was the 1990 film *Fresa y Chocolate* that brought him fame outside the island. The short story and the film questioned Cuba's policies toward gays, but what made the film successful in Europe and the United States was the realistic and sensitive portrayal of the platonic relationship between a Communist militant and an intellectual gay man. His other filmscripts include *Cosas que deje en la Habana* (1997) *Sí, quiero* (1998), *Un paraíso bajo las estrellas* (1999). *See also* Cuban Literature, History of; Gay and Lesbian Literature.

Further Reading

Bejel, Emilio. *Escribir en Cuba*. Río Piedras, Puerto Rico: Editorial de la Universidad de Puerto Rico, 1991.

—*Emilio Bejel and D. H. Figueredo*

Péan, Stanley (1966–)

Canadian Haitian Péan is a novelist, a critic, and a writer of young-adult fiction. Like many Caribbean authors who live abroad, Péan writes both about Haiti and Canada.

Born in Port-au-Prince, Haiti on March 31, 1966, Stanley Péan was raised in Jonquière, Quebec, where his parents, who had opposed dictator **François Duvalier**, had settled in the 1960s. During the early 1980s, he performed with a theatrical group called Groupe Sanguin. In 1984, he matriculated at the University of Laval, where he studied literature.

While in college, he began to write stories and articles and helped to organize the literary review *Stop*. In 1988, his collection of short stories, *La plage des songes*, was published. Three years later, he published his first novel *Le tumulte de mon sang* which was favorably reviewed by the Canadian media. Two more novels followed *Sombres allées* (1992), and *Zombi Blues* (1996). The latter novel, the story of a jazz musician, became a bestseller. In Haiti, where his books were distributed, scholars noticed Péan's pessimistic assessment of Haitian politics, a common theme in his works and lectures.

In 1999, Péan became literary critic for *La Presse*, a position from which he re-signed years later when he was asked to re-write a negative review of a book writ-ten by a popular Canadian personality. He also worked as the editor of the journal *Le libraire*. In 2000, he wrote the young adult novel *Le temps s'enfuit* for which he received the Prix littéraire M. Christie award. Péan is a music critic as well.

Further Reading

"Stanley Péan, médaille Raymond-Blais." http://www.scom.ulaval.ca/contact/automne00/art_12.html (accessed 9/23/05).

—*D. H. Figueredo*

Peasant Novel, The

A literary genre wherein the novelist records the experiences and struggles of the rural poor with the intention of exposing the abuses visited on them by politicians, capitalists, and residents from the cities. In Haiti, the peasant novel first appeared toward the end of the nineteenth and beginning of the twentieth centuries. Two popular works from this period are **Justin Lhérisson's** *Famille des Pitite-Caille*, pub-lished in 1905, and *Mimola*, written by Antoine Innocent and published in 1906.

During the first decade of the twentieth century, Haitian writers did not ex-plore this genre, since they were concerned with expanding the horizons of Haitian literature and taking their place among francophone writers. For example, poets such as **Etzer Vilare** focused on the broader themes of love, moral values, and re-flections on life and death, leaving behind topics of nationalism and of local inter-est. The **American occupation of Haiti** in 1915, however, stirred new interest in the peasant novel. It was a way of rejecting the American presence but also of celebrat-ing the peasants, who were the only people to rebel against the American forces in an insurgency that lasted two years and that ended with the killing of leader Charlemagne Peralte (1885–1919) and the death of thousands of peasants.

The elements of the peasant novel include lengthy descriptions of the Haitian landscape, the works of the peasants, and the traditions and religious practices of peasant. The overall desire, however, is to accept the culture of the peasants as equal to that of the cities and to take pride in that culture. Perhaps the best-known novel in the genre is *Gouverneurs de la rosée* (1946), written by **Jacques Roumain**. Other peasant novels include *La Drame de la Terre* (1933), *La Vengeance de la Terre* (1939), and *L'Héritage Sacré* (1945), all by Mean Baptiste Cineas; *Canape vert* (1942), *La bête de musseau* (1946), *Le crayon de dieu* (1952), and *Tous les homes sont fous* (1970), all written by the brothers **Phillip** and **Pierre Thoby-Marcelin**.

In the Hispanic Caribbean, one of the best-known peasant novels is *La llama-rada* (1935). Written by the Puerto Rican **Enrique Laguerre**, this is the story of an idealistic young man who, recently graduated with a degree in agriculture, seeks to better the conditions of the peasants and improve productivity but instead becomes a corrupt plantation overseer.

In French the term used is *roman paysan* and in Spanish *novela de la tierra. See also* Indigènisme; Plantation Society in Caribbean Literature, The.

Further Reading

Dash, J. Michael. "Introduction to Masters of the Dew." In *Masters of the Dew* by Jacques Roumain, translated by Langston Hughes and Mercer Cook. Oxford: Heinemann, 1978.

—*D. H. Figueredo*

Pedreira, Antonio Salvador (1899–1939)

In his relatively short life—he died at the age of forty—Pedreira emerged as one of Puerto Rico's most important and controversial thinkers, writing the famous book *Insuralismo* (1934), in which he traced the island's cultural roots to Spain and defined Puerto Ricans as Spanish and white. He was also a gifted poet and a professor.

Pedreira was born in San Juan on June 13, 1899. Conducting his elementary and secondary studies in his hometown, at the age of twenty-one he became a teacher. Attracted to medicine, he then went to New York City to study, but lack of economic resources forced him to return home. In 1925, he earned a BA in Spanish literature from the Universidad de Puerto Rico; the following year, he received an MA from Columbia University. While working on his doctorate at the Universidad de Madrid in the late 1920s, he was writing essays on Puerto Rican and Spanish culture, producing two books, *De los nombres de Puerto Rico* (1927) and *Arista* (1930).

Years before and during graduate school, he collected and studied works written by Puerto Ricans since the discovery of the island to the twentieth century. This labor resulted in 1932 in a mammoth volume, *Bibliografía puertorriqueña*. That same year, he published a biography of his compatriot and great writer **Eugenio María Hostos**: *Hostos, ciudadano de América*. His objective was to rescue from obscurity and introduce to Latin America the brilliant Puerto Rican thinker.

In 1934, Pedreira published *Insularismo: Ensayos de interpretación puertorriqueña*, the product of his desire to study the nature of his compatriots from a historical, social, and global perspective. Realizing that if it was difficult to comprehend the whys and hows of an individual, he observed that it would be impossible to define the collective psychology of a people. His attempt, though, enticed and excited Puerto Rican intellectuals of the era. Seven decades since its publication, *Insularismo* still provokes discussion with many Puerto Rican thinkers who criticize Pedreira's exclusion of the island's African heritage from his definition and who describe him as an elitist.

In 1935, Pedreira continued his social and nationalistic exploration with *La actualidad del jíbaro*, wherein he concluded that the white farmer from the Puerto Rican mountain was the true representative of Puerto Ricanness. In 1937, he wrote a nineteenth-century history of the island, *El año del 87: Sus antecedents y su consecuencias*.

At the time of his death on October 23, 1939, Pedreira was chair of Department of Hispanic Studies at the Universidad de Puerto Rico and was working on several books, including *El periodismo en Puerto Rico*, a history of journalism, and *Aclaraciones y crítica*, an anthology of editorials and columns he had published in the newspaper *El Mundo*—both works were published posthumously—the first in 1941, the latter in 1942. Though remembered for the book *Insuralismo*, during his lifetime Pedreira wrote poems and essays that were published in major Latin American reviews the likes of *Puerto Rico Ilustrado*, *Revista Bimestre Cubana*, and *Revista de Estudios Hispánicos*.

Further Reading

Flores, Juan. *The Insular Vision: Pedreira's Interpretation of Puerto Rican Culture*. New York: CUNY, Centro de Estudios Puertorriqueños, 1978.

Sierra Berdecía, Fernando. *Antonio S. Pedreira, buceador de la personalidad puertorriqueña*. San Juan, Puerto Rico: Biblioteca de autores puertorriqueños, 1942

—*D. H. Figueredo*

Pedroso, Régino (1896–1983)

One of the creators of the poetry of social protest in Cuba, poet Régino Pedroso was born in the town of Unión de Reyes, in the province of Matanzas, on March 3, 1896. His father was a Chinese laborer and his mother was Afro-Cuban. After the death of his father, his family suffered economic hardship, and his mother moved to Havana in search of employment. Pedroso was able to go to school until he was thirteen years old, but at that age he had to quit to find work. He relocated to eastern Cuba, where his older sister Angela and her husband had moved to work at the Cape Cruz Company. In Oriente, he met workers who wrote poetry and began to write. He read, too, building a library of paperbacks that included *Don Quixote*, *the Bible*, Greek mythology, and novels by Sir Walter Scott (1771–1832), Alexandre Dumas (1802–70), and Victor Hugo (1802–85). In 1918, he returned to Havana, where he worked at the American Steel Company. Between 1918 and 1924, he wrote Modernista poems, which were published in such Havana periodicals as *Castalia, El Figaro*, and *Chic*. He met the poets José Z. Tallet, **Nicolás Guillén**, and Ruben Martínez Villena, and in 1927 the literary supplement of the prestigious Havana newspaper *El Diario de la Marina* published his poem "La Salutación Fraterna al Taller Mecánico." This poem marked the beginning in Cuba of a poetry of social commentary.

In 1933, Pedroso published his first book, *Nosotros*, which was read widely outside Cuba and was translated into English by the African American poet Langston Hughes (1902–67). In 1934, he began to work for the newspaper *Ahora* and for *Masas*, the journal of the Cuban Anti-Imperialist League. The following year he was imprisoned together with the editors of *Masas*, accused of subversion. Pedroso was overwhelmed by this experience, and as an act of faith in Marxist fraternity, he wrote the poems compiled later in the volume *Mas allá canta el mar* (1939).

In 1940, he married Petra Ballagas, and shortly after he began working for the Cuban Department of Education. In 1945, he published *Bolívar: Sinfonía de libertad*, a collection of poems inspired by faith in freedom and in Latin American solidarity. Ten years later, he published a collection of an entirely different nature, *El ciruelo de Uan Pei You*, an evocation of Chinese wisdom and human values.

In 1959, Régino Pedroso embraced the revolutionary government, and **Fidel Castro** sent him as cultural adviser to the Cuban Embassy in Mexico City. In 1961, he was sent to the Cuban Embassy in China, where he wrote the book of poems *Ofrenda ancestral* (1964). For Pedroso, the Cuban revolutionary government represented the realization of his Marxist ideals and the achievement in Cuba of the social justice that he had sought in his proletarian years. In 1975, his *Obra poética* was published in Havana by Editorial Arte y Literatura, and in 1982 he was proposed by the Cuban Academy of Language for the prestigious Cervantes Prize in Literature. He died in Havana in 1983.

Pedroso wrote in diverse styles and formats, ranging from the modernista poetry of his youth through social commentary poetry and Negrista poems, such as "Hermano Negro," to the meditative style of *El ciruelo de Yuan Pei You*. His most significant contribution to Cuban poetry was his "La Salutación Fraterna al Taller Mecánico," which spawned sensitive poetry of social concern. *See also* Literatura Comprometida/Socially Engaged Literature; Modernismo/Modernism; Negrista Literature.

Further Reading

Navarro, Osvaldo, ed. *Órbita de Régino Pedroso*. Habana: Unión de Escritores y Artistas de Cuba, 1975.

Pedroso, Régino. *Poesía*. Habana: Ediciones Unión, 1996.

Vitier, Cintio. *Cincuenta años de poesía pura cubana (1902–1952)*. Habana: Dirección de Cultura del Ministerio de Educación, Ediciones del Cincuentenario, 1952.

—*Rafael E. Tarrago*

Peix, Pedro (1952–)

Pedro Peix is a short-story writer and novelist from the Dominican Republic; his works study the bureaucratic nature of dictatorship and the seductive capabilities of undisputed power. He is also a television journalist and commentator.

Peix was born in Santo Domingo, Dominican Republic, on March 20, 1952. He attended the Universidad **Pedro Henríquez Ureña**, earning a law degree in 1976. In 1982, he served as library director of the National Library and as associate director of Ministry of Education. He also wrote for the daily *Listín Diario*.

In 1974, he published his first novel, *El placer esta en el último piso*. In 1977, he won a national prize for the collection of short stories *Las locas de la Plaza de los Almendros*. Then he wrote two further collections of short stories that brought him international recognition: *La noche de los buzones blancos* (1980) and *La narrativa yugulado* (1981). His most famous short story, "El fantasma de la called El Conde" (1977), which uses **magical realism**, is allegorical story of economic and political corruption in the Dominican Republic.

Further Reading

Céspedes, Diógenes. *Antología del cuento dominicano*. Santo Domingo: Editora de Colores, 1996.

—*D. H. Figueredo*

Peña de Bordas, Ana Virginia de (1904–48)

De Peña de Bordas was a Dominican short-fiction writer and novelist who wrote about the Amerindians of the Dominican Republic and whose work has been neglected by scholars both in her native country and in the United States. She exemplifies the woman author who is often silenced by a male-dominated society.

Born in Santiago de los Caballeros, Dominican Republic, in 1904, Ana Virginia de Peña de Bordas was the daughter of Julio de Peña and Edelmira Bordas, and the granddaughter of the distinguished Dominican intellectual Manuel de Jesús Peña y Reynoso. She attended elementary and secondary school in her native Santiago de los Caballeros. As a young woman, she studied painting and ballet for a number of years at the Cushing Academy of Art in Boston, United States. Although as a young girl Peña de Bordas showed literary interest and promise, as an adult she kept her writings under what has been termed a strange and hermetic silence. At the age of thirty-six, she published in newspapers her children's stories "La eracra de oro" and "La princesa de los cabellos platinados." Death found Virginia unexpectedly, while she was still a young and vibrant woman, during an afternoon siesta in 1948.

Virginia de Peña de Bordas is a little-studied Dominican woman author whose work has recently received some attention in the United States. An article, "Una flor en la sombra: Vida y obra de Virginia de Peña de Bordas," written by Daisy Cocco de Filippis, has been included in the fourth volume of the *Recovering the U.S. Hispanic Literary Heritage*, edited by Silvio Torres-Saillant, et al. (2002). In addition to the aforementioned children's stories, Peña de Bordas authored *Toeya*, a novel in the Indianista tradition, and *Seis novelas cortas*, both published posthumously in 1952 and 1949, respectively, with second editions for each in 1978. Her work, however, is mostly unknown in the United States, and it is usually ignored in the Dominican Republic today. Its survival is due to the diligence and financial position of Isidro Bordas, her widower, who disconsolate about her untimely death proceeded to collect her writings and have them published posthumously, some as late as 1978, thirty years after her death. Interestingly, de Peña de Bordas's work is marked by her experience in the United States, where she lived and studied for a number of years in the 1920s. Her life and work pose very real questions about the nature of the Latino and Caribbean experience for women writers and about their place or lack thereof in literary and cultural history.

In the Archivo Nacional of Santo Domingo, there is a copy of Peña de Bordas's *Toeya* that bears a handwritten, unsigned dedication, recording the fact that the family had donated the copy of the poema indigenista (*sic*), written by their unforgettable Virginia. It is dated 1968 and it appears on the opposite side of a printed biographical sketch of the author in the 1952 publication which also explains that

> Su poema Toeya es la hija espiritual que nos lega. Educada en los Estados Unidos, la escribió primero en inglés, con el propósito de publicarla en una revista Americana; traduciéndola más tarde al castellano (5) (Her poem Toeya is the spiritual daughter she left us. Educated in the United States, she first wrote it in English with the objective of publishing it in an American journal, translating it into Spanish later on.)

A similar explanation appears in *Seis novelas cortas*, where it is also indicated that the note had been previously printed in *El Caribe*—one of the leading newspapers in Santo Domingo at that time—on September 14, 1949. In her introduction to the 1952 edition of *Toeya*, the Dominican scholar and literary critic Flérida de Nolasco indicates that Peña de Bordas "como cultora de la palabra fue una flor que vivió en la sombra" ("as an artisan of the word, Peña de Bordas was a flower who lived in the shadows"). *See also* Dominican Republic Literature, History of; Feminism in Caribbean Literature.

Further Reading

Cocco de Filippis, Daisy. *Para que no se olviden: The Lives of Women in Dominican History*. New York: Ediciones Alcance, 2000.

Peña de Bordas, Virginia. *Seis novelas cortas*. Santo Domingo: Taller, 1978.

———. *Toeya*. Barcelona: Editorial Juventud, 1952.

—Daisy Cocco de Filippis

Pepín Estrella, Ambrosia Ercilia (1886–1939)

Pepín Estrella was an educator, writer, feminist, orator, and patriot from the Dominican Republic. She was the first Dominican woman to denounce the American invasion of 1916.

Pepín Estrella was born in Santiago de los Caballeros, the Dominican Republic, on December 7, 1886. She attended the Escuela Normal de Señoritas in the late 1890s but as a result of the school's closing by the government was not able to graduate until 1913. However, her diligence, intelligence, wide knowledge, and public-speaking abilities earned her the position of director of the Escuelas de Niñas de Nibaje at the age of fifteen. She worked also as a mathematics, physics, and natural science teacher at the Colegio Superior de Señoritas, responsibilities normally assigned to four different teachers.

In 1911, Pepín Estrella began an active campaign in centers and civic associations to advance the cause of patriotism. Her speech "Juan Pablo Duarte y Eugenio María de Hostos," read only forty days alter the American invasion of 1916, brought her fame and a reputation for altruism and courage. Throughout her life she delivered numerous speeches and wrote articles in support of educational reform and suffrage. In 1928, she founded the Junta Provincial de la Acción Cultural Feminista of Santiago.

Her courageous spirit, her solidarity, and love for her motherland cost her the position of school director when she protested the death of one of the many teachers assassinated by Rafael Leónidas Trujillo (1891–1961) during the **Trujillo Era.** Her articles and speeches were regularly published in such popular publications as *La Información, El Diario, Listín Diario, La Opinión,* and *La Cuna de América.* Her works include *Por la patria y por la escuela.* (1920), *Árboles y madres* (1926), *Mi homenaje a las madres y una ofrenda al libertador Sandino.* (1926), *Ante el ara de la escuela* (1929), *Feminismo* (1930), and *Mi homenaje a los héroes y mártires de La Barranquita* (1930). She passed away in her hometown on June 6, 1939. Today a high school and numerous pedagogical awards carry her name. *See also* Dominican Republic Literature, History of; Feminism in Caribbean Literature.

Further Reading

Cocco de Filippis, Daisy. *Documents of Dissidence: Selected Writings by Dominican Women.* New York: CUNY, Dominican Studies Institute, 2000.

—*Daisy Cocco de Filippis*

Perdomo y Heredia, Josefa Antonia (1834–96)

A poet from the Dominican Republic, Perdomo y Heredia is considered one of the first woman writers to be published in that country.

Related to the romantic poet **José María Heredia y Heredia,** from Cuba, Perdomo y Heredia was born in Santo Domingo on June 13, 1834. Though she was born into a wealthy family, she suffered the loss of her mother when she was an infant and was of a sickly nature. Her uncle, the poet Manuel de Jesús Heredia taught her writing and grammar and introduced her to the literature of the period.

When she was in her teens, she began to write poetry, which she published under the pen names of Lucia or Laura in the periodical *El Oasis,* becoming one of the first women poets in the Dominican Republican to be published in the press.

Her poems were of religious nature. A typical example is the poem "A Dios" (1885):

> Y si te place ¡oh Dios! que yo padezca
> todo el rigor de mi destino impío,
> haz a lo menos que tu amor merezca
> cumpliendo fiel tu voluntad, Dios mío!

(If it pleases you, God, that I shall suffer/the pains of my irreligious destiny, / at least let me earn your love / faithfully obeying your will, my Lord!)

A collection of her poetry appeared in 1885 under the title of *Poesías de la señorita Josefa A. Perdomo*. The volume was well received by the intellectuals of the time, a major accomplishment, considering that she was writing during a period when women were not meant to display either creativity or intellect that took them beyond the realms of their homes and duties as homemakers. *See also* Dominican Republic Literature, History of; Feminism in Caribbean Literature.

Further Reading

Cocco de Filippis, Daisy. "Josefa Antonia Perdomo Heredia." In *Para que no se olviden: The Lives of Women in Dominican History*. New York: Ediciones Alcance, 2000.

—*Daisy Cocco de Filippis*

Pérez, Rolando (1957–)

A philosopher, writer, and librarian, Rolando Pérez is probably one of the very few Cuban-born writers living in the United States who is most integrated in the American culture. Most nonnative American writers living in the United States create works of art that in many different ways reminisce about or romanticize the native land, the land of their childhood, the land they had to leave behind, heartbroken. Rolando Pérez's work, on the other hand, distinguishes itself in that it portrays a world not strictly defined by the beautiful island or peninsula of his memories or by the land he lost. His work at once seems to embrace and represent a more comprehensive world: the journeys, the anguishes, the fantasies that all humans experience in general, no matter where they're from. Pérez recognizes that the world is already filled with too many boxes and that for one to continue to identify oneself as Cuban, Italian, Protestant, and so on, it is to perpetuate a categorization process that is the basis of so much hatred, prejudice, jealousy, and bloodshed throughout the world (*H Is for Box*, 1993).

The son of a pediatrician, Rolando, and his wife, Digna Casas Pérez, and the grandson of Spanish immigrants, Pérez, who has always had a special admiration for philosophy, first came in contact with philosophy with his reading of Friedrich Nietzsche (1844–1900) in high school. The writings of the German philosopher offered a "window on the world," for the would-be writer. In 1983, enthused by Nietzsche's work, he published his undergraduate thesis, *Understanding the Psychology and Morality of the Overman*, a work dispelling many of the misconceptions concerning Nietzsche's Overman. In the late 1980s, as a graduate student, impressed with the works of Cuban writer **Severo Sarduy**, he published his thesis, *Severo Sarduy and the Religion of the Text* (1988), one of the first essays on the Cuban writer written in English.

During his graduate studies, as a student of philosophy, Pérez became interested in contemporary French criticism and philosophy, particularly the works of Gilles Deleuze (1925–95) and Felix Guattari (1930–92). His attraction to their revolutionary, anarchical book *Anti-Oedipus* led him to write and publish *On An(archy) and Schizoanalysis* (1990). In 1990, he also published *The Odyssey*, a beautifully written work of poetic prose that clearly reflects the influence of Deleuze's and Guattari's idea of "plateau," where in "different" parts coexist in no particular division or strict sequential order. The world of *The Odyssey* is one that allows equal space to all views and to all forms of expression: be it that of the child, the romantic, the philosopher, the erudite, or everyman. "Picture the childlike innocence of Italo Calvino's early tales, ballasted by an alienation that invokes the lost souls of Beckett," wrote John Strausbaugh of *The Odyssey* in *New York Press* (1990).

Pérez has also written numerous plays, which have received readings and productions over the years. His plays, satirical and absurdist in tone, deal with such issues as lack of communication between people ("I Can't Open It," in Eve Ensler's *Central Park Magazine*, Fall 1986); power relations ("Playthings" in *Plays and Playthings*, 1999), sterile conformity and racial stereotypes (*H Is for Box*, 1993), and home ownership as the kind of materialism that swallows people up (*The House That Ate Their Brains*, 1992). Toward the end of the 1990s, Pérez moved in a slightly different direction, with an interest in exploring the relationship between language and images. In 1999, Cool Grove Press published *The Divine Duty of Servants: A Book of Worship*, a book based on the artwork of the Polish writer-artist and victim of the Holocaust Bruno Schulz (1892–1942). *The Divine Duty* is a reflection on Schulz's erotic drawings of masochism and foot fetishism. Here the author makes the connection between the dark myths of power and the most oppressive dictatorships of the twentieth century. According to Pérez, "These drawings—reminiscent of Goya's Los Caprichos ('The Caprices') and Los Desastres del la Guerra ('The Disasters of War')—are profoundly telling about our human, and sometimes all too human, nature," as quoted in *Contemporary Authors* (323).

Rolando Pérez's next artistic journey was *The Lining of Our Souls: Excursions into Selected Paintings of Edward Hopper*, with a foreword by renowned Edward Hopper scholar, Gail Levin. *The Lining of Our Souls* captures all the sensations, moods, and places that the colors and the images of Edward Hopper (1882–1967) evoke in the young writer. **Gustavo Pérez Firmat** has called *The Lining of Our Souls* "A powerful and disturbing performance by one of our most gifted Latino writers."

Pérez's next work, *The Electric Comedy*, is his homage to Italian medieval poet Dante Alighieri's (1265–1321) brilliant poem *Commedia*. Just as Dante's Commedia takes the reader through a journey of medieval decadence, so Pérez's *Electric Comedy* takes his readers through a journey of contemporary electric consumption and Internet capitalism, with its metaphysics of virtual realities. At the end of this journey, the reader becomes aware of the cynicism of the Internet, as it turns people into puppets of all the Bill Gateses of the twentieth century.

His most recent work involves essays on Carlo Levi, with Rosa Amatulli, Primo Levi, and Milan Kundera in *Multicultural Writers Since 1945* (2004) and "Severo Sarduy" in *The Review of Contemporary Fiction* (Spring 2004). Selections from his work can be found in the prestigious *Norton Anthology of Latino Literature* (2005). Rolando Pérez is a doctoral candidate in the Department of Hispanic and Luso-Brazilian Literatures and Languages at the CUNY Graduate Center.

Further Reading

Pérez, Rolando. Selections. *The Norton Anthology of Latino Literature*, edited by Ilan Stavans. New York: Norton, 2005.

"Rolando Pérez." *Contemporary Authors*. http://galenet.galegroup.com (accessed 5/23/05).

Strausbaugh, John. "From Cuba, With Camel." *New York Press*, August 8–14, 1990.

—*Rosa Amatulli*

Pérez de Zambrana, Luisa (1835–1922)

A romantic poet from Cuba, Pérez de Zambrana wrote poems expressing sorrow at the loss of her children and her husband. Critics have praised the sincerity of her poetry and musicality of her diction.

Born in 1835 in a farm near the town of El Cobre, in Eastern Cuba, Luisa Pérez spent her childhood in a rural environment. This early experience is reflected in her first compositions, in which she shows herself a delicate poet of nature. In 1852, her father died, and her mother moved her family to Santiago de Cuba, then the capital city of eastern Cuba, where Luisa was received in the literary circles and where she published her first collection of poems. The intellectual Dr. Ramón Zambrana read this book in 1853 and traveled to eastern Cuba to meet its author. After a brief correspondence with Luisa, Dr. Zambrana asked her to marry him, and she accepted. They married and settled in Havana, where Luisa socialized with literary figures and continued writing poetry. In 1860 she participated in the Havana festivities to welcome back from Spain the celebrated Cuban poet **Gertrudis Gómez de Avellaneda**, crowning her with a wreath of laurel at an event in her honor. Also in that year, Luisa published a second collection of poems, with a prologue by Gómez de Avellaneda.

Ramón Zambrana died in 1866, leaving Luisa with five children. She supported her family with income derived from translations and romances that she wrote for Havana literary journals. She also continued writing poetry. All her children died within her lifetime, and their deaths inspired her to write moving elegies. Toward the end of her long life, the government of the Republic of Cuba, established in 1902, provided her with a pension in recognition of her literary merit.

A compilation of her poetry was published in 1920; however, two years later she passed away in Havana.

After Luisa's death, a collection of her elegies to her children and a poem that she wrote after the death of her husband, "La Vuelta al Bosque," were published under the title *Elegías familiares* (1937). Her complete works were reprinted in the thirteen-volume collection *Los Zambrana* (1957), including her 1864 novel *Angélica y Estrella*.

The poetry of Luisa Pérez de Zambrana was celebrated by her contemporaries. In the prologue to the 1860 edition of her poems, Gómez de Avellaneda praised their sincerity, tenderness, and melancholy spirituality. Outside Cuba, **José Martí** sang her praises in an article published in the Mexican journal *El Universal* in 1876. José María Chacón y Calvo included several of her poems in his anthology *Las cien mejores poesías cubanas*, published in Madrid in 1922.

Pérez de Zambrana was a distinguished representative of the romantic movement in Cuba, remarkable for the sincerity of her tender melancholy verses. Within this romantic sensibility a literary, emotional, and intellectual development is noticeable in her poetry, going from the intuitive evocation of nature in the poems of her youth to the mature and chiseled verses of her sorrow-filled latter years. The poetic individuality and sincerity of her imagery and the musicality of her language are significant. **Cintio Vitier** did justice to this significance by including her in his anthology *Los grandes románticos cubanos* (1960). *See also* Romanticismo/Romanticism.

Further Reading

Martínez Bello, Antonio. *Dos musas cubanas*. Habana: P. Fernández y Cia., 1954.

Pérez de Zambrana, Luisa. *Poesías de Luisa Pérez de Zambrana*. Habana: Imprenta "El Siglo XX" de la Sociedad Editorial Cuba Contemporánea, 1920.

Tejera y Horta, María Luisa de la. *Bibliografía de Luisa Pérez de Zambrana*. Habana, 1955.

—*Rafael E. Tarrago*

Pérez Firmat, Gustavo (1949–)

Pérez Firmat is a Cuban American memoirist, novelist, poet, and scholar who writes on the duality of maintaining one's ethnicity while fully participating in the American experience and becoming an American. This experience is illustrated in his novel *Anything But Love* (2000), in which the narrator, probably the author himself, leaves his Cuban wife to marry an American woman who doesn't understand why he longs so much for Cuba and remains so angry at **Fidel Castro**, years after leaving the island.

Early in the revolution, Pérez Firmat and his parents fled Cuba, settling in Miami. Initially a lackluster student who didn't take his studies seriously, he attended Dade Community College, going on to graduate school and earning a doctorate from the

University of Michigan. After teaching Spanish at Duke University in North Carolina, he relocated to New York, where he is a language professor at Columbia University. It was during his stay at Duke University that he achieved recognition as a scholar and a poet.

At first, Pérez Firmat wrote in Spanish, then chose to write poetry in English, a move that allowed him to express the pathos of living in two countries and thinking in two languages:

The fact that I
am writing to you
in English
already falsifies what I
wanted to tell you.
My subject:
how to explain to you
that I
don't belong in English
though I belong nowhere else
if not here, in English.

Cuban American poet, novelist, and scholar Gustavo Pérez Firmat writes about the experience of becoming an American while maintaining an ethnic identity and culture. *Courtesy of Gustavo Pérez Firmat.*

In his scholarly work, *Life on the Hyphen: The Cuban American Way* (1994) and the memoir *Next Year in Cuba* (1995), he expressed the development of Cuban American writers, including himself, as an intellectual growth away from Cuba and toward the United States, couched on the realization that the anticipated return to a pre-1959 Cuba, a belief held by Pérez Firmat's parents as well as thousands of exiles who thought Castro would not last long in power, was not going to take place.

Pérez Firmat is credited with popularizing the terms ABC, "American-born Cubans," and "one and a halfer," meaning young Cubans who emigrated from the island as young children and reached adulthood in the United States. His literary appeal, however, extends beyond Cuban Americans to a reading audience interested in the ethnic experience in general and the poetics of assimilation. *See also* Cuban American Literature; Exile Literature.

Further Reading

Dick, Bruce Allen. "A Conversation with Gustavo Perez Firmat." *Michigan Quarterly Review* 41 (2001): 682–94.

Pérez Firmat, Gustavo. *Life on the Hyphen: The Cuban-American Way.* Austin: University of Texas Press, 1994.

———. *Next Year in Cuba.* New York: Anchor Books, 1995.

—*D. H. Figueredo*

Performance Poetry

Meant to be seen and heard, performance poetry uses rhythm, intonation, gestures, and even music. Performance poems are not to be read, thus the delivery depends on the performer's talent. Often, a performer might change the verses in response to the audience, thus endowing the verses with a sense of community participation and even mass writing. There are critics, however, who feel that performance poems do not transfer well to the written pages and lack evidence of the craft of writing. In the Caribbean, two of the best-known performance poets are **Louise Bennett** and **Mickey Smith**. In the United States, the poets who are part of the literary movement known as **Nuyorican literature** perform their poetry in clubs, in schools, and, especially, in the literary salon the Nuyorican poets' Café. One of the best Nuyorican performance poets is the Puerto Rican Jesús Abraham "Tato" Laviera. *See also* Dub Poetry.

Further Reading

Hoyles, Asher, and Martin Hoyles. *Moving Voices: Black Performance Poetry*. London: Hansib Publications Limited, 2002.

—*D. H. Figueredo*

Persaud, Lakshmi (1939–)

Persaud is an accomplished novelist who brought to a close the silence of Indo-Caribbean women who were predominantly represented by male Indian writers, or writers of other ethnicities, as marginalized, passive, idealized figures or repositories of sensuality and exotic otherness. Her fiction adds another facet to a multifaceted, shifting mosaic of representation of gendered subjectivity within the Caribbean sociocultural framework.

Born in then rural village of Pasea, Trinidad, within a devout Hindu family, Persaud lived the challenges of adaptation to creolized Trinidadian society and secondary migration to the metropolis: her grandparents, Hindus from Uttar Pradesh, were indentured Indians who had arrived in Trinidad in the 1890s. After completing her secondary education at St. Augustine Girls School Trinidad, Persaud read for a BA (Honors) and a PhD at Queen's University of Belfast, Northern Ireland; she then earned a postgraduate diploma at Reading University, United Kingdom. Upon her return to the West Indies, she worked as a teacher at prestigious schools throughout the region—Queen's College of Guyana, Harrison College in Barbados, and St. Augustine Girl's High School in Trinidad. In 1974, she moved to the United Kingdom with her husband, Professor Bishnodat Persaud, an economist, and their children.

Persaud began writing fiction in the late 1980s. Her short story "See Saw Margery Daw," was broadcast by the BBC World service in 1995. Her first novel, *Butterfly in the Wind*, was published in 1990, followed by *Sastra* in 1993. Her third novel, *For the Love of My Name*, published in 2000, sealed her reputation as a lyrical and accomplished author.

Butterfly in the Wind re-creates the idyllic childhood of a sheltered, dearly loved and protected young girl; her adaptation to the process of acculturation within modern Trinidad society provides a gendered evocation of the journey of an ethnic minority. The novel presents the many divergences between the Hindu worldview and that of mainstream Trinidadian society: the "good" colonial education administered by the Presbyterian mission school creates dissonance, and the protagonist's growing disaffection with stringent Hindu mores are revealed in a meandering and questioning of an inner voice, which she is constantly seeking to silence. Her fragility, strength, and desire for freedom are evoked in the motif of the butterfly seeking escape over a high wall.

In *Sastra*, the novelist moves away from muted dissatisfaction and ambivalence toward re-Indianization, a reach for ancestral groundings. The narrator says of a venerable, elder woman and role model, "Her religious values and her cultural values were one. Her culture was her way of life, it was all encompassing. Dharma was to her the path of righteousness." *For the Love of My Name* is based on the fictional island of Maya, which resembles Guyana from the mid-1960s to the 1980s. The novel, a mystery about a land mass and society that were swallowed, employs a multivoiced, fragmented mode to explore the potentially devastating impact of political and ethnic strife on fragile island societies.

Persaud is constantly pushing back the boundaries of the natural world, in an attempt at capturing through evocation of simple domestic gestures the essence of life: simple village women who in the act of kneading flour and preparing traditional dishes infuse the air with spiritual warmth, creating an almost mystical experience Yet because these roles, though philosophically ennobling, are in reality restrictive to women, Persaud is careful to identify that the roles are prescribed neither by genetic code nor by the transcendent elements of blood and relation, but by tradition. Ultimately Persaud's text negotiates an ambiguous space between loyalty to the traditional mores and liberation of its constraints.

Persaud's lyrical studies of gender and ethnicity and, ultimately, her characters' search for identity have found a responsive audience throughout the world. There has been increasing recognition of Lakshmi Persaud's work by academic institutions. Her novels are being used as texts in Caribbean and postcolonial literature courses in many universities and colleges. *See also* Feminism in Caribbean Literature; Postcolonialism.

Further Reading

Mehta, Brinda J. "The Colonial Curriculum and the Construction of the 'Coolie-ness' in Lakshmi Persaud's Sastra and Butterfly in the Wind (Trinidad) and Jan Shinebourne's The Last English Plantation (Guyana)." *Journal of Caribbean Literatures* 3, no. 1.

Persaud, Lakshmi. Home page. http://www.lakshmipersaud.com (accessed 5/22/05).

—Paula Morgan

Perrenal, Julio. See Lauffer, Pierre A.

Perse, Saint-John (1887–1975)

The first writer from the Caribbean to receive a Nobel Prize for Literature (1960), Perse was a poet who was born in Guadeloupe but spent most of his life in France and the United States. His actual name was Marie-René-Auguste-Aléxis Saint-Léger Léger.

Perse was born on May 31, 1887, in Saint-Leger-les-Feuilles, Guadeloupe. He was the descendant of French colonial administrators and plantation owners. His early education was informal, tutored by a Catholic bishop and by his nurse, a Hindu priestess of Shiva. At the age of twelve, he and his parents moved to France. Though he never returned to Guadeloupe, the memory of his childhood there, the countryside, and the people he met were the inspiration for his first book of poems, *Eloges* (1911).

In 1910, Perse enrolled at the University of Bordeaux, earning a law degree. In 1914, he became a diplomat, working for the French Foreign Office. He was posted in China in 1916. He traveled widely in China, befriending Chinese philosophers and writers, often retiring to the solitude of an old temple he had rented. His experiences in China were captured in his second book of poetry, *Anabase* (1924), a well-received effort that was promptly translated into English.

Perse ascended through the ranks of the diplomatic service, and in 1933 he was appointed ambassador of France. His responsibilities as a diplomat prevented him from publishing, though he did not stop writing, producing five volumes of unpublished poetry between 1933 and 1940. In 1940, when the Nazis occupied Paris, Perse went into exile. The Nazis then destroyed his manuscripts.

Perse relocated to the United States, where he worked for the Library of Congress, in Washington, D.C., as a French literature consultant. In 1944, he published *Exile*, poems that explored, in metaphysical and symbolical style, his exile condition. In 1946, he wrote *Vents*, in which he alluded to the Caribbean. In 1957, he wrote *Amers*, reflective and symbolical poems about the sea. That same year, he returned to France. Other works followed, including *Chronique* (1959), *Oiseaux* (1962), and *Nocturne* (1972).

Scholar Mary Gallagher, in "Seminal Praise: The Poetry of Saint-John Perse," in the volume *An Introduction to Caribbean Francophone Writing: Guadeloupe and Martinique* (1999), describes Perse's poetry as consisting of three phases: his sojourn in China, the poetry of exile, and the works of old age (17). Some critics from the Caribbean view Perse as detached from Guadeloupe, identifying himself only with France and French culture. Others indicate that his poetry is rich in Caribbean imagery and with a subtext that expresses displacement and nostalgia for Guadeloupe.

Further Reading

Current Biography Yearbook. 1961. New York: H. W. Wilson, 1961,1962.

Gallagher, Mary. "Seminal Praise: The Poetry of Saint-John Perse." In *An Introduction to Caribbean Francophone Writing: Guadeloupe and Martinique*, edited by Sam Haigh,17–33. New York: Berg, 1999.

—D. H. Figueredo

Phelps, Anthony (1928–)

Phelps is a poet, novelist, and short story writer from Haiti. During the 1960s, he migrated to Canada where he promoted the works of Haitian authors. Some of his fictions depict the horrors of the **François Duvalier** dictatorship.

Phelps was born in Haiti in 1928. Upon graduation from high school, Phelps traveled first to the United States and then to Canada to study chemistry, ceramics, and photography. He returned to Haiti in 1953 and began to write stories and poems that he contributed to local publications. In 1960, he founded with several poet friends, including **Davertige**, and **Morisseau Leroy**, the literary group Haïti-littéraire and the journal *Semences*. He was also a participant and moderator for a group of comic actors called Prisme and read his poetry in radio programs. During the 1960s, he concentrated on the writing of poetry, publishing several volumes, including *Été* (1960), *Présence*; poème (1961), *Éclats de silence* (1962), *Points cardinaux* (1966), and *Mon pays que voici. Suivi de: les Dits du fou-aux-cailloux* (1968). Many of his poems rejected nationalism and favored the broadest definitions of humanity, views not accepted by dictator Duvalier, who was enforcing a fascist version of **Négritude**.

In 1964, Phelps left Haiti for Montreal, where he worked in theater, radio, and television, writing the play *Le conditionnel* in 1968. For the next decade, he wrote two novels—*Moins l'infini* (1973) and *Mémoire en colin-maillard* (1976)—and in 1980 his book of poetry *La bélière caraïbe* won a prestigious literature prize from the **Casa de las Américas** in Cuba. While writing, he produced recordings of poetry readings by Haitian poets and spent much time promoting Haitian literature in Canada. During the 1990s, he wrote fiction, poetry, and recorded readings of his own poetry.

Phelps's experience with the racist Duvalier's regime, as well as his years in exile, informed his worldview. He advocates for the acceptance of writers based on nationality rather than on race, and much of his works promote an all-inclusive perspective of the Caribbean, a celebration of the diverse ethnic groups that compose the region.

Further Reading

Dash, J. Michael. "Textual Error and Cultural Crossing—Poétique de la relation by Edouard Glissant / L'Exil, entre l'ancrage et la fuite by Yanick Lahens / Eloge de la créolité by Jean Bernabé, Patrick Chamoiseau and Raphaël Confiant." *Research in African Literatures* 25, no. 2 (Summer 1994): 159.

—D. H. Figueredo

Philip, Marlene Nourbese (1947–)

A pioneer African Caribbean Canadian writer, Marlene Nourbese Philip explores how the English language was used by the colonialists to annihilate Afro-Caribbean heritage and culture. She was also one of the first Caribbean Canadians to depict the experiences of a young black girl in Toronto in her novel *Harriet's Daughter* (1988).

Marlene Nourbese Philip was born on February 3, 1947, in Moriah, Tobago. Her father was a school principal, and from him she learned the proper use of standard English, which she called "father tongue." From the common folks, she learned popular speech, which she dubbed "mother tongue." Early on, she figured how to work with the two languages, preferring the latter as an expression of solidarity with the people and a tool of liberation from colonialism. She also realized that there was a language of silence, as scholar Myriam J. A. Chancy essays in her book *Searching for Safe Spaces* (1997), a silence imposed by those

Marlene Nourbese Philip is an African-Caribbean-Canadian author who examines how language is used to foster racism and colonialism. *Courtesy of Marlene Nourbese Philip.*

in power when they didn't want to hear the voice of the oppressed, and as a silence of protest used by the oppressed. Language and silence became the dominant themes of her Philip's writings.

Philip attended elementary and secondary schools in Trinidad, where her family had relocated in the mid-1950s, and then went to the University of West Indies in Kingston, Jamaica. Graduating in 1968 with a degree in economics, she moved to Canada. She attended the University of Western Ontario where she was awarded a masters in political science. Two years later, she earned a law degree from the same school and in 1973 began to practice as an attorney. While managing a household— she had two children—and running a successful law firm, the first Canadian firm administered by a black woman, she wrote poems and stories. In 1982, she gave up law to dedicate herself to writing.

Philip's first book of poetry was *Thorns*, published in 1980. This was followed by *Salmon of Courage* in 1983. Finally, in 1988 she received critical attention with the collection of poems *She Tries Her Tongue, Her Silence Softly Breaks*, which was awarded the prestigious literary prize from the **Casa de las Américas**, in Cuba, the first time an Anglophone Caribbean woman received such an honor. That same year, Philip published the young-adult novel *Harriet's Daughter*, praised for the strong characterization of the heroine. In 1991, she combined prose and poetry to write *Looking for Livingstone: An Odyssey of Silence*, her examination of Dr. David Livingstone's exploration of Africa and the colonialist mentality that made white travelers "discoverers" of lands already inhabited by people. The book proved controversial in Canada, where some readers regarded Philip as a radical and ungrateful for the prosperity British colonialists had brought to Africa during the nineteenth century. In 1992, Philip wrote *Frontiers: Essays and Writings on Racism and Culture*. In 1993, she wrote *Showing Grit: Showboating North of the 44th Parallel*.

Philip has emerged as a literary activist, like Dominican scholar **Daisy Cocco de Filippis** and Cuban anthologist **Mirta Yañez**, who gives a voice to those who have been silenced by colonialism or repressive regimes. In doing so, she affirms the survival of Afro-Caribbean traditions. Observes Chancy that Philip's work "is part of a global, collective effort to struggle . . . against man-made destruction from one generation to the next" (101).

Further Reading

Chancy, Myriam J. *Searching for Safe Spaces: Afro-Caribbean Women Writers in Exile*. Philadelphia: Temple University Press, 1997.

—*D. H. Figueredo*

Philippe, Jean Baptiste (1796-7?–1829)

The author of a text known as *Free Mulatto* (1824), one of the earliest proclamations on racial equality in the Caribbean, Jean Baptiste Philippe was a physician, intellectual, and pioneer activist.

Philippe was born in Trinidad, the son of a free black family who were sugar planters and who had received free land, called a "cedula," from the Spanish crown upon swearing allegiance to Spain during the eighteenth century. When England took over Trinidad in 1783, the colonial power honored the cedulas, the land grants given by Spain to Trinidadians, and Philippe's family continued to prosper. Wishing for young Philippe to receive a proper education, they sent him to England in 1812 where he enrolled at the University of Edinburgh, earning a medical degree at the age of nineteen. After graduation, Philippe traveled throughout Europe, attending lectures at diverse universities, and reading the popular writers of the day such as Lord Byron (1788–1824), who became one of Philippe's favorite authors.

During the time Philippe was touring the continent, a new British governor, Sir Ralph James Woodford, (1784–1828) arrived in Trinidad. Racist and resentful of the wealthy black families, Woodford took a series of steps to undermine the freedom of the black community on the island. He taxed the land inherited by black children, demanded that residents declare their race when signing legal documents, and segregated theaters, ships, and even cemeteries. He demanded that blacks pay higher fees than whites for medical treatment and stated that no black man should be addressed as "Mister." When Philippe returned to Trinidad, he joined the militia, which was the common practice for a recently graduated physician. However, instead of signing on Philippe as an officer, as expected, the governor assigned him the rank of private and did not allow him to treat white soldiers.

In 1824, Philippe protested the abuses through a document title *An Address to the Right Hon. Earl Bathurst, His Majesty's Principal Secretary of State for the Colonists by a Free Mulatto of the Island*. Nearly three hundred pages long, the document, which became known as *Free Mulatto*, was a polemical exercise on the nature of equality, freedom, and civil law. It revealed an author who was well versed with British law, literature, and the use of logic, an author who was better educated than the general population in England and on the islands. Toward the end of the address, Philippe reminded the British Crown that the ongoing abuses and inequalities could provoke a rebellion similar to what had occurred in Haiti in 1791 and requested that the Crown "put a period to the suffering of the coloured population" (197).

Free Mulatto provoked discussions in England, and it prompted the authorities to review the governor's action. In 1829, civil liberties were reestablished in Trinidad, two weeks after Philippe had passed away.

Further Reading

Philippe, J. B. *Free Mulatto: An Address to the Right. Hon. Earl Bathurst by a Free Mulatto.* Trinidad and Tobago: Paria Publishing, 1987.

—*D. H. Figueredo*

Phillips, Caryl (1958–)

A novelist and playwright from St. Kitts, Caryl Phillips has experienced the displacement and in-betweenness of living in England while yearning for his homeland. The experience draws him to an artistic and intellectual exploration of immigration and exile.

Caryl Phillips was born in St. Kitts, West Indies, in 1958. Four years later, his parents emigrated to England, where Phillips grew up and received his education. He was the first student from his high school to attend Oxford University. Though internationally acclaimed as a novelist, Phillips's first love was theater. He had studied theater direction at Oxford, and his first work was a play entitled *Strange Fruit* (1981), which was purchased by the BBC. The characters in that play are members of a Caribbean family that has been living in England for twenty years.

Most of Phillips's work has dealt in one way or another with the historical legacy of the Atlantic slave trade and its consequences. Whether fiction or nonfiction, Phillips explores displacement, border crossing, ocean crossing, exile, return, alienation, and the conflicting versions of events, of history, that these movements engender. Many of his novels, from *The Final Passage* (1985), his first, onward, employ multiple narrators and multiple perspectives within which the reader must find him-or herself. Situated in a narrative of migration, his characters are often caught between the pull of home and the reality of existential homelessness, between the search for roots and the acknowledgement of rootlessness that characterizes the diaspora. Although his novel *A State of Independence* (1986) is contemporary, set on the eve of the independence of St. Kitts, Phillips has taken the long historical view on migration. His fourth novel, *Cambridge*, is set in the nineteenth century, on a plantation in St. Kitts with a gallery of border-crossing characters, from the absentee plantation owner and his daughter to the main character, Cambridge, a literate slave who, after his violent initial uprooting, crisscrosses the globe. It has been said of Phillips's oeuvre that, in it, he is concerned to investigate how **slave narratives**, like that of Cambridge, inform the contemporary migrant condition. His edited volume *Extravagant Strangers: A Literature of Belonging* (1987) argues by its very content that "others" have informed English literature for centuries. It includes writing by outsiders to England over a two-hundred year time frame. Phillips himself has said that he would like to be "buried" in the Atlantic Ocean, between Africa, the Caribbean and Britain.

Author of novels, the most recent being *A Distant Shore* (2003), plays, screenplays, radio plays and documentaries, Caryl Phillips has received prestigious awards for his work, among them the Guggenheim Fellowship in 1992 and the Lannan Literary Award in 1994. He has taught at universities in Africa, Asia, the Caribbean, Europe and the United States. *See also* Exile Literature; Immigrant Literature.

Further Reading

Ledent, Bénédicte. *Caryl Phillips*. Manchester, England: Manchester UniversityPress, 2002.

—Pamela María Smorkaloff

Philoctète, René (1932–95)

A cofounder, with **Franketienne** and **Jean-Claude Fignolé,** of the **Spiralist Movement,** a type of experimental writing that maintained the notion that artistic patterns occurred from random forms and that literature extended beyond social realism and nationalistic expressions, Philoctète was a politically committed author who promoted social change through literature. A poet, novelist, and playwright, he wrote in French and **Kreyòl;** for the latter language, he used the name Rene Filoktèt.

René Philoctète was born on November 16, 1932, in Jérémie, Haiti. During the 1950s, he developed the concept of "Spiralisme," or Spiralist Movement, which he, Franketienne, and Fignolé interpreted as a dialectical process of the spirit that carries the thinker beyond rigid political, artistic, or social structures. During the late 1950s and early 1960s, Philoctète cultivated poetry, publishing several volumes, including *Saison des hommes* (1960), *Margha* (1961), *Les tambours du soleil* (1962), and *Et caetera* (1967). The poems in these collections were politically engaged and advocated solidarity with revolutionary groups. During this decade, he founded with **Anthony Phelps**, and **Roland Morisseau**, among others, the movement Haïti Littéraire, named after its journal, which emphasized a universal approach to Haitian literature rather than a nationalistic emphasis.

In 1966, Philoctète went to Quebec, where he remained for six months. He also began to write dramas, of which *Boukman, ou le rejeté des enfers* is one of the best known, which were staged in Haiti. Like his poetry, his drama presented a political agenda for social change. While still writing poetry, in the 1970s he was attracted to the format of the novel and wrote *Le huitième jour* (1973), *Le peuple des terres mêlées* (1989), and *Une saison de cigales* (1993). Concerned over political corruption in Haiti, he wrote satirical essays in the journal *Le Nouvelliste*.

In 1992, Philoctète traveled to Argentina to receive a medal from the Argentine Parliament in recognition for his writings and political stance. Three years later, on July 17, 1995, Philoctète passed away. The years following his demise, Philoctète was nearly forgotten in Haiti's literary circles. But in 2003, the writer **Lyonel Trouillot** published an anthology of Philoctète's works, *Anthologie poétique*, renewing interest in Philoctète. *See also* Haitian literature in Kreyòl (the Haitian Language); Literatura Comprometida/Socially Engaged Literature.

Further Reading

Saint-Éloi, Rodney. "René Philoctète." http://www.lehman.cuny.edu/ile.en.ile/paroles/philoctete.html (accessed 9/9/05).

—*D. H. Figueredo*

Pierre, Claude (1941–)

Pierre is a Haitian poet who after spending many years in Canada, returned to his country to teach. His poetry, written in French and Kreyòl, affirms his love for Haiti and his compatriots.

Claude C. Pierre was born on February 28, 1941, in Corail en Grande Anse, Haiti. After attending primary school at Frères de l'Instruction chrétienne, he studied at the Collège Saint Louis and the Lycée Alexandre Pétion, both secondary schools. In 1965, he graduated from l'Institut Français d'Haïti with a teaching certificate. Three years later, he received an MBA from Affaires Internationales de l'École Nationale des Hautes Études Internationales. He then taught high school before moving to Canada to study literature at the Laval University, in Quebec. In 1973, he published his first book of poetry, *Coucou rouge, suivi de Charlemagne Péralte*, his tribute to Charlemagne Péralte (1885–1919), the leader of a rebellion during the **American occupation of Haiti** in 1915–34.

In 1978, Pierre received a certificate in education from the University of Quebec. He taught literature at a regional school in Ottawa and at the University of Ottawa. During the 1980s he published several books of poetry, including *Huit poèmes infiniment* (1984), winner of the literary prize Prix littéraire de l'Outaouais, *Tourne ma toupee* (1985), *Le coup de l'étrier* (1986), and *À haute voix et à genoux*it (1988). As his reputation as a poet was growing, Pierre decided to return to Haiti and in 1986 was named literature professor at the l'Université d'État d'Haïti. In the 1990s, he participated in numerous cultural and educational activities throughout Haiti.

His poetry describes the natural beauty of his country, seeking through its flora and fauna a definition of a Haitian identity. While aware of the political tragedies that have befallen his nation, his tone remains optimistic, certain that Haitians will triumph. *See also* Haitian Literature in Kreyòl (the Haitian Language).

Further Reading

"Claude Pierre." http://www.lehman.cuny.edu/ile.en.ile/paroles/pierre.html (accessed 9/9/05).

Dumas, Pierre-Raymond. *Panorama de la literature haïtienne de la diaspora*. Tome II. Port-au-Prince, Haiti: Promobank 1996.

—*D. H. Figueredo*

Pietri, Pedro Juan (1943–2004)

A writer of plays, narratives, and poetry, Pietri is best known for his book of poetry *Puerto Rican Obituary* (1973). He is one of the founders, with **Miguel Algarín**, of the **Nuyorican** literary movement.

Pietri was born in Ponce, Puerto Rico, on March 21, 1943. When he was four years old, his family moved to New York City, where Pietri attended public schools. When he was eighteen years old, he joined the army and served in Vietnam. The discrimination he experienced in the armed forces served as the inspiration for his famous book of poetry. Pietri worked as a page in the Butler Library of Columbia University, using the opportunity to teach himself literature.

Puerto Rican Obituary was first published in the journal *Palante: Young Lords Party* in 1971. Two years later, Pietri revised some of the poems for the book edition, published by the Monthly Review Press in 1973. By the time the book had come out, *Puerto Rican Obituary* was well known within the Puerto Rican community in New York City and especially within the members of the Young Lords, since Pietri was a Young Lord himself. The volume addresses the same community that the Young Lords were helping and chronicles the lives of Puerto Ricans living in Manhattan and working hard to obtain the American Dream. Pietri incorporates elements of the Caribbean traditions Puerto Rican immigrants brought to the mainland, thus alluding to the presence of Latino culture in the United States. Pietri also ridicules those who had lost their sense of Puerto Rican cultural values and who placed Anglo-American society, namely money, above everything else. The poems mix Spanish and English and are meant to be performed or read out loud.

In 1974, Pietri worked as a consultant for the El Museo del Barrio, in New York City, and worked for the Puerto Rican Association for Community Affairs. In 1979, he published *Invisible Poetry*, followed by *Out of Order* in 1980, and *Lost in the Museum of Natural History* in 1981. He also wrote numerous dramas that were staged in New York. Often anthologized, in works such as *Nuyorican Poetry: An Anthology of Puerto Rican Words and Feelings* (1975), Pietri has influenced the works of such younger poets as Jesús Abraham "Tato" Laviera. His other works include *Invisible Poetry* (1979), *Out of Order* (1980), *Traffic Violations* (1983), and *The Masses Are Asses* (1984). *See also* Code Switching.

Further Reading

Luis, William. *Dance Between Two Cultures: Latino Caribbean Literature Written in the United States*. Nashville: Vanderbilt University Press, 1997.

—*William Luis*

Pineau, Gisèle (1956–)

This contemporary novelist, essayist, and short-story writer, who first started writing at the age of seven, has become one of the most celebrated and prolific authors of the francophone Caribbean. One of the few female proponents of the *Créolité* movement, Pineau is known for the **magical realism** of her style and for her success at speaking for Caribbean women of the present and past.

Born in Paris of Guadeloupean parents, Pineau spent the first fourteen years of her life living in France. When her military father was transferred to Martinique in 1970, she began discovering the Caribbean region of her origins. Pineau would later return to France to enter the university at Nanterre, but she would have to abandon her studies because of financial difficulties. She eventually received a diploma in psychiatric nursing, a profession that she continues to practice at the Centre hospitalier Saint-Claude in Guadeloupe.

The engaging autobiographical novel *Exile selon Julia* (1996) illustrates what life was like for Pineau growing up in the Paris of the sixties. The author begins by having the nameless, bright young protagonist list a series of harmful ethnic slurs which have wounded her and have led her to believe that she is "the invisible black girl" at school. Her Creole-speaking illiterate grandmother Man Ya, the Julia of the book's title, feels even more confused and alienated in this strange land of exile. At times the older woman goes wandering like a zombie, lost in the seemingly hostile streets of Paris. Even Man Ya's own grandchildren, who have not learned Creole or any appreciation of back home, have trouble understanding their grandmother and feel the need to teach her to read and write in French. Yet, because of Man Ya's character and colorful stories about the devil and *diablesses*—she-devils—slaves and maroons, the girl finally comes to have a sense of "pride, a history, an existence, a country to love."

Pineau's writings often focus on uneducated women like Man Ya who are unable to record their own stories. The author reiterates her feelings of being marginalized as a youth in Paris in her essay "Writing as a Black Woman" in "Écrire en tant que Noire" (1995). Once more she refers to her beloved storytelling grandmother, who preferred returning to a miserable existence with her physically abusive husband in Guadeloupe rather than remaining exiled in metropolitan France. In *Femmes des Antilles* (1998), Pineau and journalist Marie Abraham offer a revised historical work, written to commemorate the 150th anniversary of the abolition of slavery. This hybrid text, which mixes historical fact and contemporary essays with fiction, seeks to give voice to female slaves as well as to modern Caribbean women.

Violence inflicted upon women in the Caribbean is a recurrent theme in Pineau's fiction. *L'Espérance-macadam* (1995), centers on Éliette Florentine, a twice-widowed, childless woman living in the small town of Savane Mulet. As Hurricane Hugo approaches the island in 1989, the sixty-eight-year-old recalls repressed memories, including the cyclone of 1928 and instances of fighting, killing, infanticide, and incest in her community. Like most the others around her, Éliette reacts with fear, silence, and cowardice when confronted with evil. The torment of her sixteen-year-old neighbor, Angela, however, provokes the older woman's maternal instincts and drives her to act. Recurring bestial imagery, referring to the savagery of people as well as nature, is especially artistic and effective. The author's first novel, *La Grande drive des esprits* (1993), is a beautifully written tragic and at times humorous story about the fluctuations of destiny. Winner of two literary prizes, the story focuses on the suffering endured by one rural family. The first-person narrator, a photographer, relates the life story of her friend Célestina, going back four generations in the woman's family tree.

Other titles by Gisèle Pineau include her most recent novel, the critically acclaimed *L'ame prêtée aux oiseaux* (1998), and the short stories of *Paroles de terre en larmes* (1987).

Further Reading

Condé, Maryse. "Femme, terre natale." In *Parallèles: Anthologie de la nouvelle féminine de langue française*, edited by M. Cottenet-Hage and J.-P. Imbert, 253–60. Quebec: L'Instant Même, 1996.

Gyssels, Kathleen. "L'Exil selon Pineau, récit de vie et autobiographie." In *Récits de vie de l'Afrique et des Antilles: Enracinement, Errance, Exil*, edited by Suzanne Crosta, 169–213. Sainte-Foy, Québec: GRELCA, 1998.

Haigh, Sam, ed. *Introduction to Caribbean Francophone Writing: Guadeloupe and Martinique*. New York: Berg, 1999.

Spear, Thomas C. "L'Enfance créole: la nouvelle autobiographie antillaise." In *Récits de vie de l'Afrique et des Antilles: Enracinement, Errance, Exil*, edited by Suzanne Crosta, 143–67. Sainte-Foy, Québec: GRELCA, 1998.

Suarez, Lucia-M. "Gisèle Pineau: Writing the Dimensions of Migration." *World Literature Today* 75, no. 3–4 (Summer/Autumn 2001): 9–21.

—Jayne R. Boisvert

Piñera, Virgilio (1912–79)

Cuba's foremost dramatist, Virgilio Piñera was marginalized by the Cuban government because he was gay. An innovator who revitalized and modernized Cuban theater in the 1940s, his plays were an expression of Cubans' sense of humor and irreverence toward political power. He helped to shape and influence the writing of numerous authors, the most famous of them being novelist **Reinaldo Arenas**.

Piñera was born in Matanzas, Cuba, on August 4, 1912. Due to economic constrains, his parents moved around the island. A sickly child, Piñera entertained himself by creating imaginary characters with whom he spoke. When he was twenty-eight years old, he relocated to Havana, where he matriculated at the university. But his relentless spirit and creative energy did not permit him to conform to a studious discipline. Though he finished his doctoral dissertation—on the nineteenth Century Cuban writer and pioneer feminist **Gertrude Gómez de Avellaneda**—he refused to submit it to his adviser and the dissertation committee. He did submit his poetry, though, to such journals as *Grafos* and *Espuela de Plata*, and by 1936 writers such as the Spanish poet Juan Ramon Jiménez (1881–1958) were reading his poetry: Jiménez included Piñera in his anthology *La poesía cubana en 1936*.

In 1941, Piñera published the poem "Las furias," which was widely welcomed by the major Cuban writers of the time and allowed him entry into Havana's literary circles. By the mid-1940s, Piñera became associated with the influential group of writers connected with the journal **Orígenes**, edited and directed by **José Lezama Lima**. It was in this journal that one of Piñera's most famous plays, *Electra Garrigó* (1943), appeared for the first time. When the play, an adaptation of the ancient Greek classic *Electra*, was staged in Havana, it drew an audience of over twenty thousand spectators.

In 1946, Piñera left Cuba for Argentina, where he stayed until 1958, working as a functionary of the Cuban consulate. In Argentina, he wrote the novel *La carne de Rene* (1952) and a collection of short stories, *Cuentos fríos* (1956). He also wrote the autobiographical drama *Aire frío* (1959), in which he told of his decision to leave Cuba and of his frustrations with Cuba's society.

When **Fidel Castro** came to power, Piñera—who had returned to Cuba a few months before the triumph of the Revolution—embraced the revolutionary regime, directing and writing for the publication *Revolución*. A collection of short stories, *Cuentos completos*, were published in 1964, and four years later, his drama *Dos viejos pánicos* received the **Casa de las Américas** literary prize for drama. It was during this period that he befriended and mentored one of Cuba's best writers, Reinaldo Arenas.

In 1971, the revolutionary regime grew intolerant of lifestyles that were divergent of the new society Castro was trying to create. Openly gay, Piñera was arrested, harassed, isolated, and never again allowed to publish on the island. When he passed away on October 18, 1979, the journal *Casa de las Américas* published a brief obituary, and Cuba's intellectuals stopped discussing Piñera's work. It would take two decades before his works were to be reissued and before it would be acceptable to study his oeuvre.

Comments scholar Tomás López Ramírez in *Spanish-American Authors: The Twentieth Century* (1992): Piñera "had a profoundly pessimistic view of the human condition. His protagonists were abandoned beings, condemned to the most absolute despair. His dark vision . . . constitutes a description of a world without alternatives . . . an unacceptable society in the face of an unacceptable human condition" (677). *See also* Cuban Literature, History of; Gay and Lesbian Literature. Hispanic Caribbean Literature, History of.

Further Reading

Abreu Arcia, Alberto. *Virgilio Piñera: un hombre, una isla*. Habana: Ediciones Unión, 2002.

Flores, Ángel. *Spanish American Authors: The Twentieth Century*. New York: Wilson, 1992.

—*D. H. Figueredo*

Piñero, Miguel (1946–88)

Piñero was one of the most troubled and talented writers to come out of the New York City ghetto environment. He emerged at a time when many Puerto Ricans were caught in a cycle of poverty. As a result, they romanticized a return to their parents' paradisiacal island. However, Puerto Ricans living in New York, also known as Nuyoricans, who did return were considered foreigners in their own land. Piñero embraced his New York City experience, with all the evils that it entailed, which he would later incorporate into his writings. Though he lived a life of crime, with his drama and poetry he made many positive contributions to an emerging form of literature that embodied both Latino and American cultures and experiences. With **Miguel Algarín**, Piñero edited *Nuyorican Poets: An Anthology of Puerto Rican Words and Feelings* (1975) and helped create the Nuyorican Poets' Café. In the final analysis, the same environment that gave Piñero a voice also consumed his life. In 1988, Piñero died of cirrhosis of the liver.

Piñero was born in Puerto Rico on December 19, 1946. Like many other families uprooted by the failure of Operation Bootstrap, the United State's attempt to industrialize the island, Piñero's family moved to the mainland to seek a better life. However, the dream turned into a nightmare when Piñero's father abandoned the family, plunging them into a life of poverty. Piñero had problems in school, fell into a life of crime, and looked for salvation in the streets. Piñero had been in and out of reform schools, and by the age of twenty-five, he was imprisoned at Sing Sing for armed robbery. In prison, he began to write poetry and later joined Marvin Felix Camillo's drama workshop, The Family. There he completed *Short Eyes*, a play about the interaction of African American, Puerto Rican, and some white inmates, one of whom was a child molester—in prison known as "short eyes." Though incarcerated, prisoners have their own code of justice, and prison represents a microcosm of society. The play was an instant success. It was performed at the Riverside Church theater, and later Joseph Papp introduced it to Broadway. *Short Eyes* won the New York Drama Critics Circle Award and an Obie in 1974. It was published by Hill and Wang in 1975 and made into a full feature film by Robert M. Young, starring Bruce Davison, in 1977.

As a playwright, Piñero also wrote other successful plays, including *The Guntower*, about two prison guards in a tower, one of whom experiences flashbacks to Vietnam; and *The Sun Always Shines for the Cool* (1984), about hustlers, street life, and warped values from which there is no escape. He also wrote one-act plays like *Paper Toilet*, describing a man asking for toilet paper in a New York subway restroom that is used for unlawful activities.

Piñero was also an accomplished poet and wrote what is known as a Nuyorican style of poetry. Written in spoken language and influenced by the Beat Generation, the Last Poets, and also by soapbox preachers, he published *La Bodega Sold Dreams* (1980), about the life and conditions in his immediate environment. Piñero's rejection of Puerto Rico in "This Is Not the Place Where I Was Born," highlights the poet's return to the island, his place of birth. Forgetting the reasons for leaving Puerto Rico, Piñero was raised with his mother's dream of an idealized Puerto Rico. However, upon his return to the island, he realized that Nuyoricans were not welcomed, nor did island Puerto Ricans share their ideas of an independent Puerto Rico. On the island, Commonwealth and Statehood parties receive more votes than do Independent and Socialist organizations. Puerto Ricans who live in New York fight for the rights of their countrymen on the island, but when returning home their efforts go unnoticed or are unappreciated. According to Piñero, Puerto Ricans in New York are more Puerto Rican than those who reside on the island. In fact, he sees more similarities among wealthy North Americans, Cubans, and Puerto Ricans. Piñero's poem is significant insofar as he comes to understand that a return to Puerto Rico, whether physical or spiritual, is no longer an option. For him, the beginning and the end are found on the Lower East Side.

Piñero was aware of the evils of the city, with its hustlers, freaks, and perverts. But he also recognized that he was a part of the environment he described. The New York experience had marked him and, in turn, he accepted and even welcomed his destiny. Unlike many of his cohorts, Piñero's compositions have a notable absence of Spanish. Puerto Rico, island culture, and its language are no longer a distant memory. Instead, they have been replaced by a speech more readily associated with those educated in the streets of New York City.

Perhaps sensing his mortality, Piñero wrote "A Lower East Side Poem" (1988), a confessional and autobiographical composition that also became his living will. In this poem, Piñero comes to term with his environment, accepts its shortcomings, and requests that when he dies his ashes be scattered throughout the Lower East Side:

> A thief, a junkie I've been
> committed every known sin
> Jews and Gentiles . . . Bums and Men
> of style . . . run away child
> police shooting wild . . .
> mother's futile wails . . . pushers
> making sales . . . dope wheelers
> & cocaine dealers . . . smoking pot
> streets are hot & feed off those who bleed to death . . .

all that's true
all that's true
all that's true
but this ain't no lie
when I ask that my ashes be scattered thru
the Lower East Side.

Piñero was proud of his environment and way of life and wanted to live and die in New York City. When that day arrived, his friends honored his wishes and scattered his ashes throughout the Lower East Side. After his death, Piñero received the unusual honor of having his life made into a film. Leon Ichaso produced *Piñero*, starring Benjamin Bratt, in 2001. The film captures with precision Piñero's troubled and self-destructive life in black and white and digital color: from the abuses he suffered as a child to those he imposed upon others as an adult, from his inability to fit into the island environment to his embrace of the Lower East Side. Indeed, Piñero was a self-destructive and unusually gifted writer. *See also* Code Switching; Kanellos, Nicolás; Marqués, René; Nuyorican Literature.

Further Reading

Kanellos, Nicolás, and Jorge Huerta, eds. "Nuevos Pasos: Chicano and Puerto Rican Drama." *Revista Chicano-Riqueña* 7, no. 1 (1979): 173–74.

Luis, William. *Dance Between Two Cultures: Latino Caribbean Literature Written in the United States*. Nashville: Vanderbilt University Press, 1997.

Piñero, Miguel, and Miguel Algarín. *Nuyorican Poetry: An Anthology of Puerto Rican Words and Feelings*. New York: Morrow, 1975.

Rossini, Jon D. "Miguel Piñero." In *Twentieth-century American Dramatists, Fourth Series*, edited by Christopher J. Wheatley, 238–44. *Dictionary of Literary Biography*, vol. 266. Detroit: The Gale Group, 2002.

—*William Luis*

Piñeyro, Enrique (1839–1911)

The author of a classic text on **romanticismo**, entitled *El romanticismo en España*, Piñeyro was an essayist, journalist, scholar, patriot, and one of Cuba's foremost literary critics of the nineteenth and early twentieth centuries. He was also an academic administrator and a judge.

Joining the movement for independence from Spain, Piñeyro left for the United States in 1868—at the beginning of the conflict known as The Ten Years' War—where he founded the periodicals *La Revolución* and *El Nuevo Mundo*; during the 1870s, he toured Latin America, seeking financial support for the Cuban cause. When The Ten Years' War ended in a truce in 1878, he returned to Cuba but left again in 1882 never to return. After Cuba became a republic in 1902, he switched from politics to the study of literature and the writing of literary criticism and biographies. He published scores of articles on such important figures as South American liberator Simón Bolívar (1783–1830), and poets **José María Herediay Heredia** and **Gabriel de la Concepción Valdés (Plácido)**. In the early 1900s, he researched the evolution of the romantic movement in Spain, penning in 1904 his famous book on the subject. The text was incorporated into the academic curriculum throughout Latin America. In 1934, it was translated into English, *The Romantics of Spain*, a text that is still being used. Some of his other books include *Vida y escritos de Juan Clemente Zenea* (1901), *Hombres y glorias de América* (1903), and *Biografías americanas* (1906). Enrique Piñeyro died in Paris in 1911.

Further Reading

Aguirre, Angela M. *Vida y crítica literaria de Enrique Piñeyro*. New York: Senda Nueva de Ediciones, 1981.

—D. H. Figueredo

Piquion, René (1906–2001)

Haitian author and promoter of black consciousness, Piquion was born in Saint Marc in 1906. While teaching at the École Normale Supérieure (ENS) in Port-au-Prince, Piquion was accused by the Vincent government of subversive activities and imprisoned for three months in late 1938. In 1941, Piquion was named "inspector-instructor" of primary schools in Port-au-Prince. He was named Haitian representative to UNESCO in 1962. He served first as director of the ENS (1963) and later as dean of the faculty of arts and sciences at the Université d'État (1968–69).

Piquion's literary studies of major black writers and artists were important in bringing African American artists and celebrities to the attention of Haitians. His *Langston Hughes: Un chant nouveau* (1935) underscored Hughes's genius and his triumph in making himself heard, first in the racist society of the United States and soon across the world. Marian Anderson's struggle for recognition furnished Piquion another occasion to celebrate African American artistic talent in opposition to prevailing racist prejudices (*Marian Anderson* [1950]). Following the publication of Léopold Senghor's (1906–2001) anthology, *La nouvelle poésie nègre et malgache* (1948), Piquion began to write about African writers who were becoming increasingly influential in European literary and political circles after World War II. He published *Négritude* (1961), *Léon Gontran Damas, un poète de la négritude* (1964), and *Les trois grands de la négritude: Césaire, Senghor, and Damas* (1964).

Although Piquion, along with the other writers associated with **Les Griots**, first underwent the influence of nationalist tendencies and ethnographic research by **Jean Price-Mars** and **J. C. Dorsainvil**, the Duvalier coterie began to diverge from those views toward a more exclusive "noiriste," or all-black, politics. Piquion expressed a desire to prostrate himself "before the shrines of the African gods." According to David Nicholls—in *From Dessalines to Duvalier: Race, Colour and National Independence in Haiti* (1996)—in texts published in *Les Griots* as the

Nazis were coming into power, Piquion favored the social order brought by a reasoned dictatorship, particularly that of Mussolini (170, 172). Piquion became the ideological spokesperson for the Duvalier regime, insisting on the evils of communism, the racism of whites and mulattoes, and the doctrine of black power. He entered into a heated exchange with Jean Price-Mars, criticizing the latter for not blaming mulatto holders of power for misery among Haitians (*Manuel de Négritude* [1966]). In "Lettre ouverte au Dr. René Piquion" (1967), Price-Mars replied that money and power, not color, were the decisive factors for keeping the masses in servitude.

Piquion was named Haitian ambassador, first to UNESCO in 1979, and then to Guinea in 1981, but was soon removed from that post. He was a founding member of the Parti National Progressiste—National Progressive Party—in 1986. He passed away in Port-au-Prince, Haiti, in 2001.

Further Reading

Berrou, F. Raphaël, and Pradel Pompilus. *Histoire de la littérature haïtienne illustrée par les textes*, vol. III. Port-au Prince: Éditions Caraïbes, 1977.

Nicholls, David. *From Dessalines to Duvalier. Race, Colour and National Independence in Haiti.* Rev. ed. New Brunswick, NJ: Rutgers University Press, 1996 [1979].

Supplice, Daniel. *Dictionnaire biographique des personnalités politiques de la République d'Haïti 1804–2001.* Tielt, Belgium: Lanoo Imprimerie, 2001.

—*Carrol F. Coates*

Plácido. See Valdés, Gabriel de la Concepción.

Placoly, Vincent (1946–92)

Placoly was a novelist and playwright from Martinique. His works promoted political and social change on the island. He criticized the establishment of the overseas department, which turned Martinique into something similar to a French province.

After primary studies at the Lycée de Fort-de-France, Martinique, Placoly went to Paris to finish his secondary education at the Lycée Louis-le-Grand. Earning a BA in French from the Sorbonne, in the late 1950s he returned to Martinique, where he taught French at his alma mater.

The plight of the poor of Martinique inspired his writing. In 1973, he published the novel *L'eau-de-mort-guildive*, a portrayal of life on the island that advocated the need for social change. The novel was well received in France but provoked little discussion in Martinique. The same year, he published *La fin douloureuse et tragique de André Aliker*, an experimental work that combined drama, press releases, and prose comments to criticize what he perceived as colonialism in Martinique. In 1983, he published a drama about Haitian liberator Jean-Jacques Dessalines

(1758–1806) *Dessalines, ou, La passion de l'indépendance*. The historic drama afforded Placoly an avenue to criticize francophone Caribbean politicians who traded ideology for political and social comfort.

Placoly's criticism of the departmentalization of Martinique, something akin to making the island a province of France, earned him respect and admiration from liberal thinkers but also distrust from supporters of **Aimée Césaire**, who promoted the creation of an overseas department.

Further Reading

"D'au-delà des mers: Placoly et le charme des Antilles." *Le Monde*, October 18, 1973.

Seguin-Cadiche, Daniel. *Vincent Placoly: une explosion dans la cathédrale, ou regards sur l'oeuvre de Vincent Placoly*. Paris: L'Harmattan, 2001.

—*D. H. Figueredo*

Plantation Society in Caribbean Literature, The

The plantation society is the subject of many literary works from the Caribbean. However, instead of offering the romanticized and glamorized vision of the plantation presented in such popular novels as *Gone with the Wind* (1936), by the American Margaret Mitchell (1900–1949), the portrayal of plantations in Caribbean literature reflect the horrors of slavery and the injustices of racism. In the plantation society, regardless of the historic period, the white owner is on top of the pyramid and the slaves or black workers are at the bottom; the lighter the skin, the higher the individual is placed on the pyramid.

Representative novels of the plantation society during slavery are *Francisco: el ingenio, o las delicias del campo*, written in Cuba by **Anselmo Suárez y Romero** in 1838–39 but published in 1880; *Cecilia Valdés o La Loma del Ángel*, written by the Cuban **Cirilo Villaverde** in the late 1830s and published in 1882; and *Die the Long Day* (1972) by **Orlando Patterson**, from Jamaica . The two works in Spanish, which are set in colonial Cuba, depict the inhumanity practiced in the sugar plantation, where the slaves are treated as beasts of burden, are tortured, and serve and live at the whims of the master, often with deadly results. In *Francisco*, for example, the hero is separated from the slave woman he loves and finds freedom and consolation only through suicide. *Die the Long Day* tells the story of a slave woman in eighteenth-century Jamaica and her efforts to stop her master from raping her daughter. It is an episodic narrative rich in details about the daily life of the slaves and in sociological insight about the relationship between master and slave. A dominant theme is the study of the process by which an individual dehumanizes another to convert that person into property.

Representative novels of the twentieth-century plantation are *La Rue Cases-Nègres*, (1950) by **Joseph Zobel** and *Demain Jab-Herma* (1967) by **Michèle Lacrosil**. Of these two, the first is probably the best known, especially since it was made into a successful film in 1983. Though *La Rue Cases-Nègres* is an autobiographical novel chronicling the author's growth and departure from Martinique, it depicts the dehumanization of the black laborers at the hands of the white or lighter-skinned bosses or owners: "a damnable place where executioners, whom you couldn't even see, condemned black people . . . to weed, to dig . . . to shrivel up . . . in the broiling sun that devoured them . . . to breathe their last breath on a dingy plank on the ground of an empty, grimy hut" (122), writes Zobel.

Other works about plantation life include *La zafra* (1926), by the Cuban **Agustín Acosta;** *La llamarada (1935),* by the Puerto Rican author **Enrique Laguerre;** Guyanese **Edgar Mittelhölzer's** *Kaywana trilogy—Children of Kaywana* (1952), *The Harrowing of Hubertus* (1954), *and Kaywana Blood* (1958); *Demain Jab-Herma* (1967), by Michèle Lacrosil, from Guadeloupe; and the collection of poems *Slave Song* (1984), by **David Dabydeen,** from Guyana.

Further Reading

Luis, William. *Literary Bondage: Slavery in Cuban Narrative.* Austin: University of Texas Press, 1990.

Ormerod, Beverley. "The Plantation as Hell: The Novels of Joseph Zobel and Michèle Lacrosil." In *An Introduction to the French Caribbean Novel,* edited by Beverley Ormerod, 56–86. London: Heinemann, 1985.

Patterson, Orlando. *Slavery and Social Death: A Comparative Study.* Cambridge, MA: Harvard University Press, 1982.

—*D. H. Figueredo*

Pluralismo, El

■

Literary movement created in 1974 in the Dominican Republic by author and musician **Manuel Rueda,** who wanted to introduce music and graphic arts into poetic works and who wanted poetry to extend beyond words into orthography. Pluralismo uses a diversity of space and medium to express an idea, combining elements of performance poetry with the plastic arts. Scholars Doris Sommer and Esteban Torres, writing in *The Handbook of Latin American Literature,* state that "Pluralism asks unanswerable questions about poetic image and suggests that the discourse writes the author, rather than the reverse" (281).

Rueda developed pluralism in the Dominican Republic to rescue poetry from the routine and the banal. An illustration of pluralism is his volume *Las metamorfosis de Makandal* (1998), in which the syntax is influenced by musical rhythm: "Macandal. Makandal. Mackandal / Proteico como tus sonidos. Secreto y rehecho. (Macandal. Makandal. Mackandal. / Protean like your sounds. Secret and remade.) Rueda acknowledged in an interview in the volume *Doce en la literature dominicana* that the precursor to pluralism was the movement known in the 1940s as the **Poesía Sorprendida.**

Further Reading

Piña Contreras, Guillermo. *Doce en la literatura dominicana*. Santiago de los Caballeros, República Dominicana: Universidad Católica Madre y Maestra, 1982.

Sommer, Doris, and Esteban Torres. "Dominican Republic." In *Handbook of Latin American Literature*, edited by David William Foster. London and New York: Garland Publishing, Inc. 1992.

—D. H. Figueredo

Poesía Negrista. See Negrista Literature.

Poesía Sorprendida, La

A literary movement created in the Dominican Republic in 1943, "the surprised poetry" challenged **costumbrismo**—regional writing or writing of local color—and traditional and realistic poetry while promoting a national poetry informed by international trends. The movement was founded by the writers Alberto Baeza Flores, Eugenio Fernández Granell, **Freddy Gatón Arce**, Mariano Lebrón Saviñón, and **Franklin Mieses Burgos**, with the latter being identified as its leader. Other writers who joined later on included **Aída Cartagena Portalatín**, **Antonio Fernández Spencer**, Rafael Américo Henríquez, and **Manuel Rueda**. The subtitle of La Poesía Sorprendida was "la poesía con el hombre universal," meaning poetry with and for the universal man, thus emphasizing its universal and global perspective. The movement used experimental devices, surrealism, and symbols. At a time when the Dominican Republic was ruled by a ruthless dictator, Rafael Leónidas Trujillo (1891–1961), and literature was censured, the symbolical and surrealist nature of the surprised poetry movement allowed, through oblique writing, criticism of social conditions of the day. The movement's organ was the journal of the same name; it was published from 1943 to 1947, publishing twenty-one issues. La Poesía Sorprendida influenced the development in the 1970s of a movement known as **pluralismo**. *See also* Dominican Republic Literature, History of; Trujillo Era.

Further Reading

Piña Contreras, Guillermo. *Doce en la literatura dominicana*. Santiago de los Caballeros, República Dominicana: Universidad Católica Madre y Maestra, 1982.

Publicaciones y opiniones de La Poesía Sorprendida. San Pedro de Macorís, Dominican Republic: Universidad Central del Este, 1988.

—D. H. Figueredo

Poetry League of Jamaica

Established in 1923, the Poetry League of Jamaica was a branch of the British-based Empire Poetry League. Its founder was the poet and critic **JEC McFarlane**, and its members included poets **Vivian Virtue** and **Una Marson** and novelist **Tom Redcam**. Considered politically conservative, and even colonialist, by such important writers as **Derek Walcott**, the league nevertheless attempted to raise literary awareness on the island and to seek a Jamaican voice. The philosophical views of the league, which emphasized patriotism and encouraged poets to write about the island's natural beauty, were published in a series of newspaper articles during the early 1930s and in book format under the title *A Literature in the Making* in 1956, all written by McFarlane. The League sponsored lectures and poetry readings, offering a generation of Jamaican writers and would-be poets a gathering place, and published a year book: the 1940 edition of the year book provided the emerging radio program *Caribbean Voices*, from London, a selection of poems to read. By the end of the 1940s, with the rise of a labor movement, social unrest, and interest in self-government and suffrage, the league ceased to be influential. *See also* Bennett, Louise; Jamaican Literature, History of.

Further Reading

Breiner, Laurence A. *An Introduction to West Indian Poetry*. Cambridge, New York, Melbourne: Cambridge University Press, 1998.

McFarlane, J. E. Clare. *A Literature in the Making*. Kingston, Jamaica: Pioneer Press, 1956.

—*D. H. Figueredo*

Pollard, Velma (1937–)

Velma Pollard is a former senior lecturer in language education in the Department of Educational Studies, Faculty of Arts and Education of the University of the West Indies at Mona, Jamaica. Her major research interests have been **Creole** languages of the anglophone Caribbean, the language of Caribbean literature and Caribbean women's writing. Articles in these areas appear in local and international journals. She has published a handbook, *From Jamaican Creole to Standard English— A Handbook for Teachers* (1994) and a monograph, *Dread Talk—The Language of Rastafari* (1994, 2000).

Pollard is also a creative writer who has published poems and stories in regional and international journals and anthologies. She has a novel, two collections of short fiction, and three books of poetry on the market. Her novella *Karl* (1992) won the **Casa de las Américas** prize in 1992. Her creative publications include *Crown Point and Other Poems* (1988), *Considering Woman* (1989), *Shame Trees Don't Grow Here* (1989), *Homestretch* (1994), *Karl and Other Stories* (1994) and *The Best Philosophers I Know Can't Read and Write* (n.d.).

Pollard's creative explorations bridge worlds, compassionately probing their strengths and their fissures. Her short story "Gran" is a lament on the ravages of aging, which transform an industrious, fiercely independent, morally upright, much-loved grandmother into a lonely, deserted woman who resorts to bothersome tricks to attract the attention of her now-distant offspring. Her highly productive homestead, which she maintained long after her husband's death, with its luxuriant garden, orchard, and home industry is reduced to a haunt of aging beggars, the most desperate of the rural poor. In this story, Pollard laments the passing of the rural extended family—its values, its hierarchies of lineage, its traditional skills, and its idyllic childhood wonderland.

Pollard's short stories have been published in such periodicals as *Jamaica Journal, Bim,* and *Focus* (1983) and in international anthologies such as *De moedervlek suite* (1987), *Her True-True Name* (1989), *Green Cane and Juicy Flotsam* (1991), *Daughters of Africa* (1992), and *The Oxford Book of Caribbean Short Stories* (1999).

Her poems have been published in *Bim, Caribbean Quarterly, Trinidad and Tobago Review*, and *Kyk-Over-Al*, and in the following anthologies: *Jamaica Woman* (1980), *Focus* (1983), *Black Women's Writing* (1989), *Women Poets of the Caribbean* (1990), *Crossing Water* (1992), *Daughters of Africa* (1992), and *The Whistling Bird* (1998). Pollard has received numerous other awards and fellowships, including a Jamaican Government Scholarship (1958), the Fulbright-Hays Senior Research Fellowship (1998), James Michener Creative Writing Fellowship, Summer Workshop Department of English, University of Miami (1991), Caribbean 2000 Rockefeller Fellowship Universidad de Puerto Rico (1998). *See also* Grandparents in Caribbean Literature.

Further Reading

Cooper, Carolyn. "Contemplating Subversion." *Third World Quarterly* 12, no. 3 (October 1990): 195–99.

—Paula Morgan

Pompilus, Pradel (1914–2000)

A Haitian literary critic and scholar, Pradel Pompilus was the author of several histories of Haitian literature. The first to write an empirical and academic study of the use of French in Haiti, Pompilus was a respected linguist and beloved college professor. He was also one of the pioneers in the promotion of the uses of **Kreyòl** as Haiti's true language.

Pompilus was born in Arcahaie, Haiti, on August 5, 1914. The son of a judge, he conducted his elementary education in his hometown and then went to Port-au-Prince to attend secondary school at the Petit Séminaire College Saint-Martial. In 1928, he matriculated at the Faculty of Law, earning a law a degree.

Pompilus taught elementary and secondary school while also active in cultural and political activities. In 1950, he was appointed undersecretary of the Ministry of National Education, a post he kept for two years. Through the 1940s and early 1950s, he pursued his passion: researching and studying Haitian literature. In 1951, he published his first major work, *Pages de literature haïtienne*. He also studied the uses of French in Haiti, publishing *Destin de la langue française en Haïti* (1952) and *Quelques particularités grammaticales du Français parlé en Haiti* (1958). He knew that French was not Haiti's mother tongue—assigning that role to Kreyòl—and therefore French needed to be taught as a foreign language, with the assumption that not all Haitians spoke French.

In 1957, Pompilus traveled to France, earning in PhD in language from the Sorbonne. In the 1960s, he wrote two studies of major Haitian writers: *Oswald Durand, études critiques et poèsies choisis* (1964) and *Etzer Vilaire, études critiques et texts choisis* (1968). In 1975, Pompilus published his masterpiece, the three-volume history of Haitian literature: *Histoire de la littérature haïtienne illustré par les texts*. This massive work, written in collaboration with Raphael Berrou, was the first attempt to document the rich literary history of the nation, from the colonial era to the twentieth century. The volumes were quickly incorporated into literature courses in Haiti and France.

During the 1970s, Pompilus taught high school and eventually founded and directed his own school, Cours Secondaires. His volume *Contribution a l'etude comparee du francais et du creole: Part I, phonologie et lexique; Part II, morphosyntaxe* (1973, 1976) was a major study of Kreyòl linguistics and advocated for the use of that language in schools in Haiti. Some of his suggestions formed the basis of educational reforms in Haiti during the late 1970s.

Scholar Albert Valdman, in "Focus on Creolists No. 13: Pradel Pompilus" (1985), described Pradel Pompilus "as the most versatile and productive of Haitian native linguists." He said: "Rather than theorize about the origin and genesis of [Kreyòl] . . . he . . . preferred to lead the bilingual minority of his country— including the educational establishment and classroom primary and secondary teachers—to understand the structure and social functions of the vernacular." Pompilus saw such an approach as crucial for the national development of Haiti. *See also* Haitian Literature, History of; Haitian Literature in Kreyòl (the Haitian Language).

Further Reading

Herdeck, Donald E. *Caribbean Writers. A Bio-Bibliographical-Critical Encyclopedia.* Washington, DC: Three Continents Press, 1979.

Valdman, Albert. "Focus on Creolists No. 13: Pradel Pompilus." www.webster.edu/~corbetre/ haiti-archive (accessed 9/26/05).

—*D. H. Figueredo*

Ponce de León y Troche, Juan (1525–90)

The author of the first crónica—chronicle—of Puerto Rico, Ponce de León was the grandson of the famous explorer and colonizer of Puerto Rico, Juan Ponce de León (1460–1521). His chronicle *Memoria y descripción de la isla de Puerto Rico*, and better known as *Memoria de Melgarejo*, was written in 1582 and described life on the island during and after colonization by the Spanish.

Juan Ponce de León II was born in San Germán and died in San Juan. When his father passed away, he inherited the posts of royal accountant and treasurer of the island. He married the governor's daughter in 1545 and in 1579 was interim governor of Puerto Rico.

In 1582, he was ordered by King Phillip II to write a chronicle of the island. Written exclusively for the monarch, the memoria was not made public until its publication in 1864. The document contained the typical elements of the genre of crónicas: salutations to the king, religious allusions, commentary on the Church, and descriptions of the island.

A few years before his death, Ponce de León, who was a deeply religious man, resigned from his posts and entered a monastery.

Further Reading

Ribes Tovar, Federico. *100 Outstanding Puerto Ricans*. New York: Plus Ultra Educational Publishers, 1976.

Rivera de Álvarez, Josefina. *Diccionario de literatura puertorriqueña*. Tomo I. San Juan: Instituto de Cultura Puertorriqueña, 1970.

—*D. H. Figueredo*

Portela, Ena Lucía (1972–)

The Cuban Ena Lucía Portela belongs to the group of writers known as members of the **posnovísimas**, an informal grouping of feminists who came of age in the late 1990s and who wrote about personal and intimate matters rather than historical themes, as practiced by most Cuban authors who grew up after the triumph of the Revolution. Her stories are populated by bizarre characters who choose to live on the margin of society.

Portela was born in Havana and attended the university there, studying classic literature. Writing at a young age, by the time she was in her mid-twenties she was awarded a grant to work on a novel. Finished in 1997, the novel, entitled *El pájaro: pincel y tinta china*, earned the **Cirilo Villaverde** prize from the **Unión de Escritores y Artistas de Cuba**. In 1999, the novel was published simultaneously in Cuba and in Spain. Two other works followed: La *sombra del caminante* (2001) and *Cien botellas en una pared* (2002).

Portela's setting is usually Havana, a decadent Havana of crumbling old houses and cemeteries frequented by drug and sex addicts, grave robbers, and practitioners of Satanic arts. Her protagonists are usually involved in abusive and destructive relationships and are often involved in tabooed affairs, such as incest, all described in a prose that is both elusive and illuminating, as evidenced in the short story "At the Back of the Cemetery," from the anthology *Open Your Eyes and Soar* (2003):

> During their siestas and even during their embrace of discovery, the cockroaches grew bold again, walking on them, contaminating and gnawing. Lavinia's hands would slide down her little brother's spine as he lay on top of her . . . a cockroach. (111)

In Portela's stories she often hints that the bizarre behavior is the result of an absence, usually that of a loved one, and while she doesn't clarify the reason for the absence the suggestion is that the missing individuals, often parents, have left Cuba for the United States, forsaking their children. The unique quality of the novels and the writing style has made Portela one of Cuba's most famous new writers. "Portela . . . is recognized for her major . . . innovations in her fiction, surely the most condensed, ambitious and impressive body of work of [the 1990s]" says Luisa Campuzano in *Open Your Eyes and Soar* (17). Portela's novels and short stories have been translated into Dutch, English, French, and Portuguese.

Further Reading

Berg, Mary G., ed. *Open Your Eyes and Soar: Cuban Women Writing Now.* Buffalo, NY: White Pine Press, 2003.

—*D. H. Figueredo*

Posnovísima

The term refers to a group of Cuban woman writers who were in their twenties and early thirties during the late 1990s and wrote narratives, specifically short stories, that veered away from social and political issues, a common practice on the island, to explore an individual's voice within a closed setting of people, either family or friends. These writers rejected the notion of literature as a political activity responding to historic circumstances or engaged in political change, as maintained by such influential Cuban critics as **Roberto Fernández Retamar**. Their themes were, according to Luisa Campuzano, writing in *Open Your Eyes and Soar* (2003), sexualities, eroticism, prostitution, domestic violence, pedophilia, and drug addiction (12). These stories were published in journals and anthologies and were meant for local consumption. Many of the stories, however, were included in international anthologies published outside of Cuba. The posnovísima writers include Nancy Alson, **Aida Bahr, Maryline Bobesleón**, Sonia Bravo Utera, **Adelaida Fernández de Juan**, Mylene Fernández Pintado, **Ena Lucía Pórtela**, Karla Suárez, and **Anna Lidia Vega Serova**.

Further Reading

Berg, Mary. G., ed. *Open Your Eyes and Soar: Cuban Women Writing Now*. Buffalo, NY: White Pine Press, 2003.

Mujeres como islas. Habana: Ediciones UNION; Santo Domingo: Ediciones FERILIBRO, 2002.

—*D. H. Figueredo*

Postcolonialism

The term *postcolonial*, although still current in literary and critical studies, presents a problem for those who wish to use it to categorize a written text or a theoretical concept: its meaning is ambiguous and controversial. Both the "post" and the "colonial" elements of the word bear scrutiny, and even assuming that the term itself is satisfactory, a debate would still exist concerning which texts should fall under the rubric of "postcolonial literature."

The problems attending the prefix "post" tend to center around understanding it as a temporal construct or an ideological construct. If temporal, "post" would seem literally to indicate a time period after the end of colonization. Even if the context for definition is clearly that, for example, of the British Empire, no single date exists to signal the beginning of this time period for all former British colonies. Furthermore, as an ideological construct, the use of "post" might suggest a clear endpoint of metropolitan political and cultural influence on the former colony, which is rarely the case. Although a country may no longer officially be under the colonial rule of another, its political, economic, and cultural relationships with many other countries may more accurately be categorized as *neocolonial*, rather than *postcolonial*.

The primary problem with the "colonial" element of the term focuses on the implication that understanding these countries (their history, literature, and people) is best achieved through the prism of colonialism. Considering that a significant portion of postcolonial writing stands in opposition to colonial oppression, using the word "colonial" as a part of the category defining this writing can seem at odds with the intents of the writing itself.

Finally, determining which texts qualify as postcolonial literature raises a number of problems as well. Using again the example of the British Empire, one might decide that all former British colonies are equally postcolonial, and, accordingly, all literature from these former colonies is also equally postcolonial. Thus, Indian, Jamaican, Irish, Australian, even American literature could be postcolonial literature. Although it may be helpful to recognize some of the commonalities between texts from former colonies, it is essential to recognize the differences inherent in the specific conditions of colonization for each individual region and people. Using the term "postcolonial literature" indiscriminately could have the effect of conflating colonial experiences, leading to an oversimplified understanding of the long-term effects of colonization.

Anthologies of postcolonial literature and theory frequently contain the work of many Caribbean writers. Seminal texts that address postcolonial issues include **Edward Kamau Brathwaite**'s *The Development of Creole Society in Jamaica*

1770–1820 (1971), **Aimé Cesairé**'s *Discours sur le colonialisme* (1950), **Frantz Fanon**'s *Les damnés de la terre* (1961), **CLR James**'s *Beyond a Boundary* (1963), **Jamaica Kincaid**'s *A Small Place* (1988), **George Lamming**'s *The Pleasures of Exile* (1960), and **Derek Walcott**'s "The Muse of History."

Further Reading

Ashcroft, Bill, Gareth Griffiths, and Helen Tiffin, eds. *The Post-colonial Studies Reader.* London: Routledge, 1995.

Durrant, Sam. *Postcolonial Narrative and the Work of Mourning: J. M. Coetzee, Wilson Harris, and Toni Morrison.* Albany: State University Press of New York, 2004.

Loomba, Ania. *Colonialsim/Postcolonialism.* London: Routledge, 1998.

Mishra, Vijay, and Bob Hodge. "What is Post(-)colonialism?" In *Colonial Discourse and Post-colonial Theory*, edited by Patrick Williams and Laura Chrisman, 276–90. New York: Columbia University Press, 1994.

—Paula Makris

Postumismo

A literary nationalist movement created in the Dominican Republic in 1921 by writers **Domingo Moreno Jimenes**, Rafael Augusto Zorrilla, and **Andrés Avelino**. These writers favored free verse and looked toward their country's history, geography, and traditions for inspiration, rejecting **Modernismo**, with its extravagant metaphors, European influences, and even claiming disdain for Greek classical literature and for such writers as William Shakespeare (1564–1616) and Johann Wolfgang von Goethe (1749–1832). Postumismo celebrated the language of the common person and saw beauty in routine events such as the act of brewing coffee.

In 1921, Avelino published the movement's manifesto as prologue to his book of poems *Fantaseos*. In the manifesto, Avelino claimed that every individual, regardless of academic preparation or economic condition, could be a poet; that the only aristocracy was that of the mind; that all words, no matter how simple or base, were beautiful and poetic. The postumistas poets believed that poetry belonged to the people, and as such, Domingo Moreno Jimenes set out to travel throughout the nation, reading his poems to anyone willing to listen. Postumista poetry was published in the journals *Cuna de America, Bahoruco*, and *El día estético*—the latter was managed by Moreno Jimenes. Today, Moreno Jimenes is considered the heart and soul of this movement. *See also* Dominican Republic Literature, History of; Poesía Sorprendida, La.

Further Reading

Piña Contrera, Guillermo. *Doce en la literatura dominicana.* Santiago de los Caballeros, República Dominicana: Universidad Católica Madre y Maestra, 1982.

—D. H. Figueredo

Poujol-Oriol, Paulette (1926–)

A novelist and short-story writer from Haiti, Poujol-Oriol is a teacher, a feminist, and a promoter of Haitian culture. She is recognized for capturing in her prose the richness and complexities of Kreyòl, the language spoke by most Haitians.

Poujol-Oriol was born on May 12, 1926, in Port-au-Prince, Haiti. She lived with her family in Paris until the age of six, when they returned to their native Haiti. She then studied at the École Normale in the Haitian capital. Her father was the founder of l'Institut Commercial Joseph Pujol, where she also studied. As a teenager, she lived first in Jamaica and then in Great Britain, where she matriculated at the London Institute of Commerce and Business Administration. Poujol-Oriol later taught at her father's school and was also an English and French professor for many years at the Collège Saint François d'Assisse. She befriended author **Marie-Thérèse Colimon-Hall**, teaching at a school owned by the writer. While dedicated to teaching, she had a passion for acting and founded the Piccolo, a school specializing in dramatic arts. From 1983 to 1991, she was an administrator of the Téâtree de l'École Nationale des Arts. Culturally and politically active, Poujol-Oriol was the president of the Ligue Féminine d'Action Sociale.

Besides her activism and teaching career, Poujol-Oriol found time to work as a creative writer. Her first novel, *La creuset* (1980), for which she received the Henri Deschamps Award, concerns the moral choices faced by a middle-class family and their struggles. The story centers on the character of Pierre Tervil, who, thanks to his family's sacrifices, grows up to be a famous doctor. *La fleur rouge* (1992), a short-story collection and its title piece, explores the dynamics of sexual relationships in Haiti and the oppression of women. *Le passage*, a second novel published in 1996, is a character study of Coralie Santeuil, a Haitian woman who reviews her life as she climbs from Port-au-Prince to the elite city of Pétion-Ville. In all her writings, Poujol-Oriol uses standard French with Kreyòl to capture the nuances of the Haitian vernacular. *See also* Haitian Literature in Kreyòl (the Haitian Language).

Further Reading

Esteves, Carmen C., and Lizabeth, Paravisini-Gebert, eds. *Green Cane and Juicy Flotsam: Short Stories by Caribbean Women*. New Brunswick, NJ: Rutgers University Press, 1991.

Hoffmann, Léon-François. *Le Roman haïtien: idéologie et structure*. Sherbrooke, Quebec: Éditions Naaman, 1982.

"Paulette Poujol-Oriol." http://www.lehman.cuny.edu.île/paroles/poujol-oriol.htm1. (accessed 4/2/05).

—*D. H. Figueredo*

Pradel, Seymour (1875–1943)

Pradel was a Haitian poet who dedicated his life to politics and public service.

Born in Jacmel, Haiti, on July 10, 1875, Pradel was sent to Jamaica for his primary education. He returned to Haiti for his high school studies, attending the Lycée Pétion in the late 1880s. He studied French literature and demonstrated an interest in teaching. He wrote poetry and essays that were published in local newspapers and such reviews as *La Ronde*. With **Justin Lhérisson**, he founded the review *La Jeune Haiti*. He also founded *L'Appel*. Involved in politics, in 1912 he was appointed Minister of the Interior, in 1915, he was elected senator, and in 1930, he was an unsuccessful presidential candidate.

While teaching at his alma mater and pursuing political activities, Pradel continued to write. His poetry was of a romantic nature and celebrated Haiti's beauty, which Pradel found mystical and sensuous. With the exception of the volume *Le docteur Destouches* (1912), Pradel passed away on April 25, 1943, without gathering many of his poems in book format.

Further Reading

Gouraige, Ghislain. *Histoire de la littérature de haïtienne, de l'indépendance à nos jours.* Port-au-Prince: Impr. N.A. Théodore, 1960, 1961.

Herdeck, Donald E. *Caribbean Writers: A Bio-Bibliographical-Critical Encyclopedia.* Washington, DC: Three Continents, 1979.

—*D. H. Figueredo*

Price, Hannibal (1841–93)

A public servant and theoretician, Price is the author of *De la réhabilitation de la race noire para la République d'Haïti* (1900), a critique of European bigotry and of the legacy of colonialism in the Caribbean. He glorified Haiti by calling the nation the Mecca and the Judea of the black race.

Price was born in Jacmel, Haiti, in 1841. He attended elementary school in his hometown and was then privately tutored. A brilliant intellectual and interested in politics, he served as an adviser in the Haitian government, was elected president of the Haitian Congress, and represented his government in Washington, D.C., from 1890 to 1893.

In 1893, he wrote *De la réhabilitation de la race noire para la République d'Haïti*. Published posthumously seven years later, the volume is a defense of Haiti and of blacks. It was the author's response to a bigoted study written by Spencer Saint-John, who in his book *Hayti or the black republic* (1884) called Haitians inferior. The work affirmed the African heritage of the Haitian people.

Price died in Baltimore in 1893.

Further Reading

Berrou, Raphaël, and Pradel Pompilus. *Histoire de la littérature haitienne.* Tome 1. Port-au-Prince: Editions Caraïbes, 1975.

—*D. H. Figueredo*

Price-Mars, Jean (1876–1969)

One of Haiti's most influential intellectuals and a pioneer in the promotion of black consciousness, Price-Mars was the author of a seminal text on Haitian culture and nationhood, *Ainsi parla l'oncle* (1928). Affectionately known as "the Uncle," Price-Mars was a physician, an orator, and an educator. He served Haiti as a minister and a diplomat. In 1966, Léopold Senghor (1906–2001), a cofounder of the **Négritude** movement and president of Senegal, called Price-Mars the "Father of Négritude."

Price-Mars was born on October 15, 1876, in Grande Rivière de Nord, Haiti. Orphaned at an early age, he was raised by his maternal grandmother and his father. Since the grandmother was a devout Catholic and the father was a Protestant, both agreed to teach tolerance to the child, an attitude that would allow him years later to respect the practice of vodouism and to promote acceptance of this religion at a time when most educated Haitians viewed vodouism as a primitive cult. His father introduced him as well to Haitian folklore and to the natural beauty of Haiti, fostering in Price-Mars an appreciation of geography that would lead him to found in 1922 the Society of Haitian History and Geography.

Around 1888, Price-Mars was sent to the northern city of Cap-Haitien to begin secondary school at Henri Grégoire Collège; three years later, he finished his secondary education at the prestigious Lycée Pétion in Port-au-Prince, Haiti's capital. Upon graduation, he enrolled at the medical school, and in 1898 the government awarded him a scholarship to study medicine in Paris. During his stay in France, he came across a book that changed his life. Titled *Psychological Laws of the Evolution of Peoples* (1894) and written by Gustave Le Bon (1841–1931), the volume presented racist views in an academic manner, claiming that people of color were by natural design inferior to whites; furthermore, the author described the people of Haiti as savages. An outraged Price-Mars promised himself to fight through scholarship and education such views as held by Le Bon.

In 1902, Price-Mars returned to Haiti and then undertook a tour of the United States, visiting the Tuskegee Institute and meeting Booker T. Washington (1856–1915). Back in Haiti, Price-Mars advocated for an educational program based on the Tuskegee's model. During the first decade of the twentieth century, he was appointed national inspector of Haiti's schools.

In 1915, the president of Haiti, General Vilbrun Guillaume Sam, was assassinated, and the nation stood on edge of civil war. Claiming the protection of American interests, the U.S. Marines landed in Haiti. This was the beginning of an occupation that would linger for three decades. To combat the humiliation experienced by

Haitians who felt their sovereignty had been violated but were not able to end the occupation, Price-Mars delivered a series of lectures on Haitian culture, folklore, and patriotism. These lectures made up two of his books, *La vocation de l'élite* (1919) and *Ainsi parla l'oncle* (1928). The latter became an overnight sensation: it affirmed and celebrated the African roots of the Haitian people, advocating for a cultural and spiritual return to Africa.

Ainsi parla l'oncle established Price-Mars as an international figure, leading to the development of Négritude in the Caribbean and influencing the writings of authors and activists for several decades, from **Aimé Césaire** in the 1930s to Stokely Carmichael (1941–98) in the 1960s, according to Jacques C. Antoine in *Jean Price-Mars and Haiti* (1981). Other works followed, including *Le sentiment de la valeur personnelle chez Henry Christophe* (1933), *Formation ethnique: folklore et culture du peuple haitien* (1939), *Jean-Pierre Boyer-Bazelais et le drame de Miragoâne* (1948), *De Saint Domingue á Haiti* (1959), and *Vilbrun Guillaume, se méconu* (1961).

Like most Caribbean writers, Price-Mars had to earn a living: he taught at different schools and institutions of higher education, worked as a country doctor, and held several government posts. But he was also active politically, running twice, unsuccessfully, for the presidency of Haiti. His patriotism and loyalty to his students and friends, including **François Duvalier**, helped him survive several revolutions and government changes. He received dozens of international honors, including La Medalla de Bronze de Cuba, Comandante de la Orden "El Sol de Peru," and the French's Academy Prize of the French Language for his books. In 1970, the Senegalese government printed a postage stamp in his honor. Price-Mars died in his sleep on March 1, 1969. *See also* American Occupation of Haiti, Literature of the; Bovaryism; Haitian Literature, History of; Roumain, Jacques.

Further Reading

Antoine, Jacques C. *Jean Price-Mars and Haiti*. Boulder, CO: A Three Continents Book; Lynne Rienner Publishers, Inc. 1981.

Shannon, Magdaline W. *Jean Price-Mars: the Haitian Elite and the American Occupation, 1915–1934*. New York: St. Martin's Press, 1996.

—*D. H. Figueredo*

Prida, Dolores (1943–)

Describing herself as "Cuba-rican," meaning Cuban and Puerto Rican, this playwright embraces the whole of the Latino immigrant experience rather than concentrating on a particular nationality. Her popular one-act comedy-drama *Botánica*, set in New York City, is a microcosm of the Caribbean universe in the United States.

Born in Caibairén, Cuba, on September 5, 1943, she and her parents left the island after the triumph of the Cuban Revolution. In New York City, Prida attended

Hunter College, studying literature and majoring in journalism. In 1969, she worked for several publishers, including Collier-Macmillan and Simon and Schuster, as well as such Spanish publications as *El Tiempo* and *Visión*. In 1977, her first play, *Beautiful Señoritas*, was staged in New York City. The play, a humorous and sarcastic exploration of Latina stereotypes—it takes place during a beauty pageant—was followed by several dramas, including *The Beggars Soap Opera* (1979), her adaptation of the *Three Penny Opera*, *Coser y Cantar* (1981), *Pantallas* (1986), *Botánica* (1991), and *Casa Propia* (1999). The plays have been performed throughout the New York area, in Florida, and in Latin America.

Prida's plays are written in English, in Spanish, and in both languages at the same time. She employs **code switching**, speaking in one language but using expressions and words from another language, as an affirmation of the bilingual and bicultural experience of Latinos. She also explores the concept of the bicultural existence, life-on-the-hyphen as critic **Gustavo Pérez Firmat** calls it. For instance, in the one-act play *Coser y Cantar*, the protagonist is represented by two actresses, one who speaks in English and likes everything American, and one who speaks in Spanish and longs for Cuba; both, however, are extension of the same person.

Prida has also written books of poetry, including *Treinta y un poemas* (1967), *Women of the Hour* (1971), and *The IRT Prayer Book*, coauthored with Roger Cabán. Critic Judith Weiss, in her introduction to *Beautiful Señoritas*, describes Prida as an author who wants to maintain her own cultural identity and heritage and that of the Latino community as well: "The author reaffirms the importance of individual consciousness in saving the group identity and the strength that the individual continues to derive from community" (15–16).

Further Reading

Kanellos, Nicolás. *Hispanic Literature of the United States.* Westport, CT: Greenwood Press, 2003.

Weiss, Judith. "The Theater Works of Dolores Prida." In *Beautiful Señoritas and Other Plays* by Dolores Prida. Houston, TX: Arte Público Press, 1991.

—*D. H. Figueredo*

Prince, Mary (1788–?)

Mary Prince was a pioneer in the writing of **slave narratives**. Her account of the horrors of slavery served as a powerful tool for the abolitionist movement in Great Britain.

Mary Prince was born in Bermuda in 1788. In Bermuda and Antigua, she worked in the salt mines, where chemicals damaged her feet. In 1826, she married a free black man but still served as a slave to her owner, John A. Wood, who abused her physically, often stripping her naked and beating her. In 1828, Wood and his wife traveled to England, taking Prince with her. Mary Prince seized the opportunity to escape, seeking shelter in a Moravian Church in London. She did not return to the West Indies, and it is believed she did not see her husband again.

Mary Prince narrated her story to Thomas Pringle, who edited the narrative into a book entitled *The History of Mary Prince, a West Indian Slave, Related by Herself*. The volume was published as an antislavery tract in 1833. It depicted the horrors of slavery from a very personal view while serving also as a document of resistance. According to scholar Sandra Pouchet Paquet, in *Caribbean Autobiography* (2002), the narrative presented "personal freedom . . . as the moral and legal right to determine one's identity as a birthright" (32).

In 1834, Prince achieved freedom when Great Britain abolished slavery. At about that time, according to Paquet, Prince disappeared from public records. Nothing else is known about her.

Further Reading

Paquet, Sandra Pouchet. *Caribbean Autobiography: Cultural Identity and Self Representation*. Madison: The University of Wisconsin Press, 2002.

—*D. H. Figueredo*

Prud'Homme, Emilio (1856–1932)

A patriotic poet, Prud'Homme was the author of the poem that became, by popular demand, the Dominican Republic's national anthem. He also wrote meditative and metaphysical poems.

A native of Puerto Plata, Dominican Republic, Prud'Homme was an attorney and teacher, preferring the second profession over the first. He was a friend of philosopher and educator **Eugenio María de Hostos**, from Puerto Rico. Together, they founded a school, Escuela Perseverancia, where Prud'Homme taught. He was also a teacher at the Liceo Dominicano and director of the Escuela Normal.

He was influenced by **romanticismo**, a literary movement that found inspiration in nature, and throughout his life he wrote numerous poems, many of which were published in local publications. A typical poem is "El sepultero," written sometime in the 1880s but published in 1946, in which he narrates the life of a grave digger from middle age to burial. Written in four-line stanzas, the clarity of language and sentiment is characteristic of Prud'Homme's style. What made him famous, though, was "Himno a la Patria." Written in 1883, the lyrical poem recounts the history of the Dominican Republic, claiming that his nation would never be enslaved again: "If she were enslaved a thousand times, as many she would break free." Prud'Homme corrected and revised the poem in 1897; with music by composer José Reyes in 1883 (1835–1905), the poem was adopted as the nation's anthem in 1934.

During the last years of his life, Prud'Homme served on the country's supreme court. His daughter collected his poems, publishing them in two volumes in 1946 under the title of *Mi libro azul*.

Further Reading

"Emilio Prud'Homme." http://www.Bnrd.gov.do/poesía/1856–1932.htm (accessed 9/9/05).

Incháustegui, Arístides. *Apuntes para la historia del Himno Nacional Dominicano.* Santo Domingo, Dominican Republic: Museo Nacional de Historia y Geografía: Asociación Jaycees Dominicana, 1982.

—D. H. Figueredo

Puerto Rican Literature, History of

Christopher Columbus sighted Puerto Rico during his second trip to the New World in 1493. During the conquest and colonization of the Americas, Puerto Rico served essentially as a garrison. Early chroniclers, however, reported on the activities of the Amerindians. One activity was the performance of **areytos**—areitos—which were musical and dramatic rituals staged to tell a story or celebrate an event. Though not necessarily a literary enterprise, the areyto was a theatrical production of sorts, serving as an early manifestation of a Puerto Rican cultural activity.

The first Puerto Rican historian was **Juan Ponce de León II**, grandson of the famous explorer Juan Ponce de León (1460–1521), who in 1508 explored Puerto Rico. In 1582, Ponce de León wrote the first full chronicle about the island, *Memoria de Melgarejo.* The first poet was **Francisco de Ayerra Santa María**, a priest who was born in San Juan but lived in Mexico. In 1691, he won a literary award for a sonnet describing a battle that took place in the Dominican Republic between French and Spanish forces when France was trying to take over the isle of Hispaniola. In 1683, his poetry was included in the anthology *Triunpho Parthénicoa: Palestra Literaria*, edited by the Mexican writer and humanist **Carlos de Sigüenza y Góngora**. In 1695, he wrote a sonnet to honor the memory of the Mexican poet and nun, Sor Juana Inés de la Cruz (1651–95). Sigüenza y Góngora himself wrote a true narrative about a Puerto Rican who had been kidnapped by pirates and led a life of adventures and misadventures. The work was entitled *Los infortunios de Alonso Ramírez* (1690), and it was the first appearance of a Puerto Rican picaresque character in literature.

During the 1600s and 1700s, numerous plays were staged in churches or outside churches. These dramas and comedies commemorated religious festivities, recalled historic events, or rendered tribute to the Spanish kings. Actual literary production, however, began in the nineteenth century with the introduction of the printing press in 1806–7. Points out Aníbal González, in the *Handbook of Latin American Literature* (1992): "The arrival of the printing press coincided with the first expressions of a national consciousness by the Creole elite that, in Puerto Rico as in most of Spanish America, had been slowly developing in the shadow of Spanish sovereignty . . . with the printing press came journalism, and the first . . . literary expressions of the Puerto Rican Creole."

The pioneer in the creation of a literary expression was a woman, **María Bibiana Benítez**, whose poem "La ninfa de Puerto Rico" (1832) celebrated, in a heroic and joyful mood, the natural beauty of the island. Published in the journal *La Gaceta de Puerto Rico*, the poem proved so popular that a copy was framed and hung at the entrance of the court Real Audiencia Territorial in San Juan. In 1843, she contributed poems to the anthology **Aguinaldo puertorriqueño**, the first book credited with inaugurating Puerto Rican literature. Beyond her writing, Benítez was also a development force: her niece **Alejandrina Benítez** was the second woman poet published in Puerto Rico, and her grandnephew **José Gautier Benítez**, Alejandrina Benítez's son, was of one the island's best romantic poets.

A poet familiar with the works of the Benítez family was **Manuel Alonso,** who in 1849 published *El gíbaro*, his attempt at creating a cultural identity. In this book, a good illustration of the genre of **costumbrismo**—literature of local color—the poems duplicated the lexicon and diction of Puerto Rican farmers and the stories depicted local events and scenery. A contemporary was **Alejandro Tapia y Rivera**, considered the great man of Puerto Rican literature. Tapia y Rivera wrote in all genres: essays, drama, fiction, and poetry. A self-taught renaissance man, he was also the father of Puerto Rican theater and the earliest to document, in *Biblioteca histórica de Puerto Rico* (1854), the island's culture before the arrivals of the conquistadores. The totality of his work explored a range of themes, from political oppression and racism to the celebration of civic duty and love of country. His play *La cuarterona* (1867) was an attack on slavery; the novel *Póstumo el transmigrado* (1879) studied Puerto Rican society; and the journal he founded, *La Azucena* (1870), was one of the first in the Caribbean published for women readers.

Though Tapia y Rivera and Alonso were abolitionists, they were not anticolonialist: They believed in autonomy within Spanish rule. Proindependence sentiments were expressed by another generation of writers of which the best known were **Salvador Brau, Eugenio María de Hostos, Manuel Zeno Gandía, Lola Rodríguez de Tió,** and **"Pachín" Marín.** Eugenio María de Hostos, a philosopher, wished not only independence for Puerto Rico but believed in the creation of a Hispanic Caribbean federation composed of Cuba, the Dominican Republic, and Puerto Rico. A selfless man of progressive ideas, he toured Latin America from 1870 to 1885, creating schools and promoting public education for all, including women— a novel idea at the time—in such countries as Chile and Peru. He served as a model of liberation that is still celebrated today, even in the United States, where several schools bear his name.

Equally selfless was the poet "Pachín" Marín, who fought for Cuba's and Puerto Rico's independence in the 1890s, dying in the Cuban jungles where he had gone to fight against the Spanish. A darker mood underlined the novels of Manuel Zeno Gandía, Puerto Rico's best naturalist writer. His internationally recognized novel *La charca* (1894) portrayed the pathetic lives of the poor of the countryside and the abuses they suffered at the hands of merchants and the elite. *La charca* is an outstanding example of **naturalismo** in Latin America.

In 1898, the Spanish-Cuban-American War broke out. The conflict lasted a few months, with Spain as the loser. Puerto Ricans saw Spanish authorities give up the island to the American forces. In the process, Puerto Ricans did not gain the independence they had pursued. To combat the growing American influence and the threat of losing Spanish heritage and language, Puerto Rican intellectuals embraced **Modernismo.** These writers did not respond to the aesthetic and artistic affectation of this literary movement but the modernist notion of culture as an artificial entity that could be shaped, that could be created. For writers like **José de Diego, Luis Llorens Torres,** and **Nemesio Canales,** Modernismo became a "conscious attempt to define the particularity of Puerto Rican culture and to find its adequate symbolic representation," according to González (565). For Llorens Torres, in *La canción de las Antillas y otros poemas* (1929), Puerto Ricanness was manifested in the figure of the Puerto Rican peasant and on the island's folklore.

Exactly what Puerto Ricanness meant became a dominant debate in the twentieth century, especially during the 1930s. The **Generación del 30** was inspired by the island's countryside, the agrarian worker or peasant, and local costumes and traditions, and opposed America's culture and political influence on the island. The members of this generation abolished the obligatory teaching of English in Puerto Rican schools, thus maintaining the Hispanic culture of the island.

The writers who composed this generation were **Emilio S. Belaval, Tomás Blanco, Enrique A. Laguerre, Concha Meléndez, Manuel Méndez Ballester,** and **Antonio S. Pedreira.** The latter, writing in the volume *Insularismo* (1934), defined Puerto Ricans as white and of Hispanic origins, denying the African presence on the island. A different view was maintained by the poet **Luis Palés Matos,** who saw Puerto Ricans as the offspring of the marriage of blacks and whites, Africa and Spain. Palés Matos was one of the creators of **Negrista literature,** which celebrated and acknowledged the African presence in the Hispanic Caribbean.

The 1930 generation was followed by **Generación del 45, or the Desperate Generation.** Consisting mainly of novelists and short-story writers, this generation broke away from **costumbrismo,** a literature of local color, and criollismo, a literature that emphasized the national and the native, to focus on urban issues, be it on the island or in the Puerto Rican communities living in the United States. Poet **Juan Antonio Corretjer,** dubbed this group the "generación desesperada" because its members expressed a sense of desperation at seeing the island plunge into economic chaos and realizing how the American influence was overwhelming Puerto Rican culture. Many of the writers who composed this generation would later form the canon of Puerto Rican and Latin American literature. In theater, **René Marqués** wrote the tragedy *La carreta* (1952), probably the best-known play outside Puerto Rico. **José Luis González** was one of the masters of the short story in Latin America. In novels like *Ardiente suelo, fría estación* (1961) **Pedro Juan Soto** studied the cultural duality and suffering experienced by Puerto Rican immigrants who found themselves rootless in the United States and Puerto Rico. These writings signaled an important shift: the emergence of New York City as a component of Puerto Rican literature and the presence of Manhattan in the lives of all Puerto Ricans, including those who did not leave the island.

Life in New York City was not a good experience. For example, for the legendary poet **Julia de Burgos,** the city translated into anonymity and death: in 1943, she was found unconscious in Harlem, and it took a few days for friends to find her body at the city's morgue. The harshness of New York City—the crime, the violence, and the discrimination—served as the subject of the writings of the activist **Jesús Colón,** who had left Puerto Rico in his youth. Highly identified with the Puerto Rican working class and staking out a piece of Manhattan as part of a Puerto Rican identity, Colón can be seen as an inaugurator of a New Yorker–Puerto Rican identity, a Nuyorican, as it were.

Nuyorican literature is the body of work produced by Puerto Rican authors born or raised in New York and/or the continental United States. This literature flourished in the 1960s and 1970s, and some of its best proponents were the poets **Miguel Algarín** and Jesús Abraham "Tato" Laviera, the novelist and memoirist **Piri Thomas**, short-story and young-adult writer **Nicholasa Mohr**, and the playwright **Miguel Piñero**. Their works captured the vitality of street life and the heroism of the average Puerto Rican surviving poverty and discrimination in the United States.

The excitement created in the literary world by Puerto Rican authors living in Manhattan paralleled the excitement in San Juan, where Puerto Rican authors who had come of age in the 1960s were writing works that matched the quality and innovations of the **Latin American Boom**. Two names shone brightly: the feminist **Rosario Ferré** and the innovator **Luis Rafael Sánchez**. In short stories like "La muñeca mejor"—translated into English as "The Youngest Doll" (1986)—and novels like *The House on the Lagoon* (1995), Rosario Ferré challenged the male dominance of Puerto Rico culture and society, criticizing the treatment of women on the island across socioeconomic levels. Sánchez, playwright, novelist, and short-story author, criticized Puerto Rico's semicolonial condition. His novel *La guaracha de Macho Camacho* (1976) placed Puerto Rican literature firmly within the universe of experimentation and innovation, redefining contemporary literature. Both Ferré and Sánchez achieved near literary stardom beyond Puerto Rico and Latin America.

Ferré's presence was indicative of the growing voices of women in the 1980s, both in the literature written on the island and in the United States. These brilliant women included **Olga Nolla**, the **López Baralt sisters**, **Magaly García Ramis**, **Esmeralda Santiago**, and **Luz María Umpierre**. The latter author, essayist, and poet expressed a perspective that prior to the 1980s had been denied or censored: homoerotic literature and accounts of the gay and lesbian experiences. Alongside Umpierre, authors such **Manuel Ramos Otero** and **Alfredo Villanueva Collado** emerged as major figures in gay writings.

Toward the end of the twentieth century, Puerto Rican authors revisited the Spanish-Cuban-American War and the end of Spanish rule on the island in 1898. The most controversial and famous reinterpretation of the event was the novel *Seva* (1983) by **Luis López Nieves**. Using ancillary documentation—maps, letters, affidavits, and photos—the author told the story of an American attack on the island before the beginning of the actual conflict in July 1898. The manipulation of information combined with fiction confused many readers, who thought the novel was an actual work of nonfiction.

Seva was an examination of Puerto Rico's participation in the historical process of the island. Another author pursuing such a course is **Edgardo Rodríguez Juliá**. One of the Caribbean's most important contemporary novelists, Rodríguez Juliá's fictional biography of **Luis Muñoz Marín**—*Las tribulaciones de Jones* (1981)—is an incisive study of the conflict between idealism and compromise.

The process of self examination continues in the twenty-first century, if not for a historical understanding of a Puerto Rican identity, at least for an awareness that Puerto Rican writers might be remaking themselves in the new century, might be taking new journeys of self-discovery. Observes Myrna Nieves in the anthology *Mujeres como islas*: "These writers . . . present Puerto Rican perspectives of that journey that is life . . . showing multiple prisms of . . . the possibilities of literature" (145–46).

Further Reading

Algarín, Miguel and Miguel Piñero. *Nuyorican Poetry.* New York: Morrow, 1975.

González, Aníbal. "Puerto Rico." In *Handbook of Latin American Literature*, edited by David William Foster, 555–81. New York and London: Garland Publishing, 1992.

López-Baralt, Mercedes, ed. *Literatura puertorriqueña del siglo XX: antología.* San Juan, Puerto rico: Editorial de la Universidad de Puerto Rico, 2004.

Mohr, Eugene V. *The Nuyorican Experience: Literature of the Puerto Rican Minority.* Westport, CT: Greenwood Press, 1982.

Nieves, Myrna. "Atisbando: Cinco Cuentos." In *Mujeres como islas.* Santo Domingo, República Dominicana: Ediciones Ferilibro; Habana: Ediciones Unión, 2002.

Rivera de Álvarez, Josefina. *Diccionario de literatura puertorriqueña.* Tomo I. San Juan: Instituto de Cultura Puertorriqueña, 1970.

Rodríguez-Seda de Laguna, Asela. *Notes on Puerto Rican Literature: Images and Identities, an Introduction.* Newark: Rutgers University Press, 1987.

—*D. H. Figueredo and Asela R. Laguna*

Q

Quiñones, Francisco Mariano (1830–1908)

Quiñones was a nineteenth-century novelist and political writer for Puerto Rico. He was an abolitionist and a political figure.

A native of San Germán, Puerto Rico, Quiñones descended from a well-known and respected family. As a young man, he traveled widely throughout Europe and the United States, where he learned English, French, and German. Upon his return to Puerto Rico, he wrote for numerous newspapers, including *El Liberal de Mayagüez* and *La Opinión*. His articles and essays advocated for the abolition of slavery and for autonomy for the island. In 1865, he was one of the founders of Liberal Party; his progressive ideals resulted twice in imprisonment, in 1868 and 1871.

In 1875, he published the novels *La magofonia* and *Nadir Shah*, narratives that took place in the Middle East, depicting exotic characters and background. In 1888, his *Apuntes para la historia de Puerto Rico*, a collection of political and historical essays was published. In 1889, he published a literary study of the Spanish author, *Emilia Pardo Bazán*. In 1892, he founded the newspaper *El Espejo*, a political publication that promoted liberal reforms for Puerto Rico.

Quiñones distinguished himself as a patriot. He was elected as Puerto Rico's representative to the Cortes, the Spanish Parliament, in 1871, and was one of the co-founders of the Puerto Rican Republican Party in 1898. He was also president of the Puerto Rican Congress and served as mayor of his hometown.

Further Reading

Enciclopedia puertorriqueña. Siglo XXI. Santurce, Puerto Rico: Caribe Grolier, 1998.

—*D. H. Figueredo*

Quiñones, Magaly (1945–)

Quinoñes is a Puerto Rican poet whose works explore colonialism and alienation. She is also a well-known artist.

Marta Magaly Quiñones was born in Ponce, Puerto Rico. While growing up, she was attracted both to literature and the graphic arts. Obtaining an MA in comparative literature from the University of Puerto Rico, she published her first book of poetry, *Entre mi voz y el tiempo* (1969), at the age of twenty-four. Though she had already published poems in journals, the publication of this book allowed Quiñones to view herself as a professional poet. In 1974, she published *Era que el mundo era*, followed by *Zumbayllu* two years later. The poems in these volumes explored a range of topics from a mythic interpretation of Puerto Rico to an understanding of the poet's voice; underlining these themes, though, is the poet's evaluation of the effects of colonization on the human condition.

In *En la pequeña antilla (1982)* she wrote about such personal issues as nostalgia, pain, and death, emphasizing the sense of isolation that can make individuals feel as if they were islands; the second part of the book concentrated on descriptions of actual islands, such as Puerto Rico. The emphasis is on the imposed loneliness of islands and those who live on them. *Razón de lucha, razón de amor* (1989) were political poems in which the author expressed solidarity for Latin America. In *Sueños de papel* (1996) she explored the craft of writing.

In 1985, Quiñones received PEN Club prize for the book of poetry *Nombrar*.

Further Reading

"Magaly Quinones." In *Jornal de poesía: banda hispánica.* www.secrel.com.br/jpoesia/bh5quinones.htm (accessed 9/12/05).

—*D. H. Figueredo*

Quiñones, Samuel R. (1904–76)

A poet and an essayist, Quiñones was a member of a Puerto Rican literary movement known as **noismo**. A major political figure, he was a tireless public servant and speaker who favored independence from the United States.

Born in San Juan on August 9, 1904, he went to elementary schools in San Juan and Mayagüez. While a student at the Universidad de Puerto Rico in 1925, he became one of the founders, with **Vicente Palés Matos**, among others, of the literary movement known as noismo, which rejected foolish and effeminate literature as well as utilitarianism and puritan values. In 1926, Quiñones received his law degree. Involved in political activities, he still found time to write poetry which he submitted to local newspapers.

During the 1930s, he was occupied with civic and political work: he was an active member of the Liberal Party; participated in a commission that studied the island's potential for independence; supported would-be governor **Luis Muñoz Marín**; directed the Democratic Popular Party; cofounded the Academia Puertorriqueña de la Historia; and was elected president of the **Ateneo Puertorriqueño**. He also directed the literary review *Índice* and the journal *La Democracia*.

In 1941, he published his first book, the collection of essays *Temas y letras*, in which he advocated the idea that only through cultural activity could a nation get to know itself. The volume received a literary prize from the Instituto de Literatura Puertorriqueña. The rest of the decade witnessed his involvement in public service, as he was elected to the Puerto Rican Congress, served as Senator on the island, was president of the Association of Puerto Rican Attorneys, and was a delegate to the Pro-Independence Congress. By the end of the 1940s, he had begun to favor complete autonomy for Puerto Rico.

A brilliant orator, in 1951, he collected his speeches in the monograph *Libertad de prensa, ética parlamentaria, ética periodista*. In 1954, he published *Puerto Rico y las Américas ante la Declaración de Independencia de Estados Unidos*. In 1956, he published *Las Naciones Unidas y el Estado Libre Asociado de Puerto Rico*. He also wrote two literary studies, *Manuel Zeno Gandía y la novela en Puerto Rico* (1955) and *Nemesio R. Canales, el humorista de Puerto Rico* (1961).

Quiñones passed away in San Juan on March 11, 1976.

Further Reading

Figueroa, Javier. "Diccionario Histórico-Biográfico." In *La gran enciclopedia de Puerto Rico*, vol. 14, edited by Vicente Báez, 281. San Juan: Puerto Rico en la Mano and La Gran Enciclopedia de Puerto Rico, 1981.

—*D. H. Figueredo*

R

Rahim, Jennifer (1963–)

Jennifer Rahim is a Trinidadian poet, short-fiction writer, essayist, and literary critic. Her poems and short stories have been widely published in journals and anthologies, including *The Caribbean Writer, Small Axe, MaComere, The Graham House Review, Mangrove, Anthurium, Crab Orchard Review, The Malahat Review, Crossing Water, Creation Fire*, and *Sisters of Caliban*. She has published three books of poems: *Mothers Are Not the Only Linguists* (1992), *Between the Fence and the Forest* (2002), and *You Are Morning in Me* (2005). She currently teaches in the Liberal Arts Department at the University of the West Indies, St. Augustine and Trinidad.

Rahim's poetry celebrates the mentors and guides who facilitate life's journeys. The poem "Song" uses the metaphor of ironing to explore the form, beauty, and artistic insight imparted by a mother's instructions on the simple daily task. "Seeds in Rich Soil" celebrates the green thumb of a father who coaxes the earth to yield its bounty and declare anew its capacity for nurturance and renewal. Rahim is interested also in searching out and declaring the lessons of in-betweeness. She claims, in an interview with scholar Paula Morgan: "Like the douen, the unbaptised child who calls us to invite us into its own darkness, perchance, to tell us its name, good writing has the power to lead people into the unknown, into pathways we would not normally traverse" (conversation with Paula Morgan, UWI, St. Augustine, May 26, 2004).

Rahim deploys grammar as a metaphor for resistance positions in her search for grammars of survival and revolt in poems such as "On Entering Airports" and "Some Uses of Punctuation." Her writing challenges readers to explore the realities on the edge. She focuses particularly on what it means to be a citizen of a small place and to claim one's right to exist and to understand the challenges and sacrifices that attend the drama of citizenship. "Revolt of the Yam," in *Between the Fence and the Forest*, addresses the potentiality of greatness in the midst of smallness. The poem invites us to marvel at the survival strategies of the disempowered who have nevertheless learned how to make their way in the world with dignity, all the while challenging narrow, prejudicial assumptions. Finally, Rahim's creative expression tugs the reader beyond pain as protest—which after all remains mere lament—by embracing a vision of pain as a gateway to transcendence, which calls us to be truly human.

Further Reading

Persaud, Sasenarine. "Review of *Mothers Are Not the Only Linguists and Other Poems.*" *Caribbean Writer* 8. http://rps.uvi.edu/CaribbeanWriter/volume8/v8p155.html (accessed 9/12/05).

Rahim, Jennifer. 2004. Interview by Paula Morgan, May 26. University of the West Indies–St. Augustine.

—*Paula Morgan*

Ramchand, Kenneth (1939–)

One of the most influential literary critics and promoters of anglophone Caribbean literature, Ramchand is a scholar and educator from Trinidad, whose texts have substantially shaped the West Indian literary canon.

In recognition of the pivotal role he has played in establishing West Indian literature as a recognized academic discipline, Kenneth Ramchand was appointed a personal professor in West Indian Literature at the University of the West Indies–St. Augustine in 1984. Ramchand acquired a PhD from Edinburgh University, Scotland, in 1968. In 1970, he published the seminal text *The West Indian Novel and Its Background*, which is seen until today as the groundbreaking text for West Indian literary study. Ramchand summarizes the impulse that has driven his lifelong literary pursuits as follows:

> My stance as a critic has always been to draw attention to the existence of books, to use my knowledge and scholarship to put books in their social and literary context, to help readers to appreciate the writer's form and style, and to do all I can to encourage people to experience the books for themselves and to learn to talk about the experience and the meaning of the experience. The main response I hope to evoke is 'I must read this book' or 'I must re-read this book.' (Correspondence with Paula Morgan, UWI–St. Augustine, March, 2005)

Ramchand's substantial body of research has spanned an extremely wide range of topics to make him a foremost postcolonial critic. He has produced some sixteen other texts, edited collections, and compilations. Since the 1990s, he has focused critical attention on the West Indian short story. In the keynote address to the International Short Story Conference, University of Northern Iowa in 1994, Ramchand theorized:

> Between 1950 and 1970, there are no West Indian novels, only clusters of West Indian short stories pretending to be novels (as required by the publishing industry). The fact that the early West Indian writers were practitioners in the shorter forms (poems and stories in ephemeral organs) has been responsible for the features of the West Indian novel that most distinguish it from novels from other countries.

As an educator, Kenneth Ramchand has been responsible for initiating Caribbean studies courses and programs at the undergraduate and graduate levels at the University of Kent; the University of the West Indies in Mona and St. Augustine; and Colgate University, in New York. Consistent with his goal of promoting study of the Caribbean and its culture, he has been a consultant to study-abroad programs at St. Lawrence University, Dartmouth College, Pacific Lutheran University, University of Miami, Florida and Colgate University. He has also delivered countless invitational lectures locally, regionally, and in the United Kingdom, North America, and Australia. Moreover, he served the University of the West Indies as its public orator for numerous years until his retirement from the institution.

Ramchand has also served as the people's educator through a *Trinidad Guardian* weekly column, which ran for extended periods in the 1980s and the 1990s. Through this medium, he interpreted the emerging corpus of West Indian literature for the Caribbean people, promoting literary sensitivity and appreciation within the common man. His efforts at preserving the literary heritage of the region are nowhere more evident than in his work with the Friends of Mr. Biswas society—named after the classic novel *A House for Mr. Biswas* (1961) by **V. S. Naipaul**—in which he played a pivotal role in persuading the government to purchase the former Naipaul residence in St. James and transform it into a museum.

As a Professor Emeritus of the University of the West Indies, he remains active in the public arena as an Independent Senator. He serves on numerous joint parliamentary committees, where he is especially vocal on issues of education, culture, and the promotion of the public well-being. He continues to advance literary development as a mentor to young writers and the director of the Ken Ramchand Literary Associates, the first literary agency to be established in Trinidad and Tobago. His other works include *West Indian Narrative: An Introductory Anthology* (1966), *An Introduction to the Study of West Indian Literature* (1976), and *The West Indies in India* (1948–49), *Jeffrey Stollmeyer's Diary* (2004), and a 2004 edition of his classic, *The West Indian Novel and Its Background*. His short-story compilations with introductions include *Best West Indian Stories* (1982), *Tales of the Wide Caribbean: The Caribbean Short Stories of Jean Rhys* (1985), *Listen, the Wind and Other Stories: The Short Stories of Roger Mais* (1986), *King of the Carnival and Other Stories: The Short Stories of Willi Chen* (1988), *Foreday Morning: Selected Prose of Samuel Selvon 1946–1986* (1989). Other edited collections include

A Return to the Middle Passage: The Clipper Ship Sheila by Capt. W. H. Angel (1995), Afterword in 'The Witness Who Would Not See' and *In Celebration of One Hundred and Fifty Years of the Indian Contribution to Trinidad and Tobago* (1995).

Further Reading

Correspondence with Paula Morgan UWI, St. Augustine. March, 2005.

Ramcharitar, Raymond. "Review of the 2004 issue of *The West Indian Novel and Its Background*." *The Trinidad and Tobago Review* (September 2004).

Williams, E. A. "The West Indian Novel and Its Background." *Choice* 42, no. 4 (December 2004): 662.

—Paula Morgan

Ramírez de Arellano, Rafael W. (1883–1974)

This historian and educator from Puerto Rico was a beloved cultural figure known as Don Rafa. He served as the historian of the city of San Juan and wrote articles and books that documented that city's and the island's history and traditions.

Rafael W. Ramírez de Arellano y Asenjo was born in San Juan on July 25, 1883. Graduating with a teaching degree from the Instituto Civil de Segunda Enseñanza in his late teens, he dedicated his life to education and the promotion of culture on the island. While teaching at the Universidad de Puerto Rico, as well as several institutions in the United States, including Glynn Institute and the University of Athens, both in Georgia, he collected Puerto Rican traditions and folklore. In 1926, he published the volume *Folklore puertorriqueño: Cuentos y adivinanzas recogidas de la tradición oral*.

Ramírez de Arellano was also interested in the preservation of San Juan and its colonial city as well as the promotion of the island's history. With that objective in mind, he founded the Museo de Historia de Puerto Rico and accepted the position of historian of the city of San Juan. In 1932, he published *Los huracanas de Puerto Rico*, a pioneer history of hurricane's trajectories in the Caribbean, and in 1935, *Cartas y relaciones históricas sobre Puerto Rico, 1493–1598*.

In 1965, the Instituto de Cultura Puertorriqueña awarded Don Rafa a medal, honoring his labor for the preservation and enrichment of Puerto Rican culture. His other works include *La procesión borincana* (1939), *La capital a través de los siglos* (1950), *Como vivían nuestros abuelos* (1957), and *La última tarde* (1964).

Further Reading

Figueroa, Javier. "Diccionario Histórico-Biográfico." In *La gran enciclopedia de Puerto Rico*, Tomo 14, edited by Vicente Báez, 286. San Juan: Puerto Rico en la Mano and La Gran Enciclopedia de Puerto Rico, 1981.

—*D. H. Figueredo*

Ramírez de Arellano, Olga. See Nolla Family.

Ramos, Juan Antonio (1948–)

A Puerto Rican novelist, short-story writer, and playwright, Ramos has written about the effects of urbanization and industrialization on the people who live on the fringes of society. He is also an educator.

Born in Bayamón, Puerto Rico, on January 4, 1948, Ramos spent his childhood in Río Piedras before he and his parents moved to New York City in 1954. Two years later, the family returned to Puerto Rico, where Ramos attended school. His mother, who was a teacher, introduced him to literature at an early age.

In 1964, he enrolled at the Universidad de Puerto Rico. At the age of twenty-two, he graduated with a BA in history and spent the next few years teaching at different public schools on the island. Returning to the university to pursue graduate studies in literature, he was tutored by two of the island's great writers: the novelist **Luis Rafael Sánchez** and the literary critic **Arcadio Díaz Quiñones**. In 1973, he traveled to the United States, enrolling at the University of Pennsylvania, where he obtained an MA in 1975 and a PhD in 1979, both in literature. During this period, he was also publishing short stories in such influential Puerto Rican journals as *Sin Nombre*, *Zona de Carga y Descarga*, and *Ventana*. In 1978, the journal *Sin Nombre* awarded him a literary prize.

Encouraged by the recognition, his creative activities proliferated, publishing several collection of short stories: *Démosle luz verde a la nostalgia* (1978), *Pactos de silencio y algunas erratas de fe* (1980), *Hilando mortajas* (1983), *Papo Impala está quitao* (1983); the last one being his best known for the introduction of the character Papo Impala, a drug addict who is representative of the social and economic ills plaguing the island. In 1986, Ramos's novel *Vive y vacila* was published in Argentina, bringing him a wider readership. A literature professor at the Universidad de Puerto Rico, his academic responsibilities prompted him to write a major analysis on Colombian novelist Gabriel García Márquez (1927–): *Hacia "El otoño del patriarca": la novela del dictador en Hispanoamérica* (1983), considered a seminal text.

Ramos was also interested in theater and in film. He wrote several one-act and full-length plays, including *Oraciones y novenas* (1987) and *Un beeper del cielo* (1996), and a film script entitled *The Disappearance of Lorca* (1997), which was a major Hollywood release about the death of Spanish poet Federico García Lorca (1898–1936). He also wrote a young-adult novel, *El príncipe de Blancanieves*. In the 1990s, many of his short stories were translated into English and German. In 1990, he received a Guggenheim Grant.

In 2003, he reintroduced, in the novel *El jockey*, the character of Papo Impala, using him as an avenue for commentary on contemporary Puerto Rico. Under the pen name of Moncho Loro, Ramos has also written sarcastic social commentaries that were published in the newspapers *Relevo* and *Claridad* during the 1970s and 1980s.

Further Reading

Minero, Alberto. "Un actor en busca de lo básico: Teofilo Torres: lo que nos trajo "La guagua aérea." *El Diario La Prensa*, November 12, 1993.

Torres, Víctor Federico. *Narradores puertorriqueños del 70: guía biobibliográfica*. San Juan, Puerto Rico: Editorial Plaza Mayor, 2001.

—*D. H. Figueredo*

Ramos Escobar, José Luis (1950–)

Ramos Escobar is an experimental playwright from Puerto Rico. A native of Guayanilla, he was raised in a family of thirteen by his widowed mother. He went to primary and secondary schools in Ponce and studied astronomy, changing later to theater and literature, at the Universidad de Puerto Rico. In 1963, he wrote his first drama, *Ya los perros no se amarran con longaniza*. He became involved with different theater groups and in 1971 finished his BA in literature. In 1977, he went to Brown University, earning an MA in theater; three years later, he received his PhD on the same discipline.

In the mid-1980s, he wrote several plays, one of them, *Mascarada* (1985), was chosen for the theater festival in San Juan. In 1989, he wrote about the plight of illegal immigrants, *Indocumentados*, an experimental drama that tells the story through dream sequences. In 1993, he received the Iberoamericana Drama-award, from the Universidad Santa Maria de la Rábida, for the play *Geni y el Zepelín*. Though many of his works are regularly performed, they have yet to be published in book format.

Ramos Escobar teaches drama at the Universidad de Puerto Rico. He is the author of the novel *Sintigo* (1985) and the collection of short stories *En la otra orilla* (1992). In 1998, the University of Wisconsin–Milwaukee staged his one-act drama *The Smell of Popcorn*, about a young actress and a burglar discussing each other's lives.

Further Reading

Quiles Ferrer, Edgar Heriberto. *Teatro puertorriqueño en acción*. San Juan: Ateneo Puertorriqueño, 1990.

—*D. H. Figueredo*

Ramos Otero, Manuel (1948–90)

Ramos Otero is representative of the gay Caribbean writer who must leave his country in order to fully express his gayness. He was a poet and a short-story writer.

Born in Manatí, Puerto Rico, on July 20, 1948, Jesús Manuel Ramos Otero was influenced by his father, who loved to recite and perform poetry, and his mother, who was a pianist; thus interest in the arts and literature came at an early age for the would-be writer. He attended private Catholic schools in his hometown until his family moved to San Juan in 1955. After graduation from high school in 1965, he matriculated at the Universidad de Puerto Rico. Despite the fact that he was already writing extensively, he chose to major in social sciences, earning his BA in 1968.

A gay man, he felt that Puerto Rican culture was homophobic and sought the freedom of New York City in 1968. In 1969, he enrolled at New York University, eventually earning an MA in Spanish and Latin American literature. In 1970, he studied drama at the Actors Studio in New York City. While teaching in different schools and colleges in the New York area, he also managed Aspaguanza, a theater company he founded.

In 1975, Ramos Otero founded a literary press, El Libro Viaje, where he published his experimental novel, *La novela bingo*. In 1979, he published the collection of short stories *El cuento de la mujer y el mar*. In 1985, he published the book of poems *El libro de la muerte*, a tour of a cemetery where many gay poets were buried. In 1990, Ramos Otero returned to Puerto Rico, renting an apartment in Old San Juan, where he wrote his meditation of AIDS and his own mortality. The volume *Invitación al polvo*, was published posthumously in 1991.

Since his death on October 7, 1990, Ramos Otero has been recognized as one of the central figures of contemporary Puerto Rican literature. *See also* Gay and Lesbian Literature.

Further Reading

Cañas, Dionisio. *El poeta y la ciudad: Nueva York y los escritores hispanos*. Madrid: Cátedra, 1994.

—D. H. Figueredo

Ramos Perea, Roberto (1956–)

Ramos Perea is a Puerto Rican dramatist who re-creates in his plays political events that occurred on the island during the 1930s and 1950s as nationalist activists attempted to earn independence from the United States. He is a drama critic and a theater producer as well.

Born in Mayagüez, Puerto Rico, on August 13, 1957, Ramos Perea studied theater and acting at the Instituto Nacional de Bellas Artes de México and at the Universidad de Puerto Rico. He worked as a journalist for several major newspapers, including *El Mundo* and *El Vocero*. In 1977, he published his first drama, *Cueva de ladrones*. This was the beginning of a literary production that would yield over twenty plays in two decades. His best-known work, however, is a trilogy examining the revolutionary process in Puerto Rico and the absence of political agreement within proindependence groups on the island. The plays in the trilogy are *Revolución en el Purgatorio o Módulo 104* (1982), *Revolución en el Infierno* (1983), and *Revolución en el Paraiso* (1983), a reworking of his first play. These dramas were staged in Puerto Rico, provoking much discussion within political and writers circles. *Revolución en el Infierno* received honorable mention from the **Casa de las Américas** literature contest in 1981.

In 1985, he wrote the treatise *Perspectivas de la nueva dramaturgia puertorriqueña*, a study on Puerto Rican modern theater. In 1987, he was awarded the journalism prize from the Instituto de Literatura Puertorriqueña. During this period, he also explored in his work the effects of AIDS on Puerto Rican society and the constant migration of Puerto Ricans to the United States.

Ramos Perea is the executive director of the **Ateneo Puertorriqueño** and an active member the National Society of Dramatic Authors. In 1992, his play *Mienteme más* received the Tirso de Molina Award from Instituto Cooperación Iberoamericana in Spain. His dramas have been translated into English and Japanese and staged in such international metropolises as Buenos Aires, London, New York, and Tokyo. His works include *Mala sangre-la nueva emigración* (1987), *A puro solero* (1989), *Las amantes pasan el año nuevos solas* (1990), *Callando amores* (1994), *Vida de un poeta romántico* (1996), *Más allá de ti* (1997), *and Miles: La otra historia del 98* (1998).

Further Reading

Betancourt, Tony. "Así es la Gente." *Impacto* 36, no. 1454 (July 1, 2003): 17.

Quiles Ferrer, Edgar Heriberto. *Teatro puertorriqueño en acción*. San Juan, Puerto Rico: Ateneo Puertorriqueño, 1990.

—D. H. Figueredo

Realismo/Realism

■

In Latin America, realism might be described as containing the following elements: minute but accurate descriptions, attention to types, customs, and language—but without accenting the picturesque the way **costumbrismo** did—and exploration of social, political, and philosophical issues. Realistic writers reflected reality as they saw it and focused on ordinary people, usually members of the middle class, and ordinary events. A representative realistic novelist was the Cuban **Nicolás Heredia**, who was born in the Dominican Republic, and his novel *Leonela* (1893), about a doomed love affair set in the Cuban countryside.

Realistic elements, such as accurate and detailed descriptions of a setting or an individual, were present in the different genres popular in the Hispanic Caribbean during the nineteenth century: costumbrismo, **the historical novel**, and to some extent **romanticismo**. Some of the abolitionist novels, such as *Francisco* (1838–39) by the Cuban **Anselmo Suárez y Romero**, had realistic descriptions of life on a sugar plantation.

In the twentieth century, realismo manifested itself as socialist realism in the works of a few Cuban writers, such as **Cesar Leante**. In New York, in the 1960s and 1970s, **Nuyorican** writers like **Piri Thomas** and **Nicholosa Mohr** wrote realistic stories about life in the United States and the struggles of minorities and the working poor.

Realism is present in the novels of many writers from the anglophone Caribbean, mostly written in the twentieth century. A prototype is **Garth St. Omer,** from St. Lucia, who in such works as *A Room on the Hill* (1968), describes in great detail how his characters view their surroundings and their political and philosophical musings. His rendering of 1950s St. Lucia evokes the realistic images of a photograph. Likewise, Trinidadian born Rosa Guy won praise for her realistic depictions of Harlem during the 1960s and 1970s. While realism might no longer be a dominant literary style, its appeal remains, and authors often include realistic descriptions in their novels. In Haiti, **Jacques Stephen Alexis** sketches in minute details the city of Port-au-Prince and its neighborhood, as well as the countryside, in his volume *Compère Général Soleil* (1955). In Martinique, **Joseph Zobel** was known for his realistic renderings of the underclass in such novels as *Laghia de la mort* (1946).

Naturalismo, which was more popular in Caribbean literature than realism, was an outcome of the latter. *See also* Magical Realism.

Further Reading

Levine, George, ed. *Realism and Representation: Essays on the Problem of Realism in Relation to Science, Literature, and Culture.* Madison: University of Wisconsin Press, 1993.

—*D. H. Figueredo*

Realismo Mágico. See Magical Realism.

Rechani Agrait, Luis (1902–94)

The author of one of Puerto Rico's most popular plays, the comedy *Mi señoría* (1940), about the clash between idealism and political compromise, Rechani Agrait was the editor of the influential daily *El Mundo.* He was also a poet.

A native of Aguas Buenas, Puerto Rico, he attended primary and secondary schools in Aguas Buenas and Río Piedras before traveling to the United States, where he studied natural science at Harvard and Richmond Universities. In 1924, he returned to Puerto Rico, accepting a position in the Department of Public Instruction. He contributed poems and short stories to *Puerto Rico Ilustrado* and *El Mundo.* In 1929, he published a collection of children's poems, *Nube en el viento.*

In 1930, he became editor of *El Mundo* and started to write for the theater. In 1939, he finished *Mi señoría*, which was staged and published in 1940. The satire explored the political compromises that a labor leader must make in order to bring about social reforms. The play was highly successful, and it has been staged several times since its debut. *Mi señoría* made Rechani Agrait, along with **Manuel Méndez Ballester**, one of the major Puerto Rican playwrights of the 1940s.

Rechani Agrait retired from journalism in 1943, devoting his time to the writing of plays: *Los descendientes de Poncio Pilatos* (1959), *¿Como se llama esta flor?*

(1966), *Tres piraguas en un día de calor* (1970), and *El extraño caso del Sr. Oblomos* (1982). In 1991, the Instituto de Cultura Puertorriqueña gathered some of his plays into the volume *Teatro de Luis Rechani Agrait.*

Further Reading

Martínez, Edgardo. "A dos años de la muerte de El Mundo." *El Diario La Prensa*, Dec. 23, 1992.

Quiles Ferrer, Edgar Heriberto. *Teatro puertorriqueño en acción.* San Juan: Ateneo Puertorriqueño, 1990.

—*D. H. Figueredo*

Redcam, Tom (1870–1933)

As a poet, Thomas Henry MacDermot chose to call himself Tom Redcam, spelling backward part of his surname. The descendant of Irish immigrants who settled in Jamaica in the eighteenth century, Redcam was a pioneer in claiming that Jamaica had a literature that was the equal of the literary works produced in Great Britain. Many of his contemporaries called him the "Father of Jamaican Poetry."

Redcam was born in Clarendon, Jamaica. Initially, he worked as a schoolteacher but switched to journalism, writing first for *The Jamaica Post* and *The Daily Gleaner* and then becoming the editor of *The Jamaican Times*, a position he held for twenty years. Desiring to create a literature written by Jamaicans and to foster a national interest in such a literature, he published from 1903 to 1909 a series of books he titled "The All-American Library," emphasizing themes from the New World and the Americas, rather than from Europe. He also befriended, mentored, and published younger writers, including **H. G. de Lisser**, and **Claude McKay**.

As a poet, Redcam was a romantic, devoting much of his literature to Jamaica's natural beauty. Typical of his production is "My Beautiful Home" (1929):

> I sing of the island I love,
> Jamaica, the land of my birth,
> Of summer-lit heavens above,
> An island the fairest on earth . . .
> Oh! Land that art dearest to me,
> Though unworthy of thee is my song,
> Wherever I wander, for thee
> My love is abiding and strong.

Redcam wrote songs that proved popular and were part of the elementary school curriculum during the 1920s and 1930s. Though in his verses there was a stirring of nationalism, Redcam was still loyal to England and imperial rule. In 1932, he wrote, "We are true to our King and Country / We are heirs of the ages to be."

Much appreciated during his lifetime, the **Poetry League of Jamaica** crowned him the First Poet Laureate of Jamaica a year after his death. The following two decades, however, proindependence scholars belittled his accomplishments and criticized his colonial outlook. But in the 1990s, a new generation of readers reevaluated Redcam's contributions, recognizing him as one the earliest writers and promoters of Jamaican literature. Observes scholar Laurence A. Breiner, in *An Introduction to West Indian Poetry*, Redcam "not only described the island's beauty, but was capable of conveying its character and especially the weight of its history" (65). Today, a public library in Jamaica bears his name. *See also* Jamaican Literature, History of; McFarlane, J. E. Clare.

Further Reading

Breiner, Laurence A. *An Introduction to West Indian Poetry*. Cambridge Cambridge University Press, 1998.

Donnell, Alison, and Sarah Lawrence Welsh. *The Routledge Reader in Caribbean Literature*. Toronto and New York: Routledge, 1996.

McFarlane, J. E. Clare. *A Literature in the Making*. Kingston, Jamaica: The Pioneer Press, 1956.

Redcam, Tom. *Orange Valley and Other Poems*. Kingston, Jamaica: The Pioneer Press, 1951.

—*D. H. Figueredo*

Reid, Vic (1913–87)

Vic Reid wrote the first novel to incorporate Jamaican diction and dialect throughout the text. entitled *A New Day* (1949), the fictionalized rendering of the island's history became a symbol of Jamaicans' affirmation of their culture and identity after independence. It was the first nationalistic novel written and published in Jamaica. Says critic Laurence A. Breiner, in *Introduction to West Indian Poetry*, *A New Day* meant that, as for literature, "the center was no longer London . . . [and] the language was West Indian and not British" (5).

Victor Stafford Reid was born on May 1, 1913, in Kingston, Jamaica. He wrote for several newspapers and worked for several publishers before turning to fiction writing. *A New Day* was his first novel. It was followed by *The Leopard* (1958), *Sixty-Five* (1960), *The Young Warriors* (1967)—both young adult novels— *Peter of Mount Ephraim* (1971), *The Jamaicans* (1976), and *Nanny-Town* (1983). He also wrote *The Horses of the Morning* (1985), a biography of Norman Manley (1893–1969), the island's first prime minister. Reid was awarded the Silver and Gold Musgrave Medal, in 1955 and 1978, the Order of Jamaica in 1980, and the 1981 Norman Manley Award for Excellence in Literature.

A New Day and *The Leopard* are his most successful novels. In the first novel, an elderly John Campbell recalls Jamaican history from the Morant rebellion in 1865—when parishioners from a Baptist church led by their minister rioted over the poor administration of the island by the British governor—to independence in 1944. The novel is poetically written and rich in allusions to the Jamaican landscape; the Campbell family, with its credible and likable characters, especially the narrator, is modeled on the influential Manley family, who produced the island's first prime minister. The second novel takes place in Kenya during the Mau-Mau uprising. It is the multilayered story of a Kenyan who has a brief affair with a white woman, his remorse at having cuckolded the husband, his complex relationship with the son produced by the union, and his violent encounter with the offended husband. While the first novel doesn't explore the nuances of the racial divide—for Reid wanted to celebrate all that was positive about independence and his hope for a "new day" in a new Jamaica—the second work addresses the complexities of racism and postcolonialism. Contrasting the two works, scholar Nilson Wilson-Tagoe interprets *A New Day* as an "optimistic sense" of political process and progress, whereas *The Leopard* studies the "contradictory impulses . . . [and] dual identities of Caribbean people," attempting to reconcile them.

Reid's inspiration came from Jamaica's history, the people he met, and the land that surrounded him, especially the mountains. His writing is filled with a genuine love that has made a *New Day* one of the most popular novels on the island. Reid was not an autobiographical writer, preferring to depict historical and political events. However, toward the end of his life he started to experiment with autobiographical poetry. He passed away in on August 25, 1987. See also Historical Novel; Jamaican Literature, History of.

Further Reading

Breiner, Laurence A. *An Introduction to West Indian Poetry*. Cambridge Cambridge University Press, 1998.

Reid, Vic. *The Leopard*. New York: Viking, 1959.

———. *New Day*. New York: Knopf, 1949.

Wilson-Tagoe, Nana. *Historical Thought and Literary Representation in West Indian Literature*. Gainesville: University Press of Florida, 1998.

—D. H. Figueredo

Revista Chicano-Riqueña (1973–85)

Founded by Puerto Rican scholar **Nicolás Kanellos** and initially published at Indiana University Northwest, this journal featured writings by Latinos from diverse backgrounds and national origins from across the United States. This was a new approach at a time when Latino publications practiced a sort of national nepotism—Chicano (of Mexican origin) publishers were interested only in Chicano authors and Cuban publishers wanted only Cuban writers. In 1979, editor Kanellos relocated to the University of Houston, where he continued publishing the journal.

In 1986, the *Revista Chicano-Riqueña* became the *Americas Review*. The publication ceased publishing in 1999, but only after providing an avenue for emerging Puerto Rican and Cuban American writers such as **Virgil Suárez** and **Judith Ortiz Cofer**.

Further Reading

Figueredo, Danilo H. "Love's Labour Not Lost: Latino Publishing." *Multicultural Review* 7, no. 3 (September 1998): 24–33.

—*D. H. Figueredo*

Revista de Avance (1927–31)

An avant-garde journal published in Cuba and edited by such major literary figures as **Alejo Carpentier** and **Jorge Robato Mañach**. The journal promoted European art while also exploring the national consciousness. The journal published creative writings and articles by Cuban authors—the likes of **Emilio Ballagas** and **Eugenio Florit**—while also accepting such foreign contributors as Federico García Lorca (1898–1936), from Spain, and José Carlos Mariátegui (1894–1930), from Peru. It also sponsored concerts of music by such emerging artists as Amadeo Roldan. In 1927, *Revista de Avance* organized the art exhibit Exposición de Arte Nuevo, the first major showing of modern Cuban painting. The journal ceased publication during the onset of the Gerardo Machado (1871–1939) dictatorship in 1931. *See also* Cuban Literature, History of; Literary Journals.

Further Reading

Manzoni, Celina. *Un dilema cubano: nacionalismo y vanguardia*. Habana: Fondo Editorial Casa de las Américas, 2001.

—*Wilfredo Cancio Isla*

Revue Indigène, La (1927–28)

Published in Port-au-Prince and edited by **Normil Sylvain,** this short-lived journal attempted to foster a national culture in Haiti, rejecting American influences as well as the imitation, then in vogue, of French literature by Haitian writers. The founders and contributors—which included such major writers as **Emile Roumer** and **Jacques Roumain**—had lived in France and were cosmopolitan. They promoted the indigenist movement and advocated for solidarity with blacks all over the world. The journal published articles on Haitian folklore and traditions and celebrated the use of Kreyòl as a national language. *See also* Haitian Literature, History of; Haitian Literature in Kreyòl (the Haitian Language); Indigènisme; Literary Journals; Négritude; Price-Mars, Jean.

Further Reading

Antoine, Jacques C. *Jean Price-Mars and Haiti*. Washington, DC and Colorado: Three Continents Press and Lynne Rienner Publishers, Inc. 1981.

—*D. H. Figueredo*

Rhys, Jean (1890–1979)

One of the most famous authors from the anglophone Caribbean, Jean Rhys wrote novels and short fiction that deal with the struggles of being an outsider: as a woman, as a white person in the West Indies, and as a West Indian woman in Europe. Her most famous novel, **Wide Sargasso Sea**, revisits *Jane Eyre*, by Charlotte Brontë (1816–55), to tell the story of Bertha, Edward Rochester's Caribbean first wife whom he keeps hidden in the top floor of his estate. In this, as in other works, Rhys brings into focus the worldview and consciousness that develop among women from the Caribbean and that provide an alternative to the British view of the empire.

Jean Rhys was born Ella Gwendoline Rees Williams on August 24, 1890, in Roseau, Dominica, to a white Creole mother and a Welsh-born father. As a child, Rhys regarded herself as an outsider. When Rhys was a girl, Dominica had long since passed from French to English rule, yet she remembered feeling left out of the French patois language in use and excluded from the Catholic rituals observed by most black people of the island. Her move to England at age sixteen began a stage of disillusionment with love, England, and European values. An early affair with an older man ended abruptly leaving her with an abortion and an allowance, two situations that shaped her bitter feelings about what she termed, in her autobiography *Smile Please* (1979), "the whole business of money and sex" and the relationship between the powerful and the powerless. After these events, Rhys began keeping a journal of, or rather reflections on, her past, in a series of black exercise books.

She married Dutch journalist Jean Lenglet in 1919 and lived with him in various European cities, finally moving back to England. During this period, she began transforming material from her journals into short fiction and publishing works under the patronage of British writer and editor Ford Madox Ford (1873–1939). In 1923, her husband was sentenced to prison for illegal currency trades, and Rhys became involved with Ford. The affair ended bitterly, but once over, Rhys began novel writing in earnest.

Francis Wyndham, one of Rhys's editors, suggests that the author's first four major novels all deal with roughly the same protagonist, all linked to different stages of Rhys's own life. In all four, the character corresponds to a type known then as the "New Woman": independent, self-reliant, and comfortable with moving through a series of sexual relationships. Her freedom is punished consistently by men in her life, who betray her and cast her off, leaving her in dire financial conditions. In the first two of these, *Quartet* (1928) and *After Leaving Mr. MacKenzie* (1930), young female protagonists fall in love with older men who try to control them and ultimately leave them lonely and depressed. In the third, *Voyage in the Dark* (1934), Rhys captures her nostalgia for the natural and human beauty of her homeland. Her West Indian protagonist, Anna Morgan, discovers she is ever more out of place in the detached English society. She is cut off abruptly by her older lover and ends up a prostitute having an abortion, suggesting the ugly results of an unnatural attitude toward love.

Between 1939 and 1958, little was heard from Rhys until a BBC broadcast of a dramatized version of the novel *Good Morning, Midnight* (1939), which brought her work back to the public eye. In 1966, she published *Wide Sargasso Sea*, undoubtedly her best-known work. Here, more than in any of her other novels, Rhys deals with her West Indian heritage. The story revolves around Antionette Cosway, the insane first wife of Edward Rochester of Charlotte Brontë's *Jane Eyre*. More than sequel or "prequel" to the Bronte story, Rhys uses the novel to explore the faulty but powerful binary systems—black-white, European-West Indian, male-female, Christian–non-Christian—that govern relationships between colonizer and colonized. The novel takes place in Jamaica, allowing Rhys to paint the backdrop of lush natural beauty that she found lacking in Europe. She captures the unique quality of race relations in an island scarred by slavery and on which the white people are in the minority. In Antionette, Rhys creates the culmination of her outsider figure; she is a woman in a world of male power, white on an island of blacks, and a crazy Caribbean wife trapped in another, colder island of England.

In her final years, Rhys received the attention and monetary success she had always hoped for. She published another collection of short stories, *Sleep It Off, Lady* (1979), and worked on her autobiography, *Smile Please*, published after her death. She passed away on May 14, 1979. *See also* Feminism in Caribbean Literature; Mother-Daughter Relationships; Postcolonialism.

Further Reading

Angier, Carole. *Jean Rhys: Life and Work*. Boston: Little Brown, 1990.

O'Connor, Teresa F. *Jean Rhys: The West Indian Novels*. New York: NYU Press, 1986.

Rhys, Jean. *Smile Please*. New York: Harper & Row, 1979.

Wyndham, Francis. "Introduction." *Wide Sargasso Sea*, by Jean Rhys, Norton Critical Edition, edited by Judith L. Raiskin. New York, Norton, 1999.

—*Angela Conrad*

Ribera Chevremont, Evaristo (1896–1975)

Alongside **Luis Palés Matos** and **Luis Llorens Torres**, this poet was one of the best-known Puerto Rican writers of the early twentieth century. He was considered both a romantic and postmodern poet. He was also a journalist.

Born in San Juan on February 16, 1896, Ribera Chevremont expressed an interest in literature at an early age, and by the time he was teenager, he had written two books of poems, *Desfile romántico* (1914) and *El templo de los alabastros*, both poetic exercises in the tradition of the romantic movement or **romanticismo**. After graduating from high school, he traveled to Spain in 1919 and lived there for five years. His stay in Spain was crucial to his development as a writer: he studied the classic works of Spanish literature, served as secretary of the Ateneo, a cultural and literary organization, and became interested in vanguard literature.

Upon his return to Puerto Rico, he founded the journal *Los seis* and published his poems in numerous publications, including *Puerto Rico Ilustrado*. His first major book, *Color*, was published in 1938. The poems in this collection explored universal themes. Other works followed: *Tonos y formas* (1943), *Anclas de oro* (1945), and *Verbo* (1947). These books brought him recognition in Puerto Rico and throughout the Caribbean.

In the 1950s, he visited Spain several times. The friendships he developed there with other writers and intellectuals helped to internationalize his reputation. By now, his poetry was becoming more personal and reflective; the sea, as demonstrated in the volumes *Tú, mar, y yo y ella* (1946) and *Inefable orilla* (1961), served as a source of inspiration.

Ribera Chevremont attempted a variety of styles and formats, from free verse to sonnets to décimas, poems written in ten lines. Critics **Margo Arce de Vázquez**, Laura Gallego, and **Luis de Arrigoitia** in *Lecturas puertorriqueñas* (1968) described Chevremont as a poet interested in the metaphysical whose preoccupation with Christian values and the encounter with death and God augmented as he grew older.

Ribera Chevremont passed away in San Juan on March 1, 1975. In Puerto Rico, the date of his birth is celebrated as the week of Puerto Rican poetry. A national literary prize is also offered in his name.

Further Reading

Arce de Vázquez, Margot, et al. *Lecturas puertorriqueñas: poesía*. Sharon, CT: Troutman Press, 1968.

Marxuach, Carmen Irene. *Evaristo Ribera Chevremont: voz de vanguardia*. San Juan, Puerto Rico: Centro de Estudios Avanzados de Puerto Rico y el Caribe y La Editorial de la Universidad de Puerto Rico, 1987.

—*D. H. Figueredo*

Riley, Joan (1958–)

Joan Riley is a Jamaican novelist who criticizes the island's social ills and who protests against women's oppression and neglect. She bases her work on her research and experience as a social scientist and as an expert on drug abuse.

Joan Riley was born on May 26, 1958, in St. Mary, Hopewell, Jamaica. The youngest of eight children, she began writing as a young child, though she preferred to spend time at the local library reading Greek mythology, Robert Frost (1874–1963), Thomas Hardy (1840–1928) and William Shakespeare (1564–1616). She entertained herself entering slogan competitions for local ads and writing poetry but stopped writing to concentrate on her studies. She left Jamaica to attend the University of Sussex, from which she graduated with honors; she then earned two masters—in arts and in social sciences—from the University of London.

During her first years in London, Riley was taken aback by racism, the climate, and the aloofness of her British neighbors. She decided to write about the experience, but rather than tell the story from the perspective of a college woman, she felt it would be better to make her protagonist a young girl on the verge of puberty; the novel, entitled *The Unbelonging* was published in 1985. Her second book was *Waiting in the Twilight* (1987), about an old Jamaican servant living in London. In this novel, Riley explored how Jamaican women are taught by society—both in Jamaica and in Europe—to be subservient and to rely for everything on their male lovers or husbands, even when these men abuse them and commit incest with their children.

In 1988, Riley wrote *Romance*, about the entrapment experienced by two sisters: one who is trapped in a physique that is homely and overweight and one who is trapped in a bad marriage. In 1992, Riley published *A Kindness to Children*, a story about a woman returning home to Jamaica only to find despair, oppression, and sexual abuse. In 1996, she edited, with Briar Wood, *Leave to Stay: Stories of Exile and Belonging*.

Many of her novels have provoked anger in Jamaica, since she portrays the men as abusive, reckless, and irresponsible, and she criticizes the Jamaican government for neglecting Jamaican women's social and sexual plight. Though Riley writes about black Jamaicans, she wants her stories to have a universal appeal, afraid that some readers might stereotype her as a black writer writing only for blacks. She told scholar Donna Perry in the book *Backtalk: Women Writers Speak Out* (1993): "It's important that a white audience can pick up [a] book and say, 'I can identify with that.' . . . People are people, with the same pains, the same hurts, the same uncertainties, regardless of class" (286). Riley has received Mind Book of the Year Award, the Voice Award for Literary Excellence, and the Voice Literary Figure of the Decade. *See also* Exile Literature; Immigrant Literature.

Further Reading

Perry, Donna. *Backtalk: Women Writers Speak Out; Interviews by Donna Perry*. New Brunswick, NJ: Rutgers University Press, 1993.

—*D. H. Figueredo*

Ripè, Soni. See Rupaire, Sonny.

Risco Bermúdez, René del (1937–72)

One of the founders of the literary group known as El Puño, this short-story writer and poet is credited with introducing the experimental techniques of the **Latin American Boom** to the literature of the Dominican Republic.

Risco Bermúdez was born in San Pedro de Macoris, Dominican Republic. He was studying law when at the age of twenty two he joined the underground plotting to overthrow dictator Rafael Leónidas Trujillo (1891–1961). Working in the clandestine organization Movimiento de Liberación Dominicana, he was one of the planners of an invasion that was launched from Cuba in the late 1950s. He was arrested by the secret service. Upon his release, he sought exile in Puerto Rico, returning when Trujillo was assassinated in 1961. He then participated in the political activities that attempted to restore a democratic regime after decades of repression.

In 1967, he published a collection of poems, *El viento frío*, reflections on the political conditions in the Dominican Republic. Dissatisfied with poetry and convinced that prose was a better avenue for the expression of political ideology, he switched to prose in 1967 and wrote a collection of short stories entitled *Del júbilo a la sangre*. From then on, he wrote numerous short stories, which were published in local journals. His best-known work is *En el barrio no hay banderas* (1974). He died in a car crash in 1972. *See also* Trujillo Era.

Further Reading

Mújica, Barbara. "Remaking a Lost Harmony: Stories from the Hispanic Caribbean." *Americas* 48, no. 3 (May/June 1996): 62–64.

—*D. H. Figueredo*

Rivera, Edward (1939–2001)

Though Puerto Rican author Edward Rivera only wrote one book, entitled *Family Installments* (1982), it established him as one of the premier writers of the Latino immigrant's experience. Like novelists **Julia Álvarez**, from the Dominican Republic, and **Virgil Suárez**, from Cuba, Rivera decided to write in English rather than in his native tongue.

Edward Rivera was born in Orocovis, Puerto Rico. After spending his childhood in the countryside, Rivera moved to New York City when he was about eight years old. He attended Catholic and public schools, and upon graduation from high school, he worked at a variety of jobs. When he was twenty-one years old, he enlisted in the army. When he was discharged, he matriculated at night school at the City University of New York. Graduating in with a BA in English in 1967, he went on to Columbia University where he earned a masters in fine arts.

Family Installments: Memories of Growing Up Hispanic tells of Rivera's family in Puerto Rico and of his move to New York City. Though it took him ten years to write the memoir, several chapters were published from 1971 to 1980 in such prestigious journals as the *New American Review* and the *Bilingual Review/La Revista Bilingüe*. The memoir, consisting of vignettes, is a prototype of **immigrant literature** and contains its classic elements: the homesick father playing on his guitar old songs from the homeland; the well-intentioned nuns assuming the narrator is poorly fed and poorly clothed and buying him clothes he didn't need; the feelings of discomfort experienced by relatives once the narrator becomes a college student; the sense of separation that acculturation fosters between immigrant parents and their children; the shock and pain of discrimination and racism. Rivera wrote in an accessible, poetic, and gentle language; his characters are memorable and likable.

Rivera died of heart failure on August 25, 2001. He was a college professor at the City College of New York and a mentor of such young Latino writers as **Junot Díaz.**

Further Reading

Rivera, Edward. *Family Installments: Memories of Growing Up Hispanic.* New York: Penguin Books, 1983.

—D. H. Figueredo

Rivera de Álvarez, Josefina (1923–)

Rivera de Álvarez is one of the greatest literary critics and a devoted professor of Puerto Rican, Latin American, and Spanish literatures. Besides a legacy of important pioneering texts, she has been an advocate and inspiration for all those interested in Puerto Rican literature.

She was born in Mayagüez, Puerto Rico. In 1945, she received her bachelor's degree in liberal arts from the Inter American University, in 1947, her masters from Columbia University, and in 1954, a doctorate in philosophy and letters from the Universidad Central de Madrid. Since 1947, she has taught at the Universidad de Puerto Rico in Mayagüez, where she also shared her dedication to literature with her husband, the well-noted Puerto Rican linguist Manuel Álvarez Nazario (1924–).

As a critic of Puerto Rican letters, she published extensively in journals such as *La Torre, Atenea, Revista del Instituto de Cultura Puertorriqueña, Orígenes,* and others. A distinguished member of the Puerto Rican Academy of Arts and Letters and the Puerto Rican Academy of History, she is best known for her pioneering book, based on her doctoral dissertation, *Diccionario de la literatura puertorriqueño* (1955), a three-volume text that became the first systematic and panoramic overview of the past and of contemporary Puerto Rican literature. That publication, like her second major book, *Historia de la literatura puertorriqueña* (2 volumes, 1969) received recognition and an award from the Instituto de Literatura Puertorriqueña. Her magnum opus is *Literatura puertorriqueña: Su proceso en el tiempo* (1983), an almost one-thousand-page text that to date is the best reference book on the subject of Puerto Rican literature. It is a well-researched book, with exhaustive footnotes, thorough bibliographies and eye-opening and suggestive analyses of authors, books, and critics. In addition, she has authored the volume of the *Diccionario de la literatura latinoamericana* (published by the Organization of American States) devoted to Puerto Rico and the volume of the *La gran enciclopedia de Puerto Rico* (1976) devoted to the Puerto Rican novel, from its origins to the seventies. Both she and her husband and have donated their private library and important literary memorabilia to the Juan M. Sama Library of the Universidad de Puerto Rico–Mayagüez.

Further Reading

Toro-Sugrañes, José Antonio. "Biografías." In *Nueva enciclopedia de Puerto Rico*. Hato Rey, Puerto Rico: Editorial Lector, 1994.

—*Asela R. Laguna*

Roach, Eric Martin (1915–74)

In 1974, after a lifetime of writing poetry in Trinidad-Tobago but obtaining little recognition, Roach committed suicide by drinking a container of insecticide and then swimming out to sea. His suicide note, "Finis," was the very last poem he wrote.

Born in Mount Pleasant, Tobago, Roach attended high school, pursuing pedagogical training that secured him a teaching position after graduation. At the outbreak of World War II, he enlisted in the army in Trinidad. During this period, he began to write poetry under the name of Merton Maloney.

When World War II ended, Roach worked as a civil servant in Tobago. In the meantime, he was writing and submitting his poems to numerous publications, such as the influential *Bim* and *Kyk-Over-Al*. In the early 1950s, he left his job, hoping to earn a living as a writer. He also participated in the political organization People's National Movement and supported historian and political personage **Eric Williams**.

Unable to make a living from his poetry, in 1973, Roach worked as a journalist. He continued to write but did not submit any works for publication. Always a nationalist, during this period, Roach expressed concern over black power which he characterized as American import rather than a true manifestation of anglophone Caribbean culture.

Many of the poems Roach wrote during the 1970s were gathered in the anthology *The Flowering Rock: Collected Poems 1938–1974*, published nearly twenty years after his death. In 1974, he was posthumously awarded Trinidad and Tobago's National Hummingbird Gold Medal. Critics today rank Roach with the likes of **Martin Carter** and **Edward Kamau Brathwaite**.

Further Reading

Breiner, Laurence A. *An Introduction to West Indian Poetry*. Cambridge: Cambridge University Press, 1998.

Griffith, Glyne. "Deconstructing Nationalism: Henry Swanzy, Caribbean Voices and the Development of West Indian literature." *Small Axe* 15, no. 2 (Sept. 2001): 1–22.

—*D. H. Figueredo*

Roberts, Walter Adolphe (1886–1962)

∎

Walter Adolphe Roberts was a Jamaican poet, historian, and novelist who advocated for Caribbean nationalism and demonstrated a preoccupation with American influence in the region. He promoted Jamaican culture, was president of the Jamaican Historical Society, and was the first editor of Pioneer Press, a Jamaican publishing house.

Born in Kingston, Jamaica, and the descendant of a wealthy Creole family, Roberts benefited from an excellent education that introduced him to a cultural experience that went beyond the confines of the British Empire. At the age of sixteen, he became a journalist for the *Daily Gleaner*, and, in 1904, he traveled to the United States, where he was a reporter for the *Brooklyn Daily Herald*. In that capacity, he covered World War I from France and later on toured Latin America. He founded several newspapers and wrote over twenty five books in different genres, two of the books written under the pseudonym Stephen Endicott, *Mayor Harding of New York* (1931) and *The Strange Career of Bishop Sterling* (1932).

Roberts's poetry was initially characterized by Greek classical motifs—*Pan and Peacock* (1928)—though eventually he essayed on the theme of Négritude— *Medallions* (1950). He cultivated the historical romance and his trilogy *Royal Street* (1944), *Brave Mardi Gras* (1946), and *Creole Dusk* (1948) traced the trajectory of Louisiana's French immigrants from Haiti to the United States, detailing their process of acculturation. His Caribbean novel *The Single Star* (1949) is centered on Cuba's war of independence in 1895. It tells the story a young Jamaican who joins the insurrection after befriending a family of Cuban patriots and falling in love with a beautiful Cuban woman fighter. In this novel, Roberts reconstructs historical events, combining the factual with the fictive in a fast-paced narrative. This novel is representative of Roberts's style and concerns: historical themes, police drama, romantic depiction of characters and situations. Roberts was also one of the first writers from the Caribbean to write a detective story: *The Mind Reader* (1929).

Some of his other works include *Pierrot Wounded and Other Poems* (1919), *The Haunting Hand* (1926), *The Moralist* (1931), *Sir Henry Morgan, Buccaneer and Governor (1933), The Top-floor Killer (1935), Self-government for Jamaica* (1936), *Semmes of Alabama* (1938), *The Caribbean: The Story of Our Sea of Destiny* (1940), *The Pomegranate* (1941), *The French in the West Indies* (1942), *The U.S. Navy Flights (1942), Lake Pontchartrain (1946), Lands of the Inner Sea, the West Indies and Bermuda* (1948), *Six Great Jamaicans* (1952), *Havana; The Portrait of a City* (1953), *Jamaica; The Portrait of an Island* (1955), and *The Capitals of Jamaica: Spanish Town, Kingston, Port Royal* (1955). *See also* Detective Fiction; Historical Novel.

Further Reading

Bennett, Wycliffe. "W. Adolphe Roberts, the Man and the Poet." *Sunday Gleaner*, September 30, 1962.

Birbalsingh, Frank. "W. A. Roberts; Creole Romantic." *Caribbean Quarterly* 19, no. 2 (June 1973): 100–107.

McFarlane, J. E. Clare. *A Literature in the Making*. Kingston: Pioneer Press, 1956.

Ramchand, Kenneth. *The West Indian Novel and Its Background*. London: Faber and Faber, 1970.

Sander, Reinhard W. "The Thirties and Forties." In *West Indian Literature*, edited by Bruce King. London and Basingstoke: Macmillan Press, 1979.

—Emilio Jorge Rodríguez

Rodolfa, Micha. See Juliana, Elis.

Rodríguez, Emilio Jorge (1947–)

A Cuban literary critic and internationally recognized scholar who has dedicated his life to introducing Caribbean literature to Cubans and promoting Cuban literature to the Caribbean, Rodríguez is one of the few scholars from the region who sees the Caribbean as one entity and not as a series of individual islands. His critical studies emphasize cultural diversity and affinities within the Caribbean.

Rodríguez was born in San Antonio de los Baños, Cuba, on April 5, 1947. He conducted his primary studies in his hometown, learning English at an early age. In 1970, he graduated from the Universidad de la Habana with a BA in Spanish literature and in 1984 was appointed Hispanic American researcher by the Academia de Ciencias de Cuba. In 1975, he anthologized the poetry of the Mexican poet Efraín Huerta (1914–82)–*Poesía*–and in 1981 he founded and managed the scholarly publication *Anales del Caribe*, one of the most prestigious in the Caribbean. Rodríguez edited this publication, which was published by the **Casa de las Américas**, until 2000.

Beginning in 1972, he dedicated himself to the research of Caribbean literature, paying particular attention to comparative literature and the relationship between literature and oral traditions. He toured the Caribbean, lecturing on the subject while contrasting Cuban literature with Latin American Literature. This was a challenging task, considering that at the time very little was known in Cuba about the literature from the region.

From 1980 onward, he participated in dozens of international conferences and seminars and contributed articles to numerous anthologies exploring Caribbean literature and culture. He also accepted the post of visiting scholar at such major institutions as Duke University, Vassar College, Universite Quisqueya, in Haiti, and Freie Universitat Berlin. In 1989, he published, with Vitalina Alfonso, *Literatura caribeña: bojeo y cuaderno de bitácora*, one of the few volumes published in the Hispanic Caribbean to study anglophone and francophone Caribbean literature. In 1991, he introduced to Cuban readers Puerto Rican authors previously unknown in Cuba with the volume *Cuentos para ahuyentar el turismo: 16 autores puertorriqueños*. In 2001, his *Acriollamiento y discurso escrit/oral caribeño* was issued in Cuba. This volume proposed a borderless conception of the Caribbean defined neither by language nor nation but by the wholeness of the region. His literary style combines sociopolitical analysis with a historical and linguistic perspective that takes his works beyond the realms of literary theory. His scholarship has earned him the distinction of being one of the few Caribbean scholars with knowledge of literary productivity across borders.

Further Reading

Rodríguez, Emilio Jorge. *Acriollamiento y discurso escrit/oral caribeña*. Habana: Ediciones Letras Cubanas, 2001.

———. 2005. Interview by D. H. Figueredo, May.

—D. H. Figueredo

Rodríguez de Laguna, Asela (1946–)

Puerto Rican scholar and essayist, Rodríguez de Laguna, like her compatriots the **López Baralt sisters,** has brought an international perspective to the study of Puerto Rican literature, contrasting and comparing the literary works of such important writers as George Bernard Shaw (1856–1950), from Great Britain, with **Nemesio Canales,** from Puerto Rico. She is also a well-known conference organizer and academician.

A native of Santurce, Asela Rodríguez de Laguna graduated magna cum laude from Universidad de Puerto Rico in 1968. Two years later, she earned an MA in comparative literature from the University of Illinois; in 1973, she received her PhD from the same university. Through the 1970s, she published numerous essays on comparative literature, focusing on George Bernard Shaw, in such influential journals as *Sin Nombre, Revista Chicano-Riqueña, Revista del Instituto de Cultura Puertorriqueña,* and Latin American Theater Review. During this period she accepted a position at Rutgers University, where she taught Spanish literature. In 1981, she published *George Bernard Shaw en el mundo hispánico,* one of the first texts to examine the British playwright's influence in the Caribbean and Latin America.

In 1983, she created and organized the first international conference to gather in one place the major Puerto Rican writers of the period, including **José Luis González, Luis Rafael Sánchez, Clemente Soto Vélez,** and **Pedro Piedri.** Called, Images and Identities: The Puerto Rican in Literature, the conference occurred on the Newark campus of Rutgers University. Two years later, she edited the proceedings into a book with the same title.

In 1986, she codirected, with her husband, Elpidio Laguna-Díaz, and Carlos Rodríguez, the first Multidisciplinary Conference on the Dominican Republic. In 1987, she wrote *Notes on Puerto Rican Literature: Images and Identities—An Introduction.* She also published numerous articles exploring Latino literature, as well as studies on Christopher Columbus (1451–1506), in anthologies and scholarly textbooks. As she gained scholarly recognition, she also befriended and mentored emerging writers as well as numerous Latino students.

Rodríguez de Laguna has edited several reference sources, including *The Global Impact of Portuguese Language and Culture* (2001). She is the acting chair of the Department of Puerto Rican and Hispanic Caribbean at Rutgers University. She has won recognition, as journalist José Rohaidy pointed out in the daily *El Diario La Prensa*, for her promotion of Latino culture in the United States.

Further Reading

"Faculty Notes." http://honorsnewark.rutgers.edu/fasn/FASN. 2001 (accessed 5/15/05).

Rohaidy, José. "Hispanos incrementan sus actividades en un mes." *El Diario La Prensa*, Oct. 11, 1998.

—D. H. Figueredo

Rodríguez de Tió, Lola (1843–1924)

The most renowned of the nineteenth-century female patriotic poets from Puerto Rico, Rodríguez de Tió was the author of the revolutionary poem "La Borinqueña" (1868). For many contemporary critics, she was among the first women authors in Puerto Rico to defy her assigned domestic role and imposed silence by conducting lectures in public gatherings.

Lola Rodríguez de Tió was born in historical San Germán, where she was educated and lived with her husband, the journalist Bonocio Tió (1839–1905). A feminist who advocated for gender equality and educational opportunities for women, Rodríguez de Tió also fought political tyranny and against the colonial status of Puerto Rico. An essayist and a poet, she is most remembered as the author of the original lyrics of the well-known "La Borinqueña" and also for her well-known poetic verses that fraternally unite both Cuba and Puerto Rico: "Cuba and Puerto Rico are two wings of the same bird / And the bullets and flowers geared towards them are received by one heart."

In 1865, when she married Bonocio Tió, both became involved in the proindependence struggle. As a result of their political views, they were banished three times from Puerto Rico. During those exiles, she spent time in Venezuela (1877–80 and in 1887), Cuba (1889–95), and the United States (1895–99). After her last exile of 1899, she spent most of her life in Havana, where her home became a pilgrimage place for other Puerto Ricans or important literary and political figures. She befriended such legendary figures as **José Martí, Eugenio María de Hostos**, and **Pachín Marín** and such major writers as **Julián del Casal**, Rubén Darío (1867–1916), **José de Diego**, and Santos Chocano (1867–1935). In Cuba, she was instrumental in establishing in 1910 the Cuban Academy of Arts and letters. Until her death in 1924, she only returned three more times to Puerto Rico. In her visit in 1915 not only the Universidad de Puerto Rico but also de **Ateneo Puertorriqueño** organized a series of events to honor the poet.

In 1868, she wrote the poem "La Borinqueña," using the tune of the song of the same name written by composer Félix Astol Artés (1813–1901) in 1867. The poem rallied Puerto Ricans to fight against Spain:

> Nosotros queremos
> ser libre ya,
> y nuestro machete
> afilado está

(We long / to be freed / and our machete / is sharpened for combat).

In 1903, poet and writer **Manuel Fernández Juncos** wrote new lyrics for this poem, a much tamer version than the original, thus it was adopted as the popular representative song of the island. By 1952, the softer version had become the national anthem of the Commonwealth of Puerto Rico.

With regard to literature, Rodríguez de Tió's poetry exhibits more than a modernist vein, verses framed within the Spanish tradition of the Golden Age and **romanticismo,** with influences also of other European romantics as Heinrich Heine (1797–1856) and Alfred de Musset (1810–57). Her thematic itinerary moves from verses that deal with love, the memories of her home town, pain, death, and religion to suffering, nationalism, and patriotism. In 1876, Rodríguez de Tió published her first book of poetry, *Mis cantares.* This volume was followed by two other collections, *Claros y nieblas (1885)* and *Mi libro de Cuba* (1893). She wrote numerous essays of which perhaps the two most famous are "La influencia de la mujer en la civilización" (1875) and "La educación de la mujer" (1886). Rodríguez de Tió denounced a patriarchal society that silenced women and criticized a mediocre educational system that favored men. Her style was direct and yet poetic, and her views provoked much discussion and controversies.

Further Reading

Birmingham-Pokorny, Elba D. "Del centro a la periferia: en el discurso de Lola Rodríguez de Tió." In *La voz de la mujer en literatura hispanoamericana fin-de-siglo*, compiled by Luis Jiménez, 157–61. San José, Costa Rica: Editorial de la Universidad de Costa Rica, 1999.

Cadilla de Martínez, M. *Semblanzas de un carácter (Apuntes biográficos de Lola Rodríguez de Tió).* San Juan: 1936.

—Asela R. Laguna

Rodríguez Frese, Marcos (1941–)

One of the founders of the literary journal *Guajana* (1962), Rodríguez Frese is a Puerto Rican poet and activist. His poetry is an example of **literatura comprometida,** socially engaged literature.

A native of Cayey, in 1962, Rodríguez Frese founded, with poets **Andrés Castro Ríos** and Wenceslao Serra, the review *Guajana*. Inspired by Marxist ideology,

Rodríguez Frese's poetry demonstrates a commitment to the betterment of the common people as well as independence for the island. While involved in political and cultural activities through the 1960s, Rodríguez Frese studied law at the Universidad de Puerto Rico, earning his degree in 1971.

In 1968 and 1969, the **Ateneo Puertorriqueño** presented him with two awards for his poetry, much of which had been published in journals or read by the poet at public readings. In 1971, he published his best two best-known works, *Arbol prohibido* and *Todo el hombre*.

Rodríguez Frese devotes much of his time to the proindependence movement on the island. Critic **Efraín Barradas**, in *Para entendernos: Inventario poético puertorriqueño* (1992), describes Rodríguez Frese's poetry as observing "little details . . . insignificant incidents . . . [and] transforming them in poetic recourses" (401).

Further Reading

Barradas, Efraín. *Para entendernos: Inventario poético puertorriqueño*. San Juan, Puerto Rico: Instituto Cultura Puertorriqueña, 1992.

—*D. H. Figueredo*

Rodríguez Juliá, Edgardo (1946–)

One of the Caribbean's most important contemporary novelists, Rodríguez Juliá is a Puerto Rican author whose works attempt to understand political development on his homeland, often analyzed through the vehicle of historical fiction. His fictional biography of **Luis Muñoz Marín**—*Las tribulaciones de Jones* (1981)—is an insightful study of the conflict between idealism and compromise.

Born on October 9, 1946, in Río Piedras, Rodríguez Juliá spent a good deal of time with his grandmother on her coffee farm in the town of Aguas Buenas. His grandmother and her friends were natural storytellers, and the young child was fascinated by stories about farm life. At the age of eleven, he and his parents moved into a middle-class neighborhood in San Juan. In 1964, he attended the Universidad de Puerto Rico. By this time, he was already writing short stories.

After earning his BA in 1968, he taught for several years at his alma mater. In 1971, he moved to New York City to study at New York University. After earning an MA in literature, he returned to Puerto Rico. In 1973, he won a short-story contest sponsored by the **Ateneo Puertorriqueño**. Encouraged by the award and by writer **Pedro Juan Soto**, Rodríguez Juliá turned to the writing of long fiction. In 1974, he published *La renuncia del héroe Baltasar*, a historical novel set in eighteenth-century Puerto Rico. In 1981, his fictional analysis and biography of poet and governor Luis Muñoz Marín, *Las tribulaciones de Jones*, where he portrayed the governor as a prisoner of his political aspirations—the creation of the commonwealth status for the island, making it neither an independent republic nor an American colony—earned him recognition and popularity.

After *Las tribulaciones de Jonás*, Rodríguez Juliá became a widely published author: *El entierro de Cortijo* (1983), *La noche oscura del Niño Aviles* (1984), *Una noche con Iris Chacón* (1986), *El cruce de la Bahía de Guanica* (1989), *Sol de medianoche* (1995), and *Mujer con sombrero Panamá* (2004), writing over twenty four books in as many years. These volumes, which ranged in genre from **magical realism** to **detective fiction**, explored the themes that characterized all his works: observations on Puerto Rican society, an understanding of a Puerto Rican identity, and the island's political ambivalence. But he also wrote books of nonfiction, including an art book, *Campeche o los diablejos de la melancolía* (1986), *Cámara secreta* (1994), on erotic photography, and a study on baseball, *Peloteros* (1997). While teaching, Rodríguez Juliá also wrote for the daily *El Nuevo Día*, beginning in 1988.

Considered one of the great Latin American writers of the late twentieth century, Rodríguez Juliá has received numerous awards: a literary prize from the Instituto de Literatura Puertorriqueña (1982), a Pen Club Award (1984), a Guggenheim Grant (1986), finalist in the prestigious Premio Planeta-Joaquín Mortiz (1993), and the Francisco Herrera Luge Award for an international novel (1995). Critic Julio Ortega, writing in the *Michigan Quarterly Review*, selected *Sol de medianoche* as one of the best novels from Latin America. Rodríguez Juliá's novels have been translated into English and French.

Further Reading

González, Rubén. *La historia puertorriqueña de Rodríguez Juliá*. San Juan: Editorial de la Universidad de Puerto Rico, 1997.

Ortega, Julia. "The Ten Best Novels from Spanish America." *Michigan Quarterly Review* 39, no. 1 (Winter 2000): 108–16.

—*D. H. Figueredo*

Rodríguez Nietzsche, Vicente (1942–)

Cofounder and editor of the journal *Guajana*, Rodríguez Nietzsche is a politically committed Puerto Rican writer who promotes social and political change through literature. The simplicity and directness of many of his verses bring to the mind the poetry of the nineteenth-century Cuban poet **José Martí**

Rodríguez Nietzsche was born and raised in San Juan. While attending the Universidad de Puerto Rico, he cofounded, with **Marcos Rodríguez Frese** and **Andrés Castro Ríos**, the journal *Guajana*, which advocated for the independence of Puerto Rico and criticized the American presence on the island. As editorial director of the journal, Rodríguez Nietzsche encouraged public discussion of political poetry. He favored the promotion of his works through public readings rather than actual publication in a book.

Nevertheless, in 1967, he published the volume *Estos poemas*, consisting of work written by several poets at once. And, in 1968, he published *Trovas lareñas*.

Then, from 1976 to 1992, he published nearly ten volumes of poetry. A typical collection is *Te digo Fidel* (1978), in which he expresses his admiration for the Cuban leader and denounces capitalism and exploitation.

Rodríguez Nietzsche's poetry, intensely political, evokes a sense of speed and oral performance. While intensely patriotic and nationalist, he nevertheless seeks solidarity with other nations, especially those whose countries and peoples he sees as opposing American imperialism. To underline his stance, in 2002, he wrote:

> En Cuba yo soy cubano.
> En Francia yo soy francés. /
> con el nativo de allí . . . /
> darle mi abrazo sincero.

(In Cuba, I'm Cuban. / In France, I'm French. / To the native from there . . . / I offer a sincere embrace.)

Further Reading

González, José Emilio. "La poesía en Puerto Rico." In *La gran enciclopedia de PuertoRico*, vol. 3, edited by Vicente Báez, 337–40. San Juan: Puerto Rico en la Mano and Gran Enciclopedia de Puerto Rico, 1981.

Rodríguez Nietzsche, Vicente. "Ciudadanía." *Editorial Poetas Anti-imperialistas de América.* http://www.poetas.com (accessed 9/26/05).

—*D. H. Figueredo*

Rodríguez Torres, Carmelo (1941–)

Carmelo Rodríguez Torres is the best-known Puerto Rican writer from Vieques, for many years the disputed site of an American military base. He has written extensively about the conflict between the residents of Vieques and the presence of the American military.

Rodríguez Torres began his literary career as a poet, writer of short stories, and collaborator on journals and literary magazines such as *Mester* in the 1960s. A professor of Spanish at the Universidad de Puerto Rico–Mayaguez, he has aligned himself with an intellectually active group of academicians and writers associated also with the Aguadilla campus, and, in general, with the literary production of the west of the island.

In 1965, he published his first book of poems, *Minutero del tiempo*, in which he totally identifies with the poetry of protest and of struggle against oppression and injustice. He became one of the pioneering voices of the new Puerto Rican novel when, in 1971, he published *Veinte siglos después del homicidio*, a highly acclaimed but complicated text that evidences renovation, engagement, and assimilation of all the literary strategies of the famous **Latin American Boom**. The mystified and magically articulated island—Vieques—of the American military bases and presence served as poetic and suggestive emblem of all the complex political and social realities of the big island—Puerto Rico.

His premier collection of short stories, *Cinco cuentos negros*, came out in 1965 and could be considered the blueprint of his future writing and thematic obsessions: the patriotism and the struggle for national representation, the assertiveness of black ancestry and contemporary presence in the cultural and racial construct of the island, racism, injustice, and sexuality. He followed this collection with several novels, including *La casa y la llama fiera* (1982), *Este pueblo no es un manto de sonrisas* (1991), and *Vieques es más dulce que la sangre* (2000), texts in which the memory of Vieques and the presence of the U.S. Marines are always present. *La casa y la llama fiera* deals with Aldo, a successful man who lives in the suburbs and is proud of his great achievements: a huge and carefully organized library, a well-educated white wife, his children, and a solid standard of living. Aldo has distanced himself emotionally and socially from his remote past as a poor child from Vieques, however, the visit of his black nieces serve to articulate the confrontation between Aldo's present and the unavoidable past. The structure of the text moves back and forth from the present to the past, and in so doing allows the narrator to bring back the historical, economical, and cultural struggle of a small, poor island affirming its identity amid America's control. The novel also explores a theme often overlooked in Puerto Rican literature—racial prejudices and clashes. These traumatic experiences are conveyed through the presentation of many characters and through a narration that often shifts from the two geographical spaces—suburbia and Vieques—two economic classes—poor and middleclass—two races—black and white—and two historical periods—the past and the present.

Further Reading

Ramos Rosado, Marie. *La mujer negra en la literatura puertorriqueña: cuentística de los setenta: Luis Rafael Sánchez, Carmelo Rodríguez Torres, Rosario Ferré y Ana Lydia Vega.* San Juan: Editorial de la Universidad de Puerto Rico, 1999.

—*Asela R. Laguna*

Rogers, Joel Augustus (1883–1966)

■

Pioneer historian of African culture and the African diaspora who during an age of belief in white supremacy dedicated his life to disproving such a belief and to celebrating African contributions to the world, Rogers was a prolific writer who was one of the first black authors to achieve popularity with the common people and to see numerous reprints of his works. He was a self-taught scholar and researcher who published and distributed his own books.

J. A. Rogers was born on September 6, 1883, in Negril, Jamaica. In 1906, he migrated to the United States and, in 1917, became an American citizen. That same year, he published the novel *From "Superman" to Man*, described by author Darryl Pinckney, in *Out There: Mavericks of Black Culture* (2002), as "a bold and unexpected discussion novel in which a Pullman porter [questions] the superiority of the Anglo-Saxon and the inferiority of the Negro" (14). During the 1920s, Rogers toured the United States, reading from his novel. In 1931, he wrote *World's Greatest Men of African Descent*, and from 1935 to 1936 he worked for the *Pittsburgh Courier*, traveling to Ethiopia and becoming the first black war correspondent to write on Italy's invasion of that African nation. In 1936, he collected his articles and columns in the volume *The Real Facts About Ethiopia*.

In 1940, Rogers wrote *Your History from the Beginning of Time to the Present*. From 1941 to 1944, he wrote and published one of his most famous works, the three-volume study entitled *Sex and Race*, wherein he traces the development of Western Civilization to Africa and asserts that historical figures such as the poet Sappho (610–580 BC) were either black or of mixed heritage. Written during the rise of fascism and Adolf Hitler (1889–1945), Rogers used *Sex and Race* as a tool to combat theories of Aryan supremacy.

Joel Augustus Rogers, who used his literary theories to combat racism, traced the beginning of Western civilization to Africa. *Source: Schomberg Center for Research in Black Culture, The New York Public Library, Astor, Lenox, and Tilden Foundations.*

In 1959, Rogers wrote *Africa's Gift to America* and numerous articles for the *Pittsburgh Courier*. He passed away on March 26, 1966, in New York City.

Further Reading

Pinckney, Darryl. *Out There: Mavericks of Black Literature.* New York: BasicCivitas Books, 2002.

—*D. H. Figueredo*

Román, Sabrina (1956–)

Sabrina Román belongs to a generation of women writers from the Dominican Republic who voices their criticism of a male-driven society. She is a poet, a dramatist, and a diplomat as well.

Román was born in Santo Domingo on August 25, 1956. She attended elementary and secondary schools in Santo Domingo and enrolled at Colegio Santo

Domingo, graduating with a BA in philosophy and literature. In 1985, she earned a doctorate in philosophy, literature, and linguistics from the Universidad Católica Santo Domingo. She has served as consulate in Miami and in Boston. From 1990 to 1992, she was deputy director of the Dominican Republic's National Library. In the mid-1990s, she became an influential official in the presidency of **Joaquín Balaguer.**

While finishing her undergraduate studies, Román published the book of poetry *De un tiempo a otro tiempo* (1978). During the early 1980s, she concentrated on her studies, but in 1983 she published her second book of poetry, *Palabras rotas.* Since then, she has written several other collections as well as the play *Carrusel de mecedoras* (1989). In her works, Román challenges the machista notion that women have no intellectual capabilities. She often writes of the contrasts between the private self and public image a woman must present. She also writes extensively about the love she feels for the Dominican Republic and asks her compatriots to look beyond political parties and slogans for true national unity.

Further Reading

"Consul dominicana en Boston realiza visita a Lawrence." *El Mundo*, Sept. 29, 1993.

"Sabrina Román." *Escritores Dominicanos.* http://www.geocities.com/alcance66/r.html (accessed 9/26/05).

—*D. H. Figueredo*

Romane, Jean-Baptiste (1807–58)

Romane was a pioneer Haitian poet and playwright who wrote about the nation's heroes. One of the earliest writers to celebrate Haiti's natural beauty, he used his poetry to help foster a national identity.

Born in 1807, there is not much written about Romane's life. He began to write at an early age, and when he was eighteen years old, he wrote his most famous poem, "Hymne a l'independence" (1925). The poem claims that the world salutes Haiti and her children for their bravery. The poem also reaffirms that though Haiti rebelled against France, the two nations were not adversaries. Thus, at the end of each stanza, the poet shouts: "Vive Haïti! Vive La France!"

Romane wrote the poem to honor a French dignitary: the Baron de Mackau, a French naval officer who was visiting the nation on an anniversary of Haiti's revolution. It was performed for the visitor at a banquet. In gratitude, the French government honored the poet with a gold medal.

Romane also wrote drama. His play *La mort de Christophe*, about Henri Christophe (1767–1820), who ruled the newly independent nation from 1806 to 1820, pleased president Jean-Pierre Boyer (1776–1850), who rewarded Romane with financial favors.

Further Reading

Berrou, Raphaël, and Pradel Pompilus. *Histoire de la littérature haïtienne*. Tome 1. Port-au-Prince: Editions Caraëbes.

—D. H. Figueredo

Romanticismo/Romanticism

Though the romantic movement originated in Europe during the eighteenth century, it found a home in the Americas, where in the nineteenth century the vastness of the land and its exoticness matched and surpassed the imagination of the romantic writers. A good illustration is the poem "Oda al Niágara," by Cuban poet **José María Heredia**, with its dramatic descriptions of the rushing waters, the clamor of the falls, the rising mist, and the shadows of the caverns behind the cascade creating a majestic panorama that dwarfs any man-made creation.

The characteristics of the European romantic movement were (1) rebellion against classical literature from Greece; (2) rejection of the use of reason and logic (3) a sense of melancholy or pessimism; (4) unrestrained passion and exaggerated attention to personal sentiments; (5) a reflection of the self in nature; and (6) allusions to Christian themes—which had been neglected by writers who preferred the Greek classics. El romanticismo, the Spanish version of the romantic movement, demonstrated interest in the Spanish Middle Ages, in nationalism, and in "costumbres," or local customs. Among the European romantics who influenced the Spanish Caribbean writers were Victor Hugo (1802–85), Walter Scott (1771–1832), and William Wordsworth (1770–1850); the Americans included Edgar Allan Poe (1809–49) and William Cullen Bryant (1794–1878). The Caribbean writers adapted European romanticism to emphasize the natural beauty of the region and to celebrate local settings, customs, and traditions. Rather than look at a medieval past for inspiration, these writers turned to the tragic fate of the Amerindians during the conquest and to the evils of slavery.

Representatives writers are the aforementioned Heredia, **Gertrude Gómez de Avellaneda** and **Cirilo Villaverde**, from Cuba; **Manuel de Jesús Galván** and **Federico García Godoy**, from the Dominican Republic; and **Alejandro Tapia y Rivera** and **Eugenio María de Hostos**, from Puerto Rico. Gómez de Avellaneda was a prolific poet, dramatist, and novelist; her romantic poem "Al partir" celebrated Cuba's natural beauty and her pain at leaving the island for Spain, whereas her novel *Sab* (1841) denounced slavery; Villaverde wrote the classic *Cecilia Valdés*, described both as a costumbrista and romantic novel. Galván wrote *Enriquillo* (1879), a combination of romantic, historic, and costumbrista work that takes place during the colonization of the Dominican Republic and García Godoy wrote a trilogy— *Rufinito* (1908), *Alma dominical* (1912), and *Guanuma* (1914)—about his country's struggles against Spain and Haiti. Tapia y Rivera, considered to be the father of Puerto Rican literature, wrote *La palma del cacique* (1852), *La leyenda de los veinte años* (1874), and *Cofresí* (1876), about Puerto Rico's early inhabitants.

Hostos was the author of *La peregrinación de Bayoán* (1863), a symbolic tale about a search for a national identity and the dream of creating one federation consisting of Cuba, the Dominican Republic, and Puerto Rico.

In the anglophone Caribbean, romanticism served as a viewing glass through which the visitor and the native could admire the tropics; a good example are the poems of the nineteenth-century Guyanese poet **Egbert Martin "Leo"** and **Tom Redcam**, from Jamaica. In Haiti, **Ignance Nau**, known for writing lovelorn poems, longing for his dead wife, and **Oswald Durand**, often called the "Victor Hugo of Haiti," celebrated Haitian landscapes, using imagery representative of the island—such as palm trees and coconuts—rather than European allusions—such as pine trees and apples.

Romanticismo spawned **costumbrismo**, writings about local traditions, and **Modernismo**, which was in fact a reaction against the romantic movement. During the twentieth century, romantic tendencies yielded to **social realism, surrealism**, and socially engaged literature. *See also* Abolitionist Literature; Historical Novel; Literatura Comprometida; Realismo/Realism.

Further Reading

Argullol, Rafael. *El héroe y el único: el espíritu trágico del romanticismo*. Madrid: Taurus, 1999.

Foster, David William, and Daniel Altamiranda, eds. *From Romanticism to Modernismo in Latin America*. New York: Garland, 1997.

Garrido Pallardó, Fernando. *Los orígenes del romanticismo*. Barcelona: Editorial Labor, 1968.

Zea, Leopoldo. *Dos etapas del pensamiento en Hispanoamérica. Del romanticismo al positivismo*. México: Colegio de México, 1949.

—*D. H. Figueredo*

Roqué de Duprey, Ana (1853–1933)

Puerto Rican teacher and feminist who was one of the island's first women journalists and editors, Ana Roqué advocated for universal suffrage while mentoring young writers and musicians. In her writings, she depicted marriage as a hypocritical institution that imprisoned wives while allowing husbands to indulge in multiple relationships. She was the first woman to found and direct a journal for women, *La Mujer* (1898).

Ana Roqué was born in Aguadilla, Puerto Rico, on April 18, 1853. Orphaned at the age of four, her father and her grandmother, who was a retired teacher, raised her and homeschooled her. Roqué married when she was nineteen years old. In her home, she and her husband hosted **tertulias**, literary salons, that attracted such important literary figures as **Alejandro Tapia y Rivera**. When she was in her mid-twenties she passed a teaching exam and became a teacher. In 1887, she was the first woman in Puerto Rico to earn a bachelor's degree. She taught at several public and private schools for more than twenty years, always promoting the need for equal education for men and women.

Roqué founded several newspapers and journals, including *La Evolución* (1902), *La Mujer del Siglo XX* (1917), *Álbum Puertorriqueño* (1918), and *Heraldo de la Mujer* (1920). Aware that at the time there were many Puerto Ricans who were illiterate, Roqué chose for her publications articles that were accessible, since her objective was to promote the reading aloud of the pieces at literary and family gatherings. Roqué also founded numerous women's organizations: La Liga Femínea Puertorriqueña in 1917, La Asociación Puertorriqueña de Mujeres Sufragistas in 1924, and La Asociación Puertorriqueña de Mujeres Votantes in 1929. She was the first woman member of the prestigious **Ateneo Puertorriqueño** and the first to join the public library.

Roqué wrote educational texts, including *Elementos de geografía universal* (1884), and *Explicaciones pedagógicas* (1894). Her two novels, *Sara la obrera* (1895) and *Luz y sombra* (1903), explore marriage and adultery. In the first novel, Sara is seduced by her best friend's husband, and while there are no consequences for the seducer, Sara is shunned by society. In the second novel, the heroine, neglected by her husband, is attracted to a former beau, however, to keep her place in society, she restrains her passion. In both novels, however, it is the men who pursue the women while the women must assume the passive role.

Roqué died at the age of eighty. While scholarly attention has focused on Roqué's feminist activism and work in education, Roqué, the writer, still beckons study.

Further Reading

"Ana Roqué de Duprey." http://www.duprey.cps.k12.il.us/Biography.htm (accessed 9/12/05).

Chen Sham, Jorge. "Sanción Moral y Castigo: Contradicciones Ideológicas en Narrativa de Ana Roqué." In *La voz de la mujer en la literatura hispanoamericana fin-de-siglo*, compiled by Luis Jiménez, 167–80. San José, Costa Rica: Editorial de la Universidad de Costa Rica, 1999.

—*D. H. Figueredo*

"Rosa Blanca, La" (1891)

"The White Rose" is the one poem loved by all Cubans, on the island and in exile. Written by patriot and poet **José Martí**, it appeared in his collection *Versos sencillos* (1891), simple verses; the poem exemplifies the simplicity promised in the volume's title. It is this simplicity—of structure, of phrasing, and of rhyme—that makes the poem so accessible and easy to memorize.

The message of the poem is simple: love thy enemy. This might be seen as a trite statement, but it must be considered that it was written at a time when the poet was organizing Cuba's war of independence from Spain; written by a man whose enemy—the Spanish government—had imprisoned him at the age of fifteen, had banished him from his country, and had separated him from his family and beloved son. The simplicity of the message also reaffirms that in tumultuous times and in moments of uncertainty, it is the commonplace, even the banal, that assures the continuity of life. The poem is about life: a rose that is blooming. It's about friendship: a rose to give to a friend. And it's about not returning hatred with hatred, pain with pain: to my enemy, I give a rose.

The collection *Versos sencillos* was the last book by Martí published during his lifetime. Four years later, the poet was killed in action in Cuba during a skirmish between Cuban rebels and Spanish soldiers. In the years before his death, Martí carried the volume with him, reading the verses to friends and presenting them the book as gift.

La Rosa Blanca was chosen for the title of a film version of the poet's life, produced in Cuba and Mexico in 1954. It's interesting to know that Martí did not title the poem; similar to a Shakespearean sonnet, the poem only bears a number: verse 39. However, over the years, the reading public assigned the title "La Rosa Blanca" to the poem.

> Cultivo una rosa blanca,
> En julio como en enero,
> Para el amigo sincero
> Que me da su mano franca.
> Y para el cruel que me arranca
> El corazón con que vivo,
> Cardo ni ortiga cultivo:
> Cultivo la rosa blanca.
>
> (I plant a white rose
> In July and in January
> For the sincere friend
> Whose hand I take.
> But for the cruel foe who uproots
> The heart that breeds me life
> Neither thistles nor thorn I plant:
> I plant a white rose.)

Further Reading

Mañach, Jorge. *Martí, el apóstol*. Habana: Organización Continental de los Festivales Del Libro, 1960.

Martí, José. *Versos sencillo: edición del centenario*. Camagüey, Cuba: Ediciones Acana, 1991.

—*D. H. Figueredo*

Rosa Nieves, Cesáreo (1901–74)

A playwright and poet from Puerto Rico, Rosa Nieves was one of the first writers on the island to explore the subject of homosexuality with the drama *La otra* (1948). A scholar and educator, his literary essays were inspired by his love for the island. He was a musician as well.

A native of San Juan, Rosa Nieves attended elementary and secondary schools in the town of Cayey where he demonstrated an early talent for music. After a short stay in New York City, he returned to San Juan, where he published his first book of poetry, *Veredas olvidadas*, in 1922. To support himself while studying for a teaching degree at the Universidad de Puerto Rico, he played the clarinet at a movie house—to accompany silent films—and was director of the ROTC band. In 1927, he earned his teacher's certificate. Writing poetry, which he contributed to numerous journals and newspapers, including *El Imparcial* and *Puerto Rico Ilustrado*, he befriended such would-be poets as **Vicente Geigel Polanco**, and was one of the founders of the literary movement, **noísmo**, which rejected frivolous literature.

In the early 1930s, he continued writing poetry but also ventured into theater, writing children's plays, including *Juan Bobo infantil* (1932). He also attended graduate school, obtaining in 1936 an MA in arts from his alma mater. That same year, **Antonio S. Pedreira** appointed him to the newly created Department of Hispanic Studies at the Universidad de Puerto Rico.

During the 1940s, Rosa Nieves continued his involvement with theater, writing historic dramas—*El huésped del mar* (1945), *Flor de Areyto* (1945), and *Román Baldorioty de Castro* (1947)—plays set in the countryside—*Nuestra enemiga la piedra* (1948) and *Campesina en el palacio* (1949)—and psychological studies—*La otra* (1948), the first work in Puerto Rico to approach the theme of homosexuality. In the same decade, he finished his doctoral studies at the Universidad Autónoma de México.

His academic responsibilities prompted him to write several scholarly works, including the literary study *La poesía en Puerto Rico. Estudio histórico-crítico del verso puertorriqueño* (1943), the biography *Francisco de Ayerra y Santamaría, poeta puertorriqueño* (1948), and *Guía para la lectura de Ramón del Valle Inclán* (1951). Yet the academic output did not curtail his productivity either as a poet or as a playwright: during this period he published three poetry collections and several staged but unpublished plays. He also edited the anthology *Aguinaldo lírico de la poesía puertorriqueña* (1957).

His love of Puerto Rican culture is evident in the mammoth work *Historia panorámica de la literatura puertorriqueña* (1963), consisting of two volumes, *Plumas estelares de las letras de Puerto Rico* (1967), and *Biografías puertorriqueñas: Perfil histórico de un pueblo* (1971). In the 1960s, he wrote a novel, *Mañana será la esperanza* (1965), and attempted poetry in the poesita **Negrista** genre, Afro-Caribbean poetry: *Diapasón negro*. To the very end of his life, he was involved in teaching and in conferences and was active in organizations such as the Academia de la Historia Puertorriqueña, Instituto Internacional de Letras, Ciencias y Artes de Italia, and the Academia de Artes y Ciencias de Puerto Rico.

Further Reading

Figueroa de Cifredo, Patria. *Apuntes biográficos en torno a la vida y obra de Cesáreo Rosa Nieves*. San Juan: Editorial Cordillera, 1965.

—*D. H. Figueredo*

Roumain, Jacques (1907–44)

One of the best writers of the French language, novelist and poet Jacques Roumain was born in Port-au-Prince, Haiti, on June 4, 1907, the son of Auguste Roumain, a wealthy landowner, and his wife, Émilie Auguste, whose father had been president of the republic from 1912 to 1913. As was usual at the time for sons of the Haitian mulatto aristocracy, Roumain was sent to boarding school abroad. He completed his secondary education in Bern, Switzerland, and later studied at the Zurich Polytechnic Institute.

Roumain returned to Haiti in 1927 and immediately became active in the resistance against the American occupation of his country, which had begun in 1915 and was not to end until 1934. He was one of the founders of *Le Petit Impartial*, probably the most virulent of the opposition newspapers, in which he published numerous articles on political and social questions. His impassioned denunciations of the occupiers, and especially of their collaborators, President Louis Borno (1865–1942) and the members of his administration, landed him in prison on several occasions. While imprisoned he contracted malaria and suffered from the disease until his death.

Roumain became influenced by Marxist ideology and founded the Haitian Communist Party in 1934. His political convictions and continuing subversive activities led to his expulsion from the country on the order of President Sténio Vincent (1874–1959). Roumain and his family found refuge in Belgium and later in France. He sent his wife and children back to Haiti just before the outbreak of World War II in 1939, but he himself was still barred from returning. He reached Martinique, then New York, and then Havana and was finally allowed to rejoin his family in 1941, once Élie Lescot (1883–1974) had replaced Sténio Vincent as president.

During his exile, Roumain had become fascinated with anthropology, which he studied in Paris and later at Columbia University. When he returned to Haiti, he founded the Bureau d'ethnologie, whose mission was to collect, study, and preserve Haitian folk culture, which until then had been ignored and despised by the country's westernized elite. He authored monographs on Vodùn, botany, and Arawak archaeology. But Roumain was soon obliged to leave his family and his country once more, when in 1942 President Lescot named him chargé d'affaires to Mexico. While pursuing his diplomatic duties he became gravely ill, returned home, and died a few days later on August 18, 1944, at the age of thirty-seven.

Today, Roumain is remembered as one of the leaders of the resistance to the occupation, as an eloquent spokesman for the exploited Haitian poor, and as one of the first to recognize the value of their culture, but, above all, as an outstanding poet and novelist and as the first Haitian author to have attained worldwide recognition.

When he returned from Switzerland, Roumain cofounded two influential literary reviews: *La Trouée* and *La Revue indigène*, in which he published poems as well as translations from the German and the Spanish. His first poetic efforts were influenced by the languorous and sentimental aesthetics of contemporary French poets, but he soon abandoned decadent elegance in favor of racially and politically committed verse. His most famous long poem, *Bois-d'ébène*, published the year following his death, begins with a lament for the sufferings of Africa and her sons everywhere and ends with an appeal for revolutionary solidarity between all the downtrodden of the world.

In the 1930s, Roumain authored a collection of short stories and two novels. The short stories in *La Proie et l'ombre* and the novel *Les Fantoches* are bitter satirical denunciations of the Haitian upper classes into which Roumain was born and against which he rebelled. Their members are depicted either as cynical sensualists or as aimless powerless youth who seek escape in drink and the company of prostitutes. With *La Montagne ensorcelée* (1931), Roumain initiated a new genre: the Haitian **peasant novel**, which deals with the country's rural forgotten, the silent majority, a subject matter ignored up to that point by Haitian novelists who had focused exclusively on the urban upper and middle classes. The seminal *La Montagne ensorcelée*, and especially in his posthumous masterpiece *Gouverneurs de la rosée*, translated into seventeen languages after its publication in Port-au-Prince in 1944, Roumain created for his peasant protagonists an original language, made up of an amalgam of French, archaic and regional French, and Haitian **Creole**. Thus, while respecting their linguistic means of expression, Roumain enabled his characters to communicate with all readers of French. His linguistic creation, as well as his ideological writings, has been the subject of much analysis and commentary by scholars from all over the world. *See also* American Occupation of Haiti, Literature of (1915–34); Haitian Literature, History of; Négritude.

Further Reading

Dorsinville, Roger. *Jacques Roumain*. Paris: Présence Africaine, 1981.

Roumain, Jacques. *Works: Ouevres completes. édition critique*, edited by Léon-François Hoffmann. Paris: Allca XX, 2003.

Thadal, Roland. *Jacques Roumain: l'unité d'une oeuvre*. Port-au-Prince, Haïti: Editions des Antilles, 1997.

—*Léon-François Hoffmann*

Roumer, Émile (1903–88)

Haitian poet Roumer was a member of the seminal group of writers who founded the journal *Revue indigène* in 1927. His poetry celebrated Haiti and its African roots, though at times he expressed universal concerns beyond his patriotism. His poem "Marabout de mon coeur" (1947), in which he compared a woman's beauty to Haiti's flora, is one of the most popular in the nation.

Émile Roumer was born into an affluent family on February 5, 1903, in Jérémie, Haiti. He was sent to England and France to study, and it was in the latter country that his writing career began. Dared by Parisian friends to submit his poetry to the prestigious journal *Les Annales*, he did, and the poems were accepted for publication. At the age of twenty-two, he gathered some of these poems into his first volume, *Poémes d'Haiti et de France*. The poems revealed the style he would use throughout his life: the fourteen-line stanza, sensuous imagery, and the subject of Haiti and Haitians, with emphasis on the nation's African heritage.

In 1927, he returned to Haiti and soon joined the group that had founded *La Revue indigène* as a response to the growing American presence and influence and an affirmation of Haitian culture. He befriended such major figures as **Jacques Roumain** and the **Marcelin** brothers and became the journal's director. He also wrote for several other reviews, including *Les Griots* and *Haïti Journal*. In 1948, the periodical *Haïti Journal* published a special edition dedicated to his writings: *Poémes en vers, octaves, contrerimes, coples*. Through the 1940s and 1950s, his essays and poems were published in numerous journals and anthologies in Haiti.

Early in the 1960s, he became interested in the use Kreyòl for poetry, writing two volumes in that language, *Le Caïman étoilé* and *Rosaire, Couronne de sonnets*, both in 1963. Despite his growing popularity in Haiti, where at least one of his poems—"Marabout de mon coeur"—was set to music, he could be shy or sarcastic about his labor as a poet. When invited by the Library of Congress to record his poetry, he turned down the invitation, stating that he didn't have anything to offer. *See also* America Occupation of Haiti, Literature of (1915–34); Haitian Literature in Kreyòl (the Haitian Language).

Further Reading

Garret, Naomi M. *The Renaissance of Haitian Poetry*. Paris: Présence africaine. 1963.

Saint-Louis, Carlos. *Panorama de la poésie haïtienne*. Port-au-Prince: H. Deschamps, 1950.

—*D. H. Figueredo*

Rueda, Manuel (1921–99)

One of the best-known cultural innovators from the Dominica Republic, Manuel Rueda was the founder of the literary movement **pluralismo**. He was a musician, poet, dramatist, and critic. His extensive music training influenced his poetry.

Manuel Rueda was born in Monte Cristi, Dominican Republic, on August 27, 1921. He studied music at the Liceo Musical and during the 1940s spent fifteen years in Chile studying music, achieving recognition as a concert pianist and befriending such important literary figures as Pablo Neruda (1904–73) and Vicente Huidobro (1893–1948). In 1951, he returned to the Dominican Republic, where he became a member of the literary group **La Poesía Sorprendida**. He was appointed music professor at the Conservatorio Nacional de Santo Domingo and was also director of the research institute of folklore at the Universidad Nacional **Pedro Henríquez Ureña**. In 1957, he received the National Prize for Literature for the play *La trinitaria blanca*—he was to receive this award on five more occasions; the drama helped to reinvigorate drama in the Dominican Republic. While writing poetry, he also toured the Caribbean as a pianist, performing with several national symphonic orchestras from Cuba, the Dominican Republic, and Puerto Rico.

In 1974, Rueda, influenced by the innovations promoted by the Poesía Sorprendida movement and concerned that literature in the Dominican Republic was becoming too banal and routine, founded the movement pluralismo, which advocated the use of a diversity of space and medium to express an idea, combining elements of performance poetry with the plastic arts and music. The poem that best expressed this literary movement was "Con el tambor de las islas" (1975), which is also his most famous poem. In 1979, he wrote the drama *El rey Clinejas* (1979) and in 1985 the collection of short stories *Papeles de Sara y otros relatos*. In 1995, his historical drama *Relato de la pasión y muerte de Juana Loca*, about the daughter of Queen Isabela (1451–1504) of Spain and her obsession with her dead husband earned him the prestigious Tirso de Molina literary award, issued in Spain. In his 1998 novel, *Las metamórfosis de Makandal*, he essayed on the possible union of the Dominican Republic with Haiti, a notion that provoked criticism from nationalists on both sides of the islands. The other themes that Rueda explored include sexual liberation, artistic freedom, and the need to develop a national literary identity in the Dominican Republic.

Further Reading

Piña Contrera, Guillermo. *Doce en la literatura dominicana*. Santiago de los Caballeros, Republica Dominicana: Universidad Católica Madre y Maestra, 1982.

Veloz Maggiolo, Marcio. *Cultura, teatro y relatos in Santo Domingo*. Santiago de los Caballeros, República Dominicana: Universidad Católica Madre y Maestra, 1972.

—*D. H. Figueredo*

Ruíz Belvis, Segundo (1819–67)

An abolitionist from Puerto Rico, Ruíz Belvis was the author of a manifesto, written in 1867, demanding the end of slavery. The rhetoric, logic of presentation, and carefully chosen vocabulary made his manifesto a brilliant example of the literature of persuasion.

Ruíz Belvis was born in Hacienda Luisa, Puerto Rico, on May 13, 1819, into a closely knit family that encouraged him to obtain a college education. After attending primary schools in his hometown, his father sent him to high school in Caracas, Venezuela. In that South American city, Ruíz Belvis was exposed to the liberal ideas of liberator Simón Bolívar (1783–1830) and began to favor the abolition of slavery. After graduation, sometime in the late 1830s, he visited his parents in Puerto Rico before going on to Spain. At the Universidad de Madrid he earned a law degree and remained in Spain for a few years where he associated with compatriots and writers.

In 1860, he returned to Puerto Rico. In Mayagüez, he founded, with **Ramón Emeterio Betances,** a secret society to end slavery. In 1867, he and other patriots formed a committee that traveled to Spain to plead for the abolition of slavery. Ruíz Belviz wrote, with other colleagues, an antislavery manifesto—*Proyecto para la abolición de la esclavitud en Puerto Rico*—where he eloquently, and with clarity, demonstrated the ill effects of slavery on economics, society, and the family structure. The document, its controlled but fiery rhetoric and the sincere expression of the author's sentiments, equaled similar documents written by the likes of **José Antonio Saco,** from Cuba, and the volume *Free Mulatto* (1824) by Trinidadian **Jean Baptiste Philippe** during the nineteenth century.

When the Spanish authorities ignored his request, Ruíz Belvis returned heartbroken to Puerto Rico. A few months later, the Spanish government banished Ruíz Belvis, along with Betances, from his beloved island. The two friends traveled to the Dominican Republic and New York. Invited by the Chilean government to seek shelter in that nation, Ruíz Belvis went to Valparaíso, where he died mysteriously on November 3, 1867.

Further Reading

Cancel, Mario R. *Segundo Ruíz Belvis: el procer y el ser humano (una aproximación crítica a su vida).* Bayamón: Editorial Universidad de América; San Juan: Centro de Estudios Avanzados de Puerto Rico y el Caribe; Hormigueros: Municipio de Hormigueros, 1994.

Ruíz Belvis, Segundo. *Informe sobre la abolición inmediata de la esclavitud en la Isla de Puerto-Rico.* Madrid: Establecimiento Tipográfico de R. Vicente, 1870.

—*D. H. Figueredo*

Rupaire, Sonny (1940–91)

Rupaire was a poet and revolutionary from Guadeloupe. A promoter of the use of Creole, a language spoken in the francophone Caribbean—in Haiti it is also called Kreyòl—Rupaire also used the Creole version of his name, Soni Ripè.

Sonny Rupaire was born on November 7, 1940, in Capesterre-Belle-Eau, Guadeloupe. The loss of his mother at an early age prompted him to find solace in reading and in writing poetry. In 1953, he attended secondary school at the Lycée Carnot de Pointe-à-Pitre, and in 1959 he studied pedagogy at the l'École Normale in Pointe-à-Pitre. In college, he joined a group of writers called the Jeux Floraux. They read each other's works and encouraged him to pursue his poetic calling.

In 1961, Algeria's revolution attracted him. He left Guadeloupe, refused to serve in the French draft, and made his way across Morocco. In Algeria, he joined the Army of National Liberation. When the war ended in 1962, Rupaire remained in the newly independent Algeria, where he taught at the school Lycée de Douera. While involved in political activities and in teaching, he continued to write poetry.

In 1967, after months of social unrest in Guadeloupe, French forces massacred eighty laborers who were on strike. Rupaire made two decisions: from then on he would write only in Creole, denouncing French as the language of the oppressors, and he would return home. Passing through Cuba, Rupaire arrived in Guadeloupe in 1969 using the name of Comrade Max. In 1971, he was one of the founders of the first labor union for farmers on the island. He also published his first collection of poems, many of them written in Algeria: *Cette igname brisée qu'est ma terre natale, ou Gran parade ti cou-baton*. Well received by his compatriots and critics in the francophone Caribbean, the volume would be published twice.

Throughout the 1970s, Rupaire participated in the establishment of several unions and edited the newspaper *Lendépandans*. His productivity in Creole augmented, and he was soon regarded as one of the fathers of Creole literature in Guadeloupe. By the time of his death on February 25, 1991, he was considered, alongside **Saint-John Perse**, as one of the seminal creators of a national literature.

Further Reading

Toumson, Roger. *La transgression des couleurs*. Paris: Éditions Caribéennes, 1989.

—D. H. Figueredo

S

Saco y López-Cisneros, José Antonio
(1797–1879)

José Antonio Saco was a Cuban economist, historian, and political writer who wrote one of the first histories of slavery in Latin America, *Historia de la esclavitud de la raza negra africana en el Nuevo Mundo y en especial en los países américo-hispanos*. He also wrote one of the first sociological studies in the Caribbean, *Memoria sobre la vagancia* (1830), and studied the cultural differences between the Spanish and anglophone Caribbean.

Born on May 7, 1797, Saco studied at the San Carlos seminary under the abolitionist Father **Félix Varela**. A promoter of Cuban identity, as separate from a Spanish identity, Saco opposed annexation with the United States—which was being offered in the 1830s by white Creoles as means to a rupture with Spanish rule—claiming that such a union would destroy Cuban culture. A friend of **Domingo Del Monte** and a regular attendee at Del Monte's **tertulias**, literary salons, he believed African slaves should be freed and returned to Africa. Today, there are scholars who see José Antonio Saco as the typical nineteenth-century white Caribbean intellectual who considered blacks inferior and favored separation of the white and black races. However, scholar **William Luis** suggests that for his time, Saco was quite revolutionary in opposing the sugarocracy (rule by sugar barons) and in recommending importing white free-wage laborers to Cuba, ending the slave trade and eventually establishing a black free-labor force. *See also* Abolitionist Literature; Cuban Literature, History of.

Further Reading

Luis, William. *Literary Bondage: Slavery in Cuban Narrative*. Austin: University of Texas Press, 1990.

Opartrny, Josef. "Jose Antonio Saco's Path Toward the Idea of Cubanidad." *Cuban Studies* 23 (1994): 36–56.

—*William Luis and D. H. Figueredo*

Sáez Burgos, Juan (1943–)

A member of the *Guajana* generation, young Puerto Rican poets who espoused Marxist ideals and wrote political poetry in the journal *Guajana*, Sáez Burgos is a writer and an attorney.

A native of Río Piedras, Sáez studied at the Universidad de Puerto Rico where in 1962 he cofounded, with **Andrés Castro Ríos**, the journal *Guajana*. The poems he published in the journal expressed a commitment to the struggle of the common people against capitalism. In the 1960s, he traveled to Spain, where he earned a law degree from the Universidad de Granada in 1969. That same year, he received a literary prize from the **Ateneo Puertorriqueño**.

In 1969, he published *Un hombre para el llanto*. In 1976, he published *Selección de poemas*. Overall, Sáez Burgos's poetry suggests that the only way to affirm a Puerto Rican identity and to reject American influence on the island is to laugh at Puerto Rican politics and social circumstances. Critic Efraín Barradas observes, in *Para entendernos: Inventario poético puertorriqueño* (1992), that "Sáez Burgos lampoons everything, including his own poetry . . . this way, the lampooning turns into . . . salvation" (407).

Further Reading

Barradas, Efraín. *Para entendernos: Inventario poético puertorriqueño*. San Juan, Puerto Rico: Instituto Cultura Puertorriquena, 1992.

González, José Emilio. "La poesía en Puerto Rico." In *La gran enciclopedia de Puerto Rico*, vol. 3, edited by Vicente Báez, 337–40. San Juan: Puerto Rico en la Mano and Gran Enciclopedia de Puerto Rico, 1981.

—*D. H. Figueredo*

Saint-Aude, Clément-Magloire (1912–71)

Saint-Aude was a surrealist poet from Haiti. His major work, *Dialogue de mes lamps* (1941), was a pessimistic view of Haitian society in particular and the world at large in general.

Born as Clement-Magloire fils on April 2, 1912, in Port-au-Prince, Saint-Aude was the son of a journalist who introduced him to literature at an early age. Saint-Aude pursued his secondary education at the Institution Saint-Louis de Gonzaque. He began to write poetry as an adolescent and published his *Dialogue* at the age of twenty-nine. This book of poetry, which has been reprinted several times, presents the musings of a disillusioned intellect. Observes Naomi Garret in *The Renaissance of Haitian Poetry* (1963): "The poet's dreams, as luminous as lamps, are contrasted with the base, vile dreams of others, dreams which appear to him as dark as his are bright" (189–90). The work is representative of the author's style. The language is elusive, filled with evasive allusions that make the text difficult for the casual reader.

In 1949, the poet wrote *Parias*, followed by a work of fiction in 1956, *Veillee*. Saint-Aude wrote for several journals, including *Le Nouvelliste* and *Haïti-Journal*. He worked for the Service d'Information et de Documentation.

Further Reading

Garret, Naomi M. *The Renaissance of Haitian Poetry*. Paris: Présence africaine, 1963.

—*D. H. Figueredo*

St. Omer, Garth (1931–)

Garth St. Omer is a novelist from St. Lucia known for writing existentialist stories about characters who lament the postcolonial conditions of their countries but who are unable to take any type of action that could improve the emerging society.

St. Omer was born on January 15, 1931, in Castries, St. Lucia. After attending the University of the West Indies, Mona, Kingston, where he received a BA in French, he taught in France and in Ghana. From 1969 to 1975 he pursued graduate studies at Columbia University and Princeton University. In the mid-1970s, he moved to California, where he is a professor of English literature and creative writing at the University of California–Santa Barbara. Before and during his university studies, St. Omer wrote the novella *Syrop* (1964), the novels *A Room on the Hill*, *Shades of Grey* (consisting of two novellas, *The Lights on the Hill* and *Another Place Another Time*), both published in 1968, *Nor Any Country* (1969), and *J—, Black Bam and the Masqueraders* (1972).

St. Omer writes in a confessional mode, describing in great detail how his characters view their surroundings and their political and philosophical musings. So much emphasis on themselves, though, makes St. Omer's heroes observers rather than participants, self-centered rather than socially committed. His prototype is John Lestrade, the protagonist of *A Room on the Hill*, the product of a dysfunctional family, an emotionally paralyzed man who is unable to develop and maintain relationships, even to the point of not helping a friend who is drowning. But with such paralysis comes a sense of guilt and fatalism. Fatalism also dominates the heart-wrenching novella *Syrop*, wherein a young man prays for a sailor to drop a coin from a ship so that he could dive and fetch the coin: the sailor drops the coin at the very moment that the ship's propellers start up, decapitating the young boy.

St. Omer's writings depict a malaise, a lament that years of colonialism in the Caribbean have fostered only poverty, self-neglect, and dependence on the outside world—in this case, tourism. A quiet man, St. Omer seldom grants interviews and prefers not to talk about his writings. *See also* Postcolonialism.

Further Reading

Bush, Roland E. "Garth St. Omer (1931–)" *Fifty Caribbean Writers: A Bio-Bibliographical-Critical Sourcebook*, edited by Daryl Cumber Dance. Westport, CT: Greenwood Press, 1986.

—D. H. Figueredo

Saint-Remy, Joseph (1819–58)

Saint-Remy was a Haitian historian and chronicler. Through his writings, he promoted a national identity. While admiring French culture and literature, Saint-Remy still encouraged Haitians not to be imitators but their own creators.

A native of Guadeloupe, Saint-Remy, arrived in Haiti as a child. He studied law in France and was involved in the antislavery movement in that country. His early poems appeared in Parisian literary reviews. When he was in his mid-thirties, he decided to write a biography of Haitian liberator Henri Christophe (1767–1820). Publishing *Christophe* in 1850, he depicted the liberator as a tyrant and criticized both the French and Haitian forces for the bloodshed during the revolution. He also published a biography of Toussaint-Louverture—*Vie de Toussaint-Louverture* (1850)—and helped to edit the general's memoirs in 1853. The research he had conducted for these biographies helped him write a five-volume history of Haiti, *Pétion et Haïti: étude monographique et historique*, published from 1854 to 1857.

Though Saint-Remy was not always a sympathetic historian, he still rallied his readers to promote a Haitian identity and to reject European racism. He encouraged the development of national literature and the use of local vernacular rather than French.

Further Reading

Bellegard-Smith, Patrick. *Haiti: The Breached Citadel*. Boulder, San Francisco, London: Westview Press, 1990.

Herdeck, Donald E. *Caribbean Writers: A Bio-Bibliographical-Critical Encyclopedia*. Washington, DC: Three Continents, 1979.

—D. H. Figueredo

Saldaña, Excilia (1946–99)

Excilia Saldaña was a Cuban poet, translator, educator, and editor of children's literature. She lived mainly in Havana and traveled throughout Europe and the Americas.

Saldaña received the **Nicolás Guillén** Distinguished Poet Award Prize given by the UNEAC—**Unión Nacional de Escritores y Artistas de Cuba**— (Cuban National Union of Writers and Artists) in 1998, as well as several awards for her children's writing: Ismaelillo Prize (1979), **La Rosa Blanca** Prize (1984, 1987) and La Edad de Oro Prize (1984). Her major literary works include several books for children, a collection of refrains, and three major autobiographical poems. These extensive poems show Saldaña's repeated attempts to draw her personal and poetic portrait, always in dialogue with the rich Hispanic literary tradition dating back to Sor Juana Inés de la Cruz (1648–95), San Juan de la Cruz (1542–91), and Quevedo (1580–1640) to the more recent voices of **José Martí**, Federico García Lorca (1898–1936), Vicente Huidobro (1893–1948), Gabriela Mistral (1889–1957), and others. In her effort to inscribe her own name at the center of Cuban letters, Saldaña also alludes to the prophetic voices of Pablo Neruda, (1904–1973), Walt Whitman (1819–92) and William Shakespeare (1564–1616)

Most central in the definition of her poetic voice, however, stands the poetic mastery of Nicolás Guillén, who established for Cuban letters the integration of both Hispanic and African traditions in the poetic idiom. Like Guillén, Saldaña plays with the traditional meter and rhyme of Hispanic poetry in conjunction with the rich narrative treasure and strategies found in Yoruba culture, as transmitted by Cuban blacks in legends called patakines in her book—*Kele, Kele* (1987). Saldaña's mastery at appropriating and integrating universal poetic traditions as a black woman of the Caribbean also appears in her collection of aphorisms *El refranero de la Víbora* (1989), a collection of refrains from La Víbora, a neighborhood in Havana, and in her "Cartas Eróticas," found in the volume *In the Vortex of the Cyclone* (2002). From her lullabies to her autobiographical poems, Excilia Saldaña places the figure of her grandmother, Ana Excilia Bregante, at the center of her poetic inspiration. Particularly in "La Noche" (1989) and "Mi Nombre" (1991), the grandmother reaches mythical dimensions to represent the experience of black women in the African diaspora as keepers of memory and as nurturers of both white and black children in the Caribbean context. Behind the figure of the grandmother looms large that of Mariana Grajales (1815–93), mother of Cuban independence general Antonio Maceo (1845–96), as well as unacknowledged black women in Cuba's history. Ultimately, in Saldaña's poetry, the personal is closely tied to the historical.

Several of her children's books have been adopted as teaching material by the Ministry of Education in Cuba. *Kele, Kele*, "Monólogo de la Esposa" (1985), and "La Noche" have been adapted for the theater in Cuba and Sweden. Her poetry, thus far available through Cuban publications and scattered translations, is now available in the bilingual anthology *In the Vortex of the Cyclone*. The collection includes a prologue by **Nancy Morejón**, a critical introduction by Flora González Mandri, and an epilogue by **Cintio Vitier**. *See also* Grandparents in Caribbean Literature.

Further Reading

Saldaña, Excilia. *In the Vortex of the Cyclone: Selected Poems by Excilia Saldaña*, Edited and translated by Flora González Mandri and Rosamond Rosenmeier. Gainesville: University Press of Florida, 2002.

———. *Jícara de miel*. Habana: Gente Nueva, 2000.

———. *Kele, Kele*. Habana: Letras Cubanas, 1987.

———. "Monólogo de la esposa." *Casa de las Américas* 26, no. 152 (1985): 86–100.

—Flora González Mandri

Salkey, Andrew (1928–95)

Andrew Salkey was a Jamaican novelist, poet, writer of children's books, editor, and anthologist. While working for BBC radio for over twenty years, he promoted Jamaican culture and literature.

Felix Andrew Alexander Salkey was born on January 28, 1928, in Colón, Panama, of Jamaican parents. When he was two years old, his parents sent him to Jamaica, where he was raised by his grandmother. From his grandmother he heard many **Anancy stories,** the mythical African spider trickster, that would serve as the basis for his some of children's writings years later. Since his father was a successful businessman in Panama who sent Salkey and his grandmother a monthly check, Salkey was able to afford St. George's College and Munro College, two of the island's most prestigious schools. In 1952, Salkey went to England to attend the University of London, earning a BA and an MA in English literature. He did not return to Jamaica, remaining in London, where he worked for BBC from 1952 to 1976 and taught literature in a public school. In 1968, he founded, along with **Edward Kamau Brathwaite** and John La Rose, the **Caribbean Artist Movement (CAM)**, an organization that hosted seminars on West Indian literature and encouraged Caribbean writers to read each other's works. In 1976, he accepted a writing professorship at Hampshire College, in Amherst, Massachusetts. His absence from his homeland was often criticized by younger writers and college students in Jamaica, who regarded him as too middle class and removed from the plight of the common people and, according to Bill Carr, writing in *The Islands in Between*, thought he presented to England a false and stereotypical picture of the island. Yet Salkey was not unique in his absence from Jamaica: he was a prototype of the twentieth-century Caribbean writer who spends much time away from his or her country but writes extensively about it—some of these writers include **Julia Alvarez, Edwidge Danticat, Rosa Guy, Eugenio María Hostos**, and **Jorge Mañach** to name a few.

Salkey's first novel, *A Quality of Violence* (1959), is set in rural Jamaica at the turn of the twentieth century. Drought conditions and poverty force a group of farmers to practice Pocomania, a religious cult that believes in the visitation of spirits but also promotes violence. The novel explores how colonialism, discrimination, and desperation pile up to foster hatred, violence, and self-destructiveness. The theme of his second novel, *Escape to an Autumn Pavement* (1960), is the alienation experienced by black West Indians in England. Autobiographical, the novel tells the story of a middle-class well-educated black Jamaican and his friendship with a gay man, who is attracted to the protagonist, and his affair with an oversexed woman.

From 1960 to 1967, Salkey concentrated on young-adult books: *Hurricane* (1964), *Earthquake* (1965), *Drought* (1966), *Riot* (1967), and *The Shark Hunters*, all depiction of natural disasters and political developments in Jamaica narrated in a clear language and depicting such memorable characters as a likable grandfather who represents an understanding of the past. In 1968, Salkey returned to the novel, writing *The Late Emancipation of Jerry Stover*, about a middle-class Jamaican disillusioned with life on the island, followed by *The Adventures of Catullus Kelly* (1969), about a black teacher in London who finds escape from discrimination and oppression through womanizing and extensive sexual encounters. His third novel, *Come Home, Malcom Heartland* (1976), is about a Jamaican who returns home only to be murdered by revolutionaries.

As a poet, Salkey wrote in 1973 the epic poem "Jamaica." In 1979 he won the **Casa de las Américas** literary prize for his book of poems *In the Hills Where Her Dream Lives: Poems for Chile, 1973–1978*. In 1980, he published *Away*, poems about exile. His Anancy stories include *Anancy, Traveller* (1988) and *Anancy and Other Stories* (1993). The numerous anthologies he edited include *Island Voices; Stories from the West Indies (1970), Writing in Cuba Since the Revolution* (1977), and *Caribbean Folk Tales and Legends* (1980).

Salkey passed away in 1995 in Amherst, Massachusetts. Despite his lengthy literary production, Salkey has not received much literary criticism. *See also* Grandparents in Caribbean Literature; Jamaican Literature, History of; Obeah Practices in Literature.

Further Reading

Carr, Bill. "A Complex Fate: The Novels of Andrew Salkey." In *The Islands in Between: Essays on West Indian Literature*, edited by Louis James, 100–108. London: Oxford University Press, 1968.

Dance, Daryl Cumber, ed. *Fifty Caribbean Writers: A Bio-Bibliographical-Critical Sourcebook*. Westport, CT: Greenwood Press, 1986.

—*D. H. Figueredo*

Sampeur, Virginie (1839–1919)

∎

Recently rediscovered by Caribbean scholars, Sampeur was a pioneer in Haitian women's fiction and the country's first woman poet. An educator, she served as the director of the National Boarding School for Women in the 1900s. She was also an essayist.

Born on March 8, 1839, in Port-au-Prince, Haiti, Sampeur began to write as a teenager, publishing her poems in local newspapers. At the age of twenty-three she married poet **Oswald Durand**. Because of their unhappy union, nine years later they were divorced. Her poem "L'Abandonnée," which tells of the failed marriage and her subsequent turmoil, is one of the best-known poems in Haiti.

Although Sampeur is said to have destroyed most of her writings at the end of her life, "L'Abandonnée" remained. Her poems were not collected in book format until 1980, in the volume *La poésie féminine haitienne: histoire et anthologie de Virginie Sampeur a nos jours*. Sampeur left an unfinished biography, *Angèle Dufour*. Her life and writings merit study.

Further Reading

Christophe, Charles. *La poésie féminine haitienne: histoire et anthologie de Virginie Sampeur a nos jours*. Port-au-Prince, Haiti: Editions Choucoune, 1980.

—Jayne R. Boisvert and D. H. Figueredo

Sanabria Santaliz, Edgardo (1951–)

Sanabria Santaliz is a Puerto Rican short-story writer. He is an ordained priest.

Born in San Germán, Puerto Rico, on September 27, 1951, Sanabria Santaliz expressed an interest in religion at an early age. He studied at the Catholic school Academia Santa Monica de Santurce and spent a year at the Seminario Diocesano de San Juan. In 1969, he matriculated at the Universidad de Puerto Rico and then traveled to Spain to study music at the Universidad de Sevilla and the Conservatorio de Madrid. In 1973, he earned an MA in literature from Brown University. In 1996, he was ordained into the Dominican Order.

Sanabria Santaliz began to write while working as a translator at the Bilingual Resource Center in San Francisco in 1975. In 1978, he published the collection of short stories, *Delfia cada tarde*. His next collections were *El día que el hombre piso la luna* (1985), *Cierta inevitable muerte* (1988), and the anthology *Las horas púrpura* (1994). In 1996, he published the collection of essays *Peso pluma*, which consisted of articles he had previously published in the newspapers *Claridad* and *El Nuevo Día*.

His short stories have won him wide readership in Puerto Rico and in Latin America. He has won numerous awards, including a Pen Club Award (1985), a literary prize from the Universidad Veracruzana (1983), and a prize from the Instituto de Literatura Puertorriqueña (1988). During the 1990s, Sanabria Santaliz devoted his creativity and energy to the priesthood, serving in a church in Bayamón, Puerto Rico.

Further Reading

Torres, Víctor Federico. *Narradores puertorriqueños del 70: guía biobliográfica*. San Juan and Madrid: Editorial Plaza Mayor, 2001.

—D. H. Figueredo

Sánchez, Enriquillo (1947–2004)

A member of the group writers who formed the **Joven Poesía Dominicana,** Enriquillo Sánchez was a poet, essayist, and short-story writer from the Dominican Republic. Through his writings he explored, often with humor, issues of national and cultural identities.

Sánchez was born in Santo Domingo on August 25, 1947. He started to write as an adolescent, interested in becoming either an essayist or a biographer. In 1966, he won a short-story contest—Concurso Dominicano de Cuentos. Influenced by the works of compatriot **Pedro Mir,** whom Sánchez considered one of the best poets in Latin America, Sánchez began to experiment with poetry while writing articles and essays for several newspaper, including *El Siglo, Hoy,* and *El Caribe,* and editing the cultural supplement *Ahora.*

During the 1970s, his poems were published in journals and anthologies. In 1983, he published his first book of poetry, *Pájaro dentro de la lluvia* (1983), which won the national poetry award and became one of his most popular volumes. In 1985, he received the prestigious Poesía Rubén Darío award, from Nicaragua, for the collection of poems *Sherif on ice cream soda.* His other works include *Convicto y confeso I* (1989), *Musiquito, anales de un déspota y un bolerista* (1993), *Memoria del azar* (1996), *Germán E. Ornes: Una vida para la libertad* (1999), and *Para uso oficial solamente* (2000). Sánchez wrote poems that were sensuous, emotional, and filled with love. His essays, allegorical and with numerous allusions to world literature, revealed a deep love for his country while expressing concern for the nation's political instability.

Sanchez passed away on July 13, 2004, of heart failure.

Further Reading

Piña Contreras, Guillermo. *Doce en la literatura dominicana.* Santiago de los Caballeros, República Dominicana: Universidad Católica Madre y Maestra, 1982.

—*D. H. Figueredo*

Sánchez, Luis Rafael (1936–)

Puerto Rican author Luis Rafael Sánchez is one Latin America's leading writers. A playwright, novelist, and short-story author, he criticizes the island's semicolonial condition while also affirming Puerto Ricans' creative spirit and love of life. His most famous work is the novel *La guaracha del Macho Camacho* (1976), celebrated throughout Latin America and in the United States, where it was published in English as *Macho Camacho Beat* (1980).

Luis Rafael Sánchez was born on November 17, 1936, in a coastal town in Puerto Rico. In 1948, his family relocated to San Juan, where he attended secondary school. Initially interested in acting, young Sánchez acted in high school productions and then went on to study drama at the Universidad de Puerto Rico, winning a competition to act in a theatrical production in Mexico. Around this time, he started to write drama. He wrote his first play for a drama class. His second play, however, found a larger audience. Titled *Farsa del amor compromedito*, it was staged at the university in 1960, drawing national attention and becoming an instant classic of contemporary Puerto Rican theater. It was soon included in theatrical anthologies and is regularly performed on the island.

After teaching at the Universidad de Puerto Rico High School and after a stint as radio actor in the early 1960s, Sánchez attended Columbia University, where in 1963 he earned a masters degree in creative writing. Ten years later, he received a doctorate in Spanish literature from the Universidad Complutence in Madrid. While pursuing his academic studies, he continued to write drama. In 1961, he wrote *La hiel nuestra de cada día*, *O casi el alma* in 1964, and *La pasión según Antígona Pérez*, a retelling of the Antigone story but set in the Caribbean. The latter play was staged at the Puerto Rican Culture theater in 1968 and then taken on a tour by the Puerto Rican traveling theater.

When not writing drama, Sánchez was writing short stories. In 1966, he published *En cuerpo de camisa*, naturalistic and grotesque stories that satirize Puerto Rico's political system and dependence on the United States. Then, in 1976, he wrote *La guaracha del Macho Camacho*, inspired by an experimental short story, "La autopista del sur," written by the Argentine Julio Cortázar (1914–84), one of the writers who sparked the **Latin American Boom** of the 1960s, when novelists devised new ways of telling stories. *La guaracha del Macho Camacho* takes place during a traffic jam in San Juan. The main characters are a senator, who is having an affair with a mulata, a traditional object of sexual desire in Latin American literature; his wealthy wife; his son who is sexually aroused by the Ferrari he owns; and a mentally retarded young boy who is the mulata's son. Desperate to get out of the traffic jam, Benny looks for a shortcut and in doing so, runs over and kills the young boy. The novel can be read as a parable, with the traffic jam suggesting that the political situation on the island is not going anywhere and that the materialism embodied by Benny can only lead to death. The diction used in the novel is everyday Puerto Rican speech, English, and **Spanglish**—the combination of English and Spanish. The story is told through a series of sketches and anecdotes. Lyrics of popular songs, ads, and vulgar languages are present throughout the text. Unlike his previous works, which had been published in Puerto Rico, *La guaracha* was published in Argentina, allowing for wider distribution in Latin America and in Spain. The literary experimentation and the criticism of capitalism and the United States were well received by critics in the Spanish-speaking world, making of the novel a best seller and of Luis Rafael Sánchez a celebrity.

In 1989, Sánchez wrote *La importancia de llamarse Daniel Santos*, a fictional biography of one Puerto Rico's most famous crooners. In this work, there is no clear chronology and plot: a song serves as the medium to tell the story of the womanizer Daniel Santos and his alcoholism. While *Macho Camacho* satirizes politics, *Daniel Santos* criticizes Latin American's macho culture, where manliness is defined by how many women a man beds.

Sánchez has participated in numerous conferences in the United States and in Europe. He teaches at the Universidad de Puerto Rico and New York University.

His other works include *La guagua area* (1983), essays and short stories illustrating the Puerto Rican experience on the island and in New York City; *Fabulación e ideología en la cuentistica de Emilio S. Belaval* (1979), a work of literary criticism; and an updated edition of *En cuerpo de camisa* (1984). *See also* Hispanic Caribbean Literature, History of; Mulata in Caribbean Literature, The; Naturalism/Naturalismo; Puerto Rican Literature, History of.

Further Reading

Nouhaud, Dorita. *Luis Rafael Sánchez: dramaturge, romancier et essayiste porto-ricain*. Paris: L'Harmattan, 2001.

Perivolaris, John. *Puerto Rican Cultural Identity and the Work of Luis Rafael Sánchez*. Chapel Hill: University of North Carolina. Department of Romance Languages, 2000.

—*D. H. Figueredo*

Sánchez Boudy, José (1928–)

∎

Sánchez Boudy is a prolific Cuban writer who has cultivated several genres: drama, fiction, poetry, reference sources, and scholarly studies. He has collected expressions and slang from Cuba, documenting the linguistic pattern of the pre-Castro era. Like many writers who have gone to live abroad, the bulk of his oeuvre is not about his adopted home but about his roots and Caribbean homeland.

Born on October 17, 1928, Sánchez Boudy's father was a Spanish businessman and his mother was of French descent. Like **Louise Bennett** in Jamaica, as a child Sánchez Boudy listened intently to the popular language used by Cubans and befriended children from diverse economic and ethnic backgrounds, from Afro-Cuban to Cuban Chinese. In 1953, he became a well-known criminal lawyer; his research took him deep into the Cuban underworld. Years later, his childhood experiences and criminal exposure would serve as the foundation for his creative writings. He left Cuba in 1961, living in Puerto Rico, where he worked as a journalist, before accepting a teaching position at the University of North Carolina, in Greensboro.

Though fluent in English, Sánchez Boudy prefers to write in Spanish. In his poetry, he laments the separation from his native land, feeling alone and nostalgic. The nostalgia allows him to hear street sounds from Cuba, and in doing so, he renders poetic tribute to Afro-Cuban vendors plying their trade in Old Havana. His interest in Afro-Cuban poetry has resulted in the books of poetry *Aché, Babalú, Ayé* (1975), *Ekué, Abanakué Ekué* (1977), and *Ritos Náñigos* (1977).

Language is the protagonist in his novels *Lilayando* (1971) and *Lilayando pal tu* (1978), in which there are no characters but a series of conversations. These novels testify both to Sánchez Boudy's attempts at preserving the way Cubans talked before 1959 and his attempt at using the experimental techniques that evolved during the **Latin American Boom** of the 1960s, when Latin American authors invented diverse ways of constructing a novel. In this style is the novel *Los cruzados de la* *aurora* (1973), an anti-Castro narrative that takes place in the twentieth and seventeenth centuries simultaneously. The anti-Castro theme is also present in his drama *La soledad de la Playa Larga* (1971), about the Bay of Pigs invasion in 1961. He has written a six-volume dictionary of Cuban expressions, *Diccionario mayor de cubanismos* (1999).

Sánchez Boudy is a popular figure in Miami, where he participates in conferences and cultural events. Though he has written over sixty books, literary studies of his works are scarce. *See also* Anti-Castro Literature; Negrista Literature

Further Reading

Hernández-Miyares, Julio E., ed. *Narrativa y libertad: Cuentos cubanos de la diáspora.* Miami: Ediciones Universal, 1996.

Kanellos, Nicolás. *Hispanic Literature of the United States.* Westport, CT: Greenwood Press, 2003.

León, René. *La poesía negra de José Sánchez Boudy.* Miami, FL.: Ediciones Universal, 1977.

—*D. H. Figueredo*

Sánchez Lamouth, Juan (1929–68)

Described as a "poeta trotamundo"—a wandering poet—Sánchez Lamouth visited the poor neighborhoods of Santo Domingo, the Dominican Republic, where he read his poetry. Despite a short life, he was a prolific poet, writing more than a dozen volumes of poetry.

Sánchez Lamouth was born in Santo Domingo, on June 24, 1929. Like the Haitian **Carl Brouard**, this poet led a bohemian life and wrote a poetry that was simple and direct, preferring short verses that allowed him to write with speed and fewer revisions. A typical poem is the autobiographical "La enfermeda" (1965):

> Mirando hacia
> el cielo obrero
> sobre el polvo
> de la aldea;
> Juan Sánchez Lamouth
> esta enfermo

(Staring at / the worker's sky / above the dust / of the village / Juan Sánchez Lamouth / lies infirm).

Perhaps because of his lifestyle—he was an alcoholic—and because of his limited education, Sánchez Lamouth was belittled by the intellectuals and critics of his era. Living in poverty and seeking recognition, Sánchez Lamouth wrote in the 1950s poems praising dictator Rafael Leónidas Trujillo (1891–1961). Such poems afforded him certain recognition from the government and some economic gains. However, the poems lacked authenticity, and many of his friends understood that Sánchez

Lamouth was playing a political game in order to improve his lot. Upon the assassination of Trujillo in 1961, Sánchez Lamouth wrote poems that celebrated the poor of the Dominican Republic, explored black themes, and contemplated his decaying health. In 1964, he received the National Prize. As his critical recognition was increasing, Sánchez Lamouth became ill and died on November 18, 1968.

His works include *Brumas* (1954), *Elegía de las hojas caídas y 19 poemas sin importancia* (1955), *Cantos a Trujillo y una oda a Venezuela* (1958), *Sinfonía vegetal a Juan Pablo Duarte y otros poemas* (1968). All of his poems were collected in 1992 in the volume *Resplandor del relampago: obra completa. See also* Trujillo Era.

Further Reading

Cabral, Manuel del. *10 poetas dominicanos: tres poetas con vida y siete desenterrados.* Santo Domingo, República Dominicana: Publicaciones América, S.A., 1980.

—*D. H. Figueredo*

Santaliz, Pedro (1938–)

A playwright from Puerto Rico, Santaliz has chosen New York City for the staging of his plays. The founder of the community theater Nuevo Teatro Pobre de América, Santaliz uses his dramas to advocate political change while illustrating the plight of the urban poor.

Pedro Santaliz Ávila was born on May 28, 1938, in Isabela, Puerto Rico, but was raised in the town of Río Piedras. In his childhood he became interested in drama and the age of six was performing in theater. After attending high school, he matriculated at the Universidad de Puerto Rico, where he joined a theatrical group and acted in a traveling theater company. In 1960, he received his BA in drama. Two years later, he traveled to Hungary and Poland to study theater.

In 1965, he went to New York, where he founded the Nuevo Teatro Pobre de América, a community theater, with the objective of introducing drama to poor neighborhoods. He not only managed the company but acted as well. From 1969 to the mid-1990s, he wrote nearly a dozen plays, which he also produced: *El cemí en el Palacio de Jarlem* (1969), *Cadencia en el país de las maravillas* (1973), *Oda al rey de Jarlem* (1974), *Historia amorosa de Evaristo y Matera* (1981), *El castillo interior de Medea Camuñas* (1984), and *Olla* (1985), among others. These dramas tended to be experimental and explore the ills plaguing urban centers: drugs, violence, and political corruption. His commitment to Latinos in New York City has garnered him praise. Journalist Tony Betancourt, from *Impacto*, has called Santaliz a "Hispanic treasure."

Further Reading

Betancourt, Tony. "Gente del Teatro: La Cartelera del mes." *Impacto* 36, no. 1350 (May 22, 2001): 24.

"Pedro Santaliz." *Fundación para la cultura popular.* http://www.prpop.org/biografias/p_bios/pedro_santaliz (accessed 9/15/05).

—*D. H. Figueredo*

Santería in Literature

Santería is a religion that originated in Cuba when African slaves from western Nigeria combined African traditions and belief systems with Catholicism. Thus they saw in the island's patron saint, La Virgen de la Caridad del Cobre, an incarnation of the African goddess of love and rivers, Ochún. The principal components of Santería include establishing and maintaining a relationship with an Orisha—a nonhuman being—practicing divination, and performing public rituals. The work of Santería is carried out through a *santero*, an ordained priest. Often, an individual trying to reach an Orisha must do so through a santero.

Through the nineteenth century and early twentieth century, white Cuban intellectuals who were more interested in exploring their European heritages and traditions distanced themselves from studying and writing on Santería. But the first decade of the twentieth century, Cuban anthropologist and ethnologist **Fernando Ortiz** began to study the subject in his book, *Hampa afro-cubana: Los negros brujos* (1917). While his initial outlook was from a racist perspective, years of research transformed him into a progressive intellectual who appreciated the complexities and sophisticated practices of Santería. In the 1930s, a second Cuban scholar, **Lydia Cabrera**, encouraged by Ortiz's works and her interest in Cuban traditions, began to publish texts on Santería. In 1940, she wrote *¿Por que? Cuentos negros de Cuba*, which emphasized Afro-Cubans' connections with natural forces as manifestations of African gods. In 1954, she wrote the seminal study *El monte: Igbo, finda, ewe orisha, vititi nfinda: notas sobre las religiones, la magia, las supersticiones y el folklore de los negros criollos y del pueblo de Cuba*, an in-depth analysis of Yoruba religion in Cuba. Similarly, the novelist and short-story writer **Lino Novas Calvo** wrote stories that included description of Santería rituals, and the poet **Nicolás Guillén** used Santería vernacular and symbols in his writings.

Nevertheless, Santería remained an exotic topic seldom approached by Cuban writers. Even after the triumph of the Cuban Revolution, which claimed racial equality and acknowledged the island's African roots, established authors maintained their distance. For example, in 1975, **Manuel Cofiño López** published the award-winning novel *Cuando la sangre se parece al fuego*, which takes place in a "solar," a tenement built like a barrack, criticizing the practices of Santería as undermining the advances made by the Revolution. During the 1980s, **Eugenio Hernández Espinosa** used Santería motifs in his play *Patakín* (1984), where African gods tell a story of love and betrayal; again, he revisited the theme in the dramas *Odebí, el cazador* (1982) and *Oba y Shangó* (1983). Poet **Excilia Saldaña** also used Santería imagery in her poetry. By this period, the revolutionary government was more receptive to the Afro-Cuban religion.

Equally receptive were Cuban writers in exile during the 1990s. **José Raul Bernardo** explored the sexuality of the African gods in the best seller *The Secret of the Bulls* (1996), and mystery novelist **Alex Abella** depicted Santería rituals and spirit possession in his thrillers *The Killing of the Saints* (1997), *Dead of Night* (1998), and *Final Acts* (2000). While these writers emphasized the exotic elements of Santería, there were two other writers who saw the acceptance of the religion as a healing process. In the novel *Dreaming in Cuba* (1992), by **Cristina García**, a character who is descending into insanity becomes a Santeria priest in order to find mental stability, and in *Going Under* (1996), by **Virgil Suárez**, the protagonist turns to Santería as way to find his Cubanness.

Santería is also known as La Regla de Ocha and Lucumí.

Further Reading

Canizares, Raul. *Cuban Santeria: Walking with the Night*. Rochester, VT: Destiny Books, 1999.

Fernández Robaina, Tomás. "Cuba." In *African Caribbeans: A Reference Guide*, edited by Alan West-Duran, 55–71. Westport, CT: Greenwood Press, 2003.

Wedel, Johan. *Santería Healing: A Journey Into the Afro-Cuban World of Divinities, Spirits, and Sorcery*. Gainesville, Tallahassee: University Press of Florida, 2004.

—*D. H. Figueredo*

Santiago, Esmeralda (1948–)

As a Puerto Rican native, Esmeralda Santiago has raised awareness and opened important critical dialogues about identity and origin in her two memoirs and one novel that tally the challenges and losses experienced by Puerto Ricans migrating to North America, specifically New York.

Born on May 17, 1948, in San Juan, Puerto Rico, in her first book, *When I Was Puerto Rican* (1994), she recounts episodes from her childhood in Puerto Rico as well as from her migration experience. The first of eleven children raised by a single mother, Santiago describes in detail the hardships, but also the comforting community, which surrounded her poverty-stricken family. With them she moved to Brooklyn, New York, when she was eleven and battled her way into a school system that favors natives and English speakers. She attended the highly selective School of Performing Arts in Manhattan. Eventually she graduated from Harvard University and embarked on her writing career. To date, she has published two memoirs and one novel and has edited two collections of nonfiction.

Santiago's first memoir has received the most critical attention. Many readers identified immediately with the sense of divided identity that she describes in the book. In addition to capturing Puerto Rico's unique cultural charms, she also highlights traditions that are painful to some members of society. For example, she describes a tender relationship with her father, who teaches her to be proud of being from the country and belonging to a peasant tradition, and yet she evidences also how her mother was mistreated by that same father. She records a traditional ritual of sending a dead baby to heaven and the more common experience of eating a ripe guava. Santiago's powerful imagery juxtaposes the squalid lifestyle in the suburbs of San Juan with the unmerciful coldness of New York's ethnic groups.

Santiago herself has reported her surprise at finding the discourse on cultural identity that her book awakened. "People accept and understand the irony of the past tense in the title," she stated on her publisher's Web site—http://www.randomhouse.com/vintage/read/puerto/santiago.htmls—noting that many immigrants recognize the feeling that "once they've lived in the U.S. their cultural purity has been compromised" and they are never fully accepted again in their original homes. In fact, the greatest audience for the book has not been Caribbean readers as much as it has been immigrants to the United States from the islands and elsewhere.

In 1997, Santiago published *America's Dream*, a novel that further develops her themes of belonging, while introducing a more in-depth look at mother-daughter relationships and domestic violence. The protagonist, America Gonzales, is a housekeeper in a hotel in Puerto Rico where wealthy North American guests ignore her. When her daughter runs away with a man, she accepts an offer to work as a nanny for a couple in Westchester, New York. By doing so, she also attempts to escape from an abusive relationship with her married boyfriend, Correa. In this work, Santiago is able to offer more beautiful portraits of Puerto Rico, while maintaining her criticism of unfair gender relationships there and the discrimination against Caribbean people in North America.

Santiago currently lives in Westchester County, New York, with her husband Frank Cantor, with whom she produces documentary films. She continues to work with organizations that provide shelter for victims of domestic violence. *See also* Mother-Daughter Relationships.

Further Reading

Hernández, Carmen Dolores. *Puerto Rican Voices in English: Interviews with Writers.* Westport, CT: Praeger, 1997.

—*Angela Conrad*

Santiesteban, Ángel (1966–)

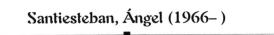

A short-story writer and film director, Santiesteban belongs to the generation of Cuban writers, known as the **novismo** generation, who came of age in the late 1980s and 90s. His short stories explore sexual abandonment and the psychological effects of the Angola war, when Cuban soldiers went to that African nation to fight against an invasion from South Africa.

As a child Santiesteban studied art. Later on, he attended military school but decided to withdraw from the academy. Beginning to write during the Periodo Especial in Cuba, when adverse economic conditions and paper shortages did not allow for the publication of full length books, Santiesteban was attracted to the short-story genre. He interviewed veterans of the Angola war, and their testimonies served as the basis for his stories.

In 1989, he won the Juan Rulfo literary award for short stories. During the 1990s, he received several honors, including being a finalist in the Casa de las Americas literary competition. In 2001, he was awarded the **Alejo Carpentier** prize. His collection of short stories includes *Sueño de un día de verano* (1998) and *Los hijos que nadie quiso (2001)*.

Further Reading

Caro, Boris Leonardo. "Vivir para narrar Entrevista al escritor Angel Santiesteban." www.cubaliteraria.com/novedades/de_la_cuba_literaria/anteriores/santiesteban.htm (accessed 9/20/05).

—*D. H. Figueredo*

Santos-Fébres, Mayra (1966–)

One of Puerto Rico's most widely published recent authors, Santos-Fébres is an educator, poet, and short-story writer. Her stories and poems draw a balance between **magical realism** and sexuality, between poetic language and vulgarity. Her writings are also characterized by a sense of humor and irony.

Born in Carolina, Puerto Rico, Santos-Fébres lived in a house surrounded by books. Since both her parents were teachers, she developed an early love of reading. Asthmatic, she was unable to play with other children, thus she idled her hours away writing. She attended a Catholic school, where a lay teacher recognized her talent and encouraged her to write and to discipline herself, writing at least an hour a day. After graduating from the Universidad de Puerto Rico, she attended Cornell University, first earning an MA in Latin American literature and then, in

Mayra Santos-Febrés is a Puerto Rican poet who combines sexuality and magical realism in her writings. *Source: Americas Society. Courtesy of Elsa M. Ruiz.*

1991, a PhD. While studying, Santos-Fébres submitted her poems and stories to numerous publications, including *Revue Noir, Latin American Review of Arts and Literature*, and *Revista Tríptico*; the latter journal presented her with the **Evaristo Ribera Chevremont** literary prize.

In 1991, she published *Anamú y manigua*, a collection of poems selected in Puerto Rico as one of the best volumes of the year. In 1995, her collection of short stories, *Pez de vidrio*, earned her the Juan Rulfo Prize, from Mexico, for one of the pieces in the volume, "Oso blanco." In 1997, the collection was translated into English as *Urban Oracles: Stories*. Her literary recognition resulted in an invitation to teach at Harvard University and to conduct conferences at numerous other institutions in the United States and in Europe.

In 1998, she published her second collection of stories, *El cuerpo correcto*. In 2000, she published the volume of poetry *Tercer mundo*. That same year saw the publication of the comic novel *Sirena Serena vestida de pena*, about a gay man who in order to trap a wealthy lover dresses up as cabaret singer. In this novel, as in her poetry and short stories, Santos-Fébres writes, as critic Myrna Nieves points out in *Mujeres como islas* (2002), in "an exuberant language . . . of tender sexuality" (140).

Santos-Fébres has won numerous international awards, including the Premio Letras de Oro, from the University of Miami, Florida (1991), a literary award from French International Radio (1996), and was a finalist in the Rómulo Gallegos Literary Prize, from Spain (2001). She currently teaches literature at the Universidad de Puerto Rico in Río Piedras.

Further Reading

Nieves, Myrna. "Atistando: cinco cuentos." In *Islas como mujeres*, edited by Olga Marta Pérez and Thelma Jiménez, 139–47. Habana, Cuba: Ediciones Unión. Santo Domingo, República Dominicana: Ediciones Feriolibro, 2002.

—D. H. Figueredo

Santos Silva, Loreina (1933–)

Santos Silva is a poet and short-story writer from Puerto Rico. Through her poetry and her work as a feminist, she has fought for women's equality in Puerto Rico and in Latin America.

Loreina Santos Silva was born in Hato Rey, Puerto Rico, on October 18, 1933. As a child, she grew up in a male-driven environment that encouraged young women to marry and not pursue academic studies. Therefore, in high school, she took both the vocational and academy tracks. In 1953, she matriculated at the Universidad de Puerto. After graduating, she conducted studies at the University of Michigan, where in 1963 she earned a masters in the teaching of English as a second language. She taught at the Universidad de Puerto Rico while working on her PhD at Brown University. She was the director of Congreso de Creación Femenina and was a member of the Unión de Mujeres Americanas.

Santos Silva wrote numerous scholarly essays and articles before publishing poetry during the 1970s. By the 1980s, she had established a reputation as a poet with such volumes as *Incertidumbre primera* (1973), *Rikelme* (1974), *Motor mutable*

(1984), and *Umbral de soledad* (1987). In the 1990s, she continued to write poetry but also experimented with prose, publishing first a memoir, *Este ojo que me mira* (1996), and a collection of short stories, *Cuentos para perturbar el alma* (2000). Influenced by mysticism, Judeo-Christian and Hindu religions, as well as the writings of Albert Einstein (1879–1955), her poems, written in a range of styles from the simplicity of haiku poetry to elusive stanzas, explore such themes as man's unity with the cosmos, evolution, feminism, and women's exploitation. In her poems she often portrays women as the embodiment of wisdom and creativity. Her prose tends to examine political issues: her memoir, for example, is also an exploration of Puerto Rico's political identity and American influence on the island.

Santos Silva retired from teaching in 1992, then devoted her time to horticultural studies and feminist mysticism. In 2003, she wrote the novel *La Bestia: cruelda mental y violencia doméstica*, a testimonial novel about spousal abuse. Santos Silva's works have been translated into English, German, and Korean.

Further Reading

Marsán, Maricel Mayor. "Conversación con Loreina Santos Silva (La eterna itinerante y el sueño independentista)." *Revista Literaria Baquiana.* http://www.baquiana.com/número%20VII_VIII/entrevista_IV.htm (accessed 9/14/05).

—*D. H. Figueredo*

Sarduy, Severo (1937–93)

Severo Sarduy was a Cuban writer whose experimental works addressed such themes as the repression of homosexuals, while also affirming and celebrating homosexuality. A brilliant novelist, poet, and essayist, Sarduy is considered one of the most gifted writers from Latin America.

Sarduy was born on February 25, 1937 in the province of Camagüey. As critic **Roberto González Echevarría** has pointed out in *La ruta de Severo Sarduy*, Camagüey was one of the most traditional of the Cuban provinces, a twist of irony given Sarduy's own aggressively modern, postmodern, and anti-traditionalist aesthetics. Also, unlike most of his Havana-born, or *habanero*, contemporaries, his family background was solidly working

Novelist and short-story writer Severo Sarduy experimented with language and narrative, while also addressing such themes as sexual oppression. *Courtesy of Roberto González Echevarría.*

class. His cultural origins were mixed: Spanish, African, and Chinese. In 1955 he graduated from Instituto de Segunda Enseñanza de Camagüey (the equivalent of high school) with honors in arts and sciences. His developing interest in literature and the publication of several of his poems in the local newspaper no doubt made his family, who had other hopes for him, feel uneasy. Convinced that he had exhausted all the educational opportunities in Camagüey, Sarduy moved to Havana, where he enrolled in medical school at the University of Havana, with little or no intention of actually becoming a doctor. But it was his ticket to the center of Cuban culture.

In Havana, author **Guillermo Cabrera Infante**, one of the first to recognize the young writer's talents, published his short story, "El Seguro" in the magazine, *Carteles*. In the course of a year he also published several poems in *Revolución*, an anti-dictator Fulgencio Batista (1901–73) newspaper, established himself as editor of *Diario Libre*, and became a regular contributor to *Nueva Revista Cubana* and *Artes Plásticas*. Sarduy, along with other writers, established *Lunes de Revolución*, and *Ciclón* as an alternative to **José Lezama Lima**'s magazine, **Orígenes**, challenging the latter's myth of a unified Cuban identity.

The next pivotal moment in Sarduy's life came in the fall of 1959 when he was awarded a scholarship to study art history and criticism at the École du Louvre in Paris. This would be the last time he would see Cuba, because by 1961 it was clear that **Fidel Castro** had betrayed the Cuban people, turning the government into a Stalinist-type dictatorship. But Paris was good to the young, experimental writer. There he established connections with many of the writers associated with the progressive magazine, *Tel Quel*; with Julia Kristeva (1941–); Philippe Sollers (1936–); Roland Barthes (1915–80); and other structuralist and post-structuralist thinkers.

In 1963 he published his first novel, *Gestos*, which he followed four years later with *De donde son los cantantes*, after a *son* (or song) by the Matamoros Quartet. This most difficult and brilliant novel explores Cuba's multiple cultures, and remains one of the few works of literature to pay special attention to the history of the Chinese in Cuba and the transgender culture of Havana night life. In fact, for Sarduy all culture was subject to simulation (*La simulación*, 1982) and transvestism (*Escrito sobre un cuerpo*, 1969), culture itself being a readable text like any other.

The 1970s were creative years for Sarduy. The intellectually sizzling Paris inspired Sarduy to write two more novels, *Cobra* (1972) and *Maitreya* (1977); six radio plays, five of which were published in 1977 under the title, *Para la Voz*; a book of poetry, *Big Bang* (1974); and a theoretical reworking of Lezama Lima's idea of the **baroque** in *Barroco* (1974), based as much on theories of art as on astrophysics. In 1984 he published *Colibrí*, his most personal novel—a work that, among many other things, depicts his father's shame and embarrassment at Sarduy's public avowal of his homosexuality. 1987 saw the publication of two books of poetry, *Nueva inestabilidad*, in which he once again incorporated astrophysics into his poetics of life and literature, and *Un testigo fugaz y disfrazado*, taking on the theme of the *disfraze* or dress-up of the *travestí* (transvestite) as an escape from the oppressiveness of univocal signification. For Sarduy the instability of the universe and the seeming similarity of humans (through clothing) and animals (through camouflaged colors) meet at the juncture of the rich, open, irreducibility of the world to one principle. But 1987 was also significant because it was the year in which Sarduy announced to the world the beginning of the end of his life. In *El Cristo de la rue Jacob* (1987), a series of autobiographical vignettes, Sarduy tells of his visit to the doctor for a wart that had appeared on his foot. As the doctor cauterizes the wart, the smell of burning flesh reminds him of the incinerated bodies of the Jewish holocaust, providing a subtle sign of what was to visit Sarduy with the onset of AIDS. Before dying he would write two more books, *Cocuyo* (1990) and *Pajaros de la playa* (1993), the latter of which dealt with the inhumane quarantine of homosexuals with AIDS by the Castro dictatorship. On June 12, 1993 at the age of 56, Sarduy died of AIDS-related complications in Paris, the city of his exile, leaving a literary treasure for all times. *See also* Gay and Lesbian Literature.

Further Reading

González Echevarría, Roberto. *La ruta de Severo Sarduy*. Hanover, NH: Ediciones del Norte, 1987.

Pérez, Rolando. "Severo Sarduy." *The Review of Contemporary Fiction* 24, n.1 (Spring 2004): 94–138.

Sarduy, Severo. *Obra Completa*. Critical Edition. Edited by Gustavo Guerrero and François Wahl. Madrid: Galaxia Gutenberg, 1999.

———. *Christ of the Rue Jacob*. Translated with a translators' afterword by Suzanne Jill Levine and Carol Maier. San Francisco: Mercury House, 1995.

———. *Cobra* and *Maitreya*. Translated with a preface by Suzanne Jill Levine. Introduction by James McCourt. Normal: Dalkey Archive Press, 1995.

———. *From Cuba with a Song*. Translation of *De donde son los cantantes* by Suzanne Jill Levine. Los Angeles: Sun & Moon Press, 1994.

———. *De donde son los cantantes*. Critical Edition. Edited by Roberto González Echevarría. Madrid: Cátedra, 1993.

———. *Written On a Body*. Translated by Carol Meir. New York: Lumen Books, 1989.

———. *For Voice*. Translated by Philip Barnard. Pittsburgh: Latin American Literary Review Press, 1985.

—*Rolando Pérez*

Savacou, Journal of the Caribbean Artists Movement (1970–)

A literary and historical journal published by the **Caribbean Artists Movement (CAM)** in Kingston, Jamaica, and London, and edited by three major Caribbean figures, the critic **Kenneth Ramchand** and the writers **Edward Kamau Brathwaite** and **Andrew Salkey**. The journal was overseen by a committee that was composed of such emerging writers and intellectuals as **Paule Marshall, Orlando Patterson,** and **Sylvia Wynter,** among others. The purpose of the journal, as expressed on the last page of the first issue, was "to bring together the work of creative writers, academics, and theoretical thinkers and so provide a forum for artistic expression and thought in the Caribbean today." Initially, the journal was published four times a year, with the fourth volume dedicated exclusively to literature, but by the 1980s, *Savacou* was dedicating some of its issues to publishing the works of one writer, as it did in 1989 with the long poem "Sappho Saky's Meditations" by Edward Kamau Brathwaite.

Further Reading

Savacou 1, no. 1 (June 1970).

————. 1, no. 16 (1989).

—*D. H. Figueredo*

Savage, Alan. See Nicholson, Christopher R.

Schomburg, Arthur (1874–1938)

A pioneer researcher of African culture who gathered the world's first archives on African culture in the Caribbean and United States, Arthur Schomburg was an activist, a librarian, and a writer. Born in San Juan, Puerto Rico, on January 24, 1874, his father was from Germany and his mother came from St. Croix, Virgin Islands.

In 1891, Schomburg migrated to New York City, where he held various jobs, including elevator operator and clerk in the mail room of a bank, while attending high school. In New York City, he befriended Cuban poet **José Martí** and Puerto Rican writer **Ramón Emeterio Betances**, becoming interested in Cuba's and Puerto Rico's revolutionary struggles against Spain. Involved in a Spanish-speaking Free-Masonry fraternity in New York City, Schomburg started to translate Masonic literature into English with the intention of recruiting African Americans. His attempts at preserving historical documents from the

Librarian and writer Arthur Schomburg created the world's first archives and library devoted to the study of African culture. *Source: Schomburg Center for Research in Black Culture, The New York Public Library, Astor, Lenox, and Tilden Foundations. Courtesy of Lisa Finder.*

Masonic lodge piqued his interest in conducting similar work on African American culture.

In 1911, Schomburg founded the Negro Society for Historical Research. In 1914, he was inducted into the American Negro Academy, becoming its president later on. Around this time, he started to collect slaves' narratives, journals, rare books, and correspondence, among other historical items. In 1926, the New York Public Library bought his collection for the newly established African American history section and appointed him curator. Schomburg curated the collection until his death in 1938. By the end of the twentieth century, the Schomburg collection, as it became known, had grown from ten-thousand documents to nearly five million items; it is housed in the Schomburg Center for Research in Black Culture, located in Harlem.

Puerto Rican journalist **Jesús Colón** recalled how Schomburg taught young African Americans and Puerto Ricans about their heritage, often making them aware for the first time of the accomplishments of their ancestors: "Arthur Schomburg discovered that Juan Pareja, one of Spain's great painters, had been a Negro slave of Diego Velázquez, the famous Spanish painter. Velázquez taught Juan Pareja how to paint. Schomburg traced one of Pareja's paintings all the way from Europe to a store-room in New York City," wrote Colón, in 1962, for the journal *The Worker*.

Some of Schomburg's works include *Is Hayti decadent?* (1904); *Plácido: A Cuban Martyr* (1910); *A Bibliographical Checklist of American Negro Poetry* (1916); and *Military Services Rendered by the Haitians in the North and South American Wars for Independence; Savannah, Georgia, 1779; Columbia, South America, 1815* (1921). *See also* Belpré (White), Pura.

Further Reading

Allen, James Egert. *The Legend of Arthur A. Schomburg*. Cambridge, MA: Danterr, 1975.

Colón, Jesús. "Arthur Schomburg and Negro History." In *The Way It Was and Other Stories*, by Jesús Colón, 98–99. Houston, TX: Arte Público Press, 1993.

—*D. H. Figueredo*

Schwarz-Bart, Simone (1938–)

Guadeloupean novelist Schwarz-Bart is devoted to revealing and making known the unexplored histories of the African diaspora, the peasantry of the Antillean islands, and most particularly of black women of the diaspora. Her most famous novel is *Pluie et vent sur Télumée Miracle* (1979).

Simone Schwarz-Bart was born in Charente in 1938. Her mother was a teacher and her father, a military man, was stationed there at the time. The family returned to Guadeloupe when Simone was thirteen years old, and she began her studies at Pointe-á-Pitre. She would continue her studies in Paris and Dakar. Her Antillean origins together with her experiences in Paris and Dakar form a triangle that has influenced her writing. Her groundbreaking novel, *Pluie et vent sur Télumée Miracle*, translated as *The Bridge of Beyond*, is set in the Caribbean countryside. Simone Schwarz-Bart fills her novel with the stories, culture, social life, and history of people not often found in official records. By her own admission, she sets out in her novel to fill the gaps left by experts. Narrated by a female protagonist, Schwarz-Bart's novel blends legend with African and Creole belief systems and chronicles local history in a work that takes on epic proportions. With this much-acclaimed novel, Schwarz-Bart places her native Guadeloupe firmly on the map and establishes her own place in literary history.

Her first novel, *Un Plat de porc aux bananes vertes* (1967), was coauthored with her husband, André Schwarz-Bart, as was the six-volume collection of essays *Hommage a la femme noire* (1989). That first novel addresses multiple themes in the complicated construction of identity for a Martinican woman experiencing alienation from French society and searching for her Caribbean roots.

Simone Schwarz-Bart met her husband, André, when she was an eighteen-year-old student in Paris. A Polish Jew who had lost both of his parents to the Holocaust, André Schwarz-Bart shares Simone's passion for political commitment. They have been partners in a long-standing creative collaboration, which has resulted in two historical novels. The couple is working on a larger, more ambitious project of seven novels that seek to explore the history of Guadeloupe, from slavery to the present and from the perspective of a woman of color.

Simone Schwarz-Bart is also the author of the critically acclaimed novel *Ti Jean l'Horizon* (1979) and the play *Ton beau capitain* (1987), as well as numerous essays. Her writings have been translated into English, Spanish, and Dutch.

Further Reading

Gyssels, Kathleen. *Filles de solitud: essai sur l'identité antillaise dans les (auto-)biographies fictives de Simone et André Schwarz-Bart*. Paris: L'Harmattan, 1996.

—*Pamela María Smorkaloff*

Scott, Dennis (1939–91)

A playwright and poet from Jamaica, Dennis Scott was also an educator, a dancer, an actor, and a stage director. Politically and socially engaged, his works explore the themes of class differences and the struggle for racial and social equality. His poetic diction drew from standard English and the Jamaican vernacular, affording him a style that had a lilting and musical quality that pleased Jamaican audiences.

Dennis Courtney Scott was born into a middle-class family on December 16, 1939, in Kingston, Jamaica. As a child he spent many hours reading. His

Episcopalian family was closely knit, and from his parents he developed a sense of loyalty that was evident later on in his poetry and dramas. On the other hand, he found boarding school—Jamaican College, which he attended for his elementary and secondary education—to be cold and impersonal. The conflict of the freedom found in familial love and the controlled environment of an institution became a theme in his writings.

Scott graduated from the University of the West Indies and then conducted graduate studies in the United States and in England. Traveling throughout the Caribbean and the United States allowed him, according to Ian D. Smith in *Fifty Caribbean Writers*, "to become aware of the commonalities that the people of the region share . . . [focusing] Scott's atten-

Popular playwright and poet Dennis Scott wrote about poverty in Jamaica and the struggle for racial and social equality. *Courtesy of Daryl Cumber Dance.*

tion on relationships between people in the peculiar social contexts in which they evolve" (429). The socioeconomic inequalities that he witnessed prompted him to use writing as a tool for political expression.

Attracted to theater from an early age, he wrote the drama *An Echo in the Bone* in 1974. The play, about a black man who murders an oppressive estate owner, and in the act avenges centuries of oppressions of slaves in the Caribbean, was performed by students at the Creative Arts Center, in Jamaica. In 1977, he wrote a children's adaptation of *Sir Gawain and the Green Knight*, which was commissioned by the O'Neill Center for the National Theater of the Deaf and was published a year later under that title. In 1981, he wrote his second major drama, *Dog*, about a sadistic middle-class man who goes hunting for dogs. The production was staged in Jamaica and Barbados. The recognition he received as a dramatist resulted, in 1983, in an invitation to teach at the Yale School of Drama.

While teaching and writing drama, Scott wrote two books of poetry, *Uncle Time* (1973) and *Dreadwalk* (1982). The latter demonstrated his interest in the Rastafarian religion. Both works were political and revealed his concerns for the poor of Jamaica: some of the poems were set in a barrack yard, a tenement centered in an open courtyard. Scott also busied himself with dancing and choreographing ballets at the university.

In 1989, Scott published his last work, the poetry collection *Strategies*. Many of the poems in this volume are written to his son. Scott died on February 21, 1991.

Scott's plays have been regularly performed but have not been published yet. During his lifetime, he received numerous prizes and recognitions, including the Schubert Playwriting Award (1970), the International Poetry Forum Award (1973), the Silver Musgrave Medal (1974), and the Jamaican Prime Minister's Award for contribution to the creative arts and education (1983). *See also* Barrack Yard Literature; Literatura Comprometida/Socially Engaged Literature.

Further Reading

Smith, Ian D. "Dennis Scott (1939–). In *Fifty Caribbean Writers: A Bio-Bibliographical-Critical Sourcebook*, edited by Daryl Cumber Dance, 428–37. Westport, CT: Greenwood Press, 1986.

—D. H. Figueredo

Seacole, Mary (1805–81)

Celebrated in her lifetime for her courage as a nurse during the Crimean War (1853–56), Mary Seacole was one of the few Afro-Caribbeans to write an autobiography during the nineteenth century and one of a handful of black women to have a book published in Great Britain. Entitled *The Wonderful Adventures of Mrs. Seacole in Many Lands*, the volume proved a best-seller at the time of its publication in 1857.

Seacole was the daughter of a Scottish army officer and a free black Jamaican woman who was a healer. From her mother, Seacole learned how to treat tropical diseases and how to nurse wounds. As a young woman, she ran a boardinghouse and offered nursing services to British soldiers on the island. In 1850, Seacole traveled to Colombia, where she set up a general store and a hotel and helped the victims of a cholera outbreak. In 1854, she moved to London. She volunteered for service in the Crimean War, but because she was black she was rejected. Undeterred, Seacole went to Crimea on her own, establishing a general store and a hotel, which she named the British Hotel, near the battlefield. The hotel served as a hospital, where she nursed wounded soldiers.

But Seacole also ventured onto the battlefields to attend to the soldiers. After the war, Seacole was received as a heroine in Great Britain, where a festival in her honor was held at the Royal Surrey Gardens.

The Wonderful Adventures of Mrs. Seacole in Many Lands was a travelogue, a narrative about life in the West Indies and Central America and an account of the Crimean War. Though some twentieth-century readers might be disturbed by Seacole's identification with the British, it is important to note that the narrative presents a black woman who rejects victimization and asserts her own persona. Observes scholar Sandra Pouchet Paquet in *Caribbean Autobiography* (2002): "Little is weak and self-effacing about [Seacole's] life and actions . . . even as she embraces British colonial values, she exerts a powerful, muscular energy that forces new parameters on her status as colonial" (71).

Further Reading

Paquet, Sandra Pouchet. *Caribbean Autobiography: Cultural Identity and Self-Representation*. Madison, WI: University of Wisconsin Press, 2002.

—D. H. Figueredo

Seaforth, Sybil (1935–)

An educator, social worker, librarian, and young-adult novelist who explores young-adult development in the West Indies, Sybil Seaforth was born in Jamaica, where she attended the prestigious Wolmer's Girls School. She subsequently read for a degree at the University College of Swansea in Wales. In 1963, she moved to Trinidad. Seaforth has published five books.

From 1989 to 1993, she worked with Caribbean Association for Feminist Research and Action (CAFRA), coordinating their Women's Creative Expression program, overseeing the publication of *Creation Fire: A CAFRA Anthology of Caribbean Women's Poetry* and CAFRA's *Publishing Handbook for Caribbean Women Writers*, as well as the hosting of two successful creative writing seminars for women writers.

The majority of Seaforth's fictions return to the experience of growing up within a complex Caribbean sociocultural scenario. Her earliest short stories include "A Letter to Santa" (1977) and "A Season to Remember" (1980). Sybil Seaforth came to prominence as a creative writer after the publication of her first novel, *Growing Up with Miss Milly*, in 1988. The novel deals with a common Caribbean family life scenario—young male protagonist who grows up with a single parent. It explores the developmental challenges that young boys must confront within this social situation if they are to successfully embrace adulthood.

Childhood experiences are also the themes of *Vilmal's Cricket Bat* (1995) and *A Voyage to a Sandy Bay* (1997). The latter is a coming-of-age narrative with a primary focus on a young girl's awakening to the first subtle stirrings of love. It also charts her awakening to a bewildering adult world of pain, loss, and difficult class and color relations. Commenting on her choice of focus for this novel, Seaforth indicates that it was during her stint at a prestigious girls secondary school that she became aware of class and color discrimination, which was then endemic to Jamaican society. The author observed that the darker-skinned girls were highly intelligent because at that time their only means of access to the school was through a few highly prized scholarships. The fair-skinned girls, who were in the majority, kept away from the darker-skinned girls, befriending them only when they needed help with schoolwork. The novel raises questions about the double standards that seem to be necessary to survive in the adult world, about how to contain joys and fears that threaten to overwhelm, and the values that young people will eventually adopt or reject.

Her novel *In Silence the Strands Unravel* (1999), written for an older audience, set in the fictional island of Cantillean, explores the responses of three long-married women who confront the dissolution of their marriages. A major issue is the creeping coldness and the lack of communication that can submerge failing marriages. The novel is written from the vantage point of middle-class Caribbean women whose hopes for a lifelong love and support are undercut and who, too late, reconsider the cultural expectations of female sacrifice and selflessness that govern such unions.

In 2001, Seaforth returned to young-adult literature with the publication of *Caribbean Short Stories for Children*. Seaforth's works frankly, yet sensitively, interrogate the issues, choices, values, personality traits, and aspirations that the young protagonists must grapple with in their quest for their niche in an adult world. Her novels carry the stamp of a socially conscious writer who is concerned with instructing young people about social pitfalls and to guide them into the practice of just and equitable social relations. *See also* Feminism in Caribbean Literature.

Further Reading

"CAFRA Launches Writer's Fourth Novel," Jan. 31, 2000. http://www.cafra.org (accessed 9/15/05).

Robertson, Ian. "Growing up with Miss Milly by Sybil Seaforth: A Review." In *Caribbean Women Writers: Essays from the First International Conference*, edited by Selwyn Cudjoe. Wellesley, MA: Calaloux Publications, 1990.

—*Paula Morgan*

Secades, Eladio (1904–76)

A Cuban journalist who wrote about local customs and traditions, Secades was noted for his quick wit and sharp observations not only about Cubans and life in Cuba but also about the world at large. His sketches, published in newspapers and popular magazines, were about three pages long, and the subject matter ranged from how buses ran in Cuba to the increase in divorces throughout the world to the nature and popularity of the tango.

A native of Havana, Secades covered sports events, but it was his humorous pieces on local events and characters that made him well known. His first sketches appeared in 1935 in the newspaper *Alerta*, of a popular nature, and were soon picked up by the more prestigious *Bohemia*, a weekly with the largest circulation on the island. As his fame grew, he became a reporter for the highly respected newspaper *Diario de la Marina*, though he continued working for *Alerta* and *Bohemia*.

Secades replicated Cuban diction and vernacular in his writings. Always meant to be humorous, the sketches treated Cuban life lightly while indirectly questioning any type of authority. After the triumph of the Cuban Revolution in 1959, Secades felt that his sense of humor was not appreciated by the new regime, especially after the closing down by the government of the humorous magazine *Zig-Zag*. In 1962, he sought exile in Mexico, relocating in 1967 to the United States, where he transferred his attention to life in exile and the struggles of assimilation. Of the subway in New York City, he observed in an article collected in *Mejores estampas de Secades*, (1983) published after his death, "To ride on the subway, you must leave behind good manners, shyness, and compassion." Of the preparations for the arrival of a winter storm, he likened it to the preparations in the Caribbean for a hurricane, noticing that if neither the snow storm nor the hurricane took place, people were disappointed. Secades collected his writings in three books, *Estampas de la época* (1941), *Estampas de la época, cuentos y greguerías* (1943), and *Mejores estampas de Secades: estampas costumbristas cubanas de ayer y de hoy* (1983). *See also* Costumbrismo.

Further Reading

Secades, Eladio. *Las mejores estampas de Eladio Secades*. Miami: Ediciones Universal, 1998.

—D. H. Figueredo

Séguy-Villevaleix, Charles (1833–1920)

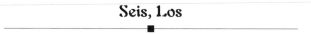

Séguy-Villevaleix was a pioneer Haitian poet. He was inspired by his country and wrote of the beauty of Haitian women rather than celebrating France and European standards of feminine beauty.

Born in Port-au-Prince, Haiti, in 1833, Séguy-Villevaleix was the son a public notary, a position of high public esteem. The young Séguy-Villevaleix was sent to study in France and upon his return assumed the post of teacher at L'École Polymathique. Séguy-Villevaleix became a journalist, contributing regularly to the periodical *Bien public*. He published his early poems in this journal.

Séguy-Villevaleix entered the diplomatic corps and served as secretary of the Haitian delegation in London. He also served in Paris during the 1860s. In 1866, he published in Paris the volume *Les Prime-vères*. Writing in rhyming verse, and influenced by the poetry of Victor Hugo (1802–85) and William Shakespeare (1564–1616), Séguy-Villevaleix wrote nature poetry that celebrated the beauty of Haiti, and in the poem "Rosita" he speaks of his love for a black woman. His glorification of the Haitian landscape and of the Haitian women was a novelty. For at the time, most Haitian writers were looking toward the French landscape and the concept of Western European feminine beauty for inspiration.

Further Reading

Berrou, Raphaël, and Pradel Pompilus. *Histoire de la littérature haïtienne*. Tome 1. Port-au Prince: Editions Caraëbes.

—D. H. Figueredo

Seis, Los

A Puerto Rican poetic movement that was founded in 1924 by **Antonio Coll Vidal, José I. de Diego Padró**, José E. Gelpi, Bolívar Pagán, **Luis Palés Matos**, and Juan J. Llovet. These writers published a journal titled *Los Seis*. The group's objective was to revitalize Puerto Rican values and identity in all areas of intellectual endeavor and to rescue the island from insularism. Later on, other writers joined the movement, including **Luis Muñoz Marín**, Pérez Pierret, and **Evaristo Ribera Chevrenont**. The latter in particular was responsible for introducing to Puerto Rico vanguard literature from Spain and the works of Vicente Huidobro (1893–1948), an avant-garde poet from Chile. As a group, Los Seis did not survive the 1920s; most members, however, went on to achieve national and literary recognition.

Further Reading

"Poesía." In *La gran enciclopedia de Puerto Rico*. Tomo 3. San Juan, Puerto Rico: Puerto en la Mano y La Gran Enciclopedia de Puerto Rico, 1976.

—*D. H. Figueredo*

Sekou, Lasana M. (1959–)

A poet, short-story writer, and essayist from St. Maarten, Sekou has received numerous awards for his writing and promotion of literature and culture in and about St. Maarten and the Caribbean.

Born in Aruba, Sekou was raised in St. Maarten. In 1982, he earned a BA in political science and international relations from the State University of New York–Stony Brook. In 1984, he received an MA in mass communication from Howard University, Washington, D.C. For his thesis he wrote the study *Political News in the People's Paper—A Content Analysis of Windward Islands Newsday (1976–1982)*.

Lasana M. Sekou has distinguished himself for his **poetry performances** throughout the United States and the Caribbean, Latin America, Africa, Europe, and Asia. In his published poetry collections—including *Born Here* (1986) and *Nativity and Monologues for Today* (1988)—he has claimed the African roots of his adopted island home—St. Maarten—while also identifying his country's similarities with other Caribbean countries and territories. In his collection of short stories, *Love Songs Make You Cry* (1989), he examines the Caribbean migrations that formed part of the economical and social reality of the twentieth century. A characteristic of his poetic production is the incorporation of oral traditions from Africa.

During the mid-1980s, he codirected and wrote for Traditions, the annual drama extravaganza that changed the face of theater in St. Maarten. He also served as editor of the periodical *St. Martin Newsday*. Since 1984, he has been director of the publishing company House of Nehesi Publishers, a major enterprise dedicated, for the first time in the history of St. Maarten, to the dissemination and distribution of books about the island. Sekou has been an active participant in debates about regional interests and the Caribbean and has collaborated with cultural and social institutions, such as the Philipsburg Jubilee Library and Council on the Arts.

Sekou was coauthor, with Oswald Francis and Napolina Gumbs, of the first compilation of political essays on the island, *The Independence Papers–Readings on a New Political Status for St. Maarten/St. Martin* (1990), and selected the topics that went into the reference volume *National Symbols of St. Martin—A Primer* (1996), a book about the historic personalities, culture, and flora and fauna of St. Maarten.

Lasana M. Sekou has received diverse awards to honor his cultural activities: the James Michener Fellow from the University of Miami, Florida (1993), the University of St. Martin Local Heroes and Heroines Awards (1998), and was knighted by the Kingdom of the Netherlands (2004).

Further Reading

Albus, Alida. "From Oral to Written Literature: St. Maarten, Saba, and St. Eustatious." In *A History of Literature in the Caribbean, vol. 2: English and Dutch-Speaking Regions*, edited by A. James Arnold, 443–49. Philadelphia: John Benjamins Publishing Co, 2001.

Badejo, Fabian A. "Introduction to Literature in English in the Dutch Windward Islands." *Callaloo* 21, no. 3 (1998): 676–79.

Combie, Valeri. "Brotherhood of the Spurs." *The Caribbean Writer* 13 (1999): 273–74.

Pereira, Joseph. "A Maturing Voice from St. Maarten." *The Sunday Gleaner*, Nov. 30, 1986.

—Emilio Jorge Rodríguez

Selvon, Samuel (1923–94)

∎

A native of Trinidad, Selvon was one of the early Caribbean writers to produce a literature in English that was read in Europe and that helped to develop international recognition of West Indian writers. Selvon wrote about immigrants and laborers, duplicating their languages in his novels. Observes Sandra Pouchet Paquet, in *Fifty Caribbean Writers*: "He [knew] their language and [used] it appreciatively and well; he was a pioneer in the use of a modified dialect as the language of consciousness" (441). He was also one of the first East Indian writers to achieve literary recognition.

Samuel Dickson Selvon was born in South Trinidad on May 20, 1923, the son of a woman who was half-Indian and half-Scottish and a man who was Indian. Though his mother wanted him to cultivate his Indian heritage, Selvon identified with the diverse cultural background of his classmates, who were African, Chinese, and European; thus he grew up with a creolized perception of himself. Though he graduated from Naparima College in 1938, he was not interested in studying and only began to read literature while serving in Royal Naval Reserve. It was during this period, from 1940 to 1945, that he first began to think about writing.

When World War II ended, he found a job as journalist for the *Guardian Weekly* and was soon appointed editor of that publication. He befriended writers who would later on become major literary figures: **George Lamming** and **Errol Hill**, to name two. He also submitted short stories to the influential journal **Bim**. In 1950, he moved to England. He stayed at a hotel where many other West Indians were living. Despite the harshness of the immigrant experience, the boarders from the Caribbean approached difficulties with a sense of humor and a zest for life. This experience would serve as the basis for Selvon's most famous work, *The Lonely Londoners* (1956).

In 1952, Selvon published his first novel, *A Brighter Sun*. This novel tells the story of an East India youth, his arranged marriage, and his move from the countryside to a neighborhood near the city. The narrative permits Selvon to study the complexities of racism—whites discriminating against anyone who was not white, East Indians discriminating against blacks—and to comment on the search for identity within a postcolonial society. The novel was well received by the critics and brought Selvon major recognition in the Caribbean's literary circles.

Equally well received was his third novel, *The Lonely Londoners*. These two novels represent the two major themes in Selvon's work, according to Sandra Pouchet Paquet: London and "the attractions and frustrations of West Indian emigrant life" there and Trinidad and "the psychic dangers that beset Caribbean life"(442). The success of these novels allowed Selvon to dedicate all his time to writing.

In 1958, Selvon published a sequel to *A Brighter Sun*—*Turn Again Tiger*—in which he explores the sexual attraction and tension the main character, Tiger, feels for a white woman. That same year, he adapted *The Lonely Londoners* for the screen.

Throughout the 1960s, Selvon visited the Caribbean quite often. The visits afforded him the opportunity to study the maturing process of Caribbean nations before and after independence in novels such as *I Hear Thunder* (1963) and *Those Who Eat the Cascadura* (1972). In the 1970s, he began writing the sequels to *The Lonely Londoners*: *Moses Ascending*, published in 1975, and *Moses Migrating*, published in 1983. In attempting to understand in these novels what it meant to be Caribbean, Selvon affirmed his own Caribbeanness.

In 1978, Selvon moved to Canada. He wrote extensively for BBC radio and published more than fifteen novels as well as plays. When he died on April 16, 1994, he had become the epitome of the writer in exile: living away from his homeland but always writing about it. *See also* Exile Literature; Immigrant Literature.

Further Reading

Looker, Mark. *Atlantic Passages: History, Community, and Language in the Fiction of Sam Selvon*. New York: Lang, 1996.

Paquet, Sandra Pouchet. "Samuel Dickson Selvon (1923–)." In *Fifty Caribbean Writers: A Bio-Bibliographical-Critical Sourcebook*, edited by Daryl Cumber Dance, 439–49. Westport, CT: Greenwood Press, 1986.

Salick, Roydon. *The Novels of Samuel Selvon: A Critical Study*. Westport, CT: Greenwood Press, 2001

—*D. H. Figueredo*

Senior, Olive (1942–)

Olive Senior is a Jamaican short-story writer, poet, lecturer, and publisher. Her writings maintain that the strength and vitality of the Caribbean is not based in the middle class but comes from the common people.

Olive Senior was born in rural Jamaica in 1942. The daughter of rural peasant farmers, young Olive lived between two environments, a dark-skinned lower-stratum village home and a light-skinned middle-class environment, where she was sent to be groomed for upward social mobility. Her early life was spent shifting between continua of worlds, and this became a major emphasis of her early fiction, which is predominantly written from the narrative perspective of children who are negotiating hazardous color and class relations.

Senior has worked with words her entire life. She studied journalism at the Thompson Foundation, Wales, 1964, and read for a bachelor of journalism at Carlton University Canada, 1967. In 1987, she studied book production at the University of the Philippines. Olive Senior began her working life as a reporter and sub editor with the *Daily Gleaner* in Jamaica from 1960 to 1964. She subsequently became an information officer with the Government Information Service and a publications editor with the Institute of Social and Economic Research, the University of the West Indies—Mona. From 1982 to 1989, Senior was the managing director of the Institute of Jamaica Publications and editor of *Jamaica Journal*. She has held numerous positions of faculty and writer in residence in tertiary institutions in the Caribbean and in the United States and Canada, including director of fiction workshop for the Caribbean Writers Summer Institute—1994, 1995—and faculty member in the school for writers in Humber College, Toronto.

Senior's publications include the collection of short stories *Discerner of Hearts* (2002), *Gardening in the Tropics* (1995), *Quartet*, a collection of stories by Maya Angelou, Alice Walker, **Lorna Goodison**, and Olive Senior (2002); *Working Miracles: Women's Lives in the English-Speaking Caribbean*, a compilation of studies of women's lives (1991); *Arrival of the Snake Woman* (stories) (1986); *Talking of Trees* (poetry) (1986); *A-Z of Jamaican Heritage* (1984); *Pop Story Gi Mi*, four booklets on Jamaican heritage for schools (1973); *The Message Is Change* (1972). Senior is currently working on an encyclopedia of Jamaican heritage—a labor of love intended to preserve the nation's indigenous cultures, which are under siege from entertainment and media-generated global cultural expression.

Her earliest short stories focused on children who are negotiating dichotomous worlds in terms of class and color relations. A gap is fixed between the free, natural lifestyle of the folk as opposed to the pressure to conform to a process of socialization, which is a prerequisite to upward mobility in Jamaican society. This latter process is portrayed as soul destroying, and the individuals who have achieved it are portrayed as stilted, false, and unnatural. In Senior's narrative, there is no linking character or principle between the dichotomy created by the two worlds. Indeed, they are often portrayed as irreconcilable entities, each with a guide who beckons or coerces, as the case may be. Senior is particularly gifted in her ability to convey the inner workings of the mind of the child, exploring complex psychosocial issues while remaining true to child's perspective

The second collection, *Arrival of the Snake Woman*, turns to a systematic and dispassionate view of Caribbean social relations. This title story explores African Indian relations in rural Jamaica as the arrivants grapple with the forces of imperialism; the constructions of gendered ethnicities and the competing ideologies of their ancestral communities and a hegemonic Christian worldview.

"The View from the Terrace" takes up the theme of class and gender relations from the perspective of an aged man confined to a wheelchair who has formed an obsessive though distant relationship with a woman who has the effrontery to squat on the hills opposite his terrace, in the centre of his favorite view. The woman becomes the focal point of the man's attention and over the years causes him to re-assess his entire life. He has carefully built an ordered, structured life based on class and other certainties—of which he was at the center and from which he controlled all around him. His right of ownership and sovereign mastery of all he surveys comes into question when he confronts the order, beauty, and simplicity of the lifestyle of a poor peasant woman. He is so conflated with his fantasy world that when it is exposed for the sham that it is, he self-destructs. Senior affirms that the strength and vitality of the Caribbean is not in the imitative pseudocultured middle class—it is in the folk. They will survive even as the illusory fantasy empires of the petty bourgeoisie fall. She also testifies of the existence of an intermediate class—an Anancy-type group that has learned to give the wealthy all that they desire, includ-ing the fantasy of subservience, but has kept a private flow of life and vitality and has learned to manipulate the two worlds.

In her poetry, Senior excels in capturing complex social and historical movements in verse. "Colonial Girls School" (1986), included in the volume *Talking of Trees*, deals with the process of indoctrination that was inherent in the British educational system and was damaging to the sexual and social identity for-mation of young Caribbean girls. In "Mediation on Yellow" (1985), in *Gardening in the Tropics*, the first persona engages both the historical civilizing enterprise of empire and the contemporary neoimperial interactions that undergird the tourism industry.

Olive Senior has received numerous awards, including the F. G. Bressani Liter-ary Prize for Poetry (1994), the Institute of Jamaica Silver Musgrave Medal for Lit-erature (1989), The Jamaica Press Association Award for Editorial Excellence (1987), and the Commonwealth Writer's Prize (1987).

Further Reading

Pollard, Velma. "Mothertongue Voices in the Writing of Olive Senior and Lorna Goodison." In *Mothertongue: Black Women's Writing from Africa, the Caribbean and South Asia*, edited by Susheila Nasta. London: The Women's Press, 1991.

—*Paula Morgan*

Serpa, Enrique (1900–68)

Serpa was a Cuban short-story writer, novelist, and journalist. He depicted the world of Cuban gangsters during the 1920s and 1930s. His crime fiction, however, drew complex psychological portraits of people on the margins of society.

Serpa was born in Havana on July 15, 1900. In the first decade of the twentieth century, he worked as a shoemaker and a typographer and eventually found a job in the office of attorney **Fernando Ortiz**, a major Cuban writer who introduced Serpa to other writers and intellectuals from Havana. Serpa then worked for several newspapers, including *El mundo*, and in the 1950s, due to his recognition as writer and journalist, he served as cultural attaché to the Cuban embassy in Paris.

His experiences in the law firm and as a journalist placed him in contact with Havana's underworld, which would serve as the basis for his novels. In 1938, he published the novel *Contrabando*. The narrative, about the smuggling of alcohol from Cuba to the United States during Prohibition, earned Serpa Cuba's National Literary Prize. In 1957, he published *La trampa*, about a gangster and a policeman and the tragic consequences of their meeting. He also wrote a collection of short stories, *Felisa y yo* (1937), exploring sexual relationships, and *Noche de fiesta* (1951), about political intrigue and persecution.

Serpa was influenced by **naturalismo**, which depicted members of the lower classes, but, according to **Antonio Benítez Rojo**, in *Dictionary of Twentieth-Century Cuban Literature* (1990), his work "shows aesthetic concerns and literary techniques that give his style a dynamism and flexibility seldom found in naturalistic novels" (433).

Further Reading

Martínez, Julio A. *Dictionary of Twentieth-Century Cuban Literature*. Westport, CT: Greenwood Press, 1990.

—*D. H. Figueredo*

Seymour, A. J. (1914–89)

◼

The founder and editor of the pioneer literary journal *Kyk-Over-Al*, Seymour was a Guyanese poet and anthologist who promoted Guyanese and West Indian literature. His poetry mirrored the nationalistic growth of West Indian poets: from works imitative of British poetry to a voice that affirmed West Indian culture and self-rule.

Arthur James Seymour was born on January 12, 1914, in Georgetown, British Guiana, now Guyana. After graduating from high school, he worked as an administrator in several government positions—such as the Bureau of Publicity and Information—most of them related to information and community services. In the early 1960s, he was the information officer at the Caribbean Organization in Puerto Rico. In the 1970s, he taught at numerous universities and schools in Guyana and in the Caribbean. He also edited a weekly radio program.

Sensing the movement toward independence in the West Indies during the 1940s, as well as the awareness of a need for a national literature, Seymour founded in 1945 the journal *Kyk-Over-Al*, named after a Dutch fortress established on the island in the sixteenth century. The journal attempted to define and foster a national identity primarily through poetry and essays. In 1951, Seymour established the Miniature Poet Series, pamphlets which featured poems by Guyanese and Caribbean writers such as **Martin Carter, Wilson Harris, Philip Sherlock**, and

Frank Collymore, introducing many of them to a Caribbean audience. Eager to promote anglophone Caribbean literature, he went on to publish several anthologies based on submissions featured in his journal: *An Anthology of West Indian Poetry, Kyk-Over-Al* (1952), *An Anthology of Guianese Poetry, Kyk-Over-Al* (1954), and *The Kyk-Over-Al Anthology of West Indian Poetry* (1957).

Seymour himself wrote several volumes of poetry that, considering limited publishing opportunities in Guyana, he printed himself. Some of the titles include *Six Songs* (1946), *We Do Not Presume to Come* (1948), *Three Voluntaries* (1953), *A Little Wind of Christmas* (1967), *Black Song* (1972), *City of Memory* (1974), and *Tomorrow Belongs to the People* (1975). As a poet, he was initially dismissed as an imitator of colonial literature, according to Lloyd W. Brown, in *Fifty Caribbean Writers*. But in the 1980s, critics became aware that Seymour evolved into a poet searching for his own Guyanese voice, even writing poems, such as "Over Guiana Clouds" (1944)—his most famous—that contained criticism of colonialism while celebrating the move toward independence. During the 1970s and 1980s, Seymour wrote his autobiography in a three volume set: *Growing up in Guyana* (1976), *Pilgrim Memories* (1978), and *Thirty Years a Civil Servant* (1982). In 1970, the Guyanese government honored Seymour with the Golden Arrow of Achievement Award. In 1974, the National Library of Guyana published a monograph listing all of Seymour's writings. *See also* Guyanese Literature, History of; Literary Journals.

Further Reading

Brown, Lloyd W. "A. J. Seymour (1914–)." In *Fifty Caribbean Writers: A Bio-Bibliographical-Critical Sourcebook*, edited by Daryl Cumber Dance, 451–55. Westport, CT: Greenwood Press, 1986.

Christiani, Joan. *A. J. Seymour: A Bibliography*. Georgetown, Guyana: National Library, 1974.

—*D. H. Figueredo*

Sherlock, Sir Philip M. (1902–)

A poet, Philip M. Sherlock was an early promoter of a national Jamaican culture. He was also a historian and an educator.

Philip Manderson Sherlock was born on February 25, 1902, in Portland, Jamaica. A brilliant student, he attended Calabar College in Jamaica before earning a BA in English from the University of London, through the external degree program. He worked as a high school teacher until 1939, when he became secretary of the Institute of Jamaica and Education Officer of Jamaica Welfare Limited. During this decade, he achieved a reputation as a teller of **Anancy**—the African Caribbean trickster—stories. In 1945, he served in a committee that recommended the establishment of the University College of the West Indies and founded the Extra Mural Department at that university. In 1960, he was appointed vice chancellor of the University of the Association of the West Indies.

While achieving recognition as an educator, he also became well known as a historian, writing several volumes on the history of Jamaica. Always keeping in mind a young reading audience, Sherlock's style was closer to his skills as story-teller rather as an academic. His history tomes, which included *The Aborigines of Jamaica* (1939), *Jamaica To-day, a Handbook of Information for Visitors and Intending Residents* (1940), *Jamaica: a Junior History* (1966), proved popular in schools. He also wrote books on the Caribbean: *A Short History of the West Indies* (1956), *Caribbean Citizen* (1957), and *The Land and People of the West Indies* (1967). For his work as an educator and public servant, he was knighted by the British in 1967.

As a poet, he was an early contributor to the influential review *Focus*, edited by **Edna Manley**. One of his most popular poems is "Pocomania" (1949), in which he celebrates Jamaica and the Caribbean:

> Black of skin and white of gown
> Black of night and candle light . . . Africa among the trees
> Asia with her mysteries.

Though he published numerous poems in literary journals, his only volume of poetry is *Ten Poems* (1953), published in the Miniature Poet Series that **A. J. Seymour** edited.

Further Reading

Brown, Lloyd W. *West Indian Poetry*. Boston: Twayne, 1978.

Donnell, Alison, and Sarah Lawrence Welsh, 58–59. *The Routledge Reader in Caribbean Literature*. London: Routledge, 1996.

—*D. H. Figueredo*

Shinebourne, Janice (1947–)

Shinebourne is a Guyanese author who explores the transition from colonialism to independence in her novels.

Of East Indian and Chinese heritage, Janice Low Shinebourne was educated at Berbice High School, New Amsterdam, and the University of Guyana, in Georgetown. During the 1960s, she wrote for several newspapers and witnessed the rapid transformation of Guyana from what she perceived as a revolutionary state to a reactionary society, where conflict arose between the Afro-Guyanese and the Indo-Guyanese. In 1974, she moved to Great Britain. In London, she wrote for and edited several journals, including the *Southall Review*. She was also an activist within the Afro-Asian community of London.

Nostalgic for Guyana and recalling her mother's life during the 1950s and 1960s, when colonialism was nearing its end and a postcolonial Guyana was attempting to define itself politically, Shinebourne began to write. Her first novel was *Timepiece* (1986)—which she actually started to write while in college—about a young reporter fighting censorship while also dealing with the loss of her parents. Her second, and best-known work, was *The Last English Plantation* (1988). It takes place in 1953, when Guyana is granted home rule by the British and when Winston Churchill (1874–1965), fearing a Communist takeover, sent the military to Guyana to remove from power the elected minister, Cheddi Jagan (1918–97), who was a Socialist. The events are seen through the eyes of a young girl.

Shinebourne travels widely, reading from her works. She is a visiting professor at New York University and writes for several journals. *See also* Postcolonialism.

Further Reading

Shinebourne, Janice. "Twin Influences: Guyana in the 1960s and Anglophone Caribbean Literature." In *Caribbean Women Writers: Essays from the First International Conference*, edited by Selwyn R. Cudjoe, 142–44. Wellesley, MA: Calaloux Publications, 1990.

—*D. H. Figueredo*

Sierra Berdecía, Fernando (1903–62)

Sierra Berdecía was a Puerto Rican dramatist, journalist, and public servant. His life was divided between his creative and literary activities and his work in numerous political and civic organizations.

A native of Ciales, Sierra Berdecía lived in New York City as a child and returned to Puerto Rico when he was in his teens. Devoted to public service and literature, he was highly productive in both spheres. As a public servant, he served in several labor-related positions, including secretary of Labor from 1952 to 1961 (some sources say 1958). He was on the board of Council on Higher Education and represented the Partido Popular Democrático, of which he was one of the founders, in the Puerto Rican Congress. He was an active member of the **Ateneo Puertorriqueño**, the Sociedad Puertorriqueña de Periodistas, and the Academia Puertorriqueña de la Lengua.

In the 1930s, he began to write articles and news stories for numerous newspapers, including *El Mundo*, and *El Imparcial*. He also published literary criticism in such influential reviews as *Alma Latina* and *Revista del Ateneo Puertorriqueño*. He wrote poetry as well, but his major literary contribution was the comedy *Esta noche juega el joker* (1939).

The play explored the popular theme of Puerto Ricans who live in New York City. But unlike René Marqués, who in his masterpiece **La Carreta** (1952) depicted the move from the island to Manhattan as a tragic event with deadly consequences, Sierra Berdecía celebrated his compatriots' ability to survive—and to laugh—in the face of adversity. The play received the 1939 literary prize from the Instituto de

Literatura Puertorriqueña. His second play, *La escuela de buen humor*, an examination of overpopulation in Puerto Rico, was staged in 1941.

In the 1940s and 1950s, Sierra Berdecía wrote literary criticism and social commentaries: *Antonio S. Pedreira: buscador de la personalidad puertorriqueña* (1942), *Fuente de trabajo* (1952), *Emigración puertorriqueña* (1955), and *La libertad de información como derecho de los ciudadanos* (1957). Like many of his compatriots, Sierra Berdecía was also concerned about the conflict between the uses of Spanish and English on the island, *El español y el inglés en Puerto Rico* (1959).

Sierra Berdecía was praised for his sense of humor and the ability to duplicate the Puerto Rican vernacular in his dramas. He endowed his characters with humility and dignity.

Further Reading

Toro-Sugrañes, José A. "Biografías." In *Nueva enciclopedia de Puerto Rico* 195. Hato Rey, Puerto Rico: Editorial Lector, 1994.

—*D. H. Figueredo*

Sigüenza y Góngora, Carlos de (1645–1700)

A Mexican **baroque** poet who wrote a true narrative about a Puerto Rican who had been kidnapped by pirates and led a life of adventures and misadventures. The work was entitled *Los infortunios de Alonso Ramírez* (1690).

Sigüenza y Góngara was a relative of Luis de Góngora (1561–1626), one of Spain's greatest poets, and grew up in a home surrounded by books. His father, who had been a royal tutor in Spain before moving to Mexico, was his teacher. At the age of fourteen he began his training to become a Jesuit but in 1667 was expelled from the Jesuit Society for venturing out at night without permission. He continued his studies at the Universidad de México and in 1672 was appointed chair of mathematics and astrology. Sigüenza y Góngara demonstrated numerous talents: he was a poet, a philosopher, a cartographer, an archeologist, and a historian, to list a few.

In the late 1680s, he met Alonso Ramírez, a Puerto Rican who narrated to Sigüenza y Góngara how he had left Puerto Rico for Cuba, had traveled to the Philippines, had then been kidnapped by pirates, and cast off in the Yucatan, surviving and making his way to Mexico City. Sigüenza y Góngara wrote the narrative and published it in 1690. The narrative was an adventure story, a biography, and travelogue. Though of humble beginnings and illiterate, Alonso Ramírez was able to express himself with wit, thus facilitating Sigüenza y Gongara's task as an interviewer and author.

Los infortunios de Alonso Ramírez was the first literary instance of a picaresque Puerto Rican character in literature; the work was also a precursor of the Latin American novel. *See also* Barroco/Baroque; Puerto Rican Literature, History of.

Further Reading

Nofal, Rossana. *La imaginación histórica en la colonia: Carlos de Sigüenza y Góngora*. San Miguel de Tucumán, Argentina: Instituto Interdisciplinario de Estudios Latinoamericanos, Facultad de Filosofía-Universidad Nacional de Tucumán, 1996.

—D. H. Figueredo

Silvestri, Reinaldo (1935–)

Silvestri is a Puerto Rican poet and journalist. A native of Cabo Rojo, Silvestri studied at the Universidad Interamericana de San Germán and the Colegio Agricultura y Artes Mecánicas de Mayagüez. Attracted to journalism, he wrote for several newspapers and magazines, including *El Mundo, El Imparcial*, and *El Diario de Nueva York*.

In 1960, he published his first collection of poems, *Poemas amargos*. In 1969, he published *Poema de un silencio azul*. In 1978, *Hombres de alma y de barro*. In 1987, he self-published *Tiempo abrupto—y aún te dejo una canción*. His poetry is romantic, expressing his love of the island while also addressing such universal themes as mortality, love, and creativity. Some of his early poems, published in the influential journal *Guajana*, address political themes.

Further Reading

Enciclopedia puertorriqueña: Siglo XXI. Vol. 6. Santurce: Caribe Grolier, Inc. 1998.

—D. H. Figueredo

Simpson, Louis (1923–)

A prolific Jamaican American poet, Simpson has received numerous awards and honors. A World War II hero and a scholar, his initial works did not reveal much of his Jamaican heritage, but his matured work as a poet and his two autobiographies render tribute to his birthplace and to Jamaicans.

Louis Aston Marontz Simpson was born on March 27, 1923, in Kingston, Jamaica, the son of a well-known Jamaican attorney and a Russian actress. Expected by his parents to be an attorney, Simpson went to New York City during World War II. He served in the army as a sergeant and was awarded the Purple Heart. After the war, he matriculated at Columbia University. Since literature, writing, and teaching beckoned him, he did not pursue a career in law.

After obtaining a BA in English literature in 1948 and finishing an MA in 1950 from Columbia, he accepted the position of editor at Bobbs-Merrill Publishing, where he worked for five years. In 1952, he published *The Arrivistes, Poems*, which consisted of verses he had written as a college student and during the war. In 1955, his second volume appeared, *Good News of Death and Others Poems*. Critics noticed his works, commenting on his mastering of traditional forms of poetry. In 1957, he was awarded the Prix de Rome for poetry.

In 1959, he published *A Dream of Governors*. That same year, he earned a PhD from Columbia University and moved to California, where he was first an assistant professor and then a professor of English at the University of California–Berkeley. The early 1960s saw the publication of two volumes of poetry—*At the End of the Open Road* (1963) and *Selected Poems* (1965)—and several major distinctions, including the Pulitzer Prize for Poetry (1964) for *At the End of the Open Road*, the Columbia University Award for Excellence (1965), and the Commonwealth Club of California poetry award (1965). The poems included in these volumes were more experimental and with more flexible stanzas, wherein the poet attempts to understand what America is and his own sense of development as a writer and as a person.

Toward the end of the 1960s, Simpson returned to New York, teaching poetry and comparative literature at New York State University–Stony Brook. In 1972, he published his autobiography, *North of Jamaica*. If many of his early poems did not reveal his love of the island and appreciation of Caribbean culture, this autobiography clearly states the opposite, as Simpson nostalgically looks back at his childhood, his father's long hours of work as an attorney, and the beauty of Jamaica. Other works followed, in diverse genres: in literary studies, he published *Three on the Tower: The Lives and Works of Ezra Pound, T. S. Eliot and William Carlos Williams* (1975) and *A Revolution in Taste: Studies of Dylan Thomas, Allen Ginsberg, Sylvia Plath and Robert Lowell* (1979); as a poet, he published *Searching for the Ox* (1976), *Out of Season* (1979), and *Caviare at the Funeral* (1980). In 1980, he was awarded the Institute of Jamaica Centenary Medal for his poetry and academic work.

Through the 1980s, he continued his poetic productivity. In 1994, he published a follow-up to his autobiography, *The King My Father's Wreck*, where he recounted his World War II experiences, which led him to oppose the Vietnam War, his maturity as a writer, and a visit to Jamaica to return a book he had borrowed from a library fifty years before. In 2003, he was nominated for the National Book Award for the collection of poetry *The Owner of the House: New Collected Poems*. In 2004, critic Peter Makuck wrote of Simpson: "There are many things to admire about Louis Simpson's work—the perfect pitch of his voice, his range, critical intelligence and serious knowledge, probing explorations, gift for imagery, wit, and humor—but I especially value his ability to look beyond the turmoil of a self and take an interest in the world and people very different from himself."

Further Reading

Lazer, Hank. *On Louis Simpson: Depths Beyond Happiness*. Ann Arbor: University of Michigan Press, 1988.

Makuck, Peter. "The Simpson House: Sixty-One Years in Construction." *The Hudson Review* 57, no. 2 (Summer 2004): 335–45.

—*D. H. Figueredo*

Sin Nombre (1970)

Journal founded by **Nilita Vientós Gastón** to promote works by Puerto Rican writers. Prior to this periodical, Vientós Gastón had published the journal *Asomante*, the organ of the Asociación de Graduadas de la Universidad de Puerto Rico, but when this association attempted to dictate what could be or could not be published in the journal, Vientós Gastón ended the relationship with the sponsoring group. However, when she attempted to continue publishing the journal, she was informed she did not have the rights to the publication. Therefore, she began to edit a new journal, and since she could not use the name of her previous publication, she decided to call the new venture the journal without a name, *Sin Nombre*, as she indicated in her first editorial.

The journal's objective was to maintain an intellectual conversation with the rest of Latin America, featuring essays and creative writings by Puerto Rican and Latin American authors and introducing new foreign writers to Puerto Rican readers. *Sin Nombre* was funded with subscriptions and ads from local bookstores and from such prestigious publishers as Editorial Seix Barral, from Spain, and Siglo Veintiuno, from Mexico. In 1975, *Sin Nombre* ceased to publish the journal, opting to become a publishing house instead. *See also* Literary Journals.

Further Reading

Sin Nombre 15, no. 1 (October–December, 1984).

—*Fernando Acosta-Rodríguez and D. H. Figueredo*

Singh, Rajkumari (1923–79)

One of the first published Indo-Caribbean women, Singh was an activist, a poet, a dramatist, and a literary mentor from Guyana.

Singh was born in Georgetown, British Guyana, in 1923, the daughter of a doctor and a cultural activist. Her parents, members of the upper class, promoted Indian culture in the Caribbean and encouraged Singh to affirm her Indo-Guyanese heritage. At the age of five, Singh contracted polio and was affected for the rest of her life, often suffering pain and walking with the help of a cane.

Singh pursued writing and the promotion of the arts from an early age. In 1960, she wrote and staged a drama, *Gitangali*. That same year she published a book of short stories, *A Garland of Stories*. During this decade, she devoted much of her time to political work within the People's Progressive Party, which promoted independence from Great Britain.

After independence in the 1970s, Singh continued her work in the arts. She edited the literary booklet *Heritage* and founded, in 1972, the **Messenger Group**, an influential cultural association that would influence the career of such emerging writers as **Mahadia Das**. She also joined the Guyana National Service with the objective of demystifying Indians to the Afro-Guyanese population. Indo-Guyanese criticized her action, believing that it was a way of betraying her Indian culture and heritage. Nevertheless, her work helped all Guyanese accept each other's heritage and contributions to the nation.

One of her most famous writings is the poetic essay "I Am a Coolie" (1973), in which like the writers of the **Négritude** movement who affirmed and rejoiced in their blackness, she reshaped the pejorative term *coolie* into an expression of Indian pride. Her other works include *Days of the Sahib Are Over* (1971) and *Collection of Poems* (1976).

Further Reading

Donnell, Alison, and Sarah Lawson Welsh. *The Routledge Reader in Caribbean Literature.* London: Routledge, 1996.

—*D. H. Figueredo*

Slave Narratives

Autobiographical texts written or dictated by former slaves from Africa, or of African descent, reconstructing their human bondage, as Charles T. Davis and Henry Louis Gates Jr. phrased it in *The Slaves Narratives* (1985). Some of the elements of the slave narratives include, according to James Olney, in the essay "I was Born: Slave Narratives, Their Status as Autobiography and Literature" (1985): a chronology from birth to freedom or old age; descriptions of cruel masters; an account of the horrors of slavery; stories about strong slaves; comments on Christianity; depiction of slave auctions where families were separated; descriptions of escape attempts; achieving freedom; obtaining a new name; reflections on slavery (152–53). Slave narratives, which were as engaging as novels, proved powerful political tools used by abolitionists during the nineteenth century.

One of the most famous slave narratives from the Caribbean—though it was written in England—was *The Interesting Narratives of the Life of Olaudah Equiano, or Gustavus Vassa, the African, Written by Himself* (1787). This volume proved a popular text that fueled the abolitionist movement in England and created the model for all nineteenth-century slave narratives. **Mary Prince** narrated her story to Thomas Pringle, who edited the narrative into a book entitled *The History of Mary Prince, a West Indian Slave, Related by Herself.* The volume was published as an antislavery tract in 1833. As popular as these works was the book *Poems by a Slave in the Island of Cuba* (1840), written by **Juan Francisco Manzano** and translated into English by Dr. R. R. Madden. Manzano had been encouraged by Cuban abolitionist **Domingo del Monte** to write the autobiography and to offer it to Madden as an antislavery text. In the twentieth century, another Cuban text gained international recognition: *Autobiografía de un Cimarró*, written by former slave Esteban Montejo and edited by **Miguel Barnet**.

The nineteenth-century narratives contained strong Christian motifs, and many were modeled on the British religious classic *Pilgrim's Progress* (1678). The twentieth-century narratives were of a more secular vein. Both types, though, served as political documents.

Slave narratives have informed and inspired countless of novels written in the Caribbean by twentieth-century writers. Some of the best known are **Lino Novas Calvo**'s *El negrero: Vida novelada de Pedro Blanco Fernández de Trava* (1933), a realistic historical novel about a slave trader; *Die the Long Day* (1972), by **Orlando Patterson**, which tells the story of a slave woman in eighteenth-century Jamaica and her efforts to stop her master from raping her daughter; *Ti Marie* (1988), by **Valerie Belgrave**, wherein the tragic lives of a slave couple is contrasted with the romantic existence of a white aristocrat and mulatto beauty; and *Ajeemah and His Son* (1992), written by **James Berry**, about the enslavement of a father and his son. *See also* Abolitionist Literature; Equiano, Olaudah.

Further Reading

Gates, Henry Louis, and Charles T. Davis, eds. *The Slave's Narrative*. Oxford: Oxford University Press, 1985.

Olney, James. "I was Born: Slave Narratives, Their Status as Autobiography and Literature." In *The Slave's Narrative*, edited by Henry Louis Gates and Charles T. Davies. Oxford: Oxford University Press, 1985.

Smith, Faith. "Beautiful Indians, Troublesome Negroes, and Nice White Men: Caribbean Romances and the Invention of Trinidad." In *Caribbean Romances: The Politics of Regional Presentation*, edited by Belinda J. Edmondson. Charlottesville: University Press of Virginia, 1999.

—D. H. Figueredo

Smith, Michael "Mikey" (1954–83)

Mikey Smith was one of the first performance artists from the Caribbean to gain international recognition. His poetry, meant to be performed rather than heard, used the language of the common people, often combining Jamaican dialect with standard English.

Michael Smith was born in Kingston, Jamaica, on September 14, 1954. His family was poor, and though he attended public schools, Smith claimed that he picked up his education on the streets. He started to write poetry as a child and read the works of **Marcus Garvey** and Langston Hughes (1902–67). Considering himself a man of the people, he developed an interest in performing poetry rather than just writing it. He began to read his poems at clubs and community centers. In 1978, he attended the World Festival of Youth in Cuba where he performed his poetry. That same year, he recorded and released three compositions, "Word," "Mi Cyaan Believe It," and "Roots." As his fame grew, he traveled to Europe to perform and in 1981, the BBC released a documentary on Carifesta, an annual cultural celebration in Barbados, featuring Smith performing.

While performing and traveling, Smith studied drama at Jamaica School of Drama, graduating in 1980 with a degree in theater. His studies disproved the impression that Smith was casual about his craft and that he often improvised his performance while on the stage; to the contrary, Smith devoted hours of practice to perfecting his delivery and rhythm, reciting lines into a recorder to listen to his voice and cadence. Politically, Smith preferred leftist ideology, was a supporter of the Cuban Revolution, and was critical of political developments on Jamaica. He was murdered on August 17, 1983, when three men stoned him to death. *See also* Dub Poetry; Performance Poetry.

Further Reading

Cooper, Carolyn. *Noises in the Blood: Orality, Gender, and the "Vulgar" Body of Jamaican Popular Culture*. Durham, NC: Duke University Press, 1995.

Hoyles, Asher, and Martin Hoyles. *Moving Voices: Black Performance Poetry*. London: Hansib Publications Limited, 2002.

—*D. H. Figueredo*

Smorkaloff, Pamela María (1956–)

One of the earliest Cuban American scholars to defy the definition of contemporary Cuban literature as either a work of the Revolution or exile, Smorkaloff is a literary critic and essayist who approaches the Caribbean from a multiplicity of views and experiences. She is a well-known lecturer and researcher.

Pamela María Smorkaloff was born in New York City of Cuban and Russian parents. Her Cuban grandmother and Cuban mother influenced her identification with Cuba rather than with Russia, and from early on in her life, Smorkaloff was attracted to Cuban and Latin American culture and the Spanish language. She received a BA in romance languages from New York University. She went on to earn an MA in 1980, concentrating in Latin American and Brazilian literature, and a PhD in 1986 in Latin American literature, both from New York University.

Approaching the Cuban Revolution from a perspective that included both the views of Cubans on the island and those outside the island, she conducted research in Cuba, publishing in 1987 *Literatura y edición de libros; la cultura literaria y el proceso social en Cuba, 1900–1987*, winner of a literary prize from the **Casa de las Américas**. Her interpretation of Cuban literature as a product of the exile experience before the arrival of **Fidel Castro** in 1959 challenged the position held by many Cuban scholars in the United States, who maintained that the Cuban Revolution was unique in uprooting writers such as **Guillermo Cabrera Infante** and **Heberto Padilla**. Smorkaloff, on the other hand, asserted that most classics of Cuban literature, such as **Cecilia Valdés** by **Cirilo Villaverde** and the works of **José Martí**, were written in exile. Furthermore, she expanded and extended this view to the rest of the Caribbean in her volume *If I Could Write This in Fire: An Anthology* *of Literature from the Caribbean* (1994), where again she demonstrated that exile and writing in exile was a characteristic of the region.

In 1997, Smorkaloff published *Readers and Writers in Cuba: A Social History of Print Culture, 1830s–1990s* (1997), a history of the relationship between publishing, institutions such as universities, and writers in Cuba. Exile again was one of themes she explored in *Cuban Writers on and off the Island* (1999) where she elaborated on the concept of Cuban literature as works produced beyond borders: a "'stretching' of the contemporary canon," as she explains it (ix). Her *Cuban Reader* (2004), coedited with Aviva Chomsky and Barry Carr, is a history of the island presented from a diversity of multidisciplinary sources.

Smorkaloff has taught at New York University and Princeton University and is an associate professor at Montclair State University, New Jersey, where she directed the Latin American and Latino Studies Program.

Further Reading

Behar, Ruth., ed. *Bridges to Cuba—Puentes a Cuba*. Ann Arbor: University of Michigan Press, 1998.

Smorkaloff, Pamela María. *Cuban Writers on and off the Island*. New York: Twayne, 1999.

———. 2004. Interview by D. H. Figueredo, Dec.

—*D. H. Figueredo*

Soler Puig, José (1916–98)

José Soler Puig was the first Cuban novelist to publish the first novel of the Cuban Revolution. Entitled *Bertillón 166*, the novel, published in 1960, describes a day during the last year, 1959, of the dictatorship of Fulgencio Batista (1901–73). A socialist realist work, it won the 1960 **Casa de las Américas** literary prize and established Soler Puig as one of the Revolution's major new writers.

Soler Puig was born on November 10, 1916, in Santiago de Cuba, Oriente. His father owned a bakery, and as a young man Soler Puig socialized with the bakers and other workers. Through these friendships, Soler Puig grew conscious of uneven social conditions on the island. In 1933, he joined the Socialist Youth Movement and became an ardent reader of Communist political works.

He was also interested in writing. Though he attended several schools, he never graduated from any one institution, thus his education as a writer evolved from his reading of the book *El arte de escribir* (1924) by Miguel de Toro y Gómez, during the 1930s, and his friendship with Cuban intellectual José Antonio Portuondo (1911–96), during the 1950s. From the manual on writing he learned the discipline of the craft, the need to write every day. From Portuondo's advice, he developed plots based on his knowledge of the struggles of Cuban workers and of the clandestine activities carried out against Batista. In 1959, he wrote *Bertillón 166*.

The novel, atmospheric and suspenseful, tells of the revolutionary struggle in the city of Santiago de Cuba. It is filled with chase scenes, encounters between young rebels and the police, and human rights violations in Batista's prisons. The success of this novel on the island and abroad allowed the author the opportunity to write full-time, though he still participated in cultural activities and conferences sponsored by the revolutionary regime. As a cultural representative of Cuba's new government, he traveled widely throughout Europe.

In 1963, he wrote *En el año de enero*, again set during the fight against Batista, and in 1964, he wrote *El derrumbe*, a naturalistic novel where the author contrasts the sexual desires of a member of the Cuban bourgeoisie with the revolutionary idealism of a young woman. His *El pan dormido* (1975) continues the analyses of the revolutionary and political process in Cuba, this time during the dictatorship of Gerardo Machado (1871–1939). *El caserón* (1976) is an experimental novel about a family and the big house, caserón, where they live. Some of his other works include *Mundo de cosas* (1982), *El nudo* (1983), *El decoro de muchos* (1983), *Anima sola* (1986), *Año nuevo* (1989).

Soler Puig also wrote dramas and radio scripts, but he is best remembered for his first novel. He died in 1998. *See also* Fidel Castro; Literatura Comprometida/Socially Engaged Literature; Naturalism/Naturalismo.

Further Reading

Torres, Edel. *Los caminos y la palabra de José Soler Puig*. Santiago de Cuba: Editorial Oriente, Ediciones Santiago, 2002.

—*D. H. Figueredo*

Soto, Pedro Juan (1928–2002)

A major Puerto Rican dramatist, novelist, and short-story writer, Soto studied the cultural duality experienced by Puerto Rican immigrants who found themselves rootless in both the United States and Puerto Rico. He was also a journalist and a college professor.

Pedro Juan Soto was born in Cataño, Puerto Rico, on July 11, 1928. His father was a barber and also a seller of coffins. His mother was an "espiritista," a spiritualist, who held séances in her home. The presence of the coffins and séances both frightened and fascinated young Soto. These incidents seeded his imagination with stories.

Soto attended elementary and secondary schools in his hometown and in the town of Bayamón, then moved to New York City to enroll at Long Island University in 1946—initially to study pre-medicine but later switching to English literature. After graduation, he was drafted into the army and served in Korea. The discrimination he witnessed in New York and in the army inspired him to write a series of short stories entitled *Spiks* (1956), the derogatory term racists used to refer to Puerto Ricans.

Once his tour was finished, he matriculated at Columbia University, earning an MA in 1953. He also wrote articles for several Spanish dailies and magazines published in New York: *Diario de Nueva York, Temas* and *Ecos de Nueva York*. That year, his short story "Garabatos," won the literary prize from the **Ateneo Puertorriqueño**.

Returning to Puerto Rico in 1954, he wrote screenplays and pamphlets for the Puerto Rico Department of Education. In 1959, he published the novel *Usmail*, which takes places on the island of Vieques, at the time an American naval base. In 1961, he published *Ardiente suelo, fría estación*, a novel about a Puerto Rican who returns home after living in New York City. The protagonist finds that while Americans do not want him because of his nationality, Puerto Ricans on the island reject him as a New Yorker. In 1969, Soto published *El francotirador*, about a Cuban exile living in Puerto Rico.

As his reputation grew, tragedy visited him: in 1978, his nineteen-year-old son was killed by Puerto Rican police officers who accused the young man of planning to sabotage a television station on a hillside called Cerro Maravilla. Though years of investigation and litigation concluded that the police had used excessive force, Soto did not find relief in the government's admission of guilt. From 1978 onward, bitterness characterized his writings, and his own health began to fail: he developed diabetes and had to have a leg amputated.

In 1982, Soto published *Un oscuro pueblo sonriente*, for which he received the prestigious **Casas de las Américas** literary award. He continued writing while teaching literature at the Universidad de Puerto Rico. Upon his death, he left an unfinished diary about his son's death and the Cerro Maravilla incident. *See also* Lugo Filippi, Carmen.

Further Reading

Ortiz Guzmá, Rosaura. "Tres grandes temas de Spiks." *Revista de Estudios Generales* 1, no. 1 (January–June 1987): 43–64.

"Pedro Juan Soto." In *Spanish-American Authors: The Twentieth Century*, edited by Angel Flores, 828–30. New York: Wilson, 1992.

Simpson, Victor C. *Colonialism and Narrative in Puerto Rico: A study of Characterization in the Novels of Pedro Juan Soto*. New York: Lang, 2004.

—*Emilio Jorge Rodríguez*

Soto Vélez, Clemente (1905–93)

Soto Vélez was a groundbreaking poet and one of the most significant and revered contemporary Puerto Rican writers. He was a mentor to many of the young artists and writers of his time. He was a founding member of a vanguard literary group known as **Atalayismo**.

Born in 1905 in Lares, Puerto Rico, Soto Vélez was orphaned when he was seven years old and was reared by his godfather. As a boy, he attended a primary school in the Lares countryside and also studied painting in Arecibo. At the age of thirteen, he went to live with his sister in San Juan and enrolled in the Ramírez Commercial School, where he studied electrical engineering and business administration. Interested in literature and the arts, he participated in intellectual circles and gatherings at the **Ateneo Puertorriqueño** and the Carnegie Library, where he met poets such as **Alfredo Margenat** and Pedro Carrasquillo. In 1928, he worked as a journalist and as editor in chief of the newspaper *El Tiempo*, but he was dismissed for publishing an editorial against sugar company interests. Also in 1928, along with Margenat and Carrasquillo, he formed a literary group called "El hospital de los sensitivos," a name under which they published their new brand of poetry. They were joined by another young, talented poet, **Graciany Miranda Archilla**, and together with **Fernando González Alberti**, Luis Hernández Aquino, **Samuel Lugo**, Juan Calderón Escobar, and Antonio Cruz Nieves they founded the group "El Atalaya de los Dioses," which turned into an important literary movement known as "Atalayismo." Their aim was to break with existing literary traditions and

Founding member of the literary movement Atalayismo, Clemente Soto Vélez was an experimental Puerto Rican poet and much-admired cultural figure. *Source: Centro de Estudios Puertorriqueños.*

be the vanguard of a new movement. This caused a great deal of controversy among other writers and intellectuals but also gained the group an enthusiastic following.

"El Grupo Atalaya" sought to connect the poetic and literary world with political action. Their emergence coincided with the rise of the Partido Nacionalista de Puerto Rico, which advocated the overthrow of American colonial rule in Puerto Rico. Subsequently, a number of the "atalayistas" were radicalized and joined the Nationalist Party. Soto Vélez was among those who became a militant member of the Partido Nacionalista and worked as an organizer for the party. He took part in an attempt to take over the capital building in San Juan in 1932 and in 1934 was arrested and jailed for helping to instigate and participate in a sugar workers' strike. In 1936, Soto Vélez and other Nationalist leaders were brought up on conspiracy charges and sentenced to seven years in prison. Soto Vélez was moved from prison in San Juan to Atlanta, Georgia. He was given a conditional pardon in 1940 and returned to Puerto Rico, where he was imprisoned once again for violating the conditions of his release. This time he was transferred to a prison in Lewisburg, Pennsylvania, where he served out the remaining two years of his sentence. While in prison, he met Earl Browder (1891–1973), Secretary General of the Communist Party of the USA, which Soto Vélez later joined in 1943. Soto Vélez was released in 1942, but because of the war and as a condition of his release, he was not permitted to return to Puerto Rico. Instead, he set up residence in New York City.

Once in New York, he immersed himself in political activity. He got involved with the American Labor Party and Vito Marcantonio's (1902–54) political campaigns. His first job in the city was with the Spanish Grocer's Association, Inc., whose goals inspired him to found the Puerto Rican Merchants Association, Inc., which he directed through the 1970s. He was also a founder of the Club Cultural del Bronx and Casa Borinquen. As President of the Círculo de Escritores y Poetas Iberoamericanos (CEPI) and a member of the Instituto de Puerto Rico en Nueva York he organized numerous literary and cultural events. Additionally, he pursued his interest in journalism working as an editor for *Pueblos Hispanos* in the 1940s and in the 1950s establishing a magazine titled *La Voz de Puerto Rico en Estados Unidos*.

Soto Vélez's early writings from 1928 to 1935 were published in newspapers and periodicals in Puerto Rico such as *El Tiempo*, *Puerto Rico Ilustrado*, *Alma Latina*, and *Armas*, which he founded and directed until 1936. He also contributed to *El Nacionalista*, the organ of the Partido Nacionalista de Puerto Rico. His first book, *Escalio*, a philosophical essay, was written in 1937 while he was incarcerated and published by friends. It was not until 1954 that his first book of poetry, *Abrazo Interno*, was published. This was followed by *Árboles* (1955), *Caballo de Palo* (1959), and *La Tierra Prometida* (1979), which are all long single poems. These works continued to explore the themes of rebellion and independence expressed in the early Atalayista writings. Soto Vélez is also known for experimenting with the spelling of the Spanish language in his writings, for example, exchanging the "c" for a "k." He was the winner of various poetry awards from the Círculo de Escritores y Poetas Iberoamericanos and its yearly competitions.

It was in New York that Soto Vélez met the Argentine Amanda Andrea Vélez, who became his second wife. A member of a well-to-do family with a father who was a Spanish anarchist, she was a political activist in Argentina and a member Argentina's Socialist Party. She came to New York in 1964. Amanda played an extraordinary role in Soto Vélez's life, becoming deeply engaged in his work, urging him to write, and promoting his work by organizing events on his behalf. She was often the sole breadwinner for the household, working mostly as a housekeeper for wealthy Manhattan families. For many years, their Upper East Side apartment was converted into a "salon" for the young poets, artists, and intellectuals who revered Soto Vélez and sought him out for advice and inspiration. He was often invited to seminars and conferences throughout the city. During the 1980s, Soto Vélez and Amanda were frequent visitors to Puerto Rico, where La Casa Aboy, run by Ramón Aboy, became their headquarters. Amanda's dream was to create an institute dedicated to Soto Vélez in Puerto Rico. Although they moved there in hopes of bringing this to pass, they did not succeed. Soto Vélez died in Puerto Rico on April 15, 1993. *See also* Literatura Comprometida/Socially Engaged Literature; Nuyorican Literature; Puerto Rican Literature, History of.

Further Reading

Kanellos, Nicolás. *Biographical Dictionary of Hispanic Literature in the United States: The Literature of Puerto Ricans, Cuban Americans, and Other Hispanic Writers.* Westport, CT: Greenwood, 1989.

Puebla, Manuel de la, ed. *Historia y significado del atalayismo.* San Juan, Puerto Rico: Ediciones Mairena, 1994.

Rodríguez, Carlos A., ed. *Simposio Clemente Soto Vélez—Simposio Klemente Soto Beles*. San Juan, Puerto Rico: Instituto de Cultura Puertorriqueña, 1990.

—Nélida Pérez and Nelly Cruz

Spanglish in Literature

This term refers to the combination of Spanish and English. The novel *Yo-Yo Boing!* (1998) by Puerto Rican author **Giannina Braschi** is a good illustration of the use of Spanglish in literature, as demonstrated in this excerpt:

> In this very room watching you looking for
> those hands five years from now. I know they're here
> somewhere—that's what you'll be saying, revolting all my
> gavetas with your hot hands . . .
> —Me sacaste de quicio . . . What do you them for anyway?(45)

Spanglish requires some knowledge of either language, but writers such as Braschi and **Luz María Umpierre**, also from Puerto Rico, master both languages.

On the east coast, Spanglish was first used by the **Nuyorican** writers, Puerto Rican authors who were born or live in New York City; one of the most famous is the poet Jesús Abraham **Tato "Laviera."** The use of Spanglish in literature is still more prevalent with Puerto Rican authors than with Cuban American writers. In the 1980s and 1990s, some Dominican American authors began to use Spanglish. The novel *How the Garcia Girls Lost Their Accents*, by **Julia Alvarez**, serves as a good example of characters grappling with both languages. There are scholars and writers in the Caribbean who perceive of Spanglish as more of social phenomenon than a linguistic exercise. Other writers who use Spanglish include **Gustavo Pérez Firmat**, from Cuba.

Further Reading

Stavans Ilan. *Spanglish: The Making of a New American Language*. New York: Rayo, 2003.

—D. H. Figueredo

Spirale, La. See Spiralist Movement.

Spiralist Movement

Haitian author **Frankétienne** (Franck Étienne) traces the beginning of "la spirale" back to the 1950s, when he, Jean-Claude Fignolé, and **René Philoctète** took partial inspiration from their reading of Marxist texts. Frankétienne also refers to Gabriel

García Márquez's (1927–) idea of a "spiraling" construction of the novel as well as to **Jacques Stephen Alexis**'s influential speech for the first International Congress of Black Writers and Artists (Paris, 1956), "Of the Marvellous Realism of the Haitians." Franketiénne conceives of "spiralism" as an upward circular movement of the spirit that never returns to the same point. It is a dialectical process of the spirit that carries the thinker beyond rigid political, artistic or social structures such as socialist realism or political dictatorships. Spiralist discourse is a "semantics without substance" that participates in the "subversion of current hierarchies." Franketiénne's conception of spiralism resembles a form of madness (schizophrenia, or "la schiozophonie"—a split form of speech), a form of "chaos" in which artistic patterns emerge from apparently random forms. The writers associated with "la spirale" have never pretended to be associated with a "school" or any form of orthodoxy, although some younger writers—Rodney St.-Eloi, for example—have been somewhat influenced by their work and thought.

Further Reading

"Franketiénne" (interview with Charles H. Rowell). *Callaloo* 15, no. 2 (1992): 385–92.

—*Carrol F. Coates*

Stahl, Agustín (1842–1917)

A beloved Puerto Rican scientist, Stahl wrote numerous essays and textbooks on the island's flora and fauna. He also conducted demographic studies.

The son of a German father and a Dutch mother, Agustín Stahl Estamm was born in Aguadilla, Puerto Rico, on January 21, 1842. After losing his mother as a young child, his father took him to Germany where he was raised. In 1864 he obtained a medical degree from the University of Prague. He returned to Puerto Rico, establishing a medical practice in San Juan and traveling throughout the island, both to offer medical services and to collect archeological artifacts and study the flora and the fauna. A talented artist, he drew over 4,000 sketches of Puerto Rican flowers and plants.

In 1873, he began to teach natural history at the Instituto de Segunda Enseñanza de San Juan and became involved with autonomist causes, joining the political parties Autonomista Ortodoxo and Unión Autonimista Liberal. His observations on sugar cane resulted in an award-winning scientific study, *La enfermedad de la caña de azucar* (1880). This work was followed by several scientific treatises, including *Catálogo del Gabinete Zoológico* (1882), and *Estudios sobre la flora de Puerto Rico* (1883–88). Toward the late 1880s, he studied the Amerindians of the islands, publishing *Los indios borinqueños: Estudios ethnográficos*. In 1890, he was the first scientist in Puerto Rico to discover and a study a patient suffering from leukemia.

Though he was highly respected, Spanish authorities nevertheless arrested him in 1898 because of his pro-independence views. He was soon deported to the

Dominican Republic where he stayed until the end of the Spanish-Cuban-American War. Returning to Puerto Rico in 1904, he was elected president of the Medical Association of Puerto Rico. He wrote essays, which were published in local publications, on a variety of subjects, ranging from fertility on the island to demographic studies.

Despite his fame as a Puerto Rican scientist, Stahl did not accumulate wealth, and the money he had, he used to support his research. Impoverished in his old age, the Puerto Rican government awarded him a modest pension. He passed away in Bayamón on July 12, 1917.

Further Reading

Figueroa, Javier. "Diccionario: Diccionario Histórico-Biográfico." In *La gran enciclopedia de Puerto Rico*. San Juan: Puerto Rico en la Mano and La Gran Enciclopedia de Puerto Rico, 1981.

Gutiérrez del Arroyo, Isabel. *El Dr. Agustín Stahl, hombre de ciencia: perspectiva humanística: lección inaugural, Facultad de Humanidades, 17 de agosto de 1976*. Río Piedras: Universidad de Puerto Rico, 1978.

—*D. H. Figueredo*

Stéphenson, Elie (1944–)

Stéphenson is a poet, a chanteur, and a public official from French Guiana.

Born in Cayenne, Guiana, on December 20, 1944, Stéphenson went to primary and secondary schools in Cayenne. In 1966, he traveled to France to attend the University of Paris. In 1967, he was elected president of the Union des Etudiants Guyanais. In 1970, he earned a BA in philosophy. Returning to Guiana, he worked in the Department of Higher Education. Two years later, he served as Guiana's representative at the famous Carifesta festival in neighboring Georgetown, Guyana.

Through the early 1970s, he published poetry in journals and in the anthology *New Writing in the Caribbean* (1972), edited by **A. J. Seymour**, and in 1975, he published his first collection of poetry, *Une flèche pour le pays à l'encant*. The poems in this volume express a philosophical questioning of his African ancestry while also exploring the more universal themes of love of humanity.

During this period, he was involved with the theatrical group Troupe Angela Davis, writing two plays for the group: *O Mayouri* and *Un rien pays*, which were staged but not published. He was appointed an officer of the Office of Economic and Social Planning of Cayenne. In the 1980s, he wrote songs that he performed in his native Guiana, as well as in British Guyana, and Paramaribo. His other works include *Comme des gouttes de sang* (1988), *La conscience du feu* (1996), and *Paysages négro-indiens: aux enfants de Guyane* (1997), all books of poems.

Further Reading

Martin, Florence. *De la Guyane à la diaspora africaine: écrits du silence Florence Martin et Isabelle Favre*. Paris: Karthala, 2002.

—D. H. Figueredo

Suárez, Virgil (1962–)

A novelist and poet, Suárez is representative of the writer from the Spanish-speaking and francophone Caribbean who chooses to write in English rather than in his native language. His novels detail the lives of successful Cuban Americans who face a sudden crisis that forces them to return to their roots. His poetry explores the duality of life-on-the-hyphen, living in the United States while maintaining Cuban culture and traditions, and evokes a sense of uprootedness and of cultural dislocation. Often, Suárez writes about his relationships with his father, a man who couldn't understand Suárez's need to write and who was baffled by the fact that Suárez wrote in English, a language foreign to his father.

Suárez left Cuba in 1974. He and his parents lived in Spain before relocating

Virgil Suárez is a poet and novelist whose fast-paced narratives and poems reflect the tempo of contemporary American society and how it affects newcomers. *Courtesy of Virgil Suárez.*

to California. A graduate of California State University–Long Beach, Suárez earned a masters degree in creative writing from Louisiana State University. Early on, he decided to be one of the first Cuban American writers to write in English. His first novel was *Latin Jazz* (1990), about the Mariel Boatlift; this was followed by *The Cutter*, an anti-Castro novel (1991). Then, in his next effort, a collection of short stories entitled *Welcome to the Oasis and Other Stories* (1992), he switched from dealing with Cuba and the Revolution to focus on the life of Cubans in the United States.

Suárez's novelistic style is realistic and fast paced with a preference for dialogue. Like Ernest Hemingway, he doesn't reveal much about his characters, inviting the readers to go underwater—as one of his characters literally does in the novel *Going Under* (1996)—to explore the hidden part of the iceberg. His poetry, on the other hand, is leisurely paced, reflective, and filled with pathos. Suárez has also written a memoir, *Spared Angola (1997)*. His books of poetry include *In the Republic of Longing* (1999) *Banyan* (2001) and *Guide to the Blue Tongue* (2002).

A professor of creative writing, Suárez is committed to promoting the works of colleagues and younger writers. In that capacity, he edited the anthologies *Iguana Dreams: New Latino Fiction* (1992) and *Little Havana Blues: A Cuban-American Literature Anthology* (1996), both edited with his wife, Delia Poey, also a writer, and *Red, White, and Blues: Poets on the Promise of America* (2004), with Ryan G. Van Cleave. *See also* Anti-Castro Novel; Cuban American Literature.

Further Reading

Smorkaloff, Pamela María. *Cuban Writers on and off the Island.* New York: Twayne, 1999.

—*D. H. Figueredo*

Suárez y Romero, Anselmo (1818–78)

At a nineteenth-century **tertulia**, or literary salon, hosted by the Cuban **Domingo Del Monte**, the host commissioned the writing of a novel about slavery on the island. The objective was to provide an antislavery document to British abolitionist, Richard Madden (1798–1886), who was visiting Cuba. The novel was entitled *Francisco*, and its author was Anselmo Suárez y Romero.

Born on April 20, 1818, in Havana, into a wealthy family, Suárez y Romero's father passed away when the would-be author was a young man, plunging the family into poverty. To support the family, Suárez y Romero began to teach in 1842. He became an attorney in 1866 but did not practice law.

A friend of Del Monte, Suárez y Romero attended the informal gatherings where literature and politics were discussed. One of the participants was the slave and poet **Juan Francisco Manzano**, who had written an account of his life as a slave. Suárez y Romero corrected the manuscript, which was then handed to Richard Madden, who translated it into English and published it in England as *Poems by a Slave in the Island of Cuba* (184). When asked to write an antislavery novel, Suárez y Romero used Juan Francisco as model, even using the name for a title; for a plot, he was inspired by a true story about doomed lovers he had heard at Del Monte's tertulias.

Francisco: el ingenio, o las delicias del campo tells the story of Francisco, a slave in love with another slave, named Dorotea. When Francisco is not allowed to consummate his relationship with his beloved, who is taken away from the sugar plantation where they live, Francisco commits suicide. Though criticized for fostering a stereotypical image of a passive slave, the novel does offer some revolutionary ideas for the time: (1) the slave woman was black and desirable, contrary to the colonial practice of depicting blacks as unattractive and portraying only the mulatas, light-skinned blacks, as comely, as in the contemporary novel **Cecilia Valdes**; (2) Dorotea falls in love with a black man, preferring him over the attention of the white master; and (3) the master himself falls in love with a black woman. The novel also accomplishes its objective: it serves as a political document that demonstrates the inhumane conditions fostered by slavery.

Suárez y Romero wrote the novel between 1838 and 1839, predating *Uncle Tom's Cabin* by at least thirteen years. The finished product was published in New York in 1880. In 1974, it was made into a film in Cuba titled *El otro Francisco*. The storyline of *Francisco* was also the subject of another antislavery novel, *El negro Francisco*, written in Chile in 1875 by another Cuban writer, **Antonio Zambrana**. *See also* Abolitionist Literature; Villaverde, Cirilo, Mulata in Caribbean Literature, The.

Further Reading

Luis, William. *Literary Bondage: Slavery in Cuban Narrative.* Austin: University of Texas Press, 1990.

Meson, Danusia L. *Historia y ficción: el caso "Francisco."* Buenos Aires: Ediciones de la Flor, 1994.

—*D. H. Figueredo*

Suro, Ruben (1916–)

Founder of a literary society called Los Nuevos, Ruben Suro is a poet from the Dominican Republic who has achieved national fame despite the fact that his poetry is published primarily in literary journals and newspapers. He was one of the first poets in the Dominican Republic to write "poesía negrista," poems that celebrate the Afro-Caribbean experience.

Ruben Suro was born in La Vega, on June 13, 1916. The grandson of the novelist and literary critic **Federico García Godoy**, he was exposed to literature at an early age and began to write as a teenager. In 1936, he and his brother founded a journal that they called *Los nuevos* to emphasize their rejection of traditional and realistic literature. The group of writers and artists the two brothers attracted with the publication became known as "Los Nuevos," the new ones. The members of this literary society did not hold formal, organized meetings, and when they met, they had no agenda, no leader, and no timeline for either the beginning or the end of the meeting.

During the late 1930s, Suro attended law school and upon graduation moved to Santo Domingo, where he worked as an attorney and taught at the Universidad Autónoma de Santo Domingo. During this period, he was briefly arrested and accused of criticizing the dictatorship of Rafael Leónidas Trujillo as a result of one of his poems "Protesta," which was published in an issue of *Los nuevos*. Upon his release, Suro chose to concentrate on his law practice.

He never gave up writing, and in 1976 he published the collection of poems called *Opúsculo, poemas de una intención*. Two years later he wrote *Poemas de una sola intención*. Suro's poetry is rhythmic and humorous, lending itself to performances by professional "declamatores," poetry performers, on television and radio. *See also* Dominican Republic Literature, History of; Negrista Literature; Trujillo Era.

Further Reading

Piña Contreras, Guillermo. *Doce en la literatura dominicana*. Santiago de los Caballeros, República Dominicana: Universidad Católica Madre y Maestra, 1962.

—*D. H. Figueredo*

Surrealism
∎

This is a movement that originated in France during the 1920s and that found its Caribbean expression predominantly in the poetry of the Martinican **Aimé Césaire**, in the influential journal *Tropiques*, and in the writings and literary theories of the Cuban novelist **Alejo Carpentier**. Surrealism rejected middle-class values, promoted automatic writing—unedited writing that allows what is in the unconscious to come to the fore—excluded aesthetic and moral concerns, celebrated the presence of the extraordinary in the mundane, and sought to find a reality beyond what was visible. The acknowledged leader of surrealism was the French poet and philosopher André Breton (1896–1966), who wrote a manifesto in 1924 explaining the movement.

It was André Breton who while visiting Martinique in 1941 on his way to New York City, escaping Nazism in Europe, read an issue of the journal *Tropiques* and proclaimed it the best expression of surrealism. Likewise, he promoted Aimé Césaire, as a result of his famous book-length poem *Cahier d'un retour au pays natal* (1939, 1947), as the best writer in the French language and one of the best exponents of surrealism. The poem *Cahier d'un retour au pays natal*, a history of French colonialism, slavery, and the final acceptance of black consciousness, consisted of long, rambling verses, repetitive patterns, a novelty of imagery, and repetition of words. The poems also rejected the pretenses of European bourgeoisie for the more spontaneous world of Africa.

In Cuba, **Alejo Carpentier** incorporated some of the liberating ideas of surrealism and its celebration of the concept of the marvelous in the ordinary into his theory of "lo real maravilloso," the natural presence of the marvelous in Latin America, as exemplified by the variety of the flora and fauna in the Americas. Other Caribbean writers who practiced surrealism were **René Ménil**, and **Suzanne Césaire**. *See also* Boom, the Latin American; Magical Realism.

Further Reading

Carpentier, Alejo. "On the Marvelous Real in America (1949)." In *Magical Realism: Theory, History, Community*, edited by Lois Parkinson Zamora and Wendy B. Faris, 76–88. Durham, NC: Duke University Press, 2000.

Celorio, Gonzalo. *El surrealismo y lo real-maravilloso*. México: Secretaría de Educación Pública, Dirección General de Divulgación, 1976.

Richardson, Michael, ed. *Refusal of the Shadow: Surrealism and the Caribbean*, Translated by Krzysztof Fijalkowski and Michael Richardson. London and New York: Verso, 1996.

—*D. H. Figueredo*

Sylvain Family

Father and siblings who were twentieth-century writers and intellectuals from Haiti. They promoted a national literature while favoring the use of the French language as a unifying tool in a culturally and politically divided Haiti—along geographical lines, North versus South, and racial lines, mulattoes versus blacks. Georges was the father; Normil was the son, and Suzanne, known as **Suzanne Comhaire-Sylvain**, was the daughter.

Comhaire-Sylvain, Suzanne (1898–1975). The first woman anthropologist in Haiti, and one of the first in the Caribbean, Comhaire-Sylvain published books of Haitian tales and scholarly studies that affirmed the nation's African roots.

Suzanne Comhaire-Sylvain was born in Port-au-Prince on November 6, 1898. After attending elementary school in Haiti, she traveled to France and matriculated at the University of Paris where she earned a BA, a masters, and a PhD—the first Haitian woman to achieve such academic distinction. In 1935, she pursued postdoctoral work at the University of London. In 1936, she published a pioneering work about Kreyòl, *Le créole haïtien; morphologie et syntaxe*, making her one of the first Haitian intellectuals to actively promote the scholarly study of such a language.

In 1937, Comhaire-Sylvain founded the school l'École des Lettres, appointing as professors such major Haitian figures as **Dantes Bellegarde** and **Jean Price-Mars**. Her husband, Jean Comhaire, taught at the school. During the 1940s and 1950s, Comhaire-Sylvain was inspector of Haitian schools, head of the Haitian delegation to a international women's conference in Argentina, member of the faculty of the Institute of Ethnology, and was a UNESCO representative. She wrote over two-hundred articles on Haitian anthropology. Comhaire-Sylvain received numerous awards, including the Alliance Française Prize, the Medal of the Royal French Academy. Her sisters were equally accomplished: Yvonne Sylvian (1907–89) was Haiti's first woman physician and gynecologist and Madeleine Sylvain was the founder of First Female League of Social Action, which advocated for women's rights.

Comhaire-Sylvain died in a car accident in Nigeria on June 20, 1975. Her works include *Les contes haïtiens, origine immédiate et extension en Amérique* (1937), *Le roman de Bouqui* (1940), *Femmes de Kinshasa, hier et aujourd'hui* (1968), *Jetons nos couteaux*, and *Contes de garçonnets de Kinshasa avec parallèles haïtiens* (1974).

Sylvain, Georges (1866–1925). Best known for his adaptation into Kreyòl of La Fontaine's fables, published under the title of *Cric?Crac!/krik? krak!* (1901), Georges Sylvain was a Haitian patriot who challenged the American occupation of his country in 1915. He was an attorney, a journalist, and a promoter of Haitian culture.

Georges Sylvain studied law in Paris and upon his return to Haiti founded a law school in 1888 in Port-au-Prince. He worked for the Department of Public Education and created the *L'Oeuvre des ecrivains*, an association for writers. He represented Haiti in Paris during the early 1900s. Though a committed nationalist, he promoted the use and expansion of the French language as way of avoiding the growing American influence in the Caribbean and maintaining a Franco-Haitian identity.

Sylvain was also conscious of developing a poetry that was controlled and re-vealed artistic and intellectual mastery, sometime concentrating more on form than on message. This was an attitude that was shared by the younger poets of the turn of the nineteenth century who made up **La generation de La Ronde**, of which Syl-vain was a member. But he also used poetry, in poems such as "Frères d'Afrique" (1901), to lash out at the injustices of slavery and to rally all black people to join forces against the European oppressors.

In 1915, Sylvain turned his talents to opposing the American intervention. He founded the newspaper *La Patrie* and the organization *L'Union patriotique* to af-firm Haitian nationalism and to challenge U.S. authority over his country. Upon his death ten years later, the whole nation mourned him.

Sylvain, Normil (1900–29). A poet and one of the founders of the influential journal *La Revue Indigène*, Normil Sylvain challenged Haitian writers to work to-gether for the benefit of the nation. Explains Naomi Garret in *The Renaissance of Haitian Poetry*: "Sylvain [called] for a concerted singing of his country by all poets, North and South, in order to know and understand their native land . . . and to show more selfless love for her" (89). Through a series of essays that Sylvain pub-lished in *La Revue indigène*, he assumed the task of guiding his country out of fac-tionalism and into the creation of a national identity. In his writings, he reminded all Haitian writers to create a positive image of their country and to seek solidarity with writers from Latin America.

Sylvain attempted to carry these ideals in his poetry. In some of his verses, such as "Moralites Insolites," he celebrates the black beauty of Haitian women, and in poems, such as "Poemes" and "Images de la mer"—both published in his journal—he pays particular attention to the Haitian landscape and flora. Sylvain's early death did not allow him to fully realize his talents. He is remembered as the eager theoretician of the founders of the *La Revue Indigène*. *See also* American Occupa-tion of Haiti (1915–34); Haitian Literature in Kreyòl (the Haitian Language).

Further Reading

Garret, Naomi M. *The Renaissance of Haitian Poetry*. Paris: Présence africaine, 1963.

Sylvain, Georges. *Confidences et mélancolies: poésies, 1885–1898: précédées d'une notice sur la poésie haïtienne par l'auteur*. Port-au-Prince, Haïti: Impr. H. Deschamps, 1979.

—*D. H. Figueredo*

T

Tapia y Rivera, Alejandro (1826–82)

Considered the great man of **Puerto Rican literature**, Tapia y Rivera wrote in all genres: essays, drama, fiction, and poetry. A self-taught renaissance man, he was also the father of Puerto Rican theater and one of the first to write about the island's native culture and Amerindian's traditions.

Tapia y Rivera was born in San Juan on November 12, 1826. He conducted his elementary studies in private schools until his family could no longer afford to send him; he then found employment in the Ministry of Interior. In 1848, he published the novel *El heliotropo*. In 1849, he dueled with a Spanish officer and was banished to Spain by the authorities. In Madrid, he spent hours in museums, libraries, and exhibits, and studying English, French, and Latin as well as science and math. He read documents and early accounts kept by Spanish authorities on colonial life, uncovering information about **areytos**, an early form of Puerto Rican theater and entertainment. He published his findings on the volume *Biblioteca histórica de Puerto Rico* (1854).

From Spain, he traveled to Cuba, where he published *El bardo de Guamaní*, a collection of legends he had gathered, short stories, and his first novel *La antigua sirena*. Upon his return to Puerto Rico in 1862, he settled in Ponce and wrote three theatrical pieces, *La cuarterona* (1867), about racial prejudices on the island, *Camoens* (1868), about Portuguese history, and *Héroe* (1869), a tragedy. In 1870, he founded and edited the journal *La Azucena*, meant for women readers. He relocated to San Juan, where again he wrote several novels and plays, including one of his most popular, the historical romance *Cofresí* (1876), about a Puerto Rican pirate, and two of his best novels *Póstumo el transmigrado* and *Póstumo el envirginiado* (1882), before traveling to Spain once more. In that country he was knighted by the royal court into the Distinguida Orden de Carlos III.

Tapia y Rivera was an active participant in **tertulias**, or literary salons, held at the **Ateneo Puertorriqueño**, of which he was a cofounder. He lectured on such subjects as literature, autonomy, and women's rights. Many of his lectures were gathered in the tome *Conferencias sobre estética y literatura* (1881). It was while giving one of these lectures at the Ateneo, that Tapia y Rivero suffered a cerebral hemorrhage, on July 19, 1882, and died on the spot.

Tapia y Rivera is highly esteemed in Puerto Rico. One of the best-known theaters in Puerto Rico, originally built in 1832, is named after Tapia y Rivera, and

November 12, the anniversary of his birth, has been designated as the Day of the Puerto Rican Writer.

Further Reading

Rivera, Angel A. *Eugenio María de Hostos y Alejandro Tapia y Rivera: avatares de una modernidad caribeña*. New York: Lang, 2001.

Rivera de Alvárez, Josefina. *Diccionario de literatura puertorriqueña*. San Juan, Puerto Rico: Instituto de Cultura Puertorriqueña, 1970.

—*D. H. Figueredo*

Tardon, Raphaël (1911–66)

Tardon was a controversial Martinican novelist who claimed **Négritude** was a form of racism and that the value of an individual emerged from actions and accomplishments and not from the color of his skin.

Born in Fort-de-France, Martinique, on October 27, 1911, Tardon was a member of wealthy family who owned land in Martinique. He studied at the Lycéee Schoelcher in Fort-de-France and then went to Paris to study at the School of Law. While he socialized with other students from the Caribbean, he maintained an intellectual distance from the supporters of Négritude, whom he saw as advocating black supremacy.

When World War II began, he served in the French army, and upon the Nazis' entrance into Paris, Tardon joined the resistance in the South of France. When the war ended, he worked as a journalist in Paris. In 1946, he published his first book, a collection of short stories entitled *Bleu des îles*. In 1947, he published *Starkenfirst*, a novel about the slave trade. This novel became his best known work. In 1948, he wrote about the eruption of volcano Mont Pelé in 1902: *La caldeira*.

Through the 1950s, Tardon occupied several prestigious government posts, including Minister of Information and Director of Information of Guadeloupe, and Chief of the Cabinet of the Prefect of Guadeloupe. During this period, he wrote a biography, *Toussaint Louverture: le Napoleon noir* (1951), and began writing the essays that would make up the study, *Noirs et blancs* (1963). After his death on January 16, 1966, Tardon was awarded in France the Literature des Caraïbes prize for his work as a novelist.

Further Reading

Tardon, Raphaël. "Richard Wright Tells Us: The White Problem in the United States," translated by Kenneth Kinnamon. In *Conversations with Richard Wright*, edited by Kenneth Kinnamon and Michel Fabre, 99–105. Jackson: University Press of Mississippi, 1993.

—*D. H. Figueredo*

Tertulia/Cénacle/Literary Salon/Soirée

These terms, in Spanish, English, and French, refer to a gathering of writers and intellectuals to discuss literature and politics in a formal or informal setting, such as an academy or a friend's house. Tertulias and salons serve as avenues for the dissemination of culture and promotion of a national literature, the publishing of particular literary works, and even the careers of writers.

The Spanish word *tertulia*, originally referring to a section of a theater, may be a form of the word *tertuliante* or *tertuliano*, which referred to a person who frequented this section. Both words appear to allude to the church father Tertullian—in Spanish: *Tertuliano*—but the origin of the allusion is uncertain. Tertulias were popular in Spain beginning in the seventeenth century and eventually replaced the more formal academies. Some well-known tertulias were described in novels and memoirs of the participants, including *La fontana de oro* (1870) by Benito Pérez Galdós. In the Caribbean, tertulias became popular in the nineteenth century. In Cuba, one of the most famous centers for tertulias took place in the home of writer and literary mentor **Domingo Del Monte**, at whose invitations poets wrote poetry and at least one novel, *Francisco* (1838, 1839) by **Anselmo Suárez y Romero**, was written. In Puerto Rico, tertulias were held at the **Ateneo Puertorriqueño**, an institution that helped to shape the career of scores of writers, including **Emilio S. Balaval**, to name one. In the Dominican Republic, informal gatherings occurred at the home of the poet **Salomé Ureña de Henríquez** during the nineteenth century, and literature and the need for education for women were favorite topics. In the twentieth century, Salomé's son, the scholar **Max Henríquez Ureña**, hosted tertulias in his home, where writers like **Manuel del Cabral** and **Juan Bosch** met to discuss poetry.

With immigration or exile to the United States came the tertulias. In the 1960s, the Cuban writer **Lino Novás Calvo** was known for hosting discussions at in his home in Syracuse, New York, where students visited him. During the same era, Puerto Rican poet **Clemete Soto Vélez**'s tertulias in his apartment in Manhattan were famous throughout the Puerto Rican literary community. Toward the end of the twentieth century, the Dominican scholar **Daisy Cocco de Filippis** sponsored tertulias where women writers from the Caribbean, especially those who were not yet published, was the focus. Such gatherings led to the publication of the book *Tertuliando: dominicanas y amiga(o)s—Hanging out: Dominican women and friends: bilingual text(o)s bilinguales, 1994–1996*, compiled by Cocco de Filippis in 1997.

In the anglophone Caribbean, toward the beginning of the twentieth century, writers like **Tom Redcam** and **Una Marson** met to discuss the need for a national culture in Jamaica. In 1923, the **Poetry League of Jamaica**, founded by **J. E. Clare McFarlane**, attempted to raise literary awareness on the island and to seek a Jamaican voice in literature. In Barbados, beginning in the 1940s, writers like **George Lamming** met with literary mentor and editor **Frank Collymore** to discuss the emerging Barbadian literature. During the same period, the Beacon Group, which included author **Alfred Mendes** and political figure **Albert Gomes**, contemplated the development of literature in Trinidad while also publishing the journal

The Beacon. In the 1960s, literary salons prospered in London as anglophone writers from the Caribbean migrated to the metropolis; many of these writers created the **Caribbean Arts Movement (CAM)**. This association began its work in some of the writers' own apartments in London, then held meetings at the West Indian Students Union building, and later on conferences and seminars on the campus of the University of Kent. Topics for discussions were varied and numerous, including "Is There a West Indian Aesthetic?" "Contribution of the West Indies to European Civilization," and "Spanish and French West Indian Literature Today."

In the francophone Caribbean, salons—which had originated in France during the seventeenth century as a space away from the king's court where literature and politics could be discussed politely and intelligently—were crucial in the development of a national literature. One such group was the "Cénacle of 1836." Major figures in the cénacle included **Émile Nau**, who would produce a *Histoire des caciques d'Haïti* (1855) and his brother **Ignace**, Céligny and **Beaubrun Ardouin**, Beauvais and Dumay Lespinasse, and others. Ignace Nau founded the newspaper *Le Républicain* (1836) and then *L'Union* (1837), both of which published poetry and prose by this group. Toward the end of the nineteenth century, the literary club "Les Emulateurs" was a center for intellectual discussions. In the late 1920s, three Haitian writers, Louis Diaquoi, **Lorimer Denis**, and **François Duvalier**, met regularly to discuss their nationalist views. In 1932, Diaquoi announced the formation of the **Griots** group, which published a literary review of the same name; their emphasis was the celebration and appreciation of African roots and the development of a black consciousness. Black consciousness was at the root of the journal *Tropiques* and at the root of the intellectual activities of its founders, **Aimé** and **Suzanne Césaire**, and **René Ménil**, during the 1940s. Suzanne Césaire conducted **soirées** in her home and school, exploring colonialism and the need for a national culture and literature in Martinique.

It is possible that the growing presence in the world scene of writers from the Caribbean would have occurred without the tertulias and soirées, but participation at such gatherings accelerated the process and helped to increase the number of works published. There is still a need for a documented history of the role of literary salons throughout the Caribbean.

Further Reading

Breiner, Laurence A. *An Introduction to West Indian Poetry*. Cambridge: Cambridge University Press, 1998.

DeJean, Joan. "The Salons, 'Preciosity,' and the Sphere of Women's Influence." In *A New History of French Literature*, edited by Denis Hollier, 297–303. Cambridge, MA: Harvard University Press, 1989.

Donnell, Alison, and Sarah Lawson Welsh. *The Routledge Reader in Caribbean Literature*. London: Routledge, 1996.

Luis, William. *Literary Bondage: Slavery in Cuban Narrative*. Austin: University of Texas Press, 1990.

Walmsley, Anne. *The Caribbean Artists Movement, 1966–1972: A Literary and Cultural History*. London: New Beacon Books, 1992.

—Carrol F. Coates and D. H. Figueredo

Testimonio

—■—

A narrative told by an individual and edited by a professional writer, a testimonio is an autobiographical account that uses techniques from the novel such as plot, character development, and chronology. The most famous example is the book *Biografía de un cimarrón*, in which an elderly former slave, Montejo, is interviewed by the Cuban writer **Miguel Barnet**. The writer provides questions to the narrator who then fleshes out answers that Barnet then edits, without altering the narrator's diction and mannerism, to create a cohesive narrative.

Testimonial narrative usually depicts the life of a marginalized individual. Exploring chapters of history and culture that had been ignored, testimonios are political statements. Though practiced by some writers during the 1950s, testimonio became popular after the publication in Cuba of *Biografía de un cimarrón*. In 1970, the **Casa de las Américas** added the category of testimonial narrative to its prestigious literary prize.

Further Reading

García, Gustavo V. *La literatura testimonial latinoamericana: (Re) presentación y (auto) construcción del sujeto subalterno.* Madrid: Editorial Pliegos, 2003.

—Pamela María Smorkaloff

Thaly Brothers

—■—

Daniel and Fernand were brothers and poets from Dominica. While aware of their African roots, which they celebrated, they identified with the French and French culture. Of the two, Daniel was the most prolific and best known.

Thaly, Daniel Desire Alain (1879–1950). Thaly was a physician and a poet. A native of Dominica, Thaly received his primary and secondary education in Martinique. He traveled to Paris in the 1890s to study medicine, graduating from the Faculty of Toulouse in 1905. While in Paris, he wrote poetry, publishing his first volume, *Les Caraïbes*, in 1899. The poems, descriptive of the islands and expressing his nostalgia and homesickness, were well received by the critics and in 1900, he was awarded a prize from the l'Acadamie des jeux Floraux de Toulouse.

Returning to Dominica, he began to write dozens of poems, which he submitted to numerous journals, including *La Phalange* and *Les Marges*. In 1905, he published *La claret de Sud*. In 1911, he published *Le Jardin des Tropiques* and *Chanson de mer et d'outre-mer*. In these poems, he again explored the nature of Caribbean culture and celebrated Africa's presence on the island. These themes were present in his other works: *Chansons lointaines* (1920), *L'Île et le voyage* (1923), and *Héliotrope ou les ammants inconnus*.

Despite his affirmation of a black consciousness and a romantic longing for Africa, Thaly remained, nevertheless, a supporter of the French language and culture, as demonstrated in the volume *Nostalgies françaises* (1923). Many critics considered him more of a French writer than a Caribbean poet.

Daniel Thaly died in Dominica on October 1, 1950.

Thaly, Fernand (1882–1947). Fernand wrote poems that served as a memoir of his childhood in Dominica and Martinique.

Thaly was born in Martinique but was raised in Dominica. When he was in his early twenties, he joined his brother in Paris. Like Daniel, he wrote poetry and felt a deep love and admiration for France. He visited Martinique in 1906 and 1908 but spent much of his life in France, where he managed a café frequented by writers.

Thaly submitted his poetry to numerous journals and newspapers. His verses were light and often depicted scenes from his childhood in the Caribbean. Much of his poetry has not been collected. Nearly twenty years after his death, a collection was published, *Le Poème des îles*. In 1976, a second volume was published, *La Leçon des île*.

Further Reading

Corzani, Jack. "Deux chantres de l'exotisme antillaises: Daniel et Fernand Thaly." In *Splendeur et misère: l'exotisme littéraire aux Antilles*, by Jack Corzani. Point-a-Pitre, 1969

"Daniel Thaly." *Literature, Music, and Art*. http://www.avirtualdominica.com (accessed 5/10/05).

—*D. H. Figueredo*

Thelwell, Michael (1939–)

The author of one of the best-known novels about Jamaica, *The Harder They Come* (1980), Michael Thelwell is a short-story writer, essayist, educator, and political activist.

Michael Miles Thelwell was born in Ulster Spring, Jamaica, on July 25, 1939, the son of a member of Jamaica's House of Representatives. When his father passed away, his mother found a job in an office and was able to send him to private schools. He attended Jamaica College and then moved to the United States, where he enrolled at Howard University. After graduating in 1964, he earned a masters in fine arts in 1969 from the University of Massachusetts. He wrote several short stories during this period and, in 1967, won the first prize in a contest sponsored by the journal *Story*. Many of the stories he wrote were about the civil rights movement in the South.

In 1980, he published *The Harder They Come*, the result of an invitation by Grove Press to novelize the popular 1973 Jamaican film of the same title. The novel is based on the exploits of the legendary Jamaican bandit Ivan-"Rhygin" Martin— something of a Robin Hood—but Thelwell uses the protagonist's life as a vehicle to portray the idyllic countryside, the ugliness of the slums, and the discrimination common people experience at the hands of the Jamaica elite and the American tourists. The novel was well received by the mainstream media in the United States and in Jamaica. Even Prime Minister Michael Manley (1924–97), according to critic Daryl Cumber Dance, applauded the work.

In 1987, Thelwell published the book of essays *Duties, Pleasures, and Conflicts: Essays in the Struggle*, an overview of the civil rights movement. Thelwell is also the author of the screenplays *Washington Incident* (1972) and *Girl beneath the Lion* (1978). His stories and essays have been published in numerous journals, such as *Black Scholar*, *Partisan Review*, and *Short Story International*.

Further Reading

Dance, Daryl Cumber. "Michael Thelwell (1939–)" In *Fifty Caribbean Writers: A Bio-Bibliographical Critical Sourcebook*, 457–61. Greenwood Press, 1986.

—*D. H. Figueredo*

Thoby-Marcelin, Phillipe. See Marcelin Family.

Thomas, Piri (1928–)

The author of the classic *Down These Mean Streets* (1967), the best-known work that describes the Puerto Rican experience in New York during and after the Depression, Piri Thomas is a memoirist, short-story writer, and poet. Raised in El Barrio—Spanish Harlem—his life mirrored that of many Nuyoricans—Puerto Ricans from New York—who lacked either economic opportunities or a political ideology and who were susceptible to drugs, gangs, and crime.

Born on September 30, 1928, in New York, of a Puerto Rican mother and a black Cuban father, Thomas considered himself Puerto Rican, an identity kept alive by his mother's dream of one day returning to the island. The racism he experienced growing up drove him to street gangs, criminality, and illicit sex. At the age of twenty-two, he and two associates

One of the most famous Latino writers in the United States, Piri Thomas is the author of *Down These Mean Streets*, a memoir that helped to popularize the genre of Nuyorican literature. *Source: Centro de Estudios Puertorriqueños.*

robbed at gunpoint a Manhattan nightclub. Thomas, who was shot in the stomach, was arrested and sentenced to prison. In jail, he passed the time reading. He also experienced a religious conversion. Then, it occurred to him that he could try writing prose. The result was the autobiography *Down These Mean Streets*.

The book portrays the life of a youngster who rebels against society and against a family he believes has ignored him. Thomas's dark skin led him to search for his identity among his African American friends. Thomas's identity crisis is centered on what he perceives to be his family's rejection, and later his hatred manifests itself against mainstream American society. The autobiography explains and justifies Thomas's life from his own point of view; his description of life in prison symbolizes his fall.

Down These Means Streets was well received by critics from such influential periodicals as the *New York Times* and the *Christian Science Monitor*. The success afforded him the opportunity to write a follow-up, *Saviour, Saviour, Hold My Hand* (1972). In this book, Thomas looks to the Pentecostal Church for salvation, and his conversion is precipitated by his aunt and Nita, his future wife. In the end, Thomas's rebellion against the church, and all institutions, results in his separation from Nita. The subject of his next book, *Seven Long Times* (1974), is his incarceration, which he describes in more details. This autobiography, along with *Down These Mean Streets*, raises the issue of the effectiveness of prison system and rehabilitation, claiming that prisons serve to intensify the criminality of prisoners. In 1978, he published a young-adult book, *Stories From El Barrio*. Thomas reads his recorded poetry to the beat of Latin jazz in *Sounds of the Streets* (1994) and *"No Mo' Barrio Blues"* (1996*)*.

Thomas has established himself as the most accomplished Puerto Rican American writer in the United States. By revisiting his own life in several books, Thomas provides a solution derived from his own fall and salvation. He finds that society must rehabilitate itself and eradicate the structures of prejudice and discrimination that forces many Latinos into a life of crime. Likewise, he makes plain that individuals cannot wait for society to change; they have an obligation to take charge of their own lives and rehabilitate themselves. *See also* Nuyorican Literature.

Further Reading

Luis, William. *Dance Between Two Cultures: Latino Caribbean Literature Written in the United States*. Nashville: Vanderbilt University Press, 1997.

—William Luis

Tió Family

■

Salvador and Elsa Tió are father and daughter writers from Puerto Rico. Salvador was a preeminent journalist and social commentator. Elsa is a poet.

Tió, Elsa (1951–). At the age of seven, Elsa Tió published a book of poetry, *Poesía*, consisting of many poems she had dictated to her father. When Cuban poet and literary critic **Eugenio Florit** read the poems, he offered to write the prologue. Twenty years later, a second edition was published to welcoming reviews.

In the interval, Elsa Tió studied literature at the Universidad de Puerto Rico, earning a BA and then an MA in comparative literature. She worked in Washington, D.C. for the Puerto Rican Commissioner's Office and for Puerto Rico's Foundation for the Humanities. In 1977, she published the collection *Detrás de los espejos empañados*, for which she received a literary prize from the Instituto de Literatura Puertorriqueño. In 1988, she published *Inventario de la soledad*. Her poetry is romantic and contemplative of the complexities found in human relationships. In the early 1990s, she edited two of her father's books, *Lengua Mayor* and *Desde el tuétano*.

Elsa Tió has been involved in cultural and political activities in Puerto Rico and in the Caribbean. In 2003, she cosigned, with many other writers and diplomats from Europe and Latin America, a letter sent to **Fidel Castro** protesting his treatment of writers in Cuba.

Tió Montes de Oca, Salvador (1911–89). Tió Montes expressed concerns over American influence on the island and the need to maintain a Spanish Caribbean identity and culture. He coined the term *espanglish* which later on, in New York, was adapted into **Spanglish** to indicate the use of Spanish words while conversing or writing in English.

Salvador Tió was born in Mayagüez, Puerto Rico, on November 20, 1911. After pursuing studies in Puerto Rico, he traveled to New York City, where he enrolled at Columbia University with intentions of studying law. From New York, he went to Madrid to continue his legal studies, but when the Spanish Civil War broke out in 1935, he was forced to leave.

In Puerto Rico, he took over the family agricultural business. He wrote articles and essays that were published in numerous local publications, including *Bohemia Puertorriqueña*, *El Diario de Puerto Rico*, *El Imparcial*, and *Puerto Rico Ilustrado*. He also founded the journal *Revista Isla*. His editorials, which poked gentle fun at social and political conditions on the island, made him famous. Throughout his work, there was a firm belief in the Puerto Rican identity, an understanding of the complex situation the island faced as neither a colony nor an independent nation, and sensitivity to the tug of war between the uses of Spanish and English in Puerto Rico. In 1948, he introduced the concept of *esplanglish*, meaning the insertion of Spanish words and phrases in English; later on, in the United States, writers used the term as Spanglish. In 1974, he published *A fuengo lento. Cien columnas de humor y una cornisa*, a collection of his editorials. The book, the only volume he published during his lifetime, carried the name of his popular newspaper column "A fuego lento."

Tió was director of Editorial Universal, the publishing house associated with the Universidad de Puerto Rico, director of the Academia Puertorriqueña de la Lengua Española, and was interim president of the **Ateneo Puertorriqueño**. A few after years his death on September 16, 1989, many more of his columns and poems were published: *Lengua mayor* (1992), *Desde el tuétano* (1993), and *Soy boricua porque soy*. *See also* Code Switching.

Further Reading

"Carta por el día de los derechos humanos." http://www.adcuba.org (accessed 12/10/03).

Fernández Méndez, Eugenio, ed. *Homenaje a don Salvador Tió Montes de Oca: humanista y patriota.* San Juan, Puerto Rico: Academia Puertorriqueña de la Lengua Española, 1991.

—*D. H. Figueredo*

Tirolien, Guy (1917–)

Tirolien was a Guadeloupean poet and novelist. His writing was influenced by the **Négritude** movement, which asserted black consciousness.

Tirolien was born in Ponte-à-Pitre, Guadeloupe, on August 13, 1917. A highly intelligent student, he attended secondary school in his hometown before traveling to Paris, where he studied at the Lycée Louis le Grand, the School of Law, and the École Coloniale, where the most promising students from the francophone Caribbean were trained to become colonial administrators. When World War II broke out and the Nazis invaded France, Tirolien was arrested. In prison, he met and befriended Léopold S. Senghor (1906–2001), one of the founders of the Négritude movement.

Tirolien and Senghor discussed literature, and the latter encouraged Tirolien to write poetry. His desire to write increased after the war ended, but professional obligations restrained his creative output. He worked in Niger as Commissioner of Information and was also appointed cultural adviser to the nation's president. In 1961, Tirolien published his first book of poetry, *Balles d'or*. The themes he explored were slavery, blacks' oppression, and the need to fight racism. His poetry was often direct, even harsh.

In the early 1960s, Tirolien worked in the French Civil Service in Mali. Later on, he was appointed United Nations representative in Mali. From Mali, he went to the Sudan, Cameroon, and Gabon. In 1977, he wrote the novel *Feuilles vivantes au matin*. His best-known poem is "Marie Galante" (1961), the story of a slave's uprising. In the poem, Tirolien rallies all men "to learn to be free."

Further Reading

Alante-Lima, Willy. *Guy Tirolien: l'homme et l'oeuvre.* Paris: Présence africaine, 1991.

Harley, E. A. "Guy Tirolien: In Search of an Attitude." *Between Négritude and Marvelous Realism: Black Images* 3, no. 2 (Spring 1974): 55–64.

—*D. H. Figueredo*

Tirso de la Torre. See Morales Cabrera, Pablo.

Torres, Edwin (1931–)

Edwin Torres is a Puerto Rican judge who has written novels that have become successful and have served as the basis for popular movies filmed within the Hollywood gangster tradition. His knowledge of the streets of Manhattan, the underworld, and the legal system lend credibility to his fictional characters and situations. Torres is one of a handful of Latino writers whose books have been reviewed in such mainstream publications as *Newsweek* and the *New York Times*.

Edwin Torres was born on January 7, 1931 in New York City of Puerto Rican parents. He attended public school in Manhattan, graduated from City University of New York, and enrolled at Brooklyn College's Law School. He was the first Puerto Rican appointed assistant district attorney for New York City and the first to serve in the state Supreme Court. In the mid-1970s, he began to write novels.

Carlito's Way was published in 1975. Spanning twenty years, from the 1940s to the 1960s, it narrates the life of a Puerto Rican hoodlum who becomes a powerful drug dealer. Similar in structure to such gangster films as *Little Caesar* and *Public Enemy*, the novel was well received by the critics and the public. Four years later, Torres wrote a sequel, *After Hours* (1979), which follows the protagonist after his release from prison. Elements of the two novels were combined for the 1993 film *Carlito's Way*, starring Al Pacino.

In between these two novels, Torres wrote a detective story, *Q & A*, about a crooked policeman and the investigation into his killing of a small-time gangster. The narrative is fast paced and presents a vivid portrayal of New York's underworld: mafia hit men, corrupt officials, prostitutes. *Q & A* is fundamentally a morality play: the villain dies at the end and the hero rises triumphantly. But Torres also addresses bigotry: the protagonist, who is Irish, breaks off his relationship with the woman he loves because her father is a black Puerto Rican. *Q & A* was made into a film with Nick Nolte (1941–) portraying the crooked policeman.

Further Reading

Figueredo, Danilo H. "The Stuff Dreams Are Made Of: The Latino Detective Novel." *Multicultural Review* 8, no.3 (September 1999): 22–29.

Hernández, Carmen Dolores. *Puerto Rican Voices in English: Interviews with Writers.* Westport, CT: Praeger, 1997.

—*D. H. Figueredo*

Torres, Omar (1945–)

Omar Torres is a Cuban playwright and novelist whose works explore the duality experienced by people in exile: the longing for a return to the homeland while realizing that they can't leave their adopted country. He is also an actor.

Omar Torres was born in Las Tunas, Cuba, in 1945. In 1956, his father left for the United States to look for better economic opportunities. Three years later, Torres and his mother joined his father. The family settled in New York City, where Torres attended Queens College but did not graduate. He took drama courses at the New York Theater of the Americas and graduated from the International Television Arts School, where he studied broadcasting. On and off, Torres worked as a radio announcer while also designing jewelry.

In 1972 he cofounded, with fellow Cuban playwright **Iván Acosta,** the Centro Cultural Cubano de Nueva York. He also founded the journals *Cubanacán* and *Inter/Cambio.* In 1979, he was awarded the best prize for an actor in Spanish production by the Association of Arts Critics of New York. During this period he wrote several plays that were staged at the Centro Cultural Cubano. The plays include *Abdala/José Martí* (1972), cowritten with Acosta; *Antes del vuelo y la palabra* (1976); *Cumbancha cubiche* (1976), which was filmed by WNET and broadcast across the United States; and *Latino* (1979), a musical comedy. Collectively, the plays examine the loneliness and nostalgia experienced by the exile and the need to break with the past.

In 1981, Torres wrote the novel *Apenas un bolero,* probably his best-known work. The novel, which takes place in Cuba, Florida, and New York, is a retelling of the *Odyssey* with a Cuban character in search of a home. Torres followed this novel with two others, *Al partir* (1986) and *Fallen Angels Sing* (1991). Torres often pokes fun at a Cuban type: the successful exile who brags about his accomplishments in the United States while also reminding his listeners about how much wealth he had in the old country, whether it is true or not. *See also* Exile Literature.

Further Reading

Kanellos, Nicolás. *Hispanic Literature of the United States.* Westport, CT: Greenwood Press, 2003.

—*D. H. Figueredo*

Trefossa (1916–75)

A poet and short-story writer from Suriname, Trefossa wrote the first poem in that country written in Sranan Tongo, the local language, rather than in Dutch, the official language. A librarian and editor, he was a promoter of Surinamese culture and identity.

Trefossa, whose actual name was Henny Frans de Ziel, was born in Paramaribo on January 15, 1916. He conducted his primary education at the school Zinzerdorfschool, in Paramaribo, and earned a teaching degree in 1934 from the same institution. Unable to find employment as a teacher, he served in the army and later on worked as a nurse. Eventually, he was able to find a teaching position in a leprosy hospital. He was also a rural teacher.

He began to write short stories in 1940. In 1944, his story "Maanavonden," written in Dutch, appeared in the October issue of the journal *Suriname Zending*. In 1951, he published the poem "Bro" in *Foetoe-boi*, a journal edited by JGA Koenders, with whom Trefossa had studied. This poem was the first attempt at composing a sonnet in Sranan Tongo, the vernacular used by the people of Suriname.

From 1953 to 1956, supported by Sticusa, a Dutch foundation for cultural collaboration, he was able to pursue library science studies in Holland. While attending school, Trefossa befriended the Dutch researcher Jan Voorhoeve, who studied the Sranan Tongo language and established contact with a nationalist cultural movement, Wie Eegi Sani, which had been founded by the politician and writer Eddy Bruma a few years before, but Trefossa did not get involved in the group. Upon his return to Paramaribo, he was appointed director of the library of the Cultureel Centrum Suriname as well as director of the institution. He resigned, however, to return to teaching.

His publication in 1957 of the volume *Trotji*, consisting of nineteen poems written in Sranan Tongo and with notes, translations, and poetical analysis of his poem "Kopenhagen" by his friend Jan Voorhoeve, proved a turning point in the development of a national literature as well as a stimulus for other writers who started to use the local language for artistic expression. In 1959, Trefossa adapted Paramaribo's national hymn into Sranan Tongo. During this period, he was also on the editorial board of the journals *Tongoni* (1958) and *Soela* (1965). In the former, he published many of his writings.

Toward the end of the 1960s, Trefossa, who was ill, returned to Holland, where he prepared the edition of the nineteenth-century diary of Johannes King, a bush inhabitant and follower of the Moravian order, also translating the work into English as *Life at Maripaston* (1973). Trefossa passed away in Haarlem, Holland, on February 3, 1975. His literary work is acknowledged as helping to develop a cultural identity of Suriname as a nation on its own right.

Further Reading

February, Vernie. "The Suriname Muse; Reflections on Poetry." In *A History of the Literature of the Caribbean, vol. 2: English and Dutch-Speaking Regions*, edited by A. James Arnold, 569–80. Philadelphia: John Benjamins Publishing Co., 2001.

Kempen, Michiel van. "Traditie en compositie; Trefossa's 'Kopenhagen' en 'Maanavonden.'" *Bhasa* 3, no. 1 (1985): 34–41; 3, no. 2 (1985): 17–221; 3, no. 3 (1985): 9–12.

Ormskirk, F. W. "Henny de Ziel." *De Vrije Stem* 18, no. 2 (1975).

Voorhoeve, Jan, ed. *Trefossa*. Paramaribo: Bureau Volkslectuur, 1977.

Voorhoeve, Jan, and Ursy M. Lichtveld, eds. *Creole Drum: An Anthology of Creole Literature in Surinam*, 195–215. New Haven, CT: Yale University Press, 1975.

—*Emilio Jorge Rodríguez*

Trinidadian and Tobagonian Literature, History of

The history of Trinidad and Tobago helps explain the extraordinary diversity of this nation's population and literature. The island of Trinidad, situated only ten miles from the northern coast of South America, near Venezuela, was sighted by Christopher Columbus's (1451–1506) crew in 1498. For the next three centuries, the island was claimed by Spain. In the 1700s, the Spanish and indigenous inhabitants were swiftly outnumbered by an influx of West African slaves, who worked on plantations. In 1797, Britain invaded and took over Trinidad; slavery was officially abolished there, as on all British Caribbean islands, in 1834. After abolition, indentured workers were brought from India, and the vast majority of them remained in Trinidad.

The nearby island of Tobago, much smaller and mostly rural, was claimed by Spanish explorers in 1502. French, Dutch, and British forces fought over control of Tobago during the seventeenth, eighteenth, and early nineteenth centuries, establishing colonial settlements and importing slaves to the island. The island was ceded to the British in 1814 and administered separately from Trinidad until Great Britain combined them into the colony of Trinidad and Tobago in 1889. Trinidad and Tobago achieved independence from Britain in 1962; today the Republic of Trinidad and Tobago is a parliamentary democracy. For the sake of brevity, the terms Trinidad and Trinidadian will be used to refer to the nation formed by these two islands.

Although the linguistic heterogeneity of these colonies may have inhibited the early development of an extensive print culture, a number of notable writers emerged during the nineteenth century and early twentieth centuries. **Jean Baptiste Philippe**'s *Free Mulatto* (1824) is an early anticolonial narrative and describes the unjust ways in which blacks were treated in society. Michel Maxwell Philip's *Emmanuel Appadocca: A Tale of the Boucaneers* (1854), a sea adventure story and antislavery novel, is also the first known novel by an English-speaking Caribbean person. Albert Raymond Forbes (ARF) Webber's *Those That Be in Bondage* (1917) concerns the plight of indentured Indian immigrants.

But the emergence of English as common language and the wider entrenchment of literacy in the early twentieth century paved the way for a period of literary prosperity, one enmeshing cultural and political concerns. In the late 1920s and early 1930s, a small, informal group of talented young men, "The Beacon Group," met regularly to share their interests in music and literature and to discuss the political and social conditions of Trinidad. Its work is often considered the first stage of the formation of modern Trinidadian literature. **CLR James** and **Alfred Mendes** founded a literary magazine called *The Beacon* (1930–33), a controversial and influential magazine that proved a major force in the emergence of modern Caribbean literature. They were joined by **Albert Gomes**, who, like Mendes, was of Portuguese descent, and **Ralph Anthony Charles (RAC) De Boissière**, a French Creole. De Boissière later wrote the novels *Crown Jewel* (1952), *Rum and Coca-Cola* (1956), and *No Saddles for Kangaroos* (1964).

CLR James, the most influential Trinidadian writer and activist of the twentieth century, prided himself on being an "outsider" who had immersed himself in the ideas of Western civilization. James's novella *Triumph* (1929) was a key example of what came to be called **barrack yard literature**—distinguished by its realistic depictions of urban squalor. James's only novel, *Minty Alley* (1936) is the best-known work in this tradition and vividly portrays the interactions of people of different classes and ancestries. Much of James's later life was spent as an expatriate in England, where he wrote about subjects as diverse as cricket, Marxism, and Pan Africanism; the latter two preoccupations found expression in his play *The Black Jacobins* (1936).

Many Trinidadian writers were influenced by such vibrant vernacular forms of culture as calypso, a musical form that emerged in the 1930s; based on simple melodies and rousing rhythms, calypso assayed, in satirical lyrics, themes that ranged from sexual braggadocio to social protest. Among the Caribbean writers whose work was inflected by such vernacular traditions was **Samuel Selvon**, notably in his short story "Trinidadian" (1952). Selvon, who left Trinidad for England in 1950, was also known for the novels *A Brighter Sun* (1952) and *The Lonely Londoners* (1956). Selvon was admired, too, for his radio shows. Indeed, the BBC played an important role for diasporic Trinidadian culture: its radio program *Caribbean Voices*, broadcast weekly from 1943 to 1958, helped pique international interest in Caribbean writing. The program was a major force in supporting and sustaining the careers of Caribbean writers, including those who elected to stay in the region.

If Selvon distinguished himself by his immersion in Trinidadian Creoles and customs, **V. S. Naipaul**, Trinidad's most internationally celebrated writer, distinguished himself by his sense of critical detachment from his native land. Naipaul, who grew up in Chaguanas, Trinidad, in an East Indian community, left to attend Oxford at the age of eighteen and has lived in England for most of his life. His novels, which invariably shun all forms of ethnic solidarity, include three set in Trinidad: *Miguel Street* (1959), *The Mystic Masseur* (1959), and *A House for Mr. Biswas* (1962), which many critics consider his finest novel. In 2001, V. S. Naipaul won the Nobel Prize for Literature "for having united perceptive narrative and incorruptible scrutiny in works that compel us to see the presence of suppressed histories." Naipaul's younger brother, **Shiva Naipaul**, though less well known, also achieved some acclaim as a novelist and journalist. He is known for the novels *Fireflies* (1971) and *The Chip-Chip Gatherers* (1973), and for *Beyond the Dragon's Mouth* (1985), a collection of stories and articles.

A younger generation of Trinidadian writers, many of whom have become expatriates, has gravitated toward new themes. The poet **Dionne Brand**, who emigrated to Canada, writes about the struggles of black women in the face of racial and sexual discrimination and about the travails and triumphs of immigration. The novelist and short-story writer **Neil Bissoondath**, who also resides in Canada, has explored themes of physical displacement and emotional alienation in his novels *A Casual Brutality* (1988) and *The Worlds Within Her: A Novel* (1998), as well as the short-story collections *Digging up the Mountains* (1986) and *On the Eve of Uncertain Tomorrows* (1990). Another Canadian who grew up in Trinidad, **Marlene Nourbese Philip**, an essayist, playwright, poet, and novelist, is known for the children's book *Harriet's Daughter* (1988) and for her poetry collection *She Tries Her Tongue, Her Silence Softly Breaks* (1989). She explores the challenges of cultural decolonization in a language she describes as a "Caribbean demotic." Her work also includes the play *Coups and Calypsos*.

Indeed, theater has played a central role in this literature tradition. Modern Trinidadian theater began in 1946 when **Errol John** (1924–88) and **Errol Hill** founded the Whitehall Players. **Derek Walcott,** the Nobel Prize–winning poet and playwright, originally from St. Lucia, produced several plays in Trinidad in the 1950s: *Henri Christophe* (1950), *The Sea at Dauphin* (1954), and *Drums and Colours* (1958); he founded the Trinidad Theater Workshop in 1959, a group that helped introduce vernacular, creolized forms of English to the stage. Errol Hill's earliest play, *The Ping Pong* (1958), was written from the point of view of steel-band players; and his short play *Man Better Man,* which was produced in England in the 1950s, was a musical that drew upon steel-band traditions. Another writer who has contributed greatly to Trinidadian theater is **Earl Lovelace,** who attended Howard University in Washington, D.C., taught in several colleges in the United States, and, in 1982, returned to Trinidad, where he still resides. He is known for the novels *The Dragon Can't Dance* (1979), *Salt* (1997), and for the plays *Jestina's Calypso* (1978) and *The New Hardware Store* (1980). *See also* Abolitionist Literature; Anglophone Caribbean Literature, History of; Literary Journals.

Further Reading

Donnell, Alison, and Sarah Lawson Welsh, eds. *The Routledge Reader in Caribbean Literature.* London; New York: Routledge, 1996.

Gilkes, Michael. *The West Indian Novel.* Boston: Twayne, 1981.

James, Louis. *Caribbean Literature in English.* London; New York: Longman, 1999.

Markham, E. A., ed. *The Penguin Book of Caribbean Short Stories.* London; New York: Penguin Books, 1996.

Patteson, Richard F. *Caribbean Passages: A Critical Perspective on New Fiction from the West Indies.* Boulder, CO: Lynne Rienner Publishers, 1998.

Sander, Reinhard W. *The Trinidad Awakening: West Indian Literature of the Nineteen-thirties.* Westport, CT: Greenwood Press, 1988.

—*Lisa Finder*

Tropiques (1941–45)

Surviving fascist censorship and representatives in Martinique from the Vichy regime installed by the Nazis in France during World War II, this literary journal propagated throughout the francophone Caribbean the ideas of **Négritude** expressed by the writer and poet **Aimé Césaire** and his wife Suzanne, as well as encouraging an anticolonialist stance.

Arriving at his native Martinique from France in 1939, Césaire founded *Tropiques* with his wife, and philosopher **René Ménil** in 1941. The journal was meant to be a cultural vehicle that celebrated Martinique's roots. The editors published essays about Caribbean culture, folklore and even articles about animals and plants from the region. Césaire published his poetry as well; Ménil wrote philosophical texts, expounding specifically on the Surrealist movement that was so popular in Paris. Literary news from the Spanish speaking Caribbean was also included.

French philosopher André Breton (1896–1966), sojourning on the island on his way to New York, came across an issue of the journal at a shop in Fort-au-France, Martinique's capital. Reading Césaire's poetry, Breton called him the best writer in the French language; of **Suzanne Césaire** and Ménil, he expressed that they were the best commentators of **surrealism**. From that moment on Breton was an enthusiastic supporter of the journal.

But despite *Tropiques*' aesthetics, its political and revolutionary tone was quite evident: Aimé Cézaire lamented the absence of art in Martinique but blamed it on the colonial condition; Suzanne Cézaire advocated cannibalizing French culture to produce a true Martinican culture; and Ménil insisted that Martinican artists could only find their voices through an immersion into their repressed African heritage. In 1943, the Vichy authorities on the island called the journal radical and destructive and attempted to shut it down by withholding paper for printing. The editors responded with a letter claiming that they were as radical and disruptive as Émile Zola (1840–1902) and Victor Hugo (1802–1885), icons of French culture, were in their times.

The journal went on for two more years, influencing such young writers as **René Depestre** and **Joseph Zobel**. A quarterly publication, *Tropiques* published fourteen issues; a special compilation was published in 1978. *Tropiques* rallied Martinicans in particular, and Caribbeans in general, toward self-assertion, as Suzanne Césaire phrased it: "The most troubling reality is our own. We shall act. This, our land, can only be what we want it to be." *See also* Literary Journals; Martinique, History of the Literature of.

Further Reading

Kelley, Robin D. G. "A Poetics of Anticolonialism" *Monthly Review* 51, no. 6 (November 1999): 1–21.

Sharpley-Whiting, T. Denfan. *Negritude Women*. Minneapolis: University of Minnesota Press, 2002.

—*D. H. Figueredo*

Trouillot, Évelyne (1954–)

Trouillot is a novelist and feminist from Haiti. She lived in exile in the United States but, unlike many writers from the Caribbean, chose to return to her native country to promote a national culture and education.

Évelyne Trouillot was born on January 2, 1954, in Port-au-Prince, Haiti. She spent her childhood and teen years in the United States, where she studied languages and education at the university level. Returning to Haiti when she was in her twenties, Trouillot divided her time between education and cultural activities and, eventually, writing. In 1996, she published a collection of short stories, *La chambre interdite*. The following year, she published *L'oiseau mirage* a collection of stories for young adults. It was the publication of her first novel in 2003, though, that brought her international recognition. Entitled, *Rosalie l'infâme*, the novel, based on true events that occurred in Saint-Domingue in the 1750s, narrated the story of a slave woman named Lisette who deforms scores of young black children to free them from bondage. This narrative portrays slaves as individuals who exhibit a variety of character traits, from passion and courage to weakness, while suffering under colonial rule.

Trouillot uses literature as a device to fight against political corruption and poverty. Her writings affirm the need for solidarity, a theme that she clearly stated in her 2002 book-length essay, *Restituer l'enfance: Enfance et état de droit en Haïti. See also* Slave Narratives.

Further Reading

Cordova, Sarah Davies. "*Rosalie l'infâm.*" *World Literature Today* 78, no.3–4 (September–December 2004): 119.

Danticat, Edwdige. "Evelyne Trouillot" (interview). *Bomb 90* (Winter 2004–05): 48–52.

—*Jayne R. Boisvert*

Trouillot, Lyonel (1956–)

A political engaged writer, Trouillot is a major cultural and political figure in Haiti who uses literature to advocate for social change. He is considered one of the leading intellectuals and novelists in the Caribbean. He writes both in Kreyòl, the Creole language of Haiti, and in French.

Born on December 31, 1956, into a family of lawyers, Trouillot studied law, as expected by the family, but was also fascinated by literature and by writing. He contributed stories and poems to numerous journals in Haiti and in the Caribbean. He also wrote songs for popular Haitian singers. In the 1990s, he directed the journal *Cultura*.

Though Trouillot began his writing career in 1979 with the publication, in Kreyòl, of the book of poems *Depale*, it was not until the 1990s when many of his novels appeared, first in Haiti and then in Paris. Probably the work most characteristic of his style and message is the novel *Rue des pas perdus*, published in 1993 and translated into English, as *Street of Lost Footsteps*, in 2003. The novel, which uses elements of **magical realism**—realismo mágico—describes the economic decline and political violence that has scarred Haiti in a brutal manner. Observes reviewer Nicholas Birns, in *Review of Contemporary Fiction*: "Trouillot is an aggressive writer. He seizes the moment, and he is not afraid to render carnage and domesticity side by side."

In 2003, Trouillot became the leader of a group of intellectuals who opposed President Jean-Bertrand Aristide (1953–). Their antigovernment activity—through writings and speeches—was one of the causes of the removal of Aristide from office. *See also* Literatura Comprometida/Socially Engaged Literature.

Further Reading

Birns, George. "Street of Lost Footsteps." *Review of Contemporary Fiction* 24, no.1 (Spring 2004): 156–58.

—*D. H. Figueredo*

Trujillo Era (1930–61)

This era is named after the dictatorship of Rafael Leónidas Trujillo, who ruled over the Dominican Republic for over three decades. Trujillo (1891–1961) assumed control of his nation's government through electoral fraud, sheer force, and, when not in the limelight, through personally selected puppets who served as either vice presidents or presidents.

Unlike **Fidel Castro**, who installed a government plan to direct and encourage a national culture through cultural institutions, think-tanks, and publishing houses, Trujillo simply treated well only those writers who supported him and silenced those who didn't. Two polar examples suffice: **Joaquin Balaguer Ricardo**, a Trujillo supporter and high official, who served as president during the Trujillo Era, published positive accounts of Trujillo's rule and was rewarded with diplomatic posts throughout the world; scholar Juan Galíndez and novelist **Ramón Marrero Aristy**, on the other hand, were murdered for expressing anti-Trujillo sentiments and providing information on how Trujillo amassed his wealth and stole money from the government.

"The Marrero Aristy Case," as it was called, made international news when it happened: the writer was killed outside the National Palace and his charred body discovered inside the wreck of his car. A similar fate awaited the legendary Maribel sisters—María Teresa, Minerva, and Patria. For opposing Trujillo and supporting the underground, in 1960, these three beautiful sisters were murdered and pushed off a cliff. Though the sisters were not writers, their lives inspired poetry by **Pedro Mir**, a film, and the popular novel *In the Time of the Butterflies* by Dominican-American **Julia Alvarez**. A third event, now seen as a horrid act of violence but initially ignored by the international press and governments, was the massacre of twenty-thousand Haitian immigrants in 1937. This holocaust is depicted in the novels, *General Soleil, mon compare* (1955) by **Jacques Stephen Alexis**, and **Edwige Danticat's** *The Farming of the Bones*.

During the Trujillo Era, writers veiled the meaning of their words to avoid persecution. **Marcio Veloz Maggiolo** wrote a poetry that was so elusive in its criticism of Trujillo that the reader did not always realize the object of the poem, and **Héctor Incháustegui Cabral**, in collection such as *Poemas de una sola angustia* (1939), wrote on universal themes—poverty and hunger, for example—which were not unique to the Dominican Republic. Such were the characteristics of the movements

Poesía Sorprendida and Los Poetas Independientes: because the dictator did not realize he was being criticized, he allowed the poets associated with those movements to continue writing. But those who did express clear criticism, and were lucky enough not to meet Marrero Aristy's fate, were either imprisoned—**Miguel Alfonseca**—or forced into exile: **Juan Bosch**, Pedro Mir, and **Abelardo Vicioso**.

Essentially, two types of works were produced in the country, pro-Trujillo literature, clearly written and obviously celebratory or supportive of the tyrant or of Trujillo's political aims. The best example of this type of literature was the novel *Over* (1939), written by Marrero Aristy at the time when he was friends with the dictator. The novel criticized American interests in the sugar industry, echoing Trujillo's own sentiments and his desires to nationalize American sugar companies. The other genre was poetry, which Doris Sommer and Esteban Torres, in the *Handbook of Latin American Literature* (1992), describe as "innovative in an intentionally difficult way . . . to vouchsafe a space for art amid the increasingly oppressive regime" (276).

The assassination of Trujillo in 1961 ended his reign. Writers like Bosh, Mir, and **Manuel del Cabral** returned home, and their works were now openly appreciated. A few poets wrote volumes critical of the era: *Los testigos* (1962) by **Antonio Fernández Spencer**; **Máximo Avilés Blonda**'s *Centro del mundo* (1962); and **Lupo Hernández Rueda**'s *Santo Domingo vertical* (1962), but for these writers, though, most of the anti-Trujillo works began to appear in the 1970s after the civil war that followed his death.

Other examples of anti-Trujillo literature include *Solo cenizas hallarás (1981)*, by **Pedro Verges**, *La tierra está bramando* (1986), by **Hilma Contreras**, probably the best-known literary account of the era. *La Fiesta del Chivo* (2002), a novel by the Peruvian author Mario Vargas Llosa (1936–). *See aso* Dominican Republic Literature, History of.

Further Reading

Crassweller, Robert D. *Trujillo: The Life and Times of a Caribbean Dictator*. New York, Macmillan, 1966.

Sommer, Doris, and Esteban Torres. "Dominican Republic." In *Handbook of Latin American Literature*, edited by David William Forster, 271–86. New York and London: Garland Publishing, 1992.

Vargas Llosa, Mario. *La fiesta del chivo*. Madrid: Alfaguara, 2000.

—*D. H. Figueredo*

U

Ugarte España, María (1914–)

Ugarte España is one of the Dominican Republic's best-known literary and art critics. She is also an essayist and a journalist.

María Ugarte was born in Segovia, Spain, on February 2, 1914. She finished her secondary education at the Instituto de Segunda Enseñanza de Segovia in 1929 and then attended the Universidad Central de Madrid, earning a masters in philosophy and literature. After teaching history at her alma mater, she moved to the Dominican Republic in 1940. Becoming a naturalized citizen of her adopted country, she then worked for the Ministry of Foreign Relations from 1944 to 1948. From 1963 to 1998, she was editor of the cultural supplement of the daily *El Caribe*.

As a journalist and a critic, she published numerous essays on contemporary Dominican writers and artists as well as Caribbean and Dominican architecture. In 1978, she published the volume *Monumentos coloniales*. She followed this study with three scholarly works, *La catedral de Santo Domingo, primada de América* (1992) *Iglesias, capillas y ermitas coloniales* (1995), and *Estampas coloniales* (1995). Her experience as a journalist allows her to treat the subject of architecture in an accessible style that has made her popular in the Dominican Republic. She has been responsible for introducing Dominican art to readers throughout Latin America and Europe.

Ugarte has received numerous honors, including Orden del Mérito Civil en el grado de Comendador medal, given to her by Spanish king Juan Carlos (1986) and Orden de Duarte, Sánchez y Mella (1990), given to her by the government of the Dominican Republic. *See also* Trujillo Era.

Further Reading

Cocco de Filippis, Daisy. "María Ugarte." In *Para que no se olviden: The lives of Women in Dominican History*. New York: Ediciones Alcance, 2000.

Escritores Dominicanos. http://www.geocities.com/alcance66/u.html (accessed 9/15/05).

—Daisy Cocco de Filippis

Umpierre-Herrera, Luz María (1947–)

Sexual identity, rebellion against machismo, and affirmation of a Puerto Rican identity and language are the themes that inspire Umpierre's poetic works. A scholar, her feminist militancy has not always been well received by college administrators, who describe her as controversial. She has also struggled against scholars who tend to favor Spanish culture over Puerto Rican culture.

Umpierre was born in Santurce in 1947 into a large household that included her parents, two aunts, and several cousins. She attended a private school in San Juan and won several scholarships to attend the Universidad del Sagrado Corazón in Santurce. She graduated in 1970 with a BA in Spanish, and though she had been writing poetry since the age of thirteen, Umpierre planned to be an attorney and matriculated in law school, first at the Universidad Católica de Ponce and then in Río Piedras. It was not an experience she liked: "I hated law school. I hated it with a passion because everything was so stifling. The readings were dry. It was too stifling. . . . So what I did was that while I was taking classes at the Law School, I took one course in Hispanic studies at a master's level. Then I decided that's what I wanted," she recalled in an interview in the journal *Melus* (2002).

In 1974, she began her doctoral studies at Bryn Mawr College, Pennsylvania. The subtle racism she encountered at the school, where her colleagues viewed anything Puerto Rican as inferior, prompted her to write her first poetry collection, *Una puertorriqueña en Penna* (1979). In the volume, she used Spanish and **Spanglish**—a combination of English and Spanish—to criticize elitist views within academia. In 1982, she published her second book of poetry, *En el país de las maravillas*.

In the early 1980s, she taught Latin America literature at Rutgers University and wrote two literary studies, *Ideología y novela en Puerto Rico* (1982) and *Nuevas aproximaciones críticas a la literatura puertorriqueña contemporánea* (1983). Her stay at Rutgers was a difficult period: she filed a complaint with the Equal Employment Opportunity Commission, accusing the university of discriminating against her when a position she sought was given to a male professor; the university attempted to remove her tenure; and her mother, with whom she was close, passed away.

In 1989, Rutgers reinstated Umpierre, but by now she had accepted the position of chair of Modern Languages and Intercultural Studies at Western Kentucky University. A year later, the Women's Alliance at Western Kentucky named her Woman of the Year.

Umpierre's best-known work is *The Margarita Poems* (1987). The volume indicates a shift from writing in Spanish to writing in English and signals the emergence of her lesbian identity. Observes critic Nancy Vosburg in *Contemporary Lesbian Writers of the United States* (1993): "[Umpierre] seeks out her lesbian muse and identifies it in an act of liberation that she invites others to share . . . nurturing and empowering support of other women, paying tribute to her literary foremothers and sisters"(553). *See also* Gay and Lesbian Literature; Puerto Rican Literature, History of.

Further Reading

DiFrancesco, Maria. *Poetic Dissidence: An Interview with Luz Maria Umpierre*. Melus 27, no. 4 (Winter 2002): 137–56.

Vosburg, Nancy. *Contemporary Lesbian Writers of the United States*, edited by Sandra Pollack and Denise D. Knight. Westport, CT: Greenwood Press, 1993.

—D. H. Figueredo

Unión de Escritores y Artistas de Cuba (UNEAC)

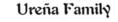

The Union of Cuban Writes and Artists was established by Cuba's revolutionary government in 1961 to direct artistic and literary production on the island. Consisting of over five thousand members, UNEAC published the journals *La Gaceta de Cuba* and *Unión*, which discuss literature, music, film, and the plastic arts, and manage the publishing house Ediciones Unión, which published the winners of the institution's annual literary award. In 1968, under the direction of the poet **Nicolás Guillén**, UNEAC awarded prizes to playwright **Antón Arrufat** and poet **Heberto Padilla**, both of whom were accused by militant members of the Cuban government as being antirevolutionaries. In the 1970s, UNEAC refused to acknowledge the existence of writers who were not supportive of the revolutionary regime: novelist **Reinaldo Arenas** recalled in his autobiography *Antes que anochezca* (1992) how a scholar from abroad was told by an UNEAC official that on the island there was no such writer named Arenas. In the 1990s, however, the institution published works by Cuban exiles. Ever changing, UNEAC began to publish two electronic bulletins in 2002, *La isla en peso* and *Bolentín electrónico Anjá*, both available through http://www.uneac.com.

Further Reading

Johnson, Peter T. "The Nuanced Lives of the Intelligentsia." In *Conflict and Change in Cuba*, edited by Enrique A. Balroya and James A. Morris, 137–63. Alburqueque: University of New Mexico, 1993.

—D. H. Figueredo

Ureña Family

Nicolas and Salomé Ureña were father and daughter poets from the Dominican Republic. They wrote during the nineteenth century.

Ureña de Henríquez, Salomé (1850–97). Called the "muse of the Dominican Republic," Salomé Ureña is one of the country's most beloved and famous poets. An educator as well, she promoted education and equality for Dominican women.

Salomé Ureña was born on October 21, 1850. Her parents were Gregoria Díaz y León and Nicolás Ureña de Mendoza. During her childhood, Salomé Ureña did not go beyond elementary school, the only type of formal education permitted to Dominican women at the time. Her father, a discreet poet and lawyer with a good reputation who held positions in the Senate and Judicial System, gave her the best literary education that could be had in those days: the reading of the classics of the Spanish language. Wise teachings and wise readings forged the intellect of this woman, who became one of the most distinguished figures in the history of literature and education in the Dominican Republic.

She started to write at young age, and by the time she was fifteen years old, she had established herself as a poet. When she was twenty-eight years old, Salomé Ureña was so well known in the Dominican Republic that she was awarded a medal, funded by the public. In 1880, she married the writer, physician, and attorney Francisco Henríquez y Carvajal (1859–1935), who later on would serve as president of the republic. Together they had four children: Francisco, Pedro, Max, and Camila, and all but Francisco would become major literary figures in Latin America. In 1881, influenced by the pedagogical philosophy of the Puerto Rican thinker and writer **Eugenio María de Hostos**, whom she had befriended, Salomé Ureña founded the Instituto de Señoritas, the first secondary school for women in the country.

Salomé Ureña published her poems in such publications as *Boletín Oficial de Santo Domingo* and *El Universal, La Opinión, El Nacional*, and *El País*. Her poems were patriotic, romantic and sentimental. She also wrote **Indianist** poetry, which celebrated the Amerindians who had lived on the island before the arrivals of the Spanish conquistadores. The clarity, lyricism, and sincerity of her poems allowed Salomé Ureña a critical acceptance seldom granted to women writing in the Dominican Republic. She occupied a favored place in Dominicans literary circles as well as receiving praises from critics outside the country. Though she never left the Dominican Republic, she received honorary membership in such prestigious cultural organizations as Cuba's Liceo de Puerto Príncipe, and Alegría from Venezuela.

She died of tuberculosis in Santo Domingo on April 6, 1897. Her life is the basis of the best-selling novel *In The Name of Salomé* (2000) by Dominican-American writer **Julia Alvarez**. Her collections of poems include *Poesías* (1880), *Poesías* (1920), *Poesías completas* (1950), and *Poesías escogidas*.

Ureña de Mendoza, Nicolás (1822–75). One of the first poets from the Dominican Republic to use **costumbrismo**, a style that emphasizes local customs and traditions, Ureña de Mendoza was an attorney, an educator, and a journalist. His daughter, **Salomé Ureña**, became the nation's best-loved nineteenth-century poet.

Ureña de Mendoza was born on May 25, 1822. He taught at one of the first public schools established in the republic and wrote for the cultural paper *El progreso*. At the age of twenty-five, the president of Dominican Republic, Buenaventura Baéz (1834–1920), dispatched him to the United States to negotiate the annexation of the Dominican Republic.

In 1850, Ureña de Mendoza became an attorney. In the 1860s, he started to write costumbrista poetry. His most famous contribution is "El guajiro predilecto" (1855), a ballad about the love a man from the countryside feels for a local beauty. The verses depict the natural beauty of the island and pay tribute to the customs of the simple country folk. The diction is simple, straightforward, meant to be easily memorized. "El guajiro predilecto," considered one of the most beautifully written poems in the Dominican Republic, affirmed nationalism and encouraged Dominicans to take pride in their nation.

Ureña de Mendoza passed away in Santo Domingo on April 3, 1875. In the novel *In The Name of Salomé* (2000), Dominican American author Julia Alvarez portrays the poet as handsome and charismatic, a loving father, who encourages his daughter to study and write, and a patriot who advocates education and liberty for all Dominicans. *See also* Dominican Republic Literature, History of.

Further Reading

Alvarez, Julia. *In the Name of Salomé*. Chapel Hill, NC: Algonquin Books of Chapel Hill, 2000.

Cocco de Filippis, Daisy. *Documents of Dissidence: Selected Writings by Dominican Women*. New York: CUNY Dominican Studies Institute, 2000.

Vicioso, Sherezada. *Salomé Ureña de Henríquez (1850–1897): a cien años de un magisterio*. Santo Domingo: Comisión Permanente de la Feria Nacional del Libro, 1997.

—*Daisy Cocco de Filippis and D. H. Figueredo*

Ureña de Mendoza, Nicolás. See Ureña Family.

Ureña de Henríquez, Salomé. See Ureña Family.

v

Valdés, Gabriel de la Concepción, "Plácido" (1809–44)

Romantic poet Gabriel de la Concepción Valdés was born in Havana on March 18, 1809. His mother was a Spanish dancer and his father was a Cuban of Afro-Hispanic ancestry. Immediately after his birth, his mother left him at la Casa de Beneficiencia y Maternidad, Havana's orphanage, where he was given the surname Valdés. Eventually, his father took him out of the orphanage, and the child was brought up by his paternal grandmother. Gabriel de la Concepción went to primary school, but at the age of twelve, he had to go to work, first as a typesetter in a printing shop, and later as a comb maker. Early in his life he began writing poetry, showing a great facility for rhyming. Using the name Plácido, he published his poems in several periodicals in the city of Matanzas, where he had gone to live as a youth.

Plácido embraced the aesthetics and the literary forms of the romantic movement. His gifts for rhyming and his ease for writing in verse made him popular at social gatherings of the Cuban elites of Spanish ancestry. But he was also popular among the Afro-Cuban middle classes of artisans and small farmers. He was known for his constant traveling in the Havana-Matanzas area, attending private social events and public festivities, where he would improvise poetry. He wrote many poems praising public figures and personal benefactors, but he also wrote poems in praise of political freedom and chastising despotic rulers. Many of his odes to monarchs and ministers can be interpreted as admonishments to govern justly or as warnings about the tragic end of tyrannical rulers. In 1844, Plácido was accused of being implicated in a conspiracy for the rebellion of blacks in Cuba, known as the Conspiracy of La Escalera. He was imprisoned, and after a trial of questionable procedures, he was condemned to death. He died by firing squad in the city of Matanzas on June 26, 1844. A romantic in his life as well as in his poetry, he read his poem "Plegaria a Dios" on the way to his execution.

Most of the published works of Plácido appeared in newspapers and magazines. In his lifetime he published one collection of poems in Matanzas, but it did not include most of his poetry. In 1886 Sebastian Alfredo de Morales published in Havana a book entitled *Poesías completas de Plácido*.

Plácido wrote in practically all literary formats, and excelled in his lyric "romanzas" and witty fables. He was an uneven but gifted poet. The superficiality of many of his poems can be ascribed to the fact that they were meant to be ephemeral, written just to enliven a celebration or to praise in homage. More justified is the criticism that the thoughts that he expresses in his poetry are too often incomplete or meaningless. But his images are brilliant, and the sounds of the words that he chose are always musical. As the purist Spanish literary critic Marcelino Menéndez y Pelayo said in his *Historia de la poesía Hispano-Americana*, "If Plácido did not always know what he was saying, whatever he said sounded good." Literary critics judge him as a genius whose output was uneven on account of his deficient academic education and his limited literary background. His poetry is significant as one of the first flowerings of romanticism in Cuba. *See also* Cuban Literature, History of; Romanticismo/Romanticism.

Further Reading

Bueno, Salvador. *Acerca de Plácido*. Habana: Editorial Letras Cubanas, 1985.

Menéndez Y Pelayo, Marcelino. *Historia de la poesía Hispano-Americana, 2 v.* Madrid: Librería General de Victoriano Suárez, 1911.

Pérez del Río, Luis ¿*Es falsa la confesión de Plácido?* Santiago de Cuba: Editorial Oriente, 1994.

—*Rafael E. Tarrago*

Valdés, Zoé (1959–)

Valdés is a feminist writer whose novels explore eroticism as a tool of rebellion against repressive regimes. In 1995, she wrote the novel *La nada cotidiana* which portrayed a poverty-ridden Cuba where the revolutionary government monitors and controls the activities of the ordinary citizen: the only avenue for temporary liberation and free expression is through excessive sex. Valdés's novels are rich in graphic descriptions of the sexual encounter, often using the kind of crude and direct vocabulary found in pornographic literature. Yet, there is a mastery of the prose and a sense of the poetics that raises the works from the mere prurient to the artistic. Critic Jennifer Schuessler, writing in the *New York Times*, describes Zoé Valdés as "fanciful and streetwise, self-consciously feminine and intensely dirty-minded."

Valdés was born in Havana of a Cuban mother and a Chinese father. She worked for UNESCO, was in the diplomatic staff of the Cuban embassy in Paris, and was assistant director of the journal *Revista Cine Cubano*. In the mid-1990s she sneaked out of Cuba two copies of the manuscript for *La nada cotidiana*; one copy reached France, the other surfaced in Florida. Upon publication, in French and in Spanish, the novel became a best seller in Europe and was translated into English as *Yocandra in the Paradise of Nothing* (1995).

In 1995, Valdés was invited to Paris to teach a course on Cuban poet **José Martí**. She didn't return to Cuba and stayed in France, where she currently lives, though she visits Miami, Florida, quite frequently. Valdés is a fervent critic of the Cuban Revolution; however, she doesn't want to be seen just as another anti-Castro writer but as an author of serious works that affirm feminism, women's rights, and the rejection of machismo, or a male-dominated society. Her novels include *Respuestas para vivir* (1986), *Sangre azul* (1993), *La hija del embajador* (1995), all written in Cuba. In exile, she has written *Te di la vida entera* (1996), *Traficante de belleza* (1998), and *Milagro en Miami* (2001). In 2002 an English translation of her 1999 lesbian love story *Querido primer novio* was published as *Dear First Love*. Valdés has also written several books of poetry, including *Todo para una sombra* (1986), *Cuerdas para el lince* (1999), and *Breve beso de la espera* (2002).

Valdés won the prestigious Planeta Award in 1997 for her novel *Café Nostalgia*. In 2003, she received the Fernando Lara Award for her novel *Lobas de mar,* a historical romance about eighteenth-century Caribbean pirates Anne Bonny and Mary Read. *See also* Anti-Castro Literature; Feminist Literature.

Further Reading

Schuessler, Jennifer. "Speak, Manatee: A Magic Realist Novel in Castro's Cuba." *New York Times Book Review*, September 1, 2002.

Strausfeld, Michi. *Nuevos narradores cubanos*. Madrid: Siruela Ediciones, 2000.

—*D. H. Figueredo*

Valero, Roberto (1955–94)

Cuban poet and scholar who was a cofounder of the literary journal *Mariel* and who wrote lyrical poetry about his experiences in Cuba under **Fidel Castro**'s regime and about his life in exile. He was a member of the **Mariel generation**, a group of Cuban writers who arrived in the United States in 1980.

Roberto Valero was born in Matanzas, Cuba. He attended the Universidad de la Habana, where he majored in Russian Language and Literature. Unable to publish in Cuba due to his anti-Castro stance, he suffered imprisonment and in 1980 participated in the Mariel Boatlift, when over 110,000 Cubans crossed the Strait of Florida on all types of sailing vessels to reach Florida. He collaborated with novelist **Reinaldo Arenas** in the founding and editing of the literary journal *Mariel* and participated in conferences that witnessed human rights abuses on the island. Early in the 1980s, he settled in Washington, D.C., where he studied at Georgetown University, earning a PhD in literature.

Though he wrote several short stories, he was primarily a poet. His books of poetry include *Desde un oscuro ángulo* (1982), *En fin, la noche* (1984), *Dharma* (1985), *Venías* (1990), and *No estaré en tu camino* (1991). Unlike other writers that make up the Mariel generation, Valero preferred not to write in anger about his experiences in Cuba. Often, nostalgia, homesickness, and his wife were the source of his inspiration. A particular image that Valero used was his grandmother:

> Abuela esta dormida en mi cartera
> Se que flota una sonrisa de recuerdo
> La ausencia de un cuerpo conocido . . .

(Grandmother sleeps in my ballet / I know she floats a smile of remembrance / The absence of a known person. . . .) For Valero, the grandmother was an archetypal link to a biblical paradise when history had not severed families.

Valero also wrote a critical study of his close friend Reinaldo Arenas titled *El desamparado humor de Reinaldo Arenas* (1991) and the novel *Este viento de cuaresma* (1994). Valero passed away in 1995. *See also* Anti-Castro Literature; Grandparents in Caribbean Literature.

Further Reading

Figueredo, Danilo H. "Ser Cubano: To Be Cuban. The Evolution of Cuban-American Literature." *Multicultural Review* 6, n. 1 (March 1997): 24–25.

Hernández-Miyares, Julio E. *Narrativa y libertad: cuentos cubanos de la diáspora*. Miami: Ediciones Universal, 1996.

—D. H. Figueredo

Varela, Félix (1788–1853)

———————————————— ■ ————————————————

A priest, teacher, philosopher, and patriot, Félix Varela might be the first author from Latin America to write and publish a novel in the United States, a trend that would continue for the next two centuries. He was the first Cuban abolitionist.

Félix Varela y Morales was born in Havana on November 20, 1788. He studied at the seminary of San Carlos and then at the University of Havana. Ordained into the priesthood in 1811, he taught philosophy at the Seminary where he had studied, befriending **Domingo Del Monte** and **José de la Luz y Caballero,** who would become influential in the antislavery movement and in the promotion of Cuban culture. In 1822, Varela was elected to represent Cuba before the Spanish Cortes—akin to a parliament—where he spoke in favor of the abolition of slavery and advocated Cuba's independence. The Spanish king Fernando VII didn't look favorably on Varela and sentenced him to death. Varela escaped, seeking refuge in Gibraltar and eventually reaching the United States; he was never able to go back to Cuba. Varela lived in Philadelphia and New York, where he taught and was named vicar of New York City. Sickly and tired of winters, he relocated to St. Augustine, Florida, in 1850; three years later, he passed away in that city.

Throughout his life he published scores of articles and essays in numerous newspapers in Cuba and the United States, including *Diario de Gobierno, Memorias de la Real Sociedad Económica de la Habana*, and *El observador habanero*. In the United States he published and edited a proindependence periodical, *El habanero*, which was regularly smuggled into Cuba, and edited *The Catholic Expositor and Literary Magazine*. Between 1835 and 1838, he wrote *Cartas a Elpidio: sobre la impiedad, la superstición y el fanatismo en sus relaciones con la sociedad*. In this epistolary, Varela criticized superstition and fanaticism. In the 1990s, the Catholic Church in the United States and Latin America promoted the canonization of Varela, a recommendation on which the Vatican has yet to act. In 1997, the United States Postal Service issued a stamp to honor his memory.

In his writings, Varela promoted freedom for Cuba and equality for all. Recently, scholars Rodolfo J. Cortina and Luis Leal attributed the authorship of the novel *Jicoténcal*, published anonymously in Philadelphia in 1826, to Varela. The story of the conquest of Mexico by the conquistadores, the novel criticized Spanish rule in Latin America.

Varela's prose was rich in allusions, psychological analysis, social commentary, and humor. His sense of duty toward Cuba, his moral views, and his proindependence stance influenced many Cuban writers, especially the Cuban poet and patriot **José Martí**. *See also* Cuban Literature, History of; Indianist Literature; Tertulia/Cénacle/Literary Salon/Soireé.

Further Reading

Céspedes, Carlos Manuel de. *Pasión por Cuba y por la iglesia: aproximación biográfica del P. Félix Varela*. Madrid: Biblioteca de Autores Cristianos, 1998.

Hernández González, Heriberto. *Félix Varela: retorno y presencia*. Habana: Imagen Contemporánea, 1997.

Varela, Félix. *Jicoténcal*. Houston, TX: Arte Público Press, 1995.

—D. H. Figueredo

Vasallo y Cabrera, Francisco (1823–67)

One of Puerto Rico's first poets, Vasallo y Cabrera wrote poems that celebrated his island and the love he felt for it. He was a romantic, though some of his poems revealed a satirical vein as well.

Vasallo y Cabrera was born in San Juan on November 19, 1823. He attended the Seminario Conciliar de San Ildefonso and in 1841 traveled first to Spain and then to France to study medicine, earning his diploma in 1847. While in Barcelona, he befriended a handful of Puerto Rican students who, like him, were homesick. Together they wrote poems that celebrated the island's beauty. The poems appear in the volume *Album puertorriqueño* (1844). In 1846, he contributed seventeen poems to a second anthology, *El cancionero de Borinquen*.

Vasallo y Cabrera returned to Puerto Rico in 1848. For twenty years, he worked as a physician at a military hospital and in the department of public health.

He also wrote numerous poems that were published in newspapers and anthologies, though he himself never published a collection of his poems. His poetry, which affirmed a Puerto Rican identity, could also be humorous, poking fun at some of the island's customs and traditions.

Further Reading

González, José Emilio. "La poesía en Puerto Rico." In *la gran enciclopedia de Puerto Rico*, vol. 3, edited by Vicente Báez, 17–18. San Juan: Puerto Rico en la Mano and Gran Enciclopedia de Puerto Rico.

—*D. H. Figueredo*

Vassa, Gustavos "The African." See Equiano, Oluado.

Vastey, Pompée Valentin (1735–1820)

The first of Haiti's essayist, Le baron de Vastey wrote memoirs and early analysis of colonialism and of his country's struggle for independence. He was secretary to King Henri Christophe (1767–1820).

Le baron de Vastey was born in 1735. Not much is written about his life except that as a child he was an avid reader and liked to observe people. He joined the Haitian revolution sometime in the 1790s. In 1804, he served as secretary of finance of the emerging new nation. After the assassination of Emperor Dessalines (1758–1806), Vastey worked for Henri Christophe, who ruled from 1806 to 1820. A defender of Christophe and of the revolution, Vastey wrote a series of pamphlets and essays criticizing articles that had been published in Europe and that were critical of events in Haiti. In a clear and strong language, he reminds readers of the atrocities that the French had perpetrated on Haitians during colonialism. For his loyalty and patriotism, King Henri bestowed on Vastey the title of baron. His books include *Le système colonial dévoilé* (1814), perhaps his most famous work, *Le cri de la patrie* (1815), *Réflexions sur les Noirs et les Blancs* (1816), *Réflexions politiques sure quelques ouvrages e journaux francais concernant Haïti* (1817), *Essai sur les causes de la Révolution et des guerres civiles en Haïti* (1819), and *Cri de la conscience* (1819).

Further Reading

Berrou, Raphaël, and Pradel Pompilus. *Histoire de la littérature haïtienne.* Tome 1. Port-au-Prince: Editions Caraëbes.

—*D. H. Figueredo*

Vedrismo

Vedrismo was a literary movement from the Dominican Republic that was founded in 1917 by poet **Otilio Virgil Díaz** and that initiated the development of vanguard poetry in that country. The term alludes to the aerial acrobatics of daredevil pilot Jules Vedrines (1881–1919) during the early twentieth century. Díaz promoted a type of poetry that was experimental and free from traditional forms and rhymes, rejecting nationalistic poetry. What was important to Díaz was the free expression of a sentiment without artificial constraints enforced by form and meter, thus allowing the use of poetic prose. The poem that best illustrates Vedrismo is "Arabesco," written by Díaz in 1919:

> Para que no coman de su lubrica carroña
> famélicos canes
> le haremos exequias griegas en la sabana.

(So they don't eat the slippery corpse/the famished dogs/will conduct a Greek funeral in the valley.)

Further Reading

Enciclopedia ilustrada de la república dominicana, vol 6. Santo Domingo, Dominican Republic: Eduprogreso, S.A. 2003.

—*D. H. Figueredo*

Vega, Ana Lydia (1946–)

Puerto Rican author Ana Lydia Vega explores the themes of colonialism, cultural identities, and feminism in the Caribbean. She is a fiction writer as well as an essayist.

Ana Lydia Vega was born in Santurce, Puerto Rico, on December 6, 1946. Having learned French at an early age, her trilingualism—Spanish, French and English—gave her a rare window onto pan-Caribbean reality. It is from that knowledge base that she explores the multifaceted problem of Caribbean and Latin American identities.

Vega attended the University of Puerto Rico, where she studied foreign languages and literatures, obtaining her BA in 1968. She was then awarded a scholarship to pursue a master's and a doctorate in French literature at the University of Provence. She ultimately completed her doctorate there in comparative literature in 1978. Given her commitment to exploring the roots and contradictions of Caribbean reality, it is not surprising that her dissertation was on the theme of the myth of King Henri Christophe (1767–1820), in Haitian literature. Ana Lydia Vega is married to French poet, Robert Villanua, and they have one daughter, Lolita. Currently she is a professor of French and Caribbean literature at the Universidad de Puerto Rico, in Río Piedras. She has been a columnist for the newspapers *Claridad* and *El nuevo día*.

Ana Lydia Vega began to achieve fame as a writer in the 1960s. By 1981, she had published a volume with fellow Puerto Rican writer **Carmen Lugo Filippi**, entitled *Vírgenes y mártires*. The collection quickly became obligatory reading for anyone interested in the problems of neocolonialism, identity, the divided self, colonial education, and feminist consciousness in Puerto Rico and, by extension, the wider Caribbean. It was not just the topics that Vega broached in her writing, but the way she approached them that made her stand out. Vega's intelligent irreverence, her willingness to attack the machismo, snobbery, and cultural paternalism of the upper classes as well as the myopia and self-hatred of the lower classes, coupled with feminism and honesty, made her voice new and unique. Ana Lydia Vega's story "Pollito Chicken," for which she won the **Emilio S. Belaval** Prize in 1978, has an epigraph from anticolonial theorist Alfred Memmi (1920–), and bears a title taken from a ditty small children in Puerto Rico memorize in order to learn to pronounce the English equivalents for basic, everyday items. The story was and is still widely read, becoming a kind of manifesto against the numbing and divisive effects of the colonized mind, Operation Bootstrap, and assimilation. Its protagonist, a Nuyorican—a Puerto Rican New Yorker—public-housing secretary, is cast as a kind of Trojan horse, a figure who breaks through and attains liberation and the beginnings of a radical, nationalist consciousness upon her return to Puerto Rico.

Ana Lydia Vega is author of the short-story collections *Encancaranublado y otros cuentos de naufragio, Falsas crónicas del sur* (1982), several collections of essays, and, in collaboration with Marcos Zurinaga, the script for the film *La gran fiesta* (1985). *See also* Feminism in Caribbean Literature; Nuyorican Literature; Postcolonialism.

Further Reading

Henao, Eda B. *The Colonial Subject's Search for Nation, Culture, and Identity in the Works of Julia Alvarez, Rosario Ferré, and Ana Lydia Vega*. Lewiston, NY: E. Mellen Press, 2003.

—*Pamela María Smorkaloff*

Vega, Bernardo (1885 or 1886–1965)

Vega was a Puerto Rican self-taught author who chronicled the lives of Puerto Ricans in New York during the early twentieth century in his autobiography *Memorias de Bernado Vega* (1977). His book was one of the first memoirs to contain information about ethnic and cultural groups excluded from many contemporary official histories of New York and of the United States.

Vega was born in Cayey, Puerto Rico, of Spanish descent. In 1916 he migrated to New York City, where he worked as a cigar worker for the next two years. After 1918, he was a life insurance agent and held a variety of jobs, though he maintained his association with cigar workers for most of his life. In 1927, he became the owner and editor of the weekly the *Gráfico* with the mission to publicize injustices committed against Latinos, regardless of national origin. During the 1930s, he was active in local New York City politics, favoring liberal politicians. In the 1940s, Vega returned to Puerto Rico, where he became involved in the independence movement.

Vega wrote his autobiography in 1947, but it was not edited and published, by writer **César Andreu Iglesias**, until thirty years later. Although Vega intended to document the lives of Puerto Ricans in New York City, neither he nor Andréu Iglesias thought that the time was right to publish it while the author was alive. The autobiography offered a chronology of one century, from the American Civil War to the post–World War II period. This is accomplished through a series of flashbacks narrated by a fictitious character, Tío Antonio, who migrates to New York in 1847, and then by Vega himself.

Bernardo Vega was the first chronicler of Puerto Ricans living in the United States in the twentieth century. *Source: Centro de Estudios Puertorriqueños.*

Vega gave the manuscript to Andreu Iglesias. The author's original intention had been to write a novel, but Andreu Iglesias convinced him to turn it into a memoir. *Memorias de Bernardo Vega* preserved Puerto Rican nationalism and identity as well as capturing some of the history of the migration of Caribbean people. *See also* Immigrant Literature.

Further Reading

Luis, William. *Dance Between Two Cultures: Latino Caribbean Literature Written in the United States.* Nashville: Vanderbilt University Press, 1997.

—*William Luis*

Vega, Ed (1936–)

Ed Vega is a Puerto Rican author who writes novels satirizing the stereotypical image of the Puerto Rican criminals or drug users popularized in works written by **Miguel Piñero** and **Piri Thomas** during the 1960s and 1970s. An activist, he is the director of the **Clemente Soto Vélez** Cultural and Educational Center, located in New York City.

Edgardo Vega Yunqué was born on May 20, 1936 in Ponce, Puerto Rico. His father was a Baptist minister who moved the family to United States in 1949 and accepted the poverty he encountered in the city by contrasting it to Christ's passion and martyrdom. The young Vega, on the other hand, rejected Christianity, became an atheist, and sought to improve his life by joining the armed forces. On furlough from the military, he visited a girlfriend who worked for a wealthy family. While helping to clean the guest house, he came across a collection of discarded books. "I picked out about one hundred of them by looking at their covers . . . I had taken William Faulkner's entire works, and those of Ernest Hemingway," he recalled years later in *Puerto Rican Voices in English* (201).

Vega was fascinated by Faulkner (1897–1962) and went on to read novels by John Steinbeck (1902–68), Albert Camus (1913–60), and his compatriot **José Luis González**. Influenced by these writers, Vega decided to become a writer himself.

Vega attended New York University, graduating in 1969 with a bachelor of arts degree. He worked for community groups and taught at different colleges, but in 1972, he dedicated himself to writing. He submitted short stories to journals and in the early 1980s wrote his first novel, *The Comeback*, which he had difficulty publishing, since editors were looking for a stereotypical work. He observed in the introduction to the novel that he was "expected to write one of those great American immigrant stories, like *Studs Lonigan, Call It Sleep,* or *Father.* . . . Or something like . . . Piri Thomas's *Down These Mean Streets*"(xix). Instead, he wrote a satire of ethnic autobiography. In 1987, he published a collection of short stories entitled *Mendoza's Dreams,* a humorous look at life in the ghetto. In 1991, he wrote *Casualty Report,*a somber fictional study of poverty. In 2003, with his experimental novel *No Matter How Much You Promise to Cook or Pay the Rent You Blew It Cauze Bill Baily Ain't Never Comin' Home Again,* Vega switched from the prestigious academic publisher Arte Público Press to the commercial, and more affluent, Farrar, Straus & Giroux.

While his novels have been distributed in Europe, he is not as well known in Puerto Rico, probably because he writes in English and not in Spanish. He has commented in *Puerto Rican Voices in English*, "In the place I was born . . . my work is not known" (203). *See also* Kanellos, Nicolás; Nuyorican Literature.

Further Reading

Hernández, Carmen Dolores. *Puerto Rican Voices in English: Interviews with Writers.* Westport, CT: Praeger Publishers, 1997.

—*D. H. Figueredo*

Vega, José Luis (1948–)

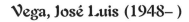

Award-winning Puerto Rican poet, José Luis Vega is known for writing a poetry that is socially engaged but not dogmatic, a poetry that emphasizes the human and the political. Scholar Josefina Rivera de Álvarez, cited in the 1992 volume *Spanish American Authors*, calls Vega a "neoromantic . . . reinvested with a tonality of warm emotion joined to the unfolding of irony, humour, and jest" (878).

José Luis Vega was born in Santurce, Puerto Rico, on June 18, 1948. He lived with his parents, his sister, and a maternal grandfather, who seemed like a literary character, "a drinker, fighter, and fabulist . . . who [insisted] . . . the world . . . was flat and . . . did not move" (877), as Vega wrote critic Ángel Flores in *Spanish American Authors*. The experience of his childhood was a source of inspiration for his book of poetry, *Las natas de los párpados* (1974).

After graduating from high school in 1964, Vega enrolled at the Universidad de Puerto Rico, remaining at that institution until the completion of a doctorate in 1983. He taught secondary school while pursuing graduate studies, then in 1988 he was appointed professor of Hispanic American literature, eventually becoming dean of the College of Humanities in 1999. In 1972, he founded the literary journal *Ventana*. In 1984, he founded a second literary journal, *Caribán*.

Vega published his first book of poetry, *Comienzo del canto* (1967), while still a teenager. This was followed by *Las natas de los párpados* and *Signos vitales* (1974), *La naranja entera* (1983), *Tiempo de bolero* (1985), *Bajo los efectos de la poesía* (1989), *Solo de pasión* (1996), *La ceniza y el viento* (1996), *Evidencia indirecta: antología personal 1967–1997* (1998) and *Letra viva: antología, 1974–2000*. His books of nonfiction incluye *Cesar Vallejo en "Trilce"* (1983) and *Emisión de obligaciones en el régimen legal de Perú* (2002). He edited a anthology of Puerto Rican short stories—*Reunión de espejos* (1983)—which has been described as "indispensable source for a better knowledge of contemporary Puerto Rican narrative," *La Prensa* (August 2002).

José Luis Vega is the recipient of the National Prize, International Pen (1983), and the Instituto de Literatura Puertorriqueña literary award of 1990.

Further Reading

Flores, Ángel. *Spanish American Authors: The Twentieth Century*. New York: Wilson, 1982.

Ortiz, Niza. "Encuentro de notables" *La Prensa*, Aug. 2002.

—*D. H. Figueredo*

Vega Serova, Anna Lidia (1968–)

Cuban short-story writer who belongs to a group of feminist authors who emerged on the island during the 1990s, sometimes called the **posnovísima** group, Vega Serova writes contemplative homoerotic sketches that challenge stereotypical images of homosexuality as well as reflecting contemporary economic conditions in Cuba and how they affect the daily lives of the common person. She has won numerous awards and is often compared to Julio Cortázar (1914–84), and J. D. Salinger (1919–).

Anna Lidia Vega Serova was born in Leningrad, Russia, in 1968, of Cuban parents and returned to the island sometime in the 1980s. At a time when economic circumstances on the island—due to the collapse of the former Soviet Bloc—discouraged the publication of books to favor the publication of short stories in journals and anthologies, Vega Serova began to cultivate the genre, and by the end of the decade she had attracted local and international attention. In 1998, she won the David prize for literature, offered by the **Unión de Escritores y Artistas de Cuba,** for her collection of short stories *Bad Painting.* The next two years, she published two more collections, *Catálogos de mascotas* (1999), and *Limpiando ventanas y espejos* (2000). In 2001, she published her first full novel, *Noche de ronda.* (2001)

As an experimental author, Vega Serova tells stories from multiple and changing perspectives, using repetition and fragmentation, as illustrated in the narrative "Retrato de mi suegra con retoques consecutivos" from the anthology *Mujeres como islas* (2002):

> . . . me la encuentro ahí, con la espuma hasta
> los codos y pienso, preocupada, en mi cuento
> y esa mujer, en su cuento, en la mujer de su
> cuento que se levanta, reocupada . . . (20)

> (. . . I find her there, with the foam up to her
> elbows and I think, somewhat worry, about
> my story and that woman in her story, the
> woman who in the story gets up, worries . . .)

Linear chronology is meaningless to Vega Serova, as are traditional values. For she rejects notions of marriage, employment, social responsibility, and sexual assumptions in a variety of relationships, be it heterosexual or homosexual. Yet she draws characters that are vivid and real, creating, what critic Olga Marta Pérez calls in the prologue to *Mujeres como islas,* "narratives with a perfect harmony" (10).

Vega Serova has received numerous awards, including Ada Elba Pérez de Plaza literary prize (1996), honorable mention in the Concurso Internacional de Cuento Fernando González, Medellín, Colombia (1999), Instituto Cubano del Libro literature prize (2000), Primera Mención en el Concurso Iberoamericano de cuentos Julio Cortázar (2002), and first honors in **Alejo Carpentier** Internacional Contest (2002). *See also* Gay and Lesbian Literature; Feminism in Caribbean Literature.

Further Reading

Pérez, Olga Marta, et al. *Mujeres como islas.* Habana: Ediciones Unión; Santo Domingo: Ediciones Ferilibro, 2002.

—*D. H. Figueredo*

Veloz Maggiolo, Marcio (1936–)

A novelist from Dominican Republic known for writing anti-Trujillo works, Marcio Veloz Maggiolo is an educator, a scholar, and a poet. He advocates the use of literature to bring about social and political change. In his volume, *Cultura, teatro y relatos en Santo Domingo* (1972) he describes an author as "a fighter whose pen is his rifle" (14).

Born in Santo Domingo on August 13, 1936, he was exposed to literature at an early age by his father who provided him with volumes written by such popular European authors as Alexander Dumas (1802–70) and Emilio Salgari (1863–1911). Later on, Veloz Maggiolo started to read works by his compatriots, especially the poetry of **Tomás Hernández Franco**, realizing that the universal themes addressed by the likes of Dumas could be combined with a literature that was nationalistic, such as Hernández Franco's.

In 1957, he wrote *El sol y las cosas*, lyrical and romantic poems written in traditional rhyming format. Three years later, he switched from poetry to prose, writing a novel that was critical of the dictatorship of Rafael Leónidas Trujillo (1891–1961). Titled *El buen ladrón*, the novel took place during biblical times but the descriptions of the abuses committed by the Roman Empire alluded to the Trujillo regime. He continued exploring biblical settings with his second novel, *Judas* (1962), for which he won the Dominican Republic's National Book Award. In 1963, he wrote the play *Creonte* (1963), a reworking of the Greek classic *Antigone*. While writing, Veloz Maggiolo attended the University of Santo Domingo, graduating in 1961 and obtaining a teaching position at his alma mater shortly after graduation. In 1968, he earned a doctorate from the Universidad Complutense de Madrid, concentrating on archaeology and pre-Columbian history.

In the mid-1960s, Veloz Maggiolo became part of the literary group known as El Puño, young writers who were critical of the American intervention in the Dominican Republic during the 1965 civil war. A decade later, the conflict inspired Veloz Maggiolo to write the novel *De abril en adelante*, a critique of the nation's middle class and their inability to prevent America's presence in local politics. Considered his most famous work, the novel employs the experimental techniques that surfaced during the **Latin American Boom** of the 1960s.

Veloz Maggiolo's novels follow a simple structural frame: a single event determines the narrative's progress and character's development. The subjects he addresses are political corruption and poverty. He has also written several books of poetry, including *La palabra reunida* (1982), *Apearse de la máscara* (1986), and *Poemas en cierne; Retorno a la palabra* (1986). As a scholar, he has achieved recognition for such academic texts as *La arqueología de la vida cotidiana* (1985) and *Panorama histórico del Caribe precolombino* (1991), among others.

Veloz Maggiolo has also served as the Dominican Republic's ambassador to Mexico (1965–66), Peru (1982–83), and Italy (1983–85). Early in 2000, he was appointed professor in residence for life at the University of Santo Domingo. *See also* Dominican Republic Literature, History of; Trujillo Era.

Further Reading

Piña Contreras, Guillermo. *Doce en la literatura dominicana*. Santiago de los Caballeros, República Dominicana: Universidad Católica Madre y Maestra, 1982.

Valerio-Holguí, Fernando, ed. *Arqueología de las sombras: la narrativa de Marcio Velo Maggiolo*. Santo Domingo, República Dominicana: F. Valerio-Holguín, 2000.

Veloz Maggiolo, Marcio. *Cultura, teatro y relatos in Santo Domingo*. Santiago de los Caballeros, República Dominicana: Universidad Católica Madre y Maestra, 1972.

—*D. H. Figueredo*

Ventura Álvarez, Miriam (1957–)

Miriam Ventura is a poet and journalist from the Dominican Republic. Though she lives in the United States, she, like many other writers from the Caribbean, focuses on cultural and political developments in the Dominican Republic. She is a feminist who promotes works by women writers from the Caribbean.

Ventura was born on December 8, 1957, in Santo Domingo, the Dominican Republic. She attended elementary and second schools in Santo Domingo and earned a BA in communications from the Universidad Central del Este. In 1986, she published *Poemas de la noche*, a collection of her poetry. Her second book of poetry was published a year later under the title of *Trópico acerca del otoño*.

In the mid-1980s, Ventura moved to New York City, where, in 1992, she became a writer for the periodical *Listín USA* and in 1997 started to write for the popular and influential New York daily, *Diario La Prensa*. As a journalist, she has paid close attention to activities of the Dominicans who live in Manhattan. In 1999, she received the Rafael Herrera Journalism Prize for her labor in New York City.

Ventura also is the secretary of the Ministry of Culture of the Dominican Republic and director of the Casa de la Cultura Dominicana en Nueva York. In 2004, she published *Memoria de la transnacionalidad*, an account of her years as director of the Casa.

Further Reading

Artists and Authors. http://www.lartny.org/biografias/vent.htm (accessed 9/15/05).

—*D. H. Figueredo*

Vergés, Pedro (1945–)

Pedro Vergés is a poet and short-story writer from the Dominican Republic. He was his country's ambassador to Spain from 1997 to 2000.

Vergés was born in Santo Domingo on May 8, 1945. He traveled to Spain to attend the Universidad de Zaragoza, where he earned a degree in literature and philology. From 1981 to 1993, he was the director of Centro Cultural Hispánico. In the mid-1990s, he was appointed president of the Casa del Escritor Dominicano.

Vergés was initially interested in poetry. In 1977, he published two books of poetry, *Juegos reunidos* and *Durante los inviernos*. Four years later he wrote the novel *Solo cenizas hallarás*, for which he was awarded the Premio de la Crítica Española. The novel, his best-known work outside the Dominican Republic, is a chronicle of Trujillo's dictatorship, which lasted from 1930 to 1961, and how it affected the lives of common citizens.

In his poetry, Vergés explores the dynamics of political power and sexual relationships, focusing on issues of control where the man sees himself in charge and the woman must manipulate him. His poetry and prose is reflective, often presenting the perspective of a single narrator. *See also* Trujillo Era.

Further Reading

Céspedes, Diógenes. *Antología del cuento dominicano*. Santo Domingo: Editora de Colores, 1996.

"Pedro Verges." http://www.escritoresdominicanos.com/verges.html (accessed 9/15/05).

—*D. H. Figueredo*

"Viaje a la semilla" (1944)

Innovative short story by Cuban writer **Alejo Carpentier,** in which the action, character development, and narrative regress in time, as if the story were a rewound video. It is not similar, however, to the science fiction novel *Time Machine*, by H. G. Wells (1886–1946), which Carpentier had read, where the character travels in time but neither his age nor physical appearance change: in Wells's work, the time traveler remains a Victorian gentleman no matter the historical period that he visits. In "Viaje a la semilla," entitled "Journey Back to the Source" in the English translation, the protagonist ages backward, from senility to the womb. Carpentier realizes this illusion by describing Marcial, the hero, as a babbling old man, a young man at a dance, a child playing with his toy soldier, and an infant experiencing sounds and sights for the first time. The surroundings are seen through Marcial's eyes: furniture grows taller and morticians return his dead father to the house and then place the body on his bed, where he regains consciousness and talks to Marcial. The house itself returns to its origins as the floors collapse onto the ground.

This seminal short story anticipated the techniques that were used later by the writers of the **Latin American Boom** and of **magical realism**: nonlinear time, multiple perspectives, and numerous literary and historical allusions. The short story was a prelude to Carpentier's best known novel, *Los pasos perdidos* (1953), where a musicologist travels back in time with each step he takes into the Amazon jungle. The return to the womb motif was used by Mexican writer Carlos Fuentes (1928–) in his masterpiece *La muerte de Artemio Cruz*, and the concept of nonlinear time and the return to the origins was also used by Nobel Prize–winner Gabriel García Márquez (1927–), from Colombia, in his best-selling novel *Cien años de soledad*; both authors acknowledge their debt to Carpentier. *See also* Barroco/Baroque; Cuban literature, History of.

Further Reading

Carpentier, Alejo. *Cuentos completos*. 3d ed. Barcelona: Bruguera, 1980.

Font, María Cecilia. *Mito y realidad en Alejo Carpentier: aproximaciones a Viaje a la semilla*. Buenos Aires, Argentina: Editorial R. Alonso, 1984.

—Pamela María Smorkaloff and D. H. Figueredo

Vicioso, Abelardo (1930–)

Award-winning poet from the Dominican Republic, Abelardo Vicioso is known for writing love sonnets as well as political poetry. In his writings, he criticized Rafael Leónidas Trujillo's dictatorship and American intervention during the Dominican Republic's civil war of 1965. He is a member of the literary generation known as **La generación del 48**. An attorney, Vicioso has also served as a diplomat in Curaçao.

Abelardo Vicioso was born in Santo Domingo. His father wrote for a local newspaper and expressed an interest in literature, sometimes writing poetry. Since the public library was near Vicioso's home, he spent many hours there, reading the poetry of Pablo Neruda (1904–73) and Walt Whitman (1819–92) as well as Shakespeare's plays. But he was also influenced by such national poets as **Pedro Mir** and **Franklin Mieses Burgos**.

Vicioso attended law school during the early 1950s, graduating in 1953. From 1953 to 1957, he served in the Dominican Republic's armed forces, which solidified his anti-Trujillo views, while also writing for the publication *Caribe* and editing the journal *La revista militar*. In 1959, he sought exile in Cuba, where he plotted against his country's government. After the assassination of Rafael Leónidas Trujillo (1891–1961), Vicioso returned home in 1963 and was appointed to the faculty at the Universidad Autónoma de Santo Domingo. In 1975, he became dean of the faculty.

In 1958, he wrote the book of poetry *La lumbre sacudida*. The book was divided into four parts, reflecting the poet's interests: (a) "cuatro sonetos sobre el amor y la vida" and (b) "Lámpara en la ausencia" were essentially love poems; (c) "Mas cerca de la tierra," were political and social poems; and (d) "Versos de la tristeza," were philosophical. The volume earned Vicioso the national poetry award. In 1979, he wrote *Santo Domingo en las letras coloniales, 1492–1800*. In 1984, Vicioso wrote *Neruda, itinerario de una poesía combatiente*.

Further Reading

Castro Burdiez, Tomás. *La Generación del 48 en el ensayo*. Ciudad Universitaria, Santo Domingo, República Dominicana: Editora Universitaria UASD, 1998.

—D. H. Figueredo

Vicioso Sánchez, Sherezada "Chiqui Vicioso" (1948–)

Chiqui Vicioso is a Dominican poet, playwright, essayist, and cultural activist.

Born in the Dominican Republic in 1948, she is the daughter of Juan Antonio Vicioso Contín and María Luisa Sánchez. After the death of her father, Chiqui Vicioso moved with her mother and three siblings to New York City, where she completed her studies. She holds a BA in sociology and history from Brooklyn College (CUNY) and a MEd from Teachers College, Columbia University. She also studied administration of cultural projects at the Getulio Vargas Foundation in Rio de Janeiro, Brazil.

In 1980, Chiqui Vicioso returned home to the Dominican Republic after having lived in New York City for eighteen years. In her homeland, Vicioso found the encouragement and support needed to publish her first collection of poetry *Viaje desde el agua* (1981). This first book is a collection of poems written mostly while living in the United States and during her many travels abroad. To Vicioso, in her early collection and in much of what she has written since, the world is indeed small. So small, in fact, that everyday survival in New York City goes hand in hand with the struggles of the African people or of a Dominican youth drifting, seeking to find direction.

In the Dominican Republic, Vicioso assumed a number of important positions, including Director of Education for Pro-Familia (1981–85), Consultant on Women and Children's programs for the United Nations, in particular UNICEF. She has had a weekly column in the *Listín Diario*, a daily newspaper comparable to the *New York Times*, has been a contributor to the daily *La Noticia* and the editor of the literary page *Cantidad Hechizada* for *El Nuevo Diario*.

At the beginning of the 1980s, Vicioso founded the Circle of Dominican Women Poets. In 1988, the Dominican Writers Association awarded her the Golden Caonabo prize, and in 1992 the National Women's Bureau awarded Vicioso a gold medal as the most accomplished woman of the year. She has published four collections of poetry, *Viaje desde el agua* (1981), *Un extraño ulular traía el viento* (1983), *Internamiento* (1991), and *Wish-Ky Sour* (1996), a poetic biography of Julia de Burgos. She has edited a collection of **Salomé Ureña**'s poems and has become one of the leading scholars on the subject. She is also a writer who travels often to the United States to share her experiences as a transnational Dominican, educated in the United States. She is the author of a script, entitled *Desvelo*, for ballet and theater. In the last decade, she has published and staged several plays, including the award-winning *Wish-ky Sour*—National Theater Award, 1996—and *Salomé U, Cartas a una ausencia*—Cassandra Award (2000). More recently, *Perrerías* was staged in Spain and Cuba. Her poems and essays have been translated into several languages and included in numerous anthologies published at the national and international levels.

Further Reading

Cocco de Filippis, Daisy. *Para que no se olviden: The Lives of Women in Dominican History.* New York: Alcance, 2000.

Gutiérrez, Franklyn. *Diccionario de la literatura dominicana.* Santo Domingo: Editorial Búho, 2004.

—Daisy Cocco de Filippis

Vidarte Brothers

Two Puerto Rican brothers, Juan Bautista and Santiago, who—with a group of young Puerto Rican writers in Barcelona—initiated the beginning of a national literature on the island. Their actual surname was Rodríguez but they chose Vidarte to honor their adoptive father, Rafael Vidarte.

Vidarte, Juan B. (1826?—?). Born in Yabucoa, Juan Bautista Vidarte studied law with his brother in Barcelona and befriended the Puerto Rican would-be poets **Manuel Alonso, Francisco Vasallo y Cabrera,** and Pablo Sáez; together, they published two volumes of poetry that reflected their homesickness and love of Puerto Rico: *Álbum puertorriqueño* (1844) and *El cancionero de Borinquen* (1846). His poem "A Puerto Rico" was the first entry in *Álbum.* In the poem, the young poet compares Puerto Rico to Eden.

Vidarte belonged to the first group of Puerto Rican writers to publish books that achieved popularity on the island. Beyond his contribution to these two volumes, not much is known about his life.

Vidarte, Santiago (1827–48). A native of Yabucoa, Vidarte traveled to Spain to study law at the Universidad de Barcelona. He befriended a group of Puerto Rican students who, homesick, decided to publish a collection of poems evocative and celebratory of their islands. The two volumes were *Álbum puertorriqueño* (1844) and *El cancionero de Borinquen*(1846).

The poems that Santiago Vidarte contributed reflect his romantic tendencies. One of the best known is "Un recuerdo a mi patria," a recollection of his father and mother, and an expression of his desire to serve his island. His "A la vida" revealed his concern with death, describing life as an early flower that is regretting that life only lasts a day.

His concern about life's brevity was both romantic and real. Vidarte died in Barcelona at the age of twenty after developing a high fever. Scholar Toro-Sugrañes, in the *Nueva enciclopedia de Puerto Rico* (1994), described Vidarte as "a poet of great inspiration and talent . . . cut down by his premature death" (215).

Further Reading

Rivera de Álvarez, Josefina. *Diccionario de literatura puertorriqueña.* Tomo 2. San Juan: Editorial del Departamento de Instrucción Pública, 1969.

Toro-Sugrañes, José A. "Biografía." In *Nueva enciclopedia de Puerto Rico.* Hato Rey, Puerto Rico: Editorial Lector, 1994.

—D. H. Figueredo

Vientós Gastón, Nilita (1908–89)

Widely admired in Puerto Rico, Vientós Gastón was the editor of two influential journals, *Asomante* and *Sin Nombre*, an essayist, and a tireless defender and promoter of Puerto Rican literature and culture. The first woman attorney to work for the Department of Justice, she won the famous "language lawsuit" of 1965, wherein she maintained that the legal language of Puerto Rico was Spanish and not English.

Vientós Gastón was born in San Sebastián, Puerto Rico, on June 5, 1908, but spent her childhood in Cuba. As an adolescent, she and her family lived in New Jersey, where Vientós Gastón attended high school. In 1923, she returned to Puerto Rico, earning a law degree from the Universidad de Puerto Rico. In 1940, she was hired by the Department of Justice, where she remained until 1967.

Literature was a major passion, and from 1946 to 1961, she was president of the **Ateneo Puertorriqueño**. In 1948, she received a scholarship from the Rockefeller Foundation to study literature at Kenyon College, Ohio. She taught literature at the Universidad de Puerto Rico and established and edited the journal *Asomante*, where all the major Puerto Rican writers of the time, as well as many contributors from Latin America, published their stories and articles. Of an independent mind, when the members of the university's Alumni Association, which funded *Asomante*, demanded more editorial control, Vientós Gastón left the journal in 1970 and formed her own publication, *Sin Nombre*. Under her guidance, *Asomante* and *Sin Nombre* became two of the most important literary journals in Latin America.

Through the 1950s, Vientós Gastón Gaston wrote a cultural column for *El Mundo*. Titled "Índice cultural," in the column she reviewed books and wrote on contemporary literature. In 1957, she collected the columns into the book, *Índice cultural*. Consisting of four volumes, *Índice* received the journalism award from the Instituto de Literatura. The year before, 1956, she had published a literary study of Henry James (1843–1916), *Introducción a Henry James*.

Vientós Gastón presided over the Pen Club of Puerto Rico in the mid-1960s. She wrote, with **María Teresa Babín**, an analysis of the island's culture and politics, *La situación de Puerto Rico* (1964). Through her life, her devotion to Puerto Rico, demonstrated in her work as an attorney and writer, earned the respect and love of such major figures as **Cesáreo Rosa-Nieves** who regarded her as one of the brightest intellects on the island.

Further Reading

Rosa-Nieves, Cesáreo. *Plumas estelares en las letras de Puerto Rico*. Vol. 1. San Juan: Ediciones de la Torre, 1967.

Vassallo, Ruth. *Nilita Vientós Gastón: una vida en imágenes*. Río Piedras, Puerto Rico: Editorial Marién, 1989.

—*D. H. Figueredo*

Vieux, Isnardin (1865–1941)

—•—

A Haitian poet and playwright who celebrated the nation's heroes and folklore, Vieux was an attorney and public servant.

Born on September 7, 1865, in Port-au-Prince, Haiti, Vieux conducted secondary studies at the Lycée Pétion and then went on law school at Faculty of Law, in the same city. After graduation, he worked as a teacher at the Secondary School for Boys and also taught law at his alma mater. While studying and during his early days as a teacher, he wrote poetry. His first collection of poems was published in 1895, *Les vibrations*. In 1896, he published a second volume, *Chants et rêves*. In 1909, he founded the journal *La Pioche*.

In the 1920s, he befriended such important writers as **Émile Roumer**, **Normil Sylvain**, and **Jacques Roumain**. He contributed to the influential journal *La Revue indigène*. During this period, he began to write dramas that affirmed Haitian identity and nationalism and rejected the American presence in the country. In 1925, he published *Mackdal, drame en 3 actes*, his rendering of the rebellion in the seventeenth century that eventually led to the Haitian revolution. Other works written during the same year were *Ogé et Chavannes* and *La fille de Geffrad*.

After the 1920s, Vieux concentrated more on public service and teaching and did not write as much. He served as a judge in Port-au-Prince's civil court.

Further Reading

Herdeck, Donald, ed. *Caribbean Writers: A Bio-Bibliographical-Critical Encyclopedia.* Washington, DC: Three Continents Press, 1979.

—*D. H. Figueredo*

Vigil Díaz, Otilio A. (1880–1961)

—•—

A lyric poet from the Dominican Republic, Vigil Díaz was the founder of the literary movement **Vedrismo**, which promoted a type of poetry that was experimental and free from traditional forms and rhymes and which rejected nationalistic poetry. He was the first to introduce vanguard poetry to the Dominican Republic and is considered a precursor to **postumismo**, a major movement which dominated much of the country's literature during the 1920s and 1930s.

Otilio Vigil Díaz was born in Santo Domingo on April 6, 1880. He attended primary and secondary schools in the nation's capital but did not continue his studies beyond high school. At the turn of the century, he visited Havana and New York before traveling to Paris. In France, he was influenced by French literature and became interested in experimental poetry. Upon his return to the Dominican Republic in 1917, he created Vedrismo, named after the aerial acrobatics of the

French daredevil pilot Jules Vedrines (1881–1919). The movement rejected traditional poetic forms, preferring free verse and poetic prose.

In 1917 he published the poem "Arabesco" which introduced vedrismo. His poems were then published in numerous journals and newspapers, including *Listín Diario, La Opinión,* and *La Nación.* In 1921, he published the book of poetry *Galeras de Pafos,* followed, in 1922, by *Del sena al Ozama,* and *Música de ayer* in 1925. Vigil Díaz also wrote a collection of short stories: *Orégano* (1922).

He passed away in Santo Domingo on January 20, 1961.

Further Reading

Cabral, Manuel del. *10 poetas dominicanos: tres poetas con vidas y siete desenterrados.* Republica Dominicana: Publicaciones Américas, 1980.

"Otilio Vigil Díaz." http://www.escritoresdominicanos.com (accessed 9/15/05).

—*D. H. Figueredo*

Vilaire, Etzer (1872–1951)

A poet from Haiti, Vilaire wrote poetry that represents the political sentiment of his peers during the turn of the twentieth century. He was a politician and a judge.

Vilaire was born on April 7, 1872, in Jeremie, Haiti, into a middle-class family—his father was a judge. Of a sickly constitution, Vilaire was frail and developed a sense of fatalism that would characterize his early poetry. Attending a Protestant school, he was attracted to literature and began to write poetry at the age of fourteen. An intelligent student, he was awarded a scholarship to study in Paris, but his failing health did not allow him to travel. He continued his studies at Saint-Martial College, becoming first a teacher and then an attorney in 1894.

When he turned twenty nine, Vilaire published one of the best-known poems of Haitian literature: "Dix homes Noirs." It is the story of ten friends who, disgusted with the poverty and political corruption of their country, agree to kill each other one by one. The survivor would then commit suicide. However, the sad spectacle of the deaths drive the last friend insane. The poem, according to Naomi M. Garret, in *The Renaissance of Haitian Poetry*, "characterized the thought of the Haitian intellectuals at the turn of the century" (26).

At the age of thirty, Vilaire published the collection, *Le filibustier* (1902). Three years later, *Poème avec mon couer* (1905) was published. In 1907, *Poèmes de la mort,* which included "Dix hommes noirs" was published in Paris. The publications made Vilaire something of a celebrity, and in 1910, the French Academy honored his poetic accomplishments. Together the poems revealed a spiritual trajectory, from the despair of the young poet who finds solace only in the thought of death to a matured, religious writer who embraces Christian resignation and a mystical optimism.

When the Americans occupied Haiti in 1915, Vilaire joined the writers and intellectuals who protested against the intervention. In the 1930s, he was appointed judge of the Haitian Supreme Court. He retired in 1946, leading a quiet life. He passed away on May 2, 1951. *See also* American Occupation of Haiti, Literature of (1915–34).

Further Reading

Garret, Naomi M. *The Renaissance of Haitian Poetry.* Paris: Présence africaine, 1963.

—*D. H. Figueredo*

Villanueva Collado, Alfredo (1944–)

A Puerto Rican poet, short-story writer, and literary critic, Villanueva Collado explores gay themes in his writings. He is also a member of a generation of authors who publish and disseminate their works not only in book format but also on the Internet.

A native of Santurce, Villanueva Collado spent his childhood in Venezuela. Returning to Puerto Rico when he was in his teens, he attended the Universidad de Puerto Rico, where he was introduced to the poetry of the gay writer Allen Ginsberg (1926–97) with whom Villanueva Collado, aware of his own homosexuality, identified. Wanting to write and teach, Villanueva Collado traveled to New York City in 1970 to attend a Modern Language Association conference and look for employment. That same year, he matriculated at the State University of New York–Binghamton, from where he earned a PhD in comparative literature in 1974.

He taught English at Hostos Community College and wrote over thirty articles and essays on **Modernismo** and the treatment of masculinity in Latin American literature. In the 1980s, his volumes of poetry began to appear: *Las transformaciones del vidrio* (1985), *Grimorio* (1989), *En el imperio de la papa frita* (1989), *La mujer que llevo dentro* (1990), *Entre la inocencia y la manzana* (1996), among others. His poems, highly personal, are written with a clear voice that vividly depicts human anatomy and sexual encounters in an elegant and telegraphic style, sometime reminiscent of Ginsberg, sometimes of Pablo Neruda (1904–73).

Villanueva Collado's short stories are autobiographical, often dealing with sexuality. However, a dominant theme is the exploration of the legacy of colonialism and American influence in Puerto Rico. One of his best-known stories, "The Day We Went to See Snow," tells of a true incident when a Puerto Rican politician had snow flown in from the Northeast so that children in San Juan could experience an American Christmas; the message was that children in Puerto Rico were not experiencing Christmas, since there was no snow on the island and were therefore inferior to children in the United States.

Villanueva Collado publishes many of his poems and short stories in electronic format, thus reaching a wider audience. He is also known for hosting **tertulias,** informal literary salons, in his apartment in New York City. Retired from teaching, he has become an expert on the art of glassmaking and sculpture.

Unlike many writers from the Hispanic Caribbean who live in the United States and write in English—the Dominican **Julia Alvarez** and the Cuban American **Oscar Hijuelos**, for example—Villanueva Collado prefers Spanish for his poetry and stories. Comments **Nicolás Kanellos**, in *Noche Buena* (2000), Villanueva Collado "hopes that his writings offer an alternative history to that proffered by the American Dream" (182).

Further Reading

Kanellos, Nicolás, ed. *Noche Buena: Hispanic American Christmas Stories*. New York: Oxford University Press, 2000.

Villanueva Collado, Alfredo. "Games at the San Cristobal." http://www.enkidu.netfirms. com/art/2004/310804 (accessed 5/1/05).

—*D. H. Figueredo*

Villaverde, Cirilo (1812–94)

The author of **Celia Valdés o La Loma del Ángel** (1879, 1882), one of the most popular novels in Latin America, Villaverde was a journalist, a novelist, and patriot who dedicated his life to Cuba's separation from Spain and whose career was framed by the writing of *Cecilia Valdés*, which he began in his mid-twenties and completed when he was nearly seventy years old.

Villaverde was born on October 28, 1812, in Pinar del Rio, Cuba, the son of a physician who worked at a sugar plantation and where the young Villaverde witnessed, firsthand, the evils of slavery. He was sent to Havana when he was eleven years old. In the capital, he first studied with his grandfather before attending formal schools. In 1834, he became a lawyer but gave up the profession in preference of teaching. He befriended literary mentor and cultural promoter **Domingo Del Monte**; joining Del Monte's famous **tertulias**, informal literary salons, Villaverde was inspired to write his first stories and novels.

In 1839, Villaverde published the first version of his famous novel, emphasizing the romantic aspects of an attraction between a beautiful **mulata**, Cecilia, and a handsome aristocrat. He followed this work with several novels and works of nonfiction, including the love story *La joven de la flecha de oro*(1841), a costumbrista story, or tale of local customs, *El guajiro* (1842), published as a serial in a journal, and *Excursión a Vuelta Abajo* (1838, 1842), a rendition of the customs and traditions of the Cuban countryside.

In the 1840s, Villaverde became involved in political activities, turning toward political journalism to advocate separation from Spain. In 1848, he joined a failed rebellion led by general Narciso López (who would invade Cuba in 1851 and raise the Cuban flag for the first time on the island), and was arrested. Escaping from prison, in 1849 Villaverde fled to the United Status, where he worked as a teacher and a translator in New York City while continuing to plot, with other patriots, Cuba's independence. In the United States he edited several periodicals, *El avisor hispano americano*, *El espejo masónico*, *El independiente*, *La Ilustración Americana*, and *La verdad*, among others, and wrote for the English language journals *Frank and Leslie's*. He visited Cuba for two years in 1858 and then again for two weeks in 1888. He died in New York City in 1894; his body was sent to Cuba.

Villaverde completed *Cecilia Valdés*, entitled **Cecilia Valdés o La Loma del Ángel: novela de costumbres cubanas**, in 1879; the novel was published in 1882. A realistic romance, as well as a **historical novel** and a classic example of the literature of **costumbrismo**, which emphasizes and describes local events, the novel transforms itself from a forbidden and incestuous love affair between a white man and a mulatto woman to a political document denouncing slavery and colonialism. Leisurely told, the novel is rich in the descriptions of all types of edifices, from a church to a theater to government buildings, clothes, and mannerisms. The author duplicates the diction of the different populations in Havana, from the ways the poor speak to the educated vernacular of the aristocracy. But while some modern readers might find the emphasis on the local somewhat tedious, two elements make the novel engaging: the passionate affair between the doomed lovers and the vivid descriptions of slavery and the suffering of the slaves. *See also* Abolitionist Literature; Exile Literature; Morúa Delgado, Martin; Romanticismo/ Romanticism.

Further Reading

Casanova-Marengo, Ilia. *El intersticio de la colonia: ruptura y mediación en la narrativa antiesclavista cubana*. Madrid: Iberoamericana; Frankfurt am Main: Vervuert, 2002.

Villaverde, Cirilo. *Cecilia Valdés o La Loma del Ángel: novela de costumbre cubanas*. Madrid: Cátedra, 1992.

—*D. H. Figueredo*

Villegas, Víctor (1924–)

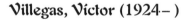

Though Villegas came to poetry relatively late, his work as a poet was immediately recognized in his native Dominican Republic and throughout Latin America. This award-winning poet is also an attorney and a literature professor.

Born on September 22, 1924, in San Pedro de Macoris, he attended public schools in his hometown. He studied law in Santo Domingo, graduating in 1948 from the Universidad Autónoma de Santo Domingo. He taught literature at his alma mater through the 1940s and 1950s while also working as an attorney. During this period, he published his poems in newspapers and literary reviews, including *La Nación*, *Listín Diario*, and *Cuadernos Dominicanos de Cultura y Testimonio*.

His first book of poetry was published when he was in his fifties, *Diálogos con Simeón* (1977). In 1982, he published *Botella en el mar*. That same year, he received the National Prize for Poetry for the volume *Juan Criollo y otras antielegías,* his most popular work. From 1982 to 1997, he published four books of poetry. Though the volumes express his concern with a Dominican identity, the clarity of his diction, his precise expression, and the depth of his sentiment appeal to readers throughout Latin America. In Venezuela, he was honored with the medal La Medalla al Merito Literario Hispanoamericano, and in Cuba he received the Medalla Literaria José María Heredia. His other works include *Poco tiempo después: poemas* (1991), *Ahora no es ahora* (1997), *Jamás* (2000), and *Muerte herida* (2002).

Further Reading

Cuevas, Julio. *Visión crítica en torno a la poesía de Víctor Villegas: ensayo.* Santo Domingo, República Dominicana: Biblioteca Nacional, 1985.

—*D. H. Figueredo*

Virtue, Vivian Lancaster (1911–98)

■

Vivian Virtue was a Jamaican poet, translator, and broadcaster. Although he was one of the most prolific of the West Indian poets, Virtue saw only one volume of his poems published during his lifetime: *Wings of the Morning* (1938), a collection of forty seven poems in a variety of verse forms. He was hailed in the 1930s and 1940s as the successor to **Claude McKay**, the Jamaican national poet and Virtue's father-in-law (in 1942, Virtue married McKay's daughter, Ruth Hope McKay; they later divorced).

Born in Kingston, Jamaica, on November 13, 1911, Vivian Virtue was educated at Half Way Tree Primary School and at Kingston College, a selective high school whose influence was long lasting. His education consisted mainly of learning Latin and other languages, Greek poetry and mythology, religion, and literature, all taught by the headmaster, Dr. P. W. Gibson. Kingston College instilled in Virtue a fondness for languages, most evident in his translations of other poets' work, including that of Charles Baudelaire (1821–67) and José-Maria de Heredia (1842–1905), into French and Spanish. Later in his career, Virtue also returned to the classics with translations from Latin, notably Virgil (70 BCE–19 BCE). Virtue's original poems are mostly classical in style and content, written in sonnet, villanelle, or rondeau form.

Virtue was the assistant secretary and librarian of the influential **Poetry League of Jamaica** and was later elected vice president. He was also a founding member and later vice president of the Jamaican Center of the International PEN Club and often represented Jamaica at PEN conferences. Virtue cofounded the New Dawn Press in Jamaica, created to encourage young black writers. Its inaugural publication was Virtue's *Wings of the Morning* in an edition of five hundred copies, an ambitious undertaking in Caribbean book production.

Virtue contributed to numerous newspapers, serials, and anthologies in the Caribbean and in Britain and America, gaining international attention but receiving decreasing recognition in his homeland. As a result, after his retirement from the Jamaican civil service in 1961, he emigrated to England and became a member of the expatriate West Indian community living in London, where he became a frequent broadcaster on the *Caribbean Voices* radio program of the BBC and wrote scripts on **Marcus Garvey**, the history of the British West Indies, and on his own poetic process. He died in London on December 17, 1998.

Virtue's works have been included in poetry anthologies and periodicals published in the West Indies, the United Kingdom, and the United States, including *Poetry of the Negro* (1949), *A Treasury of Jamaican Poetry* (1949), *Caribbean Quarterly* (1958), *Independence Anthology of Jamaican Literature* (1962), *Verse and Voice* (1965), *New Poems* (1966), *Caribbean Voices* (1966, 1970), *New Voices of the Commonwealth* (1968), and *West Indian Poetry* (1971). Many of his poems were reissued in 1991 in the volume *Wings of the Evening: Selected Poems of Vivian Virtue*, edited by A. L. McLeod.

Vivian Virtue's papers are housed at the Pennsylvania State University Libraries. The collection includes correspondence, original works, publications, translations, broadcasts, newspaper clippings, and photographs. *See also* McFarlane, J. E. Clare.

Further Reading

McFarlane, J. E. Clare. "Vivian Virtud." In *A Literature in the Making*. Kingston, Jamaica: The Pioneer Press, 1956.

—*Sandra Stelts*

Vitier, Cintio (1921–)

Cintio Vitier is a Cuban poet whose poetic range and expression has gone from the religious and hermitic to the revolutionary, writing poems that are considered among the best examples of **literatura comprometida**, or socially engaged literature. A scholar and anthologist, his critical study of Cuban poetry, *Lo cubano en la poesía* (1958), is considered the authoritative text on the subject.

Cintio Vitier y Bolaños was born in Key West, Florida, on September 25, 1921, the son of the literary critic Medardo Cintier. Returning to Cuba shortly after his birth, the family settled in the city of Matanzas, where Vitier attended a private school founded by his father. In 1936, his father was named secretary of education under the presidency of Carlos Mendieta (1873–1960), and the family relocated to Havana. In the capital, Vitier attended a private secondary school and then went on to the School of Law of the Universidad de la Habana. While studying, Vitier wrote two books of poetry, *Poemas (1937–1938)* and *Luz ya sueño*, both published in 1938. The latter book had an introduction written by the Spanish poet Juan Ramón Jiménez (1881–1958) who had befriended the younger poet while visiting the island.

During the 1940s, Vitier became friends with a group of writers who wrote for the influential literary journal *Orígenes,* founded by poet **José Lezama Lima**. The members of the group, which included **Fina García Marruz**, a young poet who would become his wife, were apolitical and believed that Cuban society could only be changed through cultural development rather than political involvement. During this period, Vitier wrote five books of poetry, all reflective of his Catholic faith. In 1947, Vitier earned a doctorate in law but chose to teach rather than practice law.

Vitier continued writing poetry throughout the 1950s. However, toward the end of the decade he wrote his seminal and probably most famous volume, *Lo cubano en la poesía.* The book, based on a series of lectures he gave at Havana's Lyceum, is an interpretation of how Cuban nationalism has been shaped by Cuban poetry; it is also one of the first critical texts to identify exile as a theme in Cuban literature. In 1959, **Fidel Castro** overthrew Fulgencio Batista (1901–73); Vitier welcomed the political change. His poetry changed as well. His verses were now supportive and complementary of the revolutionary struggle; the best work from this period is *Testimonios, 1953–1968* (1968).

During the 1960s, Vitier, along with his wife, worked at Cuba's National Library, researching the life and works of nineteenth-century patriot and martyr **José Martí,** a labor that resulted in the volume, cowritten with his wife, *Temas martianos* (1964, 1984). He also began to work on a historical trilogy about three generations of a Cuban family from the nineteenth century to 1980; the novels were *De Peña Pobre: Memoria y novel* (1978), *Los papeles de Jacinto Finalé* (1984), and *Rajando la leña esta* (1986). The 1990s saw works of poetry that were inclined more to the philosophical than the political. During the 1980s and 1990s, he traveled widely throughout Latin American and Europe as a cultural representative of the Cuban government.

The author of more than fifty books, in 1988, he was given Cuba's National Literature Award. In 2002, he received the prestigious Juan Rulfo Literary Award from Mexico.

Further Reading

Brú, José. ed. *Acercamientos a Cintio Vitier.* Guadalajara, Jalisco, México: Universidad de Guadalajara, Centro Universitario de Ciencias Sociales y Humanidades, 2002.

Saínz, Enrique. *La obra poética de Cintio Vitier.* Habana: Ediciones Unión, Unión de Escritores y Artistas de Cuba, 1998.

—D. H. Figueredo

Vivas Maldonado, José Luis (1926–)

Vivas Maldonado is a Puerto Rican short-story writer and academician.

A native of Aguadilla, Vivas Maldonado was attracted to literature and education in his youth. After earning a BA in education from the Universidad de Puerto Rico in 1948, he traveled to Colombia, where he received first an MA and then a PhD in arts from the Universidad de Los Andes de Bogotá. As he was finishing his doctoral studies, he was working on a play, *Sonrien al morir*, which was staged in San Juan in 1951.

In 1951, he taught literature at the Universidad de Puerto Rico, and in 1955 he published a collection of short stories, *Luces en sombras*, which received a literary award from the Instituto de Cultura Puertorriqueña. He then published numerous short stories in several journals and newspapers: *Alma Latina*, **Asomante**, *Paliques*, and *El Mundo*. He also participated in cultural programs and educational activities coordinated by the island's Department of Education, which encouraged him and other writers, such as **René Marqués**, to discuss literature at conferences and read their works at public gatherings. In 1971, Vivas Maldonado published some of these stories in the volume *A vellón las esperanzas o Melania*.

Essentially, Vivas Maldonado pursued two themes in his stories: the existence of Puerto Ricans who lived on the fringes of society on the island and the Puerto Ricans who tried their fortune living in New York City. As in the stories written by compatriot **José Luis González**, Vivas Maldonado's characters—such as a demented old man who lives in the garbage dump outside San Juan in the volume *Luces in sombras*—are the waste product of the island's urbanization of 1950s, disposable tragic figures. And like **Pedro Juan Soto's** works, which the author admires, Vivas Maldonado wrote stories narrating the immigrant's experience in Manhattan, criticizing the racism that Puerto Ricans were subjected to in the 1950s and 1960s but also celebrating his countrymen's ability to persist and survive.

Vivas Maldonado's major creative works were written in the 1960s and early 1970s. He collected many of these stories in the volume *Mis cuentos* (1986). He has also published a literary study on the Venezuelan author *Uslar Pietri: La cuentística de Arturo Uslar Pietri* (1963).

Further Reading

Alberto, Luis Rosario. "Festival De Cine Puertorriqueño." *La Prensa de San Antonio*, Nov. 21, 1991.

Ruscalleda Bercedóniz, Isabel María. *La cuentística de José Luis Vivas Maldonado*. San Juan de Puerto Rico: Instituto de Cultura Puertorriqueña, 1982.

—*D. H. Figueredo*

Vizcarrondo, Carmelina (1906–83)

◼

Vizcarrondo was a popular Puerto Rican poet. Many of her love poems and children's verses have been set to music.

Vizcarrondo was born in Fajardo on January 9, 1906—some sources say 1903. Attracted to literature and interested in promoting Puerto Rican culture, she was active in numerous organizations, including the Instituto de Cultura Puertorriqueña, Sociedad de Autores Puertorriqueños, and the **Ateneo Puertorriqueño**. In the late

1920s, she submitted her poetry to literary journals and newspapers the like of *Alma Latina* and *El Mundo.*

In 1935, she published her first book of poems, *Pregón en llamas.* The poems in this collection seemed influenced by **Modernismo**, with their allusions to the arts and the simple and readable structure. One of the most popular verses to emerge from this volume was "Buscame," in which the narrator chastises a lover who complains he can't find her, yet doesn't want to look for her.

In 1938, she published a collection of children's poems, *Poemas para mi niño.* Her attempt at the writing of short stories resulted in the volume, *Minutero en sombras,* which received the 1942 literary prize from the Instituto de Literatura Puertorriqueña. In these two volumes, Vizcarrondo demonstrates her love of the island.

Over the years, many of her poems were adapted to music. In 1941, composer Jack Delano (1914–97) visited the island and read *Poemas para mi niño.* From the collection, he set the playful "La Rosa y el Colibrí," about a flower and a hummingbird, to music. In 2000, "Buscame" became a popular poem shared electronically with Latina students in the United States.

Many of the poems that Vizcarrondo wrote in the 1950s and 1960s were published posthumously as *Campanerito azul* (1985).

Further Reading

"*Carmelina Vizcarrondo: Buscame.*" http://www.ciudaddemujeres (accessed 9/15/05).

Ramírez Mattei, Aida Elsa. *Carmelina Vizcarrondo: vida, obra y antología.* San Juan: Editorial Universitaria, Universidad de Puerto Rico.1972.

—*D. H. Figueredo*

Vodou in Literature

Many religions found in the Caribbean today, such as **Obeah** in English-speaking areas, **Santería** in Cuba, Candomble in Brazil, and **vodou** in Haiti, originated in various parts of Africa and came to the Americas as a result of the Atlantic slave trade. Once in the New World, a syncretism evolved as the African, Amerindian, and European beliefs entwined and became one. Like the other African-based religions of the area, Haitian vodou developed from one of the world's oldest faiths, the name itself deriving from West African words meaning *spirits* or *the unknown.* Hollywood filmmakers were later responsible for trivializing and sensationalizing the traditional belief system of the African diaspora, especially that of Haiti. Most often referred to in scholarly works by less pejorative terms such as *vodun* or *vodou,* the religion permeates nearly every aspect of Haitian creative arts, from music and painting to literature.

So Spoke the Uncle (*Ainsi parla l'oncle*), a 1928 essay by the late Haitian physician and intellectual **Jean Price-Mars**, was the driving force that prompted early-twentieth-century authors in Haiti to rethink prejudicial views of their culture imposed on them from colonial times. Price-Mars urged creative writers to abandon what he termed "dilettantist **bovaryism**," that is, the practice of portraying an inaccurate view of themselves and their country. He asked them to examine their true identity and to incorporate ancestral African aspects of their society into their works. A Haitian literary renaissance thus emerged, reawakening the country's pride by rehabilitating Haitian folklore, peasant culture, the Creole language, and, of course, vodou. One of the most outstanding authors of the so-called Indigenist Movement of the 1930s in Haiti was **Jacques Roumain**. In his fictional works, and in those of many other writers from that time to the present, there are not only literal representations of vodou practices and ceremonies, but also characters whose very temperaments exemplify various *loa*, or spirits, of the vodou pantheon.

Roumain's posthumous masterpiece, *Gouverneurs de la rosée* (1944), translated into English as *Masters of the Dew*, is a case in point. This prototypical novel reverberates with examples of vodou rituals. Near the beginning of the story, for example, there is a full-fledged religious celebration, as the community of Fonds-Rouge welcomes home the protagonist, Manuel, who has spent fifteen years working the cane fields of Cuba. Here, perfectly woven into the story line, the reader finds the setting, personages, songs, prayers, and other accoutrements characteristic of a genuine vodou ceremony. The prayers of Délia, Manuel's mother, also reveal the intricacies of the syncretic religion. She often appeals to Jesus, as well as to the Catholic Virgin, who is associated with the vodou Maîtresse Erzulie (or Ezili), and Papa Legba, the master of the crossroads, often seen as St. Peter or St. Anthony.

However, Roumain's novel, along with other Haitian works, is not simply an ethnographic display of the rites of vodou. The archetypical characters themselves illustrate types of individuals found Haitian society and, thus, resemble many of the diverse loa of its indigenous religion. Through his labor and his death, Manuel becomes the community's savior. His graceful young lover, Annaïse, represents the youthful manifestation of the beautiful, fertile vodou virgin, Erzulie Fréda, and his gentle, yet sorrowful, mother, Délia, reflects the maternal aspect of Erzulie Dantor (Dantò). The rage of Manuel's eventual assassin, Gervilen, explicitly relates him periodically throughout the story to the violent spirit of the vodou god Ogoun.

These literal and symbolic representations of vodou are found throughout the literature of Haiti: in poems and short stories as well as novels. Readers interested in the topic should explore works by Roumain, **Jacques-Stéphen Alexis**, and **Marie Chauvet**, as well as those of **René Depestre, Lilas Desquiron, Gérard Étienne**, and **Émile Olliver**, to mention but a few prominent and characteristic Haitian authors. *See also* Cabrera, Lydia; Obeah Themes in Literature; Ortiz, Fernando; Santería in Literature.

Further Reading

Boisvert, Jayne R. *The Myth of Erzulie and Female Characters in the Haitian Novel*. University at Albany, NY: Doctoral dissertation, 1998.

Déita [Mercédes Foucard Guignard]. *La Légende des loa du vodou haïtien*. Port-au-Prince: Bibliothèque Nationale d'Haïti, 1993.

Laroche, Maximilien. *La Littérature haïtienne: identité, langue, réalité*. Ottawa: Éditions Leméac, 1981.

Price-Mars, Jean. *So Spoke the Uncle*, translated by Magdaline W. Shannon. Washington, DC: Three Continents Press, 1994.

Roumain, Jacques. *Gouverneurs de la rosée*. Fort de France: Éditions Émile Desormeaux, 1977.

—Jayne R. Boisvert

Walcott, Derek (1930–)

Derek Walcott is one of the Caribbean's most accomplished writers whose international status and instrumentality in shaping the canon of modern literature is evident in his reception of the prestigious Nobel Prize for Literature in 1992. He is a poet, a dramatist, an intellectual, and an artist.

Derek Walcott was born in 1930 in Castries, St. Lucia. At the age of eighteen, he published his first collection, *25 poems* (1948). Since that modest beginning, his output as a poet, dramatist, reviewer, and essayist has been phenomenal. He is also an accomplished painter. His other books of poetry include *Epitaph for the Young: XII Cantos* (1949), *Poems* (1951), *In a Green Night: Poems 1948–1960* (1962), *Selected Poems* (1964) *The Castaway* (1965), *The Gulf and Other Poems* (1969), *Another Life* (1973), *Sea Grapes* (1976), *Star-Apple Kingdom* (1979), *The Fortunate Traveller* (1982), *Midsummer* (1984), *Collected Poems 1948–1984* (1986), *The Arkansas Testament* (1987), *Omeros* (1990), *The Bounty* (1997), and *Tiepolo's Hound* (2000).

Walcott's frequent adoption of the poet-hermit persona is not to be mistaken for social detachment. His public commitment is nowhere more evident than in his work as a playwright and director. After a year of studying theater in the United States (1957–58), Walcott moved to Trinidad, where he established the Trinidad Theater Workshop in 1959, which provided a space for serious Caribbean theater. His major published plays include *Henri Christophe: A Chronicle in Seven Scenes* (1952), *Dream on Monkey Mountain and Other Plays* (1972), *The Joker of Seville and O Babylon!* (1978), *Remembrance and Pantomime* (1980), *The Odyssey* (1993), *The Haitian Trilogy* (2002) and *The Walker and the Ghost Dance* (2002). Further, his artistic activism finds expression in his numerous essays and reviews that explore ideas on Caribbean culture, identity, literature, language, memory and the imagination, history, and politics. Several of his key essays have been published in *What the Twilight Says: Essays* (1998).

Movement has always marked Walcott's career. Apart from having traveled extensively across the globe, he spent a significant portion of his writing career in Trinidad and then the United States, where he currently lives and teaches. This itinerancy has only served to deepen his rootedness in the archipelago of his birth, the home to which his "elsewhere" going returns. Although St. Lucia, the "Helen" of his Caribbean epic *Omeros*, has emerged as Walcott's primary muse, his imagination is not provincial. In fact, the hard embrace of a single island is the ground from which his universal range takes wing. The greatness of his artistic talent and vision is borne out in the architecture of a citizenship that is as nomadic as it is rooted, global as it is local, for the world is his home, and his race is the human race, which is his fundamental commitment.

The constant themes of Walcott's work have been ancestral loss, the psychic traumas and displacement of cultural schizophrenia that are the dark legacies of a colonial history. He has been as compassionate as he has been unflinching in representing the region's condition as a civilization that endured European domination, as well as the blunders and betrayals of postindependence regimes, as is evident in such collections as his *The Castaway* and *Sea Grapes*. However, his most enduring posture, which established itself from his early collection *In a Green Night,* has been one of "elation" for the region's beauty and possibility, its peoples' miraculous emergence from a "salted" history, the patient and ingenious knitting together of the "fragments" of our myriad origins, passages, languages, traditions, memories, and faiths to create a New World whose inexhaustible "bounty" tirelessly converts his sometimes doubt. An assiduous humanism drives Walcott's desire to elevate to classical proportions the ordinary, often unrecognized people and landscape of the Caribbean as in his autobiographical poem *Another Life* and *Omeros*.

A hallmark of Walcott's career has been the transparency he risks, particularly in his poetry, wherein he lays bare the struggle to welcome and reconcile the great crosscurrents of his colonial heritage. Very early he understood and accepted this confluence of differences as a fate he was determined to make his gift, like the two languages of his craft "one so rich / in its imperial intimacies, its echo of privilege, / the other like the orange words of a hillside in drought—but my love for both wide as the Atlantic is large" (*The Bounty* 33). Walcott has not escaped criticism for his "imperial intimacies"; yet, one of his most enduring lessons has been the necessity of forgiveness, for blame is too narrow a country for literature-art and the human heart. His highest intention has been to house all the ancestors of his multicultural Caribbean heritage, and, at best, his work exists as a powerful testimony of the democratic impulse of cultures that, allowed their innocence, consort without prejudice. For, literature-art will not accept a narrow citizenship.

Further Reading

Cimarosti, Robert. *Mapping Memory: An Itinerary Through Derek Walcott's poetics.* Milano: Cisalpino, 2004.

Hamner, Robert, ed. *Derek Walcott.* New York: Twayne; Toronto: Maxwell Macmillan Canada; New York: Maxwell Macmillan International, 1993.

King, Bruce Alvin. *Derek Walcott: A Caribbean Life.* Oxford, New York: Oxford University Press, 2000.

—Jennifer Rahim

Walrond, Eric (1898–1966)

A member of the Harlem Renaissance, Walrond established early fame as an author with the publication of the collection of short stories *Tropic Death* (1926). However, he did not publish any book after that collection, and his life as a writer remains much of a mystery.

Eric Derwent Walrond was born in Georgetown, British Guiana, now Guyana, in 1898, the son of a Guyanese father and a Barbadian mother. When he was a child, his father relocated to Panama to work on the canal. When he was about twelve years old, Walrond and his mother joined his father, but the relationships did not go well. Walrond and his mother then settled by themselves in Colón, Panama. Walrond attended elementary and secondary schools in Panama, learned Spanish, and became a reporter for the *Star-Herald*.

In 1920, Walrond emigrated to New York City, seeking work as either a journalist or an editor. Racism in America shocked him: newspapers would not hire him because he was black. He then studied at City College of New York and Columbia University but did not graduate. He also worked as a stenographer for the British Recruiting Mission and as a secretary for the Broad Street Hospital. The bigotry he had encountered in the United States attracted him to **Marcus Garvey** and his Universal Negro Improvement Association. He was appointed associate editor of the *Negro World*, Garvey's journal, and began to write a series of articles and essays for several publications, including *Current History* and the *Independent*. In these writings, Walrond discusses the migration of blacks from the rural South to the urban North, life in Harlem, and black leadership in the United States.

In 1925, he became the business manager of the journal *Opportunity: Journal of Negro Life* and socialized with the writers of the Harlem Renaissance, befriending Langston Hughes (1902–67). In 1926, he published *Tropic Death*. The stories in the collection are all set in the Caribbean and are united by theme of death. Some of the stories are realistically told, such as the story of a diving boy who is eaten by a shark, and some belong in the realm of the supernatural, as the narrative about a man who rescues a boy who is in fact a vampire bat. *Tropic of Death* was reviewed in the major press of the time and earned Walrond a grant from the John Simon Guggenheim Memorial Foundation. Yet, after *Tropic of Death*, Walrond limited himself to writing essays that were published in different periodicals. He spent the rest of his life traveling throughout Europe.

Walrond married twice. He settled in London, where he died in 1966. His *Tropic of Death* and the numerous essays he wrote await critical study.

Further Reading

Bogle, Enid E. "Eric Walrond (1898–1966)." In *Fifty Caribbean Writers: A Bio-Bibliographical-Critical Sourcebook*, edited by Daryl Cumber Dance, 475–81. Westport, CT: Greenwood Press, 1986.

—*D. H. Figueredo*

Warner-Vieyra, Myriam (1939–)

A writer from Guadeloupe who has spent her life in Senegal, Africa, Warner-Vieyra writes about marriage as an institution that favors men and dehumanizes women. Her stories and novels convey the rage of silent women abused by men, either fathers who rape their daughters or husbands who are unfaithful. Often her narratives conclude with the protagonist committing violent acts or a descent into madness, the only means for her alienated and despairing female characters to find freedom.

Myriam Warner-Vieyra was born in Pointe-à-Pitre, Guadeloupe in 1939. As a child, she lived with her grandmother before emigrating to France. She attended secondary schools in France and then matriculated at the University of Dakar, Senegal, earning a degree in library sciences. She remained in Senegal, where she married filmmaker Paulin Vieyra (1925–).

In 1980, she published her first novel, *Le quimboiseur l'avait dit*, about an abused young girl who is raped by her father and who finds release through a violent attack on her mother. In 1982, she published *Juletane*, a novel about a young West Indian woman who marries an African man who was already married. The story is written in the form of a diary by a woman unaware that she has married a polygamist. Six years later, Warner-Vieyra published a collection of short stories *Femmes échouées*. One of the tales in this volume, "Le Mur ou les charmes d'une vie conjugale," deals with the solitude, muteness, and rage of a woman trapped in a marriage where she is not allowed to speak.

Warner-Vieyra is currently finishing two works of fiction and a biography. Her novels have been translated into English, German, and Swedish. *See also* Feminism in Caribbean Literature.

Further Reading

Ezeigbo, Theodora Akachi. "Women's Empowerment and National Integration: Ba's *Long a Letter* and Warner-Vieyra's *Juletane*." In *Current Trends in Literature and Language Studies in West Africa*, edited by Ernest N. Emenyonu and Charles E. Nnolim, 7–19. Ibadan: Kraft Books Limited, 1994.

—*Jayne R. Boisvert*

Waruk, Kona. See Harris, Wilson T.

Weber Pérez, Delia Mercedes (1900–1982)

Poet, playwright, narrator, cultural worker, and artist, Delia Weber is one of the most outstanding Dominican women of this century. In her eighty-two years of life, Weber participated actively in many aspects of Dominican life. A feminist, she was a member of the board of directors of Acción Feminista Dominicana, where she had the opportunity to study the condition of women and to take a stand on behalf of women's rights.

Weber was on October 23, 1900, in Santo Domingo, Dominican Republic. She attended elementary and secondary schools at the Liceo Nuñez de Cáceres, in Santo Domingo. Later on, she enrolled at the Escuela Normal de Señoritas, earning a teaching degree. Upon graduation, she spent a decade in Europe, traveling back and forth between Paris and Vienna.

Weber wrote for numerous papers throughout Latin America, including *El Diario*, from Colombia, *México Moderno*, from Mexico, and *Proa*, from Argentina. Gaining recognition as a feminist, she was one of the founders, in 1927, of Club Nosotras and Acción Feminista Dominicana in 1931.

Her short stories and poems explore the compromise between a woman's wishes for freedom and the acceptance of her position and responsibilities as a mother. However, many of her pieces, as those in the collection *Dora y otros cuentos* (1952), show the rebellion and nonconformity of characters who affirm their individualities by running away from home. Her works include *Encuentro* (1939), *Los viajeros: poema dramático* (1944), *Apuntes* (1949), *Espigas al sol* (1959), and *Estancia* (1972).

She passed away in Santo Domingo on December 28, 1982.

Further Reading

Cocco de Filippis, Daisy. *Documents of Dissidence: Selected Writings by Dominican Women*. New York: CUNY Dominican Studies Institute, 2000.

—*Daisy Cocco de Filippis*

Weekes, Nathaniel (1730–70?)

Barbados's first poet and a pioneer poet in the anglophone Caribbean, Weekes wrote one of the earliest descriptions of the West Indies and of a sugarcane plantation.

Information on his life is limited. He was well read in the English classics and started to write as a youth, imitating styles popular in England. In 1752, he published satirical verses, "On the Abuse of Poetry," probably influenced by Alexander Pope (1688–1744). Two years later, he published the pastoral poem that brought him a certain level of recognition, "Barbados." The first long poem written about a West Indian theme, "Barbados" describes the cultivation of sugarcane and presents an idyllic image of the slaves working on the field, probably not so much because he saw the plantation as Edenic but to assure English readers that he was not advocating dissatisfaction and rebellion. In 1754, he published "The Choice of a Husband, an Epistle to a Young Lady," and in 1775, he published his last work, "The Messiah; a Sacred Poem."

Weekes's "Barbados" was eclipsed by the publication of "The Sugar Cane" in 1764. Both poems were similar, but the latter was written by James Grainger (1724–67), who was white, a physician, and related to the governor of St. Kitts.

Further Reading

Breiner, Laurence A. *An Introduction to West Indian Poetry*. Cambridge: Cambridge University Press, 1998.

—D. H. Figueredo

West Indian Literature. See Anglophone Caribbean Literature, History of.

Wide Sargasso Sea (1966)

This popular novel by **Jean Rhys** challenges readers to revisit Charlotte Brontë's *Jane Eyre* through the eyes of a Caribbean reader. Rhys invents a history of Edward Rochester, beloved of young Jane, and his first wife, Bertha Mason, from Jamaica. Here the wife, renamed Antionette Cosway Mason, begins with her story about growing up dispossessed and alone as the daughter of a ruined white plantation owner in a postemancipated Jamaica. Rhys beautifully depicts the natural beauty of the islands, their rugged mountains, bright colors and lush vegetation in contrast to the cold and sterile haunts of England. She proposes an alternate view of the colonized woman; rather than seeing her as inherently mad, Rhys suggests that she is driven mad by the controlling ways of the Englishman and her new status as property, bought and sold as a mere object.

The novel contains portions narrated by Antionette and others by Rochester. With this two-sided vision, Rhys demonstrates that the two characters are similar in circumstances, though very different in perception. Both are intrigued by the appearance of the other, both forced to marry to revive decaying family fortunes. However, Antionette's love of her homeland and the different populations that compose it seem sickening to the reserved Englishman. During their time together on the islands, Rochester first indulges his appetites for Jamaica's natural abundance and freer racial and sexual relations. Finally, though, he rejects it together with Jamaica's mysterious Obeah religion; he changes Antionette's name, labeling her insane and transporting her to her English prison. There all her life becomes a horrible nightmare that transforms her into the ghoul that terrifies Jane Eyre.

Wide Sargasso Sea was made into a film in 1993. *See also* Feminism in Caribbean Literature; Mother-Daughter Relationships; Obeah Practices in Literature.

Further Reading

O'Connor, Teresa F. *Jean Rhys: The West Indian Novels*. New York: New York University Press, 1986.

Rhys, Jean. *Wide Sargasso Sea*. Norton Critical Edition, edited by Judith L. Raiskin. New York: Norton, 1999.

—Angela Conrad

Williams, Denis (1923–98)

Though Denis Williams wrote only two novels, he established a solid reputation as a provocative thinker who explored the Caribbean dilemma of creating a balance between European traditions and ancestral links to Africa, two perspectives that were often at odds with each other. In his novel *Other Leopards* (1963), he creates a prototype: the intellectual in search of a national and cultural identity in a postcolonial society. Williams was also an artist and an archaeologist who promoted the ancestral and contemporary artwork of his native Guyana.

Denis Joseph Ivan Williams was born in Georgetown, Guyana, on February 1, 1923. Raised in Georgetown, he went to London in 1946 to study painting at the Camberwell School of Art. Graduating in 1948, he was appointed lecturer at the Central School of Fine Art in Holborn and tutor at the Slade School of Fine Art. While teaching, he painted and mounted several exhibitions in London and Paris. In 1957, he moved to Africa and became an art instructor at the School of Fine Arts in Khartoum, the Sudan. But he found himself unable to follow his calling, that of the artist: "In Sudan, in the desert, you cannot paint," he recalled in a 1984 interview in the book *New World Adams*, written by Daryl Cumber Dance, "there was no colour . . . just khaki, camels, khaki. . . . And this blasting sun—and so therefore I began to write" (55).

The novel that he wrote was *Other Leopards*. Set in the Sudan, the narrative tells the story of Froad, an academic of mixed racial heritage who is torn between his European and African roots and who has accepted the stereotypes forced on him by European society. For instance, he views his African lover as almost primeval, a sex object, while he regards his European mistress as cultivated and highly intellectual. The tension that he experiences within himself—that of accepting and rejecting values deposited on him by the dominant society—maddens him to the point he attacks his boss, a white archaeologist. The novel ends with Froad hiding in a tree, uncertain of his future. An autobiographical exercise, Williams told scholar Dance that the novel was an attempt "to shed all these plagues that Europe had put on me" (55).

Upon publication the novel provoked much discussion and was quickly anthologized in several volumes published in Europe and the United States. Williams followed his success with a very different work, *The Third Temptation* (1968), an experimental novel that takes place in Europe and explores the effect an accident has on several characters who live in a small town. In this novel, the author tries to capture the multitude of sensations and events surrounding any one person at any one time. For instance, one character is watching activities on a street near him while thinking of seagulls on a faraway beach and the sound seagulls make. Numerous critics found the novel challenging but not as well crafted as *Other Leopards*.

Williams returned to Guyana in 1968, living in the jungles so he could study Amerindian art and ruins. In the 1970s, he served as director of art and culture for the Ministry of Education and as director of the Walter Roth Museum. He wrote important scholarly works, including *Icon and Image: A Study of Sacred and Secular Forms of African Classical Art* (1974), *Contemporary Art in Guyana* (1976), *Ancient Guyana* (1985), and *The Archaic of North-Western Guyana* (1989). He labored on a novel for over a decade, *The Sperm of God*, left unfinished at the time of his death in 1998. *See also* Postcolonialism.

Further Reading

Dance, Daryl Cumber. *New World Adams: Conversations with Contemporary West Indian Writers*. Yorkshire, England: Peepal Tree, 1984, 1992.

Dathorne, O. R., ed. *Caribbean Narrative: An Anthology of West Indian Writing*, 235–46. London and Edinburgh: Heinemann Educational Books, 1966, 1973.

—*D. H. Figueredo*

Williams, Eric (1911–81)

The first prime minister of Trinidad and Tobago, Eric Williams was representative of the Caribbean politician who is also a scholar and a writer. His two volumes on the history of the region, *Capitalism and Slavery* (1944) and *From Columbus to Castro: The History of the Caribbean* (1970), are classic studies of the impact of slavery on the Caribbean and on the economic development of imperial powers.

Eric Eustace Williams was born in Port of Spain, Trinidad, on September 25, 1911. His father was a civil servant who had been denied advancement because he lacked "colour, money, and education," meaning he was dark and poor, wrote Williams in his 1969 autobiography, *Inward Hunger* (26). Nevertheless, Williams's father assured the son an education by making financial sacrifices to send him to private school, the Tranquility Boys School, and then by encouraging him to win athletic and scholarly scholarships, which Williams did: the first to Queen's Royal College in Trinidad, the leading secondary school on the island, and the second, in 1935, to Oxford University. Earning a PhD in history in 1938, Williams moved to the United States to teach at Howard University. In 1944, he adapted his doctoral dissertation into a book. Entitled *Capitalism and Slavery*, Williams wrote in the preface that the volume was a "study . . . of the contribution of slavery to the development of British capitalism" (viii), and that, as such, when Britain abolished slavery it did so not out of humanitarian reasons but for economic purposes, since the practice was no longer profitable for the empire. This was a unique scholarly interpretation at the time.

Capitalism and Slavery brought Williams critical recognition. But instead of pursuing a career in academia, in 1955 he returned to Trinidad, where he founded the People's National Movement. In 1959, under Williams's leadership, Trinidad established a governmental cabinet, and, in 1960, the island was given self-rule. Two years later, Trinidad achieved full independence, and Williams became its prime minister, a post he held until his death in 1981. Always the professor, his public addresses were so informational that they were dubbed the "University of Woodford Square," referring to the plaza from where Williams spoke.

His second most famous book was *From Columbus to Castro: The History of the Caribbean*, an essay on the economic and political development of the region. The style is almost conversational, and Williams doesn't pretend objectivity, which makes the volume most endearing to the politically engaged writers of the Caribbean. He also wrote *The History of the People of Trinidad and Tobago* (1964), an official history of the islands, *British Historians and the West Indies* (1964), wherein he criticizes the historians' bigoted views of the Caribbean, as well as publishing his speeches and dozens of articles. He was criticized, though, by such East Indian scholars as Ramesh Maharaj and Roy Nehall, for neglecting to comment on the hardships suffered by indentured servants from India and for even encouraging the racial and social divide between blacks and East Indians from Trinidad.

Williams died of heart failure on March 29, 1981.

Further Reading

Boodhoo, Ken I. *The Elusive Eric Williams*. Kingston, Jamaica: I. Randle, 2001.

"Eric Williams." *Current Biography*. New York: Wilson, 1966.

Maharaj, Ramesh. "Challenges to East Indians in Trinidad and Tobago." In *IndoCaribbean Resistance*, edited by Frank Birbalsingh, 33–41. Toronto: Tsar Publications, 1993.

Neehall, Roy. "The Creation of Caribbean History." In *Indo-Caribbean Resistance* edited by Frank Birbalsingh, 1–12. Toronto: Tsar Publications, 1993.

—*D. H. Figueredo*

Williams, Francis (1700–70)

Francis Williams is an eighteenth-century Jamaican poet known for writing Latin odes to celebrate the arrivals of new governors to the island; it is also believed that he is the author of a popular ballad, "Welcome, Welcome, Brother Debtor," written sometime in the 1720s and anthologized several times in England during the 1730s and 1740s.

A free black, Francis Williams was sent to England to study by the Duke of Montague as something of an experiment—to determine how much a black man could learn—as scholar Laurence A. Breiner asserts in his volume *An Introduction to West Indian Poetry* (1998). Williams proved an excellent student, mastering mathematics, the classics, and Latin.

Upon his return to Jamaica, sometime in the 1720s, Williams set up a school in Spanish Town. Of the many odes he wrote, only his 1759 ode to Governor Haldane has survived. Though praising the governor, Williams acknowledge his blackness, mentioning the hardships endured by the black population on the island and hinting at the justified anger that would survive in the literary works of many black writers generations later.

Very little is known of Williams except for what is recorded in the book *A History of Jamaica*, written by Edward Long in 1774.

Further Reading

Breiner, Laurence A. *An Introduction to West Indian Poetry*. Cambridge: Cambridge University Press, 1998.

Drayton, Arthur. "Francis Williams (1700–1770)". In *Fifty Caribbean Writers: a Bio-Bibliographical-Critical Sourcebook*, edited by Daryl Cumber Dance. New York: Greenwood Press, 1986.

—*D. H. Figueredo*

"Within the Revolution Everything; Outside the Revolution Nothing"

This well-known phrase comes from a 1961 speech by **Fidel Castro** to the island's intellectuals, and it encapsulates the Cuban Revolution's approach toward artistic and political dissent. Cuban writers and artists must walk an intellectual tightrope between creative independence and the need to stay on the correct side of ongoing ideological debates. The degree of artistic freedom permitted by the Revolution has varied greatly during the last forty-five years, alternating between periods of great freedom and great repression.

The cause of the tension between the Revolution and its writers and artists can be, in part, explained by the series of challenges faced by the government, everything from U.S. sponsored invasions in the 1960s to the destruction of the former Soviet Union and the Communist Bloc in the 1980s, which led to the near collapse of the Cuban economy. The Revolution views art as a vehicle by which to strengthen loyalty in the citizenry. The notion that "art is an arm of the Revolution" was popularized in the 1970s. Castro has said of art, as quoted in Lee Lockwood's *Castro's Cuba: Cuba's Fidel* (1967): "It is not an end in itself. Man is the end. Making men happier, better" (207).

One of the most restrictive periods for artistic expression was the early 1970s, typified by the arrest of prominent writer **Heberto Padilla**, a critic of the Revolution. Criticism of Padilla dated back to the 1968 publication of *Fuera del juego*, a collection of poems that the government considered counterrevolutionary. After his arrest in 1971, and his subsequent release, Padilla was forced to make a staged confession before the **Unión de Escritores y Artistas de Cuba** (Cuban Union of Writers and Artists), in which he accused his wife, **Belkis Cuza Malé**, and friends of making counterrevolutionary statements. The list of Cuban writers, artists, and scholars forced into exile by the Revolution is lengthy and includes **Reinaldo Arenas, Virgilio Piñera, Guillermo Cabrera Infante** and Manuel Moreno Fraginals.

Despite the uneasy relationship between art and the Revolution, Cuban writers and artists have developed a series of survival strategies, ranging from self-censorship to circumvention and obfuscation. The eye of the government censor remains ever present in Cuban society today, but increasing European tourism, fueled by the government's need for hard currency, provides Cuban writers the flexibility to publish and exhibit their works overseas. This access to foreign markets gives many Cuban writers and artists a better standard of living than many fellow islanders. *See also* Anti-Castro Literature.

Further Reading

Art Cuba: The New Generation, edited and with an introduction by Holly Block. New York: Abrams, 2001.

Castro, Fidel. *Palabras a los intelectuales*. Habana: Ediciones del Consejo Naciona de Cultura, 1961.

Lockwood, Lee. *Castro's Cuba: Cuba's Fidel—An American Journalist's Inside Look at Today's Cuba in Text and Picture*. New York: Macmillan, 1967.

—*Frank Argote-Freyre*

Wynter, Sylvia (1928–)

An influential literary theoretician and the first black woman novelist from the anglophone Caribbean, Wynter's writings express her concerns as a woman writer and as a West Indian writer. A feminist, she was one of the first female writers to challenge such major authors and critics as **John Hearne** and **Mervyn Morris** for favoring European culture and male-driven literary perspectives.

Born on May 11, 1928, in Cuba, Sylvia Wynter's parents returned to her native Jamaica when she was two years old. She attended a private high school in Jamaica and then won a scholarship to attend King's College, University of London. She earned a BA in Spanish in 1949. In 1953, she received her MA in Spanish.

From 1954 to 1959, she traveled throughout Europe. She was involved in acting and was also writing for BBC radio, adapting into English the classic Spanish drama *Yerma*, by Federico García Lorca (1898–1936). She married writer **Jan Carew**, from Guyana, and together they wrote essays and poetry for the BBC. During this period, Wynter wrote a play entitled *Under the Sun*. The play would serve as the basis for her first novel, *The Hills of Hebron*.

The novel was published in 1962. It is the story of a religious cult based in Jamaica and the political conflicts that emerge when its leader dies and several candidates aspire to the position. Throughout the narrative, Wynter presents her views on colonialism and women's oppression in Jamaica. Though the novel was not well received by many critics, it nevertheless proved an important work that established Wynter as a major talent. Over the years, *Hills of Hebron* has remained popular. After the novel's publication, Wynter and Carew separated and eventually divorced.

In 1963, she relocated to California, where she taught at the University of California–San Diego. In 1965, she adapted the classic Jamaican novel *Brother Man* (1956), by **Roger Mais**, for the stage. That same year, she wrote the historical drama *1865 Ballad for a Rebellion*, about the Morant Bay Rebellion in Jamaica. Influenced by Marxism, she began to write articles on literary theory, often calling Caribbean literature the elitist practice of a few privileged writers. She also promoted the importance and value of folklore and popular culture. In 1968–69, she wrote one of her most influential and provocative essays, "We Must Learn to Sit Down Together and Discuss a Little Culture—Reflections on West Indian Writing and Criticism." In the essay, she advocates the need to disseminate culture and the creation of culture through the masses: "[I]t is not a luxury, not and no longer the playmate of an elite soul; it must be instead the agent of man's drive to survive in the twentieth century" (315).

In 1971, Wynter was commissioned by the Jamaican government to write about the island's heroes; the result was the book *Jamaica's National Heroes*. In 1977, she was appointed chair of African and Afro-American Studies at Stanford University, in California. Her academic responsibilities prompted her to pursue scholarly studies; she published numerous essays in anthologies and journals throughout the 1990s. Some of her best-known essays from this period are "Columbus, the Ocean Blue and Fables that Stir the Mind: To Reinvent the Study of Letters" (1997) and "Genital Mutilation or Symbolic Birth: Female Circumcision, Lost Origins, and the Aculturalism of Feminist/Western Thought" (1997).

There are critics who describe Wynter's literary essays as difficult to follow, but most scholars, such as Victor L. Chang, in *Fifty Caribbean Writers*, praise her for expanding literary criticism in the Caribbean to include a feminist perspective and for placing the analysis of race and gender on equal footing.

Further Reading

Change, Victor L. "Sylvia Wynter." In *Fifty Caribbean Writers: A Bio-Bibliographical-Critical Sourcebook*, edited by Daryl Cumber Dance. Westport, CT: Greenwood Press, 1986.

Wynter, Silvia. "We Must Learn to Sit Down Together and Discuss a Little Culture—Reflections on West Indian Writing and Criticism." In *The Routledge Reader in Caribbean Literature*, edited by Alison Donnell and Sarah Lawson Welsh, 307–15. London and New York: Routledge, 1996.

—*D. H. Figueredo*

Yáñez, Mirta (1947–)

Mirta Yáñez is a writer, scholar, and editor whose works explore the nature of feminism and homosexuality in contemporary Cuba. She has also achieved recognition for her promotion of emerging feminist writers from Cuba and the Caribbean. Cuban critic **Emilio Jorge Rodríguez** calls her "one of the most brilliant intellects of her generation."

In the 1990s, Yáñez realized that there was an absence of scholarly studies and anthologies on a generation of young Cuban women writers who had come of age during the end of the twentieth century. These women were not writing about the historical process in Cuba and were not politically engaged, as was the tradition and trend after the triumph of the Cuban Revolution in 1959; instead, they were writing short stories that essayed on the intricacies of fragile relationships among small groups of friends and relatives. Since these authors were offering a different perspective on Cuban society and politics, Yáñez felt that they should be anthologized and promoted. The result was two anthologies: *Estatuas de sal* (1996), coedited with author **Marylin Bobes León**, and *Cubana: Contemporary Fiction by Cuban Woman* (1998).

Yáñez could actively seek these authors and advocate for their writings because of the reputation she had established on the island as a writer, a scholar, and supporter of the Revolution. A Latin American literature professor at Havana University, where she earned an MA in Spanish literature in 1972 and a PhD in philology in 1991, studying under the legendary Dominican scholar **Camila Henríquez Ureña**, her books of criticism include *Recopilación de textos sobre la novela romántica latino americana* (1978), a study of **romanticismo**; *El mundo literario prehispánico* (1986) about Mayan literature; and *Album de poetisas cubanas* (1997), an anthology and study of the poems of major Cuban poets, such as **Carilda Oliver, Fina García Marruz,** and **Nancy Morejón**, among others. As a creative writer, she published her first collection of poems, *Las visitas*, about the discovery of gay love, when she was nineteen years old. At the age of twenty, she wrote the novel *La hora de los mamayes*, a narrative within the literary tradition of **magical realism**, wherein the supernatural and mundane are presented as one. This was followed, in 1980, by the collection of short stories *La Habana es una ciudad bien grande*, where again she explores, though veiled, the theme of homosexuality.

In 1988, her collection of short stories *Diablo son las cosas* was published. In 2004, the Modern Language Association dedicated a panel to Yañez's works as a critic and scholar. *See also* Cuban Literature, History of; Feminism in Literature; Gay and Lesbian Literature.

Further Reading

Berg, Mary C., ed. *Open Your Eyes and Soar: Cuban Women Writing Now.* Buffalo, NY: White Pine Press, 2003.

Rodríguez, Emilio Jorge. "Interview with Emilio Jorge Rodríguez." By D. H. Figueredo. *Interview.* April 10, 2005.

—*D. H. Figueredo*

York, Andrew. See Nicholson, Christopher R.

Z

Zambrana, Antonio (1846–1922)

Zambrana was a Cuban author who while living in Chile in the 1870s was invited by a friend to write a novel about Cuba. Zambrana chose to produce an antislavery tale based on an earlier novel entitled *Francisco* and written by **Anselmo Suárez y Romero** in Cuba in the 1830s. Both works were based on a true story about the abuses experienced by a slave in Cuba, but whereas the first attempt was of a romantic nature, Zambrana's novel, *El negro Francisco* (1876), depicted a realistic portrayal of the horrors of slavery while also creating complex characters. In a 1979 reissue of the novel, Cuban critic Salvador Bueno claimed that Zambrana initiated a new development in the antislavery narrative by humanizing the slaves and not presenting them as merely types and symbols.

Antonio Zambrana was born in Havana on June 19, 1846. Graduating from secondary school in 1861, he became an attorney at the age of twenty-one. In 1868, he joined the insurgents in Cuba's war of independence from Spain—this particular conflict was called the Ten Years' War—"La Guerra de los Diez Años"—because it lasted until 1878. In 1873, Zambrana traveled to the United States to seek support for Cuba's struggle. While in New York City, he edited the journals *La Revolución* and *La Independencia*. In 1875, he visited Chile, where he wrote the novel. Five years later, he relocated to Costa Rica.

At the end of the Ten Years' War, as a result of a truce between Cuba and Spain, Zambrana returned to the island and was elected representative before the Spanish parliament, the Cortes. In the 1880s, he went back to Costa Rica and then toured Colombia and Ecuador. After Cuba had become a republic in 1902, Zambrana settled in his homeland. He passed away in Havana on March 27, 1922.

Francisco was the only novel Zambrana wrote. Some of his other works include *La República de Cuba* (1873), *Una visita a la metrópolis* (1888), *Ideas de estética, literatura y elocuencia* (1896), *La poesía de la historia* (1900).

Further Reading

Bueno, Salvador. "Prologo." *El negro Francisco*, by Antonio Zambrana. Habana: Editorial Letras Cubanas, 1979.

Cuba en la mano. Habana: Ucar, García y CIA, 1940.

—*D. H. Figueredo*

Zenea, Juan Clemente (1832–71)

Zenea, a romantic and mysterious figure from nineteenth-century Cuba, was for many years believed by some scholars to be a traitor to the Cuban independence movement. Others supported the notion that he had been misunderstood. A poet and an adventurer, Zenea led a life more colorful than characters in an adventure novel.

Zenea began to write poetry when he was a teenager, publishing his first poems at the age of fourteen, the same age when he edited the journal *La Prensa.* Three years later, he had a love affair with the poet and actress Adah Menken (1835–68). When he was twenty, he wrote poetry critical of the Spanish government and had to leave Cuba. Relocating to New Orleans, he continued his relationship with Menken.

In 1854, Zenea returned to Cuba, where he wrote for several magazines and published the book of poems *Poesías* (1855). He then founded the journal *La Revista Habanera* (1861), but his opposition to the Spanish government forced him to leave Cuba once again. In 1870, he went to New York City, where he accepted a mission from the Cuban exiles in that city. His orders were to return to Cuba, provide information to the insurgents fighting in the jungle, and negotiate a truce with the Spanish troops on conditions that Cuba would be granted greater autonomy.

In Cuba, Zenea was captured by Spanish forces. He was imprisoned for eight months and was then executed in 1871. Documents found years later suggested that he was working for the Spanish government. But his execution disproves this conclusion. Comments scholar **Matías Montes Huidobro**, in his 1995 edition of *El laud del desterrado:* Zenea was a "victim of [political] intrigue. . . . There is no proof what so ever that Zena acted, neither for money nor for beliefs, on behalf of the Spanish cause."

Zenea's dairy and the poems he wrote in prison were published in 1972 as *Diario de un mártir y otros poemas.*

Further Reading

Lezama Lima, José. *Fragmentos irradiadores.* Habana: Editorial Letras Cubanas, Instituto Cubano del Libro, 1993.

Montes Huidobro, Matías. "Juan Clemente Zenea." In *El laúd del desterrado,* edited by Matras Montes Huidobro, 162–68. Houston, TX: Arte Público Press, 1995.

—*D. H. Figueredo*

Zeno Gandía, Manuel (1855–1930)

The author of *La charca* (1896), the first major novel in Puerto Rican literature, and a patriot who was involved in the nineteenth-century struggle for autonomy, Zeno Gandía used literature as a tool to shape a Puerto Rican identity and to attempt to solve the island's ills. A physician, a scientist, and a historian, he is considered, with **Alejandro Tapia y Rivera**, the founder of the modern novel in Puerto Rico.

Zeno Gandía was born in Arecibo, Puerto Rico, on January 10, 1855, and moved to Spain with his well-to-do family when he was nine years old. In 1875, he graduated as a physician from San Carlos University in Madrid and conducted his internship in a hospital in Bordeaux, France. In 1873, he published his first paper, a medical thesis on how climates affected people.

While in Paris he became interested in the works of Émile Zola (1840–1902) and the literary movement known as **naturalism.** During this period, he wrote in earnest: stories, poems, plays, and a first novel, *El monstruo* (1878). He returned to Puerto Rico in 1882 and a year later founded a scientific journal, *El studio.* He also contributed regularly to numerous publications, including *La azucena, La revista de Puerto Rico,* and *Revista de la Antillas.*

In the 1880s, Zeno Gandía contemplated the idea of writing a series of novels depicting the social problems plaguing Puerto Rico: greedy merchants, socially aloof citizens, and the abused and neglected poor of the countryside and small towns. He would bring together these novels under the title of *Crónica de un mundo enfermo.* Originally, he planned to write eleven novels but only wrote five: *Garduña,* written in the early 1890s but published in 1896, *La charca* (1894), and *El negocio,* all issued as books. The fourth entry, *Redentores* was serialized in the newspaper *El imparcial* in 1925. The fifth volume, *Nueva York,* unfinished, was not published. Of these books, *La charca* is the most famous.

After the Spanish-Cuban-American War of 1898, Zeno Gandía devoted most of his time to political matters, traveling to Washington, D.C., with compatriot **Eugenio María de Hostos** to lobby unsuccessfully for Puerto Rico's independence, and founding in 1912, with poet **José de Diego,** the Independent Party. He also established a newspaper, *La Opinión* (1900) and became owner of the publication *La Correspondencia* (1902).

Zeno Gandía died on January 30, 1930, in the town of Santurce. At the time, he was writing a history of Puerto Rico, to be titled *Resumpta indo-antillana.* It is said, according to Aníbal González-Pérez in *Latin American Writers,* that in his last breath, Zeno Gandía, resentful of the fact that American soldiers were governing the island, uttered: "Solicito del General de los Estados Unidos una noche de sueño." (I request of the general from the United States a good night's sleep.)

Further Reading

González-Pérez, Aníbal. "Manuel Zeno Gandía." In *Latin American Writers: Volume 1,* edited by Carlos A. Solé and María Isabel Abreu, 321 New York: Scribner's, 1989.

Sánchez de Silva, Arlyn. *La novelística de Manuel Zeno Gandía*. San Juan, Puerto Rico: Instituto de Cultura Puertorriqueña, Programa de Publicaciones y Grabaciones, 1996.

—*D. H. Figueredo*

Zequeira Y Arango, Manuel Tiburcio de (1764–1846)

Though a minor Cuban poet, Zequeira y Arango nevertheless penned the first poem to celebrate the natural beauty of Cuba and to affirm Cuban traits and characteristics that were distinct from Spain's. In his ode to the pineapple, "A la piña," he expressed intense pride in his Cubanness, describing the tropical fruit as a prize much sought by the Greek gods on Mount Olympus and suggesting that such a majestic fruit could grow only in Cuba. At a time when Spain considered itself superior to its colonies, through this ode Zequeira y Arango challenged that posture.

Manuel de Zequeira was born August 28, 1764. He attended the Seminario de San Carlos, where he befriended the scholar and writer **Félix Varela**. In 1780, he joined the Spanish army and was sent to the Dominican Republic to participate in the campaign against the French, who were trying to take over the whole island of Hispaniola—they had already colonized Haiti, on the other side of the island. He returned to Cuba in 1817.

Zequeira y Arango edited the journal *Papel Periodico de la Habana* and published a book of poetry, *Poesías* (1829). However, mental illness incapacitated him, terminating his professional life as a soldier and aspirations as a writer. He passed away on April 18, 1846. *See also* Cuban Literature, History of; Romanticismo/ Romanticism.

Further Reading

Cuevas Zequeira, Sergio. *Manuel de Zequeira y Arango y los albores de la cultura cubana*. Habana: "Tipografía Moderna" de A. Dombecker, 1923.

—*D. H. Figueredo*

Zobel, Joseph (1915–)

The author of one of the best-known novels from Martinique, *La rue cases nègres* (1950), Joseph Zobel is a short-story writer and novelist who was influenced by the **Négritude** movement, which celebrates the African heritage of the Caribbean, and whose works protest against social conditions in Martinique. Like many writers from the Caribbean, Zobel has spent much of his life away from the country of his birth.

Zobel was born on April 26, 1915, on a sugar plantation in Petit-Morne à Rivière-Salée, Martinique. He was raised by his grandmother, who instilled in him a desire to leave the sugarcane plantation and to do well in school. His grandmother was the inspiration for his novel *La rue cases nègres*. Calling her in the novel M'man Tine, the character Zobel created became "an icon of female endurance," as critic Beverly Ormerod phrased it in the 1999 volume *An Introduction of Caribbean Francophone Writing: Guadeloupe and Martinique* (103). M'man Tine is a richly developed character that is caring and dictatorial, gentle and demanding, a prototype of the strong woman who appears in many Caribbean stories. The pains and misery M'man Tine experiences are also representative of the poverty and difficulties encountered by the sugarcane workers of Martinique.

The novel was published in 1950 but banned in Martinique for the next twenty years. Its film adaptation, made in 1983 and released a year later in the United States under the title of *Sugar Cane Alley*, brought the author the recognition he deserved. During the intervening years of the writing, the publication and film adaptation of *La rue cases nègres*, Zobel left Martinique, relocating to France, where he lived until 1957. That year, encouraged by Léopold S. Senghor (1906–2001), one of the founders of the Négritude movement, Zobel moved to Senegal. When Senegal achieved independence in 1960, Zobel worked for the newly founded Ministry of Information, overseeing the development of Radio Senegal and promoting cultural activities. In 1964, he wrote the collection of short stories *Le soleil partagé*, and in 1975, he wrote *Diab'la: roman antillais*; both works explore the themes of race and class.

Zobel retired to France in 1976. In 1998, he was awarded France's Legion of Honor Award—Chevalier de la Légion d'honneur—and in 2002, he received the Grand Prix du Livre Insulair, in honor of all his works. Zobel also has written several books of poetry, including *Incantation pour un retour au pays natal* (1964), *Poèmes de moi-même* (1984), *Poèmes d'Amour et de Silence* (1994), and *Le Soleil m'a dit* (2002). *See also* Grandparents in Caribbean Literature; Plantation Society in Caribbean Literature, The.

Further Reading

César, Sylvie. *La rue cases-nègres: du roman au film: étude comparative*. Paris: L'Harmattan, 1994.

Ormerod, Beverley. "The Representation of Women in French Caribbean Fiction." *In An Introduction to Caribbean and Francophone Writing: Guadeloupe and Martinique, 101–17*. Oxford and New York: Berg, 1999.

—*D. H. Figueredo*

Bibliography

Abrahams, Roger, and John Szwed, eds. *After Africa: Extracts from British Travel Accounts and Journals of the Seventeenth, Eighteenth, and Nineteenth Centuries concerning the Slaves, Their Manners, and Customs in the British West Indies*. New Haven, CT: Yale University Press, 1983.

Abreu Arcia, Alberto. *Virgilio Piñera: un hombre, una isla*. Habana: Ediciones Unión, 2002.

Acevedo, Ramón Luis. "Pachín Marín: poeta en libertad." San Juan: Instituto de Cultura Puertorriqueña, *Cuadernos de Cultura*, no. 4 (2001): 46.

Ada, Alma Flor. *Under the Royal Palms: A Childhood in Cuba*. New York: Simon & Schuster/Atheneum, 1998.

Agostini de del Río, Amelia. *Nuestras vidas son los ríos*. San Juan, Puerto Rico: Medinaceli.

Agosto, Noraida. *Michelle Cliff's Novels: Piecing the Tapestry of Memory and History*. New York: Lang, 1999.

Aguinaldo puertorriqueño de 1843. Edición conmemorativa del centenario. Río Piedras, Puerto Rico: Junta Editora de la Universidad de Puerto Rico, 1946.

Aguirre, Angela M. *Vida y crítica literaria de Enrique Piñeyro*. New York: Senda Nueva de Ediciones, 1981.

Alante-Lima, Willy. *Guy Tirolien: l'homme et l'oeuvre*. Paris: Présence africaine, 1991.

Albala, Eliana. *El paraíso de Lezama y el infierno de Lowry: dos polos narrativos*. Morelos, México: Publicaciones del Instituto de Cultura de Morelos, Fondo Estatal para la Cultura y las Artes de Morelos, 2000.

Albin, María C. *Género, poesía y esfera pública: Gertrudis Gómez de Avellaneda y la tradición romántica*. Madrid: Editorial Trotta, 2002.

Alcántara Almánzar, José. *Narrativa y sociedad en Hispanoamérica*. Santo Domingo, República Dominicana: Instituto Tecnológico de Santo Domingo, 1984.

Alexis, Jacques Stephen. *Compère Général Soleil*. Paris: Éditions Gallimard, 1955.

———. *General Sun, My Brother*. Translation and introduction Carrol F. Coates. Charlottesville: University Press of Virginia, 1999.

———. *In the Flicker of an Eyelid*. Translation and afterword by Carrol F. Coates and Edwidge Danticat. Charlottesville: University of Virginia Press, 2002.

Alfau Galván de Solalinde, Jesusa. *Como los crisantemos lila, obra escogida*. Selection and prologue by Daisy Cocco de Filippis. New York: Alcance, Colección Tertuliando, 2000.

———. *Los débiles*. Madrid: Imprenta Artística José Blas, 1912.

———. *Los débiles*. Prologue and annotations by J. Horace Nunemaker. New York: Prentice Hall, 1930.

Algarín, Miguel, and Miguel Piñero. *Nuyorican Poetry: An Anthology of Puerto Rican Words and Feelings*. New York: Morrow, 1975.

Algarín, Miguel, and Bob Holman. *Aloud: Voices from the Nuyorican Poets Café*. New York: Holt, 1994.

Algoo-Baksh, Stella. *Austin C. Clarke: A Biography*. Barbados: Press of the University of the West Indies; Toronto: ECW Press, 1994.

Allen, James Egert. *The Legend of Arthur A. Schomburg*. Cambridge, MA: Danterr, 1975.

Alvarez, Julia. *In the Name of Salomé*. Chapel Hill, NC: Algonquin Books of Chapel Hill, 2000.

Álvarez, Nicolás Emilio. *La obra literaria de Jorge Mañach*. Potomac, MD: J. Porrúa Turanzas, North American Division, 1979.

Álvarez Borland, Isabel. *Cuban-American Literature of Exile: From Person to Persona*. Charlottesville: University Press of Virginia, 1998.

Alzaga, Florinda. *La Avellaneda: intensidad y vanguardia*. Miami, FL: Ediciones Universal, 1997.

Anderson Imbert, Enrique, and Eugenio Florit. *Literatura Hispanoamericana: Antología e introducción histórica, vol. 2*. 2nd ed. New York: Holt, Rinehart and Winston, 1970.

Andrade Coello, Alejandro. *Tres poetas de la música, la obra del dominicano Max Henríquez Ureña*. 2nd ed. Quito, Ecuador: Talleres gráficos de Educación, 1942.

Andrews, George Reid. *Afro-Latin America, 1800–2000*. New York: Oxford University Press, 2004.

Angier, Carole. *Jean Rhys: Life and Work*. Boston: Little, Brown, 1990.

Antoine, Jacques C. *Jean Price-Mars and Haiti*. Washington, DC: Three Continents Press, 1981.

Antoine, Yves. *Sémiologie et personnage romanesque chez Jacques Stéphen Alexis*. Montréal: Editions Balzac, 1993.

Aparicio Laurencio, Ángel. *¿Es Heredia el primer escritor romántico en lengua española?* Miami, FL: Ediciones Universal, 1988.

Appiah, Kwame Anthony, and Henry Louis Gates Jr., eds. *Africana: The Encyclopedia of the African and African American Experience*. New York: Basic Civitas Books, 1999.

Arce de Vázquez, Margot, et al. *Lecturas puertorriqueñas: poesía*. Sharon, CT: Troutman, 1968.

Archibald, Douglas. *The Rose Slip*. Port of Spain: Extra Mural Department, University of the West Indies, 1967.

Arenas, Reinaldo. *Antes que anochezca: autobiografía*. Barcelona: Tusquets, 1992.

Argullol, Rafael. *El héroe y el único: el espíritu trágico del romanticismo*. Madrid: Taurus, 1999.

Arnold, A. James. *A History of Literature in the Caribbean. Vol. 2, English-Dutch Speaking Regions*. Philadelphia: John Benjamins Publishing Co., 2001.

Arpini, Adriana. *Eugenio María de Hostos, un hacedor de la libertad*. Mendoza, Argentina: Editorial de la Universidad Nacional de Cuyo, 2002.

Arrigoitia, Luis de. *La ejemplaridad en Margot Arce de Vázquez*. San Juan, Puerto Rico: Fundación Felisa Rincón de Gautier, 1992.

Arrillaga, María. *Concierto de voces insurgentes: tres autoras puertorriqueñas, Edelmira González Maldonado, Violeta López Suria y Anagilda Garrastegui*. Río Piedras, San Juan, Puerto Rico: Decanto de Estudios Graduados e Investigación, Recinto de Río Piedras, Universidad de Puerto Rico; San Juan, Puerto Rico.: Isla Negra Editores, 1998.

Arrillaga, María. *Los silencios de María Bibiana Benítez*. San Juan, Puerto Rico: Instituto de Cultura Puertorriqueña, 1985.

Arrufat, Antón. *Antología personal*. Barcelona: Mondadori, 2001.

Art Cuba: The New Generation. Edited and with an introduction by Holly Block. New York: Abrams, 2001.

Arthur, Charles, and Michael Dash, eds. *Libète: A Haitian Anthology*. Princeton, NJ: Marcus Wiener Publishers, 1999.

Ashcroft, Bill, Gareth Griffiths, and Helen Tiffin, eds. *The Post-colonial Studies Reader*. London: Routledge, 1995.

Auer, Peter. *Code-switching in conversation: language, interaction and identity*. New York: Routledge, 1998.

Augenbraum, Harold and Margarite Fernández Olmos. *The Latino Reader*. New York: Houghton Mifflin, 1997.

Augier, Ángel I. *Vida y obra de Nicolás Guillén*. Habana: Editorial Pueblo y Educación, 2002.

Avila, Leopoldo. *Cuba: letteratura e rivoluzione. Le correnti della critica della letteratura cubana*. Milano: Libreria Feltrinelli, 1969.

Azougarh, Abdeslam and Ángel Luis Fernández Guerra. *Acerca de Miguel Barnet*. Habana, Cuba: Editorial Letras Cubanas, 2000.

Azougarh, Abdeslam. *Juan Francisco Manzano: Esclavo poeta de la isla de Cuba*. Valencia: Episteme, 2000.

Babín, María Teresa. *Genio y figura de Nemesio R. Canales*. San Juan, Puerto Rico: Biblioteca de Autores Puertorriqueños, 1978.

Báez, Vicente, ed. *La Gran enciclopedia de Puerto Rico*. San Juan: Puerto Rico en la Mano and La Gran Enciclopedia de Puerto Rico, 1981.

Baghio'o, Jean-Louis. *The Blue-Flame-Tree*. Manchester, England: Carcanet Press, 1984.

Bala, Suman V. S. *Naipaul: A Literary Response to the Nobel Laureate*. New Delhi: Khosla Publishing House, in association with Prestige Books, 2003.

Balaguer, Joaquín. *Historia de la literatura dominicana*. Trujillo, República Dominicana: Librería Dominica, 1956.

Balderston, Daniel, and Mike González. *Encyclopedia of Latin America and Caribbean Literature 1900–2003*. New York: Routledge, 2004.

Balroya, Enrique A., and James A. Morris, eds. *Conflict and Change in Cuba*. Alburqueque: University of New Mexico, 1993.

Balseiro, José Agustín. *Obra selecta de José Agustín Balseiro;* prólogo de María Teresa Babín; epílogo de Ángel Encarnación. Río Piedras, Puerto Rico: Editorial de la Universidad de Puerto Rico, 1990.

Banham, Martin, Errol Hill, and George Woodyard, eds. *The Cambridge Guide to African and Caribbean Theatre*. New York: Cambridge University Press, 1994.

Barnouw, Dagmar. *Naipaul's Strangers*. Bloomington: Indiana University Press, 2003.

Barquet, Jesús J. *Consagración de La Habana (Las peculiaridades del Grupo Orígenes en el proceso cultural cubano)*. Miami: Iberian Studies Institute, North-South Center, University of Miami, 1992.

———. *Teatro y Revolución Cubana: subversión y utopía en Los siete contra Tebas de Antón Arrufat—Theater and the Cuban Revolution: subversion and utopia in Seven against Thebes by Antón Arrufat*. Lewiston, NY: E. Mellen Press, 2002.

Barradas, Efraín. *Para entendernos: Inventario poético puertorriqueño*. San Juan, Puerto Rico: Instituto Cultura Puertorriquena, 1992.

Bébel-Gisler, Dany. *Léonora: The Buried Story of Guadeloupe*. Translated by Andrea Leskes. Charlottesville: University Press of Virginia, 1994.

Behar, Ruth, ed. *Bridges to Cuba/Puentes a Cuba*. Ann Arbor: University of Michigan Press, 1995.

Beiro Álvarez, Luis. *Pedro Mir en familia*. Santo Domingo, República Dominicana: Fundación Espacio Culturales, 2001.

Bejel, Emilio. *Escribir en Cuba*. Río Piedras, Puerto Rico: Editorial de la Universidad de Puerto Rico, 1991.

———. *Gay Cuban nation*. Chicago: University of Chicago Press, 2001.

Bellegarde-Smith, Patrick. *Haiti: The Breached Citadel*. San Francisco: Westview Profiles, 1990.

Bell-Scott, Patricia, et al. *Double Stitch: Black Women Write About Mothers and Daughters*. New York: Harper Perennial, 1991.

Berg, Mary C., ed. *Open Your Eyes and Soar: Cuban Women Writing Now*. Buffalo, NY: White Pine Press, 2003.

Berger, Thomas. *A Long and Terrible Shadow: White Values, Native Rights in the Americas, 1492–1992*. Vancouver: Douglas & McIntyre; Seattle: University of Washington Press, 1992.

Bergmann, E., and P. J. Smith, eds. *Entiendes? Queer Readings, Hispanic Writings*. Durham, NC: Duke University Press, 1995.

Bernabé, Jean, et al. *Eloge de la créolité*. Paris: Gallimard; Presses universitaires créoles, 1989.

Berrian, Albert H., and Richard A. Long, eds. *Négritude: Essays and Studies*. Hampton, Virginia: Hampton Institute Press, 1967.

Berrou, F. Raphaël, and Pradel Pompilus. *Histoire de la littérature haïtienne illustrée par les textes*. 3 vols. Port-au-Prince: Éditions Caraïbes, 1975–77.

Berry, James, ed. *Bluefoot Traveller: An Anthology of Westindian Poets in Britain*. London: Limestone Publications, 1976.

Bertol, Lilllian. *The Literary Imagination of the Mariel Generation*. Miami: Endowment for Cuban American Studies, Cuban American Studies, Cuban American National Foundation, 1995.

Bevan, David, ed. *Literature and Exile*. Atlanta: Rodopi, 1990.

Bisnauth, Dale. *History of Religions in the Caribbean*. Trenton, NJ: Africa World Press, 1996.

Birbalsingh, Frank, ed. *Indo-Caribbean Resistance*. Toronto: Tsar Publications, 1993.

Bobb, June. *Beating a Restless Drum: The Poetics of Kamau Brathwaite and Derek Walcott*. Trenton, NJ: Africa World Press, 1998.

Boisvert, Jayne R. *The Myth of Erzulie and Female Characters in the Haitian Novel*. PhD diss., SUNY, Albany, 1998.

Boodhoo, Ken I. *The Elusive Eric Williams*. Kingston, Jamaica: I. Randle, 2001.

Bourne, Louis, et al. *Poesía esencial de Francisco Matos Paoli: Estudio y antología*. Madrid: Verbum, 1994.

Braham, Persephone. *Crimes Against the State, Crimes Against Persons: Detective Fiction in Cuba and Mexico*. Minneapolis: University of Minnesota Press, 2004.

Braithwaite, E. R. *To Sir, with Love*. Englewood Cliffs, NJ, Prentice-Hall, 1959.

Brathwaite, Edward Kamau. *Islands*. London, New York: Oxford University Press, 1969.

———. *Rights of Passage*. London: Oxford University Press, 1967.

Breinberg, Petronella. *My Brother Sean*. Illustrated by Errol Lloyd. London: Bodley Head, 1973.

Breiner, Laurence A. *An Introduction to West Indian Poetry*. New York: Cambridge University Press, 1998.

Britton, Celia. *An Introduction to Caribbean Francophone Writing: Guadeloupe and Martinique*. New York: Berg, 1999.

Broek, Aart G. *Pa saka toro, tomo I; Historia di literature papiamentu*. Willemstad, Netherlands: Fundashon Pierre Lauffer, 1998.

Broek, Aart G. *Swirling Columns of Imagination*. Curaçao: Maduro & Curiel's Bank N.V., 1997.

Brown, Isabel Zakrzewski. *Culture and Customs of the Dominican Republic*. Westport, CT: Greenwood Press, 1999.

Brown, Lloyd W. *West Indian Poetry*. Boston: Twayne, 1978.

Brown, Stewart, ed. *All Are Involved: The Art of Martin Carter*. Leeds, England: Peepal Tree Press, 2000.

Brú, José, ed. *Acercamientos a Cintio Vitier*. Guadalajara, Jalisco, México: Universidad de Guadalajara, Centro Universitario de Ciencias Sociales y Humanidades, 2002.

Bueno, Salvador. *Acerca de Plácido*. Habana: Editorial Letras Cubanas, 1985.

Buesa, José Angel. *Año bisiesto: autobiografía informal*. Santo Domingo, República Dominicana: Universidad Nacional Pedro Henríquez Ureña, 1981.

Buhle, P. *CLR James: The Artist as Revolutionary*. London: Verso, 1982.

Burgos, Julia de. *Obra poética*. San Juan: Instituto de Cultura, 1961.

Butts, Ellen, and Joyce R. Schwartz. *Fidel Castro*. Minneapolis, MN: Lerner Publications, 2005.

Caballero Wangüemert, María M. *La narrativa de René Marqués*. Santurce: Editorial Playor, 1986.

Cabral, Manuel del. *10 poetas dominicanos: tres poetas con vida y siete desenterrados*. Santo Domingo, República Dominicana: Publicaciones América, S.A., 1980.

Cabrera, Francisco Manrique. *Historia de la literatura puertorriqueña*. Río Piedras, Puerto Rico: Ediciones Cultural, 1979.

Cabrera de Ibarra, Palmira. *Luis Lloréns Torres: ante el paisaje*. San Juan, Puerto Rico: Editorial Yaurel, 1990.

Cadilla de Martínez, M. *Semblanzas de un carácter (Apuntes biográficos de Lola Rodríguez de Tió)*. San Juan, Puerto Rico: 1936.

Callahan, Lance. *In the Shadows of Divine Perfection: Derek Walcott's Omeros*. New York: Routledge, 2003.

Cámara, Madeline. *Vocación de Casandra: poesía femenina cubana subversiva en María Elena Cruz Varela*. New York: Lang, 2001.

Campbell, George. *First Poems*. Kingston: City Printery Ltd., 1945.

Campbell, Elaine. Introduction. *The Orchid House*, by Phyllis Shand Allfrey. London: Virago Press, 1982.

Campbell, Elaine, and Pierrette Frickey. *The Whistling Bird: Women Writers of the Caribbean*. Kingston, Jamaica: I. Randle, 1998.

Canales, Nemesio R. *Obras completas*. Ed. Servando Montaña Peláez. San Juan, Puerto Rico: Ediciones Puerto, 1992.

Cañas, Dionisio. *El poeta y la ciudad: Nueva York y los escritores hispanos*. Madrid: Cátedra, 1994.

Cancel, Mario R. *Segundo Ruíz Belvis: el procer y el ser humano (una aproximación crítica a su vida)*. Bayamón, Puerto Rico: Editorial Universidad de América; San Juan: Centro de Estudios Avanzados de Puerto Rico y el Caribe; Hormigueros, Puerto Rico: Municipio de Hormigueros, 1994.

Canizares, Raul. *Cuban Santeria: Walking with the Night*. Rochester, VT: Destiny Books, 1999.

Capetillo, Luisa. *Amor y anarquía: los escritos de Luisa Capetillo*. Edited by Julio Ramos. Río Piedras, Puerto Rico: Ediciones Huracán, 1992.

Capote, María. *Agustín Acosta: el modernista y su isla*. Miami: Ediciones Universal 1990.

Carbado, Devon W., et al., eds. *Black Like Us: A Century of Lesbian, Gay and Bisexual African American Fiction*. San Francisco: Cleis Press, 2002.

Cardwell, Richard, and Bernand McGuirk. *¿Que es el modernismo? Nueva encuesta, nuevas lecturas*. Boulder, CO: Society of Spanish and Spanish-American Studies, 1993.

Carilla, Emilio. *Pedro Henríquez Ureña: signo de América*. Washington, DC: Inter-American Council for Integral Development (CIDI), 1997.

Carnegie, Charles V. *Postnationalism Prefigured: Caribbean Borderlands*. New Brunswick: Rutgers University Press, 2002.

Carpentier, Alejo. *Cuentos completos*. 3rd ed. Barcelona: Bruguera, 1980.

Carpentier, Alejo. *Los pasos perdidos*. Edited by Roberto González Echevarria. Madrid: Ediciones Cátedra, 1985.

Carpentier, Alejo. *The Lost Steps*. Translated by Harriet de Onís. New York: Knopf, 1967.

Cartaya Cotta, Perla. *José de la Luz y Caballero y la pedagogía de su época*. Habana: Editorial de Ciencias Sociales, 1989.

Carter, Martin. *Poems of Succession*. London: New Beacon Books, 1977.

Casal, Lourdes, ed. *El caso Padilla; literatura y revolución en Cuba; documentos. Introd., selección, notas, guía y bibliografía*. Miami, FL: Ediciones Universal, 1971.

Casal, Lourdes. *Itinerario ideológico: antología*. Miami, FL: Instituto de Estudios Cubanos, 1982.

Casanova-Marengo, Ilia. *El intersticio de la colonia: ruptura y mediación en la narrativa antiesclavista cubana*. Madrid: Iberoamericana; Frankfurt am Main: Vervuert, 2002.

Casey, Calvert. *Calvert Casey: The Collected Stories*. Translated by John H. R. Polt and edited by Ilan Stavans. Durham, NC: Duke University Press, 1998.

Castañeda Salamanca, Felipe. *El indio, entre el bárbaro y el cristiano: ensayos sobre filosofía de la conquista en Las Casas, Sepúlveda y Acosta*. Bogotá, Colombia: Ediciones Uniandes, Departamento de Filosofía: Alfa-omega Colombiana, 2002.

Castellanos, Jorge. *Pioneros de la etnografía afrocubana: Fernando Ortiz, Rómulo Lachatañeré, Lydia Cabrera*. Miami, FL: Ediciones Universal, 2003.

Castillo Vega, Marcia. *Catálogo de los documentos manuscritos de Camila Henríquez Ureña*. Santo Domingo, República Dominicana: Publicaciones ONAP, 1994.

Castro, Fidel. *Palabras a los intelectuales*. Habana: Ediciones del Consejo Nacional de Cultura, 1961.

Castro Burdiez, Tomás. *La Generación del 48 en el ensayo*. Universitaria, Santo Domingo, República Dominicana: Editora Universitaria UASD, 1998.

Cautiño Jordán, Eduardo. *La personalidad literaria de Francisco Lluch Mora*. San Juan, Puerto Rico: Ateneo Puertorriqueño, Ediciones Mairena, 1994.

Cazurro García de Quintana, Carmen. *Medio siglo de periodismo humorístico-satírico: el humor como fórmula artística de significación en el periodismo de Manuel Méndez Ballester.* San Germán, Puerto Rico: Universidad Interamericana de Puerto Rico, 1993.

Cella, Susana. *El saber poético: la poesía de José Lezama Lima.* Buenos Aires: Nueva Generación, Facultad de Filosofía y Letras, 2003.

Celorio, Gonzalo. *El surrealismo y lo real-maravilloso.* México, México: Secretaría de Educación Pública, Dirección General de Divulgación, 1976.

Césaire, Aimé. *Cahier d'un retour u pays natal.* Paris: Présence africaine, 1951.

———. *Notebook of a Return to My Native Land/Cahier d'un retour u pays natal.* Translated by Mireille Rosello with Annie Pritchard. Newcastle upon Tyne, England: Bloodaxe Books, 1995.

———. *Une tempête; d'après "La tempête" de Shakespeare. Adaptation pour un théâtre nègre.* Paris: Éditions du Seuil, 1969.

César, Sylvie. *La Rue Cases-Nègres: du roman au film: étude comparative* Paris: L'Harmattan, 1994.

Céspedes, Diógenes. *Antología del cuento dominicano.* Santo Domingo, República Dominicana: Editora de Colores, 1996.

Céspedes, Carlos Manuel de. *Pasión por Cuba y por la iglesia: aproximación biográfica al P. Félix Varela.* Madrid: Biblioteca de Autores Cristianos, 1998.

Céspedes, Diógenes. *Antología del cuento dominicano.* Santo Domingo, República Dominicana: Editora de Colores, 1996.

Chamberlin, J. Edward. *Come Back to Me My Language: Poetry and the West Indies.* Chicago: University of Illinois Press, 1993.

Chancé, Dominique. *L'Auteur en souffrance.* Paris: Presses Universitaires de France, 2000.

Chancy, Myriam J. A. *Framing Silence: Revolutionary Novels by Haitian Women.* New Brunswick, NJ: Rutgers University Press, 1997.

Chancy, Myriam J. *Searching for Safe Spaces: Afro-Caribbean Women Writers in Exile.* Philadelphia: Temple University Press, 1997.

Chang, Victor L., ed. *Three Caribbean Poets on Their Work.* Mona, Jamaica: Institute of Caribbean Studies, 1993.

Charles, Christophe. *La poésie féminine haitienne: histoire et anthologie de Virginie Sampeur á nous jours.* Port-au-Prince, Haiti: Editions Choucoune, 1980.

Chauvet, Marie. *Dance on the Volcano.* Translated by Salvator Attanasio. New York: William Sloane, 1959.

Chauvet, Marie (Vieux). *Amour, Colère et Folie.* Paris: Gallimard, 1968.

———. *Fille d'Haïti.* Paris: Fasquelle, 1954.

———. *Fonds des Nègres.* Port-au-Prince, Haiti: H. Deschamps, 1960.

Chávez Rodríguez, Justo A. *Del ideario pedagógico de José de la Luz y Caballero (1800–1862).* Habana: Editorial Pueblo y Educación, 1992.

Chow, Rey. *Writing Diaspora, Tactics of Intervention in Contemporary Cultural Studies.* Bloomington: Indiana University Press, 1993.

Christiani, Joan. *A. J. Seymour: A Bibliography.* Georgetown, Guyana: National Library, 1974.

Ciarlo, Héctor Oscar. *El escritor y su obra: al encuentro de Concha Meléndez y otros ensayos.* Río Piedras: Editorial de la Universidad de Puerto Rico, 1982.

Cimarosti, Robert. *Mapping Memory: An Itinerary Through Derek Walcott's Poetics.* Milan: Cisalpino, 2004.

Clemencia, Joceline A. *Het grote camouflagespel van de OPI.* Leiden: KITLV-Caraf, 1989.

Cocco de Filippis, Daisy. *Combatidas, combativas y combatientes, antología de cuentos escritos por dominicanas.* Santo Domingo, República Dominicana: Taller, 1992.

———. *Documents of Dissidence: Selected Writings of Dominican Women.* New York: CUNY Dominican Studies Institute, 2000.

———, ed. *Madres, maestras y militantes dominicanas.* Santo Domingo, República Dominicana: Búho, 2001.

———. *Para que no se olviden: The Lives of Women in Dominican History.* New York: Ediciones Alcance, 2000.

———. *Poems of Exile and Other Concerns/Poemas del exilio y de otras inquietudes.* New York: Alcance, 1988.

———. *Sin otro profeta que su canto, antología de poesía escrita por Dominicanas.* Santo Domingo, República Dominicana: Taller, 1988.

———. *Tertuliando/Hanging Out, Dominicanas & Friends.* Santo Domingo, República Dominicana: Comisión Permanente de la Feria del Libro Dominicano, 1997.

———. *The Women of Hispaniola, Moving Towards Tomorrow.* New York: York College, Executive Report No. 1, 1993.

Coll y Toste, Cayetano. *Folk Legends of Puerto Rico.* Translated by Cayetano Coll y Toste, José L. Vivas, Ulises Cadilla. Trans Caribbean Airways, n.d.

Collins, Patricia Hill. *Black Feminist Thought: Knowledge, Consciousness, and the Politics of Empowerment.* 2nd edition. New York: Routledge, 2000.

Collymore, Frank A. *Collected Poems.* Bridgetown, Barbados: Advocate Co., 1959.

———. *The Man Who Loved Attending Funerals and Other Stories.* Oxford: Heinemann International Literature and Textbooks, 1993.

Colón, Jesús. *The Way It Was and Other Sketches.* Houston, TX: Arte Público Press, 1993.

Colville, Georgiana M. M. *Contemporary Women Writing in the Other Americas.* Lewiston, NY: E. Mellen, 1990.

Commissiong, Barbara. *Mind Me Good Now.* Toronto: Annick Press, 1997.

Conde, Mary, and Thorunn Lonsdale, eds. *Caribbean Women Writers: Fiction in English.* New York: St. Martin's Press, 1999.

Condé, Maryse. *La Parole des Femmes: essai sur des romancières des Antilles de langue française.* Paris: L'Harmattan, 1979.

Cook, Mercer, ed. *An Introduction to Haiti.* Washington, DC: Pan-American Union, Department of Cultural Affairs, 1951.

Cooper, Carolyn. *Noises in the Blood: Orality, Gender, and the "Vulgar" Body of Jamaican Popular Culture.* Durham, NC: Duke University Press, 1995.

Cooper. Wayne F. *The Passion of Claude McKay: Selected Poetry and Prose, 1912–1948.* New York: Shockden Books, 1973.

Córdova, Federico. *Luis Victoriano Betancourt (1843–1885) Discurso leído por el académico de número dr. Federico de Córdova en la sesión solemne celebrada el 7 de mayo de 1943, en conmemoración del primer centenario del nacimiento de Luis Victoriano Betancourt.* Habana: Imprenta "El Siglo XX," A. Muñiz y hno., 1943.

Córdova Landrón, Arturo. *Salvador Brau; su vida, su obra, su época; ensayo histórico, biográfico, crítico.* San Juan: Editorial Universitaria, Universidad de Puerto Rico, 1949.

Corominas, Joan. *Diccionario crítico etimológico de la lengua castellana.* Vol. 1: A–C. Madrid: Editorial Gredos, 1954.

Cortés, Eladio, and Mirta, Barrea-Marlys. *Encyclopedia of Latin America Theater.* Westport, CT: Greenwood Press, 2003.

Corzani, Jack. *Splendeur et misère: l'exotisme littéraire aux Antilles.* Point-a-Pitre, Guadeloupe, 1969.

Cottenet-Hage, M., and J.-P. Imbert, eds. *Parallèles: Anthologie de la nouvelle féminine de langue française.* Quebec: L'Instant Même, 1996.

Coulthard, G. R. *Race and Colour in Caribbean Literature.* New York: Oxford University Press, 1962.

Craig, Karl. *Emmanuel and His Parrot.* London: Oxford University Press, 1970.

Crassweller, Robert D. *Trujillo: The Life and Times of a Caribbean Dictator.* New York: Macmillan, 1966.

Crosta, Suzanne. *Récits de vie de l'Afrique et des Antilles: Enracinement, Errance, Exil.* Sainte-Foy, Québec: GRELCA, 1998.

Cuaderno de homenaje a don Miguel Meléndez Muñoz. San Juan, Departamento de Instrucción Pública, Estado Libre Asociado de Puerto Rico, 1957.

Cuba en la mano. Habana: Ucar, García y CIA, 1940.

Cudjoe, Selwyn R. *Caribbean Women Writers: Essays from the First International Conference.* Wellesley, MA: Calaloux Publications, 1990.

Cudjoe, S. R., and W. E. Cain. *CLR James: His Intellectual Legacies.* Amherst, MA: University of Massachusetts Press, 1995.

Cuentos Modernos: Antología. Río Piedras, Puerto Rico: Editorial Edil, 1975.

Cuevas, Julio. *Visión crítica en torno a la poesía de Víctor Villegas: ensayo.* Santo Domingo, República Dominicana: Biblioteca Nacional, 1985.

Cuevas Zequeira, Sergio. *Manuel de Zequeira y Arango y los albores de la cultura cubana.* Habana: "Tipografía Moderna" de A. Dombecker, 1923.

Cullum, Linda, ed. *Contemporary American Ethnic Poets: Lives, Works, Sources.* Westport, CT: Greenwood Press, 2004.

Cummings, Pat. *Ananse and the Lizard: A West African Tale.* NY: Holt, and 2002.

Cuza Malé, Belkis. *El clavel y la rosa: biografía de Juana Borrero.* Madrid: Ediciones Cultura Hispánica, 1984.

Dance, Daryl Cumber. ed. *Fifty Caribbean Writers: A Bio-Bibliographical-Critical Sourcebook.* Westport, CT: Greenwood Press, 1986.

Dance, Daryl Cumber. *New World Adams: Conversations with Contemporary West Indian Writers.* Yorkshire, England: Peepal Tree Press, 1984, 1992.

Danticat, Edwidge. *Breath, Eyes, Memory.* New York: Random House, 1994.

———. *The Farming of Bones.* New York: Soho Press, 1998.

Darbouze, Gilbert. *Dégénérescence et régénérescence dans l'oeuvre d'Émile Zola et celle de Manuel Zeno Gandía: étude compare.* New York: Lang, 1997.

Dash, J. Michael. *Culture and Customs of Haiti.* Westport, CT: Greenwood Press, 2001.

———. *Literature and Ideology in Haiti, 1915–1961.* London: Macmillan, 1981.

———. *The Other America: Caribbean Literature in a New World Context.* Charlottesville: University Press of Virginia, 1998.

Dathorne, O.R., ed. *Caribbean Narrative: An Anthology of West Indian Writing.* London: Heinemann Educational Books, 1966, 1973.

Davies, Catherine. *A Place in the Sun? Women Writers in Twentieth-Century Cuba.* London: Zed Books Limited, 1997.

Dayan, Joan. *Haiti, History, and the Gods*. Berkeley, Los Angeles: University of California Press, 1995.

Dayan, Joan. *Introduction to Caribbean Francophone Writing: Guadeloupe and Martinique*. New York: Berg, 1999.

Dawes, Kwame. *Talk Yuh Talk: Interviews with Anglophone Caribbean Poets*. Charlottesville: University Press of Virginia, 2001.

D'Costa, Jean. *Escape to Last Man Peak*. Kingston, Jamaica: Longman, 1980.

Decosta-Willis, Miriam, ed. *Singular Like a Bird: The Art of Nancy Morejón*. Washington, DC: Howard University Press, 1999.

DeJean, Joan, and Nancy K. Miller, eds., *Displacements: Women, Traidition, Literatures in French*. Baltimore, MD: Johns Hopkins University Press, 1991.

DeLamotte, Eugenia C. *Places of Silence, Journeys of Freedom: The Fiction of Paule Marshall*. Philadelphia: University of Pennsylvania Press, 1998.

De Veaux, Alexis. *Warrior Poet: A biography of Audre Lorde*. New York: Norton, 2004.

Déita [Mercédes Foucard Guignard]. *La Légende des loa du vodou haïtien*. Port-au-Prince: Bibliothèque Nationale d'Haïti, 1993.

Denniston, Dorothy Hamer. *The Fiction of Paule Marshall: Reconstructions of History, Culture, and Gender*. Knoxville: University of Tennessee Press, 1995.

Desnoes, Edmundo. *Los dispositivos en la flor, Cuba: Literatura desde la revolución*. Hanover, NH: Ediciones del Norte, 1981.

Díaz de Olano, Carmen R. *Félix Matos Bernier, su vida y su obra*. San Juan, Puerto Rico: Biblioteca de Autores Puertorriqueños, 1956, 1955.

Díaz Quiñones, Arcadio. *Conversación con José Luis González*. Santa Rita, Río Piedras, Puerto Rico: Ediciones Huracán, 1977.

Dick, Bruce Allen. *A Poet's Truth: Conversations with Latino/Latina Poets*. Tucson: University of Arizona Press, 2003.

Dominique, Max. *Esquisses critiques*. Port-au-Prince, Haiti: Editions Mémoire; Montréal: Editions du CIDIHCA, 1999.

Donnell, Alison, and Sarah Lawson Welsh, eds. *The Routledge Reader in Caribbean Literature*. New York: Routledge, 1996.

Donovan, Sandra. *Marcus Garvey*. Chicago: Raintree, 2003.

Dorsinville, Roger. *Jacques Roumain*. Paris: Présence africaine, 1981.

Dorta, Walfrido. *Gastón Baquero: el testigo y su lámpara: para un relato de la poesía como conocimiento en Gastón Baquero*. Habana: Ediciones Unión, 2001.

Dumas, Pierre-Raymond. *Frédéric Marcelin, économiste, ou, Les riches dépouilles d'u ministre des finances: essai*. Port-au-Prince, Haïti: Imprimeur II, 2000.

————. *Panorama de la litterature haïtienne de la diaspora*. Tome. II. Port-au-Prince, Haiti: Promobank, 1996.

Durrant, Sam. *Postcolonial Narrative and the Work of Mourning: J. M. Coetzee, Wilson Harris, and Toni Morrison*. Albany: State University of New York Press, 2004.

Edmondson, Belinda J. *Caribbean Romances: The Politics of Regional Representation*. Charlottesville: University Press of Virginia, 1999.

Emenyonu, Ernest, and Charles E. Nnolim, eds. *Current Trends in Literature and Language Studies in West Africa*. Ibadan, Nigeria: Kraft Books Limited, 1994.

Enciclopedia Ilustrada de la República Dominicana. Santo Domingo, República Dominicana: Eduprogreso, S.A., 2003.

Equiano, Olaudah. *The Interesting Narrative and Other Writings*. Edited with an introduction and notes by Vincent Carretta. New York: Penguin Books, 2003.

———. *The Life of Olaudah Equiano or Gustavus Vassa, the African*, 1789. In two volumes with a new introduction by Paul Edwards. London: Dawsons of Pall Mall, 1969.

Espinosa Domínguez, Carlos, ed. *Teatro cubano contemporáneo: Antología*. Madrid: Fondo de Cultura Económica, 1992.

Esquenazi-Mayo, Roberto. *A Survey of Cuban Revistas, 1902–1958*. Washington, DC: Library of Congress, 1993.

Esteves, Carmen C., and Lizabeth Paravisini-Gebert, eds. *Green Cane and Juicy Flotsam: Short Stories by Caribbean Women*. New Brunswick, NJ: Rutgers University Press, 1991.

Falcón, Rafael. *La emigración puertorriqueña a Nueva York en los cuentos de José Luis González, Pedro Juan Soto y José Luis Vivas Maldonado*. New York: Senda Nueva de Ediciones, 1984.

Familia Henríquez Ureña. *Epistolario*. Santo Domingo, República Dominicana: Publicación de la Secretaría de Educación, Bellas Artes y Cultos, 1995.

Fanon, Frantz. *Black Skin, White Masks*. New York: Grove Press, 1967.

———. *Peau noire, masques blancs*. Paris: Editions Du Seuil, 1952.

———. *Toward the African Revolution*. Translated by Haakon Chevalier. New York: Grove Press, 1969.

Febles, Jorge M. Matías Montes, and Armando, González-Pérez. *Huidobro: acercamientos a su obra literaria*. Lewiston, NY: E. Mellen Press, 1997.

Feder, Lillian. *Naipaul's Truth: The Making of a Writer*. Lanham, MD: Rowman and Littlefield Publishers, 2001.

Fenwick, M. J. ed. *Sisters of Caliban: Contemporary Women Writers of the Caribbean: A Multicultural Anthology*. Falls Church, VA: Azul Editions, 1996.

Ferdinand, Joseph. *Regnor C. Bernard au naturel: sa vie, son oeuvre (de la perspectiva de l'exil)*. Montreal: Editions du CIDIHCA, 2000.

Fernández, Roberta. *In Other Words, Literature by Latinas in the U.S.* Houston, TX: Arte Público Press, 1994.

Fernandez, Ronald, et al., eds. *Puerto Rico: Past and Present: An Encyclopedia*. Westport, CT: Greenwood Press, 1998.

Fernández de la Torriente, Gastón, ed. *La Narrativa de Carlos Alberto Montaner: estudios sobre la nueva literatura hispanoamericana*. Madrid: Cupsa, 1978.

Fernández Méndez, Eugenio, ed. *Homenaje a don Salvador Tió Montes de Oca: humanista y patriota*. San Juan, Puerto Rico: Academia Puertorriqueña de la Lengua Española, 1991.

———. *Luis Muñoz Rivera, hombre visible*. San Juan, Puerto Rico: Biblioteca de Autores Puertorriqueños, 1982.

Fernández Moreno, César, et al., eds. *Latin America in Its Literature*. Translated by Mary G. Berg. Schulman, NY: Holmes and Meir, 1980.

Fernández Pequeño, José. *Espíritu de las islas*. Buenos Aires: Santillana, 2003.

Fernández Retamar, Roberto. *Caliban and Other Essays*. Translated by Edward Baker. Minneapolis: University of Minnesota Press, 1989.

———. *Calibán y otros ensayos: nuestra América y el mundo*. Habana: Editorial Arte y Literatura, 1979.

Ferré, Rosario. *Eccentric Neighborhoods*. New York: Farrar, Straus and Giroux, 1998.

Ferrer Canales, José. *Martí y Hostos*. Río Piedras: Instituto de Estudios Hostosianos, Universidad de Puerto Rico, San Juan: Centro de Estudios Avanzados de Puerto Rico y el Caribe, 1990.

Figueroa de Cifredo, Patria. *Apuntes biográficos en torno a la vida y obra de Cesáreo Rosa-Nieves*. San Juan, Puerto Rico: Editorial Cordillera, 1965.

Fisher, Jerilyn, and Ellen S. Silber, eds. *Women in Literature: Reading Through the Lens of Gender*. Westport, CT: Greenwood Press, 2003.

Fister, Barbara. *Third World Women's Literature: A Dictionary and Guide to Materials in English*. Westport, CT: Greenwood Press, 1995.

Flax, Hjalmar. *Abrazos partidos y otros poemas*. San Juan, Puerto Rico: Editorial Plaza Mayor, 2003.

Flores, Ángel, ed. *Spanish American Authors: The Twentieth Century*. New York: Wilson, 1992.

Flores, Juan. *The Insular Vision: Pedreira's Interpretation of Puerto Rican Culture*. New York: CUNY, Centro de Estudios Puertorriqueños, 1978.

Foner, Philip S., ed. *José Martí, Major Poems: A Bilingual Edition*. Translated by Elinor Randall. New York: Holmes and Meier Publishers, 1982.

Font, María Cecilia. *Mito y realidad en Alejo Carpentier: aproximaciones a Viaje a la semilla*. Buenos Aires: Editorial R. Alonso, 1984.

Foster, David William, and Daniel Altamiranda, eds. *From Romanticism to Modernismo in Latin America*. New York: Garland, 1997.

Foster, David William, ed. *Handbook of Latin American Literature*. New York: Garland, 1992.

Foster, Peter. *Family Spirits: The Bacardi Saga*. Toronto: McFarlane Walter and Ross, 1990.

Fountain, Anne. *José Martí and U.S. Writers*. Gainesville: University Press of Florida, 2003.

Fowler, Carolyn. *Philippe Thoby-Marcelin, écrivain haïtien, et Pierre Marcelin, romancier haïtien*. Atlanta, GA: Hakim's Book Store, 1985.

Friol, Roberto. *Suite para Juan Francisco Manzano*. Habana: Editorial Arte y Literatura, 1977.

Fromm, Georg H. *César Andreu Iglesias: aproximación a su vida y obra*. Río Piedras, Puerto Rico: Ediciones Huracán, 1977.

Galván, Manuel de Jesús. *Enriquillo: leyenda histórica dominicana, 1503–1533*. Santo Domingo, República Dominicana: Ediciones de la Fundación Corripio, 1990.

García, Cristina. *Dreaming in Cuban*. New York: Knopf, 1992.

García, Gustavo V. *La literatura testimonial latinoamericana: (Re) presentación y (auto) construcción del sujeto subalterno*. Madrid: Editorial Pliegos, 2003.

García Alzota, Ernesto. *Acerca de Manuel Cofiño*. Habana: Editorial Letras Cubanas, 1989.

García Cuevas, Eugenio de J. *Juan Bosch: novela, historia y sociedad*. San Juan, Puerto Rico: Isla Negra, 1995.

Garrandes, Alberto. *Tres cuentistas cubanos*. Habana: Editorial Letras Cubanas, 1993.

Garret, Naomi M. *The Renaissance of Haitian Poetry*. Paris: Présence africaine, 1963.

Garrido Pallardó, Fernando. *Los orígenes del romanticismo*. Barcelona: Editorial Labor, 1968.

Gates, Henry Louis, Jr., and William L. Andrews, eds. *Pioneers of the Black Atlantic: Five Slave Narratives from the Enlightment, 1772–1815*. Washington, DC: Counterpoint, 1998.

Gates, Henry Louis, Jr., ed. *Reading Black, Reading Feminist: A Critical Anthology*. New York: Meridian Books 1990.

Gates, Henry Louis, Jr., and Charles T. Davis, eds. *The Slave's Narrative*. New York: Oxford University Press, 1985

Gerón, Cándido. *Hacia una interpretación de la poesía de Joaquín Balaguer*. Santo Domingo, Dominicana Republic: C. Gerón, 1991.

Gerónimo, Joaquín. *En el nombre de Bosch*. Santo Domingo, Dominican Republic: Editora Alfa Omega, 2001.

Gil López, Ernesto. *Guillermo Cabrera Infante: La Habana, el lenguaje y la cineomatofía*. Tenerife, Spain: ACT, Cabildo Insular de Tenerife, 1991.

Gilkes, Michael. *The West Indian Novel*. Boston: Twayne: 1981.

Girón, Socorro. *Bonafoux y su época*. Ponce, Puerto Rico: S. Girón, 1987.

———. *Vida y obra de José Gautier Benítez*. San Juan, Puerto Rico: Instituto de Cultura Puertorriqueña, 1980.

Glad, John. *Literature in Exile*. Durham NC: Duke University Press, 1990.

Glissant, Edouard. *Caribbean Discourse: Selected Essays*. Translated by J. Michael Dash. Charlottesville: Caraf Books; University Press of Virginia, 1989.

Gomes, Albert. *Through a Maze of Colour*. Port of Spain, Trinidad: Key Caribbean Publications, 1974.

González, José Emilio. *Poesía y lengua en la obra de Francisco Manrique Cabrera*. Río Piedras, Puerto Rico: Editorial Cultural, 1976.

González, Rubén. *La historia puertorriqueña de Rodríguez Juliá*. San Juan: Editorial de la Universidad de Puerto Rico, 1997.

González Castro, Vicente. *Cinco noches con Carilda*. Habana: Editorial Letras Cubanas, 1997.

González Echevarría, Roberto. *Alejo Carpentier. The Pilgrim at Home*. Ithaca, NY: Cornell University Press, 1977; 2nd ed. Austin: University of Texas Press, 1990.

González Echevarría, Roberto, and Enrique Pupo-Walker, eds. *The Cambridge History of Latin America*. Vol. 1, Discovery to Modernism. New York: Cambridge University Press, 1996.

González Torres Rafael A. *La obra poética de Félix Franco Oppenheimer*. Río Piedras: Editorial Universitaria de Puerto Rico, 1981.

———. *Un hombre se ha puesto de pie*. Río Piedras: Editorial Universitaria de Puerto Rico, 1981.

Goulbourne, Jean. *Freedom Come*. Kingston, Jamaica: Carlong Publishers, 2003.

Gouraige, Ghislain. *Histoire de la littérature de haïtienne, de l'indépendance à nos jours*. Geneva: Slatkine Reprints, 2003.

Gran enciclopedia de PuertoRico, La: Educación, fauna, economía. San Juan, Puerto Rico: Puerto en la Mano, La Gran Enciclopedia de Puerto Rico, Inc. 1976.

Grimshaw, A., ed. *The CLR James Reader*. Oxford, England: Blackwell, 1992.

Guillén, Nicolás. *Obra poética, 2 vols*. Habana: Unión de Escritores y Artistas de Cuba, 1982.

Guirao, Ramón, ed. *Órbita de la poesía afrocubana, 1928–37 (antología)*. Habana: Talleres de Ucar, García y cía., 1938.

Gunning, Monica. *Not a Copper Penny in Me House*. Honesdale, PA: Wordsong, 1993.

Gutiérrez, Franklin, ed. *Antología histórica de la poesía dominicana*. New York: Alcance, 1997. Puerto Rico: Editorial de la Universidad de Puerto Rico, 1999.

———. *Diccionario de la literatura dominicana*. Santo Domingo, República Dominicana: Editorial Búho, 2004.

———. *Niveles del imán*. New York: Alcance, 1983.

Gutiérrez, Mariela. *Lydia Cabrera, aproximaciones mítico-simbólicas a su cuentística*. Madrid: 1997.

Gutiérrez Richaud, Cristina. *Las fronteras del erotismo y otros ensayos*. Guadalajara, Jalisco, México: Dirección General, Patrimonio Cultural, Secretaría de Cultura, Gobierno de Jalisco, 2000.

Gyssels, Kathleen. *Filles de solitud: essai sur l'identité antillaise dans les (auto-)biographies fictives de Simone et André Schwarz-Bart*. Paris: L'Harmattan, 1996.

Habibe, Henry. *Un herida bida ta. Een verkenning van het poëtisch ouevre va Pierre Lauffer*. Willemstad, Netherlands: Kòrsou, 1994.

Haigh, Sam, ed. *An Introduction to Caribbean Francophone Writing: Guadeloupe and Martinique*. Oxford, New York: Berg, 1999.

Haïti à la une: une anthologie de las presses haïtienne de 1724 à 1934. 6 vols. Compiled by Jean Desquiron. Port-au-Prince, Haiti, 1993–n.d.

Hamner, Robert, ed. *Derek Walcott*. New York: Twayne; Toronto: Maxwell Macmillan Canada; New York: Maxwell Macmillan International, 1993.

Hamner, Robert D. *V. S. Naipaul*. New York: Twayne, 1973.

Hansen, Emmanuel. *Frantz Fanon: Social and Political Thought*. Columbus: Ohio State University Press, 1977.

Harlem Renaissance. 3 vols. Farmington Hills, MI: Thomson Gale, 2003.

Harney, Stefano. *Nationalism and Identity: Culture and the Imagination in a Caribbean Diaspora*. Kingston, Jamaica: University of the West Indies, 1996.

Harris, Wilson. *Palace of the Peacock*. London: Faber and Faber, 1960.

Hartman, Carmen Teresa. *Cabrera Infante's Tres Tristes Tigres: The Trapping Effect of the Signifier over Subject and Text*. New York: Lang, 2003.

Hathaway, Heather. *Caribbean Waves: Relocating Claude McKay and Paule Marshall*. Bloomington: Indiana University Press, 1999.

Hawthorne, Evelyn J. *The Writer in Transition: Roger Mais and the Decolonization of Caribbean Culture*. New York: Lang, 1989.

Heath, Roy A. K. *A Man Come Home*. London: Longmans, 1974.

Henao, Eda B. *The Colonial Subject's Search for Nation, Culture, and Identity in the Works of Julia Alvarez, Rosario Ferré, and Ana Lydia Vega*. Lewiston, NY: E. Mellen Press, 2003.

Henderson, Helene, and Jay P. Pederson, eds. *Twentieth-Century Literary Movements Dictionary*. Detroit, MI: Omnigraphics, Inc.2000.

Henríquez Ureña, Camila. *Estudios y conferencias*. Habana: Instituto Cubano del Libro, 1971.

Henríquez Ureña, Max. *Breve historia del modernismo*. México, México: Fondo de Cultura Económica, 1954.

———. *Panorama histórico de la literatura cubana, Tomo II*. Habana: Editorial Arte y Literatura, 1979.

Herdeck, Donald E. *Caribbean Writers. A Bio-Bibliographical-Critical Encyclopedia*. Washington, DC: Three Continents Press, Inc. 1979.

Hernández, Carmen Dolores. *Puerto Rican Voices in English: Interviews with Writers.* Westport, CT: Praeger, 1997.

Hernández Aquino, Luis, ed. *Betances, poeta.* Bayamón, Puerto Rico: Ediciones Sarobei, 1986.

Hernández González, Heriberto. *Félix Varela: retorno y presencia.* Habana: Imagen Contemporánea, 1997.

Hernández Miyares, Julio E. *Narrativa y libertad: cuentos cubanos de la diáspera.* Miami, FL: Ediciones Universal, 1996.

Hernández Miyares, Julio E., and Perla Rozencvaig, eds. *Reinaldo Arenas: alucinaciones, fantasía, y realidad.* Glenview, IL: Scott, Foresman, 1990.

Hernández, Ramona, et al. *Dominican New Yorkers: A Socioeconomic Profile.* New York: CUNY Dominican Studies Institute, Dominican Research Monograph Series, 1995.

Hill, Errol, and James Hatch. *A History of African American Theatre.* New York: Cambridge University Press, 2003.

Hillman, Richard S., and Thomas J. D'Agostino. *Distant Neighbors in the Caribbean: The Dominican Republic and Jamaica in Comparative Perspective.* Westport, CT: Praeger, 1992.

Hine, Darlene Clark, and Jacqueline McLeod. *Crossing Borders: Comparative History of Black People in Diaspora.* Bloomington and Indianapolis: Indiana University Press, 1999.

Hintz, Suzanne S. *Rosario Ferré: A Search for Identity.* New York: Lang, 1995.

Hirschman, Jack, and Paul Laraque, eds. *Open Gate: An Anthology of Haitian Creole Poetry.* Willimantic, CT: Curbstone Press, 2001.

Hispanic American Almanac: A Reference Work on Hispanics in the United States. Farmington, MI: Thomson Gale, 2003.

Hoffmann, Léon-François. *Bibliographie des etudes litteraires haitienes 1804–1984.* Vanves, France: EDICEF/AUPELF, 1992.

———. *Essays on Haitian Literature.* Washington, DC: Three Continents Press, 1984.

———. *Le Roman haïtien: idéologie et structure.* Sherbrooke, Quebec: Éditions Naaman, 1982.

Hollier, Denis. *A New History of French Literature.* Cambridge MA: Harvard University Press, 1989.

Hoyles, Asher, and Martin Hoyles. *Moving Voices: Black Performance Poetry.* London: Hansib Publications Limited, 2002.

Hughes, Peter. *V.S. Naipaul.* New York: Routledge, 1988.

Incháustegui, Arístides. *Apuntes para la historia del himno nacional dominicano.* SantoDomingo, República Dominicana: Museo Nacional de Historia y Geografía: Asociación Jaycees Dominicana, 1982.

Incháustegui Cabral, Héctor. *El pozo muerto.* Trujillo, República Dominicana: Impr. Librería Dominicana, 1960

Irizarry, Estelle. *Enrique A. Laguerre.* Boston: Twayne, 1982.

Iznaga, Diana. *El estudio de arte negro en Fernando Ortiz.* Habana: Editorial de la Academia de Ciencias de Cuba, 1982.

Jackson, Richard L. *The Black Image in Latin American Literature.* Albuquerque: University of New Mexico Press, 1976.

Jackson, Shirley. *La Novela Negrista en Hispanoamérica.* Madrid: Editorial Pliegos, 1986.

James, CL R. *Minty Alley*. Introduction by Kenneth Ramchand. London: New Beacon Books Ltd., 1971.

———. *Stories from the Caribbean*. Edited by Andrew Salkey. London: Elek Books, 1965.

James, Louis. *Caribbean Literature in English*. New York: Longman, 1999.

James, Louis, ed. *The Islands in Between: Essays on West Indian Literature*. London: Oxford University Press, 1968.

January, Brendan. *Fidel Castro: Cuban Revolutionary*. New York: Franklin Watts, 2003.

Jarrett-Macauley, Delia. *The Life of Una Marson: 1905 to '65*. New York Manchester: University Press, 1998.

Jiménez, Luis, ed. *La voz de la mujer en la literatura hispanoamericana fin-de siglo*. San José, Costa Rica: Editorial de la Universidad de Costa Rica, 1999.

Jiménez Benítez, Adolfo E. *Historia de las revistas literarias puertorriqueñas*. San Juan, Puerto Rico: Ediciones Zoe, 1998.

Joassaint, Erick. Haïti, *Golimin et les autres: une lecture de Justin Lhérisson*. Port-au Prince, Haiti: Presses de l'Impr. Nouvelle,1986.

Jonas, Joyce. *Anancy in the Great House: Ways of Reading West Indian Fiction*. Westport, CT: Greenwood Press, 1990.

Jones, Bridget. *French Caribbean Literature*. Toronto: Black Images, 1975.

Jones, Edward A. *Voices of Negritude*. Valley Forge, PA: Judson Press, 1971.

John, Errol. *Moon on a Rainbow Shawl*. London: Faber and Faber, 1958.

Johnson, Scott. *The Case of the Cuban Poet Heberto Padilla*. New York: Gordon Press, 1977, 1978.

Joseph, Lynn. *Coconut Kind of Day. Island Poems*. New York: Lothrop, Lee and Shepard, 1990.

Kanellos, Nicolás. *Biographical Dictionary of Hispanic Literature in the United States: The Literature of Puerto Ricans, Cuban Americans, and Other Hispanic Writers*. Westport, CT: Greenwood, 1989.

Kanellos, Nicolás, ed. *Herencia: The Anthology of Hispanic Literature of the United States*. New York: Oxford University Press, 2002.

Kanellos, Nicolás. *Hispanic Literature of the United States*. Wesport, CT: Greenwood Press, 2003.

———. *Noche Buena: Hispanic American Christmas Stories*. New York: Oxford University Press, 2000.

———. *Short Fiction by Hispanic Writers of the United States*. Houston, TX: Arte Público Press, 1993.

Keens-Douglas, Richardo. *Freedom Child of the Sea*. Illustrated by Julia Gukova. Toronto: Annick Press, 1995.

Kennedy, Ellen Conroy, ed. *The Negritude Poets: An Anthology of Translations from the French*. New York: Viking, 1975.

Kesteloot, Lilyan. *Black Writers in French*. Translated by Ellen Conroy Kennedy. Philadelphia: Temple University Press, 1974.

———. *Les écrivains noirs de langue française: naissance d'une littérature*. Bruxelles, Belgium: Editions de Sociologie de l'Université Libre de Bruxelles, 1971

Kincaid, Jamaica. *Annie John*. New York: Plume Book, 1983.

King, Bruce Alvin. *Derek Walcott: A Caribbean Life*. New York: Oxford University Press, 2000.

King, Bruce Alvin, ed. *West Indian Literature*. London and Basingstoke: Macmillan Press, 1979.

King, John, ed. *The Cambridge Companion to Modern Latin American Culture*. Cambridge, New York: Cambridge University Press, 2004.

Klein, Leonard S., ed. *Latin American Litature in the 20th Century: A Guide*. New York: Ungar, 1986.

Kurland, Gerald. *Fidel Castro, Communist Dictator of Cuba*. Charlotteville, NY: SamHar Press, 1972.

Lair, Clara. *De la herida a la gloria: la poesía completa de Clara Lair/estudio preliminar de Mercedes López-Baralt*. Carolina, Puerto Rico: Terranova, 2003.

Lalla, Barbara. *Defining Jamaican Fiction: Marronage and the Discourse of Survival*. Tuscaloosa: University of Alabama Press, 1996.

Lamming, George. *Conversations: Essays, Addresses, and Interviews 1953–1990*. Ann Arbor: University of Michigan Press, 2000.

———. *In the Castle of My Skin*. London: Michael Joseph, 1953.

———. *The Pleasures of Exile*. London: Michael Joseph, 1960.

Laraque, Paul. *Fistibal/Slingshot*. Translated by Jack Hirshman. San Francisco: Seaworthy Press; Port-au-Prince, Haiti: Éditions Samba, 1989.

Laraque, Paul, and Jack Hirschman, eds. *Open Gate. An Anthology of Haitian Creole Poetry*. Translations by Jack Hirschman and Boadiba.Willimantic, CT: Curbstone Press, 2001.

Laroche, Maximilien. *La Littérature haïtienne: identité, langue, réalité*. Ottawa, Dntario, Canada: Éditions Leméac, 1981.

El laúd del desterrado. Edited by Matías Montes-Huidobro. Houston, TX: Arte Público Press, 1995.

Laurie, Peter. *Mauby's Big Adventure*. London: McMillan Caribbean, 2000.

Lazer, Hank. *On Louis Simpson: Depths Beyond Happiness*. Ann Arbor: University of Michigan Press, 1988.

Lehmann, Gérard. *Pages retrouvées de Constantin Mayard, poète haïtien*. Saint-Malo, France: Corlet, 2005

Ledent, Bénédicte. *Caryl Phillips*. New York: Manchester University Press, 2002.

León, René. *La poesía negra de José Sánchez Boudy*. Miami, FL: Ediciones Universal, 1977.

Leonard, Irving A. *Baroque Times in Old Mexico*. Ann Arbor: University of Michigan Press, 1959.

Lessac, Frane. *The Little Island*. New York: Harper Collins, 1984.

Levine, George, ed. *Realism and Representation: Essays on the Problem of Realism in Relation to Science, Literature, and Culture*. Madison: University of Wisconsin Press, 1993.

———. *Fragmentos irradiadores*. Habana: Editorial Letras Cubanas, Instituto Cubano del Libro, 1993.

Lezama, Lima, José. *La expresión americana*. México, México: Fondo de Cultura Económica, 1993

———. *Paradiso; novela*. Habana: Unión Nacional de Escritores y Artistas de Cuba, 1966.

Lloyd, Errol. *Many Rivers to Cross*. London: Methuen, 1995.

Lluch Mora, Francisco. *Tres estancias esenciales en la lírica de Hamid Galib: Solemnidadaes, Revoque, Los presagios, 1985–1991*. San Juan, Puerto Rico: Ediciones Mairena, 1991.

Lluch Vélez, Amalia. *Luis Muñoz Marín: poesía, periodismo y revolución, 1915–1930*. Santurce, Puerto Rico: Fundación Luis Muñoz Marín, 1999.

Lockwood, Lee. *Castro's Cuba: Cuba's Fidel; an American Journalist's Inside Look at Today's Cuba in Text and Pictures.* New York: Macmillan, 1967.

Lolo, Eduardo. *Las trampas del tiempo y sus memorias.* Coral Gables, FL: Iberian Studies Institute, North-South Center, University of Miami, 1991.

Loomba, Ania. *Colonialsim/Postcolonialism.* London: Routledge, 1998.

Looker, Mark. *Atlantic Passages: History, Community, and Language in the Fiction of Sam Selvon.* New York: Lang, 1996.

López-Baralt, Mercedes. *El barco en la botella: la poesía de Luis Palés Matos.* San Juan Puerto Rico: Editorial Plaza Mayor, 1997.

López-Baralt, Mercedes, ed. *Literatura puertorriqueña del siglo XX: antología.* San Juan, Puerto Rico: Editorial de la Universidad de Puerto Rico, 2004.

López-Baralt, Mercedes. *Sobre "ínsulas extrañas": el clásico de Pedreira/anotado por Tomás Blanco.* San Juan: Editorial De La Universidad De Puerto Rico, 2000.

López Román, Juan Edgardo. *La obra literaria de Vicente Palés Matos.* Río Piedras: Editorial de la Universidad de Puerto Rico, 1984.

Lorde, Audre. *The New York Head Shop and Museum.* Detroit, MI: Broadside Press, 1974.

———. *Zami: A New Spelling of My Name.* Freedom, CA: Crossing Press, 1982.

Lovelace, E. *Growing in the Dark (Selected Essays).* Edited by Funso Aiyejina. San Juan, Trinidad: LEXICON Trinidad Ltd. 2003.

Loynaz, Dulce María. *Antología lírica.* Madrid: Espasa Calpe, 1993.

Luis, William. *Dance Between Two Cultures: Latino Caribbean Literature Written in the United States.* Nashville Vanderbilt University Press, 1997.

———. *Literary Bondage: Slavery in Cuban Narrative.* Austin: University of Texas Press, 1990.

———. *Lunes de Revolución: Literatura y cultura en los primeros años de la Revolución Cubana.* Madrid: Verbum, 2003.

Macey, David. *Frantz Fanon: A Biography.* London: Granta Books, 2000.

Macpherson, Heidi Slettedahl. *Caribbean Women Writers: Fiction in English.* New York: St. Martin's Press, 1999.

Maes-Jelinek, Hena. *The Naked Design: A Reading of Palace of the Peacock.* Mundelstrump, Denmark: Dangaroo Press, 1976.

Magloire-Saint-Aude, Clément. *Dialogue de mes lampes et autres textes. Oeuvres complètes.* Édition établie et présentéé par François Leperlier. Paris: Jean-Michel Place, 1998.

Mais, Roger. *Brother Man.* Oxford: Heinemann, 1974.

———. *The Three Novels of Roger Mais.* London: Jonathan Cape, 1966, 1970.

Makward, Christiane. *Mayotte Capécia ou L'aliénation selon Fanon.* Paris: Karthala. 1999.

Mañach, Jorge. *Martí, el apóstol.* Habana: Organización Continental de los Festivales Del Libro, 1960.

Manicom, Jacqueline. *La graine; journal d'une sage-femme.* Paris: Presses de la Cité, 1974.

Manley, Edna. *Edna Manley: The diaries.* Edited by Rachel Manley. London: A. Deutsch, 1989.

Mansour, Monica. *La Poesía Negrista.* México, México: Ediciones Era, 1973.

Manzoni, Celina. *Un dilema cubano: nacionalismo y vanguardia.* Habana: Fondo Editorial Casa de las Américas, 2001.

Manzano, Juan Francisco. *Obras.* Habana: Instituto del Libro Cubano, 1972.

Maravall, José Antonio. *Culture of the Baroque: Analysis of a Historical Structure*. Translated Terry Cochran. Foreword by Wlad Godzich and Nicholas Spadaccini. Minneapolis: University of Minnesota Press, 1986.

Markham, E. A., ed. *The Penguin Book of Caribbean Short Stories*. London: Penguin, 1996.

Marqués, René. *La Carreta: drama puertorriqueño*. Río Piedras, Puerto Rico: Editorial Cultural, 1983.

Martí, José. *Versos sencillo: edición del centenario*. Camagüey, Cuba: Ediciones Acana, 1991.

———. *Versos Sencillos/Simple Verses*. Translated by Manuel A. Tellechea. Houston, TX: Arte Público Press, 1997.

Martin, Florence, and Isabelle Favre. *De la Guyane à la diaspora africaine: écrits du silence*. Paris: Karthala, 2002

Martin, Tony. *Marcus Garvey, Hero: A First Biography*. Dover, Ma: 1983.

Martínez, Carlos T. *Grandes dominicanos*. Santo Domingo: Editora Centenario, 2000.

Martínez, E. M. *Lesbian Voices from Latin America*. New York: Garland, 1996.

Martínez, Julio A. ed. *Dictionary of Twentieth-Century Cuban Literature*. Westport, CT: Greenwood Press, 1990.

Martínez Bello, Antonio. *Dos musas cubanas*. Habana: P. Fernández y Cia., 1954.

Martínez Carménate, Urbano. *Nicolás Heredia*. La Habana: Editora Política, 1999.

Martínez Tolentino, Jaime. *Cuentos fantasticos*. Río Piedras, Puerto Rico: Universidad de Puerto Rico, 1983.

Marxuach, Carmen Irene. *Evaristo Ribera Chevremont: voz de vanguardia*. San Juan, Puerto Rico: Centro de Estudios Avanzados de Puerto Rico y el Caribe y La Editorial de la Universidad de Puerto Rico, 1987.

Matibag, Eugenio. *Haitian-Dominican Counterpoint: Nation, Race, and State on Hispaniola*. New York: Palgrave Macmillan, 2003.

McDonald, Ian. *AJS at 70: A Celebration on His 70th Birthday of the Life, Work, and Art of A. J. Seymour*. Georgetown, Guyana: Autoprint, 1984.

McDowell, Robert E. *Bibliography of Literature from Guyana*. Arlington, TX: Sable Pub. Corp., 1975.

McFarlane, J. E. Clare. *A Literature in the Making*. Kingston, Jamaica: Pioneer Press, 1956.

Medina, Pablo. *Exiled Memories: A Cuban Childhood*. Austin, TX: University of Texas Press, 1990.

Medina López, Ramón Felipe. *Hugo Margenat, poeta agónico*. San Juan, Puerto Rico: Ediciones CIBA, 1999.

Mehrotra, Arvind Krishna, ed. *A History of Indian Literature in English*. New York: Columbia University Press, 2003.

Mejias López, William, ed. *Morada de la palabra: homenaje a Luce y Mercedes López Baralt*. San Juan, Puerto Rico: Editorial de la Universidad de Puerto Rico, 2002.

Meléndes, Joserramón. *Juan Antonio Corretjer, o, La poesía inevitable*. Río Piedras, Puerto Rico: qeAse, 1996.

Meléndez, Concha. *Antología y cartas de sus amigos*. San Juan, Puerto Rico: Editorial Cordillera Editorial de la Universidad de Puerto Rico, 1995.

———. *El arte del cuento en Puerto Rico*. New York: Las Américas Publishing, 1961.

Melon-Degras, Alfred. Preface to *Guyane pour tout dire; Le mal du pays,* by Serge Patient. Paris: Éditions caribéennes, 1980

Mendes, Alfred H. *Black Fauns.* Nendeln, Liechtenstein: Kraus Reprint, 1970. Originally published London: Duckworth, 1935.

Méndez, Roberto. *La dama y el escorpión.* Santiago de Cuba: Editorial Oriente, 2000.

Mendoza, Louis and Shankar, S. *Crossing into America: The New Literature of Immigration.* New York: The New Press, 2003.

Menéndez Y Pelayo, Marcelino. *Historia de la poesía hispano-americana, 2 v.* Madrid: Librería General de Victoriano Suárez, 1911.

Menton, Seymour. *Latin America's New Historical Novel.* Austin: University of Texas Press, 1993.

———. *Prose Fiction of the Cuban Revolution.* Austin, TX: University of Texas Press, 1975.

Meson, Danusia L. *Historia y ficción: el caso "Francisco."* Buenos Aires: Ediciones de la Flor, 1994.

Milian, Alberto. *Sorting Metaphors.* Tallahassee, FL: Anhinga Press, 1983.

Milian, Alberto, Ileana Fuentes-Pérez, and Graciella Cruz-Gaura. *Outside Cuba: Contemporary Cuban Visual Artists.* New Brunswick, NJ: Office of Hispanic Arts, Mason Gross School of the Arts, Rutgers University, 1989.

Miller, Jane Eldridge. *Who's Who in Contemporary Women's Writing.* New York: Routledge, 2001.

Miranda Archilla, Graciany. *Poesía vanguardista: 1929–1988.* San Juan: Editorial de la Universidad de Puerto Rico, 2002.

Mohammed, Patricia. *Gendered Realities: Essays in Caribbean Feminist Thought.* Barbados: University of the West Indies Press; Mona, Jamaica: Centre for Gender and Development Studies, 2002.

Mohr, Eugene V. *The Nuyorican Experience. Literature of the Puerto Rican Minority.* Westport, CT.: Westwood Press, 1982.

Molina, Sintia. *El Naturalismo en la novela cubana.* Lanham, MD: University Press of America, 2001.

Moliner, Israel M. *Indice bio-bibliográfico de Bonifacio Byrne.* Matanzas, Cuba: Atenas de Cuba, 1943.

Monserrat Gámiz, María del Carmen. *Tomás Blanco y "Los vates."* San Juan, Puerto Rico: Instituto de Cultura Puertorriqueña, 1986.

Morales, Jorge Luis. *Poesía Afroantillana y Negrista (Puerto Rico-República Dominicana-Cuba).* Río Piedras: Editorial Universitaria de Puerto Rico, 1981.

Morales Cabrera, Pablo. *Cuentos. Con un estudio biográfico-crítico de Esther Meló Portalatín.* San Juan de Puerto Rico, Instituto de Cultura Puertorriqueña, 1966.

Morán, Francisco. *Casal à Rebours.* Habana: Casa Editora Abril, 1996.

Morejón, Nancy. *Nación y mestizaje en Nicolás Guillén.* Habana: Unión de Escritores y Artistas de Cuba, 1982.

Moreno García, Bárbara. *El recorrido poético de Domingo Moreno Jimenes.* Germany: B. Moreno García, 2001.

Morfi, Angelina. *Historia crítica de un siglo de teatro puertorriqueño.* San Juan, Puerto Rico: Instituto de Cultura Puertorriqueña, 1980.

Moraña, Mabel, ed. *Relecturas del Barroco de Indias.* Hanover, NH: Ediciones del Norte, 1994.

Morisseau-Leroy, Félix. *Dyakout 1, 2, 3, 4.* Jamaica, NY: Haïtiana Publications, Inc., 1990.

Morisseau-Leroy, Félix. *Haitiad & Oddities*. Translated by Jeffrey Knapp, et al. Miami: Pantaléon Guilbaud, 1991.

———. *Kont kreyòl*. Port-au-Prince, Haiti: Imprimerie Le Natal, 2001.

———. *Les Djons d'Aïti Tonma, roman*. Paris: L'Harmattan, 1996.

———. *Teyat kreyòl*. Port-au-Prince, Haiti: Éditions Libète, 1997.

Morúa Delgado, Martín. *Obras Completas de Martín Morúa Delgado, 6 vols*. Habana: Publicaciones de la Comisión Nacional del Centenario del don Martín Morúa Delgado, 1957.

Mujeres como islas. Habana: Ediciones Unión, Santo Domingo: Ediciones FERILIBRO, 2002.

Murdoch, H. Adlai, ed. *Creole Identity in the French Caribbean Novel*. Miami: University of Florida Press, 2001.

Naipaul, V. S. *A House for Mr. Biswas*. New York: McGraw-Hill, 1961.

———. *The Middle Passage: The Caribbean Revisited*. New York: Random House, 1962, 1990.

———. *Reading & Writing: A Personal Account*. New York: New York Review of Books, 2000.

Nair, Supriya. *Caliban's Curse: George Lamming and the Revisioning of History*. Ann Arbor: University of Michigan Press, 1996.

Nasta, Susheila, ed. *Mothertongue: Black Women's Writing from Africa, the Caribbean and South Asia*. London: The Women's Press, 1991.

Naudillon, Françoise. *Jean Métellus*. Paris: L'Harmattan, 1994.

Navarro, Osvaldo, ed. *Órbita de Régino Pedroso*. Habana: Unión de Escritores y Artistas de Cuba, 1975.

Nelson, Emmanuel, ed. *Reworlding: The Literature of the Indian Diaspora*. Westport, CT: Greenwood Press, 1992.

Nicholls, David. *From Dessalines to Duvalier. Race, Colour and National Independence in Haiti*. Rev. ed. New Brunswick, NJ: Rutgers University Press, 1996.

Nofal, Rossana. *La imaginación histórica en la colonia: Carlos de Sigüenza y Góngora* San Miguel de Tucumán, Argentina: Instituto Interdisciplinario de Estudios Latinoamericanos, Facultad de Filosofía-Universidad Nacional de Tucumán, 1996.

Norris, Jerrie. *Presenting Rosa Guy*. Boston: Twayne, 1988.

Nouhaud, Dorita. *Luis Rafael Sánchez: dramaturge, romancier et essayiste porto-ricain*. Paris: L'Harmattan, 2001.

Nueva enciclopedia de Puerto Rico. Hato Rey, Puerto Rico: Editorial Lector, 1994.

Núñez, Ana Rosa, et al., eds. *Homenaje a Eugenio Florit*. Miami, FL: Ediciones Universal, 2000.

O'Connor, Teresa F. *Jean Rhys: The West Indian Novels*. New York: New York University Press, 1986.

Ojeda Reyes, Félix *Peregrinos de la libertad*. Río Piedras, Puerto Rico: Editorial de la Universidad de Puerto Rico, 1992.

Ojo-Ade, Femi. *Léon-Gontran Damas: the Spirit of Resistance*. London: Karnak House, 1993.

———. *René Maran, the Black Frenchman: A Bio-Critical Study*. Washington, DC: Three Continents Press, 1984.

Okpewho, Isidore. *African Oral Literature: Backgrounds, Character, and Continuity*. Bloomington: Indiana University Press, 1992.

Oliver Frau, Antonio. *Cuentos y leyendas del cafetal*. Yauco, Puerto Rico: Tipografía El Eco de Yauco, 1938.

Oliver Labra, Carilda. *Antología de la poesía heroica y cósmica de Carilda Oliver Labra*. Introducción, Salvador Bueno Menéndez; prólogo y análisis arquetípico, Fredo Arias de la Canal. México, México: Frente de Afirmación Hispanista, 2002.

Olivera, Otto. *La literatura en periódicos y revistas de Puerto Rico (siglo XIX)*. Río Piedras, Puerto Rico: Editorial de la Universidad de Puerto Rico, 1987.

Olmos, Margarite Fernandez, and Lizabeth Paravisini-Gebert, eds. *Sacred Possessions: Vodou, Santeria, Obeah, and the Caribbean*. New Bruswick, NJ: Rutgers University Press, 1997.

Ormerod, Beverly. *Center of Remembrance: Memory and Caribbean Women's Literature*. London: Mango Publishing, 2002

———. *An Introduction to Caribbean and Francophone Writing: Guadeloupe and Martinique*. New York: Berg, 1999.

Ortega, Alfonso C., and Alfredo Pérez Alecant. *Celebración de la existencia: Homenaje al poeta cubano Gastón Baquero*. Salamanca, Spain: Universidad Pontificia de Salamanca, 1994.

Ortega-Vélez, Ruth E. *La educación como niveladora social a través de la obra de Enrique A. Laguerre*. Santurce, Puerto Rico: Ediciones Situm, 1995.

Ortiz Cofer, Judith. *Woman in Front of the Sun: On Becoming a Writer*. Athens: University of Georgia Press, 2000.

Padura, Leonardo. *José María Heredia: la patria y la vida*. Habana: Ediciones Unión, 2003.

Paget, Henry, and Paul Buhle. *C.L.R. James's Caribbean*. Durham, NC: Duke University Press, 1992.

Pallás, Rosa. *La poesía de Emilio Ballagas*. Madrid: Playor, 1973.

Palm, Jules Ph. De, and Juian Coco. *Julio Perrenal: Dichters van het Pariamente lied*. Ámsterdam: De Bezige Bij, 1979.

Palma, Marigloria. *Cuentos de la abeja encinta*. Río Piedras: Universidad de Puerto Rico, 1975.

Paquet, Sandra Pouchet. *Caribbean Autobiography: Culture Identity and Self-Representation*. Madison: University of Wisconsin Press, 2002.

Paravisini-Gebert, Lizabeth. *Phyllis Shand Allfrey: A Caribbean Life*. New Brunswick, NJ: Rutgers University Press, 1996.

Patterson, Orlando. *The Children of Sisyphus*. Kingston, Jamaica: Bolivar Press, 1971. Originally published. London: New Authors, Hutchinson, 1964.

———. *Slavery and Social Death: A Comparative Study*. Cambridge, MA: Harvard University Press, 1982.

Patteson, Richard F. *Caribbean Passages: A Critical Perspective on New Fiction from the West Indies*. Boulder, CO: Lynne Rienner Publishers, 1998.

Pedroso, Régino. *Poesía*. Habana: Ediciones Unión, 1996.

Peña de Bordas, Virginia. *Toeya*. Barcelona: Editorial Juventud, 1952.

Pérez, Olga Marta, et al. *Mujeres como islas*. Habana: Ediciones Unión; Santo Domingo, República Dominicana: Ediciones Ferilibro, 2002.

Peña de Bordas, Virginia. *Seis novelas cortas*. Santo Domingo, República Dominicana: Taller, 1978.

———. *Toeya*. Barcelona: Editorial Juventud, 1952.

Pérez del Río, Luis. *¿Es falsa la confesión de Plácido?* Santiago de Cuba: Editorial Oriente, 1994.

Pérez Firmat, Gustavo. *Life on the Hyphen: The Cuban-American Way.* Austin: University of Texas Press, 1994.

———. *Next Year in Cuba.* New York: Anchor Books, 1995.

Pérez León, Roberto. *Tiempo de Ciclón.* Habana: Ediciones Unión, Unión de Escritores y Artistas de Cuba, 1995.

Pérez de Zambrana, Luisa. *Poesías de Luisa Pérez de Zambrana.* Havana: Imprenta "El Siglo XX" de la Sociedad Editorial Cuba Contemporánea, 1920.

Perivolaris, John. *Puerto Rican Cultural Identity and the Work of Luis Rafael Sánchez.* Chapel Hill: University of North Carolina, Department of Romance Languages, 2000.

Perry, Donna. *Backtalk: Women Writers Speak Out.* New Brunswick, NJ: Rutgers University Press, 1993.

Philippe, J. B. *Free Mulatto: An Address to the Right. Hon. Earl Bathurst by a Free Mulatto.* Trinidad and Tobago: Paria Publishing, 1987.

Picón-Salas, Mariano. *De la conquista a la independencia; tres siglos de historia cultural hispanoamericana.* Mexico City: Fondo de Cultura Económica, 1944.

Pierre-Louis, Ulysse. *L'univers poétique de Jean F. Rrierre [sic]: une obsédante quête d'identité.* Port-au-Prince, Haïti: Editions Christophe, 1997.

Pinckney, Darryl. *Out There: Mavericks of Black Literature.* New York: BasicCivitas Books, 2002.

Piña Contreras, Guillermo. *Doce en la literatura dominicana.* Santiago de los Caballeros, Republica Dominicana: Universidad Católica Madre y Maestra, 1982.

Piñero, Miguel, and Miguel Algarín. *Nuyorican Poetry: An Anthology of Puerto Rican Words and Feelings.* New York: Morrow, 1975.

Pollack, Sandra, and Denise D. Knight. *Contemporary Lesbian Writers of the United States.* Westport, CT: Greenwood Press, 1993.

Pompilus, Pradel. *Louis Joseph Janvier par lui-même: le patriote et le champion de la négritude.* Port-au-Prince, Haïti: La Presse évangélique, 1995.

Prada Oropeza, Renato. *Poética y liberación en la narrativa de Onelio Jorge Cardoso: ensayo de interpretación.* Xalapa, Veracruz, México: Centro de Investigaciones Lingüístico-Literarias, Instituto de Investigaciones Humanísticas, Universidad Veracruzana, 1988.

Praeger, Michèle. *The Imaginary Caribbean and Caribbean Imaginary.* Lincoln: University of Nebraska Press, 2003.

Press, Petra. *Fidel Castro: An Unauthorized Biography.* Chicago, IL: Heinemann Library, 2000.

Price-Mars, Jean. *Ainsi parla l'oncle.* Paris: Imp. De Compiègne, 1928.

———. *So Spoke the Uncle.* Translated by Magdaline W. Shannon. Colorado Springs: Three Continents Press, 1994.

Prida, Dolores. *Beautiful Señoritas and Other Plays.* Houston, TX: Arte Público Press, 1991.

Prono, Marta, ed. *Manuel del Cabral y su obra: comentarios y crítica.* Santo Domingo, República Dominicana: Comisión Permanente de la Feria del Libro, 2001.

Publicaciones y opiniones de La Poesía sorprendida. San Pedro de Macorís, República Dominicana: Universidad Central del Este, 1988.

Puebla, Manuel de la, ed. *Historia y significado del atalayismo.* San Juan, Puerto Rico: Ediciones Mairena, 1994.

Quiles Ferrer, Edgar Heriberto. *Teatro puertorriqueño en acción*. San Juan, Puerto Rico: Ateneo Puertorriqueño, 1990.

Rafis, Iris Fawzia. *You of age to see about yourself now! So pull up you socks!: Themes of "bildung" in select novels by West Indian women writers*. Ann Arbor, MI: University Microfilms International, 1996.

Ramchand, Kenneth. *An Introduction to the Study of West Indian Literature*. Kenya and Jamaica: Nelson Caribbean, 1976.

———. *West Indian Narratives: An Introductory Anthology*. London: Nelson, 1966.

Ramírez Mattei, Aida Elsa. *Carmelina Vizcarrondo: vida, obra y antología*. San Juan: Editorial Universitaria, Universidad de Puerto Rico, 1972.

Ramírez Morillo, Belarminio. *Joaquín Balaguer: la escuela del poder: su biografía, su pensamiento, su obra*. Santo Domingo, República Dominicana: Ediciones del Instituto de Formación, 1999.

Ramos Rosado, Marie. *La mujer negra en la literatura puertorriqueña: cuentística de los setenta: Luis Rafael Sánchez, Carmelo Rodríguez Torres, Rosario Ferré y Ana Lydia Vega*. San Juan: Editorial de la Universidad de Puerto Rico, 1999.

Redcam, Tom. *Orange Valley and Other Poems*. Kingston, Jamaica: Pioneer Press, 1951.

Reid, Vic. *The Leopard*. New York: Viking, 1959.

———. *New Day*. New York: Knopf, 1949. Reissued by Chatham Bookseller, Chatam, NJ, 1972.

Renda, Mary A. *Taking Haiti: Military Occupation and the Culture of U.S. Imperialism 1915–1940*. Chapel Hill University of North Carolina Press, 2001.

Rexach, Rosario. *Dos figuras cubanas y una sola actitud: Félix Varela y Morales (Habana, 1788–San Agustín, 1853), Jorge Mañach y Robato (Sagua la Grande, 1898–Puerto Rico, 1961)*. Miami, FL: Ediciones Universal, 1991.

Reynolds, Bonnie Hildebrand. *Space, Time, and Crisis: the Theater of René Marqués*. York, SC: Spanish Literature Pub. Co., 1988.

Rhys, Jean. *Wide Sargasso Sea*. Norton Critical Edition, edited by Judith L. Raiskin. New York, Norton, 1999.

Ribes Tover, Federico. *100 Outstanding Puerto Ricans*. New York: Plus Ultra Educational Publishers, 1976.

Richardson, Bonham C. *Igniting the Caribbean's Past: Fire in British West Indian History*. Chapel Hill: University of North Carolina Press, 2004.

Richardson Michael, ed. *Refusal of the Shadow: Surrealism and the Caribbean*. New York: Verso, 1996.

Rinner, Susanne, and Joëlle Vitiello, eds. *Elles écrivent les Antilles*. Paris: L'Harmattan, 1997.

Ripoll, Carlos. *Conciencia intelectual de América: Antología del ensayo hispanoamericano*. 2nd ed. New York: Eliseo Torres and Sons, 1970.

Rivera, Ángel A. *Eugenio María de Hostos y Alejandro Tapia y Rivera: avatares de una modernidad caribeña*. New York: Lang, 2001.

Rivera, Edward. *Family Installments: Memories of Growing Up Hispanic*. New York: Penguin Books, 1983.

Rivera de Álvarez, Josefina. *Diccionario de literatura puertorriqueña*. Tomo 2. San Juan, Puerto Rico: Editorial del Departamento de Instrucción Pública, 1969.

Rivera Rivera, Modesto. *Manuel A. Alonso: su vida y su obra*. San Juan, Puerto Rico: Editorial Caqui, 1966.

Rivero Marín, Rosanna. *Janus Identities and Forked Tongues: Two Caribbean Writers in the United States.* New York: Lang, 2004.

Rodríguez, Carlos A., ed. *Simposio Clemente Soto Vélez—Simposio Klemente Soto Beles.* San Juan, Puerto Rico: Instituto de Cultura Puertorriqueña, 1990.

Rodríguez, Emilio Jorge. *Literatura caribeña; bojeo y cuaderno de bitácora.* Habana: Editorial Letras Cubanas, 1989.

Rodríguez-Luis, Julio, ed. *Re-Reading José Martí (1853–1895): One Hundred Years Later.* Albany: State University of New York Press, 1999.

Rodríguez Correa, Awilda. *Juan Martínez Capó, crítica literaria: índice bibliográfico.* San Juan, Puerto Rico: Instituto de Cultura Puertorriqueña, 1997.

Rodríguez Monegal, Emir, ed. *The Borzoi Anthology of Latin American Literature.* 2 vols. New York: Knopf, 1977.

Rodríguez Pagán, Juan Antonio. *Julia en blanco y negro.* San Juan, Puerto Rico: Sociedad Histórica de Puerto Rico, 2000.

Rogziński, Jan. *A Brief History of the Caribbean from the Arawak and the Carib to the Presents.* New York: Meridian Books, 1992.

Romeu, Raquel. *Voces de mujeres en las letras cubanas.* Madrid: Editorial Verbum, 2000.

Rosa-Nieves, Cesáreo, ed. *El costumbrismo literario en la prosa de Puerto Rico.* San Juan, Puerto Rico: Editorial Cordillera, 1971.

Rosa-Nieves, Cesáreo. *Del contorno hacia el dintorno; notas sobre el libre de ensayos: Contornos de Félix Franco Oppenheimer.* San Juan, Puerto Rico: Editorial Yaurel, 1961.

———. *Plumas estelares en las letras de Puerto Rico.* Vol. 1. San Juan, Puerto Rico: Ediciones de la Torre, 1967.

Roses, Lorraine Elena. *Voices of the Storyteller (Contributions to the study of world Literature, no. 14).* Westport, CT: Greenwood Press, 1986.

Roumain, Jacques. *Gouverneurs de la rosée.* Fort de France: Éditions Émile Desormeaux, 1977.

———. *Masters of the Dew.* Translated by Langston Hughes and Mercer Cook. Portsmouth, NH: Heinemann International, 1944, 1978.

———. *Works: Ouevres completes: édition critique.* Edited by Léon-François Hoffmann. Paris: Allca XX, 2003.

Ruíz Belvis, Segundo. *Informe sobre la abolición inmediata de la esclavitud en la Isla de Puerto-Rico.* Madrid: Establecimiento Tipográfico de R. Vicente, 1870.

Ruíz del Vizo, Hortensia. *Antología del costumbrismo en Cuba: prosa y verso.* Miami, FL: Ediciones Universal, 1975.

Ruscalleda Bercedóniz, Isabel María. *La cuentística de José Luis Vivas Maldonado.* San Juan, Puerto Rico: Instituto de Cultura Puertorriqueña, 1982.

Ruscalleda Bercedóniz, Jorge María. *La poesía de Manuel Joglar Cacho.* San Juan, Puerto Rico: Editorial Lea, 1998.

Rutgers, Wim. *Beneden en bowen de wind: Literatuur van de Nederlandse Antillen en Araba.* Amsterdam: De Bezige Bij, 1996.

Saakana, Arnon Saba. *Colonization and the Destruction of the Mind: Psychosocial Issues of Race, Class, Religion and Sexuality in the Novels of Roy Heath.* London: Karnak House, 1996.

Sacoto, Antonio. *Siete novelas maestras del boom hispanoamericano.* Quito, Ecuador: Casa de la Cultura Ecuatoriana, 2003.

St. James Guide to Crime and Mystery Writers. Detroit: St. James Press, 1996.

Saínz, Enrique. *La obra poética de Cintio Vitier*. Habana: Ediciones Unión, Unión de Escritores y Artistas de Cuba, 1998.

———. *Silvestre de Balboa y la literatura cubana*. Habana: Editorial Letras Cubanas, 1982.

Saint-Louis, Carlos. *Panorama de la poésie haïtienne*. Port-au-Prince, Haiti: H. Deschamps, 1950.

Saldaña, Exilia. *In the Vortex of the Cyclone: Selected Poems by Excilia Saldaña*. Edited and translated by Flora González Mandri and Rosamond Rosenmeier. Gainesville: University Press of Florida, 2002.

———. *Jícara de miel*. Habana: Gente Nueva, 2000.

———. *Kele Kele*. Habana: Letras Cubanas, 1987.

Salick, Roydon. *The Novels of Samuel Selvon: A Critical Study*. Westport, CT: Greenwood Press, 2001.

Sánchez, Luis Rafael. *Fabulación e ideología en la cuentística de Emilio S. Belaval*. San Juan, Puerto Rico: Instituto de Cultura Puertorriqueña, 1979.

Sánchez, Reinaldo, ed. *Homenaje a Enrique Labrador Ruiz: textos críticos sobre su obra*. Montevideo, Uruguay: Editorial Ciencias, 1981.

Sánchez de Silva, Arlyn. *La novelística de Manuel Zeno Gandía*. San Juan, Puerto Rico: Instituto de Cultura Puertorriqueña, Programa de Publicaciones y Grabaciones, 1996.

Sander, Reinhard W. *The Trinidad Awakening: West Indian Literature of the Nineteen-thirties*. New York: Greenwood Press, 1988.

Sanga, Jaina C. *South Asian Literature in English: An Encyclopedia*. Westport, CT: Greenwood Press, 2004.

Santiago, Esmeralda. *When I Was Puerto Rican*. New York: Random House, 1993.

Santovenia y Echaide, Emeterio Santiago. *José Victoriano Betancourt: estudio biográfico*. Habana: Imp. "La Universal," de Ruiz y Comp., 1912.

Schmidt, Hans. *The United States Occupation of Haiti, 1915–1934*. New Brunswick, NJ: Rutgers University Press, 1971.

Schwarts, Kessel. *A New History of Spanish American Fiction*. Vol. 1: From Colonial Times to the Mexican Revolution and Beyond. Coral Gables, FL: University of Miami Press, 1972.

Secades, Eladio. *Las mejores estampas de Secades*. México, México: Medinas Hermanos, 1969.

Seguin-Cadiche, Daniel. *Vincent Placoly: une explosion dans la cathédrale, ou regards sur l'oeuvre de Vincent Placoly*. Paris: L'Harmattan, 2001.

Sención, Viriato. *Los que falsificaron la firma de Dios*. Santo Domingo, Dominican Republic: Taller, 1991.

Serafin, Steven R., ed. *Encyclopedia of World Literature in the 20th Century*. 4 vols. Detroit: St. James Press, 1999.

Shannon, Magdaline W. *Jean Price-Mars, the Haitian Elite and the American Occupation, 1915–1935*. New York: St. Martin's Press, 1996.

Shapard, Robert, and James Thomas, eds. *Sudden Fiction (Continued): 60 New Short Stories*. New York: Norton, 1996.

Sharpley-Whiting, T. Denean. *Négritude Women*. Minneapolis: University of Minnesota Press, 2002.

Shell, Marc, ed. *American Babel: Literatures of the United States from Abnaki to Zuni.* Cambridge, MA: Harvard University Press, 2002.

Sheppard, Jill. *Marryshow of Grenada: An Introduction.* Barbados, West Indies: Letchworth Press, 1987.

Shepherd, Vincent, and Hilary McD. Becklers, eds. *Caribbean Slavery in the Atlantic World: A Student Reader.* Princeton: Marcus Wiener Publishers, 2000.

Showalter, Elaine, ed. *The New Feminist Criticism: Essays on Women, Literature, and Theory.* New York: Pantheon Books, 1985.

Sierra Berdecía, Fernando. *Antonio S. Pedreira, buceador de la personalidad puertorriqueña.* San Juan, Puerto Rico: Biblioteca de autores puertorriqueños, 1942.

Simón, Pedro. *Dulce María Loynaz: Valoración múltiple.* Habana: Ediciones Casa de las América y Editorial Letras Cubanas, 1991.

Simpson, Victor C. *Colonialism and Narrative in Puerto Rico: A Study of Characterization in the Novels of Pedro Juan Soto.* New York: Lang, 2004.

Sirias, Silvio. *Julia Alvarez: A Critical Companion.* Westport, CT: Greenwood Press, 2001.

Sklodowska, Elzbieta, and Ben A. Heller. *Roberto Fernández Retamar y los estudios latinoamericanos.* Pittsburgh, PA: Instituto Internacional de Literatura Iberoamericana, Universidad de Pittsburgh, 2000.

Sloat, Susanna, ed. *Caribbean Dance: From Abakuá to Zouk. How Movement Shapes Identity.* Gainesville: University Press of Florida, 2002.

Smilowitz, E., and R. Knowles, eds. *Selected Papers from West Indian Literature Conference 1981–1983.* Parkesburg, IA: Caribbean Books, 1984.

Smorkaloff, Pamela María. *Cuban Writers on and off the Island: Contemporary Narrative Fiction.* New York: Twayne, 1999.

Smorkaloff, Pamela María, ed. *If I Could Write This in Fire: An Anthology of Literature from the Caribbean.* New York: The New Press, 1994.

Solé, Carlos A., and Maria Isabel Abreu, eds. *Latin American Writers.* 3 Vols. New York: Scribner's, 1989.

Sollors, Werner, ed. *An Anthology of Interracial Literature: Black-White Contacts in the Old World and the New.* New York: New York University Press, 2004.

Soto, Francisco. *Reinaldo Arenas.* New York: Twayne, 1998.

———. *Reinaldo Arenas: The Pentagonia.* Gainesville: University Press of Florida, 1994.

Souza, Raymond D. *Lino Novás Calvo.* Boston: Twayne, 1981.

Stavans, Ilan. *Spanglish: The Making of a New American Language.* New York: Rayo, 2003.

Stone, Judy S. J. *Curtain Rise. The Pioneers of West Indian Theatre 1900–1950: Errol Hill in Theatre.* London: Macmillan Press, 1994.

Strausfeld, Michi. *Nuevos narradores cubanos.* Madrid: Ediciones Siruela, 2000.

Suárez, Virgil. *Little Havana Blues: A Cuban-American Literature Anthology.* Houston, TX: Arte Público Press, 1996.

Suárez Díaz, Ada. *El doctor Ramón Emeterio Betances y la abolición de la esclavitud.* San Juan, Puerto Rico: Instituto de Cultura Puertorriqueña, 1980.

Supplice, Daniel. *Dictionnaire biographique des personnalités politiques de la République d'Haïti (1804–2001).* Tielt, Belgium: Lanoo Imprimerie, 2001.

Swanson, Philip. *The New Novel in Latin America: Politics and Popular Culture After the Boom.* New York: Manchester University Press, 1995.

Sylvain, Georges. *Confidences et mélancolies: poésies, 1885–1898: précédées d'une notice sur la poésie haïtienne par l'auteur*. Port-au-Prince, Haïti: Impr. H. Deschamps, 1979.

Takaki, Ronald. *A Larger Memory: A History of Our Diversity, with Voices*. Boston: Little, Brown and Company, 1998.

Taylor, Ula Y. *The Veiled Garvey: The Life & Times of Amy Jacques Garvey*. Chapel Hill: University of North Carolina Press, 2002.

Tejera y Horta, María Luisa de la. *Bibliografía de Luisa Pérez de Zambrana*. Habana, 1955.

Temple, Bob. *Guyana*. Philadelphia, PA: Mason Crest Publishers, 2004.

Terligen, J. *Las Antillas Neerlandesas en su vecindad: lengua y literatura Española en las Antillas Neerlandesas*. Willemstad, Curaçao: Ministerio de Asuntos Culturales de las Antillas Neerlandesas, 1961.

Thadal, Roland. *Jacques Roumain: l'unité d'une oeuvre*. Port-au-Prince, Haïti: Editions des Antilles, 1997.

Tillery, Tyrone. *Claude McKay: A Black Poet's Struggle for Identity*. Amherst: University Massachusetts Press, 1992.

Toledo Sande, Luis. *Tres narradores agonizantes: tanteos acerca de la obra de Miguel de Carrión, Jesús Castellanos y Carlos Loveira*. Habana: Editorial Letras Cubanas, 1980.

Torres, Edel. *Los caminos y la palabra de José Soler Puig*. Santiago, Cuba: Editorial Oriente, Ediciones Santiago, 2002.

Torres, Víctor Federico. *Narradores puertorriqueños del 70*. San Juan, Puerto Rico: Plaza Mayor, 2001.

Torres-Ríoseco, Arturo. *La gran literatura iberoamericana*. Buenos Aires: Emece Editores, 1945.

Torres-Saillant, Silvio, and Ramona Hernandez. *The New Americans: The Dominican Americans*. Westport, CT: Greenwood Press, 1998.

Toumson, Roger. *La Transgression des couleurs*. Paris: Éditions Caribéennnes, 1989.

Trouillot, Ernst. *Hommage à Luc Grimard*. Port-au-Prince, Haiti: Impr. de l'État, 1955.

Trouillot, Hénock. *Beaubrun Ardouin, l'homme politique et l'historien*. Port-au-Prince, Haiti: Pan-American Institute of Geography and History, 1950.

Valerio-Holguím, Fernando, ed. *Arqueología de las sombras: la narrativa de Marcio Velo Maggiolo*. Santo Domingo, República Dominicana: F. Valerio-Holguín, 2000.

Varela, Félix. *Jicoténcal*. Houston, TX: Arte Público Press, 1995.

Vassallo, Ruth. *Nilita Vientós Gastón: una vida en imágenes*. Río Piedras, Puerto Rico: Editorial Marién, 1989.

Vázquez, Lourdes. *Aterrada de cuernos y cuervos: Marina Arzola, el testimonio*. San Juan, Puerto Rico: Ediciones El Gallo Rojo, 1990.

———. *Hablar sobre Julia: Julia de Burgos: bibliografía 1934–2002*. Austin, TX: SALALM Secretariat, 2002.

Vega, José Luis. *Reunión de espejos*. Río Piedras, Puerto Rico: Editorial Cultural, 1983.

Veloz Maggiolo, Marcio. *Cultura, teatro y relatos in San to Domingo*. Santiago de los Caballeros, República Dominicana: Universidad Católica Madre y Maestra, 1972.

Vicioso, Sherezada. *Salomé Ureña de Henríquez (1850–1897): a cien años de un magisterio*. Santo Domingo, República Dominicana: Comisión Permanente de la Feria Nacional del Libro, 1997.

Villaverde, Cirilo. *Cecilia Valdés o La Loma del Ángel: novela de costumbre cubanas*. Madrid: Cátedra, 1992.

———. *Cecilia Valdés*. Translated from the Spanish by Helen Lane; edited with an introduction and notes by Sibylle Fischer. New York: Oxford University Press, 2004.

Villaverde, Fernando.*Crónicas del Mariel*. Miami, FL: Ediciones Universal, 1992.

Vitier, Cintio. *Cincuenta años de poesía pura cubana (1902–1952)*. Habana: Dirección de Cultura del Ministerio de Educación, Ediciones del Cincuentenario, 1952.

———. *Lo cubano en la poesía*. 2nd ed. Habana: Instituto del Libro, 1970.

Voorheve, Jan, ed. *Trefossa*. Paramaribo, Surname: Bureau Volkslectuur, 1977.

Voorheve, Jan, and Ursy M. Lichtveld, eds. *Creole Drum: An Anthology of Creole Literature in Surinam*. New Haven, CT: Yale University Press, 1975.

Walcott, Derek. *The Castaway*. London: Cape, 1965.

———. *Omeros*. New York: Farrar, Straus and Giroux, 1990.

Walker, Keith L. *Countermodernism and Francophone Literary Culture: The Game of Slipknot*. Durham, NC: Duke University Press, 1999.

Walmsley, Anne. *The Caribbean Artists Movement 1966–1972*. London: New Beacon Books, 1992.

Walvin, James. *An African's Life: The Life and Times of Olaudah Equiano, 1745–1797*. London; New York: Cassell, 1998.

Wambu, Onyekachi, ed. *Hurricane Hits England: An Anthology of Writing About Black Britain*. New York: Continuum, 2000.

Webhofer, Gudrun. *Identity in the Poetry of Grace Nichols and Lorna Goodison*. Lewiston, NY: E. Mellen Press, 1996.

Wedel, Johan. *Santería Healing: A Journey Into the Afro-Cuban World of Divinitie Spirits, and Sorcery*. Gainesville, Tallahasee, Tampa: University Press of Florida, 2004.

Weiser, Nora. *Open to the Sun: A Bilingual Anthology of Latin American Women Poets*. California: Perival Press, 1980.

Weiss, Judith. *Casa de las Américas: An Intellectual Review in the Cuban Revolution*. Chapel Hill, NC: Estudios de Hispanófila, 1977.

West-Durán, Alan. *African Caribbeans: A Reference Guide*. Westport, CT: Greenwood Press, 2003.

Whitson, Kathy J. *Encyclopedia of Feminist Literature*. Westport, CT: 2004.

Williams, Emily Allen. *Poetic Negotiation of Identity in the Works of Brathwaite, Harris, Senior, and Dabydeen: Tropical Paradise Lost and Regained*. Lewiston, NY: E Mellen Press, 1999.

Williams, Joseph J. *Voodoos and Obeahs: Phases of West India Witchcraft*. New York: Dial Press, 1932.

Williams, Patrick, and Laura Chrisman, eds. *Colonial Discourse and Post-colonial Theory*. New York: Columbia University Press, 1994.

Wilson, Andrew, ed. *The Chinese in the Caribbean*. Princeton, NJ: Markus Wiener Publishers, 2004.

Wilson-Tagoe, Nana. *Historical Thought and Literary Representation in West Indian Literature*. Gainesville: University Press of Florida, 1998.

Yáñez, Mirta. *Camila y Camila*. Habana: Ediciones la Memoria, 2003.

Zambrana, Antonio. *El negro Francisco*. la Habana: Editorial Letras Cubanas, 1979.

Zamora, Lois Parkinson, and Wendy B. Faris, eds. *Magical Realism: Theory, History, Community*. Durham, NC: Duke University Press, 1995.

Zea, Leopoldo. *Dos etapas del pensamiento en Hispanoamérica. Del romanticismo al positivismo*. México, México: Colegio de México, 1949.

Zeno Gandía, Manuel. *La charca: crónicas de un mundo enfermo*. Ponce, Puerto Rico: Est. Tip. de M. López, 1894.

———. *The Pond*. Translated by Kal Wagenheim. Princeton, NJ: Markus Wiener Publishers, 1999.

Zips, Werner. *Black Rebels: African Caribbean Freedom Fighters in Jamaica*. Princeton, NJ: Marcus Wiener Publishers; Kingston, Jamaica: I Randle, 1999.

Index

Morejón, Nancy, 204, 397, 550–552, 714, 837
Morel, Lise, 196
Moreno Fraginals, Manuel, 835
Moreno Jimenes, Domingo, 52, 257, 396, 407, 552–553, 653
Morgan, Paula, 648, 668, 669, 670, 736, 743, 879
Morfi, Angelina, 275
Morgan, Pamela, 401
Morgan, Paula, 32, 76, 111, 404, 434, 443, 517, 547, 627
Morgan, William, 1
Moriso-Lewa, Feliks, 366
Morisseau, Roland, 314, 365, 634
Morisseau-Leroy, Félix, 314, 365
Morisseau-Leroy, Félix/Feliks Moriso Lewa, 553–554
Morocco, 708
Morovis, P.R., 418, 537
Morpeau, Louis, 289
Morrell, Charlie, 242
Morris, Mervyn, 113, 221, 554–556, 835
Morrison Fortunato, Mateo, 421, 556
Morrison, Toni, 95
Morro Castle, 119, 79
Morte de Christophe, La (Romane), 698
Morte de Lamarre, La (Dupré), 267
Morten Dauwen Zabel Award, 427
Morton Publishers (Trinidad), 167
Morúa Delgado, Martín, 556–557
Morúa, Francisco, 556–557
Moscow Is Not My Mecca (Carew), 134
Moscow, 236, 600
Moses Ascending (Selvon), 741
Moses Migrating (Selvon), 741
Mosquetazos de Aramis (Bonafoux), 94
Mother Poem (Brathwaite), 105
Mother-Daughter relationships, 292, 558–559
Mothers Are Not the Only Linguists (Rahim), 668
Motivos de Son (Guillén), 353, 572
Motor mutable (Santos Silva), 728
Mourir pour Haïti, ou, Les croisés d'Esther (Dorsinville, R.), 262
Mourt d'Oluweni d'Ajumako (Condé), 185
Movements
    "Back to Africa," 324, 325
    abolitionist, 2, 189
    abolitionist (Great Britain), 658, 752
    anti-American, 108
    antislavery (Cuban), 797
    antislavery (Guadeloupen), 713
    Black Arts, 521
    black consciousness, 211, 286, 488, 580
    See also Négritude
    Black Power, 109, 565
    civil rights, 75, 101, 147, 586

Caribbean Artists (CAM), 715, 730, 772
Cuban independence, 55, 87, 817, 840
Dominican independence, 265
feminist, 382
Guyanese independence, 580
independence, 104, 117, 156
Indigenist, 365, 680
Indigenist, Haiti, 823
Integralismo, 383, 384
labor, 563
Les Griots, 234
liberation, 314
literary. *See* Literary movements.
Pan-African, 415
political, Négritude, 10, 25, 56, 95, 108, 125, 127, 154, 155, 156, 159, 196, 211, 212, 234, 286, 313, 314, 315, 333, 347, 373, 456, 457, 460, 488, 508, 509, 521, 531, 573–575, 580, 605, 629, 656, 752, 778, 842, 843
proindependence, 537
Puerto Rican independence, 87, 587, 802
Rastafarian, 325, 565
revolutionary, 265
See also Cuban Revolution
socialist, 417
Socialist Youth, 755
Trotskyite, 415
underground, 684
women's (Dominican Republic), 525
Women's Liberation, 109
women's, 101, 292, 375
Movimiento de Liberación Dominicana, 684
Moya Pons, Fran, 559–560
Moyers, Bill, 199
Mr. Ives' Christmas (Hijuelos), 389
Mr. Jimmy and the Blackpudding Man: A Short History of Immigrants (De Haarte), 226–227
Mr. Potter (Kincaid), 427
Mr. Stone and the Knight's Companion (Naipaul, V.S.), 569
Muchas gracias por las flores; cinco alegres tragedias (Morales, J.), 548
Mudanza de los sentidos (Hernández, A.), 382
Muerte anduvo por el Guasio, La (Hernández Aquino), 384
Muerte de Artemio Cruz, La (Fuentes), 95, 808
Muerte en el Eden (Incháustegui Cabral), 407
Muerte herida (Villegas), 818
Muerte no entrará en palacio, La (Marqués), 497
Muerte, La (Belaval), 74
Muestras de folklore puertorriqueño (Palma), 606
Muet Poems (Hendriks), 373

Mujer boricua (Corretjer), 190
Mujer con combrero Panamá (Rodríguez Juliá), 694
Mujer del Siglo XX, La (Puerto Rican journal), 701
Mujer en el arte, La (Eulate), 283
Mujer en la historia, La (Eulate), 283
Mujer en traje de batalla (Benítez Rojo), 81, 82
Mujer y la cultura, La (Henríquez Ureña, C.), 375, 376
Mujer, La (newspaper), 132, 282
Mujer, La (women's journal), 700
Mujer que llevo dentro, La (Villanueva Collado), 815
Mujer, y la cultura, La (Henríquez Ureña, C.), 254
Mujeres Como Ilas (Pérez, O.M.), 294
Mujeres como islas (Neives, M.), 663, 727
Mujeres como islas (Vallejo), 42, 382, 398
Mujeres Como islas, 805
Mujeres en la coyuntura catual: algunas reflexiones, Las (Hernández, A.), 382
Mulata, 154, 816
    Cuban, 385
    in Caribbean Literature, 560–562
Mulattos, 56
Multicultural Review (journal), 5, 320, 476
Multicultural Writers Since 1945 (Pérez), 623
Multiculturalism, 457
Multiple Presence (Camille), 128
Munco, El, 821, 822
Mundo abierto (Margenat, H.), 492
Mundo alucinante, El (Arenas), 39, 40
Mundo de cosas (Soler Puig), 756
Mundo y Palabra/The World and the Word (Espaillat), 276
Mundo, El (newspaper), 23, 103, 205, 206, 228, 245, 290, 295, 322, 384, 417, 432, 466, 467, 491, 506, 513, 536, 538, 592, 604, 616, 674, 676, 744, 747, 749, 812
Mundo literario prehispánico, El (Yáñez), 837
Muñeca de crepé envuelta en celofán, La (Carrero), 139
Muñeca, La (Eulate), 283
Muñoz Family, 563–565
Muñoz Marín, José Luis Alberto, 563
Muñoz Marín, Luis, 15, 28, 58, 396, 440, 514, 563–564, 666, 693, 738
Muñoz Rivera, Luis, 527, 564
Muñoz, Elías Miguel, 347, 562–563
Munro College, 555, 715
Murder of Pito, The (Algarin), 16
Murderer, The (Heath), 372

About the Editor and Contributors

Editor

D. H. Figueredo is the coeditor (with Luis Martínez Fernández, Louis A. Perez, and Luis González) of the award-winning *Encyclopedia of Cuba* (2003) and the author of the popular *Complete Idiot's Guide to Latino History and Culture* (2002). A children's and young-adult writer, Figueredo is the author of the picture books *When This World Was New* (1999) and *The Road to Santiago* (2003), among others, and editor of Latino studies for the journal *The Multicultural Review*. Recipient of an MA in Latin American studies from New York University and an MLS from Rutgers University, he was the Latin American bibliographer for the research libraries of New York Public Library System and the creator of the bilingual program for Newark's public libraries. An independent researcher, he is the director of the Bloomfield College Library in Bloomfield, New Jersey.

Advisory Board

Jayne R. Boisvert, who holds a master's degree in French literature from Boston College, received her PhD from the Department of French Studies at the University of Albany. Under the guidance of Dr. Eloise Brière, she wrote a dissertation entitled *The Myth of Erzulie and the Female Characters in the Haitian Novel*. Boisvert has published several articles on Haitian history and literature as well as a study of the French film *The Baker's Wife*. She has served for many years as the Caribbean book reviewer for *The Multicultural Review*.

From September 1999 until May 2001, Dr. Boisvert held the position of the Harder-McClellan scholar in the humanities at Russell Sage College in Troy, New York. Since that time, she has continued teaching at the school as assistant professor of French and comparative literature. She has also acted as program coordinator of the Modern Languages Department since 2001.

Carrol F. Coates is professor of French and comparative literature at Binghamton University–SUNY, where he teaches courses in French syntax and phonetics and in francophone Haitian, Caribbean, and African literatures. He has translated two novels by Haitian novelist Jacques Stephen Alexis *(General Sun, My Brother*, and, with the collaboration of Edwidge Danticat, *In the Flicker of an Eyelid)*, one by René Depestre *(The Festival of the Greasy Pole)*, and one by Ivoirian novelist Ahmadou Kourouma *(Waiting for the Vote of the Wild Animals)*. He is series editor of CARAF Books (Caribbean and African Literature translated from French;

published by the University of Virginia Press) and an associate editor of *Callaloo, a Journal of African Diaspora Arts and Letters* (the Johns Hopkins University Press).

Daisy Cocco de Filippis is a native of the Dominican Republic who has lived in New York City since 1961. As have many immigrants, Dr. Daisy Cocco de Filippis studied at the City University of New York, where she received her BA summa cum laude in Spanish and English literatures. She earned an MA in Spanish literature from Queens College and a PhD in Hispanic literature from the Graduate Center. A prolific writer, Dr. Cocco de Filippis has written or edited a total of eighteen books on Caribbean and Latino literatures, with special emphasis on the literature written by Dominicans and by women from the region. She has served the City University of New York with distinction for three decades. A tenured professor of Spanish at York College, she has taken a leave to serve as provost and vice president for Academic Affairs at Eugenio María de Hostos Community College, beginning in January 2002 to the present.

Peter T. Johnson's career includes twenty-five years at Princeton University as its bibliographer for Latin America, Spain, and Portugal and also in its program in Latin American studies, teaching a seminar on research trends and methods as well as being its interim director for 2002–03. His research deals with the process of political change, with studies on censorship under military governments, Sendero Luminoso, and intellectuals in Cuba. He was a member of the advisory board of the *Encyclopedia of Cuba* (2003) and is the author of *Cuba, from Colony to Revolution: A Bibliography of Microforms* (1996).

Nicolás Kanellos is the Brown Foundation professor of Spanish at the University of Houston. He is founding publisher of the noted Hispanic literary journal *The Americas Review* (formerly *Revista Chicano-Riqueña*) and the nation's oldest and most esteemed Hispanic publishing house, Arte Público Press. Among his books are *Hispanic Literature of the United States: A Comprehensive Reference* (2003), *America's Hispanic People: Their Images Through History* (1997), the *Hispanic-American Almanac* (1993), and *Biographical Dictionary of Hispanic Literature of the United States* (1989). Dr. Kanellos is the director of a national research program: Recovering the U.S. Hispanic Literary Heritage of the United States from the Colonial Period to 1960.

Asela R. Laguna is the acting chair, Puerto Rican and Hispanic Caribbean studies and professor of Spanish at Rutgers University. With a PhD and an MA from the University of Illinois and a BA magna cum laude from the Universidad de Puerto Rico, she is the author of *George Bernard Shaw en el mundo hispánico* (1983) and editor of *The Global Impact of Portuguese Language and Culture* (2001), *Images and Identities: The Puerto Rican in Two World Contexts* (1987), and *Imágenes e identidades: El puertorriqueño en la literatura.* (1985). She has published numerous articles in such journals as *Journal of Hispanic Literatures, Linden Lane,* and *Sin Nombre,* as well in chapters in such volumes as *The Christopher Columbus Encyclopedia* (1992) and *U.S. Latino Literature—A Critical Guide for Students and Teachers* (2000).

William Luis is professor of Spanish and English at Vanderbilt University. He earned a BA from the State University of New York–Binghamton, an MA from the University of Wisconsin–Madison, and a second MA and a PhD from Cornell University. Luis has published eleven books and more than one hundred scholarly articles. His books include *Literary Bondage: Slavery in Cuban Narrative* (1990), *Dance Between Two Cultures: Latino Caribbean Literature Written in the United States* (1997), *Culture and Customs of Cuba* (2001), *and Lunes de Revolución: Literatura y cultura en los primeros años de la Revolución Cubana* (2003). Also, he is the editor of the *Afro-Hispanic Review*. Born and raised in New York City, he is widely regarded as a leading authority on Latin American, Caribbean, Afro-Hispanic, and Latino U.S. literatures.

Lyn Miller-Lachman is the editor of the journal *The Multicultural Review*. An expert on children's literature and multicultural studies, she edited *Our Family, Our Friends, Our World: An Annotated Guide to Significant Multicultural Books for Children and Teenagers* (1992), *Global Voices, Global Visions: A Core Collection of Multicultural Books* (1995), and a anthology of Latino short stories, *Once Upon a Cuento* (2003). She is the author of a novel to be published by Curbstone Press in 2006.

Paula Morgan is a lecturer in the faculty of humanities and education and an associate of the Centre for Gender and Development Studies, the University of the West Indies–St. Augustine. Her primary area of research, teaching, and publication is in women's literatures of the Caribbean and the African diaspora. Dr. Morgan, a former deputy dean of Distance and Outreach, has authored *Language Proficiency for Tertiary Level* and *Writing About Literature* (with Barbara Lalla). Her most recent research project is on Trauma and Violence in Caribbean Discourse. Paula Morgan is the coordinator of UWI Literatures in English program.

Emilio Jorge Rodríguez is a critic, researcher, and editor. He is the author of the following volumes: *Literatura caribeña: Bojeo y cuaderno de bitácora* (1989); *Cuentos para ahuyentar el turismo; 16 autores puertorriqueños*—in collaboration with Vitalina Alfonso (1991), and *Acriollamiento y discurso escrit/oral caribeño* (2001). He is a member of the editorial boards of the journals *Revista Mexicana del Caribe* and *Mango Season* and serves on numerous academic committees, including Comité Académico de la Biblioteca del Caribe (Puerto Rico), and teaches at the Centro de Investigación y Desarrollo de la Cultura Cubana Juan Marinello, in Cuba. Rodríguez has traveled widely throughout the Caribbean and has taught at numerous universities in Haiti, Puerto Rico, Spain, and the United States, among others.

Daniel Shapiro is the author of "The Red Handkerchief and Other Poems" (unpublished), and translator of *Cipango*, by Chilean poet Tomás Harris. *The American Poetry Review* (Sept.-Oct. 1997) presented a selection of these translations as the cover feature. Others have appeared in *BOMB, Chelsea, Grand Street, Marlboro Review,* and *Review: Latin American Literature and Arts*. His poems have appeared in *Black Warrior Review, Confrontation,* and *Poetry Northwest*. He is director of literature, and managing editor of *Review: Literature and Arts of the Americas*, at the Americas Society in New York. He has received an NEA fellowship to complete the translation of *Cipango*.

Pamela María Smorkaloff has taught at New York University and Princeton University and is an associate professor at Montclair State University, where she directed the Latin American and Latino studies program. A graduate of New York

University, where she earned a PhD, an MA, and a BA magna cum laude, she is the author of several books, including *The Cuba Reader* (2004), *Cuban Writers on and off the Island: Contemporary Narrative Fiction* (1999), *Readers and Writers in Cuba: A Social History of Print Culture, 1830s–1990s* (1997), and the recipient of a Casa de las Américas literary prize for *Literatura y edición de libros: la cultura literaria y el proceso social en Cuba, 1900–1987* (1987). She is also the editor of the anthology *If I Could Write This in Fire: An Anthology of Literature from the Caribbean* (1994, 1996). She has written numerous articles and reviews and was a contributor to the *Encyclopedia of Cuba* (2003).

Contributors

Fernando Acosta-Rodríguez is the librarian for Latin American, Iberian, and Latino studies at Princeton University Library (since 2003). He has a BA in political science from the University of Massachusetts–Amherst and an MA in political science from the University of Texas–Austin, where he later received his MLIS. Before Princeton, he was bibliographer for Latin America, Spain, and Portugal at the New York Public Library.

Rosa Amatulli is a doctoral candidate at the Graduate Center of the City University of New York. She teaches comparative literature at Queens College–CUNY. She is the author (with Rolando Pérez) of an essay on Carlo Levi in *Multicultural Writers Since 1945* (Greenwood, 2004). Amatulli has written on Renaissance Italian and Golden Age Spanish literature and is presently working on a dissertation on the politics of humor in Ariosto, Cervantes, Twain, Calvino, and Kundera.

Frank Argote-Freyre is an assistant professor at Kean University. He received his PhD in history from Rutgers University in 2004. His forthcoming book, *Fulgencio Batista: The Making of a Dictator*, vol. 1, is scheduled to be published in early 2006. Argote-Freyre is involved in many social causes, including the struggle for immigrant rights. He was a contributor to and conducted research for the *Encyclopedia of Cuba* (2003). He serves as policy adviser for the Hispanic Directors Association of New Jersey and sits on the executive committee of the Latino Leadership Alliance of New Jersey.

Emilio Bejel, a poet and critic, is professor and chair of the Department of Spanish of the University of California–Davis. He has published several scholarly books, including *Literatura de Nuestra América*; *José Lezama Lima, Poet of the Image*; and *Gay Cuban Nation*. The titles of his latest poetry collections are *Casas deshabitadas* and *El libro regalado*. He has also published his fictionalized autobiography, entitled *The Write Way Home: A Cuban-American Story*.

Wilfredo Cancio Isla taught at the School of Communications, Havana University (1983–94), and was theater and cinema reviewer for many cultural publications on the island. He was also a member of the editorial board of the magazine *Cine Cubano*. He came to the United States in 1994 as part of a special program of the McArthur Foundation and the University of North Carolina–Chapel Hill and taught at Barry University, Florida, from 1995 to 1997. He acted as reporter in Miami for Radio Bilingüe, California, and the International Press Service (IPS) until 1998, when he obtained a PhD in information sciences from the University of La Laguna,

Spain, and started working as a reporter with Miami's *El Nuevo Herald*, where he currently covers Cuban affairs. He was part of the group of editors and consultants of the *Encyclopedia of Contemporary Latin American Culture* (Routledge, 2000), and of *Cuba: An Illustrated Encyclopedia* (Oryx Press, 2002). His book about the newspaper career of writer Alejo Carpentier is awaiting publication.

Reginald Eustace Clarke, Senior Librarian I (Senior Lecturer Status) on Tenure, Main Library, the University of the West Indies, is the author of numerous articles on Trinidadian culture as well as studies on librarianship in the Caribbean. He has taught courses on African history and Caribbean culture.

Angela Conrad is an assistant professor of English and women's studies at Bloomfield College in Bloomfield, New Jersey. She is the author of *The Wayward Nun of Amherst: Emily Dickinson and Medieval Mystical Women* (2000) and other critical works. She serves on the Board of Trustees of the New Jersey Council for the Humanities and teaches at Drew University's Caspersen School of Graduate Studies.

Nelly Cruz has an MA in Latin American and Caribbean studies from New York University. She served as the Centro's first project archivist. She was also the director of the General Archives of Puerto Rico. Currently she is the director for Public Relations of the Puerto Rico Tourism Company.

Belkis Cuza Malé is a poet and the editor and founder of the literary journal *Linden Lane*. A native of Cuba, she has received honorary mentions in several literary competitions sponsored by the Casa de las Américas. She moved to the United States in 1980. She is the author of *El clavel y la rosa: biografía de Juana Borrero* (1984), *Elvis: la tumba sin sosiego o la verdadera historia de jon burrows*, and several books of poetry.

Juan Pablo Dabove is assistant professor in the Department of Spanish and Portuguese at the University of Colorado–Boulder. He is the author of *La forma del Destino (on El beso de la Mujer Araña)* (Beatriz Viterbo, 1994) and *Nightmares of the Lettered City: Banditry, Literature and the Nation-State in the Latin American Long Nineteenth-Century* (forthcoming). He is also coeditor *of Heterotropias: narrativas de identidad y alteridad latinoamericana* (IILI, 2003) as well as author of articles on nineteenth- and twentieth-century Latin American literature, published in journals such as *Revista Iberoamericana, Revista de Critica Literaria Latinoamericana, Estudios,* and *Hispanic Review,* among others.

Daryl Cumber Dance, a graduate of Virginia State College and the University of Virginia, is professor of English at the University of Richmond in Richmond, Virginia. She has also taught at Virginia State College, Virginia Commonwealth University, and the University of California–Santa Barbara. She is the author of *Shuckin' and Jivin': Folklore from Contemporary Black Americans* (Indiana, 1978), *Folklore from Contemporary Jamaicans* (Tennessee, 1985), *Long Gone: The Mecklenburg Six and the Theme of Escape in Black Folklore* (Tennessee, 1987), *New World Adams: Conversations with Contemporary West Indian Writers* (Peepal Tree, 1992), and *The Lineage of Abraham: The Biography of a Free Black Family in Charles City, Virginia* (1998). She edited *Fifty Caribbean Writers: A Bio-Bibliographical-Critical Sourcebook* (Greenwood, 1986), *Honey, Hush! An Anthology* *of African American Women's Humor* (Norton, 1998), and *From My People: 400 Years of African American Folklore: An Anthology* (Norton, 2002).

Lisa Finder is the Serials Librarian at Hunter College. She received her MLS from Columbia University and her MA in liberal studies from the Graduate Center of the City University of New York. She was the Serials Librarian at the Schomburg Center for Research in Black Culture from 1995 to 2000.

Janet Fullerton-Rawlins is the director of the library of the School of Education at the University of the West Indies. An expert on anglophone Caribbean writers, she has lectured and written extensively on the subject.

Alfonso J. García Osuna is the chairperson of the Department of Foreign Languages at City University of New York. He received his PhD (1989) from the Graduate School and University Center of the City University of New York. He has published several articles in scholarly journals, and among his most recent books are *Incidents of Travel on the Road to Santiago* (1998), *The Cuban Filmography, 1897–2001* (2002), and *La filmografía cubana, 1897–2003* (2003).

Flora González Mandri is professor of writing, literature and publishing at Emerson College in Boston. She and Rosamond Rosenmeier translated and edited *In the Vortex of the Cyclone: Selected Poems by Excilia Saldaña* (University Press of Florida, 2002). Her forthcoming book *Afro-Cuban Women: Guardians of a Nation's Memory* will be released spring 2006, published by the University Press of Virginia.

Susan Greenbaum is professor of anthropology, University of South Florida. A PhD from the University of Kansas (1981), her current research is on displacement of public housing residents in Tampa and is funded by the National Science Foundation. Her other interests include urban ethnicity and economics, Cuban immigration, and historic preservation. Her book *More than Black: Afro-Cubans in Tampa* (2002) won four prizes, all in 2003: Theodore Saloutos Award; Harry T. & Harriet V. Moore Award; ALA Choice Award; and USF Outstanding Research Award.

Roger E. Hernández is a syndicated columnist for King Features whose articles and columns appear in over forty newspapers across the United States, including the *Washington Post, Dallas Morning News, Seattle Post-Intelligencer* and *Portland Oregonian.* He teaches writing at the New Jersey Institute of Technology and has been a visiting scholar and writer at numerous institutions. He is the author of *Cubans in America: A Vibrant History of a People in Exile* (2002), *Cuba* (2004), *Cuban Immigration* (2004), among others, and a contributor to the reference volume *Encyclopedia of Cuba* (2003).

Claudia Hill is the Art and Architecture Cataloger for Avery Library, Columbia University, New York, New York.

Léon-François Hoffmann, Professor (Em.) of French at Princeton University, is the author of several books on French romantic literature and on Haitian literature and culture. His many books include *Haitian Fiction Revisited* (1999), *Bibliographie des études littéraires haïtiennes, 1804–1984* (1992), *Haïti: couleurs, croyances, créole* (1990), and *La nègre romantique; personnage littéraire et obsession collective* (1973). The latter volume received a literary prize from the Académie française.

Paula Makris specializes in the study of colonial education and cultural inheritance in Caribbean literature and the classics. She has published articles and essays in such publications as the *Revista/Review Interamericana*. She has been visiting professor of English at the University of Tulsa, Oklahoma, and Messiah College, Pennsylvania. She is assistant professor of English at Wheeling Jesuit University, West Virginia.

Gladys Markoff-Sotomayor is Iberian-Latin American Cataloger Emeritus, Columbia University, New York, New York.

Ian H. Marshall is professor of English at William Paterson University, Wayne, New Jersey. Dr. Marshall has written articles on the connections between writing, literature, and whiteness and has edited a collection of essays that examines the intersections of composition and critical whiteness studies. The book is pending publication.

Sintia Molina, whose research focuses on women's issues, migration and identity, education, language, and literature, is the author of two books and many articles. Dr. Molina has also done research and lectured on her topics of interest and has been awarded grants to further her research and writing. She is the author of *Dominican Migration: Transnational Perspectives* (2004) and *El Naturalismo en la novela cubana* (2000). Her works have appeared in journals such as *Callaloo, Revista de Estudios Sociales, Latino Studies Journal, Baquiana*, and others.

Nélida Pérez has an MLS from Columbia University and an MA in history and archives from New York University. She is the associate director for Library and Archives, Centro de Estudios Puertorriqueños, Hunter College–CUNY.

Rolando Pérez, born in Cuba, has published in a variety of disciplines, ranging from philosophy and literary criticism to poetry and fiction. Some of his books include *Severo Sarduy and the Religion of the Text* (1988), *The Odyssey* (1990), *On An(archy) and Schizoanalysis* (1990), *The Divine Duty of Servants: A Book of Worship* (1999, based on the artwork of Bruno Schulz), *The Electric Comedy* (2000, a modern version of Dante's *Divine Comedy*), and *The Linings of Our Souls: Excursions into Selected Paintings of Edward Hopper (*2003). He is also the author of a number of encyclopedia and academic essays on such literary figures as Carlo Levi (with **Rosa Amatulli**), Primo Levi, and Milan Kundera (in *Multicultural Writers Since 1945*, Greenwood, 2004); Severo Sarduy; Jose Asunción Silva; Alejandra Pizarnik; Octavio Paz; and others. Selections from his creative work will appear in *The Norton Anthology of Latino Literature* (2006).

Jennifer Rahim, born in Trinidad, is a poet, short-fiction writer, essayist, and literary critic. Her poems and short stories have been widely published in journals and anthologies, including *The Caribbean Writer, Small Axe, Creation Fire*, and *Sisters of Caliban*. She has published three books of poems: *Mothers Are Not the Only Linguists* (TNV, 1992), *Between the Fence and the Forest* (2002), and, *You Are Morning in Me* (2005). She currently teaches in the Liberal Arts Department at the University of the West Indies, St. Augustine, Trinidad.

Cherrell Shelley-Robinson is a senior lecturer at the Department of Library and Information Studies at the University of the West Indies. She is an expert on Caribbean children's and young-adult literature and has written several children books, including *Manny and the Mermaid* (1987) and *Jójo's Treasure Hunt* (2003). She has written for children's radio programs and magazines and is the managing editor of *Scribbles*, a magazine for Caribbean children.

Sandra Stelts is Curator of Rare Books and Manuscripts in the Special Collections Library at the Pennsylvania State University Libraries. She has published articles in the fields of art history and the history of photography.

Rafael E. Tarrago was born in the city of Holguín, in eastern Cuba. He holds a master of arts degree in Ibero-American studies from the Catholic University of America, in Washington, D.C., and he is the author of several books and articles on Cuban and Spanish American history and culture, including *Experiencias políticas de los cubanos en la Cuba espanola, 1512–1898* (1996) and *La libertad de escoger: Poetas afrocubanos*, to be published in Madrid by Ediciones del Orto in 2006. At present Mr. Tarrago is librarian for Iberian and Ibero-American studies at the University of Minnesota–Minneapolis.